Bird in a Cage

LEGAL REFORM IN
CHINA AFTER MAO

Bird in a Cage

Legal Reform in
China After Mao

STANLEY B. LUBMAN

Stanford University Press
Stanford, California

Stanford University Press
Stanford, California
© 1999 by the Board of Trustees
of the Leland Stanford Junior University

Printed in the United States of America
CIP data appear at the end of the book

For Judith, Sarah, and James,
of course

Acknowledgments

A portion of chapter 2 was previously published in "Studying Contemporary Chinese Law: Limits, Possibilities and Strategy," vol. 39 of the American Journal of Comparative Law (1991), pp. 293–341. Portions of chapters 2 and 3 were previously published in "Mao and Mediation: Politics and Dispute Resolution in Communist China," in vol. 55 of the California Law Review (1967), pp. 1284–1359.

Portions of chapter 4 were previously published in "Form and Function in the Chinese Criminal Process," in vol. 69 of the Columbia Law Review (1969), pp. 535–575, and in "Methodological Problems in Studying Chinese Communist 'Civil Law'" in Contemporary Chinese Law: Research Problems and Perspectives, by J. A. Cohen, copyright © 1973 by the President and Fellows of Harvard College, reprinted by permission of Harvard University Press, pp. 230–260.

Contents

Tables

THIS VOLUME GROWS OUT of a career devoted to Chinese law that has enabled me to observe China for over thirty years from the perspectives of both scholar and practicing lawyer. I was fortunate to be invited in 1962 by Willis Reese, my former professor at the Columbia Law School, and A. Doak Barnett, who was teaching at Columbia, to be trained to specialize in Chinese law. I had already become interested in studying foreign legal systems, and after graduating from Columbia in 1958 I had studied French law for two years, first at Columbia and then in Paris. These studies led me to non-Western, especially socialist, legal systems, and in Paris I had also begun to read what I could find about China, although I had not previously studied China or Chinese. At the time, of course, there was almost no communication between the United States and the People's Republic of China (PRC). The extent of Sino-American estrangement had been brought home to me in one vivid image during the summer of 1959 when I was in Vienna while a Communist youth festival was taking place: I turned a street corner one day to see a large delegation from the PRC, well over a hundred Chinese men and women wearing identical trench coats, marching up the street toward me—to this American, they seemed to have come from another planet.

The birth of my interest in China coincided with the emergence of concern at a number of American foundations and universities about the need to revive Chinese studies, which had been demoralized by the absence of Sino-American relations and by McCarthyism. A four-year program of training was improvised for me, supported by grants from the Rockefeller Foundation, the Foreign Area Fellowship Program (itself funded by the Ford Foundation), and the Parker School of Foreign and Comparative Law at Columbia. At that time Americans could not travel to China, and I had no choice but to be trained in the language and undertake my research without being able to travel to the country that was my chosen subject of study. I spent the first two years of my training at

Columbia immersed in full-time study of Chinese language and institutions, and then spent the following two years pursuing research at the Universities Service Centre in Hong Kong. From 1967 to 1972 I taught courses on Chinese law as a member of the faculty of the University of California School of Law (Berkeley).

Soon after Sino-American détente surprised the world in 1971, I left full-time teaching to practice law, specializing exclusively in advising foreign clients on China-related transactions while continuing research, scholarship, and teaching on China. I traveled to China for the first time in the fall of 1972 to negotiate on behalf of clients first at the Guangzhou Export Commodities Fair and then in Beijing, and I have been traveling there continuously ever since. I found no law firm that would hire a lawyer to work only on matters involving China, so I practiced for five years on my own. Thereafter I headed the China practice at first one and then a second San Francisco law firm and, more recently, at an English law firm. For over twenty-five years I have been assisting American, European, and Asian clients in their negotiations and disputes with Chinese counterparts. The eventful course of history since my travels to China began has enabled me to observe the end of the Cultural Revolution, the onset and expansion of economic reforms, the launching of China's policy of "opening" to the West, the beginning of Chinese legal reforms, and the remarkable ongoing transformations in Chinese society produced by reform. I have also been able to study the dilemmas and contradictions that reform continues to spawn for China and the rest of the world.

The practice of law in the specialized context to which I confined it has added much to my education about China. My change in career brought with it an opportunity to combine the experience of law practice with the intellectual interests that had first brought me to the study of China. I have specialized in helping clients to negotiate and implement contracts for sales of capital goods, direct investment, and the transfer of technology. In more recent years I have also represented clients in a variety of disputes with Chinese counterparts. Drafting and negotiating documents, discussing pending transactions or disputes, and advising clients on strategy have required me to seek to understand not only new laws but also the uncertainties of practice, policy, and dealing with the Chinese bureaucracy. In an environment in which the gap between law (when there is any) and practice is great, the challenges have been endless.

I have necessarily had to relate my experiences as a lawyer and those of my clients to broader issues that transcend our specific daily preoccupations. The practical details of specific transactions also present more elusive issues such as coping with the use and abuse of bureaucratic discretion, understanding the links between law and policy, and trying to reconcile Western and Chinese ways. Transactions often reflect the larger forces that both support and obstruct the growth of legality, as well as the extraordinary fundamental transformations that are occurring in the Chinese economy and society.

The process of legal development has literally been going on before my eyes since the late 1970s. One day in 1978, for example, it suddenly became possible to perceive the onset of legal reform: While I was in Beijing for negotiations on the sale of an off-shore drilling platform, a headline in the *People's Daily* signaled adoption of a policy of reestablishing the legal institutions that had been effaced by the Cultural Revolution and had for the previous decade been mentioned only in denunciations.[1] And then, later that year in Tiananmen Square on the night before the "Democracy Wall" was closed down, I listened to Chinese students talking about their hopes for Chinese democracy, but the next night I felt the hostility of the workers' militias that arrived on the Square to carry out a crackdown.

In the 1980s, as Chinese legal education revived, I was able to meet many Chinese law professors and students; as the legal profession has begun to grow, I have encountered many Chinese lawyers. Throughout the years since I first went to China I have also talked with ordinary Chinese whenever possible and formed some impressions about their notions of law. Dialogues with Chinese legal professionals and other knowledgeable Chinese have helped me gain personal impressions of the dilemmas of Chinese law reform and the operation of Chinese legal institutions, some of which developed from one visit to the next. Travels with my wife, Judith, on her business trips added further dimension to my study of China.

Despite the demands of full-time law practice I have also continued my research, writing, and teaching on Chinese law at the law schools of the University of California (Berkeley), Yale, Harvard, Stanford, and Columbia as well as at Heidelberg University and the School of Oriental and African Studies of the University of London. My search for whatever insights I have been able to obtain into Chinese legal institutions and the society that lies behind them has gained much from the stimulation of colleagues and students at these institutions. I have especially benefited from the wisdom, collective and individual, of fellow members of the Committee for Legal Educational Exchanges with China (established and maintained by grants from the Ford Foundation from 1982 until its untimely demise in 1996), which administered a program that brought many Chinese law professors and legal scholars to the United States for research and study.

Both my law practice and scholarly activities constantly remind me of the difficulties that Chinese and Westerners have comprehending each other and surmounting the cultural barriers between them. These problems have become even more visible as reform has transformed China. The welter of social forces that has been unleashed by reform has made China much less orderly than it was when I first went in 1972, and although much more information has come into reach, in many ways China has become more rather than less difficult to understand.

The rapid growth of Chinese law within such a short period of time offers a pale illustration of the problems of comprehending a society in transition. When I began my studies in the 1960s, Chinese law was a shrunken and politicized token of Communist Party legitimacy, Chinese legal scholarship hardly existed, and very few Chinese law books had reached the West. Chinese efforts at institution-building during the 1980s and 1990s have been so extensive that it is now impossible to specialize in Chinese law as such. The flood of available legislation and commentary is so large that it is now necessary to choose areas of concentration such as civil and economic law or criminal law or procedure. Lawyers who specialize on matters related to foreign investment have seen their libraries grow at an extraordinary pace.

While I was working on this book, updating earlier research and undertaking new inquiries, ongoing Chinese legislative activity was changing the institutions I was trying to understand and write about. During 1994–1999 alone, for example, the criminal procedure code and criminal law were revised; laws on judges, lawyers, and administrative penalties were enacted; the system for arbitrating disputes between Chinese and foreigners was changed; new arbitration organizations for purely domestic disputes were created; and the principle of "governing the country according to law" was elevated for the first time into the Constitution. The fluidity that marks Chinese legal institutions blurs whatever snapshots I can take of this fast-paced social change, and it has sometimes induced despair at the effort of trying to understand the processes unfolding before me. At the same time, although the influence of Chinese tradition and the legal culture that predates Communism is less visible than the new laws, they are still forceful and must always be kept in mind.

Because China itself has been in constant flux for two decades, I sometimes find it difficult to imagine how my attempt to take stock of institutions in 1999 might be useful to anyone even a few years later. In my more pessimistic moments I wonder if today's foreign students of Chinese law can be compared to their predecessors in the 1930s, who studied the laws of a republic and entertained excessive hopes for Chinese legal development. My hopes are, by comparison, much more limited. China may develop something like the rule of law in the future and I perceive fragile harbingers of that possible future in China today, but the reader will discover that I remain a cautious pessimist about the future of legality in China.

It is against this background of the career described here that this book is offered to the reader, who will occasionally notice identifiably different perspectives at various places. I have been able to wear two hats, as a lawyer and as a legal scholar, and the voice in which the book is written speaks at different times from under each of those two hats.

I am pleased to acknowledge my gratitude for the encouragement and the assistance that I have received during my career as a specialist in Chinese law.

I begin with expressions of deep gratitude to two unusual professors at the Columbia Law School who encouraged and supported my interest in foreign and comparative law in general and in Chinese law in particular, Willis L. M. Reese and Walter Gellhorn.

Also at Columbia, Charles Szladits was at first my tutor on comparative law and then a supportive friend, and John Hazard encouraged me to study Chinese law and to assist him in preparing comparative teaching materials about socialist legal systems.

A. Doak Barnett, prescient in foreseeing the significance of Chinese law, was the catalyst who simultaneously stimulated Columbia's and my interest in Chinese law.

The Rockefeller Foundation, the Foreign Area Fellowship Program, and the Parker School of Foreign and Comparative Law supported me and my family for four years. The Universities Service Centre, at that time supported by the Carnegie Corporation, afforded a stimulating and congenial place at which to do research in Hong Kong in 1965–1967 and the summer of 1969.

Fellow scholars of Chinese law who have been constant sources of intellectual stimulation combined with friendship for many years are William Alford, Robert Berring, Donald C. Clarke, Anthony R. Dicks, R. Randle Edwards, James V. Feinerman, Sharon Hom, William C. Jones, Victor H. Li, and Pitman Potter. Gregory C. Wajnowski has shared with me both the travails of law practice in China and high spirits in the midst of search for insight. Phyllis Chang, Jonathan Hecht, and Randall Peerenboom have been very helpful to my research in various ways. Clark (Sandy) Randt and Neal Stender have been stimulating colleagues in law practice.

I have benefited enormously from the friendship and scholarship of a large number of China-watchers. Scholars of modern China who have been particularly helpful include Steven Goldstein, Father L. LaDany, Roderick MacFarquhar, Kevin O'Brien, Jean Oi, Michel Oksenberg, Richard M. Solomon, Ezra Vogel, Frederic Wakeman Jr., and Andrew Walder. Diplomats who have been kind enough to share much of their knowledge of China with me include Emrys Davies of HM Foreign Office and Morton Abramowitz, Donald Anderson, Stanley Brooks, Scott Halford, Arthur Hummel, Nicholas Platt, William Rope, and J. Stapleton Roy, all of the United States Foreign Service. Among journalists I am particularly indebted to Amanda Bennett, David Bonavia, Frank Ching, Loren Fessler, Stanley Karnow, Robert Keatley, Sydney Liu, Collina Mac-Dougall, and Takashi Oka. Many clients and other men and women in business too numerous to mention have kindly shared interests, questions and information.

I am particularly grateful to two scholars who shared unpublished materials with me on the eve of my departure for two years of research in Hong Kong. Jerome Cohen gave me a copy of the teaching materials he was using in his first course on Chinese law at the Harvard Law School, and Ezra Vogel displayed dazzling generosity in throwing open to me his files of interviews with hundreds of former residents of Guangzhou. Thanks to these two, I arrived in Hong Kong much more knowledgeable than I otherwise would have been, and my research benefited greatly.

Chinese who have taught me much about their country are Cao Jiarui, Dong Shizhong, Fu Hualing, Jiang Ping, Sun Jianyi, Wang Chenguang, and Ye Lin. I have benefited greatly from the scholarship of He Weifang, and Liu Hainian and his colleagues at the Institute of Law of the Chinese Academy of Social Sciences in Beijing have been generous with their time and insights. A number of Chinese judges and lawyers were kind enough to speak with me in confidence about a wide range of matters relating to the Chinese courts and Chinese law in general.

In addition to the scholars of Chinese law, Western and Chinese, whom I have thanked personally here, I owe great debts to many others, named in the bibliography and notes, whose published research has been indispensable in the course of my research. When I began the study of Chinese law, there were very few Western scholars in the field. Although the field still remains underpopulated, the scholars who have been active in it have produced a considerable body of scholarly literature that helps to illuminate a most disorderly frontier of legal knowledge. The frequency with which I have cited their work testifies to my gratitude for the insights that they have provided.

I owe special thanks to William Alford, R. Randle Edwards, James V. Feinerman, Randall Peerenboom, John Stuart Service, and Madeleine Zelin, who read all or part of the manuscript of this book.

Throughout my research and writing I was assisted by a succession of dedicated research assistants to whom I am grateful for their help and their patience with my disorganization—David Bachman, Kate Sears, and Joanne Tan during the 1980s, more recently Joshua Guo for five years at two law firms and, in 1996–1999, three graduate students at the University of California at Berkeley, Peter Gries, Imre Galambos, and Jay Dautcher. Jay gave me extraordinary support with his impressive language and research skills and his organizational abilities, first during a six-month period of intensive effort in 1996–1997 when I finished a first draft, and thereafter during its revision. Anne Banks and Jenny Starr cheerfully provided expert secretarial assistance.

I am grateful to Muriel Bell, whose interest in Chinese law made Stanford University Press a natural home for this book, and to Stacey Lynn for shepherding it through the publication process. I am pleased also to thank the law firms at which I have specialized on China and which encouraged my scholarly activities, Heller, Ehrman, White & McAuliffe and Thelen, Marrin, Johnson & Bridges in San Francisco, and Allen & Overy in London, Hong Kong, and Beijing.

Students over the years at all of the institutions at which I have taught have been an endless source of stimulation in thinking about China. I am grateful, too, for support and encouragement of my research and teaching by the Law Schools of Harvard and Stanford universities, and for assistance of the John King Fairbank Center for East Asian Research at Harvard University in gathering research materials (with special thanks to Nancy Hearst of the Center Library), the Center for Chinese Studies of the University of California at Berkeley, where I have been a Research Associate in recent years, and the remarkable staff of the Crown Law Library at the Stanford University Law School.

Special friends, generous in sharing their wisdom about China, have been John and Caroline Service.

My deepest thanks, of course, go to my wife, Judith, and our children, Sarah and James, who have borne and shared the vagaries of a career devoted to understanding China. The extent, constancy, and depth of the support and encouragement that Judith has given me, which include editing the manuscript of this book and taking me dancing, inspire my awed gratitude.

S.B.L.
Berkeley, California
February 1999

Abbreviations Used in the Text

ALL	Administrative Litigation Law
APL	Administrative Punishment Law
BLPC	Basic Level People's Courts
CCP	Chinese Communist Party
CIETAC	China International Economic and Trade Arbitration Commission
CLEEC	Committee on Legal Educational Exchanges with China
CPL	Civil Procedure Law
ECL	Economic Contract Law
EDMC	Economic Dispute Mediation Center
EU	European Union
FDI	Foreign Direct Investment
FECL	Foreign Economic Contract Law
FIE	Foreign Investment Enterprise
GATT	General Agreement on Tariffs and Trade
GPCL	General Principles of Civil Law
HLPC	Higher-Level People's Courts
ILPC	Intermediate-Level People's Courts
MFN	Most Favored Nation
MOFTEC	Ministry of Foreign Trade and Economic Cooperation
NIL	Negotiable Instruments Law
NPC	National People's Congress
OLA	Office of Legislative Affairs of the State Council
PLA	Peoples Liberation Army
PRC	People's Republic of China

RMB	Renminbi, Chinese currency (1 RMB = US$0.1208 [June 1999])
SAIC	State Administration of Industry and Commerce
SCL	State Compensation Law
SEZ	Special Economic Zone
SOE	State-Owned Enterprise
SPC	Supreme People's Court
TVE	Township and Village Enterprise
TVLSO	Township and Village Legal Service Office
WTO	World Trade Organization

Bird in a Cage

LEGAL REFORM IN
CHINA AFTER MAO

CHAPTER 1

Introduction: Understanding China
Through Chinese Law

Purpose of the Book

THIS BOOK seeks to enhance Western understanding of China by studying its contemporary legal institutions. It surveys the Chinese legal reforms fueled by the economic reforms that began in 1979 and focuses on current institutions for resolving disputes.

Studying the links between legal institutions and economic reform in post-Mao China can help us to better understand relations between state and society generally. The institutions studied here are among those that would be most essential in China were the Chinese Communist Party (CCP) and government to separate and the grip of the planned economy to continue to loosen further. From studying how Chinese law works today, we should be able to gain knowledge of China's present and speculate about China's future as well as gain insights that may assist the formation of U.S. policy toward China.

For hundreds of years, Western ideas about law have influenced Western views of China. Both history and today's events suggest the need to understand clearly the operation of Chinese legal institutions, the legal culture that influences them, the policies that are embedded in them, and their functions. Before this century, China seemed to have less law than foreigners thought a country should have. Differing conceptions of law were among the causes of the Opium War, which had disastrous consequences for the Chinese empire.[1] Throughout the second half of the nineteenth century and well into the twentieth, the Western powers and Japan made China agree to enforce foreign laws on Chinese territory and resisted surrendering extraterritorial privileges until China created a legal system satisfactory to them. China's rejection of the use of law as an instrument of governance under Mao contributed to Western disapproval, and today the People's Republic of China (PRC) is often criticized for lacking the rule of law and thereby failing to meet Western standards.

Since 1978, when China's leaders undertook to reform the Chinese economy and "open" the country to the outside world, they have promoted the development of formal legal institutions that would shape newly reformed activities of the Chinese economy and the Chinese state. They had little to work with: Chinese legal institutions had either been largely neglected or politicized by the end of the 1950s, long before the Cultural Revolution. Reform has brought about the creation of legal institutions that depart—at least in theory—from more than thirty years of well-established Maoist practice. Although Deng Xiaoping launched legal as well as economic reform, he also placed limits on reform that remained firmly in place on the eve of the millenium. The contradiction is expressed in the metaphor that has been used as the title of this book, an expression originally coined in 1982 by one of China's senior economists at the time, Chen Yun, to express his distrust for market forces when the economic reforms began,[2] but apt for Chinese law today. The economic bird has already escaped from its cage, the economic plan, but the legal bird remains in its own cage, although it is stirring and the dimensions of the cage may be changing.

The accomplishments of the legal reform to date are impressive given the need to overcome the burden of Chinese tradition, thirty years of Maoism, and the hostility of the institutional environment in which reform must take place. Law has gained more importance than it has ever possessed in Chinese history. China's emergent legal institutions have begun to define and protect expectations arising out of economic transactions among Chinese citizens, to settle an increasing number of disputes among them, and to generate new conceptions of legal rights. A complex legal framework for foreign trade and investment in China has also been created and continues to grow. However, given the novelty of the legal institutions created or revived since the late 1970s, it is no wonder that their development has been limited, hesitant, and uncertain.

This book assesses the achievements of the legal reforms, but also suggests the constraints on their scope and future development. Many of the problems they face stem from the ideology and organization of the Chinese Party-state, that hybrid in which the apparatuses of the CCP and government are entwined. Serious constraints on effectiveness arise out of the Party's determination to retain political control. The avowed policy of increasing legality has not been carried out firmly and consistently; law and the courts are still expected to be secondary to Party policy. The local Party-state seriously influences the day-to-day work of the courts.

The dictates of ideology are manifested in limits on the power of the courts. One of the most striking defects of legal reform is the failure to raise the position of the judicial system from its current level; it remains at the same level as other bureaucratic hierarchies of the state and lacks authority over them. The courts, as we will see, are severely restricted in interpreting legislation and administrative rules and decisions. Because of the lack of a unifying concept of law, and even more so because of the fragmentation of authority that marks China today, I have nowhere in this book referred to a Chinese legal *system*, only to Chinese legal institutions.

Both the Chinese state and Chinese society create difficulties for the courts. Economic reform has considerably weakened the central government's control over localities, and new configurations of power are appearing that are based on growing webs of relationships between local businesses and local governments. Critical problems for the courts arise out of the strong hold exercised by local governments, which are responsible for their budgets. These relationships, centering on personal ties and reciprocal exchanges of favors and benefits, weaken the force and impact of legal rules. Also, China is presently undergoing a crisis of belief in an ideology that has become irrelevant and in a Party whose legitimacy is in doubt. These symptoms of decay limit the effectiveness of the new legal rules and institutions.

The reforms have generated an enormous volume of Chinese legislation since 1979 and created a wide range of legal institutions, all of which cannot be studied in one volume. Some institutions are so new that little is known about their operation in practice. Some, such as China's emerging capital markets, are incomplete and in flux. Others, such as large state-owned enterprises, have for years posed increasingly worsening problems while policy on their future is debated. Further complicating the choice of institutions on which to focus—and the clarity with which they can be seen—is the pace of recent Chinese economic growth and the speed of the social change that whirls around the new legal institutions.

My principal emphasis in this book is on institutions for settling disputes among Chinese, which include informal neighborhood mediation, arbitration, and adjudication in the revived courts. The courts are resolving millions of non-criminal matters yearly, and this book gives them close attention from a variety of perspectives. Because the criminal process is still in the grip of CCP authoritarianism, I do not study criminal law and procedure closely, although in noting recent reforms I do address some of the principal defects in the criminal process that reforms have not remedied and that have implications for other institutions.

I have been concerned with identifying the principal influences that shape the new Chinese legal institutions, which simultaneously bear the imprint of values and institutions flowing from Chinese tradition, the Chinese revolution, Maoism, and the reformist aftermath that began in the late 1970s. Attempting to capture the imprint of history on China can be a truly dismaying enterprise. The history is long; the languages are difficult; the cultural distances between Westerners and Chinese are vast and their perspectives on each other are complex.

To make matters more difficult, the view changes constantly. Beginning with the mid-nineteenth century, China's long-lived institutions were subjected to a stream of powerful Western influences that brought about unprecedented change. The entire second half of the twentieth century has been marked by the transformations brought about by the CCP. The intensity and depth of those changes have obscured the configuration of the former institutions, making it all the more difficult to perceive continuities and breaks between them and their successors. As hazardous as the enterprise might be, I have sometimes sought to identify influences on the operation of legal institutions that seem to stem from roots in the pre-Communist past, as well as others traceable to the organization and dynamics of the modern Party-state.

The Maoist prologue to reform is especially important. Before the advent of reform, Maoist mobilizational tactics and a complex bureaucracy had been used to govern the Chinese Party-state, and legal institutions had been both few and symbolic. Precursors or outlines of many of the legal institutions that have recently been strengthened or created had existed previously, but attempts to make them meaningful during the previous thirty years were weak and sporadic. This study probes the continued influence of Maoism and Maoist approaches to governance on the operation and effectiveness of the new legal institutions in the Party-state.

If my concerns were only with the rules and doctrines of Chinese law, my study would be hollow, because the realities of Chinese politics still permit law to play only a secondary role in the governance of China. But the institutions studied here have a larger potential significance. They have remained in place despite the grim events around Tiananmen Square in June 1989 and despite the tenacity with which the CCP has refused to surrender any political power. The years immediately following the suppression of the "democracy movement" have demonstrated that reform cannot be undone and that pressure throughout Chinese society for further reform is strong.

Chinese reforms, economic and legal, have begun to do nothing less than redefine basic relationships among state, economy, and society. Some institutions that exercise governmental power operate in a realm considered, at least by some, to be a legal realm. Their mere existence is significant, but more so is the life that some of them are beginning to acquire.

Once in place the new legal institutions help to shape, and are acted on by, the perceptions and values of officials and the general population. The doctrine that the current leadership espouses, which urges replacement of the "rule of man" by the "rule of law," implies that the relations between state and Party must change and that the CCP must surrender at least some of its authority to law. Whether that transformation can occur and, if so, how, is at the moment unclear.

The crushing of the "democracy movement" in China and the subsequent groping in the United States for clear and consistent U.S. policies toward China dramatize the challenges presented by law reform, not only to China but also to Western understanding of China. Those challenges, which would have existed even if the bright spring of 1989 had ended in a more benign summer, are clear. The sharp swings in American popular attitudes toward China that have marked Sino-American relations for more than a century continued in the 1980s. American views of China, in particular, have been marked in the past by high expectations that the Chinese would become more like us, and by great disappointment when that has not happened.[3]

Although the 1990s have not seen similar swings between euphoria and disappointment, American policy toward China has been uneven and confused. Conflicting impulses in American foreign policy prompt some Americans to become judges of the progress of Chinese reform. Economic forces impel us to engage China benignly while only gently nudging China in the direction of greater legality. Moral forces, exhibiting the blend of legalism and moralism that has long marked American foreign policy, urge protest against the injustices of one-party authoritarian rule. Ideas about law have influenced both varieties of sentiments. Among domestic political consequences in the United States have been acrimonious debates over economic sanctions that, originating at various times in the White House or Congress, are intended to punish or reward the PRC on the basis of its attachment to the rule of law, including but not limited to Western concepts of human rights. In October 1997, U.S. policy took a constructive turn when presidents Jiang Zemin and Bill Clinton signed an agreement to promote legal exchanges in six areas of concern[4]—although in 1998 Congress refused to appropriate funds needed to support the exchanges. In the light of what we know about Chinese law reforms, it is appropriate and necessary to reexamine the expectations that Americans and other foreigners entertain when they ask questions about Chinese law and the future of the Chinese polity. By reflecting on the state of Chinese law, Americans may be able to broaden their own perspectives on China.

These, then, are some of the problems that Chinese law presents to Western observers, and which I have attempted to address in this book.

Overview of the Book

In chapter 2, I address the problems of perspective that confront Westerners studying Chinese law by considering the very different paths of legal development in China and the West before the twentieth century. I stress that the West's characteristic emphases on rights and on the ideal of an autonomous legal system are historically contingent and unmatched by similar concepts in Chinese history. After introducing the different legal traditions, I then articulate the approach I have followed, which regards the rule of law as a basic source of perspective, supplemented by emphasis on studying legal institutions in terms of their intended and latent functions and the legal culture that conditions their operation. It is too early in the period of post-Mao Chinese legal development to attempt to formulate any broader theory.

In chapters 3 and 4, I address the Maoist precursors of the institutions of post-reform China. China's economic reform since 1980 has so impressed the West that the three previous decades of PRC history have often been ignored. That history, together with traditional influences antedating it, shaped policies and practices before post-reform institutions took on their current configuration and continues to shape them today. Chapter 3 is a condensed version of "Mao and Mediation," a study that I published thirty years ago of mediational dispute resolution before the Cultural Revolution. It traces the origins of the post-1949 insistence on mediation as the principal means of resolving disputes and examines the practice of mediation by political activists. It compares the functions of Maoist and traditional mediation and finds that the Maoist variety succeeded in politicizing dispute settlement and in suppressing rather than resolving disputes, but that the traditional preferences for compromise solutions survived.

Chapter 4 condenses two essays that were published in 1969 and 1970, respectively, and addresses characteristics of the Maoist institutions that linger in the face of reform, in particular the refusal to acknowledge any functional differentiation between law and administration. The first, on the criminal process before the Cultural Revolution, found two rival models of that process, one stressing obedience to policy and to the Party and the other emphasizing a professionally bureaucratized administration of the criminal process; the conflict between the two still continues. The second essay described the politicization of civil law in practice and in theory before the Cultural Revolution and the resulting conversion of civil law concepts and contracts into administrative devices. Traces of pre-reform practice and the impetus to control transactions, rather than create a framework within which they might thrive unregulated, survive today.

Depiction of the earlier state of civil law also provides an idea of the doctrinal starting point at which China had to begin when legal reforms were undertaken.

Chapter 5 turns to the present: I first summarize the essential elements of the economic reforms that created the need for legal reform. I then note changes in relations between state and society and in values among the populace that seem critically significant for current and future legal development. Against this background chapter 5 then examines CCP policy toward law, emphasizing the inescapable contradiction between the avowed goal of attaining the rule of law and the ideological limits that Deng Xiaoping set on attempts to reach that goal, which his successors have maintained.

Chapter 6 moves from policy to examine the building of basic institutions. First discussed is a fundamental change in 1979 that prepared the way for other legal reforms, the decision to legalize governance by using legislation rather than policy statements as the basic sources of rules. Chinese legislative practice under reform is then examined. It is found to be in remarkable disorder, marked by the failure of central agencies to interpret legislation and administrative rules and by the continued use of broadly drafted wording that leaves wide scope for bureaucratic discretion. Institution building is then further addressed in a summary of the reestablishment of the bar and legal education, which serves as a preliminary to later discussion of dispute resolution. It continues the survey by examining the criminal process. Although, as already noted, this book does not focus on criminal law or procedure, regularization of the criminal process is part of the foundation for other law reform. Discussed here are the continued close links between the criminal process to policy and to policy-dictated campaigns against crime, recent reforms in criminal procedure, and the continued use of extensive police power to inflict serious sanctions without participation by the courts.

Chapter 7 reviews legislation that has created legal institutions in three important areas. One is the framework for commercial transactions in the nonstate sector, even while legality is lacking in the still-substantial state sector. I then assess the environment for foreign direct investment by placing the legal framework in the context of administrative practice and the investment contracts negotiated by foreigners and their Chinese partners. Although this book is not directly concerned with foreign investment, that area of activity affords excellent examples of the accomplishments and problems of legal reform all over China. Finally, because the vast discretion of Chinese officials hangs over all transactions whether they involve only Chinese or foreigners as well, the chapter concludes with a summary of efforts to control bureaucratic discretion using nascent administrative laws.

In chapters 8 and 9, I study the contemporary institutions for settling disputes among Chinese. Chapter 8 looks closely at the fate of extra-judicial "people's" mediation, a near-monopoly under Mao, as other institutions have been revived or created to address the growing number of civil and economic disputes. Now much less politicized than it was previously, its functions are both blurred and changing. The number of cases handled by mediation committees has declined, and more civil and economic cases are being brought to the courts. But mediation continues to be supported both by the leadership and by Chinese legal culture. The leadership is reluctant to abandon mediation because it augments strained judicial resources and is seen as a means of preventing social disorder and crime by using activists, especially in rural villages, to identify and defuse potentially violent situations. Mediation also continues to reflect traditional legal culture, with its emphasis on compromising to resolve differences and restoring ruptured relationships rather than on legalities.

Chapter 9 is devoted to the increasingly busy Chinese courts. Decision-making processes at the trial level and in higher courts are examined, including mediation in the courts, which is still used to conclude more cases than adjudication. The responsiveness of the courts to policy is considered: As in Mao's time, the courts are supposed to be obedient agents of national policies, although politicization in non-criminal matters is less intense and is indeed weaker. The formidable power of localism has been emphasized: Although the formal table of organization of the judicial system is a neat pyramid topped by the Supreme People's Court (SPC) in Beijing, in fact courts are funded and judges appointed by local people's governments. As a consequence, judges are exposed to heavy local pressures that threaten the efficacy of the courts and the coherence of Chinese law.

The chapter examines tensions in the sources of the rules that the courts apply in specific cases. Courts are forbidden to interpret the general validity of legislation or administrative rules and, moreover, must defer to administrative agencies' interpretations of their own rules. At the same time, the Supreme People's Court is engaged in a creative law-making process, despite Constitutional prohibitions against it, by issuing interpretations of national legislation that are binding on the lower courts and circulating judicial decisions chosen to provide "guidance" to the courts. Chapter 9 also looks at some reported decisions in economic and civil disputes for an indication of how rights are asserted and vindicated. The educational level and professional outlook of judges are appraised. Although propaganda still celebrates the judge in the manner that revolutionary cadres were hailed under Mao, interviews with judges, especially younger ones with good legal educations, offer evidence of a rising professional consciousness among some judges. The chapter concludes that judicial decision-making seems to more closely resemble a bureaucratic process than adjudication in the West.

Chapter 10 concludes the book with a discussion of the likely development of Chinese legal institutions in the light of constraints imposed by tradition, by the Maoist past, and by values and institutions newly generated by economic reform. Although economic reform cannot be turned back and legal reform has acquired a perceptible momentum of its own, the future of the rule of law remains highly problematic in China, at least in the short term, partially because the strength of particularistic relationships in the nonstate sector threatens to slow progress toward greater legality.

Chapter 10 also raises the possibility that despite the obstacles, the rule of law could itself become an increasingly appealing alternative ideology to many Chinese as Communist ideology becomes ever more irrelevant and the legitimacy of the CCP weakens. A rising consciousness of law and of the promise of law to limit and control administrative arbitrariness, now promoted as Party policy, has begun to appear among the Chinese people, and it may continue to grow.

I end chapter 10 by reviewing some of the implications of legal reforms for American perceptions of China and policy toward China. If my assessment of the current state of Chinese law and the probable future of Chinese legal institutions is accurate, the United States is likely to continue for some time to face a government and a political system that most Americans will find unattractive, and with only weak legal institutions. Yet the United States and China are inextricably linked, because of growing mutual economic dependence and the shared need to address trade, security, the environment, and a host of other issues, some of which will emerge as China increasingly demands to be treated as a great power. The view of Chinese legal development presented here suggests that the United States should reappraise the tone and aggressiveness of American insistence on rights-based solutions to problems that trouble Sino-American relations. At the same time, a centerpiece of U.S. policy should be to hold the PRC to performance of its international obligations.

Finally, chapter 10 envisions the possibility that China may become obligated to maintain its legal institutions according to standards set, at least generally, by international treaty. The General Agreement on Tariffs and Trade (GATT) requires member nations to promote transparency by the way they publish, interpret, and apply their laws, and this study of China suggests that the PRC is far from meeting the most minimal standards under the GATT. The requirements that China would have to meet as a member of the World Trade Organization (WTO), which implements the GATT, will have to be the outcome of negotiation, because the GATT does not spell out the standards in detail. Regardless of what is agreed, after China joins the WTO its compliance is still sure to raise problems. The issue here is not the terms of China's accession, but the likely consequences if the PRC fails to adhere to requirements to which it agreed upon becoming a member. In the future, China's legal institutions may come to be more of an international concern than at present, which is all the more reason why they ought to be better understood now.

CHAPTER 2

Eye at the Telescope or Face in the Mirror?
Approaching Chinese Law

Seen from China, the political history of the West appears altogether original, and one might even say exotic . . . not only are
the institutions, with their particular mechanisms, different, but
our notions, our patterns of thought, and even the idea of man
which we have forged in the course of our historical experience differ from those of China.[1]

CONTEMPORARY Chinese legal institutions must be understood against a
background of traditions and ways of thought that long antedate the People's Republic and markedly differ from their Western counterparts. The
rule of law was alien and unknown throughout thousands of years of authoritarian rule. Concepts central to both contemporary Chinese and
Western law, such as the creation of rights and the use of formal legal institutions to vindicate rights, were unknown in traditional Chinese law.
Certain claims were enforced by private groupings and supported only
indirectly, if at all, by legislation and by the apparatus of the state.

Analyzing the impact of Chinese culture on Chinese legal development from a Western perspective raises basic questions about the perspective itself. Among the most distinctive differences over the centuries between Chinese and Western history, thought, and culture is the manner in
which the two characterized the functions that in the West are performed
by legal institutions. The domain of activity that is regarded as "legal" and
the way it is differentiated from other domains are unique products of
Western history. The Chinese institutions that managed state-society relations and social conflict reflect very different perceptions. The differences shape both the questions that Westerners ask about Chinese legal institutions and practice and Westerners' interpretations of the answers.

This chapter approaches the study of Chinese legal institutions by emphasizing some of the principal differences between the two legal tradi-

tions, especially with regard to the concepts of rights and to the use of formal legal institutions to vindicate rights. It then presents my own perspectives on modern Chinese law, offering them tentatively and aiming at no grander result than providing background for, and orientation toward, understanding contemporary Chinese law without skewing inquiry either by insisting on adhering to Western models or by totally accepting Chinese concepts.

The Face in the Mirror? Studying Traditional Chinese Law

China is so distant, culturally as well geographically, that the metaphor of gazing outward through a telescope seems natural. Unless we focus well, however, another metaphor may better describe what takes place: If our gaze searches for what our preconceptions suggest we should find, we may see only Others, who are reverse images of ourselves.[2] As Westerners, our own assumptions about the nature of law, its historical development, and its impact on relationships among the state, society, and the individual uncritically shape our observations about Chinese law. This would be true of any comparative legal study, but the difficulties increase as the cultural distance between the observer and the system being studied widens. Chinese and Western legal institutions sometimes appear so disparate that comparing them "seems hardly appropriate."[3]

Law, of all the disciplines that can be used in the West to study China, seems the most difficult for Westerners to use meaningfully because it is so rooted in Western values. Legal institutions are so powerful and visible in contemporary Western societies, so rooted in local cultural values, that Western scholars and policy-makers often assume their universality and use them as standards in understanding non-Western legal institutions. Witness, for example, U.S. rhetoric in the mid-1990s on China's failure to raise the level of protection to intellectual property and American assumptions that Western intellectual property law is "normal" and must provide the measure of Chinese practice.[4]

Because of the great danger of unthinkingly accepting Western preconceptions when studying Chinese law, we must examine these preconceptions carefully. Views about the nature of law held by lawyers, legal scholars, social scientists, and the general population are diverse and sometimes contradictory. The spectrum extends from orientations that emphasize legal rules—as if law were completely autonomous from society—to those that look at "social and legal forces that, in some way, press in and make 'the law'."[5] I have tried to include those historical-cultural or contemporary forces in Chinese society that seem to exert a powerful influence over the operation of legal institutions.

In the face of the complexity and power of Western assumptions about law, where do we begin? History seems a helpful muse. The credo of the greatest historian of English law was that "history involves comparison,"[6] but the reverse seems equally true. We begin by considering the historical background of Chinese and Western law. Our discussion will juxtapose some principal characteristics of Chinese and Western legal history, grouped around six clusters of concepts, in order to underscore the differences and the surprising commonalities. Recent scholarship suggests that some of the differences are not as stark as they had seemed, and the juxtaposition of the two systems suggests that both depend on historical contingencies.

RELATIONS AMONG LAW, PHILOSOPHY, AND RELIGION

The West: Early Differentiation Among Law, Custom, Religion, and Morality

In Europe up until the eleventh century, custom, religion, and morality were blended.[7] Practices, rules, and procedures were embedded in the society and were not treated as belonging to an autonomous and specialized sphere of "legal" activity that was differentiated from other social spheres. In the eleventh century "the old symbiosis of religious and secular authorities was seriously weakened."[8] A struggle between Pope and king over appointments to church offices, known as the Investiture Controversy, ended with reciprocal acknowledgments. The Pope would not share responsibility for the governance and guidance of the Church, and the king would retain "the duty of secular rulers to see that justice was dispensed to the people,"[9] even if the Church still defined justice.

The early separation of secular and sacred authority in Europe gave impetus to the notions that the state was founded on law and that the ruler was bound morally and often politically by it. The separation from the state's domain of matters of "creed and cult" is the basis of today's distinction between state and society.[10]

China: Dependence of Law on a State Cult

Traditional China, by contrast, was characterized throughout its history by a remarkably close and enduring relationship between the state and the dominant cult and philosophy of Confucianism.[11] Confucianism postulated the existence of a harmony extending throughout heaven and earth, which manifested itself in a hierarchical order that began with the emperor and extended downward to the lowest level of society. The aim of government, and indeed of all human relations, was to preserve natural harmony through the promotion of ethical behavior.

In the traditional Chinese view, government was best conducted by men who behaved like the ancient sages and set high moral examples for their subjects to follow. Law was but one set of norms and was inferior to principles of nature, heavenly reason, religious canons, ethics, and rules of propriety.[12] Primary ethical rules lay in the *li*, a variety of moral and customary principles for ceremonial or polite behavior, differentiated according to status as determined by age and rank in family and society.[13] As William Alford has written, "Public, positive law was meant to buttress, rather than supersede, the more desirable means of guiding society and was to be resorted to only when these other means failed to elicit appropriate behavior."[14] In this scheme, the law "loses its independent existence," as one contemporary Chinese scholar has put it, because "law no longer has boundaries distinct from moral demands, such as ceremony and ethics, and thus is combined conceptually with them."[15] The divergence from Western doctrine can be seen in the absence of any bar on retroactive criminal legislation. Since the legislation was believed to implement higher laws according to which all human behavior was to be judged, a law was only "a revelation of a higher norm which has been in existence since an infinitely earlier time,"[16] thus raising no problem of retroactivity when the imperial law codes were periodically revised.[17]

STATE AND SOCIETY: HIERARCHY
AND LIMITATIONS ON STATE POWER

The West: Rights-Based Limitations on Power of the Sovereign

Western legal development was shaped first by feudalism and thereafter, beginning in the twelfth century, by the nation-state. Some aspects of feudalism, which influenced the later development of natural law theory, assumed great importance in Western political and legal thought. Although the mutual bonds of lord and vassal were unequal, they did involve a limitation of the lord's power. Grants of rights over land and population carried with them the notion of the vassal's immunity from assertions of power by the lord in violation of their agreement. This was true even though most of the population of Europe had no voice in these matters and were regarded by the parties to the feudal relationship "essentially as the objects of rule, and occasionally and incidentally as the beneficiaries of rule, but never as the subjects of a political relationship."[18]

The emergence of powerful kings brought with it the problem of defining limits on kingly power. An external standard of justice had been regarded as a limit on royal power, and from the Greco-Roman tradition came concepts of natural law, which became divine law in Church doctrine. As early as the thirteenth century the notion of the social compact was advanced, which conceived of government as founded on a contract among men who, formerly having no government, had chosen one. Later, as a result of the Reformation and the Renaissance, the intellectual authority of reason was substituted for the spiritual authority of divine law.[19] As Unger has pointed out, the growing social pluralism of Europe came together with a belief in higher law derived from religion, displacing natural law with the notion of natural rights. These rights were conceived of as "powers of the individual to act within a sphere of absolute discretion, rather than as entitlements to definite substantive goods."[20]

Rights-based doctrine eventually created conflicts between different conceptions of law. As their power grew, monarchies began to use law to supplement and then supplant custom so that law was "transformed . . . from a *framework of* into an *instrument for* rule."[21] In contrast, the rising propertied classes based in the towns represented a new political force, outside feudalism, which asserted the rights of the collectivities in which they were based. The crown needed the cooperation of the new classes to govern, and the two often struggled over legal issues such as taxation. The propertied classes insisted on defining and enlarging their privileges by means of law formulated to be general, abstract, and distinguishable from royal administration.[22] The continued assertion of power by the towns led to the establishment of assemblies created to represent aristocracy, clergy, and the towns; the three came to be called generically estates. The system of estates was later to grow into the modern liberal state along two routes, through parliamentarianism (as in England and France) or autocracy (as in Germany).

China: Absence of Rights Under Authoritarian Rule and a Hierarchical Society

Benjamin Schwartz has written that the "centrality and weight of the political order" is "one of the most striking characteristics of Chinese civilization," because in the Chinese conception, public order was ruled by "all encompassing authority"[23] and Chinese political culture was "unambiguously authoritarian and based on a positive evaluation of hierarchy and status."[24] As I have already noted, Confucianism emphasized moral authority. Legalism, the philosophical school that rivaled it briefly, regarded *li* and all ethical principles as irrelevant to government and stressed the need for harsh penalties that would use law (*fa*) to deter wrongdoing. The Confucians viewed *fa* as a clumsy system of punishments directed only at strengthening the state that lacked proper regard for "an ordered world of peace, harmony and simple contentment," and the cultivation of the individual.[25] However, both schools shared a vision of society in which individual lives were led within hierarchies and social distinctions and proper behavior derived from an individual's status in those hierarchies.

Codified law in traditional China, which was principally penal and represented a synthesis of the two schools, emphasized the supremacy of the hierarchy over the individual.[26] It reinforced the state philosophy of Confucianism and the hierarchical social order that that philosophy served to justify. Three basic relationships—between emperor and subject, parents and children, and husband and wife—reflected the status relationships that defined modes of proper conduct. For example, the punishments prescribed by the criminal code for murder varied according to the difference in status between murderer and victim. In all societies, law reflects and supports dominant ideological and ethical systems, but the extent to which traditional Chinese law unambiguously reinforced ideas of hierarchy and subordination made it arguably unique, especially by contrast to modern Western legal systems that insist on formal equality.

As absolute as the power of the emperor appeared to be in theory, it was limited in practice by the thinness of the imperial resources available to govern a country as immense as China. The Chinese state never penetrated Chinese society to the same degree as royal power did in England and France, and much rule was exercised indirectly through local élites. Limitations on the power of the state to administer justice have existed in every society, and the Chinese response to the problem, which endured for centuries, should be understood in contrast to the West. Before I discuss the operation of law in the Qing dynasty, China's last (1644–1911), a brief excursus is necessary on the importance of the social structure of China.[27]

In traditional China a great gulf divided state and society. The formal apparatus of government extended downward from the emperor in Beijing through provinces and smaller subdivisions to some 1,200 counties, the lowest governmental subdivisions, each with between 100,000 and 250,000 inhabitants.[28] A magistrate presided over each county, directing and controlling all functions of government within his jurisdiction. Magistrates, untrained in administration, joined the élite by passing literary examinations on the Confucian classics, which tested a candidate to determine if he "possessed the ways of thought suitable to a cultured man and resulting from cultivation in literature."[29] Over the centuries, magistrates came to acquire a considerable number of clerks and other assistants, who supplied the *main d'oeuvre* of government.[30]

Magistrates' power was buttressed by the local gentry, who had passed the same examinations as the magistrates although they held no office.[31] Gentry families commanded great respect among the commoners. They also enjoyed privileges under the imperial codes such as reduced liability for taxes and immunity from certain kinds of punishment and obligations. The gentry acted as intermediaries between officialdom and the common people. Officials often needed their assistance in governing, and the gentry often needed the magistrates to maintain their prestige. In addition, the gentry also had personal and local interests to protect and sometimes resisted officials on such issues as taxation.[32]

A small but significant quantum of power over China's peasantry was exercised by rural headmen and village leaders appointed by the magistrate. Other informal leaders were respected for their age, learning, and reputation for probity or were feared for their aggressiveness and unscrupulousness.[33]

The basic unit of traditional Chinese society was not the individual, but the collectivity. Family, clan, village, gentry, and officials dominated the individual. Most basic of all was the family, whose rules of customary behavior emphasized the precedence and authority of older over younger generations. Families were themselves organized into clans, which instructed members on Confucian morality,[34] assisted poor and aged members, maintained schools and ancestral halls, and settled disputes among members.[35] Another collective grouping was the guild, an organization of merchants or artisans in the same trade or craft. Guilds controlled prices, competition, training, and access to local markets. They also engaged in some charitable ventures and represented common commercial interests in dealing with government officials.[36]

The society had a "vast substratum of heterogeneous local communities based on a morally oriented social order and the informal primary group"[37] in addition to a national bureaucratic apparatus that emphasized centralization and an organized hierarchy of authority. Confucian ideology was one of the elements that held state and society together. The state had to rely on the gentry, family heads, and village elders to enforce local customs, whereas in the West these tasks were transferred over the centuries to courts applying rules of civil law.[38]

It is striking that the Chinese tradition did not address the problem of imperial or bureaucratic power in terms of individual rights. Imperial power was theoretically limited by certain important doctrines.[39] The emperor was obligated to carry out the requirements of the cosmic order, which were set down in the classics, and he could be admonished by officials for violating traditional norms.[40] Intricate codes governed bureaucratic behavior and prescribed punishments for violations, with the aim of maintaining clarity and consistency in the laws and accountability of officials; their incorrect decisions were punishable.[41] In practice, though, "in traditional China the limits of authority were not strictly defined, but the duty to obey authority was."[42]

The extent to which Chinese and Western political traditions differed is illustrated by noting that since the beginning of the twentieth century, every document of a constitutional nature proposed or adopted in China has consistently treated rights as *contingent*. Common to all of them, Andrew Nathan has observed, are the ideas that "rights are granted by the state and can be changed by the state; rights are goals to be reached rather than prerogatives of personhood; and government can limit rights by legislation, and is not itself restrained by law."[43] He adds that the treatment of rights in Chinese constitutions of the twentieth century expresses a "philosophy of law as the state's will and rights as the state's creation" by emphasizing the following:

First, if rights are created by the state, it is reasonable for rights provisions to be programmatic. . . . Second, it is reasonable for the state to grant rights only to those who are friendly or loyal to it or who are its 'members,' and to deprive of rights those who are hostile to its purposes. . . . Third, since the state creates rights it is reasonable that it have full powers to restrict them, so long as it does so in the same way that it grants them—by legislative enactment. . . . Fourth, since the state acts legitimately when it restricts rights by law, no law can be invalid because it restricts rights, and no procedure is needed to determine whether particular laws do violate rights.[44]

Long-standing Chinese views on the relationship between the state and the people reflected the subordination of the individual to the collective, which can be seen also in the way economic and interpersonal conflicts among Chinese, not involving the state and its representatives, were handled. I explore this point below.

RIGHTS AND THEIR ANALOGUES

The West: Rights, Choice, and Facilitative Law

In England and Europe, rights-based theory maintained a sphere within which individual activity was protected from the power of the sovereign and rested on an individualism that is characteristic of the West. As one scholar has said, "reduced to its essential elements, the modern state rests on the authority of law, and law rests on the authority of personal choice."[45] Western culture exalts the personal autonomy of the individual, emphasizing choice, consent, and contract. The relationship between rights based on choice and legal rules established by the state becomes apparent when law, in addition to limiting state power, is used to protect economic activity. Law is a set of institutions for allocating rewards and punishments, sometimes directly, but also indirectly, when it "sustains, defines and limits the area in which the free market operates,"[46] as in facilitating private arrangements such as contracts. In this way it functions as "a living process of allocating rights and duties and thereby resolving conflicts and creating channels of cooperation."[47]

The West: Modernity and Limitations on Rights

It is important to recall that although rights-based theory is at the core of Western political and legal traditions and derives from Greek and Roman philosophy, it arose late in Western history. It was, moreover, soon modified by notions of social duty,[48] and law began moving toward the limitation of private rights in contracts; property, and the relations between master and servant. In the late nineteenth century, all Western legal systems began to undergo fundamental changes that were accelerated in the twentieth. Legislation proliferated over new areas of concern, and statutes became the primary source of law as they had not previously been in the common law countries. Legislation became much more detailed and specific than the general principles laid down in traditional codes. Since the nineteenth century, administrative law has grown enormously and has, in fact, become the source of the laws that most directly affect ordinary people.[49] However, despite these transformations, the notion of individual rights remains central in defining the relationship between the citizen and the state.

China: Relationships Rather than Rights

If we look for rights in Chinese tradition, we encounter the most striking difference between Chinese and Western thought and institutions. Western thought makes the individual the bearer of rights and bases rights on the fundamental dignity and equality of every being. There were no such concepts in Chinese thought, and in the Confucian view "identity constantly changes, varying with the context; duties and, correspondingly, rights/rites are also constantly being redefined as other actors change."[50] In China, rights and duties are contextual, depending on the relationship of individuals to each other, and each conflict must be addressed in terms of the alternative consequences with a view to finding a basis for cooperation and harmony.[51] Negotiation and compromise are preferable to insistence on one's own rights. We should recall that the goal of the penal law was to express rules that would uphold the moral values embedded in relationships and the ideals toward which society should aim, and would thereby preserve social harmony.[52]

These philosophical concepts were reflected in the realities of daily life. A paucity of rules in the law codes pertained to commerce, because the codes focused on punishment and governmental resources were limited.

Economic transactions arose and were enforced largely in the context of familial and other custom-governed relationships. There were, however, many customary rules rich in detail that have largely been ignored by Western students. Compilations of local customs were prepared by the Japanese colonial government on Taiwan in the early twentieth century and later by the Republican government on the mainland.[53] The body of customs, full of detailed rules, was extensive, concerned with practicalities and different from the abstraction associated with the German and French reception of Roman law.[54]

Research on the Chinese economy in the Qing dynasty has yielded evidence of an extensive volume of commercial transactions that were made within the framework of customary rules. For example, households contracted with each other to lease or transfer land, or to pool assets in order to start a business. Often the agreements were written, negotiated through a middleman, and required eye-witnesses.[55] Transactions were also carried on not just within villages but also at longer range—between Taiwan and the mainland, for instance—often involving merchant guilds.[56] Customary rules evolved to handle problems such as the risk of loss after goods had been sold but before they were delivered, the rights of third parties, the buyer's duty to inspect, and other issues that are fundamental concerns of the conventional Western law of sales. The rules were simple—risk passed with possession, payment was made at delivery, and a strict right of inspection was enforced on buyers. Mechanisms of self-enforcement were employed, including reliance on receipts, adherence to established forms, strict inspection requirements, partial performance by payment of large deposits, and requirements of simultaneous performance. In some contracts, particularly for loans of money, third-party guarantors were used.

In traditional China, as in all traditional societies, commercial transactions were frequently entwined with noncommercial relationships, and both were distant from the mechanisms of the state. The transaction known as *dian*, a transfer of land by the landowner in return for a cash loan, is an illustration.[57] The lender received the full possession and use of the land, but not ownership, and the borrower reserved the right to redeem the land. Throughout most of Chinese history, *dian* transactions were unregulated by law. Indeed, *dian* arose by custom, in response to a long-standing prohibition against full alienation of land, which would have violated the obligation to pass land on to the owner's descendants. The transaction was not a mortgage, because the land was not security for the loan, there was no absolute obligation to repay, and the borrower did not pay interest. For the first time, Qing law required registration of *dian* transactions, imposed a ten-year maximum on the duration of the transaction, and provided for the right of redemption to lapse if not exercised within thirty years of the original transaction. Up until the Republican period, the land could be redeemed, in practice, at any time. In *dian* practice, as elsewhere, clan and customary rules were more influential than legislative rules or governmental regulation. The land could not be the subject of the transaction without the consent of family members, because it was jointly owned. Certain family members also had rights to the land, further limiting its alienability. As a result, "transfers such as the *dian* transaction greatly increased the difficulty of conducting property transactions; instead of a simple, decisive business deal between seller and purchaser, they were bound up in an ongoing arrangement which could continue for decades."[58]

Customary rules and family relations did not forbid commercial transactions, of course, but—in the absence of the kinds of claims that in the West are classified as rights—they did shape them. The Chinese analogues might usefully be considered *claims that were grounded in relationships*, whether familial, communal, or commercial. They were not defined in objective rules promulgated by the state (despite the existence of the fragmentary legislation noted above), and they were not ordinarily vindicated by agencies of the state. Rights in the West, in contrast to grounded claims in China, were theoretically, but not always, more secure, and the outcomes of disputes over rights arising out of commercial transactions in the West were, in theory, less dependent upon the personal relationships among the disputants and the persons involved in settling the disputes.

We move now to dispute resolution, and the contrast between Chinese and Western institutions that has often impressed Western observers, especially lawyers.

STATE POWER AND INSTITUTIONS FOR DISPUTE RESOLUTION: DELEGATION OF STATE AUTHORITY

The West: The Evolution of Courts as Instruments of Royal Power

The centralized legal systems that characterized post-feudal Europe arose from the expansion of royal judicial systems, enlarged by kings eager to expand royal power and increase royal revenues. England's was the first to develop. The unification of the English state in the tenth and eleventh centuries created the political foundation for construction of the Common Law,[59] but even before the Norman Conquest England's territorial organization and national unity had been greater than that of any European state.[60] England's small size, then, was an important factor: "An active king could visit most parts of his realm with some regularity."[61] The expansion of royal jurisdiction also occurred before medieval Roman law had been systematized and could exert a powerful influence. In the thirteenth century, with the fusion of the Normans and English into one nation, the Common Law became truly English and, therefore, distinct from continental law.

The dispensing of royal justice was an extension of feudal ideas, but in the hands of English kings it became a major means of expanding royal power.[62] As the king's courts began to supplant the popular assemblies, they also regularized the customs that had been applied by them before.[63] The earliest and most successful expansion of royal jurisdiction and royal power took place during the reign of Henry II. Henry began both the systematic visitation of localities by royal justices and the use of a central court of justice.[64] He established judicial machinery that had never been seen before, with hundreds of judges touring and sitting at Westminster.[65] Faced with such an "overpowering display of central justice"[66] the old local courts sank into insignificance.[67] Law became a function of royal power rather than of the power of local notables.

The expansion of royal courts in England is associated with an increased reliance on the use of the jury as the preferred mode of proof. From the assembly of local landholders called upon by the local lord to apply local custom grew the conception of the jury as an inquest summoned by royal judges; from this grew a legal system that ingeniously combined proceedings before central courts with verdicts rendered by local juries[68]; it became "probably the most centralized trial court system of any major nation in history."[69]

On the Continent, centralization of justice and the formation of nation-states occurred later and more slowly than in England. Local and regional custom "reigned supreme and even the central courts judged according to local custom in appeal cases."[70] In France the central monarchy emerged only slowly; no single jurisdiction was powerful enough to elaborate a common law. France remained a patchwork of different jurisdictions applying different bodies of law until the Code Civil was adopted in 1804.[71] Germany did not become politically unified until the late nineteenth century, and lacked a single code until 1900.

From the towns came pressures that shaped Western law in important ways. As commerce expanded from the twelfth century on, townsmen sought principles of commercial law that would fit their transactions and undertakings better than the law applied by local and royal courts, which focused on land tenure and the exploitation of land. In response to these pressures, commercial transactions came to be the subject of the jurisdiction of specialized commercial courts, both on the Continent and in England.[72]

China: Underdevelopment of State Institutions
for Resolution of Civil Disputes

Law in China was not formally differentiated from other forms of exercise of state power, in striking contrast with the West. Chinese law was a form of what Roberto Unger has called bureaucratic law, consisting of "explicit rules established and enforced by an identifiable government"[73] and distinguishable from the Western legal order, which is "institutionally autonomous to the extent that its rules are applied by specialized institutions whose main task is adjudication."[74] It was addressed to officials, not to the populace. No distinctions were made between criminal and civil liability, and law was always conceived of as operating "in a vertical direction from the state upon the individual, rather than on a horizontal plane directly between two individuals."[75] Chinese law was administered by magistrates, who had no special legal training, as part of their general duties to govern on behalf of the emperor. As Max Weber commented, "Chinese administration of justice constitutes a type of patriarchal obliteration of the line between justice and administration."[76]

Formal law and legal processes were principally concerned with punishment. Law was identified with retributive punishments that restored order and also served as a deterrent to others. Traditional China had intricate penal codes as early as the Tang Dynasty (A.D. 618–906); the most recent was that of the Qing, compiled in definitive form in 1740.[77] Records of past cases were preserved and compiled into official and unofficial commentaries; although past cases had no binding precedental authority, they provided guidance to judges. At the county level, local magistrates were assisted by legal secretaries with specialized knowledge, while specialized legal officials in provincial capitals and in Beijing reviewed all serious cases.

The obligations of lesser officials were written in detailed codes intended to limit their discretion and to provide penalties for improper decisions. Magistrates were required to discover the truth in each case brought before them, which led to numerous appeals at higher levels.[78] This system emphasized substantive justice, which meant that the outcome of a case had to meet the requirements of both law and Confucian morality.[79] The concerns for procedural justice and for finality that have come to mark Anglo-American law were absent.

Litigation was time-consuming, degrading, and costly. Litigation also meant dangerous involvement with magistrates and their staffs. The magistrate's *yamen*, or office, was usually far from the disputants' residence. Because the magistrates were, at best, inexpert and, at worst, "corrupt, cruel, and lazy,"[80] they relied heavily on their clerks and other underlings for assistance. The reputation of these "tigers or wolves"[81] for corruption and greed was "legendary and frequently well-deserved."[82] The "customary fees" which had to be paid to the *yamen* employees imposed extraordinarily heavy burdens on litigants.[83] Extraordinary, too, were the delays and "errors" that could beset a litigant hapless enough to fall afoul of a *yamen* employee.[84] Trials could be humiliating for witnesses as well, occasionally involving the use of torture to obtain evidence.[85] It was no wonder that "to involve someone in a lawsuit was a way of ruining him,"[86] and that, according to a Chinese saying, "to enter a court of justice is to enter a tiger's mouth."[87] The perils of litigation, widely publicized in popular lore,[88] undoubtedly restrained many persons from bringing suit at the magistrate's *yamen* and impelled them to settle disputes through extra-judicial mediation closer to home.

Most civil disputes were settled extra-judicially rather than through litigation in traditional China.[89] The official philosophy stressed the virtue of yielding (*rang*) and the superiority of noncontentiousness, and produced very strong social pressure against conflict and in favor of mediation and compromise, especially if conflicts threatened to go beyond the families, clans, villages, or guilds that were the basic social groupings of traditional Chinese society.

The basic nuclei of traditional Chinese society—family, clan, village, and guild—combined with the dominant ethic—the hazards of litigation and widespread fear of involvement with government officials—to cause disputes to be settled, as much as possible, within those nuclei. These social units exercised considerable independence from the *yamen*, particularly in the settlement of disputes. If disputes could not be settled within the unit, then relatives, friends, and local leaders outside the group, but still closer to the disputants than the magistrate, would often resolve them by mediation. The participation of government officials in settling quarrels was avoided.[90] Recourse to the magistrate without prior attempts to settle disputes within groups was actively discouraged and sometimes, as in the case of clans and guilds, prohibited by the group's internal regulations.[91] In sum, "the local group generally required the parties to exhaust their remedies within the group before looking to the magistrate for relief."[92]

Disputes within families were settled by elders, no doubt with much mediation by older relatives, friends, and clan leaders, while disputes between members of a clan were settled by clan leaders and sometimes by other respected local leaders.[93] Disputes within a village not coterminous with one clan were mediated not only by relatives, friends, and neighbors, but by official village headmen and unofficial leaders, whether gentry or other respected figures.[94] Within the guilds, disputes between members were settled if not by friends, witnesses of a transaction, or middlemen, then by guild officers.[95]

The devices used to resolve disputes ranged from "completely private mediation at one end of the scale to public adjudication at the other, the one shading into the other almost imperceptibly as public opinion was felt to be more strongly involved."[96] Often, mediators had to shuttle between the parties in an effort to reach a mutually satisfactory compromise.[97] In the clans and guilds, if informal mediation had failed, procedures akin to arbitration and adjudication were sometimes used.[98] Settlement of a dispute by clan members might involve a formal hearing in the clan hall before a group of clan leaders and, perhaps, other respected members assembled for the occasion.[99] Similarly, disputes between guild members were sometimes heard in the guild hall by a group of guild officers.[100] On occasions like these, parties and witnesses would give testimony, and then a decision would be reached. The "peace-talkers" or guild or clan leaders tried to bring the parties to compromise without imposing a decision on them.

These institutions for dispute settlement did not always function as smoothly and evenhandedly as idealized descriptions suggest. Just as the magistrate was often not a model Confucian gentleman, so the extra-judicial mediator was not always an exemplar of Confucian virtue. Often mediators stirred up disputes in order to mediate them and be rewarded by successful parties. Furthermore, the informal justice obtained at the hands of mediators was sometimes unfair. Favoritism and bribes were common, as were other perversions of the mediation process, especially when a relatively wealthy and respected party was pitted against a much poorer opponent or when members of wealthy and powerful clan branches opposed less favored relatives.[101] Because conflict was frequently embarrassing and disliked, parties anxious to end a dispute would sometimes agree to a compromise that was unsatisfactory to both. As a result, "the disagreement was merely driven below the surface and went on simmering, and the situation was ripe for explosion or provocation."[102] Finally, it was difficult for an unsuccessful disputant who thought he had been wronged by a village, clan, or guild to obtain redress from the magistrate, for he was challenging not merely his opponent, but the social group which initially resolved the dispute. Public opinion in village, clan, or guild, and the threat of ostracism as punishment for flouting it, were often strong enough to deter "appeals" to the magistrate.[103]

On the whole, however, extra-judicial dispute settlement by mediation offered considerable advantages to litigants and government alike. Mediation allowed parties to avoid expensive and possibly disastrous litigation while affording them "a method of terminating disputes that was socially acceptable in the light of the Confucian ethic and group mores."[104]

Mediation also avoided rupturing the tightly woven web within which many transactions took place. Ordinary social and commercial relationships between persons unrelated to each other by family or common membership in a group had a distinctive quality—different from friendship—known as *ganqing*.[105] The existence of *ganqing* between two persons meant that they had regard for each other and could ask favors from each other. In these relationships, persons did not want to lose "face"—their reputation for integrity and dignity.[106] Because prevailing social values stressed the importance of saving face and reaching a compromise satisfactory to both parties, disputants were better able to bargain with each other during mediation than in more formal proceedings.

In addition, because mediation emphasized the necessity of avoiding conflict, observing proper rules of behavior, and relying on the social group to resolve differences, it provided auxiliary support for the dissemination of Confucian standards and values. Finally, extra-judicial mediation eased the government's burden of work and helped avoid friction between magistrates and the persons and groups in their jurisdiction.

Considerable Western scholarship emphasizing the importance of mediation has tended to obscure the litigation that was carried out despite popular reluctance. Recent archival research in both China and Taiwan suggests that formal legal rules "made up the frame within which compromise took place"[107] and that litigation was more frequent than was previously supposed, even though commencement of a lawsuit often galvanized the parties to reach a compromise settlement. Magistrates sometimes became involved in resolving civil disputes. Huang has documented the importance both of the magistrate as a catalyst who promoted settlement and of the interaction between community leaders and the magistrates in a "semi-formal" realm of justice that lay between the formal and the informal.[108] The long-accepted view that litigation was shunned is contradicted, at least in the eighteenth century, by the "often overwhelming burden local and provincial officials shouldered to resolve the civil litigation cases they had accepted."[109] Even if litigation was used as a tactic to provoke settlement, the volume of litigation suggests the need to qualify the long-accepted view that Chinese shunned it. Moreover, a class of "litigation brokers" that flourished in the late Qing assisted persons involved in litigation by providing services to litigants, although such practitioners were frequently denounced by Chinese officialdom.[110] These findings in turn should prompt a more nuanced view of Chinese rights-consciousness: Although notions of rights against the state were lacking and claims against persons were not characterized as "rights," their functional analogues appear to have existed in some depth and were asserted by Chinese against each other.

These patterns of dispute resolution survived the overthrow of the Qing dynasty, and chapters 3 and 8 will show their tenacity both under Mao and today. Following an interregnum of warlordism and civil strife, the Nationalists succeeded in establishing a central government in 1928. Although they established organs of local government below the county level,[111] in the countryside "the national government failed to substantially alter the traditional, decentralized pattern of local government in which the village political life operated largely by its own local power structure and was but weakly integrated into the system of central authority."[112] A modern court system was organized, but it never functioned effectively.[113] Traditional, informal, extra-judicial mediation remained the characteristic mode of dispute settlement throughout the years of Nationalist rule.[114]

LEGAL PROFESSIONALS

The West: The Dominance of Lawyers

In Western societies law is inseparably linked with a class of legal professionals—the lawyers. Their importance arose out of the formal autonomy of the law and the development of specialized legal reasoning that was differentiated from other discourse. In England, the common law developed around procedure centered on the writs, which were standardized procedural commands from the king telling a judge of a dispute and instructing him to settle it in court. Judicial interpretation of the writs, and the development of substantive law under the rubric of each writ, inhibited the development of general legal rules and led to the common law's becoming a highly complex body of traditional practices understandable only by adepts "steeped in the tradition."[115]

Under the Chancellor, the Court of Chancery and new doctrines were developed to relieve the inflexibility of the common law courts, but the rules of equity became as rigid as those it had been designed to avoid. The writ system, a system of special procedures rather than a body of substantive rules, was so complex that it could only be learned at the Inns of Court, where the pleaders skilled in the system worked and lived. Out of the latter evolved a formal class of barristers who specialized in arguing cases before the courts. Meanwhile, a large body of rules dealing with contracts for the transfer of land, or conveyancing, took shape, and it too was highly technical and complex. From the specialists who handled this work evolved the solicitors. By the sixteenth century, judges had to come from the ranks of the barristers and as such were "both officers of the crown and leaders of an independent profession that saw itself as the maker and guardian of the law—a law so complex that no non-lawyer could understand it."[116]

On the continent of Europe, the emergence of a specialized class of lawyers is linked with the "reception" of Roman law. Roman law, specifically the extensive body of rules that had been compiled under the reign of Justinian in the sixth century, embodied and systematically organized principles that justified the centralization of power in a decentralized Europe, while also supplying concepts that were welcome to the commerce and industry that had begun to grow in Western Europe in the twelfth century. Roman law was "received" into the laws of the Italian cities during the eleventh and twelfth centuries, only later and to a considerably lesser extent (varying greatly from region to region) in France, and extensively in Germany in 1495.[117] It proved congenial to Church and kings alike, given Roman law's emphases on centralization, hierarchy, and rationalization from above.[118]

Roman law was taught at the universities, in what later came to be called a cultural "renaissance." Students came largely from the nobility and the upper bourgeoisie, and after graduation joined the administration and the professions. The law taught at the universities was a professors' law, theoretical, highly abstract, and remote from actual practice. Schools of legal scholars interpreted the body of Roman law around which the principal legal systems of the continent came to be centered.[119] They produced a "systematic conceptual legal structure that is still taught in the faculties of law of the universities."[120] It is this structure that influenced Chinese law under the Republic and, more recently, when a partial civil law code was adopted in 1986.

The increased dominance of courts in both the English and Continental systems transformed the basic sources of law and disputants' access to the courts. In the early Middle Ages most law had been oral and its principal source had been custom.[121] In England, custom had been assumed to be the basis of law, but whether or not a practice was customary had to be proven, and as society changed such proof became more difficult. As courts asserted their functions more aggressively, they mounted an attack on custom.[122] On the Continent, there was movement away from popular participation after the late Middle Ages.[123] Custom was in some places replaced by Roman law, although in fifteenth-century France, by contrast, customs were reduced to writing in official collections, which continued in use until French law was unified after the Revolution. These changes in the rules of both Roman and customary law also meant that law became increasingly specialized and that popular participation in its application diminished. As procedure became more and more Romanist, it became more difficult to understand. Common and civil law systems alike became increasingly complex and specialized, leading to the rise of legal professionals on both sides of the English Channel.

China: Law Without Lawyers

Chinese legal institutions, for their part, lacked both the functional specialization and the autonomy developed in the West. The officials who administered justice were generalists, chosen because of their success in the imperial examinations on the classics. Cultivated in the Confucian classics and untrained in administration, they took office without legal training or expertise. Legal specialists were generally officials in central agencies in Beijing, while others were simply legal secretaries to magistrates and prefects. Legal professionals did not develop the use of law on behalf of individuals, and any tendency for legal specialists to act as intermediaries between the individuals and the state was actively discouraged. The Qing code, for example, provided for punishment of "litigation tricksters" who encouraged litigation,[124] but they flourished nonetheless, as already noted.

LEGAL PLURALISM IN THE WEST AND CHINA

Western scholars of Chinese law have consistently remarked on the Chinese preference for extra-judicial dispute settlement, to the extent that it is often taken as the defining characteristic of Chinese law. By comparison, the history of Western law is not exclusively that of courts, and the importance of extra-judicial dispute settlement in Western tradition should be kept in mind.[125] The current-day importance of courts of law in Western societies skews Western views of extra-judicial dispute resolution, whether in the West or abroad, illustrating a frequently encountered problem in historical interpretation: "The past must be led up to a known present, and in the journey one encounters very grave dangers that the known present may get unhistorically projected backwards. In addition, such parts of the past as did not make it into the known present are liable to get discarded."[126] The problem is compounded when modernized societies are compared with traditional ones, because then "the traditional features of the former either disappear from view or 'are pictured as residual categories that have failed to yield, because of some inefficiency in the historical process, to the imperatives of modernization'."[127] Finally, it may be that the desire of foreign observers to "overcome their American biases and attempt to understand alien legal practice as a native would"[128] has increased their appreciation of Chinese culture and caused them to overlook some characteristics of their own. The present ubiquitousness and dominance of courts in the West obscure the long historical process of this evolution and the continued strong presence of extra-judicial means of dealing with disputes.

The West: Slow Consolidation of National Legal Systems

In Europe, the centralization of royal justice was an incremental, slow, and partial process. We should recall that "the practice of resolving disputes through extra-judicial compromise—whether by direct negotiation, mediation by third parties or arbitration—was widespread and common-place throughout medieval Europe."[129] As the courts evolved, they displaced the less formal, more compromise-oriented methods of dispute resolution. The growth of the jurisdiction of the king's courts in England, for example, meant not only the displacement of baronial courts but the growth of principles of rights rather than compromise as the basis for the resolution of disputes.

In England in the late Middle Ages most lawsuits were not ended by judgments, and recent research suggests that arbitration was extensively used by clergy who were nominated by city and borough courts in commercial disputes and other matters. Arbitration was voluntary, its procedure more flexible and faster than that of the ordinary courts, and arbitrators could aim at achieving lasting settlement of a dispute rather than its resolution in terms of limited issues of law.[130] Merchants' preference for arbitration over litigation in the law courts grew during the nineteenth century in England, a feature that has survived to the present day.[131] In France, long before the Revolution, merchants' desire to avoid the law and courts led them both to seek arbitration and to establish their own courts.[132] The law was insufficient and the courts inefficient, and after the legal system was centralized much later, mediation and arbitration survived into the twentieth century. It was not only in China, therefore, that the state lacked the resources to extend its power further into localities and that intrusions of central power were strongly resisted.[133]

The West: The Tenacity of Traditional, Compromise-Based Dispute Settlement and Legal Pluralism

Although the entwined histories of the centralized nation-state and unified legal systems of Europe are symbolized in the imposing buildings in which Western nations conduct judicial proceedings, most disputes never came to the attention of the judges and lawyers in those buildings. Even though the decisions of the king's courts supplanted customs in society at large, most people in England lived according to customs and never came before the courts at all. The world of the law courts was at the apex of a social pyramid, and most of the general population lived their lives without contact with that world.[134] It is well to recall that

Not until relatively modern times in Western societies has a single dominating and comprehensive legal system, coterminous with the territorial reach of the state, come to appear typical. In earlier times systems of religious law applied by ecclesiastical courts, mercantile law of trading communities, and local or personal law of particular regions or categories of people could co-exist in a complex array of jurisdictions within particular territories.[135]

Comparisons between China and the West must take into account that extra-judicial settlement of disputes has continued to a substantial degree, silent, relatively uncelebrated, but persistent nonetheless. And although it is conventional in the West to assume a continuum of dispute resolution institutions from mediation through arbitration to adjudication, the boundaries between them are not distinct, and informal mediation often permeates into more formal processes.[136]

China: Weak Courts and Continued Existence of Compromise-Based Institutions

The contrast between Western and Chinese judicial systems was sharpened in the late nineteenth and early twentieth centuries. While Western nation-states became more centralized and their judiciaries grew more powerful, the grasp of imperial rule over the vastness of China declined. The deepening differences between judicial systems are dramatized by the fate of the efforts at law reform during the Republic of China's brief rule on the Mainland.

The legal history of the Republic from 1912 to 1949 was marked by sporadic and inconsistent attempts to transplant legal institutions from the West and Japan, transplants that failed to flourish in their new Chinese setting. Before China became nominally unified in 1928, civil war and warlordism prevented any progress on law reform.[137] New codes based on Western models were adopted in the 1930s but had little effect on Chinese life, especially outside the cities. These codes were often too complex and irrelevant to Chinese conditions and were adopted and studied in an abstract and mechanical spirit.[138] The motives for hasty codification were in part political; China wanted to end the extra-territorial rights of foreigners but could do so only if it assured the countries whose nationals enjoyed those rights that China had a modern, i.e., Western, legal system. Legal education in Republican China illustrates the irrelevance of Republican law to Chinese conditions.[139] China did establish its first professional bar, but the lawyers' training and qualifications were uneven, their standards of professional behavior were low, and the government failed actively to promote the growth of the bar.[140]

Although plans were made for a modern court system, the judicial system never functioned effectively. New Western-type institutions were established, but most counties had no courts and justice was handled by a judicial section of the county government that was dominated by the magistrate.[141] China's judges were both few and poorly educated, and judicial professionalism and independence were undercut by corruption and favoritism.[142] The new Western-type legal institutions existed side-by-side with other institutions, established by the authoritarian Nationalist Party, which contradicted the spirit of the new legal reforms.

In civil and commercial matters the new laws were basically ignored, especially in rural China, by the persons who might have used them prospectively as guides for conduct. Disputes, of course, continued to occur. They were dealt with by the established institutions for mediation that remained in place during Republican rule, sometimes augmented by new governmental and communal institutions. One study of Republican-era dispute resolution in a Sichuan municipality demonstrates continued use of the kind of customary contractual practices that have been described above, an aversion to litigation that prompted merchants to specify in their contracts contingencies that might cause difficulty in performance, and the evolution of the local chamber of commerce as a mediation institution.[143] Another study of disputes in north China suggests that the number of civil cases rose during the Republic, but that village-level justice, with its characteristic emphasis on mediation, did not much change from the late Qing until the end of the Republican period.[144] The operation of mediation after its incorporation into the institutions of CCP control is discussed in chapter 3.

Devising Research Strategies for Studying Contemporary Chinese Legal Development

THE CHALLENGE

This overview of salient differences between Chinese and Western legal development suggests how different the two paths have been. In the West, the past tendency to look for law primarily in courts has contributed to a widespread view that traditional China lacked law. So, too, has the tendency to use Western legal history as a defining standard, which has led Western observers to emphasize characteristics of Western history as criteria for fulfilling perceived lacks in other legal systems such as a belief in divine law, differentiation of administrative commands from laws, a legal profession, a distinction between law and morals, and, of course, a strong conception of rights.[145]

But practices not characterized as "legal" in the West performed functions similar to those of some Western "legal" institutions, even though they were not specialized or differentiated from other fields of activity in the same way as in the West. Furthermore, although the imperial regime delegated to elements within Chinese society activities that a government with more extensive resources might have conducted itself, the state's reliance on those institutions did not mean that functions were neglected.[146] Indeed, research into traditional custom and practice has yielded additional evidence that these informal institutions protected the grounded claims mentioned above that could be characterized as functional equivalents of the rights created by Western jurisprudence.[147]

The very different paths that legal development and legal theory have followed in China and the West compound the difficulties of using Chinese law as a medium for understanding China today. The literature of what is conventionally called "comparative law" offers little to help foreign observers avoid making uncritical assumptions, or otherwise to aid them in comprehending foreign legal institutions in their social context.[148]

Foreign observers who seek to understand contemporary Chinese law are not only denied clear guideposts by the past, but are also challenged by the incompleteness, novelty, and fragility of current institutions. Uncertainty about the operation and significance of legal institutions is deepened by the extent and rapidity of recent social change, especially in the countryside. Reform has dramatized the existence of many Chinas, in which diverse institutional patterns of economic and governmental activity will affect and be affected by newly emergent legal rules. China's dramatic economic growth and its "opening" to foreign investment have also obscured for many in the West the influences of both Chinese tradition and Maoism on contemporary institutions and practice, although attitudes and practices shaped by both continue to weigh heavily.

The difficulty of trying to understand how Chinese legal institutions function is aggravated by the limits on accessibility to them by foreign scholars. Although American lawyers and law professors have traveled to the PRC to lecture and teach on American law and, sometimes, to discuss proposed Chinese legislation, the continued overt links between law and politics make legal research particularly sensitive and potentially controversial. Americans have attended courses at Chinese law schools, but their access to libraries has been obstructed, in part because many legal books and journals are *neibu*—for internal use only. Reflecting a general reluctance to permit field research by foreign scholars,[149] research outside universities, such as at law courts or law offices, was almost impossible to arrange before June 1989, and, since then, it has been practically nonexistent.[150] At the moment of writing, foreign observers still cannot gain sustained access to observe the operations of formal Chinese legal institutions.

Despite these difficulties, because the future of Chinese legal institutions is so important both to China and to the West, I have sought insight into their operation in Chinese society. The balance of this chapter outlines the essentials of the approach that I have taken. I have not attempted to set forth a unified theory, or even any theory at all; rather I have described a number of perspectives that have been useful, including a view of law frankly rooted in the West.

The Rule of Law

My perspective is informed by certain basic principles customarily subsumed in the West under the concept of the rule of law, which I take to be the following:

legal rules, standards or principles must be capable of guiding people in the conduct of their affairs;

the law should, for the most part, actually guide people;

the law should be stable;

the law should be the supreme legal authority;

the courts should be able to do their work impartially and without direct interference from the political system.[151]

These principles define the initial vantage point from which I have studied Chinese legal institutions. As Randall Peerenboom has observed in a nuanced discussion of the applicability of rule of law theory to contemporary China, a considerable range of differences exists between those who would insist that the rule of law must be associated with capitalism, democratic government, and liberal concepts of human rights, and others who prefer "a more limited understanding . . . that emphasizes its formal or instrumental aspects—those features that any legal system allegedly must possess to function effectively as a system of laws."[152] The principles that I have stated above are associated with such a limited or "thin" theory of the rule of law. Even so, readers must remind themselves that the rule of law is both a Western ideal that is often departed from and a concept whose content is much disputed.[153] There are, however, adequate reasons for my choice. First, the rule of law has been accepted as an ideal by most of the nations of the world. Second, as I will show in chapter 5, the leadership of the PRC professes adherence to the principle of the rule of law. Third, adherence to the rule of law is also an obligation that Article

X of the General Agreement on Tariffs and Trade (GATT) implies for sig-natories to that treaty,[154] and China would have to assume such an obliga-tion by joining the World Trade Organization, which implements the GATT. Finally, although I have used the rule of law to help define my perspective I have also looked at Chinese law from other vantage points that I have described below. Moreover, I have not tried to use the West as a standard of normality toward which China must evolve.[155]

Overcoming Exegesis

Since 1979 China has been a legislative laboratory. As chapters 6 and 7 will show, a vast array of rules made by legislatures and administrative agencies are being used to establish institutions that did not exist before economic reforms began. Most Western study has necessarily focused on the texts of the rules, which tell nothing about their impact on practice.[156] In the chapters that follow I have avoided such a narrow approach and have preferred to concentrate on some salient aspects of significant rules. The intentions of legislators and policy-makers have been considered, for example, in discussing the extensive use of legislation to legalize the Chi-nese state.[157] Secondary Chinese legal literature such as law school text-books and books intended for Chinese judges and mediators, although they too often echo rather than analyze legislation, have sometimes been useful in outlining underlying policies.[158] In addition, I have been pleased to use a number of excellent analyses by Chinese scholars. I have also re-lied on many conversations with Chinese in situations informal and for-mal, as well as a series of interviews with Chinese legal scholars and judges.

Studying Law in Action

To understand Chinese law, it is obviously necessary to venture beyond both legal rules and legal institutions. Long-standing and continuing ties between law and policy, which are reviewed and explored below, require studying the impact of other government and Party organizations on legal practice. The very novelty of Chinese legal institutions makes their place among longer-established political and bureaucratic institutions uncertain, and the impact of bureaucratic politics on new formal legal institutions must be considered. Since 1949, policy implementation by the Chinese bureaucracy has been characterized by a striking combination of cellular-ity and mutual interdependence, interagency negotiation, and consensus-building that often depends on personal associations and influence.[159] Does the new prominence of law affect previous long-standing commit-ments of personnel to particular organizations and policies? It is likely that administrative units will resist inroads of new agencies into their previously unchallenged power. The creation of a new legal infrastructure imports into Chinese administration concepts such as jurisdiction, procedural regularity, and legal rights that are fundamentally alien to the existing political culture. Established patterns of bureaucratic behavior reinforce resistance to legal reforms, and one example discussed in chapter 6 is the persistence of pre-reform attitudes toward the criminal process, both among the leadership and the organizations that administer the process.

Searching for Function

I have tried wherever possible to identify the function of the legal rules and institutions that are studied here. Functional analysis has been rightly criticized for leading the researcher to "make assumptions about the way social systems function in terms of postulated needs which imply the way such systems *should* function,"[160] and, further, to assume that Western legal systems have in fact so responded.[161] Some students of comparative law have long suggested that cultural frontiers can be surmounted by seeking to understand the functions of legal institutions in contexts that transcend the formal legal realm,[162] but they have been able neither to define the concept of function with much exactness nor convincingly to establish the objectivity that functionalism implies.[163] I am suggesting a far more restrained perspective, one that "merely tries to analyze the relationship between particular closely defined social phenomena"[164] in a search for what the great comparatist Ernst Rabel called the "social purpose" of legal institutions.[165] Over thirty years ago, when I was just beginning research on Chinese law, I thought that there was promise in analyzing legal and administrative practices and arrangements "in terms of the functions they perform, recognizing that several functions may coexist, that apparently similar institutions may have different functions, and that apparently dissimilar institutions may perform similar functions."[166] I believe that this approach continues to be helpful in understanding the institutions of China, and that the analyses above of the different trajectories taken by Western and Chinese legal development suggest its usefulness.

A functional approach may be helpful, for example, in understanding the operation of legal institutions that are recent legislative creations. As these are put into practice, differences inevitably appear between the functions that their creators intended to be primary or manifest and those that, unintended and unrecognized, appear in practice to be latent.[167] In the study of the effect of bureaucratic politics on new institutions, emphasizing functions means asking how the new institutions are made to work by the officials who staff them, and how they may mesh or clash with other institutions that existed before the new ones were created. Searching for such functions has helped to expose ambiguities about attempts to regularize the formal Chinese criminal process, both before and after reform.[168] This approach seemed useful, too, in explaining mediational dispute resolution in chapter 3, and it has informed chapters 8 and 9, which bring early studies of Chinese dispute resolution down to the present day.

But we must go further. The formal legal realm is transcended by the symbols to which the legal institutions are supposed to give legitimacy and by the ideologies that they support, with all the contradictions that Chinese ideology presently contains. Outside the formal legal realm, other institutions of the Party-state are also undergoing great change. In and around these institutions is legal culture, including popular notions of what is right. Considering these will lead us back into Chinese society itself, where the study of Chinese law must be grounded.

Legal Culture and Thick Description

In addition to examining policy toward law, legal rules and doctrine, and the behavior of legal and economic actors, our study must aim at illuminating interactions in Chinese society among law, politics, social structure, and culture. To turn to this last-named and elusive subject, we must consider available evidence that bears on law-related values and expectations among officials and members of the populace. The approach that has been used in the studies of dispute resolution in this book is aimed not at high-level theoretical "explanations," but at intermediate-level speculation about relationships among social facts. These social facts include formal legal rules, the structure and operation of the institutions that implement them, and practices and attitudes that arise from a variety of sources that here have been grouped together under the rubric of "legal culture."

Legal culture has been used to mean, "those parts of general culture—customs, opinions, ways of doing and thinking—that bend social forces toward or away from the law and in particular ways."[169] The concept of legal culture, imprecise and amorphous, could arguably include any cultural practice or value that may affect perceptions of law-related institutions. At this stage of inquiry, so much the better. This breadth of approach is appropriate to Chinese society, in which law is marked by an absence of techniques and reasoning different from those used in Chinese culture and life generally.[170] Here, I have focused attention on resolution of civil disputes by studying the organization and animating policies of extra-judicial and judicial dispute resolution, published information about disputes including judicial decisions, and attitudes among the Chinese populace and the judiciary toward settling disputes.

I do not assume here that legal culture is either readily knowable or static. I have already referred to widely held traditional cultural values that discouraged litigation.[171] The values related to social harmony and

conflict interacted with family and social structure and with political institutions to form a rich and mutually reinforcing blend of attitudes that
contributed to Chinese "legal culture" as it related to disputes. We should
also keep in mind, however, that, as I mentioned earlier, recent research
suggests that these values have been exaggerated and that traditional legal
culture was more complex. Whatever the mix of attitudes, they are changing as a result of the extensive social and economic changes unleashed by
reform.

In framing research into the dynamics of Chinese legal institutions, it
seems desirable to avoid high levels of abstraction and to be self-conscious
about the simplest of concepts that are the basic building blocks of Western legal analysis. Suggestions for a useful approach come from Clifford
Geertz, who advocates restraining the level of conceptualization that is
appropriate to use in order to develop cross-cultural understanding, characterizing it as "thick description."[172] The foreign student of Chinese law,
is like Geertz's ethnographer, and Geertz's suggestion is apposite here: The
foreign student must begin close to the perspective of the participants
themselves and keep analytical concepts grounded in thick description of
the specific details of the institutions under study.

The student of Chinese law, like the anthropologist or sociologist, must
inquire not only into the values and expectations of participants in the activities of the institutions involved, but also into those of the general populace. For example, the discussion of dispute resolution in the chapters
that follow has benefited from recent studies by Chinese researchers on
dispute resolution and attitudes toward disputes involving alleged violations of rights. The rise of the concept of legal rights in China today raises
issues of legal culture. When Chinese disputants assert claims today, they
may be more ready to compromise than Western claimants, although they
may be characterizing their rights in a terminology that is entirely recognizable to Western lawyers.[173] In addition, the means used to resolve disputes, such as mediation in mediation committees or courts, may dilute or
"soften" the rights.

I hope that my approach will aid the understanding of what the architects
of China's new legal institutions hope to accomplish, how those institutions work, and the relationships among the purpose of the institutions,
their operation, and the results. It ought to also make us conscious of the
difficulties inherent in attempts to arrive at a cross-cultural understanding
of China through law, but it cannot inoculate us against infection by un-
conscious assumptions. Worse yet, although the problems would be great if
we were studying the legal institutions of an open society, China presents
additional problems. Years ago I participated in a negotiation with a par-

ticularly opaque Chinese counterpart who avoided answering many questions about issues important to the prospective project under discussion. Amused at the frustration he was causing, he reminded me of the tale of the ten blind men who were unable to agree on the shape of an elephant. China was like the elephant, he said. I disagreed, saying: The elephant could not speak, but China could—if it wanted to. Until China speaks, we will have to depend more than we like on approaches like the one that has been fashioned here.

CHAPTER 3

Law Under Mao, I: Mediation

Model Mediation Committee Member *Aunty Wu*:

If mediation isn't successful once, then it is carried out a second, and a third time, with the aim of continuing right up until the question is decided. Once, while Aunty Wu was walking along the street, she heard a child being beaten and scolded in a house. She went immediately to the neighboring houses of the masses, inquired, and learned that it was Li Guangyi's wife, Li Ping, scolding and beating the child of Li's former wife. She also learned that Li Ping often mistreated the child this way. After she understood, she went to Li's house to carry out education and urge them to stop. At the time, Li Ping mouthed full assent, but afterward she still didn't reform. With the help of the masses, Aunty Wu went repeatedly to the house to educate and advise, and carry out criticism of the woman's treatment of the child. Finally, they caused Li Ping to repent and thoroughly correct her error, and now she treats the child well. Everyone says Aunty Wu is certainly good at handling these matters, but she says, "If I didn't depend on everyone, nothing could be solved."[1]

Introduction

THE INSTITUTIONS established under Maoism form part of the complex background to the legal reform that began in 1978 and 1979. In later chapters we will see that some institutions, like mediation, would undergo significant transformations. Others, like the formal criminal process, shaped by Leninist-Maoist totalitarianism, seem able to change only very slowly. Still others, like conceptions of contract formed under state economic planning, may linger to influence contemporary thought and practice.

This chapter analyzes mediation, for centuries the dominant form of civil dispute resolution in China, as it was reshaped by Maoism. It examines the resolution of disputes between individuals in China, relying on documentary sources and on interviews conducted by the author in Mandarin with approximately fifty Chinese émigrés in Hong Kong from 1965 through 1967. This chapter is a concise version of a longer article published in 1967.[2] Although it has been condensed, the references and notes are taken from the original article and have not been updated. Visits to China and further research since 1967 suggest to me that the analysis is relevant to dispute resolution in China today, which is the subject of chapters 8 and 9.

Even though the essay on which this chapter is based was written thirty years ago, this version is also offered here in the belief that it has continued relevance to the effort of defining Western approaches to studying Chinese law. When it was written, the essay attempted to define and isolate functions performed by mediational dispute resolution and to identify influences that seemed more traceable to newer, CCP-inspired practice rather than to traditional practice. It also suggested that, although new institutions and a new vocabulary of concepts were superimposed on traditional attitudes toward social conflict, those traditional attitudes persisted. A similar functional approach has been employed in chapter 8, which analyzes contemporary mediation.

Dispute-Resolution and Maoist Ideology

No Maoist-era Chinese institution is comprehensible without appreciating the impact of Mao's ideology on it. Mao's views of society, social control, and social conflict decisively influenced dispute resolution and are briefly described below as a necessary preface to the analysis that follows.

MOBILIZATIONAL LEADERSHIP

For the CCP Maoism was not simply a way of viewing the world, but a program for changing it. Maoist political style was characterized by the use of campaigns (*yundong*), that is, orchestrated movements intended to arouse mass enthusiasm, increase production, and eliminate enemies. These techniques evolved during the 1930s and 1940s in response to the need for a tiny minority of revolutionaries, isolated among hundreds of millions of politically inert peasants, to create a vast, Party-led revolutionary army. The use of these recurring methods throughout the 1950s, during the Great Leap Forward (1958–1960) and up through the Cultural Revolution, reflected the CCP's strong commitment to leadership through mass mobilization.[3]

THE PARTY, THE 'PEOPLE,' AND THE 'ENEMY'

During the Maoist era the Party strove to conform to the Leninist ideal of a disciplined, elite body of professional revolutionaries leading the proletarian masses. The Chinese version of the dictatorship of the proletariat distinguished the "people" from the "enemy." The "people" included workers, peasants, and certain members of the bourgeoisie, and it was to them that the revolution belonged.[4] Their dictatorship was to be wielded for them by the Party over the "enemies," the former exploiting classes and counter-revolutionaries in thought and deed. From this dichotomy emerged a principle central to all methods of social control: problems within the "people" must be resolved by methods of "democracy," "persuasion," and "education," but problems between the "people" and the "enemy" had to be resolved by methods of dictatorship, including "punishment according to law."[5]

The class basis of this distinction between people and enemy is strikingly illustrated by the administrative categorization of "class origin" (*jiating chushen*). This designation, indicating economic position and degree of affiliation with the former Nationalist government, labeled each person as "landlord," "bourgeois," "[former Nationalist] bureaucrat," "rich peasant," or "upper-middle peasant"—all bad "class origins"—or as "lower-middle peasant," "poor peasant," or "worker"—all acceptable or good class origins. These classifications—entered in every person's dossier and taken as basic indicia of his or her loyalty and reliability—were important determinants of the individual's career.

THE MASS LINE, CADRES, AND ACTIVISTS

The Maoist approach to administration relied on the celebrated "mass line,"[6] a term denoting various techniques—propaganda, discussion, persuasion, and exhortation—that the Party used to measure and shape popular support for Party policies and to enlist participation in their implementation. In the countryside, large meetings of peasants were used during the land reform campaign to denounce and punish landlords and distribute their property. In the cities, organizations of urban inhabitants were formed to carry out public welfare schemes, sanitation work, and surveillance and control of counter-revolutionaries and criminals. The mass line approach emphasized mass participation in the execution rather than the formulation of policy[7] and embodied the Party's preference for leading the masses through nonbureaucratic, if not antibureaucratic, measures of persuasion.

The mass line also obscured the distinction between governmental and nongovernmental organizations and their activities. When the Party sought direct contact with the masses, the state apparatus was only one channel for contact; mass organizations and propaganda media were alternatives. The quality of participation that the mass line sought to elicit was fervently emotional rather than reasoned and deliberate, and the Party maintained a wide range of sanctions for passivity or opposition.[8] The mass line, "invest[ed] acts that [were] not in themselves political with an aura of civic obligation . . . open[ing] up a much broader sphere for the display of political activism."[9]

The process of policy implementation was led by the cadres—persons, often Party members, who held paid administrative posts in the government hierarchy and in the mass organizations such as the Young Communist League, the All China Federation of Labor Unions, and the Women's Federation.[10] Cadres, the nucleus of political leadership,[11] were assisted by activists—non-Party members willing to act as the Party's unpaid propagandists and general assistants.

'THOUGHT' AND CONTRADICTIONS: EARLY DEVELOPMENT

Behind the strategies aimed at the behavior of the masses stood Maoism's fundamental concern with transforming the thought of individuals.[12] In the Maoist view, political action was incorrect unless it proceeded from and applied correct thought (*sixiang*).[13] Only when the individual combined correct thought and action and had arrived at a correct "standpoint," could he or she see things from a proletarian point of view. If thought was incorrect, it had to be "reformed." Correct thought was not static, however; like all things in the Maoist view, it contained internal contradictions that had to be resolved through continuous and intense struggle in order to remain correct. The tools of that struggle included "criticism and self-criticism" and "thought reform."[14]

As the CCP established political control over larger and larger areas of rural China in the late 1930s and the 1940s, it needed to administer justice,[15] and the policy of the mass line became "probably the most prominent feature of 'people's justice'" of that era.[16] In several of the largest "newly liberated areas" from 1942 to 1944 legislation was promulgated requiring mediation in civil and some criminal cases,[17] and the press hailed the development of mediation.[18]

The decisive impact of politics on mediational dispute resolution is demonstrated by a 1946 report on judicial work in the Taihang district of Shanxi province.[19] The report hailed the improvement of judicial cadres who had formerly been divorced from the masses. After a major "rectification" campaign and intense self-criticism, many cadres reformed their "thought" and matured their "viewpoint" and left their offices to serve the masses and work among them. Rectification included such measures as simplifying procedures, abolishing litigation costs, and conducting on-the-spot trials, and it generally expanded the participation of the masses in "legal work." The report extolled mediation as the primary method of resolving civil disputes, in preference to judicial proceedings.

The report stressed the superiority of mediation as an instrument for "protecting the democratic interests of the great masses of people," and as a weapon of "struggle" against efforts to injure the masses. To be correct, however, mediation could not merely aim at compromise, it had to be "principled," that is, grounded in the policies and goals of the Party. For example, mediation should promote the policy of "educating" landlords to reduce rents and interests, while peasants should be encouraged to contest landlords' demands. The report stressed that mediators should "bring people around to a correct attitude" (*datong sixiang*) by developing disputants' "positive factors." When a woman cadre who had had adulterous relations sought a divorce, mediators reminded her of the "glory" of being a cadre. Knowing she feared losing her cadre status, mediators used this "positive factor" in her "thought" to educate her; her "problem" was "solved," and there was no divorce.[20]

The report stressed the need to expand the role of activists and the participation of the masses in mediation work. The more activists and members of the masses participated in mediation, the more people would be convinced that the Party was truly promoting their interests. That support would help maintain order and ensure that disputants abided by mediated settlements.

The Maoist commitment to using struggle, conflict, and changing of "thought" to aid political development was brought to the work of dispute resolution, and these innovations were not forgotten after the Communist victory.

Mediation in the Maoist Era, 1949–1967

After their victory in 1949, the Chinese Communists consolidated their control and mounted extensive programs of economic reconstruction and social change. They substantially reintegrated and reorganized a society that had been torn apart and ravaged by decades of war. To understand dispute resolution in post-1949 China, we must first consider its larger context—the Communist reorganization of Chinese society.

MEDIATION IN RESIDENTIAL AREAS

The Organizational Context

Hierarchies of power in Maoist China were organized in formal apparatuses of state and Party; mass organizations, such as those for youth and women; and the networks of activists who served as extensions of formal organizations. The organization of authority in Maoist-era China and its effect on dispute resolution are most clearly understood from the point of view of an urban resident at the time. The description may look labored, but the basic structures that are described continue to exist.

Consider the hypothetical Mr. Lu, who lived with his wife and two children in a large room in a city of several million people. The city was divided into districts (*qu*) of several hundred thousand persons; each district had a People's court, a procuratorial office, a public security (police) subbureau,[21] and offices for supervision of economic and other routine urban activities. These district-led organizations were responsible to a municipal-level superior. Each district was itself divided into smaller areas, with populations of several tens of thousands; each of these had a police station and a "street business office."[22] It was these local organizations and their representatives that the Lus encountered in their daily lives.

The local police station, headed by a station chief and a deputy chief, had a complement of around thirty-five men. Ten men investigated disturbances, crimes, and suspicious behavior; another ten investigated political crimes and checked on the "ideological level" and political reliability of the other policemen; five handled the dossiers that were maintained for most adults in China.[23] The remaining ten men patrolled regular beats and were charged with maintaining close knowledge of residents and their visitors.[24]

Cadres at the street business office were responsible for activities such as mediation of disputes, distribution of food ration coupons, public health, propaganda, culture and education, women's work, registration of marriages, and so forth. This street business office was not, however, the lowest-level agency of *de facto* municipal government. Each street had a residents' committee staffed by activists rather than cadres. Although it was called a mass, i.e. nongovernmental, organization, it was supervised by both the street business office and the police station.[25] Some members of the residents' committees were also active in the street mediation committees described below. Within the residents' committee, all residents were organized into "small groups" of fifteen to forty households each, led by an activist "small group" leader.[26] Every household had to send its representative to regular small group meetings for political study, discussion, and criticism and self-criticism.[27] The small group leader observed the political attitudes and personal problems of group members and cooperated closely with local policemen and residents' committee activists.[28]

Another kind of activist network was comprised of security defense committees.[29] These committees had members in each residents' small group who watched fellow members for suspicious activities and reported to policemen and committee chairmen. Other organizations, such as the Young Communist League and the Women's Association, also had activist networks that extended down to the street level and transmitted Party policies to the groups they represented.

The formal Party organization[30] was embedded in each unit described above, forming a vast Party hierarchy parallel to, but distinct from and su-

TABLE I. "Basic–Level" Organization: The Urban Control System

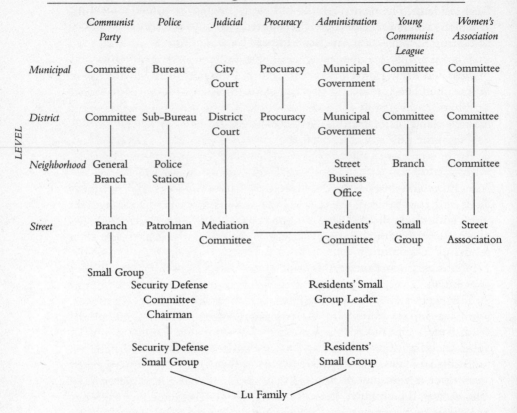

LEVEL	Communist Party	Police	Judicial	Procuracy	Administration	Young Communist League	Women's Association
Municipal	Committee	Bureau	City Court	Procuracy	Municipal Government	Committee	Committee
District	Committee	Sub–Bureau	District Court	Procuracy	Municipal Government	Committee	Committee
Neighborhood	General Branch	Police Station			Street Business Office	Branch	Committee
Street	Branch	Patrolman	Mediation Committee		Residents' Committee	Small Group	Street Asssociation
	Small Group	Security Defense Committee Chairman			Residents' Small Group Leader		
	Security Defense Small Group				Residents' Small Group		
			Lu Family				

perior to, the formal government hierarchy. Thus, residential area small groups composed solely of Party members were organized in each street or group of streets and were responsible to neighborhood-level Party branches. These local branches were subordinate to general branches, which were led in turn by the district and municipal Party committees. Each unit from branch upward was led by a Party committee headed by a Party secretary. These Party groups provided the leadership core for all activities. Thus, the chief of Mr. Lu's neighborhood police station and many of the policemen were Party or Young Communist League members, as was the head of the street business office, several of the cadres who worked for it, and some members of the residents' and mediation committees.

At weekly small group meetings, Party members discussed application of current Party policies to their work.[31] When a nationwide campaign was launched to remind the people of the need to engage in revolutionary struggle, Party members among the residents' committee members and small group leaders in the Lus' street convened propaganda meetings of local residents. The next week the Lus were "invited" to attend a meeting at which "volunteer" storytellers recounted past battles against the forces of Chiang Kai-shek and American imperialism.[32]

The Lu family members frequently encountered these representatives of state and Party power: their small group leader, security defense committee members, residents' committee members, mediation committee members, cadres from the street business office, policemen, and Party members and secretaries.[33] The interrelation of most of the important people in the Lus' city is schematized in Table 1.

At the street committee level, this apparently comprehensive system of urban control was termed "basic-level" organization. Although the control apparatus could work with astonishing efficiency, it often worked imperfectly. For example, many people in China's cities were not properly registered with local police stations, and their movements apparently went unobserved. In general, however, the apparatus was quite successful in consolidating Communist control during the early years of the People's Republic and maintaining that control up to the advent of the Cultural Revolution.

The organizational authority I have described also provided the framework for dispute resolution. In crowded Chinese cities, disputes of all kinds were—and of course still are—common: children fight; neighbors argue about noise, communal sanitary facilities, insults fancied or real, minor debts and sales, and alleged damage to property; lodgers and landlords argue over unpaid rent or unexecuted repairs; husbands and wives argue over money, the children, innumerable domestic concerns, or divorce. If Mr. Lu or his family became involved in any such disputes, quite probably an attempt to resolve them would have been made by at least one, and probably several, of the persons identified above.

Establishment and Purposes of Mediation Committees

After founding the People's Republic in 1949, the new government did not rush to establish a uniform system of mediation committees throughout the country, although some attempts were made to institutionalize dispute settlement outside the courts. In some cities "mediation sections" of full-time cadres within municipal governments handled the disputes of the urban population.[34] District-level mediation sections, which consulted with the district courts,[35] were established in 1950 as part of Beijing's district governments. In some cities, groups of citizen mediators were set up within the newly established residents' committees.[36]

Then, in mid-1952, the CCP launched a nationwide campaign to "reform law" (sifa gaige).[37] Party spokesmen proclaimed that the courts lacked ideological and political purity and a proper class point of view. They accused large numbers of "retained judges"—those who had served the Nationalist regime—of a wide range of ideological errors. The new campaign sought to reform judges through "criticism and self-criticism" encouraged by the masses, dismissal or transfer of "unreformed" judges, and punishment of the counter-revolutionaries among them. Cadres and activists with proper political attitudes and class origins were installed in the courts. The extensive application of the mass line to legal work meant that judges mediated—not adjudicated—disputes.

During the campaign, judicial cadres classified cases according to subject matter and selected activist mediators particularly suited to settle each kind of case. For example, housing disputes were to be mediated by activist street residents, commercial disputes by activist merchants.[38] The cadres then lectured the chosen activists on the policies they were to apply. After this preparation, meetings of disputants were convened, at which cadres and activists discussed the necessity of avoiding contentiousness and litigation. Only then did mediation small groups, led by the chosen activists, mediate the disputes. Cases that could not be settled forthwith were brought before large meetings, where the parties were criticized for not ending their disputes, and the cases were then returned to small groups for further mediation. If a case could not be settled, it was sent to judicial cadres. Occasionally, small groups persuaded disputants to sign "patriotic pacts" promising to avoid the conduct that had begun the dispute. Especially difficult cases were used as examples for the masses. In Shanghai, for example, two women workers accused their husbands of mistreatment. The men were brought before the entire workforce of a factory for a "large meeting for the pronouncement of judgment" (xuan-pan dahui), divorces were announced, and the two men were given prison sentences for mistreating their children.[39]

The new institutions for mediation received much praise.[40] Mediators were extolled for going directly to the disputants to investigate the causes and circumstances of disputes. The "political consciousness" of masses and cadres alike was raised, and litigation, which interrupted production, was avoided. But there were also problems.[41] Mediation was disorderly, it was often carried out with insufficient preparation, and courts frequently neglected to assist mediators. Links between policy and mediation were often ambiguous, cases were often settled without attention to policy, solely for the sake of reconciliation,[42] and some cadres forced disputants to settle.[43]

During the "legal reform" movement, mediation small groups and committees were extended across China. With China's first Five-Year Plan in 1953, Beijing began to articulate a new and different link between mediation and policy—China was embarking on a phase of economic construction, and activities such as legal work and mediation would have to support that program. This new emphasis led to promulgation of regulations on the nationwide organization of "people's mediation committees" in March 1954.[44]

The new regulations mandated mediation committees to "make timely settlement of civil disputes, strengthen education of the people on patriotism and observance of the law, and create unity among the people in order to benefit the people's efforts for production and national construction" (Art. 1). The committees were subordinate to the "basic-level" government and to "basic-level courts." The committees were to settle "civil disputes and minor criminal cases," and "carry out propaganda and education on national policies and laws" (Art. 3).

Mediation committees of three to eleven members were to be established in each area or street in the city and each township (xiang) in the countryside.[45] Committee members elected by "representatives of residents," should be "politically upright" persons with "close links with the masses" and be "enthusiastic" about mediation work (Art. 5). They were enjoined to carry out mediation "according to policy and law," and to mediate cases only when the parties voluntarily agreed to mediation (Art. 6). They were ordered not to prevent parties from going to the courts if they wished, and were prohibited from accepting bribes or showing favoritism, punishing or detaining parties, and "oppressing or retaliating against parties" (Art. 7). They were further obliged to "utilize leisure hours of production [to] listen to the views of the parties concerned, conduct penetrating investigation and study, fully acquaint themselves with circumstances of the case and adopt a polite and patient attitude and method of persuasion" (Art. 8). Cases were to be registered, and documents embodying the parties' agreement were to be issued to the parties "when necessary" (Art. 8).

Between 1954 and 1966, mediation committees continued their work in residential areas, providing an organizational means to deal efficaciously with disputes without interfering with production, thus freeing cadres and courts for more important tasks.[46] Mediation committees occasionally underwent temporary changes.[47] In some places they were merged for a time with the security defense committees. During the first years of the rural communes (1958–1960), mediation committees in some areas were transformed into "adjustment committees." As such, they organized meetings at which peasants adopted patriotic pacts vowing to obey Chairman Mao, the CCP, labor discipline, policies, law, and Communist morality; to protect public property and public order; to maintain good relations with family and friends; and to watch for "bad persons" and maintain public health.[48] After 1960, however, "adjustment committees" disappeared from sight.

Mediational Style

Mediation committees were expected to link dispute settlement with the Party's attempts to reorder society by making settlements that conformed to the needs of socialist construction. Published reports about the work of model mediators made explicit the intended role of mediation committees, suggesting the qualities which mediators were *supposed* to possess and the values they were *supposed* to foster.[49] To determine how mediators actually conducted their activities, interviews with Chinese émigrés were both more informative and more reliable.

Mediator Aunty Wu, introduced at the beginning of this chapter,[50] illustrates a Maoist mediator's ideal attributes. She hurried to investigate a disturbance she heard while walking along a street. She consulted with neighbors before investigating directly, and she later involved them in resolving a case. When she encountered a difficult case, she consulted the head of the local street business office and the local people's court; afterward she reported again, asking for cadres' opinions.[51] By maintaining close relations with cadres, she was simultaneously able to settle disputes and to "raise her own political consciousness."

Another exemplar of these traits is female mediator Li Erma.

One day, Li Erma, chairman of a mediation committee in Nanjing, heard about recurring fights in the home of Wang Ying. The next morning, Li went first to the Wangs' neighbors. She learned that Wang's wife was quarreling with Wang's co-resident mother and younger sister about sharing housework duties. Li then went next door to the Wang house, where Wang's mother admitted that she did not get along with her daughter-in-law. Li said to her: "You and I are alike. I've been a mother-in-law and in the past I, too, had a little of the old ideology. Now society is different, and we must treat daughter and daughter-in-law alike." Just then Wang's wife came home, and while Li helped her prepare lunch, she congratulated her on having a mother-in-law who helped, too. "They only eat and scold all day, and don't do anything," replied the wife. Li explained that younger children and older generations had mutual responsibilities, and owed each other respect. Later, Mr. Wang came home, and Li helped the family hold a "family unity and reconciliation meeting" in which each member of the family discussed his or her errors.

Days later, Li Erma was still concerned about the Wang family. When she met Mr. Wang on the street and asked him how the family was getting along, she was not convinced by his hesitant reply that things were all right. She returned to the Wang house, and conducted another meeting to exchange opinions. Ten days later, she returned again, and the Wangs said: "Li Erma is so concerned about unity and reconciliation in our house! This is really extraordinary devotion. From now on, we won't fight."[52]

Mediators were particularly commended when they combined dispute settlement with propaganda activities. One model mediator was praised for being "not only an activist mediator, but a very good propagandist. Through mediating disputes, or using large or small meetings, she correctly propagandizes national policies and laws to the masses."[53]

Many mediators were activists (*jiji fenzi*), who participated in other Party-sponsored work as well, for example with youth or women. Indeed, their enthusiasm and commitment in other work may have led to their selection as mediators. Mediators in cities were frequently unemployed housewives with time on their hands to stay at home—or pry into their neighbors' affairs. It should be noted that "activism" was a relative term. In some cases, "given the relatively low level of political consciousness among urban housewives, willingness to serve [was] in itself sufficient 'activism' to receive Party acceptance."[54]

Émigré interviews confirm some of the practices noted in the idealized accounts provided above. For example, former residents of Canton agreed that it was inevitable, under crowded conditions, for small group leaders or other activists to learn quickly about disputes, often just as they erupted. They also agreed that mediators maintained close links with cadres. The beat policeman circulated on the streets of his area, stopping frequently to talk with street activists. When an activist, such as a small group leader, security defense committee member, or mediation committee member, was unable to settle a dispute, he or she would report it to the police, to the residents' committee, or to the street business office and ask them to send someone to take over mediation. Even if one organization was notified, representatives of several usually came. Consider the following account, based on an émigré interview:

In a large Southern city, a woman lived with her grown son in several rooms, renting one to a lodger. Her relatives in Hong Kong occasionally sent food packages, which included cooking oil. The son discovered that some oil they received was missing, and accused the lodger of being the thief; the lodger replied by calling his accuser a "bourgeois." The two men began to argue violently, and set about destroying each other's possessions.

Their small group leader heard the commotion, and came running. She tried to calm the two, and succeeded in persuading them not to fight any more. She did not, however, solve the issue of the alleged theft, and the same evening the argument broke out again.

This time, the small group leader went directly to the street business office, and returned with a policeman and the chairman of the street mediation committee, who "invited" them to come to the street business office. There, the activists and the policeman heard the two parties' accusations. When the lodger again called the other a "bourgeois," the policeman replied that he knew the family was receiving packages from Hong Kong, but that no violation of law or policy was involved, and that it was wrong to call people "bourgeois." He lectured to the lodger on the impropriety of taking other people's belongings, and of scolding and quarreling with people. The mediation committee member lectured to both disputants on the unseemliness of their conduct; both men were comrades, he told them, and must also obey the law and not fight. Afterwards the two men returned home together.

This and other similar émigré accounts indicate that in crowded Chinese cities, the net of "basic-level" organization was tightly meshed. Disturbances and disputes were given close attention by activists and mediators, and by the cadres with whom they maintained close contact. Although mediation was formally differentiated from other activist responsibilities, activists other than mediation committee members and policemen frequently became involved in settling disputes. In fact, émigrés frequently did not distinguish between mediators and other persons likely to handle disputes. Their accounts suggest that a small group leader, a security defense committee member, a residents' committee member, or a policeman was as likely to handle a dispute as a mediator.[55]

JUDICIAL MEDIATION

If mediation by neighborhood mediators or cadres proved unsatisfactory, one or both parties would request that the local people's court settle the matter. Extra-judicial mediation was not a formal precondition to submitting a dispute to the courts,[56] but once the issue reached the courts, mediation—not adjudication—was most likely to follow.

The Politicization of Judicial Mediation

The emphasis on mediation in the courtroom increased during the "legal reform" movement of 1952–1953. Judges both practiced mediation inside the courts and supervised mediation outside the courts. A graduate of one of China's major law schools recalled participating in one such judicially directed mediation during his last year of law school, in 1952:

The local district court would send the files in a batch of civil and minor criminal cases to the law school, where a team of judges supervised the students in handling the cases as practical exercises. A cadre from the court would lecture the students beforehand on the type of cases they would hear, and on the laws and policies applicable to those cases. For marital disputes, for instance, he would urge students to be attentive to the bad influences of the old society, the oppression of women before the Revolution, the equality of women and men, and the necessity to protect women. After the lecture, the students were paired and sent to rooms already crowded with litigants, witnesses, spectators, and other law students.

The students alternated as judge and recording secretary. The "judge" would read the file in a case, and then question the disputants and witnesses, if any. After the issues were clear, the students would try to mediate the dispute in an effort to "educate the parties and the spectators."

In one case, a newly married couple requested a divorce. The husband worked in a factory by day, while the wife was employed at night. The husband wanted to have sexual relations with his wife in the evenings. She frequently refused, because she had to go to work, and the husband often beat her. The student "judge" to whom this dispute was submitted talked to the couple about women's rights, the valuable service the wife was performing to aid "national construction," and the couple's need for the wife's income. The husband protested that none of these considerations were relevant to his problem. The student told him that he would not grant a divorce, and that the couple must think of a way to settle it themselves. The parties went away.

This account shows how the emphases on resolving disputes in terms of general policies, and on educating parties and spectators, led to the inconclusive handling of disputes.

Other émigré accounts attest to the politicization of judicial mediation:

In a large Chinese city, a house owner of "bourgeois" class origin rented several rooms to a high-ranking cadre, who then failed to pay his rent for a long period of time. The landlord eventually overcame his reluctance, as a person of "bad" class origin, to become involved in a dispute with a cadre, and went to the street business office, to have the dispute mediated. Landlord and tenant agreed that the rent was owed and unpaid, but the tenant stated that he had a large family to support, and very little money. He agreed, however, to pay a fraction of the rent monthly thereafter, and to think of a way to pay the balance. Three months elapsed without any payment, and the landlord returned to the street business office. Again, the mediator could not resolve the dispute.

The landlord then explained his dispute to a judge at the local people's court. Landlord and tenant were summoned to appear together. After each stated his position, the judge noted the landlord's "bourgeois" origin and the tenant's "worker" origin and cadre status. He stated that it was the duty of "bourgeois" to help "worker," and that therefore it would be incorrect for the landlord to take money from his tenant. He added that if the tenant could pay at a later date, he would be ordered to do so, but since he could not pay at that time, he would not be ordered to pay anything at all.

The mediational style of the courts is further illustrated by divorce disputes, which comprised the bulk of civil cases handled by the courts.[57] Extra-judicial mediation usually preceded judicial disposition of divorce cases, but courts, once involved, engaged in intensive efforts to mediate.[58] In one divorce case in which the wife complained of frequent beatings by her husband and his family, the judge attempted to reconcile the couple, blaming their troubles on the father-in-law's "old-fashioned mentality." Even when the wife refused to be reconciled, the judge refused to grant a divorce unless the couple first attempted to live apart from the husband's family.[59] In another case, a well-educated husband and the wife he had

mistreated were reconciled after the husband admitted his "bourgeois attitude" and promised to correct his "erroneous attitudes."[60]

The Differences Between Judicial and Extra-Judicial Mediation

The above accounts suggest that courts settled disputes in the same
manner as mediation committees, but that their style of mediation was
perhaps more intimidating to the parties, since the courts wielded more
power than neighborhood mediators. Judges also received a more systematic instruction in policies than did street activists. These differences between judicial and extra-judicial mediation suggest that mediation, often
discussed in Chinese sources as a single, well-defined method of resolving
disputes, could vary significantly with the type of mediator. Additional
evidence of such variation is found when considering mediation in another forum, the factory or place of work.

MEDIATION WITHIN ORGANIZATIONS AND RURAL COMMUNES

"Rely on the organization, believe in the organization" was a well-
known slogan in the Maoist era. A person's organization, also called his
work unit (or simply unit), was his place of employment or other affiliation. It could be a government ministry or bureau, a factory, railroad, department store or other economic enterprise, a university, or a school.
Most Party members who were not full-time employees of the Party also
belonged to organizations in their capacities as cadres or workers, although they owed their primary commitment and allegiance to the
Party.[61]

The organization was much more than a place of work or study in
Maoist China. For the majority, who lived in quarters managed by their
unit, it was a home. Organizations also played key roles in mobilization.
As arenas for disseminating values consistent with national goals,[62] they
were expected to provide meaningful experience in the collective work of
constructing a strong, socialist China. The political and social roles of organizations, which included dispute settlement, dominated the lives of
their members.

The Organizational Context

When the first regulations for the nationwide organization of mediation committees were promulgated in 1954, mediation committees were
also established within some economic enterprises—particularly in their
residential quarters.[63] Thereafter, very little information appeared concerning the activities of such committees. Furthermore, émigrés who
spent time in economic enterprises or schools did not associate mediation
committees with such organizations.

Despite the absence or inactivity of formal mediation committees in organizations, mediation was nonetheless used to resolve the many disputes that arose among organization members and between members and nonmembers. Unlike mediation in residential units, mediation in organizations was not formally differentiated from other tasks performed by persons with official authority.

We return to the hypothetical Mr. Lu, whose neighborhood was introduced above, to illustrate the organization of authority in the work environment. The control apparatus at the neighborhood had its counterpart in Mr. Lu's factory, office, or school. In a large factory or bureau, for instance, a Party hierarchy extended downward from a Party secretary and Party committee to Party branches in workshops or offices, then to Party small groups at the lowest level.[64] All workers, whether Party members or not, were organized into small groups with the same indoctrination functions as the residents' small groups.

Every organization contained units for "security" and "personnel." In smaller organizations they were often merged, but in larger organizations, personnel and security units were separate and large. The cadres who worked in these sections were expected to be politically reliable Party or Young Communist League members or activists. Personnel sections had custody of the dossiers of all persons in the organization. Job assignments and salaries turned largely on political considerations weighed by Party cadres; thus, personnel sections were usually mere extensions of the unit's Party committee. Security sections investigated and controlled disturbances within the physical confines of the organization, reporting to and receiving directions from local police subbureaus.

Supervisors such as section chiefs in offices and workshop foremen in factories worked closely with the people they supervised. Units of such national groups as the Women's Association and the Young Communist League also conducted mobilizational work within organizations. The labor union functioned as an important adjunct of the Party in economic enterprises.[65] Again, small group leaders were the lowest level of the control apparatus. In short, if Mr. Lu worked in a factory, his contact was with an organizational apparatus closely resembling that in Table 2.[66]

Mediation in Urban Organizations

Within urban organizations, leaders dealt with social conflict ranging from petty disputes to major disturbances. If cadres or workers stole, habitually came late to work, worked poorly, were involved in accidents, fought, or argued with each other, such incidents were handled, at least initially, by supervisors, personnel or security cadres, administrative cadres,

TABLE 2. Lines of Authority in a Chinese Factory

LEVEL	Administration	Police	Communist Party	Young Communist League	Union	Police
Municipal	Municipal Bureau or Peking Ministry or Provincial Bureau [District Office]	Bureau	Committee	Committee	Committee	Committee
Intermediate	Factory Administration; Chief; Deputy Chiefs	District Sub-Bureau	Committee	Committee	Committee	Committee
Factory	Functional Sections (i.e., accounting, transport, purchasing, engineering, repair, production, etc.)	Security; Personnel	Secretary	Secretary	Committee	
	Workshop Foremen		Committee	Committee	Committee	
			Branch	Branch		
	Small Group		Party Group	YCL Group	Union Representative	

and small group leaders. Dispute resolution was little differentiated from other aspects of administration and discipline.

Disputes could be settled within the organization even if they were unrelated to the work-related duties of the disputants or the activities of the organization. For instance, a landlord not belonging to the organization could complain that a tenant employed by the organization had not paid his rent. Personnel sections and work supervisors investigated such complaints and could order monthly garnishments of a portion of the tenant's salary. Supervisory personnel also settled disputes between organization members and outsiders, who could and did make complaints.

Labor union cadres in particular handled many disputes. Cadres in charge of union welfare programs were often asked by workers or workers' dependents to settle disputes over debts, petty thefts, or damage to property. When workers wanted divorces, union cadres, like mediators in residential areas, conducted investigations, sent persons to talk with the parties, their friends, and their neighbors, and held meetings of fellow members to "assist" a comrade seeking a divorce to desist. As with disputes in residential areas, unsuccessful attempts to mediate were taken to the courts. Once in court, neighborhood and organization mediators were often called to appear. The court might conduct further fact finding and investigation in conjunction with a variety of organizations before it attempted to mediate the dispute. A case recalled by an émigré informant will illustrate:

In 1964, a worker discovered that his wife had been having extra-marital relations. He arranged for several fellow workers, including his labor union representative, to follow the wife to a rendezvous with her lover. They followed her to a hotel, and noted that she entered and remained for several hours before coming out again. The next day, he notified his neighborhood mediation committee that he wanted a divorce. The mediators held three sessions to try to reconcile the couple.

At these mediation sessions, the wife admitted that she had male friends, but denied that she had had sexual relations with them. No reconciliation could be effected. After the third mediation session, the husband wrote to the district people's court requesting a divorce and punishment of the wife's lover. His fellow workers also signed the letter.

In court, a judge and several jurors[67] heard the testimony of the couple, the fellow workers, and the mediation committee's chairman, who stated his opinion that the evidence of adultery was insufficient. The judge agreed, attempted unsuccessfully to reconcile the couple, and then adjourned the court.

Afterwards, the Party secretary of the husband's work unit wrote to the alleged lover's Party secretary, asking him to investigate. The response came back that the alleged lover had a history of associating with married women. The husband's Party secretary also wrote to the Party secretary of the factory which employed the wife, urging that she undergo "education." Several meetings were held with the wife's fellow workers, who attempted to convince her of her errors, but she was unrelenting. A second session of the court was then convened.

The judge related investigation results that showed the alleged lover had had numerous adulterous affairs. Jurors had also spoken to the couple's neighbors and fellow workers, and to their respective work unit Party secretaries. The judge reviewed the evidence and concluded that the wife had misbehaved. Later the parties were summoned to a third and final session of the court, where the judge granted the divorce and awarded custody of the child to the husband.

Mediation Within Rural Communes

Mediation in the countryside was generally similar to mediation in the urban context. In the rural communes, rural households were grouped into production teams. A number of teams formed a production brigade, and a number of brigades made up a commune.[68] Team, brigade, and commune were administered by committees headed by team, brigade, and commune chiefs. Along with divisions responsible for agricultural production, finance, culture and education, and so forth, each commune had a political-legal department and a police station, comparable to the urban neighborhood police station.[69] Each brigade and team also had security defense committees and activists responsible for public security work.[70] Few police cadres were permanently stationed in brigades or teams, so the tasks they normally performed were handled by security defense committeemen and brigade and team leaders. The Young Communist League and the Women's Association also had organizations in the commune.[71] Party organization, of course, also permeated the commune and all of its subordinate units.[72]

Although communes had mediation committees with members from each brigade, most civil disputes were handled by team and brigade leaders or by security defense activists.[73] Even when mediation committees met, team and brigade leaders were able to greatly influence the outcome of the dispute.[74]

COMPARISON OF MEDIATION IN DIFFERENT CONTEXTS

Dispute resolution in both urban organizations and rural communes was formally differentiated from other tasks far less than it was in urban residential areas. Other differences arose because organizations had focused purposes, unlike urban neighborhoods, and because the barriers between organizations and society were relatively distinct. The nature of the organization affected the extent to which political considerations were injected into dispute resolution.

Organizations such as the Party and the Young Communist League — which displayed great cohesiveness and maintained a distinct distance from other sectors of Chinese society[75]—subjected dispute resolution to overt and intense politicization, most intensely when disputes involved organizations' internal discipline or external relations. Disputes between police and ordinary citizens, for example, were taken very seriously, because such disputes involved basic questions of relations between police and the masses. At one provincial Party school for high-ranking members, all disputes were seen as potentially threatening. Even marital disputes of cadres attending the school could lead to administrative punishments or expulsion from the Party.

However, in some organizations the political significance of issues raised in disputes could also be attenuated. Neighborhood mediators had ample time to talk with the residents—to penetrate the masses, in Party jargon. Cadres and activists in economic enterprises, occupied with achieving the productive goals of their enterprise, were less likely to engage in lengthy attempts to persuade disputants of error or to mobilize other workers to engage in such activities. Such cadres treated disputes as administrative matters, to be decided like any others.

The Functions of Mediation in Maoist China

One function of mediation was to resolve disputes, thereby maintaining order in social and economic activity. Mediation was also intended to end bad feelings between individuals by offering them a readily available and highly informal mode of settling disputes. However, mediation in Maoist China also served three other identifiable functions that often worked at cross-purposes with resolving disputes. First, it was used to articulate and apply the ideological principles, values, and programs of the Party and to mobilize popular commitment to Party policies and goals. Second, it suppressed rather than settled disputes, which were seen as interfering with socialist construction. Third, it supplemented other means of control exercised by the state and Party apparatus.

MEDIATION AND MOBILIZATION

Role of Mediation Committees in Implementing Policies

In the first years of their existence, rural mediation committees were used by the CCP to support a policy of agricultural cooperativization. After the 1950–1952 land reform redistributed land among 300 million peasants, the Party began to organize peasants into mutual aid teams to raise productivity by pooling labor, implements, and draft animals.[76] Mediation committees were acclaimed for their role in benefiting production by quickly settling disputes within and between mutual aid teams over allocation and usage of water, timber, and tools.

After the promulgation of the "provisional rules" in 1954, the role of mediation committees in supporting production and implementing economic policies was emphasized. Later, from 1955 to 1957, when rural collectivization was accelerated in China and peasants were organized into rural cooperatives, the collectivization campaign was announced as the "central work" that mediation was required to support.[77] The resolution of disputes in which peasants accused each other of neglecting collective interests was popularized by mediators.[78] Mediation committees aided "unity" by "persuading" doubters of the advantages of cooperativization.[79] When China's agriculture was further collectivized with the creation of rural communes in 1958–1960, mediation committees were used to extol communal living, increase peasants' commitment to communalization, and reduce disputes that interfered with commune administration.[80] In the mid-1960s, commune mediators were encouraged to curb "spontaneous capitalism" among peasants and to assist cadres in mobilizing the masses to sign public pacts.[81]

Politicization of Mediation Standards

The political objectives of mediation changed from time to time, as did the intensity of efforts exerted to attain them. Regardless of such variations, however, the explicit politicization of standards was consistently maintained. Issues between parties, proposed solutions, and even the very occurrence of disputes, all were invested with political significance, producing a range of effects on dispute resolution. As a result of politicization, dispute "resolution" often meant not the settlement of disputes, but rather their oversimplification into abstract political generalizations. To "resolve" can mean to "answer" or to "solve," but it can also mean to "reduce to simpler form." Both meanings are pertinent here. Thus, a husband who mistreated his wife could be labeled by a judge as "feudal," a mother-in-law who squabbled with her son's wife might be told that the disagreements were caused by "old ideology," and a young married couple unable to adjust their married life to their employment schedules might be told that they must "serve national construction." In each case, the disputants' personal grievances were transcended and overwhelmed by a larger issue of political policy. In some other cases, of course, politicization of a dispute was not necessarily inconsistent with its resolution in a manner acceptable to one or both disputants.

Variability of Politicization

The Maoist ideal of politicization and its realization in practice were, of course, divergent, as are goals and practice in any legal system. Politicization was never total and in some cases may have been absent altogether. Not all mediators were persistent and patient model mediators, ready to mobilize neighbors or fellow workers to "educate" disputants; some mediators neglected political considerations, showed favoritism, accepted bribes, or attempted to settle disputes through compromise, without resort to political standards. Such "defects" in "work style" were extensively discussed and condemned throughout the Maoist era. Deviant, "incorrect" styles of mediation may have produced solutions satisfactory to disputants even if they were, in the Party's views, "unprincipled."

Even when political factors were infused into disputes, the effect was often quite insignificant, as the following dispute illustrates:

In a large city in South China in 1959, an employee of an enterprise rented a room from the agent of an overseas Chinese for ten *yuan* monthly.[82] It was understood that the tenant would have the use of a second room in the same apartment, except when the landlord's agent wished to use it. Soon afterwards, additional members of the tenant's family moved into the second room. The agent demanded that the rent be increased to twenty *yuan* monthly. The tenant refused, arguing that the agent could still sleep in the second room whenever he wanted. The agent demanded that the family vacate the premises and refused to accept the additional ten *yuan*.

When the tenant's family refused to move, the agent asked the local street business office to mediate the dispute. A mediator, "Sister" Chang, listened to the parties' positions. She suggested that she did not think that it was right for the tenant to pay no rent for the second room; nor did she think it was right for the agent to make them all move because of the disagreement. She suggested that it would be best if both sides "yielded a little" (*rang yidian*) to arrive at a compromise. The agent refused, and initiated proceedings in the district People's Court, which summoned both parties.

In a courthouse office a cadre identified himself as the person in charge of mediation (*tiaojie zhuren*), and listened to each party's explanation, interrupting to ask questions.

The cadre proposed that since the tenant was a cadre and the landlord an overseas Chinese, the two men had obligations to help and understand each other in the interests of the revolution. He proposed that the tenant pay an additional four *yuan* monthly for the use of the second room, and that the parties continue to observe their agreement that the tenant and his family would move out of the room whenever the agent wished to use it. The parties agreed to this proposal, and their dispute was thus resolved.

In this dispute, street mediator Sister Chang sought to effect a compromise without reference to any political considerations. The court mediator articulated political criteria, but since neither party had a "bad" class or political background they had no effect. If disputes in which politics were neglected are taken together with disputes in which politicization was superficial, a considerable amount of mediation may have been, for all intents and purposes, "unprincipled."

On the other hand, when some policies were implemented with a heavy hand, disputes may have been so deeply politicized that political issues determined the outcome and produced further consequences for disputants. Persons stigmatized as "enemies" or "bad elements" with a "bad class origin" could find resolution of their disputes a most unpleasant experience. Husbands of "landlord" or "bourgeois" background accused of mistreatment by wives of "worker" or "peasant" origins risked severe criticism, sometimes in large groups led by the women activists in urban mediation committees. Indeed, émigrés indicated that aggressive wives of "better" class origin than their husbands used this political factor in seeking divorce.

MEDIATION AND DISPUTE SUPPRESSION

Due to the politicization of disputes, conflicts that individuals viewed as personal and centering on narrow issues could be perceived quite differently by mediators, who applied generalized values stressing commitment to Party and national goals. Mediators might give more time and effort to fashioning a political solution—changing the "thought" or "standpoint" of the disputants—than to settling the actual issues that precipitated the dispute. Consequently, disputes could be suppressed in two ways. Primary dispute suppression occurred when resolution of the parties' differences was submerged in mediators' application of abstract principles. Thus, spouses who themselves could not reconcile their sexual life with their hours of work were told by a judge that they could not obtain a divorce, but were given no reason or alternative solution. When parties could not obtain a meaningful settlement of their original controversies, such an outcome amounted to suppression rather than resolution. Secondary dispute suppression occurred when disputants avoided mediation by activists or cadres because they felt it would not resolve their difficulties. Some émigrés told of personally avoiding mediation because they disliked mediators' lectures and exhortations. They did not wish street activists to be involved and regarded them as meddlesome agents of a feared control apparatus. Such anxieties may sometimes have led parties to seek to resolve their disputes through private rather than official mediation, or to avoid mediation altogether.

MEDIATION AS AN INSTRUMENT OF CONTROL

An important goal of the state and party apparatus to which mediator activists and cadres belonged was to maintain and strengthen Party control. The closeness of activist mediators to both the urban police and the Party was frequently stressed by the Chinese press[83] and corroborated by émigrés. Mediators were intended to provide information on the activities and "ideology" of disputants and to act as agents to locate and inhibit antisocial conduct. In this way they would help repress "enemies" of the "people," and "persuade" "bad elements" to reform.

The degree of control exercised by mediators varied with their power to invoke sanctions, and generally to exercise a range of devices used by the Party to elicit a voluntaristic response from China's people:

If a citizen is reluctant to volunteer, the regime first attempts to persuade. The citizen who does not respond to the appeal for volunteers is presented with rational arguments on why the regime needs volunteers. The arguments presented in a citizen's small group and the visits of numerous activists urging him to volunteer may arouse some anxiety, but in voluntarism, properly practiced, there is nothing to suggest the use of force. The citizen being persuaded understands perfectly that threats lie behind these rational arguments, but they remain implicit.[84]

Sanctions—deliberately kept in the background—that backed up the Party's persuasive efforts included further and more intense persuasion of a citizen who refused to volunteer, criticism at small or large meetings, adverse entries in a dossier he was never permitted to see, denial of welfare benefits, or more formal penal measures.[85] Once activists or cadres noticed a dispute and "requested" the parties to accept their mediation, they were loath to decline, fearing that renewed and insistent "requests" would follow.

There were considerable variations in mediators' persuasiveness and authority to invoke sanctions. Urban neighborhood mediators might be unheeded by disputants who had been told repeatedly by the Party that they may take their disputes to courts. Some urban mediators were poorly educated, often barely literate, and thus lacked authority and respect in their neighborhoods among younger and better educated residents. However, while mediators themselves lacked coercive power, their ties to policemen and other cadres could trigger more authoritative action. In rural communes and organizations, mediation was done by cadres who had the power to invoke sanctions such as demotions, reductions in salary, transfers, or entries of demerits in employees' dossiers. Thus, mediation and control were more closely merged in organizations than in urban neighborhoods. Regardless of milieu, however, mediators were integral parts of the mechanism of Party rule.

Dispute Resolution in Traditional and Maoist China Compared

In the Maoist era, the Party preached a revolutionary rejection of the past, insisting that contemporary mediation owed nothing to China's her-

1980s judges were cadres, administrative and mobilizational leaders of a universal type. We shall see below in chapter 9 that this view continues to a considerable extent. The continued commingling of functions had definite implications for the role of law in the CCP's efforts to modernize China.

Max Weber's influential theories on bureaucracy suggest that modernization means increasing specialization of function and differentiation of roles in bureaucracies.[98] Under this theory, dispute resolution by officials should become differentiated from their other functions.[99] However, in countries ruled by Communist parties, whether in the Soviet Union, Eastern Europe, or China, modernization and industrial development were promoted by a bureaucracy that remained highly politicized and undifferentiated.[100] China's traditional blending of law and administration conditioned, in part, the CCP's lack of inclination to separate these activities. This blend persisted not because Mao thought like China's former rulers, but because they left behind no institutional separation that might have been continued.

DISCONTINUITIES

Despite these continuities, the changes wrought by the CCP both in ideology and institutions were even more compelling. Preoccupied with ideas of struggle and change, the CCP radically transformed the processes of dispute resolution.

Differing Organizational Context of Mediation

Mediators in traditional China were clearly not regular members of a tightly knit state apparatus. The traditional Chinese state reached down imperfectly to the society it governed, and dispute resolution lay largely outside the activities of the magistrates. The gentry, to be sure, shared the intellectual background and values of the officials and had vital interests in the stability of a government which protected their own wealth and prestige. Therefore, when settling disputes, advising magistrates, or helping to enforce magistrates' decisions, the gentry acted in a sense as auxiliaries to the formal apparatus of government. In addition, they participated in propagating Confucian ideology, as did the village, clan, and guild leaders who also acted as adjuncts to government. These dispute-settlers, however, were not formally responsible to the magistrates and, moreover, sought to protect and further their own interests, which sometimes conflicted with the interests of officialdom; clans, villages, and guilds settled disputes among their own members in part to increase their chances of being left alone by the government.

In Maoist China, state and society were much more closely integrated.

The apparatus of control penetrated much more deeply into Chinese society than in the past; mediators were either cadre members of the official apparatus or its activist extension. The CCP apparatus, the Party-state, clearly exercised greater control over China than did its traditional predecessor.

The contrast suggested above is not absolute. Whoever has ruled China from Beijing, whether as emperor or chairman, has had to reinforce and supplement an elite with its own auxiliaries. The magistrate was assisted by gentry, village headmen, clan leaders, and other local notables; the cadre was assisted by the activist. In both societies the agents of indirect rule were mediators. This correlation is not accidental, but probably indicates that dispute resolution was by and large, generally, ordinarily less important than other affairs of government. The affairs to which pride of place was given in imperial and Maoist China differed, of course. Yet, because dispute resolution was placed low on the scale of priorities and was handled by auxiliaries in both political systems, there is necessarily a similarity between administrative techniques. It would be dangerous to assume that because the CCP to some extent has ruled indirectly, it was continuing an old tradition; it simply encountered an old problem—the need to rule a huge country with a limited elite—and responded to it by seeking reliable auxiliaries to implement policy. The techniques of indirect rule changed so much—the auxiliaries were no longer passive agents of the elite, and more mediation was done by the elite itself—that Maoist mediation could be said to have involved new techniques and values.

In sum, while mediation in traditional China was generally a means of avoiding official representatives of the state, mediation in Maoist China directly involved representatives of the state. Although both were extrajudicial, traditional mediation was unsupervised by officials, while Maoist mediation was conducted and supervised by representatives of the state and the Party.

Different Philosophical and Ideological Attitudes Toward Disputes and Their Resolution

Confucian and Communist views of social conflict present an obvious and dramatic contrast. In the traditional view conflict was a regrettable and possibly dangerous rending of a desired harmonious continuum of relationships. Moreover, conflict, especially face-to-face, was unseemly and embarrassing. Dispute resolution aimed at repairing relationships rent by the unfortunate occurrence and therefore sought compromise and a reasonable result rather than absolute victory for one party.

Maoist ideology not only regarded social conflict as inevitable, but considered it the very stuff of social and political progress. Individual disputes were regrettable, not because they impaired the relationships between the disputants, but because they interfered with important national tasks. The CCP's objective in handling these interferences was not merely to repair damaged relationships or even to improve production, but to use the dispute by resolving the contradictions it represented, "correcting" the disputants' "ideology" and "standpoint," and reaching results that were consistent with national policies. These different concepts of disputes radically changed mediators' views of their role.

Differing Priorities of Dispute Settlement and Didactic Functions

Although mediation in traditional China was considered primarily a mode of settling disputes, it discharged another, very secondary, "didactic" function when mediators instructed disputants, witnesses, and onlookers in the virtues of compromise and other related Confucian virtues.[101] In Maoist China, mediation supplemented other didactic administrative techniques, especially the "mass line," in reinforcing mass commitment to policy. It would be erroneous, however, to assume that the CCP merely reordered the relative priorities of didactic and dispute settlement functions. It sought, rather, to change fundamentally the very nature of dispute resolution. The significant reduction of disputants' opportunities to bargain with each other and negotiate for a mutually satisfactory compromise of their disagreement shows clearly the extent of the change.

"Mediation" in traditional China ranged from the highly informal private attempts of mutual friends to end a dispute to the imposition of a decision by an extremely powerful and respected mediator who "proposed" a solution backed up by strong public opinion. Generally, however, even in a context of powerful group pressures, the traditional mediational style emphasized compromise and facilitated negotiation between parties. In this way Confucian virtue was supported, group solidarity maintained, and social harmony restored. The parties lost no face by either arrogantly insisting on total victory or encountering total defeat, and tolerable compromises were often reached.

The Maoist mediational style condemned compromise as "unprincipled mediation." The Maoist imperative to resolve contradictions through struggle dictated the use of the face-to-face conflict that traditional mediation sought to avoid. Communist "self-criticism" should not be confused with Confucian self-cultivation, despite occasionally similar rhetoric.[102] So-called "self-criticism" was more often than not "assisted," was more intense than Confucian self-cultivation, and aimed at a more political result.

Maoist mediators were required to identify and solve correctly political and ideological factors in disputes, and they were encouraged to conduct their duties in the presence of onlookers so that they would be educated together with the disputants. For education to be correct, nothing

in the proceedings was to confuse or create doubts in the minds of onlookers. As a result, disputants' opportunities to bargain were reduced or
eliminated, decreasing the chance that the parties could obtain redress
they considered adequate.

The CCP's emphasis on suppressing bargaining was obviously linked to
its imposition on China of an authority structure that depended on and
promoted national values. Traditional mediation depended on the willingness of disputants and mediators to take into account personal characteristics and to make a highly personal evaluation of the dispute. Maoism
aimed at replacing these smaller perspectives with a larger, national perspective. Cadres were supposed to lead rather than conciliate; they were
to mobilize rather than instruct.[103] The CCP sought to repress any personal values and allegiances inconsistent with the individuals' obligations
to society.[104] In attempting to change these values and the authority relations that maintain them, the CCP replaced mediational bargaining with a
mode of dispute settlement that reflected national values and interests.[105]

Differing Relations Between Court and Extra-Judicial Mediators

In traditional China, mediation offered disputants a desirable alternative to litigation; for its part, the government welcomed the reduction in
the volume of official work. In Maoist China, mediation as a mode of dispute resolution no longer differed greatly from the judicial mode, although
the Party did promote mediation in order to lighten the workload of judicial and nonjudicial cadres. As we have seen, the actual attempts of mediators to inject political factors into a dispute varied considerably with
the context of mediation. It is clear, however, that the Party made mediation of civil cases the primary mode of resolution, rather than adjudication
in the courts.

Conclusion

While there may have been "resonances" between traditional and
Maoist dispute resolution,[106] the mediational devices used by the CCP
seem more directly traceable to the Party's own development than to the
tradition it so resolutely opposed. The CCP had considerable success in
altering the nature of courts, unifying judicial and extra-judicial methods
of resolving disputes, politicizing the mediation process, and, in general,
changing and redistributing the functions of mediation. Examination of
official Party objectives and actual practice indicates frequent and substantial correlation between the two. While it may be tempting to regard
Maoist mediators as "successors to the gentry and other prestige figures
who settled most of the disputes of village, clan, and guild,"[107] it would be

dangerous to yield to this temptation. The purposes that the CCP assigned to mediation and the mediators and the style they were expected to use in resolving disputes contrast sharply with traditional dispute resolution.

Further study may be benefited by comparing Chinese dispute resolution with dispute resolution in other modernizing Asian nations, such as Japan and Taiwan, where traditional forms of mediation coexist with elaborate codes of law.[108] Future comparative inquiry may show the effects on dispute resolution in China not only of Maoism, but of forces of modernization common to all developing nations. Studies on Taiwan, for instance, indicate that traditional mediation has decayed because land reform and urbanization disrupted traditional hierarchical relationships and reduced the respect formerly commanded by traditional mediators.[109]

When the article on which this chapter is based was originally written, I suggested that further investigation would show more accurately the effects of CCP innovations in dispute resolution, and that such innovations were only part of an extraordinary revolutionary flux. It was possible, I thought, that they were also obscuring persistent traditional practices, and could give way to an amalgam of traditional and newer CCP-influenced practice or even to practices that might resemble Western institutions. As the later chapters in this book indicate, all three of these possibilities have come to pass. Before moving to the contemporary scene, however, we should consider next another aspect of law under Maoism, the use of formal legal institutions or their analogues.

CHAPTER 4

Law Under Mao, II: Law as Administration

THE PARTY DID NOT neglect legal forms after its victory in 1949, but it allowed them little substance. Although the Cultural Revolution that exploded in 1966 is today often regarded as epitomizing the politicization of Chinese life, legal institutions had been either largely rendered irrelevant or politicized by the late 1950s, long before the Cultural Revolution ultimately swept them aside. This chapter discusses the pre-reform criminal process and the much smaller domain of non-criminal, "civil" law, and, like the preceding chapter, distills the major points of earlier articles on these subjects. Notes and references are those in the original version. A brief note on the Cultural Revolution has been added. Taken together with the preceding chapter, this chapter recalls for the reader the institutional background that heavily conditions current legal reform.[1]

The Criminal Process Under Mao

Before the Cultural Revolution, the courts' principal activities centered on the formal criminal process. The criminal process in the 1990s, although it has undergone reform, still displays greater continuity between current institutions and practices and those of the Maoist period than any other area of the law. Because it continues to operate as a tool of changing Party policies, its continuities with the period preceding reform are strong and striking. As a result, too, earlier practice in criminal matters affects judicial activity in non-criminal areas today.

In "Form and Function in the Chinese Criminal Process," published in 1969, I reviewed the policies and institutions that marked sanctioning processes from 1949 until the Cultural Revolution began. At the time, the activities of the courts in the formal criminal process seemed to reflect notions of bureaucracy rather than legality. The courts were not considered to be different from other hierarchically organized government organizations because of their functional specialization but were viewed as a constituent part of a larger sanctioning bureaucracy.

Today, as I argue in chapter 6, although legality has become valued in its own right by Chinese leaders, some of the notions of bureaucracy that competed for dominance before the Cultural Revolution continue to influence legal institutions and policies toward them. Because pre-reform practice in the criminal process has been especially long-lived and durable, an understanding of sanctioning processes in China before the Cultural Revolution is highly desirable. This chapter presents my analysis at the time, condensing the original article without substantially revising it. Enough detail has been included to explain its relevance to understanding the Chinese courts today, and to permit comparison with the current-day sanctioning institutions discussed in chapter 6.[2]

Sanctioning Processes, 1949–1965

"Form and Function" began by tracing the origins of a Chinese Communist leadership style that emphasized organizational techniques centered on mobilizational leadership and the "mass line." This style frequently blurred or obscured the distinction between governmental and nongovernmental organizations and activities, and the CCP used the state apparatus as only one means for transmitting and implementing policy. Law and regulation were required to be flexible and responsive to policy, and law enforcement was required to aim at mobilizing mass support for the Party. In Yenan and other "liberated areas" before 1949, adjudication was blended with mobilizational tactics such as mass meetings and rallies.[3]

When the Party came to power in 1949, law fell within the sphere of "political-legal work" and was linked with the mass line. At the same time, the Party recognized that some orderliness in procedure had to be assured and that methods had to be provided for reviewing cadres' exercise of discretion in applying the flexible policies that, in the absence of law codes, defined prohibited conduct only generally. Conflict between contrasting emphases on the mass line and regularity was to sharpen over the years.

1949–1953: CAMPAIGNS AND THE RESTRUCTURING OF SOCIETY

During the first four years of Communist rule the Party applied its revolutionary techniques to restructuring Chinese society. A succession of violent mass movements was launched to redistribute land and shatter the power of rural landholders, eliminate "counter-revolutionaries," and break the power of the urban bourgeoisie. Legality, of course, was ignored. The

Nationalist codes were abolished and no move was made to adopt new ones; some penal norms punishing counter-revolutionary activity and corruption were adopted in the course of campaigns, but they were broad and imprecise. Regulations establishing formal judicial and procuratorial hierarchies were promulgated, but the courts were used merely to implement specific campaigns and were at times displaced by special tribunals created for campaigns.

Law itself became a target. In 1952 and 1953, a nationwide campaign to "reform law" purged most of the considerable number of law-trained judges and clerks who had previously worked for the overthrown Nationalist regime, replacing them with politically reliable cadres. The campaign stressed the role of law as an instrument of class warfare, and criticized the purged judges for their unwillingness to wage such warfare against enemies of the people. Significantly, the "reform law" campaign also attacked "legal procedures," which were denounced as reactionary. Procedural and substantive rules and principles, such as prohibitions against retroactive criminal legislation, and even the notion that cases should be decided on the merits, were directly and sharply criticized.

The Use of Invidious "Class" Distinctions

We saw in chapter 3 that during the first years of rule, the CCP classified all adults by "class origin," a designation indicating the economic position of each family and its affiliation with the Nationalists at the time of Communist victory. In addition to class-designated labels, supplementary classification stigmatized some persons as members of "other groups which, while not class groups in any strict, traditional sense, were nevertheless identifiable opponents of the regime or were considered by the Communists to be undesirable elements for a variety of reasons."[4] Often grouped together in the "four bad elements" were "landlords," "rich peasants," "counter-revolutionaries," and ambiguously "bad elements." These classifications, noted in each person's dossier and used as an index of loyalty and reliability, remained critically important in the operation of all sanctioning schemes developed by the Communist Party until the onset of legal reform.

Creation of Police and Party Networks of Control

During the early years, the Party also created the elaborate apparatus for surveillance described in chapter 3. The police, dominated by the Party, administered serious "criminal" sanctions, which ranged from confinement in police-run "labor reform" camps to the death sentence. Trials were not usually held unless, in conjunction with some campaign, Party officials felt that a public trial would have particular educational importance. The police also administered sanctions for less serious offenses entirely without the courts. These included fines and short periods of confinement in police-run "detention centers." A police-administered regime of "control" was first applied to former landlords and minor counter-revolutionaries not linked with serious crimes, then extended to other persons deemed to deserve punishment and surveillance without prison confinement.

In every economic, educational, and government unit, police and Party cadres were charged with handling "personnel" and "security" matters and labor discipline, and they applied "administrative" sanctions such as dismissal, demotion, entry of demerits in dossiers, and reductions in salary and job assignments. The Party and its adjunct, the Young Communist League, created their own internal mechanisms for discipline. And, finally, in every urban street and less effectively in the vast Chinese countryside, the activist-augmented cadre apparatus directly controlled or influenced application of an assortment of informal punishments, such as public criticism of varying intensity in small or large groups.

Courts and Procuracy figured little in decision-making and were used chiefly to formalize the most serious punishments in order to propagandize Party policies and educate the masses on desired behavior. Although some attempts were made to regularize procedures and cadres were urged to be careful in their work, at the same time legal cadres were also constantly reminded to link ideology and legal work and were criticized for undue use of formal procedures. Generally, the Chinese leadership was reluctant to regularize judicial procedure, since making criminal law a matter for experts was incompatible with mass line notions of political leadership. The conflict between regularization and the mass line became more explicit in ensuing years.

1953–1957: TENTATIVE REGULARIZATION OVERCOME BY MASS LINE POLITICS

Legality as Discipline: Law and Politics

By 1953 the Chinese leadership had consolidated its control, and it shifted its aim to industrialization under Soviet-style five-year plans. Professing adherence to more regularized Soviet institutional models, the leadership showed greater interest in a formal judicial system. An emphasis on building new legal institutions, consistent with its Stalinist inspiration, stressed not legality but the discipline required in the drive for "economic construction."

Cadres were cautioned against thinking that law was above class and that law could restrain the revolution, as in this 1955 newspaper editorial:

'Henceforth no one can bother us'—this deviant error on the independence of adjudication must be criticized. Naturally, to understand the independence of adjudication [to mean] that when adjudication work is being done the masses do not have to be depended on, that there are no contacts with relevant departments, and that cases are handled in isolation [i.e., without reference to current policies], is extremely erroneous.[5]

Cadres were frequently reminded that law must serve policy; thus they should decide cases so that the outcomes promoted specific short-term goals, such as reducing industrial accidents or fulfilling quotas for the purchase of grain from peasants. There was never any doubt that the mission of the newly regularized institutions was to serve the construction of socialism.

Formal Steps to Regularization

In 1954, a constitution was adopted, organizational legislation was promulgated for the courts and Procuracy, and rules on arrest and detention were promulgated.[6] New policies on the administration of law were evidenced by a tripartite division of functions. The police were to investigate suspected offenses and make arrests that had been approved by the Procuracy. The Procuracy—made formally independent, as in the Soviet Union, rather than attached to the courts, as in the Nationalist system and in the Jiangsi Soviet—was not only to approve arrests but to verify evidence and make formal accusations. The courts were to determine guilt in public trials before one judge and two citizens acting as "people's jurors" in which the accused had a "right to defense." At various times between 1954 and 1957 sporadic attempts were made to implement these new measures. Law schools and university law departments were established or expanded; procuratorial offices were opened or enlarged, modest numbers of cadres were trained, and courts were enlarged; small lawyers' offices patterned after Soviet lawyers' collectives were opened, usually in large cities; experiments were conducted by the Ministry of Justice and the Supreme People's Court in administering trials under uniform rules of civil and criminal procedure. In 1957, under circumstances and with results described below, experiments with a formal criminal process were abruptly ended, but the trajectory of these experiments illustrates important tensions in Chinese attitudes toward formal legal institutions.

Continued Politicization of Formal Sanctioning:
Police and Party Disregard of Adjudication

Chinese commitment to socialist legality was far from total. Soon after the first small steps were taken to regularize the system in 1954, further political campaigns were launched that approached the intensity, although not the violence, of the campaigns of the previous five years. In 1955 and early 1956 these campaigns, particularly one to suppress counter-revolutionaries, involved mass action and direct police and Party sanctioning, principally through ad hoc teams of cadres and activists formed throughout the country. The activity of the courts continued to be linked to promoting specific policies. For example, courts were directed to "expedite" cases involving violations of government decrees on grain purchases from peasants; "thieves and swindlers" had to be severely dealt with; persons who opposed agricultural collectivization had to be persuaded or punished.

To the extent that courts participated in sanctioning, the criminal process was adjudicatory only in form, and was dominated by the police and by Party officials within the "political-legal" system, as the three organs of police, Procuracy, and courts were called. The formal procedures established by the legislation of 1954 for processing suspects and resolving disagreements among the police, Procuracy, and courts on the disposition of cases were largely disregarded. In most cases, the Procuracy and courts confirmed the police recommendation for disposition of the case. Although the official model of the process stressed procuratorial interrogation and public trials, in practice Procuracy and courts relied on the file assembled by the police in the case. Émigré interviews suggested that in approximately 15 percent of all cases the three organizations disagreed; these differences were resolved by informal consultations between the organizations involved, sometimes with the participation of Party officials (Party Committees had "political-legal departments" to oversee the work of police, Procuracy, and courts). Only "important" cases were reviewed as a matter of course. These involved counter-revolutionary crimes, homicides, large-scale thefts, or cadre misdeeds. The public trial, if held, confirmed the antecedent decisions by police and Procuracy and was generally intended to serve as an educational demonstration of the defendant's guilt. If there was a doubt about guilt the case was not tried at all, but dismissed or returned to the Procuracy or police.

Although defendants were entitled to be represented at their trials by defense counsel, the lawyers' offices that were opened intermittently in 1955–1957 during a period of experimentation with a Soviet-style bar were both small and ineffective. Defense lawyers were not widely used and were generally distrusted by cadres such as judges, who associated them with the "enemies" who were the objects of the criminal process. After conviction, defendants could theoretically appeal, but very few did; some reviews of convictions, however, were conducted by the trial court itself, higher-level courts, the Ministry of Justice, or the police. Within police bureaus, special cadre groups were formed to investigate cases of persons recently sent to labor camps. If the investigation disclosed errors, the prisoners involved would be released by orders transmitted through the police apparatus, sometimes with the formal assent of the courts.

Available sources strongly suggest the existence of deep ambivalence about the formal criminal process from the leadership to legal cadres. The leadership was not greatly concerned with maintaining fidelity to their Soviet models. Mao himself, complaining of the reluctance of rural cadres to accelerate agricultural cooperativization in 1955, said, "What we should not do is to allow some of our comrades to cover up their dilatoriness by quoting the experience of the Soviet Union."[7] Judicial cadres were similarly accused of being more concerned with following bureaucratic Soviet models than with punishing "enemies." Low-level cadres also had little commitment to legality. Many lacked education and most lacked legal training. The legal education that did exist was curiously abstract; well into 1956 it consisted of little more than mechanical teaching about the Soviet Union without attempting to apply Soviet experiences to China.[8]

The police, who had administered sanctions without meaningful judicial or procuratorial interference during the first years of Communist rule, resented the creation of procedures that, if implemented, would limit the extensive discretion and power they had grown accustomed to exercise. They continued to exercise their considerable power to punish violations of "public order" as a matter of police discretion that did not even fall within the province of the formal criminal process. Indeed, these powers were augmented during 1955–1957 as the police responded to large-scale peasant migrations into the cities by rounding up "vagrants" and putting them to work at selected work sites.[9]

Within the courts and the Procuracy, enthusiasm for the new procedures was not much greater than within the police. Many procurators were ex-policemen who shared the views of their former colleagues. Judicial cadres, conscious that the police dominated sanctions and that Party policy determined their application, also remembered the "judicial reform" movement of 1952–1953, which had sought to discredit professionalization. Reflecting Party officials' continued distrust of legal professionals, only a small percentage of law school graduates were assigned to the courts as judges after they were graduated. Most were put to work as court clerks, teachers, Procurators, or administrative cadres in ministries.

Opinion on the work of the courts, however, was not uniform. Early in 1956 the vice-president of the Supreme People's Court criticized "some cadres" who thought that timeliness and legality in deciding cases were incompatible, because it took too much time to deal with enemies according to the law.[10] On the other hand, in October 1956, two professors at Beijing University criticized judges who refused to follow the mass line and make on-the-spot investigations and who preferred to "rely on their own 'seasoned' experience, take a look at the files, and listen to what the concerned parties have to say."[11] In partial reply, an appellate judge wrote that "in handling cases [judges] cannot be divorced from the masses but judges ought to know, that in some circumstances, the things generally recognized by the masses are not necessarily all true."[12] Sentiments in this vein were soon to become unacceptable, when currents in Chinese politics then flowing in the direction of liberalization were reversed. First though, for one moment, that current became stronger.

Debates about policy toward law took place in the midst of a new movement toward liberalizing the entire political life of the nation. Adherence to legality and institutionalization of an adjudicatory model of the criminal process were most emphasized from mid-1956 until mid-1957, a period also characterized by indecision over the future course of China's revolution and industrialization. In the face of widespread nationwide fatigue and restiveness from successive political convulsions, the Chinese leadership made some explicit concessions. In the spring of 1956, the government had announced a new policy of leniency to persons accused as "counter-revolutionaries." At the same time intellectuals were told that thenceforth "freedom of independent thinking, of debate, of creative work; freedom to criticize and freedom to express, maintain and reserve one's opinion would be permitted."[13] In the newly relaxed political atmosphere of 1956, the operation of legal institutions came under criticism publicly, and the CCP responded.

The Eighth Congress of the Communist Party in September 1956 signaled a new emphasis on legality, although it also exposed a fateful lack of consensus among China's leaders on the values essential to a regularized legal system. Mao himself, in a brief speech, complained of bureaucratism and repeatedly stressed the need to preserve the unity of the Party with the people. In contrast, Premier Liu Shaoqi, although concerned with excessive bureaucratization, sought greater Party control over state organs and increased bureaucratic regularity. Liu went further, and juxtaposed an emphasis on legal institutions with the most explicit departure from the mass line by a high-ranking Party leader up to that time. He stated that "the period of revolutionary storm and stress is past . . . and a complete legal system becomes an absolute necessity."[14] Dong Biwu (then Chief Justice of the Supreme People's Court) expressed even stronger opinions. Not only did he call for criminal, civil and procedural codes,[15] he specifically addressed himself to the "serious question":

A few of our Party members and government personnel do not attach much importance to the legal system of the state, or do not observe its provisions. At the same time, Party committees at various levels have not yet paid sufficient attention to exposure and correction of this state of affairs.[16]

Dong specifically enumerated significant problems: Party committees that made no distinction between the Party and the government; certain Party members who considered "that they themselves were over and above the law"; the failure to "[see] that legal procedure is strictly observed"; and the absence of "a single fairly good book explaining the legal system of our country." Then, after criticizing those who "say that the state's legal system is a formality, or that it creates too much trouble, and its practice hinders work," Dong traced the origins of this disregard for law to the Party's long past as an outlawed revolutionary party, its hatred for the old legal system, and the mass movements of the early years of Communist rule, which had encouraged "an indiscriminate disregard for all legal systems."[17] He concluded by calling for the drafting of more laws, and for seriously observing them.

Liu Shaoqi's call for "a more complete" legal system and Dong's speech signaled the ascendancy of views more explicitly tolerant of bureaucratic regularity. From September 1956 until June 1957, the regularity of the legal system's operation was increased with official approval. A new stress on the legal system, which was defined as including "serious observance of the law,"[18] was evidenced in the press. Through the winter of 1956 and the spring of 1957, with increasing intensity, criticisms were raised against the lack of promulgated and coherent legal rules, Party supremacy over law, the inferior position of the courts vis-à-vis the police, and general carelessness, prejudice, and reliance on suspects' "class status" by courts and police alike.

1957–1966: REGULARIZATION ABANDONED

The regularization of criminal procedure that began in 1956 did not go beyond tentative and uneven steps, mostly in China's largest cities, nor did it last long. Public criticism of the Party became so intense by June 1957 that in the face of what looked to Mao and other leaders like the beginning of an anti-Party movement, debate was abruptly ended, and a furious "anti-rightist" campaign began during the summer of 1957. A prominent casualty of the Party's response to "rightism" was the discernible movement toward differentiation of police, Procuracy, and judicial functions in the formal criminal process. During the anti-rightist campaigns of 1957–1958, procurators who had refused to approve arrests and detentions in previous years were severely criticized. Defense lawyers were criticized for losing their "standpoint," and they saw their offices largely disbanded. Close cooperation among courts, Procuracy, and police was urged, insistence on following formal rules and procedures sharply criticized, and Party supremacy reaffirmed. Whatever regularization had been accomplished was undone, and after 1958, the three ostensibly separate agencies which administered the criminal process were "in fact . . . constituent units of a single administrative structure."[19]

During the Great Leap Forward of 1958–1960, many cases were disposed of by teams of cadres from the three agencies working together; public trials were again used to heighten ideological fervor. However, during the ensuing "three bad years" (1960–1962), while China recovered from the Great Leap, the combination of police, procuratorial, and judicial cadres faded and the separate hierarchies reappeared, although interagency consultation remained strong. From late 1962 to the beginning of the Cultural Revolution in 1966, articles on law reasserted emphasis on class warfare, on applying the mass line to legal work, and on the subservience of law to policy. One aspect of legal practice deserves special attention, the use of police-administered sanctions.

The negation of the courts meant that the role of the police increased greatly. Two statutes promulgated in 1957 declared the power of the police to administer minor punishments such as fines, warnings, and short periods of confinement for minor breaches of public order,[20] and to confine to labor camps for indeterminate periods of labor rehabilitation a variety of antisocial persons, including those who "do not engage in proper employment . . . hooligans . . . [petty criminals] whom repeated education fails to change . . . counter-revolutionaries and anti-socialist reactionaries [expelled from their school or place of employment]" and persons who refused to work or refused labor assignments.[21]

The statute on police-administered sanctions is the closest the PRC ever came to promulgating a criminal code during the first thirty years of CCP rule. However, it would probably be a mistake to conclude that the promulgated statute furnished the criteria for police punishment of petty crimes for any considerable length of time after it was promulgated in 1957. Evidence suggests that the administration of such sanctions did not remain stable, but was subjected to the politicization that touched most aspects of Chinese life at the time. It is important to note, too, that the sanctions administered by the police that were established during the 1950s have endured until today and still constitute areas of police power that remain outside judicial control.[22]

More generally, the police-administered sanctions express the dominance of the criminal process by the police at all times before legal reform began in 1978, except when it became a target of the Cultural Revolution.

PERSPECTIVES ON THE MAOIST CRIMINAL PROCESS

The Maoist criminal process presents patterns that were more fluid than those to which Western observers might be accustomed. In a number of areas, foreign expectations have to be reappraised.

THE FUNCTION OF FORMS

Although the Chinese Party-state has utilized formal norms such as statutes and regulations to express policies and direct the conduct of cadres and populace, by Western standards these norms have often been quite vague. For instance, a "provisional measure" promulgated in 1952 by the Government Administration Council (a predecessor of the current State Council) provided that if the seriousness of the "evil acts" of "counter-revolutionaries" such as "backbone elements of reactionary parties . . . does not require that they be arrested and sentenced," then they could be subjected to the regime of "control"[23]; the 1957 statute on "labor rehabilitation" punished, inter alia, "those counter-revolutionaries and anti-socialist reactionaries who, because their errors are minor, are not pursued for criminal responsibility [and are expelled from an educational or work unit]."[24]

The drafting of Chinese norms, and Chinese practice, suggests that throughout the Maoist period the CCP used statutes less as specific guides or prescriptions than as general and exhortative policy statements. (We shall see that this style of drafting has persisted into the reform era and continues to be a major source of uncertainty in Chinese law.) The purpose of Chinese statutes has not merely been to define the rights and duties of the persons affected by them. During the period under discussion they were used to summarize policy decisions already made[25] and to stimulate action by lower-level officials or the populace to implement policies that were themselves expressed in broad and general language. Leaders may have expected only partial compliance and were prepared to abandon the norm if the policy at which it was aimed lost priority. Secret directives and regulations were commonly used to guide cadre discretion, although these were often just as ambiguous as publicized statements.

THE GRADING OF SANCTIONS

The manner in which Chinese sanctions were formulated and enforced during the Maoist period does not suggest great concern for rational gradation. Penal legislation commonly aims at scaling criminal offenses and the consequences of their commissions. Most legal systems assume that there are legal and moral reasons for making punishments proportionate to crimes.[26] Although Chinese sanctions were not completely arbitrary before the Cultural Revolution, they were administered in a disorderly fashion.

The range of sanctions applied could of course be classified, as the Chinese scheme itself did, in ascending order of severity and formality, beginning with the mildest of rebukes by a cadre mounting through more intense forms of group criticism, and extending to formal trial and the death sentence.[27] Police-administered sanctions such as "control," short-term detention, warnings, and fines for minor offenders and indeterminate confinement in labor camps for more serious offenders fell between non-judicial criticism in residential or work units and sentences imposed through the formal criminal process.

This tripartite arrangement of sanctions—discipline within work units, police-administered punishments, and formal adjudicatory punishments—had only a limited analytical use, however. In practice, sanctions were applied in a considerably less measured fashion than the analytical scheme might suggest. For example, although persons punished by "control" or "supervision by the masses"—a regime of surveillance and restriction at work and residential units much used during the years just prior to the Cultural Revolution—were less disadvantaged than persons sent to labor camps, émigré accounts indicate that such persons often formed a class of political and legal pariahs. Their permanent stigmatization meant that they were frequently arrested, interrogated, and made to confess to crimes because police cadres assumed that they were more crime-prone than members of "the people." The permanent effects of the punishments could be just as drastic in one situation as in the other, and indeed "from the point of view of the regime the two are of comparable magnitude."[28]

THE IMPORTANCE OF POLITICIZED STANDARDS FOR DECISIONS

Class Background

Sanctioning processes were made less rational because all persons were identified in terms of their particular socioeconomic class and their general attitude toward Communist rule. Persons stigmatized as "landlords," "bourgeoisie," or "rich peasants" were regarded as putative enemies of the people and therefore as potential saboteurs and criminals. During campaigns such persons were often selected as targets for sanctions. For instance, a man identified as a "landlord" in 1949 continued to be characterized as a "landlord" even after he had long since been deprived of his land. If he stole grain during a period when no political campaign was under way, he might have been simply criticized. For the same crime committed during political campaigns, he might have been much more seriously punished. The "class background" of the individual and the level of mobilizational activity thus interacted to determine the punishment.

Campaigns

Even when campaigns did not specifically focus attention on "class background," they frequently disrupted the operation of sanctioning processes. Campaigns to "rectify" thought, for instance, such as those against "counter-revolution" in 1955 and against "rightists" in 1957, involved the formation within most organizations of ad hoc groups of Party members and activists who selected a number of persons to be criticized and a smaller number to be more severely sanctioned. The reform-era criminal process continues to be marked by the use of campaigns, as we will see below.

OFFICIAL DEVIATION FROM NORMS

The Party-state permitted much more disorder in its legal processes than Western observers might have expected from a "totalitarian" regime. Broad concerns over changing revolutionary priorities frequently overrode rules and procedures, which policy changes caused to be altered or abandoned. In general, normative language and official conduct were often very inconsistent. Police-administered sanctions seem prime examples. Much police sanctioning was imposed without formal authority, the rare relevant statutes were consistently disregarded, and direct punishments decided by ad hoc groups during political campaigns often preempted police action. Although police sanctions were formalized in a 1957 regulation, the police subsequently administered unauthorized punishment and punished conduct not specifically prohibited by the regulation. At all times since 1949, police activities were intimately connected with the politics of the Chinese Revolution, and their relationship remained bound up with politics even though that revolution is over.

The Maoist Criminal Process
and Alternative Visions of Bureaucracy

The fluidity and dispensability of formal standards and procedures described here suggest that to understand fully the Chinese criminal process of the 1960s, we must venture beyond formal legal categories. It may be tempting to dismiss the criminal process because "it no longer qualifies as a *legal* procedure,"[29] but it is still necessary to understand its dynamics. As obvious as its arbitrariness and politicization may have been, the criminal process under Mao had important characteristics besides disdaining legality.

THE CRIMINAL PROCESS AS AN
ADMINISTRATIVE DECISION-MAKING PROCESS

It has been suggested that the disposition of cases in the American criminal process can be understood better if conviction is viewed in conjunction with many other equally important but less visible decisions, including "decisions to: search or seize or grant bail; prosecute; order a psychiatric examination; allow the defendant to stand trial; permit a plea of guilty, *nolo contendere* or not guilty; raise a particular defense such as insanity, self-defense, or provocation."[30] In the Maoist criminal process there was indeed a series of similar decisions, but the essential participant in all of them was the police, which retained predominance over Procuracy and courts throughout the period before the Cultural Revolution. One indication of police predominance was the general practice of Procuracy and courts to negotiate informally with the police rather than return a case for insufficient evidence. Moreover, the police retained power to reinvestigate cases and release "erroneously" convicted persons. Even the release of many persons in 1956 reflects the continued exercise of power by police officials to decide the length of confinement.

The fact that Procuracy and courts generally operated to confirm antecedent police decisions suggests that procuratorial and judicial decisions were not permitted to differ essentially from police decision-making, in terms of purpose, doctrine, or style. A leading Chinese judge, writing in 1956, characterized police, Procuracy, and courts as "three workshops in one factory";[31] and an article written in 1962 makes no distinction among police decisions that a suspect should be formally arrested, procuratorial review of the case, and adjudication of guilt.[32] In this view, legal decision-making is undifferentiated from other bureaucratic activities.

THE CRIMINAL PROCESS AS AN ARENA FOR COMPETING VALUES

Herbert Packer suggested that the American criminal process exhibits an opposition between "crime control" and "due process"[33] models, and he expressed their difference through two competing metaphors, the "assembly line" and the "obstacle course."[34] Chinese analogues of these two conceptions have also existed and conflicted with each other. For example, some cadres seem to have regarded the criminal process as the routinized processing of putatively guilty suspects, while other cadres (especially in the Procuracy and the courts) attempted to build into the process checks that would prevent unjust convictions, even if these slowed administration. During the period of liberalization in 1956, the Chinese police were sometimes criticized for their readiness to arrest persons whose only connection with an offense was that they were thought prone to antisocial conduct by reason of their "bad" class background. When Chinese lawyers briefly participated in the formal judicial process between 1955 and 1957, there was considerable public debate over whether they aided the courts to get at "truth" or impeded them from punishing bad people.

COMPETING FUNCTIONS: MOBILIZATIONAL AND BUREAUCRATIC MODELS OF LEGAL INSTITUTIONS

A critical difference between Packer's competing models and their Chinese analogues is that the contrasting values in China, even though arising in a legal context, seemed to derive less from notions about law than from ideological issues related to larger questions about the management and leadership of Chinese society itself. The Party owed much of its original success to the mobilizational tactics that it developed during its long struggle for power. But the means used to forge a great revolution were not necessarily appropriate to modernizing a nation; new tasks called for new talents. The Party soon found that daily administrative tasks required greater routinization than had the tasks of revolutionary mobilization; as a result, the role of cadres was transformed. After victory, cadres "spent less time with 'the masses' and more with fellow officials."

As the division of labour evolved, they were given a narrower range of responsibilities and were expected to acquire more specialized skills. . . . Revolutionaries who had been provoking disorders became functionaries preserving order. . . . The qualities required were no longer fearlessness and bravery, but literacy and administrative skill. The cadre, in short, was well on his way to becoming a bureaucrat.[35]

Much in the working style of a bureaucrat differs from that of a revolutionary. The cadre making revolution by mobilizing the masses was supposed to live and work with them, share their hardships, and lead them by means of face-to-face encounters; a cadre-bureaucrat necessarily spends more time in an office away from the masses. The style of a cadre is that of a "combat leader, in intimate relationship with his followers."[36] The contrast in style with bureaucrats is evident:

Bureaucrats strive for routinization, for the creation of stable predictable environments. Cadres . . . live in a changing world and accept change as the norm. . . . The manager thinks in terms of techniques, both technological and organizational; . . . he likes rules because he knows he can bend them to his will, to enforce compliance from his workers. The cadre, however, is a leader who thinks in terms of human solidarity. He knows how to "solidarize" men so that goals can be achieved; he can manipulate their thoughts and sentiments.[37]

The conflict between mass mobilization and bureaucratic regularity within Chinese legal institutions also reflected a long-standing controversy over the value that the Party should place on the skills of intellectuals, experts, and technicians. Although the famous slogan "red and expert" balanced the two clusters of opposed values,[38] Party policy before reform generally prized "redness" over "expertness" even at the cost of lost skills and increased bureaucratic irrationality. Functional specialization conflicted with the Maoist notion of the cadre as a revolutionary generalist. Like the erosion of mobilization by bureaucracy, an increase in functional specialization was seen by Mao as weakening the will of the masses and cadres to engage in revolutionary struggle and as interfering with the solidarity of the Party with the masses. These conflicts became major issues in the Cultural Revolution.

They also highlight two opposing conceptions of the criminal process that, although not made explicit in Chinese debate, can be distilled from published discussion and émigré interviews. In one view, a politicized criminal process was mobilizational; it stressed disposing of cases as exercises in mass education in order to disseminate new values, support policy implementation and maintain revolutionary fervor. The competing model was of a routinized criminal process that stressed handling cases within the political-legal hierarchy in a manner less explicitly oriented toward policy considerations and more attentive to applying legal skills, increasing rationality, and reducing cadre arbitrariness.

The contrast between these two models is best understood in the light of controversy over bureaucracy in China generally. Even when the Chinese experimented intermittently with Soviet-style institutions, public debate clearly illustrated an opposition between mobilizational and bureaucratic models of the criminal process. If judges were urged to use care in convicting, they were also instructed not to be bureaucratic and to follow the less orderly but more familiar mass line. Thus, cadres were sometimes asked to substitute legal-bureaucratic for revolutionary values.[39] One writer objected to comparing the political-legal organs to "three workshops in one factory," because doing so tended to demean the position of the defendant and reduce the importance of the courts.[40] Regularity and bureaucratic orderliness were values that were difficult to make dominant. Most judicial cadres lacked both formal education and strong identification with regularized legal institutions. Veteran cadres had been schooled in revolution and class warfare, and younger cadres were often chosen for political activism. All were aware that the Party and the police retained decisive power over sanctions. All were familiar with mobilizational campaigns, while few were familiar with more regularized modes of sanctioning "bad people."

The coexistence of these two models was strikingly illustrated by an attempt in late 1955 to harness them together in order to implement the organizational legislation of the previous year. To implement the legislation, a "campaign" to emulate a model court in Beijing was launched.[41] To justify the use of a campaign in the courts, a newspaper article said that not only in "production departments" did some groups possess more "advanced experience" than others. In other words, emulation campaigns were as appropriate for courts as for factories.[42] Later, however, a Ministry of Justice spokesman admitted that "judicial work involves a high degree of thinking and policy and is different from production work in a factory or mine. If emulations are launched, careless conclusions of cases and decrease of quality of dealing with cases are very likely."[43] This campaign illustrates an ambivalence about the extent to which courts could be considered different from other administrative units. To Western eyes the campaign is striking because it involves an attempt to regularize and improve judicial work using a revolutionary-style and antibureaucratic device.

The history of the period was marked by alternation and competition between mass line and bureaucratic models of administration, and not only in the legal sphere. During periods of relative politicization, official policy emphasized the links between implementing policy and the criminal process, which during such periods was used instrumentally to help mobilize the masses to carry out policy. During intervening periods of post-politicization consolidation, recovery, and retrenchment, bureaucratic efficiency and the reduction of arbitrariness and mistakes were stressed. Thus the two functions of the criminal process reflected competing strains of fundamental importance in the policies of the Chinese leadership.

When we turn to the contemporary Chinese criminal process, we will see that it is the legal institution that continues to reflect the greatest continuity with its Maoist counterpart, despite recent reforms. It will therefore be necessary to ask whether policies toward the criminal process continue to echo the concerns and debates that surfaced under Mao or if, and how far, they have gone beyond conflict over bureaucracy.

"Civil" Law Under Mao

If criminal law was politicized under Mao, hardly any scope at all existed for civil law. When legal reform in the domain outside criminal law began, it had to start from a legal wasteland more bare than that in criminal law and procedure. I have here retraced my early hesitant steps in search of law-like institutions under Mao because the history of these institutions contains some lessons for the present. For example, considerable tension can be seen today between different attitudes toward civil and commercial law. One stresses controlling the behavior of economic actors, as by requiring that they be licensed to engage in business and by examining their contracts for fairness. Another view is more willing to allow transactions to be unmonitored, generally, within a facilitative framework. By looking back to pre-reform legal institutions, we can perceive the extent to which they were both politicized and undifferentiated from other administrative institutions. We can also see that the history of contract under Mao echoes the more distant past, because both traditional and CCP practice lacked strong notions of legal rights arising out of contracts.

In both periods rights were "soft," although for different reasons. As a result, the soil in which post–Mao concepts of legal rights arising out of contracts can be planted is not very fertile. At the same time, traditional notions of contract enforcement under customary practice may also be present. In the discussion of legal reforms that follows in later chapters, I will return to these issues.

In the earlier article on which this discussion is based I examined some of the analytical difficulties that Western students encountered when studying China's legal and administrative institutions and suggested the functional approach that has been introduced in the previous chapter.[44] It concentrated on Chinese institutions that seemed analogous to Western "civil law" institutions, particularly contract, as they were constituted before the Cultural Revolution began in 1966.

That article was an indirect response to an invitation to write a conference paper titled "Some Problems of Translating Chinese Legal Language: Contracts." To my mind the topic reflected two questionable assumptions: that a specialized terminology—a "legal language"—existed in China, and that Chinese contracts were recognizably distinct from other arrangements. It further implied that "contract" was a legal institution, with a unique content, bounded, and directly comparable to Western institutions with similar functions. That neither of these assumptions was justified in China dramatized how careful Western observers had to be to avoid relying uncritically on Western notions about legal institutions when they attempted to understand Chinese law.

LAW AS POLITICS

The Western notion that private or civil law *facilitates* transactions contrasts sharply with an implacably different Maoist view. In the West, legal rules define rights and duties, and indicate the circumstances in which claims arising out of transactions can be asserted and vindicated by official, that is, judicial, action, thereby providing a framework for relationships such as contracts. Chinese theory under Mao began from altogether different premises. It saw law as the tool of a ruling class placed in the service of politics and rejected sharp differentiation among judicial, legal, and administrative processes. In the Soviet Union and Eastern Europe, legal theory with common ideological roots did not prevent the development, albeit uneven, of increasingly close-textured doctrine in some areas of social and economic activity, in a context of arrangements regarded in those countries as "legal," and differing in form and function from administrative and political activities. Thus, in the Soviet Union and Eastern Europe, certain relationships were not only defined by normative rules and standards, they were enforced and applied in a relatively principled manner by specialized judicial or quasi-judicial institutions. While to critical Western observers the area of "legal" activity in those countries seemed smaller—and the regularity of official acts within that area more variable—than in the West, their boundaries and internal complexities were perceptible. Moreover, other kinds of activities considered not "legal" but administrative, such as inter-enterprise contracts, had also been characterized by the development of legalistic doctrine and practice.[45]

In China, however, the close intertwining of law with rapidly changing policies throughout the 1950s and 1960s greatly inhibited the development of judicial and quasi-judicial institutions and interfered with regularized rule-making and dispute settlement by nonjudicial institutions. Although, during a brief period of political relaxation in 1957, some Chinese theoretical discussion implied that civil law might be made to play a role in adjusting production relationships,[46] no such role was recognized before reform.

POLITICIZATION OF CIVIL LAW: SOME EXAMPLES

Notaries

The politicization of civil law institutions was illustrated by the distortions of what in Continental practice is the pallid and plain office of the notary. In European civil law countries, notaries are (and, in the former Soviet Union, were) trained legal officials whose duties include verifying the legality of certain transactions between individuals. Chinese notarial bureaus were established in the early 1950s and were discussed occasionally in the press during the mid-1950s. The manipulation of these bureaus to promote policy ends illustrates the attempt of the leadership to politicize civil law.

During the First Five-Year Plan (1953–1957), but before the Party completed the "socialist transformation" of industry and commerce in 1956, notarial bureaus were used to supervise and control privately managed enterprises that entered into contractual relations with state-managed enterprises.[47] Notarial bureaus were charged with ascertaining the legality of contracts and their consistency with policy. For example, a notary might have to determine, together with the labor union at the private enterprise and with government departments, whether the private enterprise had the productive capacity to fulfill the contract. After making the appropriate determinations, the notarial bureau was to approve the contract and "educate" the parties on their contractual obligations and on the need for performing contracts according to their tenor. In this way, notarial bureaus could help increase privately managed factories' and commercial establishments' sense of responsibility before carrying out contracts and improve their ability to handle their tasks according to the state plan. To further strengthen close supervision of capitalists, notarial bureaus were to send copies of contracts to the labor union at the privately managed factory. Thereafter, both the union and the notarial bureau were charged with investigating the enterprise's performance. This activity of the notarial bureaus was hailed as a form of supervision by the masses of the bourgeoisie, as an aid in reducing the latter's cheating the state, and as a weapon in "elevating [the bourgeoisie's] law-abiding thoughts." Although the principal task of the notarial bureaus was to maintain contract discipline and thereby help supervise and reform the bourgeoisie,[48] other functions more consistent with those performed in the West were apparently also contemplated. Temporary regulations on notarial work issued in Canton in June 1955 provided for notarization not only of contracts between state and privately owned enterprises, but also of transactions between private individuals involving such matters as power of attorney, succession, wills, sales, and divisions of jointly owned property.[49]

Supervision of the bourgeoisie became less important after 1956, following the drive, launched by the Party the previous year, for the socialist transformation (i.e., nationalization) of all industrial and commercial enterprises that remained in private hands. The possibility then arose of notarial bureaus discharging other functions, such as supervising performance of contracts between state enterprises. By late 1956, articles on notarial work began to stress the notaries' role in facilitating remittances to China from abroad. Notaries could help overseas Chinese transfer assets to the People's Republic by authenticating their identity and their right to dispose of the property. In this manner, the notarial bureaus could aid the People's Republic to obtain assets owned abroad by overseas Chinese and could also help attract interest and support among overseas Chinese by allowing them to enjoy property rights within China.

Reflecting these policies, numerous cases were reported in which residents of China signed and notarized powers of attorney or other documents in order to dispose of or gain possession of property situated abroad.[50] Notarial bureaus were also reported to have facilitated the enjoyment by overseas Chinese of property interests within China. Examples include granting a landlord a certificate affirming that an agent was acting for him in collecting rents, authenticating the right of an heir residing abroad to inherit a house situated in China that had been bequeathed to him by his overseas Chinese father, and notarizing the will of another overseas Chinese who had returned to China temporarily.[51]

Notarial work reflected yet another policy shift in 1956–1957, a period that proved to be an interlude of relative relaxation, stabilization, and retrenchment after a succession of intensive political campaigns over the preceding seven years. Policy briefly emphasized legality and, with it, the enjoyment by citizens of rights to own, enjoy, and dispose of property.[52] Several articles published during this brief period stressed how notarial bureaus could prevent litigation arising out of property transactions such as purchase and sale of houses, debts, pledges, and entrusting property to the care of another, by authenticating documents such as wills.[53] After June 1957, however, with the end of the Hundred Flowers period, notarial bureaus were rarely mentioned in the press. The political atmosphere, which had briefly encouraged enjoyment of property, turned explicitly hostile to such anti-socialist behavior, and notarial bureaus thereafter had little function. They were largely abolished in 1959, although some token bureaus were retained.[54]

The extent to which legal and administrative activities were politicized, as suggested by these examples, is striking. Whatever their resemblances to Western and Soviet institutions with the same labels, during the 1950s the notarial bureaus functioned less to maintain and preserve civil law relationships than to assist in shaping these relationships to fit policy.

Tensions in Legal Theory

Civil law institutions under Mao, to the extent that they existed at all, were far from the autonomous or semiautonomous institutions that bear similar labels in the West. It is a measure of the extraordinary cultural distance between China and the West that in 1969, when the original essay on which this discussion is based was written, only one Chinese textbook on post-1949 civil law, published in 1958, was available in the West.[55]

That textbook was perhaps most striking because its discussions of policy reflected conflict over major issues within the Party, issues no smaller than the aims of the Chinese revolution and the means by which cadres ought to lead China's masses in that revolution. As noted above, an aspect of this ideological conflict with enormous import for legal institutions involved the conflict between mass line leadership that aimed at mobilizing the masses, and more regularized, bureaucratic means of decision-making and leadership.

In 1956–1957, after the Eighth Party Congress signaled a new political stabilization, civil law institutions began to reflect a nascent functional specialization. Debates were conducted over whether the mediation committees were needed;[56] the new institution of the "people's lawyer" was publicized and endorsed, not only as an aid to defendants charged with crime, but also to claimants involved in disputes over family matters and private property;[57] and the notarial bureaus were hailed as protectors of citizens' rights.[58]

Reflecting the new stress on institutions that promoted stability rather than mobilization, greater interest was shown in legal theory in 1956–1957 than ever before. In 1957 textbooks were compiled on both civil and criminal law.[59] The civil law textbook contains extensive discussions of obligations, and of contracts in particular. The text plainly reflects the politicization of civil law, however, in asserting that civil law is "a regularization of politics and policies" and is "at the service of the politics of our state."[60] Civil law was to assist the Party to implement policy by helping to realize economic plans.[61] Most of the text is devoted to obligations, which were said to be used "to strengthen the economic relations among socialist organizations and to concretely realize the national economic plan."[62] The book's general arrangement resembles that of the Russian Federated Soviet Republic Civil Code of 1922, which was still in effect in the Soviet Union when the book was published (a new Soviet codification appeared in 1960). Because drafters of the earlier Soviet legislation had themselves borrowed broadly from West European codes such as the German Bürgerliches Gesetzbuch, the general plan of the text strongly resembles that of West European civil codes, moving as it does from the general to the specific, discussing first the general concept of "juristic relations" and then proceeding to obligations, to contracts in general, and finally to specific types of contracts.

Nevertheless, the effects of politicization can be seen. Regardless of how familiar the general arrangement of the text might be to Western lawyers, important concepts were blurred or poorly defined. "Administrative documents" were said to be an important source of civil law obligations although documents such as distribution plans generally did not directly create obligations;[63] mortgages were discussed as administrative conveniences for bank supervision of socialist enterprises but not as legal devices, because state enterprises were said never to fail to repay to state banks obligations that they secured,[64] and banks did not foreclose on mortgages that secured loans to handicraft cooperatives.[65] A particularly interesting intrusion of political considerations into legal technicalities was the discussion of void and voidable juristic acts.

The text enumerated the grounds on which voidable juristic acts may be invalidated as follows: fraud, mistake, threat of physical or mental harm, objective unfairness, and defrauding of principals by their agents.[66] These grounds are plainly similar to the grounds used in Western legal systems to declare transactions such as contracts void. However, to these the text added "all acts made under compulsory order,"[67] which was defined as "the compulsory method employed by a state worker who, in conducting civil law activities to carry out state duties, forces the other party to accept his order."[68] This criterion of voidability was plainly different in kind from the other criteria with which it was included. The other criteria pertained to the relations of the contracting parties between themselves regardless of the extent to which they represented the state. The last criterion, however, which flowed from "improper use of the means of administrative organization" or "incorrect methods of mobilization,"[69] was linked with the use of coercive state power by cadres in their relationships with individuals or legal entities and addressed essentially political relationships.

This last-mentioned criterion of voidability reflects not only the impact of politics on legal theory but the larger conflict between mass line and bureaucratic conceptions of political leadership. In the Party's lexicon of the era, "bureaucratism" and "commandism" described undesirable cadre relations with the masses, bureaucratism because it implied aloofness and commandism because it suggested coercion rather than persuasion.[70] Commandism thus represented the negation of the face-to-face contact and solidarity with the masses that the mass line requires. More important than the legal transactions entered into through cadres' efforts was cadres' maintenance of politically correct modes of leadership. The authors of the text had to alter radically the tidiness and consistency of the formal legal criteria of voidability in order to give expression to a desired political virtue. Thus the law of obligations could reflect not only the impact of ideology but also some of that ideology's internal tensions. These conflicts point up the difficulties that the Chinese had in adapting civil law concepts to meet ideological demands and the difficulties that Western observers encountered in their search for civil law relationships in Chinese administrative practice. Many years later, after I had begun to travel to China frequently, a Chinese law professor friend explained these intrusions of ideology into an otherwise orderly arrangement of concepts: The textbook discussed here had first been written in 1957 but had been revised in 1958, when the political winds shifted to the left. To make the textbook politically correct, statements had been inserted regardless of the violence they did to the logical structure of the concepts discussed.

LAW AS ADMINISTRATION

Chinese institutions before reform extensively transmuted legal forms into relatively more fluid administrative ones. Decision-making by cadres was denominated "legal" but involved no unique doctrine or decision-making processes. Cadres not only lacked professional "legal" skills; the cultivation of such skills was politically unacceptable. As a result, "legal" institutions did not differ in style or method of operation from any other administrative activities; all were tools to implement changing political policies.

The first part of this chapter has shown how the criminal process was dominated by the police. Yet although rule-making and rule-following in the Chinese criminal process were frequently disrupted by changing policies, sanctioning processes were not wholly irrational. Émigré interviews suggested that legal institutions (especially between major political campaigns) often operated with considerable, although variable, administrative coherence. Thus, although Chinese sanctioning institutions were disorderly, they were nonetheless bureaucratized.

Similarly, although China had not yet developed rules and institutions that were classified as part of "civil law," in the public sector of the economy contract practices took shape that were analogous to more formal Western and Soviet "legal" institutions.[71]

THE ADMINISTRATIVE USES OF CONTRACTS

Industrial Contracts

Beginning in the early years of the People's Republic, basic transformations in economic relationships and rules for their management were expressed in promulgated legislation. Among these, contracts had not been neglected.[72] In 1950, for instance, legislation governing the use of contracts to carry out the annual plans of state-owned enterprises was promulgated.[73] It emphasized the necessity for clarity of contractual terms and the duty of the obligor to perform contracts. Such early legislation channeled contract disputes primarily, though not exclusively, to an administrative hierarchy: disputes were to be "handled"[74] by financial and economic commissions, either in the region where both parties were located, if they were in the same region, or the central commission, if the parties were located in different regions. If the "handling" was "ineffective" the parties could in theory take the matter to a People's Court, although in practice this did not happen.[75]

Later legislation and regulations closely linked plans with some contracts, and these links were maintained despite shifts in policy that centralized management of industry during the First Five-Year Plan, decentralized it during the Great Leap, and then recentralized it somewhat thereafter. Enterprises made contracts to deliver industrial goods and essential raw materials, thereby translating into legal obligations the state plans that governed the allocation of important goods.

The contracts were standardized, as by "temporary basic clauses" issued by the Ministry of Heavy Industry in 1956, which provided for the conclusion of delivery contracts by enterprises and other units under the ministry's supervision, pursuant to the distribution plan drawn up by the ministry and other departments.[76] The "clauses" specified detailed provisions that the contracts had to include for such matters as packaging, delivery, transportation, inspection of quantity and quality, and price of goods. They also contained provisions for specific procedures in the event of faulty performance or nonperformance by the supplier, and payment of fines as well.[77] When a supplier was prevented from performing the contract because the supplier's superior unit had ordered that the products involved be allocated in a manner at variance with the contract, or because of a "natural disaster that could not have been prevented by human effort,"[78] the supplier was required to notify both its superior and its contractual partner immediately; in such cases, it could avoid paying the fines.

These "clauses" provided for payment of compensation and specific performance of duties. In addition, they provided in detail for terms of payment, for computing fines for suppliers' late delivery, failure to meet standards of quality, purchasers' delayed payment or rejection of goods in violation of the contract. However, despite the intricacy of these provisions and the use of legalistic terms such as "bear responsibility" and "reimburse," and a legalistic approach to drafting,[79] the "clauses" failed to identify any third party that might resolve disputes arising out of the contracts. Thus, the section on fines mentioned only the contracting parties; it stated only that if one party violated the contract, it must reimburse the other, but it did not mention who might decide such issues. A supplement to the "clauses" provided that "[i]f in executing the contract, losses that cannot be compensated by fines, or serious disputes occur before state arbitration organs have been established, the parties may report to their superior for arrangement and decision."[80] At that time, then, whatever disputes enterprises could not settle between themselves came to the attention of the industrial bureaus to which they were responsible and were resolved entirely within ministerial hierarchies.

This section is of historical interest because it shows that in 1956–1957 Chinese legal scholars considered following the Soviet example by establishing arbitral institutions to settle industrial contract disputes.[81] By 1958, evidently, Chinese economic planners decided to retain a wholly administrative mode of settling contract disputes. The 1958 civil law textbook states:

At present, our country still has no public arbitration organ. Any dispute between socialist organizations, before conclusion of a contract or during its execution, which the parties themselves cannot solve through negotiation, should be submitted to higher authorities for consultation and settlement and the party who violated the law shall bear pecuniary responsibility or receive administrative punishment.[82]

Evidently, arbitration Soviet-style was considered too rigid and legalistic.

Liu Shaoqi, later the chief target of the Cultural Revolution, was criticized, among other reasons, for his alleged plans to organize the Chinese economy along "revisionist" Soviet and, worse yet, Yugoslav lines.[83] One charge was that Liu wanted to restrict the role of state organs administering the economy to "the role of an 'arbiter' in disputes arising between industrial enterprises."[84] There is evidence that some progress was made along precisely these lines by expanding the roles of planning and financial institutions.

In 1962 the Central Committee and the State Council announced their joint decision to regularize means of resolving inter-enterprise differences by making contract disputes subject to arbitration by local economic commissions at each level. The People's Bank or the Construction Bank in each area was to be responsible for executing decisions of the economic commissions by withholding or paying the price of the goods involved.[85] This reflected a post-Great Leap leadership concern with increasing supervision of enterprises' use of working capital.[86] Banks were authorized to make special investigations of enterprises, and their control was buttressed by their power to sanction poor financial management by disapproving loans needed to enter into transactions. Branches of the bank exercised some power to decide inter-enterprise disputes that arose when they were notified by dissatisfied customers not to pay suppliers.[87] Thus, a text on banking states that because the bank must have the agreement of the purchaser before it can debit the purchaser's account, the bank can carry out "supervision of performance of the contract."[88] The book adds: "In this way [the bank] can enforce the supplying unit's necessary serious observance of the contract in supplying goods according to quantity, quality and time, and protect the proper interests of the purchasing unit."[89] Chinese economic planners gave economic commissions and banks the power to function in a manner analogous to that of Western courts and arbitration and Soviet arbitration. These efforts were necessitated by the continued extensive use of inter-enterprise contracts, both to implement "general" agreements signed by ministries[90] and to establish direct links between factories.[91]

When Chinese planners rejected third-party adjudication of inter-enterprise contract disputes in favor of administrative mechanisms, they demonstrated a more flexible view of economic administration than that supplied by the Soviet model. In addition, they took a much more flexible view of the "legal" obligations created by contracts. One discussion of inter-enterprise agreements stated that

an economic contract has legal efficacy, and it cannot be cancelled unilaterally. The party which does not fulfill a contract must bear political and economic responsibility . . . [and] must recognize error and compensate the other party's economic losses.[92]

This statement, however, was immediately followed by the qualification that a party injured by its partner's contractual breach should handle economic problems arising from the breach "in the spirit of seeking truth from facts," implying that enterprises should not rely legalistically on a contract as the exclusive source of the parties' duties to each other and to the state.

Even if contracts were flexible, who was charged with settling disputes arising from them? The superiors of enterprises were urged to maintain close supervision over them in order to deal with problems which arise or to make "readjustments" in their "cooperation."[93] Interviews in Hong Kong during 1965–1967 with fifteen émigrés, all of whom had formerly served in managerial or technical capacities in industrial enterprises or in state or Party bureaus concerned with transportation or industry, suggested that when difficulties arose in the course of attempting to carry out contracts, enterprise managers usually attempted to work out the matters themselves through some compromise solution, such as altering a delivery schedule. If they could not handle the matter in this manner, their superiors probably became involved, and, possibly, Party industrial bureaus. Enterprise Party secretaries and representatives of Party bureaus also participated in conferences aimed at resolving disputes. They sometimes politicized these meetings by lecturing to enterprise managers, pressing them to "confess errors," and publicizing their "errors" in bulletins circulated to other units. Because of the variety of participants and the frequent intersections of Party and state lines of authority, however, it was impossible in 1970, when the original version of this essay was written, to generalize about when inter-enterprise contracts were resolved in ways that involved participants other than the enterprises themselves.

At the same time, evidence available at that time suggested that if the enterprises could not work out the matter themselves, their superiors in the state industrial hierarchy, economic commissions, and the bank might become involved—singly or together—as might Party industrial bureaus. All evidence indicated that enterprises tried to resolve failures to perform contracts through flexible, pragmatic attempts to adjust problems without fixing "legal" blame. Inter-enterprise contracts might have been useful devices of economic administration, but they were not considered to be sources of legal rights and obligations.

Years later in China, discussion of these issues with enterprise managers and economic planners confirmed these impressions. Although the system seemed to have a high degree of uncertainty, performance of contracts was encouraged by the economic plan and by the constant possibility that economic obligations could become politicized. Recent Western scholarship has also shown that the Chinese central plan covered a considerably smaller share of economic activity than its Soviet counterpart, that it was less efficiently managed, that beginning in 1963 successive waves of decentralization placed increasing numbers of enterprises under local control, and that under these circumstances extra-plan barter trade developed, often in violation of state regulations.[94] Hindsight suggests that in this environment, legal rules and concepts of contractual obligation had even less than the minor significance that Western observers supposed.

Commercial Contracts

Contracts called "commercial contracts" essentially cloaked in voluntarism the extraction by command of agricultural production from the countryside. Commercial departments such as supply and marketing cooperatives "purchased" agricultural commodities from units of agricultural production such as rural communes and their constituent units. Contracts were used to implement plans for production of commodities, such as grain, which were completely controlled by state plans, and to control production of other commodities whose production was unplanned.

Under "unified purchase contracts," commercial units generally bought all the output of an agricultural commodity from producers, pursuant to the state plan, paying a state-fixed price; producers could retain part of their production for self-consumption, although not for sale. Under "unified purchase and supply contracts" the commercial units also sold needed inputs to the agricultural producers. When the state purchased a fixed quota of an agricultural commodity and permitted the producer to sell some of what it retained, the contract could be termed a "fixed" or "decided" purchase contract. "Order contracts" were used for commodities that were outside the plan. In such cases the producer might have some opportunity to negotiate over the quantity to be delivered and the contract price, although the price was not permitted to exceed the rural market price.[95]

These contracts were technical expressions of commands directed to the peasants to sell all or most of their production of certain commodities to the state, in quantities and at prices fixed by the state. Campaigns were conducted to convince lower level cadres and the masses that the masses wanted contracts,[96] to urge cadres to respect the principle of voluntarism,[97] and to remind all that the performance of contracts was not only an economic but a political duty.[98] State commercial agencies exercised administrative power over their contractual partners, the agricultural producers, as when commercial cadres "penetrated" into rural units in order to investigate local conditions before signing contracts.[99] In practice this meant deciding the amounts that could be extracted from the communes and persuading peasants of the gravity of contracts and the obligations they created.[100] Commercial departments were urged to supervise performance by the agricultural producers, and also to "assist" them.[101] Legalistic terminology was occasionally used, as when commune and other cadres were referred to as "supervisory and witnessing organs"[102] echoing the use of notarial bureaus in industry.

The subservience of contract notions to more fundamental issues of managing production of agricultural products was illustrated when all or part of output was delivered even though contracts had not been signed, thereby performing the obligations that the contracts would have expressed.[103] Years after the commercial "contract system" was established, reports appeared that a system of fines for nonperformance had been "instituted," implying that no such sanctions had existed before, and, perhaps, that there were no other legal sanctions for nonperformance. In short, commercial contracts were precatory and exhortative devices, and reflected even more clearly than industrial contracts the commands on which they were based and the manipulation of legal labels. To some extent, this has continued in the countryside today.

SOME IMPLICATIONS: THE INAPPLICABILITY OF WESTERN CATEGORIES

For many Western lawyers, the flexible administrative arrangements that were denominated as contracts before reform, but which did not seem to create binding "legal" rights and duties, were not contracts at all. The absence of clearly designated institutions or rules for dispute settlement further complicate analysis. In the West, formation of a valid contract is assumed to have legal consequences, by creating enforceable duties; if such duties are not performed, the aggrieved party may invoke the assistance of an official institution which will determine whether a duty existed, whether it was breached, whether the breach caused any damage, and the remedial consequences. Contracts are important, among other reasons, because they anticipate to some extent the remedies which the parties have against each other for failure to perform. Furthermore, it is assumed that the official institution will decide these questions according to articulated rules and standards that have antecedently been recognized as applying to such problems.

In Maoist China, by contrast, the duties created by contracts were not closely linked to the possibility of remedial action; nor was there evidence of the existence of well-articulated principles conditioning the remedies for violation of a contract. Contracts expressed duties, to be sure, and, if they were violated, the aggrieved party could invoke the assistance of an official institution—or such an institution could intervene—to bring about remedial consequences. Then again, the aggrieved party could decide not to do anything of the sort, and the breach could lead to no remedial consequences whatsoever.

The ambiguities of Chinese contracts stemmed from their administrative and managerial nature. The use of contracts in the planned economy had floated far away from the conceptual moorings to which Western notions of contract are normally tied, such as declarations of intent, agreement of wills, and creation and enforcement of obligations according to known, universal rules applied in a disciplined fashion according to clearly defined procedures.

Yet, in Mao's China just as in the West, contracts plainly shared the function of solemnizing duties and obligations. Solemnization is separable from creating the basis for a remedy, and in the Chinese case both were separated from the resolution of any disputes arising out of the contracts. To complicate analysis further, functions that appear similar may have underlying differences. Solemnization in the West is considered important for a variety of ethical and legal reasons, while in China it was more closely related to political mobilization and persuasion. Almost thirty years after the original version of this discussion was published, it serves to recall that before legal reform, Chinese industrial and commercial contracts were not regarded as creating duties enforceable by remedial action that could be invoked by an aggrieved party. Rather, the state created certain obligations, and contracts were useful secondary tools for expressing them. Recent legal reforms do try to introduce very different conceptions of contract, as later chapters will show, but these may have to compete with earlier notions embedded in pre-reform practice described above.

This discussion of contract use raises an issue that transcends economic management: What conception of law is implied by the rules and practices discussed? Reference has been made above to the "administrative and managerial" use of contracts. The rules involved are instructions, from higher-level bureaucrats to lower-level ones, on how to manage the state assets that they control. When we turn to recent legal reforms, we will have occasion to ask about the extent to which law is still conceived of in China as *vertical*, an ensemble of rules intended to deal with internal management of bureaucracy, rather than as *horizontal*, creating relations among legal actors who are on the same plane.

The Cultural Revolution

This chapter and chapter 3 have been included here partly because they demonstrate how far China has had to go to effect legal reform. The distance that must be traveled is even greater than indicated by these discussions of legal institutions under Mao, because they have not included the effects of the Cultural Revolution. The Cultural Revolution, a catastrophe for all of China, rendered totally irrelevant these already politicized legal institutions. The formal criminal process, which years earlier had already been emptied of whatever content it once possessed, disappeared. Before the Cultural Revolution, the Chinese police had exercised immense power and were a major instrument of coercion. By 1970 many police cadres had been purged; in some places the army was directly supervising the police, the courts, and the Procuracy; and some police functions had been distributed to new activist organizations. Between 1966 and 1969, the police, the Procuracy, and the courts were first severely criticized and their activities virtually suspended, and then they were partially reorganized. During the same period, too, China's cities and some areas of the countryside experienced a general disruption of public order that included widespread violence and many deaths. New and flamboyantly named organizations of young people, all claiming to be supporters of Chairman Mao's continuing revolution, attacked persons considered to be bourgeois and fought bitterly among themselves, sometimes to the death. Crime appeared to an extent unknown in China since 1949, and the army had to intervene to maintain order.

With the end of the Cultural Revolution, the army's role in peacekeeping receded. Army leader Lin Biao's attempt to seize power reaffirmed the determination of Mao and other Chinese leaders to maintain control over the army, and by 1972 the police again patrolled the streets. Parapolice groups, which had appeared in the cities during the Cultural Revolution, were disbanded, gradually assimilated into urban militia forces, or placed under the latter's control. Courts resumed their activities, although certainly no more vigorously than before the Cultural Revolution. A new constitution adopted in 1975 contained only limited references to judicial activity, and the Procuracy disappeared from view. However, with the overthrow of the "Gang of Four" in 1976, a new stage was inaugurated. After several years during which the power of a newly pragmatic leadership was consolidated, formal legal institutions began to receive attention that they had not known for more than twenty years. The damage done to China by the Cultural Revolution moved some Chinese leaders—and many Chinese citizens—to believe that the regularized formulation and application of known rules should have a prominent role in the government of China. An era of reforms began, in which law has risen to greater prominence in the governance of Chinese society than ever before in Chinese history. The chapters that follow explore the nature and significance of those reforms.

CHAPTER 5

Foundation: Economic Reform
and a New Role for Law

CHINA'S LEGAL INSTITUTIONS today are more vigorous than any that China has ever known. Legal reform has been driven by economic reform, and virtually every element of Chinese law today was either revived or newly created in the course of two decades of extraordinary economic and social change that have begun to transform Chinese society. Without understanding the social context in which legal institutions such as the courts must operate, it is impossible to assess legal reform and its future. There is also a policy context: In order to carry out legal reform, the leadership must redefine the role of law, raising it from its insignificance under Mao; this it has not found easy to do. As the vital prerequisite to understanding the institutions for dispute resolution that are analyzed in chapters 8 and 9, in this chapter I have considered both the impact of the economic reforms and the new policy toward law.

I begin by describing certain elements and consequences of economic reform that affect the content, operation, and social impact of legal institutions and will influence legal development in the future. These include the political and economic decentralization that is transforming the Party-state, the rise of a nonstate sector of the economy, the persistence of the state sector, emergent patterns in state-society relations, and wide-ranging social and cultural changes. Against this background, the chapter then addresses basic policies that underlie the legal reforms. Although the Chinese leadership has articulated concepts of legality and the function of law that are consistent with Western concepts, they also continue to use law as an instrument for the short-term implementation of policy. These policies, and the tension that they create, are examined here.

The Economic, Political, and
Social Context of Legal Reform

ECONOMIC REFORM

The first and the most far-reaching reforms began in the countryside in the late 1970s, when rural communes were dismantled and their functions divided between townships and economic committees. A "production responsibility" system, which collectively assigned land to households, revived family-based farming and leases of land and expanded the discretion of 185 million peasant families to decide the crops they would grow. The creation of small-scale enterprises was allowed, and restrictions on peasant mobility were eased; peasants could move to towns and establish businesses, and many others could travel to the cities to work.

In industry, the scope of the state plan was greatly reduced, price controls loosened, and much of the power over budgets and administration decentralized. The economy was transformed into a "dual-track" system in which goods produced by state-owned enterprises (SOEs) according to plan are sold at planned prices, while above-quota production by those units is sold at higher prices, some set by the market and others set by the state. As a result of further decontrol of prices, by 1997 more than 95 percent of industrial output was being sold at market prices.[1]

EMERGENCE OF A NONSTATE SECTOR UNDER
THE CONTROL AND INFLUENCE OF LOCAL GOVERNMENTS

Economic reform has changed the allocation of power in the Chinese Party-state, initially through fiscal reform. The planned sector of the economy has declined since the late 1970s and is now rivaled by a growing and increasingly differentiated nonpublic sector composed of enterprises under widely varying degrees of control by local governments and private owners.[2] At the beginning of reforms, the central government gave local governments the right to retain certain tax and nontax revenues and minimized its own claims to revenues generated locally. New commercial entities including vigorous collective enterprises were created in the countryside when many township and village enterprises (TVEs) were transferred to private entrepreneurs in exchange for cash payments to the local governments that had formerly administered them. Rural industry was encouraged first to take over agricultural processing, then allowed to produce for consumer markets, and finally permitted to engage in any lawful profitable activity. A nonstate economic sector has been fostered in which private and collective enterprises have grown.

Economic reform has expanded the power of local governments over productive enterprises. Decollectivization of agriculture and fiscal reform were two key factors that transformed local governments from providers of administrative services into economic entrepreneurs. Decollectivization took away their income from the sale of agricultural products; fiscal reform gave localities a share in tax revenues, and thus the incentive to act efficiently. Local governments could raise revenues by taxing the rural collective enterprises, but they could also go into business themselves.

In addition, the involvement of local governments in TVEs has frequently continued after the enterprises were transferred, because many private firms were allowed to register as collectives in return for payments to local officials. Such officials have sometimes become entrepreneurs and formed alliances with private enterprises; in other cases, they benefited from the ambiguous legal status of private firms to peddle influence and protection. By the end of the 1980s, "many rural firms that were nominally collective had in fact become private firms operated with the cooperation of local officials."[3] Although the share of China's industrial output contributed by state enterprises has gone down because of reform, the total *public* sector, including urban and rural collectives, is over 85 percent, and the output share of private domestic firms is less than 10 percent.[4] By the mid-1990s, a new form of political relationship had begun to appear in the countryside. In most TVEs:

Officials appoint the managers, determine the size and composition of the labor force, provide investment capital, promote production, and protect from competition. . . . The upshot is that in the semi-reformed system both the major cities and the small townships are developing more a negotiated economy than a competitive market-driven system.[5]

It is important to emphasize that the decentralization of power that marks these developments has continued a tendency in Chinese socialism that not only distinguished it from the far more centralized Soviet variety but also facilitated the piecemeal reform undertaken in the PRC. Long before reform, localities acquired administrative expertise because they managed many Chinese enterprises, and "local cadres took advantage of China's 'sporadic totalitarian state' which was unable to maintain consistent supervision of the nation's localities. As central control weakened, cadres not only promoted illicit activities, they also skirted fiscal and budgetary regulations in order to increase local development."[6] When the reforms began, the previous experience that localities had gained administering economic enterprises also made it possible to create a parallel economy alongside the state economy.

The relationships between local governments and enterprises have been characterized as "local state corporatism,"[7] a term whose implications are explored below. Local governments, while remaining agents of central industrial policy, have also, at the same time, gained the power to promote local policies more intensively and effectively than before reform. Local officials help local enterprises obtain raw materials and information about new products, markets, and technology. More generally, their control over rural enterprises allows them to redistribute revenues from those enterprises, using the profits of one to assist another. Jean Oi writes, "[As] the holders of the rights over income flows, local governments can decide, much like a corporation, how to use the profits from its various enterprises and how to redistribute income."[8] They also control sources of local credit, which are essential in an economy that has been based on credit rather than capital.

As local governments have increased their revenues through participation in economic enterprises, they have also expanded the resources that they can expend for non-economic purposes. They are more able to distribute subsidies to local residents, allowing their officials "to be not just businessmen but also overseers of community well-being" who can "take social need into consideration when making economic decisions."[9] They may also place local interests ahead of national priorities: In the late 1980s, when the central government put pressure on local governments to close some enterprises, local governments protected their enterprises through mergers and other forms of evasion.[10] As their economic power increases, so also does the parochialism of their rule and the fragmentation of state authority.

Although the economy has grown so substantially out of the plan that it can be characterized as "a market economy with a mixed ownership base,"[11] the extensive involvement of local government in the economy raises questions about the future evolution of markets. As Oi has noted, "markets are a key part of the local economy but government coordination and intervention continue. . . . Local officials have assumed new roles as entrepreneurs, selectively allocating scarce resources to shape patterns of local economic growth."[12] State organizations still play an important role in the new mix of economic relationships, but local governments now have "a greater ability to monitor firms and enforce their interests as owners."[13] As a result of their involvement, they often decide to shed relatively less profitable enterprises by leasing them out or by outright divestment.[14]

The growth of the nonstate sector has brought with it problems, of course. By early 1998 declines in consumer demand and in investment had caused the number of loss-making TVEs to increase.[15] The property rights of local governments, TVEs, and their employees and managers are poorly defined,[16] with troubling implications for legal development that are explored below. Relationships between the governments and businesses have not yet settled down. During the mid-1990s, in some places, local governments realized that privatization need not diminish their control over enterprises. They exercise their influence not only by direct supervision, as in the licensing process, but also by selecting some enterprises as beneficiaries of their support with credit, tax breaks or exemptions, allocations at market prices of scarce goods, and access to information about new products, technology, and markets.[17] They have, therefore, increased the pace of privatization. The revenues generated by local enterprises, in turn, contribute mightily to the extra-budgetary resources of local governments, which have risen under reform to the extent that 45 percent of government-controlled investment is financed by extra-budgetary resources that are monitored either poorly or not at all.[18]

THE STATE SECTOR REMAINS OUTSIDE THE LEGAL DOMAIN

Industrial reform, more complicated than its rural counterpart, has been carried out incrementally, experimentally, and incompletely.[19] The scope of mandatory planning has been reduced and most prices adjusted. Enterprise management has been formally separated from government functions. Managerial autonomy and responsibility have been increased, wages and profits have been linked, and objective criteria for profits and retained funds have been set. State-owned enterprises have gained some freedom to market their products, stock ownership and domestic joint ventures have been created and enterprise bankruptcy permitted, private enterprises have been recognized, and some small state enterprises have been privatized through sale or lease. Enterprise targets have sometimes been the subject of long-term contracts that require bureaucrats to commit themselves to less interference in enterprise operation and focus on profit remittances from local enterprises. By 1992, state enterprises were responsible for only 48 percent of China's industrial output, compared with 76 percent in 1980,[20] and, as noted earlier, almost all products are now sold at market prices.

The state sector of the economy, only partially reformed, continues to face difficult obstacles to economic and legal reform.[21] Twenty years after reform began, bargaining rather than rules still determines outcomes in relations between center and locality and between administrative superiors and inferiors.[22] In planning projects, the center must bargain with localities to match funds. Local governments wish to maximize both investment from the center and their own control over resources and finances. Local officials, who wish to enhance their own resources to promote economic growth and protect the welfare of local citizens, allow tax evasion, give tax holidays and relief, and use negotiations on tax payments to their advantage. Complex and continuous bargaining between managers and officials leads to extraction of taxes from the most profitable enterprises and protection from taxation of necessary but less profitable or loss-making enterprises.

Relations between SOEs and their superiors are also marked by negotiations. Enterprises face bureaucratic pressure to avoid price increases; they seek to reduce taxes, buy goods at concessionary prices (including consumption goods sold to the workers), and collect benefits for key individuals through corrupt transactions. These forces lead to intense bargaining over enterprise profits subsidized by the state and taxes. One observer has noted:

There are as yet no clear standards about what is legitimately the central government's or the city's or the enterprise's share of industrial profits. There are only customary practices and situational standards, which must be revised case by case. It is only out of the bargaining process that a "fair" determination of these matters can be reached.[23]

Another has noted that "almost any parameter can be altered through negotiation between superiors and subordinates."[24] In this environment, enterprises and superiors "face a vast realm of indeterminacy, in which everything—price, plan, supply, tax, credit—is subject to change and negotiation."[25] SOEs and their superiors are locked in an inextricable embrace in which they must bargain with each other, while in the bargaining process accountability fades away.

The current situation intensifies conditions that long antedate reform. Extra-budgetary funds had expanded under Maoism, and subsequent recentralization efforts never succeeded in returning fiscal flows to their prior state. By further decentralizing control over enterprises, reform has increased the ambiguity of the relationships between enterprises and the state.[26] After reform began, although enterprise resources were expanded by increasing retained depreciation funds, repair funds, and retained profits, no universal formulas were set and outcomes were left to bargaining. Monitoring has become more difficult, and managers and local officials have incentives to increase extra-budgetary funds for such items as housing and bonuses.

Further reform of the SOEs has continued to be a major concern of the central government. They are often grossly inefficient and as many as one-third of them are sustained only through government subsidies. Because the large SOEs are responsible for many aspects of the lives of their workers, reforming them presents social and political as well as economic challenges. Dismantling them would threaten to throw huge numbers of workers into unemployment, and a nationwide safety net does not exist. As the most visible embodiments of state ownership ("by the whole people"), SOEs present ideological reasons that discourage dismantling and privatizing these fundamental symbols of the revolution. Paradoxically, at the same time, many SOEs are controlled not by the state but by their managers, who, sheltered by decentralization, lack of accountability, and continued government support of SOEs, are generating losses by making poor investment decisions, authorizing excessive increases in wages and benefits, and engaging in extensive asset-stripping.[27]

Reform of the SOEs, which was much debated and conducted in a piecemeal fashion during the 1980s, slowed for several years after the repression of the "democracy movement" in 1989. Deng Xiaoping made a dramatic visit to southern China in 1992, during which he made a series of pro-reform remarks that led to a further push by reformers. In July 1992 the State Council issued a decree intended to enable state enterprises to loosen state controls over their activities.[28] In 1993, a centrally directed policy of contracting out or leasing small SOEs was announced, which has been implemented by local governments since then.[29] In September 1997 Jiang Zemin, in his report to the Fifteenth Party Congress, expressed a commitment to reduce government ownership over large and middle-size industrial enterprises by "corporatizing" them. In March 1998 newly elected Premier Zhu Rongji announced an energetic program of transforming SOEs through sell-offs, mergers, or reorganizations,[30] but the slowing of China's economic growth also slowed implementation of the program.

UNCERTAINTIES ABOUT FUTURE REFORM

The Chinese economy that we see today has been shaped—and is still being shaped—by a struggle between conservative Chinese leaders, who would have continued to rely on the primacy of ideology and the economic plan and who were apprehensive about opening China to the outside world, and reformers (led by Deng Xiaoping until his death) who wanted to reduce the influence of ideology, move away from the plan, and open wide to the outside.[31] The Chinese leadership undertook economic reforms, without any consensus on their goals, even on such basic issues as the extent to which economic levers should replace planning, or on which prices, taxes, and interest rates should be changed.

Throughout the 1980s, struggle between the two views generated a cycle. When the reformers were directing policy, they loosened controls over the economy, thus permitting lower-level officials to take advantage of the changes for their localities and stimulate growth (and inflation), as well as engage in excessive investment and corrupt practices. In response, conservatives would urge retrenchment, consolidation, renewed administrative control, and credit restraints. Further loosening of governmental controls over the economy would follow, and the cycle would begin anew. Conservatives, however, never succeeded in completely rolling back the accomplishments of previous periods of reform. Although the stated goal of reform was first a state-guided semi-market economy, in practice the market elements in the economy steadily increased at the expense of the planned elements.[32] The goal has evolved through intermediate stages until the Fourteenth Party Congress, when it was declared to be a "socialist market economy," the first time that the leadership committed itself unambiguously to aim for a market economy.[33]

Twenty years after reform began, China has two different types of economic systems. One is managed from Beijing, the other system remains local. In the near term, it seems likely that the economy will be "marketized, but not privatized,"[34] but even so the Chinese economy's future trajectory will take it far from its Maoist origins. At the moment of writing, the leadership appears committed to increased marketization but their goals remain undefined and their efforts will be affected by forces beyond their control, as was demonstrated in 1997–1998 by a slowdown in Chinese economic growth and the collapse of economies all around Asia. Moreover, other critical economic sectors await decisive actions, including fiscal and banking reform and the creation of true capital markets. In the meantime, changes in the Chinese economy are affecting some of China's basic political institutions, as the following sections of this chapter will show.

CHANGES IN THE CHINESE PARTY-STATE:
POST-TOTALITARIAN BUREAUCRATIC AND POLITICAL STYLES

The economic reforms have been accompanied by, and in some cases have caused, considerable changes in the organization and management of the Chinese Party-state[35] that raise important questions for the future of a variety of Chinese institutions. In one view,

In a space of fifteen years or so, the Chinese political structure has been transformed from one that was once reputed for its high degree of centralization and effectiveness into one in which the center has difficulty coordinating its own agents' behavior. Because power and resources are dispersed, the exercise of central control now depends to a large extent upon the consent of the sub-national units whose actions are slipping from central control.[36]

It is clearer than ever that instead of considering the Chinese "state" as a single entity, greater attention must be paid to the distinctions between local and central levels and to the growth of power at the lowest levels. Furthermore, decentralization has not been uniform. Some localities have not wrested power from the central government, but have been favored by it. At the same time, local responses to decentralization have not been consistent.[37]

Whatever the variations may be, the future of central-local relationships is in question. Some observers believe that "a serious decline in China's central state capacity . . . threatens macroeconomic stability, the organizational integrity of the state and potentially even national unity";[38] others see it as a harbinger of an informal federalism in which the rights and powers of local and central governments would be defined in a stable arrangement. Little more can be said at this juncture other than that there is a remarkable lack of clarity in China today in the division of administrative responsibilities between powers of local and central governments—which in turn suggests the secondary roles of rules and the extent to which following them is unimportant in practice. The bargaining and the looseness of rules that mark economic activity will be shown below to be highly relevant to understanding the operation of the courts and to speculating about the future of legal development. First, however, it is necessary to continue to describe forces outside formal legal institutions that are conditioning their operation.

With the decline of central power (which had never before been exercised monolithically) bureaucratic decision-making has now become so subject to inter-unit bargaining that Chinese authoritarianism has become, in one suggestive view, "fragmented."[39] Although bargaining goes on in all political systems, Chinese decision-making is distinctive because of the frequent need to build consensus among many individuals and organizations.[40]

CHANGING POWER RELATIONS IN THE CHINESE COUNTRYSIDE

The economic reforms summarized above have profoundly affected the society that legal reform is intended to serve. Village governance, for example, is changing. One study of a north China village suggests that cadres have ceased to care about ideology and have become increasingly interested in economic benefits generated in the village rather than political rewards bestowed by the state.[41] They are less inclined to enforce unpopular policies and more inclined to act as mediators when national policies conflict with local interests. Although the reforms have ended cadres' previous power over peasants, their increased power over resources has created new income opportunities that have transformed their political role from "tyrannical 'little emperors'" to "prudent middlemen."[42] The exercise of power by cadres has come to involve more bargaining and compromise than before reform, but at the same time increased corruption has also reduced their ability to exercise power. The populace, for its part, conforms outwardly to policies while turning cynical about ideology and cadre corruption. A popular slogan describes cadres as "cheating the state and coaxing the villagers" (*pian shangbian, hong xiabian*).[43]

If local governments have benefited greatly from economic reform, some of their gains have been at the expense of peasants who have remained on the land. Farm incomes have either remained stagnant or declined during the early 1990s.[44] Income disparities have appeared and continue to grow between rural communities with a substantial number of collective enterprises and those that depend on agriculture, and between rural communities in the south and those in provinces less well endowed with natural resources and less benefited by foreign investment.

State-society relations in the countryside do not show a uniform pattern. Some studies have found that peasants are less subject to cadre commands. A comparison of relatively well- and poorly-endowed counties found that in well-endowed areas "leaders cannot capriciously order farmers around."[45] Another study, of a poor county in Sichuan province, also found that a "new stratum" of powerful entrepreneurs was emerging that could resist state control.[46] It may be, though, that in communities with relatively more collective enterprises or nonagricultural businesses, entrepreneurs' need for guarantees that cadres will not cause trouble for them increases the value of officials' discretionary protection.[47]

Although some peasants have become relatively wealthy as a result of the reforms, one analysis of popular resistance in the countryside finds ample reasons for peasant discontent, including limited social mobility, growing economic inequality, and arbitrary taxes and exactions.[48] One observer notes that,

As gatekeepers to the boundaries of income-enhancing opportunities—such as small shops, factories, or factory jobs—cadres are extremely powerful vis-à-vis China's common man. They can take peasant land to build their own homes, and there is little peasants can do. No doubt, wealthier peasants or those with strong family alliances possess resources to confront cadre authority. But atomized individuals, stripped of their collective protection, remain in a highly vulnerable and inferior status in their confrontation with formidable bureaucratic forces.[49]

In some places peasants have rioted against diversion of funds by officials who have given them IOUs for agricultural produce rather than cash payments and have also imposed an array of taxes, fees, and levies. Such riots have provoked considerable concern in Beijing.[50]

Cadres have also begun to encounter resistance from peasants in a manner that may bear particular significance for Chinese legal development. Although the great majority of rural residents may be compliant, out of their ignorance of legal institutions and the latter's perceived weakness, there are also peasant "resisters," who "use laws, policies, and other official communications to defy local leaders. They accept their duty to observe laws and policies but also insist it is their right to observe only laws and policies."[51] Informing themselves through the media and personal acquaintances, they may decide, for example, whether payments they are asked to make are legal, and then remit only what they think is required by law or policy. They may also complain to higher levels, as when one group protested against a rigged village election in Liaoning. Strikingly, these "policy-based resisters" are said to regard local cadres as "bound by policies and laws to respect the interests of villagers," and to view themselves as acting on the basis of policies and laws "as if they have a right to due process."[52] The rights on which the protesters rely are still contingent because they are derived from the government and depend on the tolerance of local cadres. Moreover, complainants must adapt "their strategies of resistance . . . to the contour of a reforming authoritarian state,"[53] and win not on the strength of their legal arguments but because they have obtained the support of backers more powerful than their adversaries.[54] Nonetheless, the protests signify the emergence of rights consciousness in the countryside that could lead to broader resistance to policies that are perceived to be unjust.[55]

These developments suggest that the central Party-state's power to govern by dictatorship is so much reduced that in some places, at least, it has encountered difficulty in governing the countryside and has begun to retreat. In response, when the decline of cadre-peasant relations began to manifest itself in mid-1980s, central authorities decided to create elected Village Committees, hoping to strengthen cadre accountability and better define the respective authority of village cadres and townships.[56] To this end the Standing Committee of the National People's Congress (NPC) passed a trial Organic Law in November 1987.[57] The law provides for elected Village Committees that are responsible for maintaining public order, implementing laws and policies, and managing village land and collective property. They are not under the leadership of Party or government organs, but are subject to their guidance, support, and assistance.

Village Committees were intended to increase villagers' participation in government and to assist the central government in carrying out tasks assigned to the villages. The Ministry of Civil Affairs has also promoted the creation of Villagers' Representative Assemblies—smaller than the cumbersome Village Councils—which have adopted village "charters" and "codes of conduct." In the most successful villages, those made "demonstration villages" by the ministry, the Assemblies have raised the level of participation in government affairs and assisted in dispute resolution. Outside these few villages, however, many problems have been encountered, especially the dominance by local Party organizations and the widespread lack of interest by cadres in promoting the Organic Law. As a result, many villages can be classified as "paralyzed" (in which the villagers resent cadre intrusiveness), "authoritarian" (Party-dominated), or "run-away" (governed by cadres who resist performing state-assigned tasks).[58]

The success of experiments at promoting democracy in the villages has been very mixed; it is unlikely to grow without strong support both from the center and from local cadres. One Western commentator has observed of some of the elections that they "are the real thing—competitive, clean, with significant stakes and results that stick," and notes the enthusiasm of the Ford Foundation, the International Republican Institute, the Asia Foundation, and the United Nations Development Program for this "glint of democratic change."[59] His sensitive reading of Chinese debates on the subject, however, also suggests that increased self-government faces much opposition, from lower-level cadres who feign compliance with the policy of promoting the experiment, and from elements within the CCP who insist that the Village Committees operate under Party guidance. Perhaps most illuminating at this point is the instrumentalism of the partisans for and against greater village self-government, who seek it not because democracy is seen as an end in itself but because it will serve some other end, such as implementation of government policies or support for relief from the policies.

One possible outcome, clearly related to the future of legal development, is that institutions once put in place may, for whatever reason, begin to fulfill functions other than more limited ones their architects had in mind. Remonstrance and resistance against policies or implementation methods that are perceived as unfair could also lead to other forms of political participation and assertion of rights, especially as peasants are freer to establish relationships among themselves.[60] In chapter 9 we will see that litigation, including suits against administrative agencies, is rising, and recourse to litigation may increasingly serve to channel popular discontent.

THE EMERGENCE OF CLIENTELISM AND CORPORATISM

Clientelism

The economic reforms have also generated new patron–client relationships that benefit *local* business and bureaucratic interests, and shift power downward to the lowest, local levels in society at which business and bureaucracy intersect. A compelling study of relations between entrepreneurs and local bureaucrats in Xiamen, for example, shows how entrepreneurs provide benefits to officials in return for the use of officials' personal ties within the bureaucracy to assist the entrepreneurs.[61] Other studies show rural officials, who head village "corporations," earning salaries,[62] and a study of a neighborhood in Chengdu demonstrates similar interactions between private business and local bureaucracies to their mutual benefit.[63] The conduct involved here ranges from the exchange of favors among persons who are known to each other to outright bribery.

The emergence of these patterns raises questions about the impact and effectiveness of legal rules. Heavy emphasis on personal relationships (*guanxi*) has been a feature of Chinese life for centuries, of course, and has flourished under Communist rule both before and after reforms began. Analysis of *guanxi* is beyond the scope of this brief note on social change, but suffice it to say that traditionally the concept has been more nuanced than the crass exchange of favors and bribery with which it is often confused in the West. It has involved the entire web of family, kin, and communal relationships in which persons are ordinarily involved and has been based not on instrumental conduct but on *renqing* or "human feelings." It constitutes a "local moral world."[64] When persons come in contact with each other outside the usual web of personal relationships, particularly in economic life, *guanxi* can change, and in the new economic environment generated by reform it may be transmuted into highly instrumental relationships.[65]

The weakening of the totalitarian grip on individual lives has caused the emphasis on personal relationships, traditionally so important in Chinese society, to reemerge. The possible future impact of *guanxi* networks on economic institutions is unclear. The continued rise of clientelism that is reflected in the involvement of bureaucracy in business at the local level suggests to some observers that the thrust of the economic reforms is not toward the creation of markets.[66] It has also been argued that business based on clientelist ties could also help accelerate marketization. In this view, use of clientelist connections may stimulate competition by facilitating capital accumulation among persons connected to each other, by reducing uncertainty, and even by encouraging bribery in order to get business permits.[67]

The growth of clientelism raises other political and economic issues that have direct implications for Chinese legal culture. The rise of the local Party-state has reduced the power of the central state by weakening lines of authority and encouraging deviation from central policies. The discussion below looks further into the political domain by speculating on the implications of the growth of the local Party-state for the emergence of "civil society" in China. It then moves to a question that straddles the line between economics and law by inquiring into the future of property rights.

Corporatism

In analyzing state-society relations, we must take into account the emergence of what has been called corporatism, which arises out of ownership patterns fostered by economic reforms in the nonstate sector of the economy.[68] As local officials in rural areas become entrepreneurs,[69] there has also emerged a unique "interpenetration" of cadres and new merchants, both of them sharing dependence on the state.[70] As has already been suggested, new kinds of alliances have arisen between officials and entrepreneurs, and tax and other regulations are enforced through negotiations between entrepreneurs and officials.[71]

The growth of corporatism is not the same as the emergence of a civil society that some have hoped would be fostered by economic reform.[72] The essence of civil society has been defined as involving

the idea of the existence of institutionalized autonomy for social relationships and associational life, autonomy vis-à-vis the state . . . a well-formed civil society implies a degree of separation in the relationship between state and society, such that much social life goes on without reference to state dictates and policies.[73]

The economic reforms have caused the state to withdraw its involvement in the economic activities of individuals; could they also lead to creating a "zone of indifference" to other, non-economic activities?[74] The resurgence of religious belief, secret societies, sects, and affinity groups suggests the "growth of nonstate sources of moral authority and spiritual well-being."[75] One scholar, writing after the repression of the "democracy movement," was optimistic that "a nascent civil society will survive to provide potential for a more democratic China in the future."[76]

The concept itself may be too narrowly rooted in Western European history to be applicable to China past or present. For example, the concepts of "civil society" and legal rights are intimately related, since the autonomy from the state that is enjoyed by society in the West is often a matter not merely of tolerance but right. The weakness of concepts of individual rights in traditional China, especially against the state, has already been noted in chapter 2. Frederic Wakeman has suggested that "Chinese citizens appear to conceive of social existence mainly in terms of obligation and interdependence rather than rights and responsibilities."[77]

Even if rights-consciousness grows, the retreat of Party-state institutions from zones of activity that they dominate is braked by past practice, current structure, and governing ideology. The authoritarianism of Chinese Communism and its ambition to penetrate and control society, expressed in the term "Party-state" that is used throughout this book, has persisted in the midst of economic reform. In the West, the tension between state and society postulates a struggle of assertive elements outside the state to limit its reach, but in China "society at large is stirring but still tightly locked in the embrace of local officialdom, including local unit leaders of state organizations and enterprises."[78] The Party-state does not seem likely to recede in the near future[79] although its forms are changing and some of the local Party-state's claims over society will differ from those of the center.

It is the corporatism described here that seems to be the strongest current flowing in relations between the Chinese state and Chinese society. In civil society, the state becomes limited by society when it permits the "relatively unfettered development" of "autonomous associations," while in corporatism the state sets "ground rules for the emergence of such associations and the participation of its representatives."[80] New nongovernmental social organizations and economic associations have begun to appear in China that seem to be closely linked to the state;[81] however, these should probably be viewed not as "autonomous Western-style interest groups" but as bridges between society and government, intended to assist Party and government.[82] These newly appearing associations are by no means uniform and already seem to vary considerably in the extent to which they function to carry out state policy or, by contrast, serve to articulate the interests of their members.[83] Whatever their difference at the moment, they suggest the emergence of a "hybrid form of state-societal interdependence"[84] and give rise to long-term doubts about the development of individual autonomy.

These developments could possibly augur well for a fluidity in central-local and state-society relations that was not previously known in the PRC. Corporatism, it has been suggested, could lead to a "symbiotic tension" between the Party-state and new associations,[85] or support for evolution away from authoritarianism toward a looser form of government,[86] which has even been compared to federalism.[87] In another view, China may be approaching the "limits of gradualist reform" and further progress requires nothing less than that Chinese leadership "reinvent government."[88] This debate, still necessarily inconclusive, bears on legal reform because it highlights the unsettled nature of the environment in which legal development must take place. A further sign of the flux in the society around legal institutions is the imprecise nature of many of the relationships that have been generated by the economic reforms.

THE WEAKNESS AND AMBIGUITY OF PROPERTY RIGHTS

A striking feature of economic reform key to the future of legal reform is the ambiguity of rights over the acquisition, management, and disposition of property. Chinese economic reforms have been successful to date despite the absence of any systematic attempt to clarify what economists call (and what lawyers would also term) "property rights."[89] Chinese economic success defies conventional theory, which requires, as one economist has observed, that, "To function anywhere near its potential, any economic system must have property rights that are much better defined and enforced than is true of China's mixed economic system today."[90] As a number of economists have noted, the owners of TVEs, which are technically "nonstate enterprises" and represent a signal success of Chinese economic reform, have only ambiguous property rights that are poorly protected.[91]

The movement of assets from state ownership has come about not through a uniform and well-defined process of transfer, but through a disorderly variety of devices including the contracting or leasing of public assets, sale to private parties, illicit transfer of ownership to élites, and investment of public funds.[92] As a result, the status of property transferred to TVEs remains unclear. One analysis concludes that rural collective property is currently best thought of as "rural local government property" and that most urban collective property is "also quasi-state-owned-property controlled by various supervising bodies, not enterprise personnel."[93] Not only have these uncertainties, at the very least, done "surprisingly little" harm to Chinese reform,[94] but they may have a longevity that will surprise Western observers. In one view, the local corporatism model that has been discussed here suggests that "individuals may not need to have property rights over enterprise profits for economic growth to occur."[95] More specifically, it has been argued that clientelist networks of state officials and private entrepreneurs both allocate and enforce property rights in an effective and efficient manner that is not necessarily transitional but stable.[96] The mechanisms of allocation include using *guanxi* to obtain licenses, undervaluing state assets, and otherwise diverting state assets to legal private ownership. Enforcement mechanisms include strong concepts of personal honor, property, reciprocity, and shame; *guanxi* and *ganqing*, which have been mentioned above; and invocation of the state administrative apparatus—while avoiding formal legal institutions. What is remarkable about this argument is the extent to which the enforcement mechanisms echo those that were used among businessmen in the late Qing.[97] No great leap of imagination is required to recall the "softness" of rights that characterized traditional China.

It should be noted that the practical ambiguity surrounding property rights does not mean that the state has entirely neglected the need to define such rights. The discussion of civil law in chapter 7 will show that considerable effort has been made to address the issue of property rights in the legal domain by creating new areas of substantive and procedural law intended to define rights in various kinds of property and to enable holders of rights in such types of property to enforce and protect their rights by calling on agencies of the state to assist them. However, such formal legal institutions will have to struggle against the cultural and social forces in Chinese society that tend to weaken and undermine property rights. Illustratively, an important study of business–government relations in a South China city in the 1990s finds a trend in "the waning of conscious distinctions between legal public and private property. . . . This declining attention to public and private status reflects not the increasing clarity of legal property boundaries but rather the greater legitimacy of arrangements that do not conform to legal distinctions between public and private property."[98]

Social and Cultural Changes

Chinese legal reform is being attempted in the midst of extraordinary social changes that began in the early 1980s, and necessarily within the limits imposed by the political, economic, and bureaucratic setting that I have just summarized. Although the pace and amplitude of social change defy attempts to assess current trends and the paths they may follow, we can at least note some characteristics of present-day Chinese society that are likely to affect attitudes of both cadres and populace toward state and law and, therefore, are also likely to affect the function, significance, and effectiveness of legal institutions.

IMPROVEMENT OF THE MATERIAL LIVES AND
ENLARGEMENT OF PERSONAL FREEDOMS FOR MANY

The economic reforms have clearly improved the lives of many millions of Chinese and dramatically transformed many cities and some parts of the countryside. An annual growth rate of 9 percent for over a decade has brought to many a level of material comfort unimaginable in China twenty years ago.

The reforms have created conditions favorable to the enlargement of personal freedom for many Chinese. Before reform, the work units (*gongzuo danwei*)—state enterprises and state offices, organizations, rural communes—had enormous power over all who worked in them and who were dependent on them for many aspects of life outside the workplace. Privatization has created employment alternatives in the nonstate sector, encouraging some to "jump into the sea" (*xiahai*) of private enterprise and entrepreneurship. With the decline of the economic hegemony of the work unit over the lives of its members, its once-suffocating embrace has otherwise also been loosened. Chinese have become more able to communicate with each other without fearing surveillance, criticism, or denial of access to social welfare for political reasons by agents of the police in their work unit.[99] At the same time, the state is beginning to channel social services such as housing, social security, and medical services through local governments rather than through work units. The expansion of economic opportunities and relationships, as well as the decline of the work unit and the multiplication of other routes for the delivery of social services, could all increase pressure to develop the legal system.

Reforms have led to relaxation of state control over the lives of the Chinese populace in some other noticeable ways.[100] In matters of dress, home decoration, and use of leisure time, for example, all severely constricted under Maoism, personal choice has begun to flourish. Although under Mao the very concept of "private life" was unacceptable, under Deng it not only grew but became depoliticized. Simultaneously, China's opening to the West has brought greater access to Western media and other foreign cultural influences and the Chinese media has become partially depoliticized; the combined effect of these dramatic departures from Maoist China is to make available to many Chinese much more information about the rest of the world—including law—than they have ever had.

INCOME DISPARITY

Not all have benefited equally from reforms, and some have not benefited at all. In May 1998, reports indicated that China's poor numbered 300 million. Even for those who live outside the poorest regions, which have not shared in the boom of coastal China, urban-rural inequality is great and has been aggravated by the continuation of state subsidies of rent and staples, provided to urban residents since 1949 and only now being reduced or abolished.[101] In the meantime, demographic pressures and the lure of increased income have prompted a huge number of peasants to leave the countryside in search of employment in the cities. This population flow, formerly forbidden, has created a "floating population" of as many as 100 million in China's cities, people who have no work unit and who constitute "swelling armies of impoverished rural floaters."[102] The economic changes alluded to above have caused changes in China's social fabric that appear both momentous and irreversible.

THE FRAYED CHINESE SOCIAL FABRIC

One of the most dramatic changes in Chinese life is the new importance of wealth as a key to social status, which is an extraordinary reversal of Maoist egalitarianism. Many Chinese perceive that others are more blessed with material goods and economic opportunity than they, and the growth of "red-eye disease" (jealousy) has been much discussed in the Chinese media and noticed by foreign observers. The sudden importance of wealth has upset the long-held and widely shared perceptions of many Chinese about how society should be organized.[103] Traditional Chinese society was hierarchical, and social stability was deemed to depend on all knowing their place. China under Mao was also hierarchical, although categories of rank and status were politicized. Economic reform has totally upset former hierarchical orderings of society, causing alienation and anxiety. Older persons, for example, who sacrificed much, willingly or otherwise, to build and maintain socialism in China now see individualistic young people making fortunes without expecting to bear responsibilities toward the state.

RISING DISCONTENT, CRIME, AND CORRUPTION

Scholars and journalists alike report continuing rural discontent among peasants angry at their exploitation by local cadres, high unemployment (over 200 million), and considerable alienation among young people.[104] Since the beginning of economic reform all kinds of crime, violent and otherwise, have risen, leading the Chinese leadership to launch numerous anti-crime campaigns. The crime increase has also led to great concern on the part of the leadership and ordinary citizens alike about social order, with the "floating population" often blamed for most of the rise in urban crime. Ten years ago it was possible to walk almost anywhere in Beijing at any time of night; now, local residents are concerned about venturing into certain areas because people from "outside Beijing" have become concentrated there and make them unsafe.

One of the most striking products of reform has been increased corruption. The economic reforms have created many institutional settings in which government officials can use their power to affect economic outcomes, and as a result: "Granting licenses and loans, forgiving debts, allowing tax breaks, and providing access to needed electricity, water, telephones, and transportation are only a few of the types of decisions for which PRC officials now expect 'tea money', or bribes."[105] One Western scholar concludes the following in his study of an urban neighborhood:

Almost any business practice seems possible if adequately paid for. The reputation for cheating, selling fakes, and so on that the private sector has gained among many ordinary citizens has been steadily nourished by some of its unscrupulous representatives. . . . When confronted with such irregularities, the local bureaucracy remains passive. If it acts, it is only to secure a share of the profit gained through illegal means.[106]

He adds that people who have been cheated generally can obtain no recourse and that the Public Security Bureau claims it lacks the power and personnel to investigate outside of its territorial jurisdiction.

Corruption thrives today in China because distinctions between state and nonstate concerns, property, and interests are vague and undefined. It is not coincidental, either, that among the major beneficiaries of the rise in corruption have been high-ranking officials and their families. More basically, though, the economy is currently "semireformed, neither subject to a disciplined plan nor driven primarily by the market via activities constrained by law."[107] Political processes that could differentiate among the welter of ambiguous relationships involved have not been allowed to develop, and standards of appropriate conduct, whether ideological, legal, or moral, are lacking.[108]

IDEOLOGICAL VACUUM AND LACK OF MORAL COMPASS

Perhaps the most significant social change brought on by economic reform has been the loss among many Chinese of whatever faith they may have had in the ideology of Marxism-Leninism-Mao Zedong Thought. Together the Cultural Revolution and the great hardships caused by Mao's policies had already begun to weaken belief in the ideology, and the economic reforms have further accelerated its decline. The Party's legitimacy will increasingly be questioned, especially if a stall in Chinese economic growth brings hard times.

Even as the ideology that justifies the Party's rule declines, the opening of China to the rest of the world has helped to inform the Chinese people about many values and ideas that had long been denied to them. One observer has described how watching American TV programs helped educate residents of a north Chinese village about such matters as the powers of the U.S. Supreme Court and the independence of the judiciary.[109] In the current atmosphere, interest in politics and belief in the virtue of the officials of the Party-state have declined, and the leadership's call for national efforts to create a "spiritual civilization" has not evoked much popular enthusiasm. No alternative system of belief has appeared to challenge an increasingly hollow Communism, and at this moment China seems to be drifting ideologically. One disillusioned Communist has written of "the widespread spiritual malaise among people from all walks of life, a growing mood of depression, even despair, a loss of hope for the future and of any sense of social responsibility."[110]

Economic reform has created the need to build legal institutions that will define, guide, and regulate new relationships, not only in the economy but between state and society. The institution-building effort must simultaneously contend with the effects of ongoing economic and social changes generated by the economic reforms, influences flowing from traditional Chinese culture and the imprint of the Chinese revolution itself. The impact of all of these on legal reform will be selectively noted in later chapters. At this point, by way of beginning to consider legal reform, it is necessary to examine the basic leadership policy that has moved law from an ornamental appurtenance of Party policy to a more authoritative body of rules and doctrine.

China's Legal Reforms: Policies Toward Law

THE BEGINNING

China's law reforms formally began in early 1978. After a new Constitution was adopted by the First Session of the Fifth National People's Congress, a harbinger of a new policy appeared in an article in the *People's Daily* that urged "Smash Spiritual Shackles—Do Legal Work Well." The author, Han Youtong, was identified as the deputy director of a "Legal Research Institute"—an organization that had not been heard of since the beginning of the Cultural Revolution, more than a decade earlier. She called for "reviving and establishing necessary legal organs and legal institutions" and drafting law codes—and even quoted the late Chairman Mao on the need for law.[111] Other articles soon followed, linking orderly economic development with the growth of a legal system and warning that unless "explicit and standardized provisions" were enacted, progress toward attainment of the Four Modernizations—newly announced as a goal of the Party and nation—would be hampered.[112]

Han Youtong had directed the Institute of Law of the Chinese Academy of Sciences before it was abolished early in the Cultural Revolution. Some months after her article appeared in 1978, the first delegation from the American Bar Association to visit China since 1949 met with her one summer afternoon. A frail and dignified elderly woman, she spoke sadly of how her institute's library had been dispersed at the beginning of the Cultural Revolution. She and her husband, Zhang Youyu, were among a small number of legal scholars, who, well educated before the Revolution, had hoped that their professional talents and expertise would be used to build a post-revolutionary society. Disappointed for twenty years, they were then presented with an unexpected opportunity to help build a new legal order. Some of their hopes have since been realized.

When China's leadership, victorious after the overthrow of the Gang of Four, decided to overcome the chaos of the Cultural Revolution and restabilize Chinese society, they looked back to the relative stability of China before the Great Leap Forward. China had already developed, however invisible to most outsiders, a basic stratum of legal institutions and rules. By 1979, however, they were like crude buildings gone to ruin, but for which the architectural plans still remained. When the current legal reforms began, the first impulse of some Chinese officials was to reconstruct the institutions of the 1950s. They were powerfully reinforced in this idea by the planned economy that was still in place, and by the absence of any desire to engage in political reform.

The earlier period to which they referred had left behind a vocabulary of concepts and institutions that was easily accessible to the reformers. Some progress toward the creation of a legal system had been made intermittently between 1949 and 1966 under the influence of Stalinist and post-Stalinist Russia. Chinese scholars and legal drafters, heeding the Chinese leadership's instruction to "learn from older brother," had derived most theory about the nature and functions of law from Soviet models. Before the Cultural Revolution law had been regarded as a means to formalize discipline rather than to create rights. This, then, was the original theoretical basis for the ancestors of the legal institutions that have been emerging since the early 1980s.[113] Although legal reform has indeed recreated and consolidated some institutions and rules on models that they had been intended to follow decades ago, the reforms have since had to go much further.

Even the terminology that was used to describe legal reform when it began in the late 1970s suggests that it was plain to many at the outset that more ambitious efforts were required. Published discussions spoke of "reforming" economic institutions, but often described "constructing" legal institutions, suggesting a perception of how underdeveloped legal institutions had been during the first three decades of CCP rule. Whatever the views about legal reform might have been when the process began, the scope and speed of economic reform have relentlessly pressed law reform far beyond reestablishing the incomplete systems of the 1950s. Pre–Cultural Revolution institutions were inadequate to meet the challenge of reform, and China's law reformers have had to engage in considerable innovation to create institutions to fill legal vacuums. Not the least of these challenges was to define the policy of the Party toward law.

THE POLICIES UNDERLYING LAW REFORM

Two conflicting principles have been bound together at the core of Party policy since legal reform began. Party policy dictates that law must serve the Party-state, but at the same time it declares that China must be governed by law and aim to attain the rule of law. These two principles have coexisted uncomfortably since the inception of legal reform.

Endorsement of the Rule of Law as a Goal

In 1978, Deng Xiaoping declared that "democracy has to be institutionalized and written into law, so as to make sure that institutions and laws do not change whenever the leadership changes or whenever the leaders change their views."[114] Other formulations by leaders have not been much more specific than Deng's. China's leaders have invoked law as an alternative to the arbitrariness of the Cultural Revolution. They have, however, expressed their aims only imprecisely. Their public references to legal institutions are often exhortations to improve every major aspect of the system—such as attacking criminal activity, administering justice in economic disputes, and providing legal advice—and to eliminate major problems such as local protectionism and the arbitrary misuse of power.[115]

Others, especially Chinese legal scholars, have ventured beyond the leadership's general pronouncements on law to advance more specific ideas. They have argued, for example, that rights are universal rather than class-based, although Marxist dogma on the class nature of law has not been specifically disavowed.[116] The notion that all, including officials, must obey the law is frequently endorsed in the press.[117] Numerous scholars have used general expressions by the leadership in support for legality to endorse the supremacy of law over the CCP and the state both before and after the tragic events of June 1989 ended the "democracy movement's" idealistic spring. A notable articulation of scholarly views appeared just before the Tiananmen events. In late April of 1989 the journal of the Legal Research Institute of the Chinese Academy of Social Sciences published a summary of discussions by leading legal scholars at a conference earlier in the year. Their sentiments and proposals amount to a clear call for establishment of the rule of law based on principles familiar in the West:[118]

> law is not a tool of class dictatorship, and legal institutions such as the legislature, the Procuracy and the courts must be independent;
>
> the state and the Party must be subject to law;
>
> the Party may not supplant the state and policy may not supplant the law;
>
> the NPC must not be a "rubber stamp" and its members should be elected in public campaigns;
>
> political power must be divided by a system of checks and balances, and laws should be enacted to establish a system of constitutional government that will define procedures for amending the constitution;

administrative agencies must be permitted to act only within their
legal competence, and an administrative court and administrative
procedure should be established to exercise control over official
arbitrariness;

legislation and implementation of law must be aimed at maximizing
citizens' rights and freedoms and restricting government powers;

citizens' rights and freedoms may not be restricted except through
the exercise of due process.

These views are not just the product of a transitory moment in Chinese
history. Since 1989 and down to the present day, Chinese scholarly legal
journals continue to be filled with discussions of legal institutions and legal theory that are plainly consistent with the rule of law as that concept
is understood in the West today.[119]

Perhaps of more interest is impressionistic evidence that suggests that
many ordinary Chinese, not just legal scholars, endorse the ideal of the
rule of law. One study based on interviews and survey research in China
concludes that within the Chinese populace many persons believe that
justice is substantive fairness.[120] The sentiments of the persons who participated in the research are complex and mixed; popular views also value
personal ties and clientelist relationships but at the same time can criticize
economic and social injustice and the Party-state's support of privileged
status for its élite.

These conclusions resonate strongly with my own personal impressions,
gathered in more than twenty-five years of travel and work in China.
Since the onset of reform, when Chinese have learned of my interest in
Chinese law they often spontaneously offer their opinions on law. No
body of research exists to document these attitudes, but the subject is too
important to avoid simply for that reason. Attitudes toward law that I have
gathered from passing encounters with Chinese, largely urban residents
not professionally involved with legal matters, are direct and expressive:

laws should convey adequate notice to citizens of the consequences
of their acts;

laws should be administered consistently over time and their application should not be varied because of changes in policy or by the
arbitrary exercise of official discretion;

the acts of government and Party officials should be reviewable for
legality;

disputes should not be decided by Chinese judges, as they often are
today, on the basis of social connections, personal relationships, or
bribery.

Many have exclaimed that China has no law at all, or, as one daughter of a high official said to me, Chinese law is "like a baby that has not grown up yet." Chinese often express cynicism about the relationship between law and policy, and skepticism about the fairness of the courts, especially when cases involve persons with considerable power and influence over the judges. Most interesting of all is the fact that the standard against which they measure the performance of the Party-state in legal matters, one that is entirely understandable to the West, embodies the essence of the rule of law. Although that concept is often said to be a unique product of Western civilization and many Chinese have learned of it as an imported idea, it has roots in Chinese circumstances. The perception that they have been ruled for decades by arbitrary and frequently hypocritical cadres has led many Chinese to believe that government should be based on universally applicable rules, and that under such a government certain rights ought to be recognized and protected by the uniform application of rules. These sentiments about the rule of law suggest a heightened interest in legal institutions, and Chinese seem to be increasingly willing to litigate disputes. Recent research by Chinese legal scholars into attitudes among the Chinese populace toward disputes and litigation, discussed further in chapter 9, as well as increases in the number of civil and economic cases brought to the courts, suggest that some are increasingly more conscious of their rights under law and willing to consider the possibility of using formal legal means to protect their rights.

Competing Notions of the Rule of Law

Despite general endorsements of the rule of law by the leaders and amplification of that theme by some Chinese scholars, Chinese policy also looks in the opposite direction. Law and law reform are bounded, at least formally, by outer limits that were succinctly expressed in the Four Cardinal Principles laid down by Deng Xiaoping. These are the adherence to the socialist road, proletarian dictatorship, the leadership of the CCP, and Marxism-Leninism-Mao Zedong Thought. Speaking prior to the Tiananmen disturbances, Deng explained his rationale for these principles.[121] He opposed the wholesale introduction of capitalism, cautioning that China absorb only useful things. He condemned the copying of Western institutions, such as elections and the separation of powers, because these bourgeois institutions would nullify Party leadership and thereby bring disorder to China. Economic development was possible only in a stable political environment, and the need for stability remained paramount.

In recent years, Jiang Zemin and other leaders have echoed Deng, as in Jiang's talk in 1992 to representatives attending a national meeting on "judicial and public security work."[122] The two emphases were not paired by accident; Jiang simultaneously emphasized the importance of strengthening the socialist legal system and "performing a good job in public security work," because political and social stability were needed while the new economy was being built. The *leitmotif* of his talk was control. Thus, building a socialist market economy meant that

> we should strengthen the state's macroeconomic regulation and control through the necessary economic, legal, and other administrative means. Whether it is market regulation or macroeconomic regulation and control by the state, we should constantly sum up our experiences and gradually incorporate them into the law. We cannot possibly foster good order in the socialist market economy in the absence of a sound socialist legal system.[123]

The invocation of "control," "regulation," and "good order" in these three sentences makes Jiang's emphasis unmistakable. He also calls for strong attacks on criminal activity and cautions Party committees and governments at all levels to "act exemplary in enforcing the constitution and the law" and prevent arbitrary and illegal conduct by "people in authority." Jiang's choice of words, at the same time banal and authoritarian, marks the constraints on the rule of law under Deng, constraints that have not been disavowed by his successors.

The leadership has tried unsuccessfully to find further philosophical justification for the continuation of one-party rule beyond simple affirmation of the need for unity and stability. For a brief time before the "democracy movement" of 1989 appeared, the doctrine of "neoauthoritarianism" seemed useful for the purpose. A number of intellectuals, including some affiliated with institutes and think-tanks studying reform, expressed concern about the difficulties generated by reform. These include a growing ideological vacuum; spreading corruption; the migration of many peasants to the cities and the resulting growth of crime, disorder, and strain on resources; nationalism; and the need to address growing socioeconomic disparities. Although they varied in their emphases and points of view, they all espoused what one observer has called a "populist authoritarianism,"[124] which holds that reform can only be carried out under a strong authoritarian government that can ensure the stability and order required to protect society during a period of intense change. Some of the writers were influenced by theories of Harvard political scientist Samuel Huntington and by what they perceived to be the success of authoritarian leadership in presiding over the economic development of the "Four Dragons"—South Korea, Taiwan, Hong Kong, and Singapore. The theory fell into disfavor after 1989, however, perhaps because it was linked to the ousted Zhao Ziyang himself. It was also likely to have been unacceptable to many leaders and officials who realized that at least some of its proponents intended it to serve as an ideological basis for transition to democracy at some time in the future. Some of the overtones of neoauthoritarianism were heard again some years later, in attempts by the leadership to promote an especially Chinese "spiritual civilization." Under this rubric, supposedly informed by the spirit of Confucius, the leadership has focused on restraining economic inequality, strengthening central political control (particularly over the Chinese media), and resisting decadent Western moral values.[125]

But while Deng and other leaders looked to Confucian authoritarianism and cast their references to law in Marxist-Leninist jargon, other Chinese are formulating more sophisticated and nuanced conceptions of the possible role of law in China. Despite the boundaries set by the Four Cardinal Principles, legal scholars have debated issues that might seem to be foreclosed by the principles themselves.

Both the range of possibilities that has been envisioned for giving the rule of law new meaningfulness in China and the straitjacket that confines contemporary Chinese thinking about law are illustrated by a recent Chinese law journal. In February 1996, Jiang Zemin spoke at a Party conference at which the theme was "issues of theory and practice with regard to administering the country according to law, and establishing a socialist legal system in China."[126] In his talk, Jiang used a four-character slogan, "govern the country according to law." The journal of the Legal Research Institute of the Chinese Academy of Social Sciences contained two lengthy articles discussing the implications of Jiang's words. However, Jiang's slogan was actually uttered as part of a sentence, in which his invocation of law was offset by a longer phrase that urged "protect the nation's long-term peace and stability." Jiang also said that the idea of "strengthening the legal system, governing the country according to law" is part of Deng Xiaoping's theory of building socialism with Chinese characteristics. Under this policy, all aspects of work would become "legal-systematized" (*fazhihua*) and "standardized" (*guifanhua*) in order to "legal-systematize" (*fazhihua*) and "legalize" (*falühua*) socialist democracy.

One of the articles published after Jiang's talk summarizes a meeting at which legal scholars discussed the implications of Jiang's slogan. They could only offer interpretations, because apparently Jiang had said nothing else in that speech or in any other that added any detail to his slogan. Several did remark on the difference between creating a "*legal system*" and creating "legality," and Jiang's statement did seem to emphasize systematization and regularization as much as legality. Of more interest are the scholars' views on implementing the rule of law in China. In a separate article in 1996, Liu Hainian, deputy director of the institute, expressed his personal vision of the steps that had to be taken and the attitudes that had to change in order to make meaningful progress toward attaining the rule of law for China.[127]

Liu's article reviewed Deng's call for laws and the steps taken to establish a legal system during the 1980s. He noted, though, that some "high cadres" had interfered with justice, that the old habits of "substituting instructions for law" had reappeared, and that there was considerable official disregard of the law. He called for establishing the legal system that is required by the "socialist market economy," one that would guarantee the equality of all participants in the economy, protect property rights, and differentiate between the rights of the state as a legal entity and those of property owners. He urged that in perfecting the legal system China should look to the experience of Hong Kong and Taiwan as well as to other countries. He called for further exercise of supervisory power by the NPC and local national people's congresses; adherence to procedure; independence of the judiciary; a better-trained and professional judiciary; the absolute superiority of the law over all political parties, organizations, and individuals; and, finally, a transition from rule by administration (i.e., bureaucracy) to rule by law. Although Liu called for a moral society, "spiritual civilization" was conspicuously absent.

Liu's themes, and those in the conference summary, closely resemble views expressed at a similar conference in 1989 discussed above. In 1996, much as in 1989, scholars urged controlling administrative discretion and maximizing individual rights, emphasized procedural justice and an independent judiciary, and affirmed the superiority of law over both state and Party. These two sets of views also differ: In 1989 more specific proposals for legal reform were advanced, including some calling for more transparent legislative and judicial processes and for an abundance of public information on the activities of leaders so that citizens could form better ideas about the latter's fidelity to law (and about their finances!); Marxism was assailed much more directly. The proposals advanced in 1996 were more restrained, with less emphasis on the need to clarify the relationship between the Party and law, and more focus on the need to create a legal framework for the developing socialist market economy. Since 1996, debate among Chinese legal scholars has intensified, with some showing interest in pluralism as a basis of law to succeed the narrow emphasis on class dictated by slavish following of Marxist theory.[128]

Conspicuously absent from the speculations of the scholars in 1996 was any attempt to counterbalance Jiang Zemin's call for the rule of law with the exhortation "protect long-term peace and stability," as Jiang himself had done.[129] "Stability" is shorthand for continued Party control, and despite the Party's continued endorsement of government by law it has continued to use law as an instrument to maintain and carry out Party policies, as shown in the examples below.

The Primacy of Policy and the Instrumental Use of Law

A genuine CCP commitment to establish the rule of law would require the Party to depart from a principle it has followed since the PRC was established; policy, as defined and implemented by the CCP, must be supreme over law. Flexible policies were more appropriate to China's revolutionary needs than laws, which were criticized under Mao as so rigid that they could "bind the hands and feet of the revolution." With the rule of law a newly avowed goal of post-Maoist policy, Chinese officials and intellectuals must try to define the relative roles of policy and law and, if possible, to reconcile them.

The idea that all officials, organizations, and individuals must obey the law has been expressed often in recent years, supported not only by legal scholars but by certain leaders, notably Peng Zhen, who emphasized the need to "systematize" (*zhiduhua*) and "legalize" (*falühua*) democracy.[130] Peng also, however, noted the boundaries and limits of legalization. In a speech in May 1987,[131] he noted that although the greater use of law is necessary, new guidelines for the correct relationship between law and policy were needed; this relationship he located in the four principles enunciated by Deng Xiaoping in 1979, which would help prevent an unhealthy drift toward "total westernization," that is, bourgeois liberalization.

Although throughout the 1980s Chinese doctrine asserted that law must still be subservient to policy,[132] reform has softened the terminology that is used to express their relationship. Shen Zongling, a prominent legal scholar, stresses their complementarity and mutual support. He notes that the former practice of substituting policy for law has been condemned and argues that neither can substitute for the other, although he is obviously reluctant to articulate the concept of law's supremacy.[133] Old habits die hard, he adds. The limits set by policy on law are further suggested by the equivocating response of one judge to the question of what to do when new policies contradict current laws:

In [my] opinion, the principle for handling such instances is to start from actual realities and seek truth through facts. That is to say, on the one hand, that one must observe the principle of handling matters in accordance with law, and on the other, one must correctly apply the laws on the basis of the policies, the two must be combined organically.[134]

Still, there is no doubt that law must be subservient to policy. The judge continues:

For those laws and regulations which are not suited to reform and economic construction, one must promptly advise the national legislative organs to revise or discard them through legal procedures and methods, [and] to establish new laws that are suited to the new policies, so that the country's laws and policies can develop in harmony.

The subservience of law to policy further aggravates the tentativeness with which Chinese policies are usually formulated and implemented. Continuing a pre-reform style of administration, policies are often both generally expressed and experimentally applied. We shall see below that one Chinese writer has criticized the uncertainties created by the continued use of what he calls "policy law," which contributes to an uncertainty that law is not yet capable of dispelling. The assumption still seems to prevail that the Party alone should decide how to apply general policies and local experiments on a national scale. Reliance on Party authority to preempt legislation by dictating variations in its application suggests, as one Western scholar has observed, that many officials prefer that the legal system derive its consistency and coherence from the dictates of policy made by a supreme CCP.[135] As a result, the boundaries of positive law become blurred:

Chinese legislation is perpetually in half focus as it fades into its background context of Party decisions and policy documents. It consequently fails to achieve a separate identity as the formal source of Chinese law. The continued reliance of Chinese decision makers on policy directives and makeshift regulations to introduce reforms clearly compromises any movement towards a legislative model in which the formal sources of law provide a coherent foundation for interpretation and doctrinal elaboration. It also underscores the ambivalence of many Chinese legislative officials towards such a model.[136]

When policy is primary, law becomes only its instrument. The *instrumental* conception of law in current Chinese thought and practice has been remarked on by a number of scholars, Western and Chinese. Of course law is used to promote policies in every society and to some extent is therefore a tool everywhere, but the manner in which it is used in China, as William Alford has noted, reflects "the willingness of states or individuals to use legality as an instrument to achieve their policy objectives but to depart from it when compliance with the law no longer serves the attainment of such ends."[137] Use of law in this manner marked Maoist administration, which enlisted the courts in efforts to support a succession of mass campaigns used to promote particular policies. Since Mao's death, the overt use of campaigns has certainly declined and public administration has become more regular and rational, but the echo of revolutionary style is far from stilled.

THE INSTRUMENTAL USE OF LAW IN PRACTICE

The Lingering Mobilizational Style

The Chinese populace has long been accustomed to hearing CCP calls for urgent efforts to attain specific policy goals, and the CCP continues to use propaganda and exhortation to promote support for legal institutions and procedures and new policies toward laws. In the post-Mao era much propaganda on legal matters has been restrained in tone, as in articles or broadcasts seeking to inform citizens of their rights under the law. The use of mobilizational campaigns was expressly eschewed at the beginning of the reform period, but reliance on them has not been easy to abandon.

Popularization of the new legal institutions through the Party-led propaganda apparatus—a standard administrative device since 1949—was widespread during the early years of legal reform. Typically, after the National People's Congress adopted a cluster of new laws in 1979, the Anhui Provincial Party Committee called for a campaign to observe "publicizing the seven laws month" throughout the province for the thirty-day period beginning the twentieth of August, and then held a telephone conference "calling on all places to further whip up an upsurge of studying and publicizing the seven laws to make them known to every household and person."[138] Similarly, Shandong province launched a campaign featuring special classes for members of the three agencies administering the criminal process to study the new laws, as well as propaganda materials prepared specially for the campaign (e.g., an article entitled "Communist Party Members Should Play an Exemplary Role in Enforcing and Upholding the Law"), radio broadcasts, theatrical performances, and lectures. In this case, as elsewhere, a goal for the campaign was announced that assumed that rapid transformations were possible in the area of concern: "all cadres in political and legal departments and all policemen must be trained by the end of September."[139]

Since the earliest days of reform, campaigns to educate the populace about law have been mounted, especially under the rubrics of two five-year plans adopted in 1986 and 1991, respectively.[140] Aimed at the entire population, the campaigns have also particularly targeted Party and cadre schools, youth, and the military. For example, all schools at all levels were instructed to formulate legal curricula, mass organizations and enterprises were instructed to impart legal knowledge to their members, and the media and cultural activities were used to disseminate legal knowledge. Although the term "campaign" has not been used to describe these and other activities organized to carry out the two five-year plans and no rallies have been held to inspire public enthusiasm, these efforts constitute a considerable campaign-like attempt by the Party to disseminate legal knowledge and to promote "correct" thought about law. Moreover, while pressing for greater regularity in administration and reducing cadre arbitrariness, these campaigns like their pre-reform predecessors have had a political goal. Rather than aiming to promote development of an autonomous legal order, the campaigns have instead emphasized the function of law in perfecting Party policy and supporting Party leadership in promoting China's development.

In the exhortatory style of the Party-controlled media, propaganda has long been used to emphasize the urgency of fulfilling a particular key task. We may question, however, how appropriate it is to quantify targets in the legal realm, such as in reporting the number of officials at certain levels who completed their legal studies. Such mechanical efforts were not necessarily successful in the past, when the objective was to raise more pigs or manufacture more steel, and to Western eyes do not seem well suited to raising popular awareness of the existence and significance of legal institutions.

It might be hasty, however, to dismiss such attempts to support law reform. Is it possible to use propaganda to change the legal culture of the populace? Some Chinese and Western scholars would argue that legal education campaigns are both necessary and consistent with Chinese political culture. In conversation, the late Tong Rou, the Chinese law professor in charge of the drafting of the General Principles of Civil Law that were promulgated in 1986, asserted that popular behavior could be changed faster in China than in other countries because the Chinese government possessed the ability to persuade the populace. He expected, therefore, that once the new civil law rules were disseminated, they would rapidly become effective. One Western scholar of Chinese law has suggested that China's cultural tradition facilitates the acceptance of ideas "sown by an authoritarian system of education."[141] The reports mentioned earlier of peasants relying on their knowledge of laws and policies to protest cadre arbitrariness, and the popular sentiments about law and justice noted above, suggest that campaigns to popularize not only new laws but the idea of legality itself may help to raise the rights-consciousness of many ordinary Chinese—though not necessarily in the manner intended by Party propagandists.

Campaigns

The courts continue to be the focus of concerted efforts to mobilize resources to maintain and improve public order and to advance other policy goals. Campaigns against crime in particular have at times recalled similar Maoist drives. The persistence of the leadership's willingness to use mobilizational efforts to support law becomes clearest when the population is exhorted to join in a war on crime. At such times, the tone of propaganda greatly resembles the heavy-handed and didactic tone that has marked Chinese propaganda since 1949. From the beginning of legal reform to the present day, explicit judicial priorities have been announced for the criminal law. For example, the president of the Supreme People's Court in 1980 called on the courts to "severely punish active criminals" by taking "sterner measures against such serious criminals who commit murder, arson, robbery and rape."[142] In the early 1980s, as the reforms helped generate new types of criminal behavior, drives against economic crimes were launched. Directives treated as having the force of law and explanatory policy statements explicitly called for the courts to focus upon economic crimes. In January 1981, for instance, the State Council issued a circular attempting to define illegal speculation, "profiteering" and trade in prohibited goods such as precious metals and foreign currencies and called for a crackdown on smuggling.[143] Amidst ongoing propaganda, provincial and local instructions followed.[144] The leadership's concern was further signaled when the NPC Standing Committee amended the criminal code by increasing penalties for certain crimes,[145] and the Central Committee of the CCP and the State Council issued a decision on "dealing blows at serious criminal activities in the economic sphere."[146] Reports of judicial decisions punishing conduct of the type discussed in the circular, not surprisingly, proliferated soon after it was promulgated.[147]

These special mobilizational efforts to deal with crime have continued down to the present day. In 1992 a Central Committee for the Comprehensive Management of Public Security was formed, with Ren Jianxin, president of China's Supreme People's Court, as director. The committee was described as "the leading organ of the movement" and included representatives of the judiciary, police, and other departments. Ren called for focusing its activities on areas in which public security had been poor for a long time.[148] Ren referred in his annual report on the work of the Supreme People's Court in 1993 to a three-year "anti-theft campaign" that had been decided by that committee.[149] Later that year he urged courts to launch special anti-crime campaigns and to hand down severe sentences.[150] His annual report to the NPC on the work of the Supreme People's Court in March 1995 heavily emphasized "intensify[ing] the struggle against serious criminal offenses to maintain social stability."[151] Later in 1995, in an interview he emphasized that "courts at all levels should cooperate closely with public security and procuratorial organs"[152] to fight crime. More recently, another nationwide campaign to "Strike Hard" at criminals was begun in 1995 and carried out well into 1996,[153] and by October 1996 a successor campaign was announced by the Ministry of Public Security.[154]

The use of campaigns imparts an especially irregular quality to the work of all agencies of the central and local governments, including the courts and police,[155] and seems to force agencies to oscillate between campaigns and inaction. As a result, "what is tolerated or even positively approved by officials today may be subject to harsh penalties tomorrow."[156] Enforcement is made sporadic by the use of "policy laws," noted above, which announce general goals without specifying stable procedural arrangements that should serve as the basis for official acts. Only when cases multiply is action taken, and then by "putting together a group of people to mount an intensive investigation," which is usually followed by punishment of offenders during a short period of time. This usually means punishing a small number of major offenders while neglecting minor ones, and then ending the crackdown.[157] The unevenness in administering the criminal law that results from the frequent use of campaigns is clear to many ordinary Chinese citizens, and part of a long pattern of swings in policy since 1949. Moreover, the campaigns that have been conducted as part of a "war on crime" have adversely affected the morale of the police, who are discouraged by the ineffectiveness of the technique.[158]

When the legal reforms were just being initiated, the leadership was sensitive to questions about the significance of using campaigns to promote law-related goals. For example, in the midst of the crackdown on economic crimes in early 1982 the *Beijing Review* stated that "no purge will ever happen,"[159] and a *Xinhua* article distinguished the drive against economic criminals from the leftist "expansion of class struggle."[160] The boundary, however, between desirable mass action and inappropriate mass violence is difficult to locate as long as the CCP looks back to its revolutionary past. The April 1982 decision of the Central Committee of the Chinese Communist Party and the State Council mentioned above said in part:

In dealing blows at serious criminal activities in the economic sphere, we are resolutely against making the work a mass movement. . . . However, in dealing with major and key cases which are relatively complicated and which involve more people, we must completely follow the mass line; that is, we must, within a definite scope, mobilize the masses knowing about the cases to factually expose and inform against those who have committed serious crimes.[161]

By the 1990s, the leadership no longer felt it necessary to justify its use of campaigns to give the criminal law special force. Nevertheless, their use demonstrates that the leadership remains committed to the instrumental use of law and to techniques of mobilization associated with the mass line.[162] Although these Maoist techniques are much more muted now than before reform, they continue to express adherence to an instrumental notion of law that is subject to Party policy.

Suppressing Dissidence

The Maoist legacy that burdens Chinese law most heavily is the treatment of dissent. It has been noted in chapter 3 that Mao distinguished between "antagonistic" and "nonantagonistic" contradictions within Chinese society, the former between the "people" and the "enemy," the latter within the "people." Methods of "dictatorship" were appropriate for the former, methods of "democracy" were to be used to solve the latter. Political dissent was, of course, consistently treated as an antagonistic contradiction for which exercise of the heaviest measures of dictatorship was appropriate.

The Maoist Party-state waged a relentless war against "counter-revolutionaries," "bad elements," and "rightists," using a politicized, Party-dominated criminal process to punish persons suspected of disloyalty or of vaguely denominated "counter-revolutionary" crimes.[163] Under Deng, although the Codes of Criminal Law and Criminal Procedure that were adopted in 1979 contained provisions protecting rights of persons accused of crime and created safeguards against arbitrary detention, expressions of dissent were severely punished. After workers began posting wall posters on the "Democracy Wall" in Beijing in the fall of 1978 a crackdown followed and the courageous Wei Jingsheng, who had written a wall poster calling for democracy as the "fifth modernization," was tried and sentenced to fifteen years in prison for "counter-revolutionary propaganda" and revealing military secrets. The determination of the leadership not to tolerate expression of dissent was manifested in the severe punishment of dissidents throughout the 1980s,[164] and exhibited in all its repressive cruelty in the crushing of the "democracy movement" in June 1989 and the trials and convictions of demonstrators thereafter,[165] and has continued in the 1990s as well. The second conviction of Wei Jingsheng in 1996 further expressed the leadership's fear of dissent and its determination to crush it with no concern for legality.[166]

Dissent, inconceivable under Mao, became an issue in China only once economic reforms began and political control over Chinese society started to relax. The leadership's view has been that for the sake of maintaining social order, Chinese democracy must be a disciplined democracy in which the centralized leadership of Party and State are upheld.[167] "Democracy" could be used as a pretext by individuals to violate the basic principles of organization and discipline in China. Thus, those who "understand freedom of speech as the freedom to say whatever they want to say and to do whatever they care to do in disregard of the state and the people's interests exceed the limit of the law."[168] Such persons were warned in the early days of reform: "We will not adopt a *laissez-faire* attitude."[169] Another newspaper article was more direct: "Opinions which are anti-party and anti-socialist and which sabotage the unity of the mother-land and the Nationalities must be prohibited."[170] Typically, in a lengthy discussion, *Red Flag*, the theoretical journal of the Chinese Communist Party, went to great lengths to criticize and reject the concept of "absolute freedom of speech," which it found to be a tool of enemies of socialism.[171] More than a decade later, a British delegation visiting China in 1992 con-cluded that "the expression of political dissent [is] not permitted."[172] Some debate has occurred on the issues of the criminalization of free speech and related freedoms, both before and since June 1989,[173] but there seemed no prospect of any change in the Party-state's willingness to use its power to crush speech and conduct that are deemed threatening to Party rule.[174] This determination was underscored at the end of 1998 by the conviction, in three separate trials, of four dissidents and the conviction in another trial of an entrepreneur who had given the addresses of Chinese com-puter users to a journal published in the United States by dissidents.[175]

From the inception of legal reform, its permitted scope has been limited, as this review of Party policy shows. These limits, combined with forces generated by economic reform and the burden of both distant and recent history, seriously obstruct future legal development. Despite these hin-drances, however, two decades of institution building have made a definite beginning in the effort to bring legality to China. In the chapters that follow, it will be seen that the initial efforts have initiated processes and set institutions in place that could grow in vigor. Their promise merits an effort to understand the aims and accomplishments of legal reform.

First Steps: Legalizing the State, Reinventing Lawyers, Regularizing the Criminal Process

Introduction

THIS CHAPTER ANALYZES three institution-building efforts. Each in some important way bears on the law reforms that will be discussed later in the book.

The first is the attempt to employ legislation and administrative rules as essential tools in governing China. The Chinese leadership, departing from their previous reliance on policy declarations and their disregard of formal legal rules, have moved to elevate such rules into primary sources of authority. We will discuss their allocation of power to legislate and to interpret laws, which laid a foundation for the extensive legislation that has been needed to implement economic reforms as well as the institutional framework within which the courts operate. The arrangements produced by these efforts are currently disorderly, often to the point of incoherence, and further reforms will be required.

The second area of institution-building includes efforts to revive legal education and to recreate the Chinese bar. Legal education faces the difficult task of designing instruction on areas of law that are both novel to China and changing, even while the overall mission of law itself remains unclear. Creating a bar requires that lawyers and the Party-state define the legal profession, and in so doing negotiate the role of lawyers in Chinese society and their autonomy. Reforms of a basic nature are involved, because the energy and imagination of lawyers will be essential to vindicating and making meaningful the rights created by the flood of reform-generated legislation.

The third effort is to construct a substantive criminal law and criminal procedure. These are freighted with multiple and inconsistent purposes, because they seek both to preserve social order and stability and to regularize the administration of sanctions that have long been and fundamentally remain dominated by the police and the CCP. This book is concerned with the courts' handling of civil and economic disputes; consequently, the criminal process is not closely addressed. The criminal law and criminal process are considered here as basic institutions that define the parameters within which, bounded by the organizational power of the state, other legal processes take place. They therefore form part of the background necessary to understanding the courts. The criminal process and the organization of the courts still bear the strong stamp of pre-reform sanctioning practices, and the courts' current participation in the Party-state's efforts to maintain social order and punish deviance colors the courts' activities in resolving civil and economic disputes.

LEGALIZING THE CHINESE STATE

Legal reform has enlarged the importance of legislation far beyond the minor role it played when the entire Party-state was directed and guided by policies articulated and applied by the CCP. Formal legislation has emerged as a significant, if still frequently secondary, framework for the organization and operation of the Chinese government and for the implementation of new policies.

Legalization has also brought new problems. The manner in which authority to make rules has been allocated has led to an extensive diffusion and overlapping of powers among central and local legislative organs and the bureaucratic agencies that generate administrative rules. The need to interpret and apply the growing volume of these norms has also raised questions about the distribution of power in the Chinese state and about law itself, which echo issues that have long troubled both Anglo-American and Continental legal systems.

The CCP wields supreme authority in China, and although legislation has grown more important, defining the relationship of legislation to policy continues to trouble Chinese legal reformers. The 1982 Constitution requires all organizations to obey the law, but it also expresses the supremacy of CCP authority. The conventional approach in Chinese doctrine today acknowledges CCP supremacy and treats legislation as an expression of CCP policies and as an instrument to implement those policies. Even after policies have been given legislative expression, they are frequently modified in practice by CCP directives, speeches by leaders, and newspaper editorials. Legislation, then, is at all times dependent on and potentially secondary to CCP formulation of specific policies. More-over, the Chinese approach to legislative drafting often fails to distinguish laws and regulations clearly from general statements of policy.

Both law-making and interpreting law have become extremely disor-derly. The task of maintaining coherence and consistency between law and policy, which would be challenging enough in a country the size of China, is made more difficult by the growing complexity of Chinese soci-ety resulting from the reforms. Even before reform, the fragmentation of Chinese authoritarianism, which has already been described, required ex-tensive inter-unit negotiation and consensus-building. Under reform the problem has been made more acute. The devolution of power from the center to provincial and local governments has fostered local experimen-tation that gives rise to inconsistencies between central and local policies and interregional variation. Some Chinese legal scholars would like to en-hance the role of the legislature and limit that of the Party, moving legis-lation closer to the primary position that the Constitution formally as-signed to it. The discussion that follows identifies the principal sources of laws and indicates some of the major problems.[1]

ALLOCATION OF POWER TO ISSUE CENTRAL GOVERNMENT LEGISLATION AND RULES

Three principal law-making agencies share the central government's legislative power in Beijing. Under the Constitution adopted in 1982, the National People's Congress has the power to promulgate "basic laws," its Standing Committee has authority to promulgate and amend "laws" with the exception of those enacted by the NPC, and the State Council may enact "administrative measures . . . administrative laws and regulations . . . and orders" as well as "temporary legislation." This scheme is only general, and key terms (such as "basic laws" and "temporary legislation") are nowhere defined.[2] Questions of jurisdiction among these three are likely to increase because the range of problems that laws must address will grow more complex. In practice, the respective jurisdictions and relation-ships of the three bodies are worked out through informal negotiations. As a result, these bodies must negotiate among themselves on each law that is adopted, resulting in a system that has been aptly described as "chaotic."[3]

The National People's Congress

Although the CCP remains supreme in the Party-state, the growing number and complexity of problems that are constantly appearing de-mand specific legislative solutions rather than general policy pronounce-ments. Consequently, Party-state interactions on legislative matters are changing. CCP approval must precede enactment of major legislation, but that approval is often only very general or incomplete. The NPC has had a strong leadership in the recent past when Politburo member Qiao Shi was chairman of its Standing Committee;[4] however, CCP leadership over the NPC seems to be growing more generally supervisory and increasingly less focused on the details of specific pieces of legislation. The staffs of the NPC and the State Council, who are engaged in drafting legislation, have developed into sizable bodies of specialists. Debate on proposed legislation in the NPC is also becoming more active and outspoken and now sometimes influences the legislation under discussion. Although the NPC is a weak legislature, one Chinese scholar notes that "it has changed from a low quality rubber stamp to a good quality rubber stamp,"[5] while an American observer sees it as becoming an "extremely significant political arena."[6] Its rising political significance stems in part from the elderly leaders who are shifted to it in their old age.[7]

Still, as I noted above, major pieces of legislation must receive prior Party approval, and much of their content is decided before the NPC becomes involved. Moreover, after legislation is enacted by the NPC, the State Council exercises its power to draft implementing legislation, which may distort or pervert the law on which it is purportedly based. Basically, both policy and laws are determined by consensus among senior leaders, and consensus is often difficult to reach and maintain.

China's legislative institutions are in the midst of an evolutionary process, and they may be able to overcome the narrow limits that ideology has imposed on their scope of action.[8] Legislation has become a major avenue for expressing policies, and the very disorderliness of the jurisdictional arrangements among the major law-making bodies has created opportunities for innovation.[9] At the same time, the NPC has also become a forum for senior and conservative leaders who can slow or deflect reform through legislation. Although it is basically unrepresentative, activities by deputies on behalf of a variety of local and national interests have become more common.[10]

The State Council

Most legislation originates in the State Council, which stands at the head of the executive branch of the central government, and the ministries, commissions, and bureaus that are subordinate to it. As we have seen, the State Council has the power to issue laws, regulations, and orders that are characterized as "administrative." In addition, the NPC has also granted it authority to promulgate "empowered legislation," referred to as "quasi-law" (*zhun falü*).[11] In practice, the boundary between the "administrative" legislation that is the responsibility of the State Council and the "legislative" activity that is reserved to the NPC is obscure, in part because "the State Council enjoys too much power in relation to its legally mandated role."[12]

Legislative drafting work is led by the State Council's Office of Legislative Affairs (OLA). A predecessor had been abolished at the end of the 1950s and was revived in 1982 as the Bureau of Legislative Affairs. It was upgraded to an office in 1998. The Office faces the demanding task of determining long- and short-term priorities and then coordinating the drafting of specific pieces of legislation, usually with the ministry that will be responsible for implementation. The OLA has worked hard at becoming a professionalized legal drafting agency; however, the handicaps it must overcome are enormous.[13] The drafting process inevitably involves extensive negotiation and consultation among the OLA and the various ministries that may be concerned with the proposed legislation. Precise legislative drafting is impaired by the generality, imprecision, and hortatory tone of much Chinese legislation, by the fragmentation of authority, and by the long-standing practice of flexible administrative interpretation unconstrained by judicial review. Regardless of the final text of a law or regulation, the organizations that implement them can, by issuing regulations, depart from or ignore the intent of the drafters. This breadth of administrative discretion at all levels, which will be discussed below, is a basic structural flaw that runs through the Chinese Party-state.

Sometimes OLA drafters have been tempted to focus excessively on copying foreign laws and declaring abstract rights and duties divorced from the social realities involved in implementing legislation. One explanation lies in the quality of Chinese legal education, which is formalistic and fails to teach law graduates the skills necessary to investigate the "social facts" that shape the behavior toward which their legislation will be directed.

Law-Making by the Chinese Bureaucracy and by Provincial and Local Governments

In addition to law-makers at the national level, provincial and local governments and more than twenty functional bureaucracies of the central government are empowered to exercise law-making powers that they lacked before reform. The formal hierarchy of legislation includes "primary" laws, consisting of "basic laws" (*jiben falü*) enacted by the NPC and "laws" (*falü*) promulgated by its Standing Committee. "Secondary" legislation includes regulations by the State Council (*xingzheng fagui*, "administrative regulations") and local People's Congresses (*difangxing fagui*, "local regulations"), while "tertiary" rules are the rules (*guizhang*) of central ministries and regional and local governments (*difang zhengfu guizhang*, "local government rules").[14]

Beneath this apparently simple general classification lies a large and confusing range of documents, which in practice blur the distinctions among some of the types of laws mentioned above and between rule-making and implementation. For example, central-local demarcations of legislative jurisdiction are absent, and scholars are apparently divided on whether "regulations" (*fagui*) issued by State Council departments or "rules" (*guizhang*) issued by sub-provincial localities are "laws" (*fa*). Some attention has been given to drafting legislation that would better define the jurisdiction of State Council and provincial-level organs over "rules" issued by departments under their jurisdiction.[15] In the meantime, the respective jurisdictions of legislative and administrative organs remain badly defined.

This general introduction of a fundamental problem with deep structural and cultural roots fails to do justice to its dismaying complexity. However, it will suffice to focus attention on the rule-making power of the Chinese bureaucracy and the major structural difficulties it presents for the organization of the Chinese state and the future of the rule of law in China.

Administrative Rule-Making

The State Council supervises more than sixty departments, including ministries and commissions referred to here as "central administrative agencies." These have emerged as immensely powerful sources of rules. Central administrative agencies possess authority to issue regulations to implement specific legislation under grants of power by a legislative body, such as the NPC Standing Committee. They also exercise a technically distinct type of authority to execute their general administrative responsibilities. This second broad category of general rule-making power is deemed to be *inherent* in the agencies, and it enables them to issue any rule that is necessary to carry out their functions.[16] No procedures govern the issue of these important rules, which may be issued or modified by any agency with exclusive jurisdiction over the subject matter. When agencies share jurisdiction, rules must be either issued jointly or, with the permission of the State Council, by one of them. Some academics question their power to issue regulations based solely on the grounds that they are within their administrative competence, but, in practice, agencies exercise it because there is no central authority to delimit their power.[17] A foreign observer has written that the wide array of "departmental rules," all of which have general binding authority, is superior to all local enactments and is also the most numerous.[18] A Chinese specialist on administrative law with whom this was discussed in November 1998 disagrees, noting that the Constitution says nothing clearly about the relative effects of "departmental rules" and "local governmental rules," and adds that in practice, local governments usually employ "local rules" as a weapon to resist the central control that is asserted through "departmental rules"; he adds that local rules become tools of "local protectionism." Further confusion arises because local governments and central bureaucracies that issue rules of various types possess the exclusive power to interpret these rules.

An additional problem exists at the local level. Local governments are also authorized to add specificity and detail to the rules and regulations issued by higher-level people's governments; these are called local regulations (*difang xingzheng fagui*), local rules (*difang guizhang*), or local measures (*difang cuoshi*). There are no uniform rules for enactment of the documents used for this purpose, which are called "administrative documents" (*guifanxing wenjian*), and oversight for legality and consistency is exercised only "nominally" if at all by the next highest administrative authority.[19]

The import of the situation described here should not be overlooked. Chinese administrative agencies have the power to issue and interpret their own rules and *to require the courts to enforce them.*[20] This power is deep-seated, drawn from the power of administrative bureaucracies within the CCP, and extensive because most laws originate in the state bureaucracy rather than in the legislatures. Administrative agencies wield their law-making powers to protect or increase their jurisdictions and to advance their policies. A Chinese specialist has written that

the tendency to legislate in a manner that promotes departmental interests is severe. It is relatively common [for departments] to ignore the reasonable distribution of benefits and the reasonable allocation of authority, and to consider only the expansion of the authority of one's own department or the protection of the interests of one's own department.[21]

As localities increase their control over their own economic resources, their power to broaden their own jurisdiction becomes increasingly problematic for the central government.

The extent of the power of Chinese administrative agencies to make and to interpret laws presents an astonishing picture to the Western lawyer. The allocation of authority to interpret promulgated laws is a basic issue that any legal system must resolve to develop and maintain coherence, but China's policy and law-makers have yet to address it closely. These difficulties reflect the even more basic problem of "excessive fragmentation" of jurisdiction and of the law itself,[22] and that no legal institution has "either the authority or the desire to impose order on the legal system."[23]

Legal Interpretation and Legislative Supremacy

Every legal and political system has had to formulate doctrine and concepts that define and rank various sources of law. All Western legal systems assign the basic task of law-making to legislatures, and, in all of them, administrative agencies make rules within boundaries set by legislation, and courts apply both legislation and rules issued by administrative agencies. All Western systems have had to grapple with the problem that "legal norms . . . do not provide single determinate answers to the questions that judges must answer,"[24] and have struggled to distinguish acceptable techniques of interpretation from judicial legislation that violates the divisions of powers that are typically defined in a basic constitutional document.

THE DISORDERLY STATE OF LEGAL
INTERPRETATION IN CHINA TODAY

According to Chinese law and doctrine, the sole source of legal rules is legislation, which includes statutes enacted by the NPC, local People's Congresses, administrative regulations lawfully adopted by the State Council and the ministries and commissions subordinate to it, and similar administrative rules adopted at the local level. The Chinese Constitution gives the Standing Committee of the NPC the power to interpret the Constitution and its statutes (Art. 67 (1), (4)), but although the NPC Standing Committee is empowered to annul acts of the State Council and local regulations or decisions of the central bureaucracy that violate the Constitution, it has never formally exercised its powers of constitutional interpretation. The strengthening of constitutional supervision has been much debated, but its future will turn on more basic political reforms.[25] The Organic Law of the People's Courts states that the Supreme People's Court has the power to "carry out interpretation of any problems of the concrete application of laws or regulations in the course of litigation" (Art. 83). A 1981 resolution of the Standing Committee of the NPC[26] restricts the authority of the Supreme People's Court to interpret the law only in "questions involving the specific application of laws and decrees in adjudication work [i.e., trials]." The Procuratorate may exercise the power in "questions involving the specific application of laws and decrees in the procuratorial work of the procuratorates." In addition to dividing interpretative power between the Supreme People's Court and the Supreme People's Procuratorate, the same 1981 resolution granted to the State Council a residual power, that is, to interpret laws and decrees "in areas unrelated to judicial and procuratorial work." It retained for the Standing Committee the power to interpret laws when "the limits of laws and decrees need to be defined or additional stipulations need to be made."

These formal legal provisions, and theory elaborated on the basis of them, give legislative organs a near-monopoly over the interpretation of legislation. So strong is the opposition to interpretation that a recent Chinese study concludes that the "function and effects of legislative interpretation" by the Standing Committee "still have not been fully realized," apparently because its constructions are treated as materials "for consideration" without direct legal effect.[27] Although the study recognizes that interpretation is carried out by courts as well as by administrative agencies,[28] it proposes to strengthen the legislative function by formalizing the power of the Legislative Supervision Commission of the NPC, organs under the State Council and Provincial People's Congresses to interpret, respectively, laws, "administrative regulations" (*xingzheng fagui*), and "local regulations" (*difang xing fagui*). Pressing needs created by the economic reforms have placed great pressure on the Supreme People's Court to take on a strong role in interpreting laws and administrative rules (to be explored in chapter 9). As legislation continues to pour forth to manage an increasingly complex Chinese economy, the institutional disarray described here will continue to generate disorder that could be a serious impediment to continuing economic reform.

Bureaucratic Discretion in Implementing Laws

Bureaucrats enjoy enormous discretion in applying laws and administrative rules within their fragmented spheres of authority to make and interpret rules. Although the Standing Committee of the NPC has the power to rescind local regulations, it has not done so. It furthermore lacks the resources to oversee the consistency of regulations.[29] In practice, only the legislative or administrative body that promulgated a rule interprets it. Apart from the looseness and generality of the formal legal arrangements that make this possible, other factors combine to aggravate the legal uncertainties that mark the formulation and application of formal rules in China today.

The Continued Frequent Use of Internal Legislation

In pre-reform China, administrative discretion was close to unassailable because the rules that were being applied were usually secret. Increased reliance on promulgated laws has caused some revision of long-standing and characteristic Chinese notions about publicizing laws. Before 1979, many if not most laws and administrative regulations were not promulgated at all; they were for internal (*neibu*) circulation only. To Westerners the idea of secret laws is self-contradictory. Past Communist practice, however, echoes traditional Chinese ideas about law. As noted in chapter

2, law was formerly undifferentiated from other forms of administration, and rules that in the West would be regarded as "legal," such as the penal code, were intended to guide bureaucrats in their administrative activities rather than to give notice to the populace of crimes and punishments. For the first thirty years of the PRC's existence, the CCP ruled without any legal codes at all and promulgated only scattered formal legislation of limited scope; bureaucrats relied on Party policies and internal rules to guide them in their daily work.

Considerable progress has been made in the direction of greater transparency, although the bureaucratic attitudes that produced and relied on secret rules are changing very slowly. Some Chinese officials have been sensitive to foreign complaints. In October 1988, it was announced that "all administrative laws and regulations issued by the State Council" would be signed by the premier and published in the Bulletin of the State Council and the People's Daily and distributed by the Chinese news agency Xinhua. A Chinese official said, "The publication of regulations signed by China's Premier will help people learn exactly what they are being asked to adjust to, follow or enforce. Their legal rights and interests will also be made clearer."[30] Considerable progress has been made in promulgating central government legislation including ministerial regulations, especially in major cities such as Shanghai. Many norms, however, of various types issued by ministries, provinces, and local governments remain internal or difficult to obtain even when they are technically public.[31]

THE INFLUENCE OF DRAFTING TECHNIQUES

The role of legislation cannot grow in China unless the CCP changes some fundamental aspects of its administrative style. Party rule is marked by a tentativeness, rooted philosophically in the Maoist emphasis on experimental policy innovations and the need to adapt policy implementation to specific local conditions. Partly for this reason, "flexibility" has long been an essential goal of Chinese legislative drafting. Whatever the reason, the language and phrasing of Chinese legislation and rules create wide scope for administrative discretion in interpreting them. At all levels Chinese legislation is intentionally drafted in "broad, indeterminate language" that allows administrators to vary the specific meaning of legislative language with circumstances.[32] Standard techniques include the use of general principles, vagueness and ambiguity, undefined terms, broadly worded discretion, omissions, and general catch-all phrases.[33] Vague higher-level legislation enables lower-level officials to enlarge their discretion—which is not effectively controlled.

FORMALISM AND POSITIVISM

In the eyes of Western lawyers, Chinese attitudes toward the implementation of law are marked by a pronounced formalism, which is used here in a limited sense to mean an inclination to regard legislative texts as equivalent to practice.[34] Chinese legal formalism is buttressed by a positivism that, as already noted, has established the legislature as the sole source of law and denies the courts any law-making role. As a result of the combination, although progress has been made in publishing collections of laws,[35] it is difficult for Chinese and foreigners alike to determine their application and interpretation in practice. From these attitudes flows inattention to practice and to the *de facto* interpretation of legislation by the courts and by administrative agencies. Theory denies binding and precedental force to judicial interpretations of laws, and published reports of decided cases offer little guidance on their underlying reasoning.[36]

THE USEFULNESS AND DANGERS OF FOREIGN INFLUENCES

Chinese legal scholars and officials and their Western counterparts alike have speculated on the extent to which Chinese legal development benefits from knowledge and use of foreign institutions. While attempts by any society to transplant foreign legal institutions present obvious difficulties, they are especially problematic for China, whose history, culture, traditions, and language differ so markedly from potential foreign sources of legal models. Moreover, borrowing from abroad could have serious ideological implications. Some officials have endorsed accelerating Chinese development by borrowing institutions already deemed to be both ripe and useful, rather than by improvising and experimenting. For example, Qiao Shi, while chairman of the Standing Committee of the NPC, said in December 1996, "in formulating and amending China's economic laws, we have paid full attention to the matter of linking up with international practices."[37] Equally understandable, others have argued that China, with its own traditions and unique problems, should be cautious about borrowing foreign institutions; still others have objected to looking abroad on ideological grounds. During the 1980s, "bourgeois liberalization" was a label that could be pinned to developments or proposals deemed undesirable. The views of the late Deng Xiaoping can also be invoked for different reasons, either to favor borrowing from abroad whatever China can put to its use, or to reject alien transplants infected by ideology inconsistent with Chinese-style socialism.

Whatever the doctrinal argument, China's legal reformers have been extremely attentive to foreign institutions. The most notable example is the General Principles of Civil Law, a partial codification of civil law that came into force in 1986 (discussed in chapter 8), and which is derived from the German Civil Code.[38] The Chinese Company Law, in creating two types of limited liability entities and adopting the institution of a supervisory board in addition to the normal board of directors, also shows the heavy influence of European corporate law.

Advocacy of the use of foreign examples reveals how far Chinese attitudes toward law have come since reform began. Traditional Marxist views have been turned upside down, with law being treated as a factor in bringing about social change rather than as a mere reflection of society. The use of foreign concepts also sometimes reflects a formalistic approach, one in which law is regarded as a body of rules that can be "transplanted" and can exist independent of time and place.[39] But formalism, although it dies hard, can also yield to more sophisticated views of law. My own personal impressions from encounters with Chinese legislative drafters suggest that they and Chinese legal scholars are asking far more sophisticated questions about law than those they posed in 1979.

CONTINUING LEGISLATIVE INCOHERENCE AND ITS UNDERLYING CAUSES

Our discussion has ranged over a variety of characteristics of Chinese law-making and interpreting. However, the striking disorder and potential for arbitrariness that mark the system should be kept constantly in sight. Lawmakers currently exercise the power to interpret their own rules, which are couched in indeterminate language. It is no wonder that one writer has concluded that "the disparate mass of laws and regulations which makes up the formal written sources of Chinese law does not possess sufficient unity to be regarded as a coherent body of law. In their disarray, the sources of Chinese law seem barely capable of providing the basic point of reference which all complex systems of law require."[40]

A draft law on legislation that was intended to address some of the problems that have been mentioned here was circulated in 1997. It would have demarcated the respective jurisdictions of the NPC and its Standing Committee and specifically provided for the authority of provincial People's Congresses and their Standing Committees to legislate in areas that had not been preempted by the NPC and its Standing Committee, although it was unclear about how preemption would work in practice. The draft law also proposed mechanisms for coordinating drafting among agencies with conflicting views about their jurisdiction over matters that were the subject of pending legislation, and classified the different types of interpretations of legislation.[41]

While such a law might succeed in formally clarifying the allocation of power to legislate and to issue rules, it cannot resolve the problems that underlie the confusion. One problem, previously discussed, is insistence on what some Western students have called the instrumental use of law. By contrast, some writers and officials are interested in creating "a rationally ordered and internally consistent legislative order. For some officials and academics, the reorganization of positive law on a more coherent basis is essential if law is to become the pre-eminent framework for public and private life."[42] While some Chinese legal scholars favor a clear distinction between law and politics, declarations by high leaders, as we have already seen, do not meet the issue directly. In practice, their concern to maintain the legitimacy of the CCP impels them to insist on CCP superiority and, consequently, the subservience of law to the Party and its policies.

Close study of Chinese legislatures, central and local, suggests that since 1979, these bodies have been able to expand their jurisdiction and their capacity to influence policy outcomes.[43] The scope of law-making has expanded and the resources available to legislatures have grown. If legislatures become more deeply embedded in the Party-state, they may be able to increase their role as a rationalizing force.

At present, however, much Chinese legislation is still being interpreted and applied in the same manner as before reform. It is likely that bureaucrats may have difficulty in distinguishing laws from policies because they did not have to make such distinctions before; in applying laws, they may be more concerned with complying with their spirit than with crafting precise rules.[44] Reference has been made to the existence of what Meng Qinguo has called "policy laws," which are policy statements, administrative regulations, reports of meetings, notices, instructions, and speeches that are given legal effectiveness because they emanate from authoritative government and Party bodies.[45] Meng Qinguo further argues that reliance on "policy laws" is undemocratic, disorderly, and a source of instability; in addition, policy laws undermine legality because they do not precisely define legal and illegal behavior, they fail to define the legal consequences of failure to comply, and they are procedurally unclear. Meng's remarks parallel the common criticism by Western observers that when Party policy takes precedence over law, law loses its rationality and the need to be internally orderly and consistent.[46] If the norms intended to guide the behavior of the Chinese populace are to function as legal rules, their language must be changed. To provide clear guidance, the rules should no longer be the exhortative generalities that CCP statements of policy generally have been, but precise and specific statements about the conduct to which they are addressed and procedures for their implementation.

REESTABLISHING LEGAL EDUCATION AND THE BAR

In the midst of this complex background—of social and economic change, differing and unclear conceptions of the functions of law, and incomplete arrangements for the promulgation and interpretation of norms—China has undertaken extensive institution-building to realize legal reform. The law reformers undertook to revive the courts, reestablish legal education, and resurrect the bar. Each of these institutions had already appeared in some fashion—and had then been politicized—before the Cultural Revolution. The reformers recalled and retraced the outlines and structures of a formal, if Stalinist, legal system that had already existed during the 1950s. A central task, of course, was revival of a judicial system. Scorned as "rightist" at the end of the 1950s and as "bourgeois" during the Cultural Revolution, courts now have been given an increasingly meaningful and credible role in resolving civil and economic disputes. Judicial reform will be examined in detail in chapter 9. Two other areas of fundamental importance that had to be addressed were legal education and the bar, which we look at below.

Legal Education Reestablished

On the eve of the Cultural Revolution, Chinese legal education was already so politicized and shrunken that only a small number of university-level institutions offered law degrees. Of these, the most noted were Beijing University and Fudan University in Shanghai. Legal education was divided between (1) small law departments at universities under the jurisdiction of the Ministry of Education (which has since become the State Educational Commission) and (2) schools for the training of "political-legal cadres" (i.e., cadres for the courts, the police, and Procuracy), which were administered by the Ministry of Justice until it was abolished in 1959. All of these schools were closed in 1967, and they were among the very last university-level institutions to be reopened.

The first Chinese law schools reopened in 1979 and began to graduate students in 1982.[47] Over thirty full-time institutions of legal education existed by the end of the 1980s, and by the mid-1990s over seventy universities and other institutions of higher learning were awarding law degrees. Of these, the largest number are under the jurisdiction of the State Educational Commission; fourteen law departments at universities are directly under the commission, and an additional thirty-three are under its provincial affiliates. Since the Ministry of Justice was reestablished in 1979, it has supervised a group of schools for "politics and law" (*zhengfa xueyuan*), which train personnel for the courts, the police, and Procuracy as well as lawyers. There are now five such institutes, including the largest law school in the country, the University of Politics and Law in Beijing. In addition, there are other institutions run by the Chinese Academy of Social Sciences in Beijing and its provincial affiliates, the Ministry of Finance, the Ministry of Foreign Trade and Economic Cooperation, and other ministries.

Altogether, over 30,000 students are registered for the full-time study of law in four-year undergraduate programs. Some 5,000 students are also enrolled in graduate programs leading to master's and doctor's degrees in law. However, legal education extends considerably beyond these first-tier institutions. Students whose scores on the national college admission test are only slightly below the level required for enrollment in a degree program may attend two- or three-year courses at the same institutions leading to a general education diploma (*dazhuan*), and, if they do well, they may earn a regular academic degree. Students in these programs are very numerous, often outnumbering regular degree candidates. In addition, students may earn degrees by means of various correspondence courses, from adult education or part-time universities, or by passing an examination after "self-study." Moreover, aside from these programs, shorter-term training programs leading to certificates of various types have proliferated at local levels, run by national, provincial, and local agencies; universities; enterprises; and other bodies not directly supervised by the state.

The quality of Chinese legal education has not kept pace with this expansion. Law teaching usually involves recitation and exposition of legislative provisions. One foreign observer has commented that "students are given few if any opportunities to analyze fact patterns by reference to legal and regulatory norms,"[48] and another notes that Chinese law students "reify their experience through highly abstract units of legal thought."[49] The significance of these observations goes far beyond the classroom. Emphasis on rote learning reinforces the perspective that "the law on the books is and should be the main focus of inquiry, with little concern for actual legal behavior and practice."[50] The educational level of instructors at Chinese law schools varies greatly, and a 1994 study found that fully one-quarter of all teaching personnel at top schools lacked bachelor's degrees.[51] Moreover, life as a law professor is marked by low salaries, inadequate libraries, and little or no support for research in which full-time instructors are nonetheless expected to engage. The universities generally, not just law schools, are notoriously under-funded. It is no wonder that throughout the 1990s, visiting foreign legal specialists were told that numerous law teachers were leaving their law schools or departments to enter the more lucrative practice of law.

Personal observation as well as the testimony of others suggests that

Chinese legal education has generally not been able to fashion courses that rise above repetition of codes and statutes. To some extent, this is true of any code-based legal system, and the lecture courses that I attended during my own year at the Faculty of Law in Paris in the early 1960s were generally no more stimulating than several representative lectures that I attended at Chinese law schools almost thirty years later. A report on Chinese legal education written by two law professors, one American and the other Chinese, called for more training in legal analysis. It also suggested giving attention to the training of lawyers on a range of subjects, from practical details of court administration to professional ethics; such training seems appropriate, given the extraordinary pressures on the legal profession in a society in sharp transition. The report also called for the enhancement and support of faculty research to raise the level of legal education at universities, and hence the quality of law graduates.[52]

Chinese legal education has received some Western influence through legal exchanges. Several hundred Chinese law teachers have done research or attended classes in foreign law schools, the majority in the United States under the sponsorship of the Committee on Legal Educational Exchanges with China (CLEEC). CLEEC was established in 1982 with support from the Ford Foundation and later obtained additional funding from the Luce Foundation (for development of law libraries at law schools) and the U.S. Information Agency (for summer programs for Chinese law teachers and researchers preparing to study in the United States). Chinese participants were placed in American law schools with supervision for visiting scholars and instruction for degree candidates; an in-country course on American law was offered since the mid-1980s, staffed by American law professors and lawyers on an unsalaried basis. After June 1989 Chinese were not allowed by the Chinese educational authorities to pursue degree programs abroad, but otherwise the program continued until it was suspended for lack of funding in 1995. Congressional cuts in the budget for the U.S. Information Agency meant the end of the summer program, although sufficient funds were restored to make possible a summer program in 1998.[53]

The Chinese Bar Reestablished

Early History. No feature of China's contemporary legal scene better embodies both the novelty and the aspirations of legal reform than the recently reestablished Chinese bar. Traditional Chinese culture weighs heavily on it. The concept of a legal profession acting as an intermediary between the populace and the state was essentially unknown in traditional China, and the small Westernized bar that emerged in China's cities during the Republic was unknown to most Chinese. Later, Communist attitudes and policies were hostile to the bar. An experiment with a Soviet-style bar began in 1954 but was ended in 1957, when lawyers were among the targets of the Anti-Rightist campaign against bourgeois attitudes and institutions. Not only were the legal advisory offices closed (there were some 800, with 3,000 lawyers, by then) but, as noted earlier, the Ministry of Justice itself was abolished in 1959.

Initial Attempts to Define the Lawyers' Role. China remained without a legal profession for over twenty years, until the reforms began. The Chinese bar was formally reestablished at the beginning of the 1980s, and its growth and the extent to which it has been accepted as an institution of Chinese society are illustrated by the legislation that has been enacted to regulate the new profession.[54] "Provisional Regulations" on lawyers were adopted by the Standing Committee of the National People's Congress in August 1980 and became effective on January 1, 1982.[55] These early regulations reflected an ambivalence toward the legal profession that itself embodied basic Chinese tensions about law. In these regulations, lawyers were characterized as "legal workers of the state" and were organized into legal advisory offices supervised by the Ministry of Justice (reestablished in 1979), effectively recreating the legal profession as it had been organized in the mid-1950s. The regulations further instructed Chinese lawyers to "serve the cause of socialism" and "protect the interests of the state and the collective" on the one hand, and, on the other, to protect the "legitimate rights and interests of the citizens." The tension is, of course, a basic one, which had already been given stark expression in the 1950s, when energetic lawyers who urged courts to find their clients innocent were later criticized for protecting criminals.

Lawyers were given an explicit though limited role in defending persons accused of crimes. Under the Criminal Procedure Code adopted in 1979 they were, "on the basis of facts and law," to provide material bearing on the defendant's innocence or lack of responsibility, the degree of his crime, and the gravity of punishment,[56] although in practice their role has been much more limited. In addition, the lawyer's role in civil law transactions and in "foreign-related matters" of trade and investment has grown steadily as activity in each of these areas has expanded.

Under the Provisional Regulations, lawyers did not have to pass a bar examination to be qualified to practice. They could be certified as qualified by the Ministry of Justice if they had college educations and additional relevant work experience, which, in the case of candidates with no law degrees, was only vaguely defined. Applicants with minimum amounts of education, experience, or both were qualified when they were approved by agencies of the Ministry of Justice. The newness of the profession was underscored by the slowness with which a nationwide system of bar examinations was established; the bar examination was first given in 1986, offered biannually after that until 1993, and only since then has been administered annually. In 1988 the Ministry of Justice established a two-step qualification procedure that requires candidates to pass the bar examination and successfully complete a one-year internship in a law office, although the alternative method of certification was retained. Educational levels remain low. Only about one-fifth of all Chinese lawyers in 1994 had earned undergraduate degrees by successfully completing a full four-year course of study,[57] and as of 1996, almost 30 percent had no formal education beyond high school.[58] It is unlikely that half of China's lawyers would have law degrees by the year 2000.

Further Growth; the Lawyers Law. The organizations in which lawyers practiced in the early 1980s were first called "legal advisory offices"; the term "law office" came into use by the middle of the decade. By that time some offices, particularly those involved in trade and investment-related transactions with foreigners, were organized not by the Ministry of Justice but by other ministries and state organizations. As a flood of promulgated laws appeared during the 1980s, the demand for legal services grew rapidly, which brought about changes in law firm organization. Cooperative law firms were first authorized in 1988, and partnerships and individual law firms have been added.[59] By 1990 there were approximately 3,700 law firms; by 1995 there were approximately 75,000 trained and registered lawyers in the PRC, of whom only 40 percent were working full-time as lawyers. The number of law firms grew to 7,200 by mid-1996, of which 5,500 were state-funded, 500 cooperative, and 1,200 partnerships.[60] By 1997, the numbers had risen to 8,300 law firms and over 110,000 lawyers; foreign law firms, first permitted to register in 1992, numbered 67.[61] Lawyers have increasingly been involved in representing clients in litigation, although in 1996 clients were represented by counsel in only about 17 percent of the 5,682,363 cases resolved by the courts in that year.[62] As foreign investment accelerated during the first half of the 1990s, Chinese law firms expanded their services to foreign investors.[63]

Further evolution of Chinese concepts of the lawyer and of lawyers' roles in society is suggested by the Law on Lawyers, promulgated by the Standing Committee of the NPC on May 15, 1996; it became effective on January 1, 1997.[64] The new law, which supersedes the earlier regulations, has a much less overtly political tone. References to lawyers' duties to serve socialism and the state have been deleted, and lawyers are now defined simply as "personnel who have obtained a business license for setting up practice of a lawyer in accordance with the law *and [who] provide legal services for the public"* (emphasis added) (Art. 2). The Lawyers Law falls short, however, of defining lawyers as independent professionals, a formulation that was rejected by the drafters. It sets forth requirements for qualifying as a lawyer by taking the national examination and receiving a license to practice. A legal education is not mandatory, and a college education or a vaguely defined equivalent suffices as the minimum educational requirement. The law also still permits candidates to be qualified without law degrees, although the rules have been tightened so that this route to qualification is essentially open only to law teachers, judges, and members of the Procuracy.

The law recognizes the three types of law offices that had been previously approved—state, cooperative, and partnership; it requires fee contracts to be signed with clients; and it enumerates the tasks that lawyers may carry out for their clients (such as acting as legal advisers, representing clients in disputes, and otherwise giving legal advice). Lawyers are required to "maintain the legitimate rights and interest" of clients, may be discharged by their clients, and may not refuse to act for clients once they have accepted a fee (Art. 27).

The law states that lawyers may not be interfered with in carrying out their duties under procedural laws—the right to meet with clients "whose personal freedom is under restrictions" is specifically mentioned (Art. 30)—and they may conduct investigations on behalf of their clients if the "relevant units or individuals" approve (Art. 31). Some effort has been made to define ethical standards, at least negatively, by prohibiting lawyers from such acts as representing both sides in litigation; accepting things of value from the other side in a litigation; meeting with judges, procurators, or arbitrators "in violation of regulations" or entertaining, bribing, or attempting to bribe them; and providing false evidence (Art. 35).

The bar is formally regulated jointly, by the All China Lawyers Association, which is supposed to educate lawyers and supervise their professional ethics and discipline, and by the provincial judicial bureaus, which hold the most power. The latter have disciplinary powers over lawyers, may suspend lawyers for violating the ethical rules itemized above, and may revoke their licenses for a variety of listed offenses. The devolution of authority to provincial judicial bureaus and to the All China Lawyers Association had already begun earlier in the decade,[65] but regardless of formal separation of responsibilities the association remains closely tied to the Ministry of Justice. The Lawyers Law no longer treats that ministry as the "department in charge" of lawyers, but it still retains basic responsibility for qualifying lawyers and reviewing all law firms annually.

The 1990s saw the emergence of legal aid schemes, including *pro bono* programs initiated and funded by law firms, and legal aid programs established and funded by local governments and lawyers' associations.[66] In the principal type of arrangement, lawyers volunteer or are required under licensing agreements to take on cases for no or low fees; in some cases they are reimbursed in full or in part by legal aid funds provided by a variety of sources (local governments, private sector, and international NGOs). A small number of local governments have also established permanent staffs of legal aid lawyers. The Lawyers Law provides generally for a legal assistance scheme for litigants unable to afford lawyers' fees. The details of the scheme are promised in subsequent legislation and will likely build on several pilot projects already in place. One of these, the Center for the Protection of the Rights of the Disadvantaged, in Wuhan, has been providing legal assistance to women, children, and the handicapped since 1992. The Minister of Justice announced in early 1995 that a legal aid scheme would soon be created, and legal aid offices have already begun to operate in Beijing, Guangzhou, and Shanghai.[67] The construction of legal aid schemes has encountered difficulties caused by administrative and Party interference and the localism that infects the entire judicial system.

The expansion of legal aid also faces another problem, one that derives from a much broader set of considerations. A Chinese lawyer who has studied legal aid has observed that the legal profession has shown some ambivalence toward it, and "instead of challenging the authority of the government under the CCP leadership . . . has opted to reorganize its apparatus within the authoritarian structure [of the CCP]," rather than seeking autonomy from the state.[68] Although it is not possible to explore here either the mentalities of Chinese lawyers or Chinese officialdom, hesitations and uncertainty in each about the role of the profession should be noted.

Continuing Ambiguities in the Role of Lawyers. China's lawyers still encounter substantial limits on the expansion of their roles. Their numbers are few and their professional qualifications and educational standards remain low; as one close observer has commented, "barely one-fifth of Chinese lawyers have earned law degrees and many of them studied law in a centrally planned economy, much of which has been superseded, and in a manner hardly conducive to the cultivation of analytical skills."[69] In my own encounters with Chinese lawyers, from whom I have had to obtain opinions on Chinese law for clients, I have noticed that Chinese legal education tends to produce lawyers who have difficulty applying law to complex factual situations and too often confine their opinions to descriptive repetition of legislative provisions without analyzing their applicability to the facts at hand.

The Party-state has not yet completely recognized lawyers' functions. A clear example of the limits on the role of the lawyer has been the criminal process, in which lawyers have generally lacked a meaningful ability to assert their clients' innocence. Although the lawyer's role has been expanded in the latest revision of the Criminal Procedure Law, it remains restricted by a number of serious limitations.[70]

Other problems arise from the recent explosion of materialism in Chinese society. Lawyers, judges, and officials encounter enormous temptations to engage in bribery and a variety of corrupt practices that currently pervade their professional activities. The use of personal contacts with judges or other officials to attempt to influence the outcomes of cases, for example, is pervasive, according to practicing lawyers with whom I have discussed the problems. There is every reason to believe that in the near future the pressures on lawyers to use personal connections on behalf of their clients will continue.

Can China's lawyers transform their mentality into that of an independent profession? Even under the best of circumstances, such an evolution can occur only very slowly. Prepared more to work as "state legal workers" than as autonomous lawyers, China's lawyers are caught between the need to define standards for a post-totalitarian society and the persistence of totalitarian institutions and ways of thought. One of the many contradictions caused by this tension is the beginning of efforts to build a legal aid system even though almost all criminal defendants who are brought to trial are convicted.[71]

Basically, the bar must be invented as a profession without any guidance from Chinese tradition or China's recent history. Unfortunately, the dilemmas of the legal profession reflect the profound philosophical, moral, and ethical problems that trouble Chinese society in the midst of a number of remarkable and simultaneous transitions. The economy has moved away from planning to considerable marketization, and the state has passed from totalitarianism to a system that, although authoritarian, has also begun to accept lawyers in a manner inconceivable to the drafters of the first regulations on lawyers in 1980. In light of the speed and extent of these transitions, the progress that has been made in recognizing the role of the bar is noteworthy, although the strains are powerful. Alford notes, in particular, that:

If . . . the function of legal professionals is to reconcile public and private interests, the absence of clear, broadly shared understandings of what these interests are at a time when the contents of the Party's core ideology and of morality itself are increasingly open to contest and manipulation leaves lawyers without more than a highly personalized basis for framing such reconciliations.[72]

At the same time, Western standards cannot be strictly applied, given that many of the ethical problems that confront Chinese practitioners are difficult even for Western lawyers to solve. The high ideals claimed by the legal profession in the West have also been impaired as the profession becomes "just another business."[73]

As long as the CCP rules China, the role and position of the bar will be hedged about by political necessities, even if they have become noticeably less suffocating than when the bar was reestablished at the beginning of the 1980s. The CCP, or at least elements within it, can still be counted on to hark back to its Maoist past: After the Lawyers Law was promulgated, the Ministry of Justice issued a notice that not only emphasized the need for lawyers to place the interests of "society" first, but, more pointedly, required all law firms with three or more CCP members to form a Party cell.[74] The ministry's notion of proper professional behavior is illustrated by a 1997 article in *Chinese Lawyer*, a magazine published by the ministry. It celebrated a model lawyer who told of how, whenever he was involved in foreign-related cases, he respected the principle that "the national interest is higher than anything . . . a lawyer handling foreign-related cases . . . absolutely must not allow the national interest to be illegally infringed upon."[75]

Finally, among the basic problems embedded in Chinese political and legal culture that confront the bar is the unresolved contradiction between a legal profession and CCP opposition to autonomous organizations and professions. An example is a letter to a legal monthly published just several weeks after the Lawyers Law was enacted.[76] The writer tells of a lawyer in a Hainan county law office, who represented two elderly men in their appeal of a local police decision to impose detention for fifteen days. Their offense was failure to register an "Old Fishermen's Society" that they had organized. The lawyer wrote a statement, used by the two men in their appeal to the next higher-level police bureau, which argued that their "society" had no organization, charter, manager, or seal, did no business with anyone, and generally did not meet the criteria for an organization that should register. The decision to impose punishment was reversed, but soon thereafter the secretary of the county CCP Organization Department ordered that a meeting be assembled at which he criticized the lawyer for representing the two men and being at odds with the police. This was followed by an Organization Department decision forbidding the lawyer from practicing. It is a measure of the progress that has been made by the bar that the aggrieved lawyer could petition county, province, and central authorities, citing laws and regulations that provide that lawyers shall not be interfered with in the lawful conduct of their profession, and reminding them, "In a certain sense, the lawyer system is a gauge of the legalization (*fazhihua*) of society."[77] By his standard, the progress of the Chinese bar since 1980 has been considerable, but by the same standard a long road lies ahead.[78]

REFORM OF CRIMINAL LAW AND THE CRIMINAL PROCESS

The last of the basic reforms that this chapter addresses is the effort to give increased definition to both the substantive and procedural rules of the criminal process. The three institutions that administer the criminal process—Public Security (police), Procuracy, and courts—have had great continuity with their pre-Cultural Revolution predecessors. From the early history of those institutions summarized in chapter 4, we recall that when Maoism was infused into Stalinist-inspired structures during the decade before the Cultural Revolution, the Chinese criminal process came to be marked with a unique flexibility. Although its institutions were far from maintaining standards of legality, they were also the only ones that the Chinese leadership had known when officials in charge of legal reform began to consider how to construct institutions for the criminal process after Mao.

Reform, however, has brought with it increased perception of the need for regularity and control of arbitrariness. Reform presents the Chinese leadership with the contradiction between continuing politicization of the criminal process to support CCP rule and attaining the rule of law that is also a goal of CCP policy.

Criminal Law and Criminal Procedure

Codes. When the Criminal Law and the Criminal Procedure Law were promulgated in 1979, they were the first China had known since the abrogation of the Nationalist Codes in 1949.[79] Although these codifications formally replaced rules that had been extraordinarily fluid under Maoism, they still reflected their Maoist ancestry. The Criminal Law made a notable departure from earlier reluctance to define substantive crimes, but remained faithful to a politicized view of the criminal law. One study of the new law compared the Chinese code and the Soviet criminal code at the time: Chinese laws were "much more simple . . . much more programmatic, and much more moralistic."[80] The 1979 code retained the concept of "counter-revolutionary crimes," conspicuous because of the detail with which they are defined as compared to other offenses. The code also employed the principle of analogy, although offenders could only be punished by analogical application of the code after approval by the Supreme People's Court.

After the code was adopted, it was amended and modified by a considerable number of laws and regulations, as well as by interpretations by the Supreme People's Court and the Supreme People's Procuratorate. Many other laws issued since the reforms began contain provisions imposing criminal liability on a wide range of offenses. Consideration of amendments began in 1988, but was suspended after the Tiananmen events in June 1989, and then resumed again in 1993. The Criminal Procedure Law was revised in 1996, and an amended criminal law was adopted in March 1997, which became effective on October 1, 1997.[81] Although many new provisions have been added, the fundamental structure and organization of the previous Criminal Law have not been altered. It remains divided into two parts, devoted respectively to "General Principles" and "Special Provisions."

Some notable changes reduce the overt politicization of Chinese criminal law. The principle of analogy has been removed, and the 1997 Criminal Law states that an act is not criminal unless it is defined as such by law (Art. 3). The crime of counter-revolution has been abolished, although it has been replaced by "crimes of endangering national security," a phrase that can be interpreted and applied at least as broadly as the older offense, and which includes many activities that were formerly characterized as "counter-revolutionary." The list of such offenses against the state is somewhat shorter than in the 1979 Criminal Law.

Much more extensive change has been made to the Special part of the Criminal Law, to reflect the enormous economic changes that have resulted from reform. Thus many new economic crimes have been added, such as counterfeiting goods, smuggling, making various types of false statements in corporate or financial documentation reported to government departments or to the public, insider trading, market manipulation, and defrauding investors. A list of crimes against social order has also been expanded, and liability of state personnel has been added for various offenses. The crime of "speculation," previously undefined, has been abolished; "hooliganism," which was defined only broadly and vaguely, has disappeared, only to be replaced by four specific offenses including two against women and two involving fighting in public. Punishments continue to reflect the strong emphasis on inflicting severe sanctions for their deterrent effect, and there has been only a small reduction in the crimes punishable by death.

Chinese substantive criminal law continues to present some serious problems, not only to Western observers but to some Chinese legal scholars as well.[82] Among the most prominent issues are the extensive continued use of vague terms such as "under special circumstances" to define the seriousness of a crime; the Supreme People's Court's use of its power in order to issue prospective and sometimes broad interpretations of legislation in order to extend the definitions of criminal offenses analogically, despite the abolition of the analogy provision in the 1979 Code, which has already been mentioned in this chapter and is further discussed below; and the failure to place within the scope of the criminal law reeducation through labor, an administrative punishment introduced in 1957, which is discussed below in this chapter.

The greater attention to non-political crimes in the substantive criminal law reflects the considerable depoliticization of Chinese life since the onset of reforms, with direct implications for sanctioning processes. The classification of all persons according to their socioeconomic class and the designation of classes of political pariahs—hallmarks of the Maoist era discussed in chapters 3 and 4—have disappeared. Whereas campaigns are still used to implement the criminal law, as noted earlier, the targets are not political "enemies" but the perpetrators of ordinary and economic crimes. At the same time, although politicization has receded, the institutions that implement the criminal process still bear the strong stamp of the political forces that shaped them during the three decades before reform.

The Formal Criminal Process: Principal Characteristics. The Criminal Procedure Law of 1979 followed previously established laws. It continued the tripartite division of functions that had been established in the 1950s and given legislative expression in 1979.[83] Public Security organs are responsible for investigation of crimes, detention, and formal arrest of suspects; the Procuracy is responsible for approval of arrests, investigation leading to formal accusation, and prosecution of the accused; the courts must hold public trials at which accused persons have the right to be defended by a lawyer or other persons designated by them. Cases are to be decided by a panel, comprised either entirely of judges or of one judge sitting with two "assessors" chosen from the masses; since 1983 courts have had discretion to use either type of panel, but in practice most appear to be entirely composed of judges.[84]

Discussions in the popular press following the 1979 promulgation of the Criminal Procedure Law reflect some recognition of the need to resist the blurring of functions that is caused by politicization and to affirm the distinctions among the functions of the three agencies that administer the formal process. One article, for example, urged that each of the three agencies carefully observe the limits placed on their activities by law and, without specifically referring to the obscuring of jurisdictional lines and the police dominance of the criminal process that had marked the 1950s and the 1960s, criticized by implication that earlier perversion of the scheme:

[The] operating ranges and limits of authority [of police, Procuracy, and courts] must not be confused. They are not interchangeable, nor can they go beyond the limits of the law. Only thus can they act in accordance with the law and enforce it strictly.[85]

Although the drafters of this early legislation reestablished the pre-reform institutions, they were not only looking backward at familiar institutional patterns. They also attempted to make the criminal process more rational and coherent by means of the Criminal Procedure Law, China's first comprehensive criminal procedure code.

Stability and Campaigns Against Crime. Law had generally been identified with social control throughout the history of the PRC until economic reform required the leadership and drafters of law to broaden their views on law's role. But even as the leadership has created many other legal institutions and imported many legal concepts in order to respond to the needs of expanding nonstate sectors of the economy, they have retained their concern to use law as an instrument of proletarian dictatorship. They have frequently called for more laws and a strong legal system to maintain "political stability and good social order."[86] Even when Jiang Zemin urged that the nation "be ruled by law," as he did in February 1996, he emphasized the need for stability and order just as strongly.

Soon after the Criminal Procedure Law was promulgated in 1979, the leaders turned their attention to expanding the powers of the police, and as a result the Criminal Procedure Law was amended a number of times during the early 1980s. The effect of these changes was to weaken the procedural safeguards of persons accused of crimes. In 1980 and 1981 the NPC Standing Committee adopted legislation that allowed provincial-level People's Congresses to extend temporarily the time limits for investigation, prosecution, trial, and appeal.[87] In 1983 the NPC passed an amendment diluting the rights to defense and to appeal of persons accused of certain violent crimes,[88] and in 1984 it permanently extended the period of time during which persons accused of certain "major" or "complicated" cases could be held in custody to encompass the entire handling of their case, from investigation to appeal.[89] At the same time that these legislative moves expanded the powers of the police to deal with rising crime and social disorder, the Party initiated campaigns to "strike hard" (*yanda*) at crime. The first of these began in 1983,[90] and by 1996, "Yanda [had] become a permanent feature of Chinese life."[91] As noted in the previous chapter, reform has not reduced, down to the present day, the conspicuous use of the courts in nationwide campaigns to punish crime, repress dissidents, and join in the general struggle to maintain social order.

Police Domination, Court Passivity. The formal criminal process has been dominated by the police, who have found it easy to avoid the limits on their power articulated by the Criminal Procedure Law. Thus, although the length of time for which the police could detain a suspect without formally arresting him (which requires approval by the Procuracy) was limited, the police have employed a variety of types of detention that were not included under the Criminal Procedure Law at all. Detention can be extended, and limits are inapplicable to "complex cases."[92] In practice, before the Criminal Procedure Law was reformed, the police used a form of detention called "shelter and investigation" to detain suspects indefinitely, and there were no limits on the number of times the Procuracy could also request "supplementary investigation" by the police.[93] The Procuracy also has had the power to dispose of minor criminal cases by deciding that it would not prosecute—although Procuracies could announce their decisions in a way that "[conveys] a clear determination of guilt."[94] As we will see below, reform has diluted, but not abolished, the power to cause these determinations.

The trial process had been marked by a strong tilt in favor of the prosecution. Defendants were not permitted access to counsel until their case had been handed over to the court for trial by the Procuracy, which was tantamount to a finding of guilty, and the court was only required to give defendants seven days' notice of the date of trial. Generally, public trials have not been held in China unless the court is convinced on the basis of its pretrial investigation that the facts alleged will be proven in open trial. As noted earlier, almost all defendants brought to trial are found guilty. If there is doubt about the defendant's guilt, the public trial most probably will not take place. Since the 1950s, whenever public hearings revealed important inconsistencies in evidence, the courts would adjourn to continue their investigation in private. The function of the trial has been to demonstrate guilt, rather than to inquire into guilt or innocence.

The procedure that has been followed in practice has come to be called, expressively enough, "decision first, trial later." In 1995, prior to reform of the Criminal Procedure Law, officials from the agencies charged with administration of the criminal process met to discuss upcoming changes. No more convincing description of the criminal trial process exists than the succinct one offered by the Supreme Procuratorate:

The main problem [in adjudication] . . . is the practice of decision first, trial later, first making the ruling, then conducting the trial; internal instructions are implemented and positions coordinated, the Court President and the Division President, even officials of higher courts, determine guilt and set the punishment, then begin adjudication in the courtroom, turning what in reality is two adjudications into one. This practice causes the division of the courts into levels to exist in name only, causes adjudication activities in court to become merely formalistic appearances, and to a certain extent deprives defendants of their right to trial.[95]

In this process, the participation of lawyers, not surprisingly, has been minimal. According to one recent Chinese study, most defendants do not engage lawyers (one estimate is that no more than 30 percent of criminal defendants have been represented by counsel), and when lawyers do participate they have often been limited to arguing for light sentences.[96]

Moreover, the judges do not give great weight to lawyers' arguments, because by the time the case has come to trial, the court has already decided the outcome and may even have already drafted its decision.[97] The defendant's right to appeal, although provided for in the Criminal Procedure Law, is sharply curtailed in practice by a variety of means. For example, the appellate court may send the case back to the trial court because the facts are unclear, and on retrial, the defendant's penalty may be increased. Or, the appellate court, exercising the power of "judicial supervision" that it possesses as the administrative superior of the trial court, may retry the case.[98] For such reasons, one Chinese legal scholar finds an "obvious trend" toward expanding the powers of the public security and judicial organs to facilitate investigation, prosecution, and adjudication while restricting criminal defendants in their rights, and he concludes that Chinese legislators are more concerned to strike hard at crime than to protect the rights of persons accused of it.[99]

Significant Legal Reforms. Although the dominant policy has emphasized the fight against crime and the need to preserve order, China's interest in reforming the criminal process had grown.[100] The reasons included:

an upsurge of crime and the appearance of new crimes;

the development of legal institutions in other areas;

a desire for greater regularity and rationality;

increased professionalization and institutional differentiation within the three agencies that administer the criminal process;

growing rights-consciousness among Chinese; and

the influence of international practice and the sting of international criticism.

In 1996, after years of discussion, the National People's Congress amended the Criminal Procedure Law.[101] Among the principal actions taken, the NPC did away with "shelter and investigation" and limited to two the number of times the Procuracy could request "supplementary investigation" by the police. However, it authorized pre-trial detention for thirty days by the police, with the Procuracy's agreement, of defendants suspected of committing crimes in different places, repeatedly or jointly with others—precisely those who were formerly held under "shelter and investigation." It has also increased the limits on extensions of detention: In "major, complicated cases where the scope of the crime is broad and gathering evidence is difficult," a two-month extension is allowed, and a further extension of two months is permitted if the crimes involved are punishable by sentences of ten years or longer.[102] On balance, although the revised Criminal Procedure Law does "show some movement toward greater protection of the rights of suspected criminals . . . [it] actually weakens restrictions on the use and length of pre-trial detention."[103] The NPC also lowered the standard for authorization of an arrest from demonstrating that the "principal facts of the crime have already been clarified" to providing "evidence to prove the facts of the crime."[104]

The rule on notice of trial has been changed from seven days' notice to ten.[105] The NPC has expanded the right to counsel. Lawyers now have the right to begin to act on their clients' behalf as soon as the case has been sent to the Procuracy—in the past the case first had to reach the court—and criminal defendants must be informed of this right. Lawyers may also assist clients at earlier stages while the case is still being investigated by the police after the accused persons have been questioned or have been detained under one of the forms permitted by the law; the police, however, need not inform them of this right. It is important to note, though, that the remedy for infringement of this right lies exclusively with the Procuracy.[106] The police are permitted to deny suspects access to a lawyer if "state secrets" are involved, and they have apparently used this power often enough to prompt the Ministries of Justice, Public Security, and State Security, the Legal Work Committee of the NPC, the Procuracy, and the Supreme People's Court to issue a joint "regulation" ordering police not to use the "state secret" rule as an excuse to refuse suspects' requests to meet with their counsel in cases not involving state secrets.[107]

The trial is now more formally differentiated from police and Procuratorial involvement in a number of significant respects. The reform limits the Procuracy's power to dispense with or simply forgo prosecution in cases where it indicates that the accused was guilty; this power may still be exercised, however, when the crimes involved are "minor." The decision will still be publicly announced and directly communicated to the suspect's work unit, and the Procuracy can also recommend non-criminal sanctions or confiscation of "illegal income."[108]

These reforms attempt to reinforce the adjudicatory nature of the trial by limiting the extent to which the trial court judges should consult internally with those senior judges who form the court's Adjudication Committee (see chapter 9 for discussion of this committee's often decisive role in civil and economic cases). Under the revised Criminal Procedure Law, "difficult, complicated or important cases" may be referred to the adjudication committee at the request of the trial court, which must otherwise hear and decide the case. In practice, the effectiveness of this change is doubtful. As we will see in chapter 9, the court president has extensive powers, individual judges are not independent, and, in practice, the courts are subject to considerable outside influence, of which campaigns are only the most obvious manifestations.

The revision has also made clear that the court should not review criminal cases before the opening of the trial and that it must not send cases back to the Procuracy for further investigation. The new rules also place the burden of arguing the case on the prosecutor and defense counsel. Taken together with the expanded participation of lawyers, the new rules promise to make the criminal trial more meaningful.

The reform also takes a step toward adopting the presumption of innocence. Article 12 of the 1996 Criminal Procedure Law states that "In the absence of a lawful verdict of the people's court, no person should be determined guilty."[109] Chinese legal scholars had in the past advocated adoption of the principle.[110] The 1996 Criminal Procedure Law now refers to the "suspect" before the decision to prosecute and to the "defendant" thereafter.

The revised law also ends the practice under which the court could send a doubtful case back to the Procuracy for supplementary investigation when the evidence was insufficient to warrant proceeding to trial. It creates a new category of verdict. In addition to the verdict of not guilty "on the basis of the law," the court may now issue the verdict of "not guilty due to insufficient evidence and inability to establish the crime charged." As a detailed study of the revision argues, this implies that defendants found not guilty because of insufficient evidence are "somehow *less* not guilty."[111] In addition, the study notes that the revision has not given persons accused of a crime the rights associated, in Anglo-American law, with the presumption of innocence, including among others the right to remain silent and not to testify against oneself.[112] Chinese discussions have spoken of adoption of the principle as a step forward.[113] Others go further; one discussion states that the criminal procedure revision "draws on the rational portion of the criminal procedure laws of the Western countries and overcomes the disadvantage of China's original criminal procedure,"[114] and another notes that the criminal procedure revision meant that "the concept of 'procedure first' has become the hallmark in developing socialist civilization and that to handle cases by following the procedure and observing the law has become an important sign of civilization and democracy."[115]

Assessment. In chapter 4 I discussed the relevance of two competing metaphors for legal process: the obstacle course and the assembly line. The two jostle for precedence daily in the Chinese criminal process, although recent reforms have made the outcome of the grinding of the assembly line somewhat less predictable than before. As the preceding summary indicates, although the powers of the police have been limited because of reforms and the right to counsel has been expanded, the Procuracy still retains the power to stigmatize the accused by "exempting" him from prosecution, which denies his right to trial and limits his right to appeal to the Procuracy itself. Changes in trial procedure may expand the function of the trial, but notice to the defendants is still likely to be inadequate and counsel's rights to introduce new evidence or call witnesses are contingent on court approval.

The 1996 revisions of the Criminal Procedure Law express a concern for defendants' rights that goes beyond all previous PRC legislation. Although the debate over the revision of the Criminal Procedure Code suggests that increased functional differentiation among the agencies that administer the criminal process is emerging, albeit slowly, the terminology and concepts of the Maoist era have been left behind. Critical issues of legality have surfaced, displacing the previous competition of different approaches to bureaucracy. A fundamental problem is the continued force of constraints on judicial autonomy. The Party-state requires the courts to obey it so that order as the Party leadership defines it will be maintained. Thus, one function of the courts both before and after the Tiananmen tragedies has been to formalize decisions to punish dissidents that are made elsewhere.[116] Moreover, "if past history is any guide, the Chinese government will not necessarily abide by the revised law at all times, particularly in politically sensitive cases," and in ordinary criminal cases the courts will continue to prefer to "strike hard" at crime rather than protect the rights of persons accused of crime.[117] The subservient role of the courts in criminal matters cannot be changed merely by revising the rules of criminal procedure, but only by fundamental political decisions about the allocation of power within the Chinese state.

On balance, the assembly line will remain the dominant metaphor unless the Chinese leadership manifests strong and sustained support for changing the balance between the forces of the Party-state and the defendant when they clash in the formal criminal proceedings. At the same time, the recent reforms can be viewed as a stage in a long evolutionary process of functionally differentiating the three agencies of the criminal process. Professionalization of the judiciary, addressed in chapter 9, may work to deepen these distinctions quietly and over the long run.

Nonjudicial Aspects of the Criminal Process

Police-Administered Sanctions. Despite recent revisions of the Criminal Procedure Law and continued discussions of procedural reform, significant sanctioning processes exist from which courts are still virtually excluded, just as they were under Mao. This review of the critical areas of nonjudicial sanctioning will illustrate the enormous power that the police and the CCP continue to wield, and, conversely, the restraints placed on the courts.

Police-administered sanctions have existed alongside the formal criminal process in China since long before reform, and this extensive sanctioning power of the police has remained constant since its codification in the late 1950s. Under the 1987 Security Administration Punishment Regulations (SAPR),[118] the police may punish any "disruptions of public order" that they decide do not warrant disposition by the formal criminal process by issuing a warning, imposing a small fine, or ordering detention for up to fifteen days.[119] Formerly the only means of recourse was to appeal to the police hierarchy itself; however, since 1986 citizens have been able to appeal police sanctions to courts, and court decisions reversing police-administered SAPR sanctions have begun to appear in published reports.[120]

The police also enjoy the virtually uncontrolled power to impose much longer "re-education through labor" sentences to labor camps for acts the police determine to fall between minor violations and serious offenses.[121] Labor re-education should not be confused with "labor reform," which is a sentence of penal servitude imposed after trial. It was formally established by a 1957 statute that was reissued in 1979.[122] Rightly called a "loose cannon" by two American scholars, labor re-education is used on a wide range of offenders, from "minor" "counter-revolutionary and anti-Party, anti-socialist elements" to persons who refuse to work for a long period of time, "stir up trouble, disrupt the lives of those around them, and do not respond to admonition."[123] Not only may confinement be imposed for as long as four years, but the police may decide to detain offenders whose sentences have been completed and require them to work at designated places indefinitely (*liuchang jiuye*, "forced job placement"). This sanction, too, has become appealable to the courts under recent legislation, and a small number of decisions have been published.[124]

If sentiment in favor of expanding controls over administrative discretion grows, police discretion to sentence offenders to labor re-education would be an obvious candidate for restraint. Labor re-education is only one of a larger group of sanctions that may be imposed by administrative agencies, and until recently very little legislation imposed any controls on such sanctioning activity. An article published in the official Ministry of Justice newspaper in September 1995 noted that administrative agencies were imposing punishments without legal authority, arbitrarily imposing penalties, punishing persons who objected with a second penalty for their "attitude," setting quotas for the imposition of fines, and forcing units to depend on the fines they collected for their operating revenue.[125] These problems were addressed in the Administrative Punishment Law,[126] promulgated in March 1996, which attempted to standardize penalties and sentencing. The law states that administrative punishments may only be decided in accordance with laws (Art. 9), and that only the police may impose punishments that involve restrictions on personal freedom (Art. 10). Very general procedural rules requiring notice and opportunity to raise a defense are provided. Although the new law is so general that it does not limit police discretion significantly, it does express a desire to restrain arbitrariness in the imposition of such punishments, hitherto unregulated, and may reflect concern among some, at least, to control and limit administratively imposed sanctions. In this regard, it resonates with other legislative efforts that have begun to establish administrative law in China.[127]

The Maintenance of CCP and Cadre Discipline. The subordination of the courts to higher political concerns is also demonstrated by the limits on their jurisdiction in cases involving Party members. Courts do not hear many cases in which the accused is a CCP member, and the CCP has long used its own Discipline Inspection Commission. Before the Cultural Revolution, if it was determined that a cadre had committed serious offenses against discipline, Communist morality, law, or all three, his punishment—if there was one—was usually limited to standard administrative sanctions. These included "demerits," warnings of various degrees of severity, demotion, transfer, or dismissal. Suspension of Party membership or dismissal from the Party were additional serious sanctions. These sanctions continue to be applied today by the Discipline Inspection Commission as well as the Ministry of Supervision, which was abolished in 1959, reestablished in 1986, and may administer minor sanctions. Any punishments more serious than warnings or demerits must be approved by the commission.[128]

The use of extra-judicial agencies to punish CCP members who have committed crimes continues, often in conjunction with recurrent campaigns to curb and punish corruption. For example, a Hong Kong newspaper reported in April 1994 that the CCP would grant "sweeping" enforcement powers to CCP officials investigating corruption, including the rights to confiscate travel documents, videotape suspects without their knowledge, and freeze bank accounts.[129] The new measures were announced by the Central Discipline Inspection Committee. The article further stated that these powers were formerly granted only to the Public Security Bureau, the Procuracy, and the Ministry of State Security. In matters involving Party discipline, it said, there seems to have been little hesitation to mingle formal legal and Party mechanisms, although "some jurists have questioned whether allowing Communist Party bodies to operate directly with law enforcement powers complies with China's state constitution."

Equality of all before the law is a principle expressed in China's Constitution and Criminal Procedure Law and much discussed in the Chinese media. Under this principle, Party cadres are not above the law and offenders—including, some emphasize, the wayward children of senior cadres—who violate the law must be punished according to the law.[130] It has been argued that administrative sanctions are insufficient punishment for officials who violate the law because, as one article puts it, "'dismissal in lieu of punishment' is a reflection of the influence of a feudal privilege-seeking mentality."[131] Assertion of these principles has led to judicial trials of Party members who have committed crimes, and intermittent press reports have told of criminal punishment being inflicted on Party officials for crimes of corruption. Reports suggest that CCP and government officials are willing to cover up offenses and are reluctant to accuse other officials.[132] When cadres are punished by means of the criminal process, those prosecuted are most likely to be low-ranking officials.[133] Regardless of the mechanisms employed, corruption continues to plague the CCP. The continued separation of Party discipline from legality not only keeps the CCP beyond the reach of the law, but it also illustrates the continuing refusal—or inability—to raise the courts above other elements of the Chinese Party-state.

Concluding Note

This brief survey of the participation of the Chinese courts in the criminal process suggests the limits on their powers and, therefore, on their functions and meaningfulness. The treatment of accused persons as they pass through the formal process may turn on negotiations among the courts, Procuracy, and police. The breadth of the areas that lie *outside* the jurisdiction of the courts raises more fundamental problems of creating a legal order. The courts have little power to affect sanctions imposed entirely by the Party or the police, or by both together, acting as agents of the Party-state in a sphere that is not even viewed as "legal." A major reduction in the power of the CCP would be necessary to expand the legal realm meaningfully by extending the power of the courts to punish Party members and officials and reducing the scope of exclusively police-administered sanctions.

The Chinese criminal process remains dominated not only by the police, but by a blatant instrumentalism that puts it at the service of the CCP and political leaders when they wish to use it. Reforms both in substantive criminal law and criminal procedure have edged the system toward greater tolerance for the rights of criminal defendants, but have not yet adequately institutionalized protection for those rights. Although there has been perceptible movement toward placing administrative sanctions under some control, controls over police-administered sanctions remain woefully weak. Overall, the first measures that have been taken to raise formal legal challenges to administrative action are limited. The Chinese leadership has taken its first steps toward building institutional limits on arbitrariness in the application of sanctions, but more are needed—as is the will to go further.

In this survey, I have touched on institutions created since 1979 that are basic to Chinese legal reform. The courts will be treated below in greater detail. Before passing to them, however, we must pause to understand other aspects of the reform effort. The first part of this chapter focused on the leadership's decision to rely more on law than on policy as an instrument of governance. Leaders have followed that first step by extensive law-making for whole areas of the economy and the society that did not exist before the reforms began. The next chapter will survey the general contours of three new areas of law that illustrate some of the accomplishments of law reform and some of the issues that continue to challenge it.

CHAPTER 7

Creating a Legal Framework
for Economic Reform

TO IMPLEMENT economic and legal reforms, the Chinese Party-state has had to generate a vast assortment of legislation and administrative rules for every conceivable area of activity that could be addressed by a government. It has responded to the challenge by producing, within an extremely short period of time, an extraordinary outpouring of rules that constitutes one of the most extensive attempts of the twentieth century to legislate the institutions of a state. This chapter attempts to capture some of the accomplishments of the legislative explosion that reform has generated, as well as some of the difficulties it has created. It would be impossible to catalogue all of the legislation that has poured forth, not only from Beijing but from provinces and localities all over the country, and I have instead chosen to present an overview of entirely new legislation in three substantive areas. These are

a framework of legal rules for domestic economic transactions;

a framework of legal rules for foreign trade and investment transactions; and

the first rules that attempt to regularize administrative decision-making and control administrative arbitrariness.

The first two areas have been chosen not only for their obvious economic significance, but also because in each, struggles over policy issues that transcend the specific area of economic activity are clearly visible. The third bears on the first two, because the discretion of Chinese officials casts a shadow over almost all economic transactions, whether they involve only Chinese or foreigners, and because administrative discretion so threatens progress toward the rule of law in China.

Law and the Economy: Creating a Basis for Expectations

LEGAL INSTITUTIONS FOR A MARKET ECONOMY

With the decline of economic planning, the number of economic actors and their transactions has increased each year. The Chinese leadership has encouraged legal institution-building to construct the socialist market economy that is their declared goal. Officials and scholars often claim that China needs a more developed legal system because "a market economy is an economy governed by law," in which law provides rules like those in athletic contests.[1] Neither the game nor its rules, however, seem to be free from ambiguity. Qiao Shi, a vigorous advocate of legislation to further reform when he was chairman of the NPC, said that "the power of the State should count in removing obstacles to the reforms and opening up, and thus the establishment of the structure for a socialist market economy can be promoted."[2] He also urged that China "borrow other countries' legislative experiences and learn about those that are useful to China . . . [and] dare to assimilate that in foreign laws which is good and useful to us."[3] Other official discussions, like this one from a Xinhua release, are less bold: "Since the convocation of the Fourteenth [CCP] National Congress, a consensus has been established among many people: *To a considerable extent*, market economy means economy operated under a legal system [emphasis supplied]."[4] Still others have retained a distinctly pre-reform cast of mind by stressing the state's power to control and to regulate,[5] as will be illustrated in the discussion of contracts later in this chapter.

For two decades—despite differences in emphasis from time to time—leadership policy has aimed at creating a market economy. The task is a monumental one, of course, and not made any easier by the understandable difficulty that the leadership has had in defining and agreeing on the characteristics of the economic system that is their professed goal. Before embarking on the analysis of some of the institutions that have been put into place to give structure to transactions, we should recall the model of a market economy legal system. In the West, the market economy relies on "private" law to serve as a framework to facilitate transactions defining the rights and duties created by voluntary economic arrangements. The framework provides the rules under which the institutions of the state will protect transactions upon request. The legal rules constitute the "background" for the contractual transactions that arise from the activities of economic actors who operate within a zone of choice, and whose individual autonomy is supported by the law. The effectiveness of such a framework has to be assessed in terms of how it defines and protects legal rights whether or not the parties to transactions want to assert them.[6] The parties to a contract need to know, for example, the legal consequences of a breach by either party.

Both Chinese reformers and Western observers must of course keep in mind that this model is only a model, and sometimes it is only a myth. It is not necessary to discuss at length and support with citations a pithy truth about contract law in the United States stated by an acute observer: "Imagining that rules of law create a high degree of predictability, and that, as a result, we gain freedom, is a rich fantasy."[7] In reading the discussion that follows in this and later chapters, the reader should keep in mind the power of the model just described and its frequent elevation to myth.

The balance of this chapter examines the extent to which Chinese institution-builders have established a legal framework for the economy they are reforming. Chapters 8 and 9 discuss dispute resolution in contemporary China and explore the institutions that have been devised to protect rights created in the effort to marketize the economy.

EMERGENCE OF SUBSTANTIVE LAW

This section examines the development of rules that are intended to stabilize the expectations of parties to economic transactions. Development has been especially dramatic because it began in a vacuum that had existed since the 1960s. The areas discussed here are emblematic of the overall legislative efforts to build a legal framework for commerce.

Threshold Issues in the Formulation of Legal Rules

Chinese policy-makers and drafters of legislation were challenged at the onset of reform to devise legal rules to govern commercial transactions that had previously been forbidden. The Chinese situation seems anomalous when compared with the development of commercial law in the West, where legal rules emerged out of centuries of commercial custom and practice. In China today, by contrast, rules are being adopted even while new transactions are themselves emerging and before much experience has been accumulated about them. Sometimes, even, the legislators have had to create new institutions of the most basic nature, such as the limited liability company.[8] The Chinese experience demonstrates the difficulties of introducing new legal institutions that are at best unfamiliar and at worst inconsistent with the political and social context into which they have been thrust. Recent history has also seen some striking interactions among pre-reform ideology, new commercial transactions, the new legal rules applicable to them, and attitudes shaped by culture. It has also seen the infusion of contract principles familiar in the West, notably in the most recent attempts to achieve legislative coherence.

The reformers' commitment to reducing the scope of economic planning made it necessary to create rules governing extra-plan transactions such as contracts. Since the mid-1950s, contracts had been used between SOEs to implement orders expressed in the economic plan. Although such contracts were viewed as creating strong obligations, they were not understood as creating rights in the contracting parties. Economic managers used personal relations to try to reach goals set by the state in the face of widespread shortages and bureaucratic rigidities.[9]

When decentralization of the system was introduced as an essential aim of the reforms, the contract was seen as the means to embody the shift of considerable decision-making responsibility from bureaucracy to individual enterprises, and rules were required that would apply to these contracts. When the reforms began, most industry was state-owned and most legislation, therefore, was drafted to regulate relations between state-owned enterprises. A theoretical issue had to be resolved, however. These enterprises, because they were owned "by the whole people," had relative rather than absolute rights over their assets. Their ownership was limited, and, in the thirty years since the establishment of the PRC, little thought had been given to clarifying the nature of their rights. Moreover, "ownership by the whole people" was a dogma that could not be questioned. Within the constraints imposed by this dogma, how were transactions involving state enterprises to be defined? And what legal principles were to govern these newly recognized and approved legal relationships outside the economic plan?

Chinese contract law reflects the struggle of Chinese scholars and law drafters to shake free from the grasp of Stalinist theory. During the 1950s Chinese legal theory had only mirrored Soviet theory, which at that time rejected the notion of private law. In the 1980s, Chinese scholars, echoing debates that had gone on for decades in the Soviet Union and Eastern Europe while Chinese legal scholarship had been frozen under Maoism, pondered a core issue: Should relationships among state enterprises be governed by "civil law," a body of rules applicable to all persons and entities regardless of whether they were state-, collective-, or privately owned, or by "economic law," which would apply exclusively to transactions among state-owned enterprises? The debate went on for years, but as reform progressed it became necessary to enact rules for the contracts that were being entered into not only by state enterprises but by new nonstate economic actors as well. The first major contract law embodying these reforms was promulgated in 1981 and was revised after the emergent unplanned sector had become dominant.

The Economic Contract Law of 1981

The law on domestic "economic contracts" (ECL) was adopted on December 13, 1981, by the National People's Congress.[10] The economic contracts to which it applied were agreements between "legal persons" for achieving "a certain economic purpose and for defining [their] rights and obligations." The new law looked both to the past and to an uncertain future: It did not define the "legal persons" or parties to the contracts and thereby remained faithful in form to the requirement that every contracting party had to be registered with the government. At the same time, the new rules applied not only to state enterprises but to any independent entity that had a budget, was authorized to possess capital, and was registered with a local branch of the State Administration of Industry and Commerce (SAIC). The idea that not only state enterprises but others could be parties to contracts was expressed in Article 54, which hung at the end of the law like an afterthought and states that individual businessmen and rural commune members could conclude contracts "with reference" to the ECL. Curiously, although the term "economic law" has generally been applied to contracts that implement the economic plan, the ECL also encompassed transactions *outside* the plan.

The ECL states basic principles and enumerates provisions that all contracts must contain and otherwise provides a general framework for these transactions, including responsibility for breach, which may lead not only to civil but administrative and criminal penalties. The law emphasizes the importance of carrying out the state economic plan, though it also stresses safeguarding "the legal rights of the parties." It provides that if contracts were breached, damages had to be paid, although it also requires specific performance of the contract as well, continuing use of the favored remedy in planned economies. Before the ECL was promulgated, contract disputes could only be mediated by ministerial committees, local economic committees, or the SAIC, or arbitrated by the latter two.[11] The ECL moved contracts into the formal legal domain by providing for adjudication of contract disputes by the People's Courts.

Enactment of the ECL did not settle the debates among officials and scholars about the direction and content of law reform. Contracts could still be used as administrative devices to regulate enterprises, as illustrated by provisions for the certification of contracts at the SAIC and notarization by notaries, whose functions had been revived. Legislation on their activities clearly expressed policy-makers' interest in supervising commercial transactions. Notaries were required to investigate the legal capacity and registration of the contracting parties and to determine if the contract was within their business scope and the authority of the representative, if it complied with the ECL and other relevant regulations, if it was "practical," and if it was made according to the spirit of "equality and mutual benefit." After the contract was signed, notaries were required to provide "frequent field supervision to ensure . . . unfailing performance."[13]

After the ECL was promulgated, laws for specific types of contracts followed, such as those for technology transfer and insurance. As part of the evolving process of creating a framework for foreign investment, the 1985 Foreign Economic Contract Law (FECL) was adopted to cover contracts involving foreign nationals, entities, or organizations[14]; and it has since been augmented by China's adherence to the Vienna Convention on Contracts for the International Sale of Goods.[15] As rules proliferated, debate continued on whether China should adopt a civil code and, if so, what model might be used.

The General Principles of Civil Law (1986) and Revision of the Economic Contract Law (1993)

China moved toward partial codification of civil law when the General Principles of Civil Law (GPCL), a body of rules comparable to the general part of a European civil code, was adopted in 1986.[16] The debate over "civil" and "economic" law was won by the civilians, and a sphere of civil law was recognized. The GPCL is based on the principle that all parties to "commodity" economic transactions enjoy equal status under the law, and the GPCL is intended to apply to their "horizontal" relationships. By virtue of the GPCL, contract and property relations are now formally regulated by the Chinese equivalent of Western "private law," which treats all parties to contracts as independent legal actors.[17] Consistent with this, as will be seen immediately below, the ECL has been modified so that it now applies only to extra-plan contracts.

In form as well as content, the GPCL reflects the intellectual debt that Chinese law and legal theory owe to continental European law.[18] More specifically, it legislates certain basic notions of legal institutions that are the foundation for market-economy transactions, namely contract, legal persons, and property rights. The GPCL begins by defining all those natural and legal "persons" with legal rights. As William Jones has stated, by identifying these parties as entities entitled to legal protection, the drafters of the GPCL made a political statement that recognized the economic activities in which they were engaged.[19] The GPCL then articulates the "acts" that create, modify, or terminate legal rights and subsequently defines property rights.

Ownership is defined as "an owner's right in accordance with law to possess, use, benefit from and dispose of his own property."[20] Under this definition "in China as elsewhere, ownership is necessarily a composite of a range of potentially discrete and severable rights in property."[21] The following specific property rights are governed by the GPCL:

rights of neighboring users of land;

rights to use and obtain benefits from state-owned land and other natural resources;

rights to mine state-owned mineral resources;

rights to operate state-owned land under collective responsibility contracts;

rights to operate state enterprises.

Despite its undeniable utility in beginning to fill a vacuum, the scheme is also notable for its generality and incompleteness. For example, the GPCL recognized the basic rights created by responsibility contracts—a major vehicle of the rural reforms—under which peasant households could use land in return for payment in kind or cash, but it did not address specific rights and duties under this system that have been largely handled by other legislation.[22]

Although it created a discrete legal domain, the GPCL was a compromise between the two schools of thought that had contested for theoretical dominance. Having defined basic legal relationships, the drafters did not follow the German model by creating "special parts" to regulate specific types of transactions such as contracts.[23] It is, therefore, not a comprehensive civil code, but rather is like the first half of a German-type legal code. It has since been supplemented by separate pieces of legislation devoted to types of transactions or areas of the law that it does not address directly. By codifying the principles of legal personality and defining basic concepts of ownership and property rights, it supplied a foundation for further elaboration of the various branches of law required for a market economy.[24] Along with the decline of the state sector of the economy, the debate between the "civil law" and "economic law" schools has receded from view.

The extent of the retreat from economic planning was carried further, first by revision of the ECL in 1993 and, much more definitively, by enactment in 1999 of a comprehensive contract law, which is discussed below.[25] The 1993 revision removed all references to the economic plan from the ECL, such as one that had linked economic contracts to fulfillment of the plan and another that had exempted parties from liability for nonperformance caused by changes in the plan. The revision also broadened the definition of parties to contracts, referring to a range from individual businessmen to legal persons and including them all as "equal legal subjects."[26] Article 5 required parties to "abide by the principles of equality and mutual benefit and of achieving agreement through consultation." The 1981 ECL had included a requirement of "compensation for equal value" as a necessary element of a valid contract, but this requirement was dropped, perhaps because courts had used this last phrase in the old law to overturn price terms for unfairness even though they had been freely negotiated.[27]

The Contract Law of 1999

The Contract Law of the People's Republic of China was enacted by the NPC in March 1999 after a lengthy drafting process.[28] It is noteworthy because it further redefines the doctrinal contours of the laws that are being developed to undergird a marketizing economy. It codifies contract law by elaborating on the principles of the GPCL, beginning with general principles and then articulating rules that apply to fifteen specific types of contracts including sales, loans, leases, and construction. It repeals and replaces the ECL, the Foreign Economic Contract Law and the Technology Contract Law.

The general provisions cover such over-arching topics as contract formation, and in this regard vary notably from the Foreign Economic Contract Law in not setting down rigid requirements for validity. Parties to contracts are "individual citizens, legal persons, or other organizations who are equal subjects" (Art. 2). Other principles govern such matters as offer and acceptance, the capacity of the signatories, and transfer of contractual obligations. State planning did not, of course, disappear, but references to it are minimal; the essential provision states that when the state has "in light of its needs" issued "mandatory plans or purchase plans" to enterprises, contracts flowing from such plans must be consistent with "relevant laws and administrative regulations" (Art. 38). The state remains a visible hand elsewhere, too, since the Law also states that contracts must comply with approvals or registration required by other laws (Art. 44).

Damages are specifically provided for: The parties may provide for liquidated damages, a remedy that had not been authorized by the ECL, and those may be calculated in a manner similar to that employed under the Foreign Economic Contract Law, which permits anticipated profit to be included. Parties may petition courts or arbitration organizations for specific performance, but grounds for denial have been specified, marking a further departure from the prior dominance of this remedy. Specific performance can be denied if it is impossible as a matter of fact or law; if "it is not difficult" to obtain the subject matter of the contract on the market; if the subject matter of the contract is "unfit" for the remedy or the cost would be "excessive"; or if such performance has not been demanded within a reasonable time (Art. 110). *Force majeure* has been defined as "objective circumstances that are unforeseeable, unavoidable, and insurmountable" (Art. 117). Consistent with existing legislation, the Contract Law provides that disputants should first attempt to settle disputes

through mediation and failing that, through arbitration; litigation is authorized only if the parties do not have a valid arbitration agreement (Art.
128).

The Contract Law unifies the rules applicable to contract that previously were classified as "civil" or "economic," domestic or foreign-related,
under laws that have now been repealed. It appears to give greater recognition to freedom of contract than prior legislation, as in setting forth
rules on offer and acceptance and allowing rescission in a less restrictive
manner than was provided for in the ECL. It attempts to enlarge protection for creditors' rights, for example, by allowing unilateral termination
when a debtor is unable to fulfill its obligations.

The Contract Law, then, represents a further step forward in the attempts of China's law drafters to establish legal institutions that are more
compatible with a market rather than with a planned economy. Moreover,
its structure and concepts reflect heavy Western influence, as in its importation of rules consistent with the Convention on the International Sale of
Goods. Practice under the law will henceforth determine the extent to
which it can stimulate reliance on the legal rules underlying the law of
contract. How quickly such a new law can change the mentalities of economic actors, judges, and administrators is yet a different issue. While the
Law was being prepared, one of the draftsmen told me in private conversation that the process had been long delayed because of indecision among
the drafters about the extent to which the draft should promote freedom
of contract. As the next section will show, other institutional changes will
have to follow adoption of unified contract legislation.

The Contract: Expression of Party Autonomy or Instrument of Management?

More than a trace of the mentality of the pre-reform planned economy
remained in the ECL after its revision in 1993. It provided, for example,
that even if contracts stipulated monetary penalties for breach, the party
damaged by breach could require the breaching party to perform the contract in addition to paying the stipulated penalty.[29] This provision, retained
from the original ECL, reflected the planned economy's emphasis on specific performance of contracts. In a second example, although the 1993 revision changed an original ECL provision that excused a party for breach if it
was caused by a change in the state plan, an act of *force majeure* (*buke kangli*)
could serve as an excuse. It has rightly been pointed out that the Chinese
doctrine of *force majeure* is ambiguous, that actions of state agencies could
still be comprehended under that doctrine, and that enterprises and ministries could still collude to use it to relieve enterprises of their obligations.[30]

The rule on specific performance has been changed by the Contract

Law of 1999, as discussed above, and the spirit of the Law, anyway, arguably discourages the invocation of changes in the state plan to excuse breach of contract. A more profound tension suggests the existence of continuing ambiguity among certain elements of the Party-state about core concepts of market-oriented "private" law. In administering the planned economy, "managing" contracts was emphasized to ensure that enterprises would carry out their plan-imposed obligations, and this concern has survived into the reform era. Early in the 1980s, the State Administration of Industry and Commerce was given responsibility for "contract supervision," which was expressed in the original ECL along with "inspection."[31] Although "inspection" was omitted from the revised ECL, "supervision" was retained, as was a system of arbitrating contract disputes that has now been replaced by local Arbitration Commissions.[32] In the course of carrying out its "supervision" functions, the SAIC has from time to time issued notices intended to attack fraud in economic contracts.[33]

Other systems, little noticed in the West, have also been introduced that in practice could permit considerable government interference with contracts. In 1990, for example, the State Council Office issued a notice on promoting the use of contract forms in all "economic contracts";[34] the SAIC then issued an opinion specifying that such contract forms could only be printed by designated printers.[35] The system was still in use six years later, when the SAIC issued a notice aimed at the use of contracts in transactions involving fraud.[36] Local bureaus were instructed not only to ascertain the authority of the parties and the validity of permits and other plan-related documentation, but to determine that the parties were using only authorized contract forms and to certify the contracts.

These regulations have a broad reach. They apply to contracts that are outside the economic plan and, therefore, to transactions involving parties with equal legal status who are acting autonomously.[37] The possible involvement of the SAIC in contract "management" reflects the desire of some officials to retain, in the armories of the state, weapons that can be used to constrain contractual autonomy. This issue is likely to remain , as the Contract Law suggests. During the debates on the draft, the SAIC evidently took the position that it should be able to "supervise and manage" contracts in which one party is a state or collective enterprise and which could injure "state interests,"[38] and the Contract Law of 1999 affirms the responsibility of the SAIC and "other relevant authorities . . . to monitor and deal with any illegal activity which, through the conclusion of a contract, harms the State interests and the public interests" (Art. 127). The scope of private autonomy is likely to remain contested.

Other Commercial Legislation

In related and vital areas, progress has been made toward developing a modern system of commercial credit and commercial law. After some local experiments, the Negotiable Instruments Law (NIL) came into effect in 1995.[39] The NIL sets forth provisions applicable to bills of exchange, promissory notes, and checks, and it generally reflects principles well-known in the West with regard to negotiable paper.[40] At the same time, some current Chinese concerns shape its reach. Although the NIL deals with transactions in which banks participate, it does not deal with promissory notes between private parties, and one study suggests that this reflects the leadership's intention to restrain private transactions.[41]

The PRC Security Law, which became effective in October 1995,[42] created a basis for the development of a uniform system of standard forms of security for the payment of debts. The law applies to guaranties and to four forms of security—namely, mortgages on real property, pledges of movable assets or intangible rights, liens over assets of which the creditor has already taken possession, and deposits of funds. Whether the new law can function as effectively as its drafters hope will depend to a large extent on the energy and efficiency with which it is implemented. Under the law, for example, all mortgages must be registered before they can be effective against third parties. Local governments must establish and maintain a uniform countrywide registration system to make mortgages effective devices to encourage expansion of credit. The difficulty of maintaining consistency in implementing other rules suggests that this can be achieved only with some difficulty.

PROPERTY: LAND

After two decades China's economic reforms were successful without stabilizing property rights. Uncertainties over the definition and security of property rights in TVEs, for example, are clearly apparent. At the same time, recent legislation reflects recognition of a need to define and protect property rights if they are to provide a firm underpinning for economic reform. Further recognition of new property relationships and rights derived from them was expressed in an amendment to the Chinese Constitution adopted by the NPC in early 1999. The non-public sector of the economy, formerly characterized as a "complement to the socialist public economy," was newly designated as an "important component" of the socialist public economy.[43] I have noted below several major achievements and continuing uncertainties.

China's evolving land law is an increasingly complex structure of rules on administration of land, transfer of interests, valuation, and other matters that flow from the creation of property interests where none of any significance existed prior to reform. Here, as with contracts, the GPCL established a conceptual framework out of which have been evolving more detailed rules on land use rights. Before 1988, all land was owned by the state or by collectives. The right to use is one of the four basic rights recognized by the definition of ownership rights in the GPCL (the others are rights to possess, to benefit, and to dispose).[44] In practice, however, the system is focused on the right to use rather than on ownership of the land itself, and the drafters have thereby avoided abandoning the Marxist principle of state ownership. Under the current system, the governmental agencies administering most of the land in the PRC since the 1960s have been granting transferable land-use rights in exchange for land-use fees, in arrangements conceptually similar to the lease of real estate in the West. Even the principle of the theoretical inalienability of the land itself is "in some respects . . . analogous" to ownership by the crown in England, where the rights in a piece of property "may be only nominally inferior to ownership."[45]

Legislation adopted in 1990 established a distinction between rural and urban land;[46] rural land was to remain under the ownership and control of collectives for agricultural use and was in principle not subject to commercial transactions. Since then, rights to use rural land have been broadened. In 1993 the CCP Central Committee issued a decision that permitted peasants to obtain rights for as long as thirty years after the expiration of any rights obtained under an earlier decision, one which had permitted peasants to hold rights of use in land granted them by collectives for fifteen years. Experiments have also been conducted in using auctions and negotiations to grant rights and to develop uncultivated but reclaimable land that is classified as "wasteland."[47]

Urban land can be placed in commerce provided it fulfills certain conditions. Urban land-use rights are either "allocated" (acquired without any payment) or "granted" (acquired for value); granted land-use rights can be transferred, sold, leased, or mortgaged provided that they have been the subject of a land-use rights contract between the local Land Administration Bureau and a grantee who has paid a fee in full. The term of use may be as long as seventy years, depending on the type of use involved, and subsequent transfers will be valid only for the period of time remaining under the original grant contract. At the moment, the extent and definition of these rights are so uncertain that little can be conjectured about the fate of an investment in urban land once the term of use has expired. "Allocated" land-use rights may be converted into "granted" use rights by payment of a grant fee. Subsequent legislation has added further detail to this basic system.[48]

These new laws have been supplemented by additional legislation specifically addressed to urban real estate. Statutes have defined urban housing ownership, authorized housing development companies, established registration and recordation of property titles, and regulated the sale and transfer of housing rights including the advance sale (i.e., before construction) of such housing.[49] Although these rules exhibit the leadership's continuing concern to exercise administrative control over the use, transfer, and price of land-use rights, they nonetheless create and define the outlines of an urban real estate market that did not exist before the 1980s. This, however, is only the beginning. William Soileau notes that "statistical indicators of ownership and investment indicate that these policies [of vesting property rights in urban real property] have enjoyed some success, but that public ownership and control of urban public housing still predominates by far."[50] Soileau emphasizes that Chinese policy-makers in this field are constantly faced with problems caused by vague and general legislation and by the lack of administrative resources, expertise, and will to implement legislation. He argues that further development of mortgage rights is needed to promote public housing reform, but that enhanced mortgage rights require further changes such as granting independence to lenders and devising accurate property valuation methods. Comprehensive progress is needed in all areas of the law to make urban real property law workable: "In short, property rights reform ultimately depends upon the institution of the rule of law in all relations impinging upon the exercise of those rights."[51] Progress toward this goal can only be piecemeal and slow, but some encouragement can be taken from the gradual addition of more specific legislation to the legislative scheme, such as a recently established nationwide and uniform land registration system and amendments to an earlier land administration law intended to protect arable land.[52]

LEGAL PERSONS GENERALLY; COMPANY LAW

When the GPCL partially codified principles of legal personality and partially defined ownership and property rights,[53] it thereby established the rights of natural and some legal persons to enjoy property. It defined new lawful property holders, the private entity known as the "individual industrial-commercial household," which confirmed an innovation already in practice. The law on legal persons has continued to expand since they were first defined in the GPCL, and, apart from foreign-invested enterprises (discussed separately), Chinese law recognizes the forms of business described below.

Private Enterprises

Under regulations promulgated in 1988,[54] private enterprises that employ eight or more persons whose property is privately owned can be sole proprietorships (owned by one person with unlimited liability), partnerships (owned by two or more owners whose liability is joint and unlimited), or limited liability companies (with two to thirty owners whose liability is limited). Sole proprietorships may not have more than eight employees, only certain classes of persons may operate them, and they are regulated closely by the SAIC.[55] However, only the limited liability company is a legal person, while the owners are the legal representatives of the other two forms. These forms of business organization may operate autonomously within the scope of business approved when they registered, although limitations are imposed by law on managerial salaries and on profit distribution.

The GPCL provided for partnerships in only a preliminary and general manner.[56] Although partnerships had to be evidenced by written agreements, there was no express requirement that they register with any government agency. The law on partnership enterprises promulgated in 1997[57] is more comprehensive than the previous skeletal legislation. It adds considerable certainty to the rules, specifying the matters that must be addressed by partnership agreements and stating procedures for dissolution of partnerships. Noteworthy, once again, is the impulse to regulate private economic activity. The law requires that all partnerships register as a prerequisite for carrying out their business activities, and it contains other clauses that caused one commentator to describe it as a "rigid structure peppered with mandatory provisions."[58] Moreover, in a pattern common to Chinese legislation, the law uses numerous general terms to express vague legal standards, such as requiring that partnerships be based on "principles of voluntariness, equality, fairness and good faith," which would seem to permit administrative or judicial determinations as to whether those principles had been respected in a particular partnership (Art. 4).

Collectively Owned Enterprises

Collectives were recognized long before the reforms, but have been adapted to a reforming economy. The starting point was the simple fact that the central government exercised less control over collectives than over SOEs because collectives, which were outside the economic plan, were locally controlled. Considerable experimentation has been crystallized in a succession of regulations on both rural and urban collectives[59] that provide for the establishment, registration, management, operation, and termination of these forms of business organization. In urban collectives a workers' assembly seems to exercise ownership rights, while in rural collectives the powers of the peasants' collective are not as well defined.[60]

Ownership patterns and structures of these collectives vary so much that it is difficult to generalize about them. Some rural collectives are entirely private. In others, as I already noted in chapter 5, local governments may be large investors, an arrangement that may be formalized by village or township ownership of a considerable percentage, if not a majority, of shares. In still others, shares may also be owned by other economic units, including state enterprises. The variations are so extensive that it is sometimes difficult to determine the extent of public or private ownership. In assessing these entities, outside observers seem to be divided on their strengths and weaknesses: some stress government interference and poorly defined property rights, others regard them as functional equivalents of profit-conscious Western corporations.[61] In practice, they seem to combine strong managers with worker participation.

The central Party-state has become "well aware that clearly defined ownership rights will be a major factor in the further development" of rural enterprises,[62] and in 1997 a new law on "town and township enterprises" attempted to clarify ownership rights, limit the power of local governments to exact fees, and define the obligations of rural entrepreneurs regarding land use, pollution control, counterfeiting of goods, and product quality.[63] The law attempts further to separate local enterprises from local governments, by requiring that enterprises establish an independent accounting system. As with all new Chinese laws purporting to regulate an area of economic activity marked by a lack of clarity in the rights of enterprises and local governments, the future effectiveness of the law on rural enterprises cannot be predicted.

State-Owned Enterprises

The troubled state of SOEs, already mentioned, will not be pursued here. An attempt was made to give autonomy to SOEs by a law enacted in 1988 that purported to allow them to control their assets and to give managers stronger directing roles.[64] Little effective change occurred. Because the law was ambiguous, SOEs remained dependent on soft budget constraints and susceptible to administrative intervention in their management. Additional regulations that were promulgated in 1992 and 1994 illustrated a trend "toward a supervisory role as opposed to involvement in the day-to-day affairs of the SOE."[65] Corporatization became the chosen route of reform. At the end of 1993, after experiments had begun with stock exchanges in Shenzhen and Shanghai and several provincial company laws had been enacted, the current Company Law was adopted.[66]

The Company Law authorized the formation of two types of companies, the limited liability company and the company limited by shares. Although the two types differ as to minimum capitalization, complexity of governance structure, and transferability of shares (in any event, workers' shares are nontransferable outside the enterprise), they exhibit common characteristics. Management decisions are reached by means of the shareholders' meeting, the chairman of the board, a specific manager, and a supervisory board. The powers of the shareholders' meeting go beyond those of American shareholders. According to one American scholar of corporate law, "given the concern about managerial asset stripping, it is surprising that the Company Law constraints on managerial self-dealing are as brief and vague as they are."[67] At the same time, the power of the shareholders is limited, since by virtue of state ownership of the majority of shares, the power to control the company's direction remains in administrative agencies of the state.[68] Moreover, given the continuing desire of the Chinese leadership to maintain the primacy of state ownership in the SOEs,[69] the silence of the Company Law on such matters as the percentage of ownership that will be reserved by the state and the absence of provisions that could help to settle disputes between private shareholders and the state create potentially disquieting gaps for private investors. It is too early to tell whether the new law will release enterprises from responsibility for the extensive range of non-wage housing and welfare benefits that they have formerly provided to their workers.

It is also too early to predict the extent to which, in practice, wholly owned SOEs, transformed into companies, will be directed by state agencies. Article 67 of the Company Law states that the assets of such a company will be supervised by an authorized government body; thus, as one observer has pointed out, it will be possible to frustrate the supposed purpose of the Company Law, which is to allow companies to make decisions on the basis of economic rather than political factors.[70] This problem—and the many others like it raised by the Company Law—is only emblematic of a much larger and fundamental issue: the question of how much control over state assets the Party-state will be willing to relinquish to market forces. It has long hesitated to decide, and meanwhile, a World Bank study in 1997 called attention to the serious implications of the control over SOEs by insiders, especially managers, who were engaged in extensive asset-stripping by means of various devices: transforming SOEs into other forms of business; using state assets to establish "income-generating" businesses; under- or over-invoicing of transactions with private entities; and other means.[71] The Company Law reflects a continued commitment to state control. One Western scholarly analysis concludes about the Company Law that

it is . . . replete with inconsistencies and odd concepts which are a direct expression of the state's resistance to what has been advertised as the new system: a market economy employing increasingly private capital. Thus, while on its face the Company law promises the creation and organization of a semi-independent group of economic actors, in fact it both expresses and enables continuing state control over the economic and industrial system in China. . . . the state is merely changing the form, but not the substance of economic relationships.[72]

SOEs and Nascent Capital Markets

Parallel with experimentation in corporatizing SOEs, tentative beginnings have been made with securitization and the establishment of capital markets.[73] Local and central government experiments with issuing shares in the mid-1980s led to the emergence of local markets, and, in 1990, stock exchanges were opened in Shenzhen and Shanghai. By 1991 shares had been differentiated between "A" shares denominated in *renminbi* (RMB), which could be held only by Chinese nationals, and "B" shares, restricted to foreigners (and overseas "compatriots") who had to pay foreign currency for them. In 1992 the China Securities Regulatory Commission was established, and the State Council attempted comprehensive regulation of securities markets by delineating the jurisdiction of the national and local authorities that are involved in the issuance and sale of securities. Since then, several further regulations on share issue and trading have been issued by the State Council. However, there seems little reason to doubt the accuracy of one assessment published in late 1997: "The regulatory framework for the secondary market has been quite ineffective. Although national rules and regulations have been in place for some time, they have not been enforced effectively. Consequently, violations of the rules are prevalent in the securities market."[74]

Several institutional factors still need to be resolved in this area of law and administration. Various bodies have tried to assert authority over securities-related issues. The People's Bank of China, the State Planning Commission, the Ministry of Finance, the State Commission for Restructuring the Economy, and the two stock exchanges are only among the most obvious contenders for power over such questions as the selection and approval of SOEs that wish to issue shares and the precise role of government ownership. Chapter 6 has already touched on the inadequacy of delineation between the relative jurisdictions of Chinese legislative and rule-making authorities; these difficulties are particularly problematic in the relatively new field of securities regulation.

The issue of securitization provokes conflicting views. Some view it as a welcome alternative to privatization because it can be used to maintain the precedence of public ownership. At the moment, shares are distinguishable according to their owner: the state, other enterprises or organizations ("legal person" shares), employees of the enterprise ("employee" shares), members of the public, and foreigners. Of all the Shanghai corporations listed at the end of 1992, 62 percent of share value was held by the state, 24 percent by "legal persons" (predominantly other state enterprises), 7 percent by domestic individuals, and 7 percent by foreign capital.[75] Legal person shares, encouraged in 1992 as "a barrier against privatization," led to disappointment because institutional investors had little interest in them. The Shanghai and Shenzhen stock markets did not permit trading in those shares and they threatened to dilute the value of individual shares.[76] In response to the opposition to privatization, some scholars and policy-makers believe that shareholding could be used to separate management from the state, but as we have seen above, the Company Law suggests that the issue of how the state's shareholder rights might be exercised is as yet unresolved.

OTHER EXAMPLES OF THE CREATION OF RIGHTS

Chinese lawmakers have also created new rights and strengthened concepts of existing rights outside the area of contract and commercial law. In the realm of property, for example, one of the principal aims of a 1995 inheritance law is the protection of private rights over property that not long ago would have been considered "means of production" and, therefore, could have only been owned by the state.[77]

Tort liability, too, has been expanding. The GPCL articulated principles of tort responsibility, including product liability, which are now cited in a wide variety of cases before the Chinese courts.[78] A statute enacted for the protection of minors gives them the right to sue parents for violating parental duties or infringing upon their "legitimate" rights.[79] These are but a few illustrations of a willingness to enforce legal duties by empowering claimants to sue for violation of their rights, which is a major departure from Chinese tradition.

ASSESSMENT

The legislation summarized here responds to needs for new legal institutions that have been generated by the economic reforms. It also demonstrates the breadth of those needs and the speed with which Chinese economic development has come to require legal underpinnings. From straddling the growing divide between plan and market, the legislation on contracts has moved to expressing more forthright support of the concept of contracts between formal equals. New rights are being created and new concepts of property and business organization continue to develop, often at an uneven and uncertain pace. At the same time, the Party-state retains enough power to regulate many activities very closely, and the mix of rules that facilitate market relationships is still offset by rules attempting to control what is perceived as harmful economic behavior. The clash between these different viewpoints is likely to cause continuing tensions in the drafting of laws applicable to the nonstate sector.

The future of the SOEs remains unresolved. Among the many questions is how SOE reform will affect the extent to which law will be able to facilitate economic activity. For example, the integrity of market-driven legal rules will be impaired if the SOEs or their descendants remain extensions of the state, subject to different regulations than the nonstate sector. The future of SOEs illustrates a broad issue that has been addressed here in other contexts, such as contract law and the law on partnerships. They all reflect the stamp of the earlier reform-related legislation of the 1980s, which appeared while the state sector of the economy was dominant and the scope of nonstate economic activity had not grown to its present size. In the face of the new—and still changing—configuration of economic institutions, China's leaders and law-makers must decide on the extent to which they will continue to emphasize the regulatory, controlling approach of pre-reform China or will revise their most basic conceptions of the relationship between law and the economy. At the moment, their laws reflect their indecision. Another illustration, bankruptcy law, involves a related issue that is not explored in this book. Bankruptcy remains an issue freighted with intense political significance because of leadership concerns and popular anxiety about unemployment and social unrest that could be caused by large-scale bankruptcies. The state of the Chinese economy will necessarily influence the judgment of the Chinese leadership and their ability to undertake reforms in this and other areas such as banking and finance, as was demonstrated when the slowing of economic growth in 1998 stalled the pace of economic reform.

Creation of a Legal Environment for Foreign Investment

The legal environment for foreign direct investment (FDI) in China that has emerged since 1979 should compel particularly close attention not only by foreigners interested in investment matters but by any observers who wish to understand Chinese legal development. FDI is an arena in which fundamental characteristics and problems of Chinese legal institutions are visible with particular clarity, because many foreigners have experienced and related their encounters with them. I have not attempted here to describe legislation or practice in detail,[80] but have instead distilled major features of law-related FDI issues that are relevant to the emphases of this book.

When the drafters of legislation came to the task of defining and regulating foreign investment, they faced a great vacuum. Foreign direct investment had been unknown in China since the early 1950s. The results of their efforts should become more comprehensible when viewed against the general background of legal development that has already been surveyed.

LEGISLATIVE ACCOMPLISHMENTS

When the Chinese leadership made its unprecedented decision to "open" China to foreign direct investment in 1979, many in the West wondered whether the PRC would be able to erect a credible legal framework that would encourage foreign investors to expect that their investments would be adequately protected under Chinese law. Over the years, Chinese legislators and administrators have indeed created a framework that provides guidance of a general nature to foreign investors and their Chinese counterparts, although the overall investment environment remains marked by considerable day-to-day uncertainty because of changing policies and extensive and often unreviewable bureaucratic discretion.

China's law drafters slowly began to address foreign investment matters with a skeletal law on Sino-foreign joint ventures in 1979 that was followed by implementing regulations in 1983, but they soon picked up speed and have produced a prodigious amount of legislation on many aspects of FDI. Following promulgation of the initial law in 1979, China's Constitution was amended to declare that the lawful rights of foreign investors would be protected by law, and during the 1980s legislation defined the vehicles that could be used for Sino-foreign investment, that is, three different forms of joint venture (the equity joint venture and two forms of contractual joint ventures, one in which a separate legal person was created and another that was in essence a partnership) and the wholly foreign-owned enterprise. Provisions were made for representative offices of foreign corporations not involving investment, while legislation in the 1990s added holding companies and foreign investment in joint stock companies. Taxation of FDI profits was introduced, and special economic zones and economic development zones with tax incentives for investors were created in fourteen coastal cities. China has entered into a number of bilateral investment treaties and acceded to multilateral treaties whose rules have entered into Chinese law, such as the Convention on Contracts for the International Sale of Goods. Legislation also addresses other areas related to foreign investment such as technology transfer contracts, patents and trademarks, labor, customs, foreign exchange, bank lending and guaranties, and export and import licenses, as well as joint venture issues such as approval, capitalization, and debt. Much local legislation has also appeared.

Many gaps and ambiguities persist in FDI legislation, and implementation is not only uneven but often creates additional questions. Nonetheless, the mere creation of this framework is a considerable legislative accomplishment. FDI legislation provides some guidance on many important questions for foreign and Chinese parties negotiating joint venture agreements, although some general characteristics of the Chinese legal environment and Chinese bureaucracies continue to create difficulties.

Reflecting the general Chinese approach to legislation, FDI regulation has been tentative, general, and flexible and has depended on the broad discretion of various agencies regulating foreign investment enterprises (FIEs) for its practical application. All foreign investment projects must be approved by the Ministry of Foreign Trade and Economic Cooperation (MOFTEC) or by delegated agencies under local, provincial, or municipal control. Other agencies, such as those responsible for foreign exchange control, customs, taxation, and labor, may also regulate FIEs.

Laws and regulations on foreign investment, not surprisingly, share important characteristics with other Chinese legislation and administrative rules. FDI regulations are usually drafted in general language and are often followed by incomplete implementation guidelines. Sometimes the rules appear in "tentative" or "provisional" measures, with no indication of when or even if they will become permanent. Bureaucrats exercise considerable discretion in interpreting all of these rules, and foreign investors frequently complain about bureaucratic arbitrariness and the lack of guidance. Local legislation is often inconsistent with national legislation. For example, provincially approved tax incentives for investors have sometimes varied so greatly from national rules that the central government has issued declarations forbidding adoption of local legislation offering incentives more generous than those authorized under national law.[81]

Other difficulties arise from the formalism of the policy-makers' approach to law, treating the texts of promulgated laws as representations of reality. Although rules may be established on paper, in practice little attention may be paid to enforcing them or ensuring uniformity of implementation. The real meaning of any rule turns on policies and the discretion given to the implementing agencies, which often fail to enforce the law. Perhaps the most visible example has been the failure of Chinese officials to enforce Chinese legislation and bilateral U.S.-Chinese agreements on protection of intellectual property.[82]

The major problems encountered by foreign investors stem not from lack of formal legislation but from the combined effect of a number of factors. The legal institutions for FDI are best analyzed in terms of the forces that most significantly affect their operation and meaningfulness— policy, practice, investment contracts, and legal culture.

MAJOR INFLUENCES ON THE LEGAL ENVIRONMENT FOR FDI

Policy Indeterminacy

Just as changes in policy have marked China's uncharted economic reforms generally, policy changes have consistently created uncertainty in the foreign investment environment. The problem attracts particularly keen attention outside China not only because of widespread foreign interest in the Chinese market, but also because of the closeness with which FDI is regulated. In addition to the approval process for investment contracts, FIEs must satisfy requirements set for them with regard to foreign exchange, taxation, labor, and other areas.[83] A small number of examples of significant changes in policy that have affected the expectations of foreign investors are discussed below.[84]

Changes in Favored Investments. From 1979—when the first law on joint ventures was promulgated—until 1986, greater incentives were offered to equity joint ventures than to either contractual joint ventures or wholly foreign-owned enterprises. The 1986 regulations, the "Provisions for the Encouragement of Foreign Investment," classified all FIEs into three categories that differentiated incentives according to the desirability of the proposed investment. The most advantageous incentives were offered in the first category, "export-oriented" and "technologically advanced" enterprises, in the second category were all other "productive" enterprises, and in the third were "non-productive" joint ventures such as hotels. In 1995, new investment guidelines classified projects as "encouraged," "permitted," "restricted," and "discouraged" and added some types of enterprises that had not previously received favorable treatment to the most favored category of the 1986 regulations. Further guidelines were issued in January 1998 that emphasized the importance of employing high technology in order to qualify projects as "encouraged," added high capacity of output to the requirements for "encouraged" projects, and moved some projects to the "restricted" category.[85]

Changes in Taxation Policy. Beginning in 1979 FIEs had been exempt from import duties, but in 1996 imported capital equipment became dutiable. The policy was first announced in mid-1995, but after many foreign investors complained about the added cost of investment that the duty would impose, some official hesitation began to be expressed publicly. The date on which the new policy would come into effect remained in doubt until the latter part of 1995, when April 1, 1996, was finally chosen. This date, however, turned out to be less decisive than might be supposed. Grace periods were announced, during which joint ventures approved before that date could import capital goods duty-free—until December 31, 1996, for joint ventures with total investment under $30 million, and until December 31, 1997, for those with total investment above that figure. The new policy came at a time when purely domestic enterprises were complaining about competition from joint ventures. In late 1996 published reports suggested that the grace period might be extended, once again complicating the need for prospective investors to take tax burdens into account when planning their investments. At about the same time it was also reported that many of the projects that had been approved before April 1 were being reviewed, and that some approvals were being withdrawn by MOFTEC.[86] Yet, some investors were also being told by local authorities that even though their projects had not been approved before April, their joint venture would receive the duty-free treatment that had supposedly been terminated by the central government! On December 31, 1996, the General Administration of Customs announced that projects approved at the local level between October 1, 1995, and April 1, 1996, would receive a six-month extension to June 30, 1997, for projects under $30 million, and to June 30, 1998, for larger projects.[87] Then in December 1997, the State Council promulgated new regulations that restored the duty exemptions for certain classes of "encouraged" investment projects.[88]

Other variations in tax policy have involved VAT. The value-added tax rebate for exports was cut from 17 percent to 9 percent in 1996, a change that reportedly has operated to deter the formation of export-processing ventures, which have been characterized as "the preferred form of much Hong Kong and other Asian investment in China."[89] Faulty coordination among Chinese agencies appeared when an assistant minister of MOFTEC stated in December 1996 that the VAT on exports of FIEs would soon be eliminated, only to be contradicted by officials at the State Tax Administration. More serious has been the gradual imposition of VAT on FIEs after it was announced that their exports would be tax-free.[90]

Uncertainties in Policy Toward Technology Imports. Chinese policy-makers decided to welcome FDI because they hoped that it would be a medium for transferring advanced technology. The high priority of this goal, and the concern that investors might not bring appropriate or advanced technology, prompted the creation of a regulatory scheme under which contracts for technology transfer such as technology licenses must be approved under regulations issued by the State Council, whether or not they involve an investment contract.[91]

Uncertainties in policy toward Chinese importation of technology from abroad have appeared on a number of occasions. According to one report, for example, in March 1996 MOFTEC announced "Provisional Measures for the Administration of Technology Introduction and Equipment Import Trade Work," which apparently relaxed controls on the importation of technology by making technology contracts effective when they were registered rather than after they were approved.[92] It turned out, however, that the new measures are subject to the above-mentioned new Regulations, which require approval, and which have greater authority than the Measures because they were issued by the State Council rather than a ministry—another illustration of the lack of coordination among rule-making agencies.

The same report told of disagreements within MOFTEC over basic policy. In the past, for example, when contracts for technology transfer were negotiated, MOFTEC was sometimes willing to accommodate licensers by approving contracts with clauses stipulating that products manufactured by joint ventures using the imported technology could not be exported. MOFTEC officials now apparently want to restrict approval of such clauses. Basic uncertainty within MOFTEC has been reported over tightening the controls on technology import contracts as well.

This uncertainty over technology policy may prove to be an issue of minor importance, but it symbolizes the kinds of variations in policy that create investor uncertainty. Furthermore, the lack of transparency in Chinese policy implementation means that foreign investors must keep on the alert for hints and signs of developments that often do not rise above gossip but may be, nonetheless, the most reliable portents of policy available.

Policy: The Most Important Extra-Legal Factor. Changes in investment policy are understandable, given the novelty of FDI in China. Encouragement of FDI is a component of an overall economic program that has been improvised from its inception and continues to be improvised. To be fair, some government actions have been intended as responses to investor attitudes and complaints. This was true of the 1986 regulations mentioned above, which embodied attempts by the Chinese government to respond to criticisms of the inadequacy of the legal framework put in place by that time, disappointments of investors caused by inconvertibility of the Chinese *yuan*, and frustrations caused by local bureaucratic arbitrariness. In addition, though, and transcending foreign investment matters, broader cycles of "reform, overheating and retrenchment" in the economy at large have necessarily affected policies toward that area of economic activity.[93] Since ad hoc changes in the reforms are likely to continue, changes in policy, with varying effects on the content and implementation of laws and regulations related to FDI, are bound to occur.

FDI in Practice

The next major influence on the investment environment is practice, which is difficult to ascertain and not uniform throughout the country. A report on conditions in Shanghai in 1994 stated:

there is no distinction between official policy and officials' references. . . . Lawyers report that when they contact the tax bureau to ask about changes in the law . . . they are advised to consult the bureau's consulting company [for a substantial fee]. . . . In the absence of laws, there are rules and then clarifications. And because these often appear contradictory to confused foreign businessmen, it seems that there are no rules at all, just the arbitrary interpretation or whim of the official asked.[94]

A number of illustrations may be helpful to show the difficulties caused by uncertainties and variations in practice.

Internal Regulations. At the time FDI first appeared on the legislative landscape, policy toward law was just beginning to emerge from its Maoist coma. The National People's Congress had barely begun to meet regularly again, law was no more than a *post hoc* expression of policies, and its implementation was just as flexible. A standard feature of Chinese governance, mentioned earlier, has long been the use of secret directives or regulations, addressed principally to officials charged with implementation. Throughout much of the 1980s, foreign investors and their lawyers constantly encountered problems in negotiations caused when their Chinese counterparts or their superiors claimed that a particular position on an issue of importance to the parties' cooperation was required by an internal directive that could not be shown to foreigners.

One example of this problem was a secret limit on the percentage of registered capital of an FDI project in the form of technology. In another example, for several years during the early 1980s Chinese negotiators told foreigners that foreign investors had to invest a minimum amount of cash as capital, which varied according to the total investment of the joint venture.

Toward the end of the 1980s, central government officials concerned with legislative drafting indicated that China would rely less on internal regulations, and it does appear that some steps have been taken toward greater transparency. The problem has certainly not disappeared, however; Pitman Potter observed that "[internal regulations] remain an important yet invisible component of the regulatory system. Foreign investors face the quandary of being told that regulations prohibit certain activities, but then being refused access to those regulations."[95]

Application of Rules by Analogy. Another aspect of the incompleteness of the legislative framework for FDI has been the need to apply legislation by analogy. For example, from 1979 to 1995, in the absence of implementing rules to spell out sparse reference in legislation to cooperative joint ventures, the rules applicable to equity joint ventures were applied by analogy.

Formalism. Formalism in Chinese legislative practice has already been mentioned as a problem; the difficulties it may cause for FDI are illustrated by an example of how a formally promulgated rule may have little practical effect if the means to implement it are not created. In the mid-1980s, in response to investor concern, a new rule was promulgated that would enable joint ventures to alleviate foreign exchange shortages—they were allowed to sell "urgently needed" products for foreign exchange on the domestic market. In practice this rule never became meaningfully effective because Chinese buyers had to have administrative allocations of foreign exchange, which were not made available in any greater amount after the rule became effective. Also, local authorities were reluctant to approve the sale of products that competed with Chinese products, and the FIEs could only be paid in non-convertible currency.[96]

Uncertainties Resulting from Decentralization. More difficult for investors are the uncertainties that result from the decentralization of bureaucratic power which has encouraged provinces and lower-level localities to adopt practices that are often different from those mandated by legislation promulgated in Beijing. One prime example throughout the 1980s involved the "balancing" of the foreign exchange of joint ventures. When FDI policies were first developed, the Chinese leadership made it clear that each joint venture had to earn its own foreign exchange and could expect no assistance from any government agency to convert RMB earned on the domestic market. Thus, most joint ventures would have to earn all the foreign exchange they needed through exports, which was often impossible. The implementing regulations for the joint venture law promulgated in 1983 stipulated that provincial or local governments could aid joint ventures to resolve their foreign exchange imbalances if they had been approved to sell their goods on the domestic market. No more specific guidance than this was contained in the law or elsewhere. Such assistance was rarely given, and any that was given was provided on an ad hoc basis that was usually not very public.

A different source of inconsistency in policy implementation arises not from failure to exercise discretion, but from use of discretion as part of a strategy devised at the local level to take advantage of the central government's inability to review every joint venture. For example, under Chinese law, the appropriate agency for granting approval of a joint venture contract varies according to the amount of total registered capital.

MOFTEC in Beijing must approve all projects involving over $30 million; provinces, autonomous cities, coastal cities, and Special Economic Zones (SEZs) are allowed to approve joint ventures involving $30 million or less; and other provinces and major cities are allowed to approve projects of up to $10 million. In order to evade these limits, Chinese partners and local investment authorities frequently attempt to divide a contemplated project into stages, so that the investment for each stage falls beneath the permitted ceiling. The local desire to act as autonomously as possible creates an area of potential uncertainty about the consequences if the subterfuge should be discovered in Beijing.

Another example of localism is the frequent desire of local Chinese partners, with or without the cooperation of local officials, to conceal the fact that they are undervaluing state-owned assets that are being contributed to a joint venture in order to induce foreigners to invest. Concerned with the loss of assets involved, the central government established assets valuation agencies all over the country whose involvement in the approval process for joint ventures is required by law.[97]

An excellent example of the dynamics of central-local relations is provided by the confusion over licensing of FIEs to conduct retail operations. Until 1992, foreigners were not permitted to invest in Chinese retail enterprises, but in that year the State Council issued a decision (the 1992 Reply) that provided that "one or two joint venture retail enterprises" would be allowed "on an experimental basis" in six named cities and in the five SEZs. Each enterprise would have to be approved by the State Council after it had been qualified by the Ministry of Internal Trade.[98] Many foreigners, especially Hong Kong Chinese, were attracted by the prospect of investing in retail sales on the huge Chinese domestic market. By 1995 it was common knowledge that in Shanghai alone the number of retail joint ventures approved had exceeded the limit set by the 1992 Reply, and that in one northern province alone approximately ten had already been established. In none of these cases had the requisite State Council approval been obtained. Informal discussions with MOFTEC personnel at the time suggested that retail joint ventures were being established all over China in disregard of the State Council's policy and that no official action would be taken to stop evasion of the policy, which had continued on a significant scale.[99] The State Council came to think otherwise, however. It conducted a review of "non-experimental commercial businesses involving foreign investment" in late 1997, and a year later new measures were ordered, requiring all Sino-foreign foreign-invested retail enterprises in which foreign investors had majority ownership to be "reorganized" in order to render Chinese partners the majority owners.[100]

Localities disregard central policies so extensively that Article 14 of the

1995 investment guidelines was specifically aimed at punishing local officials who approve projects inconsistent with national laws and policies.
Chinese and foreign investors who, knowingly or otherwise, rely on assur-
ances from local approval authorities risk having their joint venture declared illegal and their contract to establish the venture invalid. The danger has apparently not deterred many investors or their local counterparts.

Contract

A third element of major importance in the legal environment for FDI
is the contract to establish the joint venture. Because the foreign investor
lacks control over both policy and practice, the contract remains the principal instrument for stabilizing his expectations about the operation of the
FIE in which he proposes to invest. Given the variations in policy and the
large amount of discretion available to local officials, the foreigner is well
advised to draft and negotiate a carefully drawn contract that addresses in
detail such matters as the markets on which the FIE will sell its products,
management and control, technology transfer, staffing, the number and re-
cruitment of workers and staff, wages and benefits, exit by the partners,
criteria for dissolution and liquidation of the FIE, and dispute settlement.

In view of the forces operating to vary contract and laws alike, it is cu-
rious that some foreign observers caution businesses not to take contracts
too seriously. The Centre for International Business and Management at
Cambridge University, after studying over sixty Sino-foreign joint ventures, suggested that foreign investors should "rely less on the legal rights
embodied in equity and contracts than they would in a western context.
Legal [sic] contracts *tend to have a negative connotation* in China."[101] It is
true that in the Chinese investment environment, expectations created by
contracts are not as secure as they would be in a Western legal environment. Some characteristics of the Chinese system may make it arduous to
achieve agreement on such contracts; nevertheless, it would be ill-advised
to assume that there is something "negative" in China about carefully negotiated and well-drafted contracts.

Not One China but Many

Local powers are considerable and growing, regional differences are
substantial, and sophistication and experiences vary widely around the
country. The Chinese "system" is hierarchical, and higher-level authorities
can crucially shape or thwart the plans of lower-level counterparts. At the
same time, China was never so authoritarian that orders issued from
higher levels were always obeyed. Thus, as I have already suggested, lower
levels hide information from their superiors. Since this problem extends
throughout the entire system, negotiations for a joint venture at any given

level of government, for example, will most likely be subject to uncertainties caused by bureaucrats at that and other levels who may not agree or may not even tell each other the truth. The foreigner may have to engage in contacts up and down the hierarchy, while maintaining the best possible relations with those authorities he will deal with most frequently after the joint venture is up and running.

In addition, the "system" is cellular, with different organizations at the same level keeping information from others and pursuing their own agendas without mutual consultation. Agreement among these bodies often requires much time and effort, and this factor more than anything causes the delays in negotiations that foreigners have often believed were designed to make them impatient and, therefore, careless. Other complications are created by the frequent disunity among Chinese counterparts, especially if the Chinese joint venture partner is itself a joint venture or an amalgamation of a number of Chinese enterprises. Not only may Chinese and foreigners have very different basic ideas about how to run a business, but serious differences of opinion between older and younger managers may plague the Chinese side. The foreigner can only try his best to ascertain the various interests and differing views on the other side of the table.

Negotiation and implementation of the contract are themselves subject to the impact of Chinese legal culture. James Feinerman concludes that although the legal infrastructure for foreign investment continues to become more complex, "Chinese conceptions of contract are a good deal more flexible than those shared by most investors from the developed countries of the industrial world."[102] The dynamics of relations between Chinese and foreign investors are a rich source of thought-provoking material for research on differences between Chinese and foreign views of contract and law. The observations here present aspects of legal institution-building in the foreign investment area that resonate with the purely domestic institutions discussed in this chapter.

Legal Culture

Foreign investors may have more power to determine the content of contractual obligations than to affect Chinese law, policy, or practice; however, contractual negotiations with their Chinese counterparts are inevitably shaped by strong cultural attitudes on both sides toward contracts and the rights and duties created by contracts.

Differing Timetables. Foreigners used to think that their Chinese counterparts acted as if they had infinite patience, and indeed in Sino-Western negotiations some years ago Westerners, especially Americans, frequently became frustrated, even furious, at time-consuming negotiations while the Chinese seemed unperturbed by the amount of time that was being expended. In recent years, however, the positions have been reversed. It is often the Chinese, especially at the lowest levels, who are anxious to sign the contract and have it approved before policies change or other uncertainties frustrate their plans. They may be concerned to consummate the transaction before the economy slows down. They also may believe that foreigners don't and won't understand their system and are pressed to invest in China, and therefore ought to negotiate quickly even if in ignorance.

Differing Views of the Function of the Contract. Western investors usually view the investment contract as a charter and a constitution for their joint venture. Chinese, on the other hand, often seem to consider the contract as a form to be filled out—in part because they usually insist on using as the discussion draft a model contract issued by the predecessor of MOFTEC in the early 1980s. Negotiations often take on a pattern marked by the foreigner's attempts to embellish and clarify the badly drafted form with varying degrees of success.

Regardless of whose draft the parties begin with, the contract that they will finally sign, together with Chinese law, constitutes a framework or cage within which the FIE must operate. The conventional foreign approach is to try to use the contract as the device that adjusts the dimensions of the cage. The Chinese side and Overseas Chinese intermediaries may, however, believe that the cage can be unlocked by a key which they alone possess. That key is represented by relationships with important individuals, such as officials high in the local—provincial or city—governments within whose jurisdiction the FIE is to be established.

Foreign investors have discovered that these two approaches must be reconciled. The investor must determine that the project is consistent with law and policy. In addition, the project must be economically feasible. A feasibility study jointly conducted by the parties must be attached to the contract when it is submitted for approval, and the foreign investor should participate actively in its preparation. It is impossible to overestimate the importance of a good feasibility study. Local officials and the State Administration of Exchange Control may take the projections of the feasibility study as predictions expressing obligations that the FIE must fulfill, such as to export products. More fundamentally, joint preparation of the feasibility study should require the parties to expose their assumptions and expectations about the proposed joint venture, and to identify potentially dangerous misunderstandings.

Differing Attitudes Toward Interpretation of the Contract. Regardless of how the parties arrive at a final joint venture contract, once the FIE has been established the parties are likely to discover that some of the assumptions, habits, and attitudes they have toward their joint investment and toward business relations in general differ considerably. For example, Westerners like to think that the contract both definitively disposes of some issues and predicts how differences between the parties or other problems will be handled by the parties. Chinese may place more value on the general obligations to cooperate, of which the contract may be regarded as only an incomplete expression of the first stage in ongoing negotiations to establish long-term relationships that transcend the contract. As a consequence, very general expressions of the foreign party's intentions or hopes, such as those expressed in a "whereas" clause at the beginning of the contract, are often taken by the Chinese side to mean the creation of obligations rather than general expectations. The Chinese, in other words, may place the contract in a larger relational context—although they are fully capable of interpreting the contract legalistically when it suits them. Moreover, the Chinese party to a contract may view the agreement as implying that it is subject to continued modification in the light of changed circumstances, while the foreign partner may view the contract as affording guidance to the parties on how to cope with specifically identified problems.

The Current Crisis of Values in China. Legal culture is bound to reflect the profound cultural crisis that China is experiencing today. As noted earlier, traditional values as well as those associated with Chinese Communism are threatened by the effects of the economic reforms. With socialism and the old ideology dead and the legitimacy of the CCP fading—at least in the cities—there is no value system to replace the old one. Corruption and bribery are extensive and growing. Although over the last fifteen years the formal legal framework for foreign investment has increased the predictability of investment transactions, the moral vacuum encourages opportunistic behavior.

Assessment

The legal institutions that China has created to define and regulate foreign investment share problems similar to those that are found in other Chinese legal institutions. Variations in policy, the extensive discretion that officials outside Beijing exercise in implementing centrally decided policies and centrally promulgated laws, and a lack of transparency in the system are among the most notable characteristics of the foreign investment environment that present problems for foreign investors.

Although difficulties have not prevented foreigners from investing in China on a large scale, by 1999 some foreign investors were beginning to reassess China. China's economic growth slowed, the Asian economic cri-

sis reduced investment from the rest of Asia to China, and some disen-
chantment set in among foreign investors.[103] There seemed to be some objective reasons to wilt the prior optimism of some Hong Kong businessmen and Westerners, who earlier had frequently looked beyond legal issues to the overall accomplishments of reform to date and the momentum
of forces for market capitalism that reform has unleashed.[104] Indeed, at the
end of 1998 a well-known Chinese financial institution, the Guangdong
International Trust and Investment Company (GITIC), defaulted on well
over $1 billion of loans from foreign bankers. The central government
showed no inclination to come forward to make good on the loans, to the
consternation of the Western bankers.[105] The problem illustrated the unfortunate confluence of Chinese hunger for foreign capital and the bad
judgment of the bankers, who had relied on handshakes and "letters of
comfort" that lacked the legal significance of a formal bank guarantee
properly registered with the central government according to Chinese
law. Other provincial institutions like GITIC were also reported to be in
trouble, and it was likely that many loans to these other floundering bor-
rowers similarly lacked proper guarantees. These problems threatened to
fuel foreign investors' disappointment.

Regardless of changes in foreign images of China from time to time,
the issues discussed here present genuine problems for foreign investors,
and not only because they bear the latter's hopes of receiving adequate
protection under Chinese law. The future path of economic reform remains uncharted, some Chinese ambivalence toward foreign investment is
evident, basic contradictions exist between a market economy and the intentions of the ruling Party to maintain control, and the power of China's
central government was sure to be less at the millennium than at the beginning of the previous decade. These are all forces that could converge
unpleasantly to hamper foreign investment and endanger the legality and
stability that have been attained so far.

Controlling Administrative Arbitrariness by Law

This section surveys the institutions of Chinese administrative law that
have grown out of the reform. Chinese legal reformers have been groping toward using legal institutions to control the exercise of power by
government agencies, a different function from using law to define economic actors and transactions but no less critical to the development of a
marketized economy.

Reform must overcome decades of the absolute supremacy of the
Party-state bureaucracies, during which citizen protest against administrative arbitrariness had few regularized channels. Both before and since re-

form, citizens could complain personally or in letters to administrative authorities, or they could invite the attention of the press to abuses. Such tactics pit complainants directly against the bureaucracy. The task is made more difficult, too, by the continued existence of an administrative apparatus that directs the planned sector of the economy.

The Chinese leadership has recognized the need to control bureaucratic arbitrariness, despite ideological barriers and decades of practice. As already noted in chapter 5, it has also come to accept that nonstate economic activity is hampered by government interference. The lawlessness of much of the Maoist period, especially during the Cultural Revolution, emphasized for the leadership the need to control arbitrary officials. A field of administrative law has begun to emerge. Its scope, however, remains limited and its enemies many, because Party policy continues to hinder development of the rule of law and too many bureaucrats prize their power.

The discussion of the allocation and implementation of law-making activity in chapter 6 noted the generality with which Chinese legislation is drafted and the broad rule-making authority of administrative agencies. The courts' lack of power to interpret laws and rules has also been noted in earlier discussion. It must be recalled here that Chinese law does not formally deal with judicial interpretation of administrative rule-making, unlike administrative law in the West. In the very disorderly Chinese bureaucracy, only the agency that formulated a rule may interpret it in the absence of an inclination of either the State Council or the NPC to exercise the interpretive powers given them by the Constitution. These practices are emphasized here at the outset because they so fundamentally limit the scope of administrative law in China.

The extent to which courts may be used to control administrative agencies is central to the existence of the rule of law itself. Without going into great detail here, I have distilled the essential issues from the available sources. In the discussion that follows, I introduce the institutions that have been established and speculate on their operation.

THE ADMINISTRATIVE LITIGATION LAW

The Constitution of 1982 states that "Citizens who have suffered losses through infringement of their civil rights by any state organ or functionary have the right to compensation in accordance with the law" (Art. 41); this principle was reaffirmed in the GPCL (Art. 121). Many Chinese laws and regulations specifically provide for the right of persons affected by decisions of administrative agencies to appeal to local People's Courts,[106] and during the early 1980s a modest experiment used administrative chambers in some local courts to hear citizens' complaints against alleged arbitrariness by administrative officials.

During the 1980s serious interest in enlivening this novel institution was expressed in high places. After Party Secretary Zhao Ziyang called for the creation of an administrative law in his report to the Party Congress in October 1987, a draft law on administrative procedure was published in late 1988. A revised draft was adopted by the National People's Congress in April 1989 as the Administrative Litigation Law (ALL)[107] and went into effect on October 1, 1990.[108] The effectiveness of this legislative innovation, which purports to allow recourse to the courts to citizens protesting acts of "state agencies," is obviously limited. Yet the new law reflects the existence of strong support within the Chinese leadership for institutions that foster bureaucratic responsibility, and it represents a kernel out of which could grow more legal means to limit the official arbitrariness that plagues China today.[109]

The ALL established procedures for challenging administrative acts in Administrative Adjudication Chambers of the People's Courts, which were given the power to quash illegal orders, compel administrative action, or modify unfair administrative sanctions.[110] Among the acts that may be challenged are orders restricting persons or property, actions that infringe on lawful business activity, denials of licenses or permits, and acts infringing upon personal or property rights. Any person or legal entity may institute a proceeding against any administrative agency, but not against the Party, which is not a "state agency" that can be sued under the statute.[111]

The basic scheme of the ALL is simple. A citizen may institute suit in the courts to protest an administrative decision. As already noted, the validity of administrative rules (known technically as "abstract administrative acts") may not be challenged;[112] the only acts that may be challenged are "concrete administrative acts," which are the applications of a rule in a particular case.[113] If the regulations governing the decision require that protest against a decision must be heard at a higher level of the agency that rendered the decision, such an administrative review is a prerequisite to the judicial action. If administrative reconsideration proves unsuccessful or if the agency does not respond within two months, the complaining party may sue in the People's Court directly.[114]

Under the ALL, the agency whose action has been challenged in a suit has the burden of proof to show that it was lawful. As under the Civil Procedure Law generally, there is great tolerance for various kinds of evidence. Unlike the heavy emphasis on mediation in ordinary civil litigation, mediation is not permitted in administrative litigation. Parties may also bring civil tort actions against administrative agencies, although they must show that they have first attempted to obtain redress from the agencies themselves. Although the ALL permits applicants to challenge a wide range of administrative actions, its effectiveness is severely limited by a number of constraints on the power of the courts.

First, the courts may inquire into only the legality of administrative actions, not their appropriateness within the discretion of the agency involved. Since most Chinese regulations are intentionally drafted to grant the implementing agencies the broadest discretion, as long as administrative action is technically lawful, the administrative use of discretion to take the challenged action may not be reviewed by the courts. The ALL does permit a court to order an agency to "withdraw" wholly or in part and to reconsider an act involving "violation of legal procedure,"[115] but it does not establish procedural rules that all agencies must follow in their decision-making. Although Chinese administrative decision-making is sometimes conditioned on procedural requirements, cases in which agency actions have been successfully challenged on procedural grounds are still rare,[116] and so procedural due process is effectively absent as a governing standard from this scheme of judicial review.

Second, as noted in chapter 5, since administrative agencies alone may interpret and determine the inherent validity of their own regulation, the courts may declare administrative action invalid only when the agency has violated its own rules, and only if the law involved by its own terms makes administrative action final and non-reviewable.[117]

Third, the courts may modify administrative imposition of penalties only when they are "manifestly unfair" (Art. 54).

Fourth, the courts have the authority to review administrative acts if the agency has "misused [its] authority" (*lanyong zhiquan*) or has acted outside its authority (*ultra vires* would be the conventional Anglo-American term), but apart from a few isolated cases these powers do not seem to have been much used.[118] The effect of these limitations is, as others have noted, that a decision by an administrative agency can be overturned "only if the decision violates the agency's own rules, while the legality and interpretation of these rules remain the province of the agency, not the court."[119]

Fifth, the courts may refuse to hear actions brought under the ALL.

In addition to these substantive limitations on the power of the courts under the ALL, there are procedural limitations as well. For example, administrative action may not be suspended unless the public interest would otherwise suffer and irreparable harm would occur. Also, agencies may declare documents for "internal" (*neibu*) use and thereby avoid public hearings under the rule that such hearings need not be held when "state secrets" are involved.

TABLE 3 · Administrative Cases by Disposition, 1990–1997

YEAR	ACCEPTED	CONCLUDED	UPHELD	RESCINDED	MODIFIED	REFUSED	WITHDRAWN	OTHER
1990	13,006	12,040	4,337	2,012	398		4,346	947
1991	25,667	25,202	7,969	4,762	592		9,317	2,562
1992	27,125	27,116	7,628	5,780	480	2,116	10,261	851
1993	27,911	27,958	6,587	5,270	430		11,550	4,121
1994	35,083	34,567	7,128	6,547	369		15,317	5,206
1995	52,596	51,370	8,903	7,733	395		25,990	8,349
1996	79,996	79,537	11,549	11,831	1,214		42,915	12,028
1997	90,557	88,542	11,230	12,279	717	7,501	50,735	6,080

Number of cases indexed to 1990, and case results by %

YEAR	ACCEPTED	CONCLUDED	UPHELD	RESCINDED	MODIFIED	REFUSED	WITHDRAWN	OTHER
1990	100	100	36.0%	16.7%	3.3%	36.1%	7.9%	
1991	197	209	31.6%	18.9%	2.3%	37.0%	10.2%	
1992	209	225	28.1%	21.3%	1.8%	7.8%	37.8%	3.1%
1993	215	232	23.6%	18.8%	1.5%	41.3%	14.7%	
1994	270	287	20.6%	18.9%	1.1%	44.3%	15.1%	
1995	404	427	17.3%	15.1%	0.8%	50.6%	16.3%	
1996	614	660	14.5%	14.9%	1.5%	54.0%	15.1%	
1997	696	735	12.4%	13.6%	0.8%	8.3%	56.0%	6.7%

SOURCE: *Zhongguo falü nianjian* (Law Yearbook of China) 1991 (p. 935), 1992 (p. 856), 1993 (p. 937), 1994 (p. 1029), 1995 (p. 1065), 1996 (p. 959), 1997 (p. 1057), 1998 (pp. 134, 1240).

Despite the limited cases in which the ALL recognizes the right of the accused to challenge administrative agency decisions, its significance "lies mainly in the fact that it was even enacted."[120] Although the scope of judicial review is limited and an overall standard of procedural due process is lacking, as has already been noted, the ALL makes a small inroad into the previous extraordinary lack of external supervision over these agencies. Given the weakness of Chinese courts, these limits make the ALL a frail weapon against administrative arbitrariness.

Some officials have not been enthusiastic about the development of administrative law, designed to curb their heretofore unlimited power and discretion. Tanner observes that:

Given the strong historical orientation toward separate sector-by-sector administration in China, the prospect of making policy through a law which purports to universal applicability creates special fears amongst ministry bureaucrats. . . . a law such as the Administrative Litigation Law is greatly feared by many bureaucrats, since it can potentially grant courts and other bureaucratic 'outsiders' the authority to intervene in a massive range of in-house ministerial activities.[121]

Despite bureaucratic resistance, however, the ALL at least offers a mechanism individuals or organizations can use to challenge arbitrariness rather than accept perceived injustice or seek influential friends to undo or modify administrative decisions.

Cases brought under the ALL have increased, especially in recent years (see Table 3). In 1991, the first full year the law was in force, 25,202 cases were concluded; in each of the two succeeding years the number of cases did not reach 30,000, but then it climbed, reaching 88,542 in 1997. Statistics on the outcomes of these cases raise some interesting questions. The percentage of cases in which the courts rescinded a challenged administrative decision has remained below 20 percent since 1990 except for one year, and it fell as low as 15 percent in 1995–1997. By subject matter, cases against the police have been the largest category in every year except 1996 and have fallen steadily, from 34 percent in 1990 to 16 percent in 1997; the single other major category has been cases involving land, which has shown a similar decline, from 32 percent in 1990 to 14 percent in 1997. The only other categories with over 5 percent of the total number of cases in any year have been forestry and urban construction. In the statistics on the disposition of cases, the largest single category is those withdrawn by plaintiffs, and their number is remarkably high, close to 60 percent in 1997.

Minxin Pei argues that in many of the withdrawn cases, government agencies unilaterally rescinded or changed the challenged administrative action,[122] but his research relies on an annual collection of reported decisions that were probably selected for publication because they represent an ideal, rather than reality.[123] It seems clear, for example, that the volumes reproduce decisions in which the plaintiffs prevailed against police in a far higher percentage of cases than that reported in the overall statistics.[124] In 1997, almost 25 percent of all the cases concluded were reported as ended after the administrative agency involved changed its illegal conduct.[125] Regardless of how one interprets the withdrawn cases, the available statistics do suggest that for plaintiffs "there is a higher probability of losing the case than winning it in the courts."[126]

Even if these reported cases are not representative, they do give a qualitative impression of the promise that the ALL offers for the future, because their flavor is interesting: Police decisions to impose administrative sanctions were rescinded in a number of cases after the court's review of the evidence. More interesting, perhaps, are cases in which police failure to follow procedure was faulted, such as:

> acting outside their jurisdiction (ordinary police had imposed fines for misconduct of a type under special forest police jurisdiction)[127]
>
> otherwise acting illegally (a deceased traffic policeman was held partially liable for his own death at a checkpoint because the checkpoint was unauthorized)[128]
>
> failing to follow procedural requirements (police silence beyond statutory period in response to request for gun permit held to be a denial of the permit).[129]

These published cases provide fairly complete summaries of the facts involved, but all discuss in only the most conclusory fashion the legality or illegality of the questioned conduct. Despite the lack of legal analysis, the reader can sense the persistence of some plaintiffs and speculate whether greater numbers may be inclined to sue in the future.

Plaintiffs undeniably face formidable obstacles. Litigation is costly, their chances of losing are great, even if they prevail they may have difficulty in enforcing the decisions, and they face the danger of retaliation. Chapter 9 describes in detail the hold that the local Party-state has over local courts. The tightness of the grasp suggests that if plaintiffs are successful, the government agencies involved may retaliate against the courts as well. It is difficult to foresee the courts becoming meaningful participants in punishing unlawful exercise of power by agencies unless they are given extremely strong support at the highest levels of Chinese leadership. To do so, however, could lead to charges of weakening the Party by rendering it hostage to accusations by anti-socialist non-Party enemies who could pervert the law to weaken Party rule, and, therefore, socialism itself. Chinese legal scholars have expressed interest in creating an administrative law in China that would use quasi-judicial or judicial bodies to control arbitrary cadre behavior and have spoken of the Administrative Procedure Act, which since 1946 has governed administrative procedures and judicial review in the United States, as a model. Bureaucratic arbitrariness is endemic in Chinese society, and the use of courts suggests that Party self-discipline has been recognized as inadequate. How far the courts will be allowed to participate, however, is in doubt. Legislators and legislative drafting staffs at the NPC and the State Council are concerned about expanding administrative law, and both its substantive content and implementation need to be addressed in the future. How far the courts will be allowed to participate, however, is in doubt, and here is a fundamental dilemma that law reformers face: How can they press for incremental reform—such as by enacting laws on licensing—that involves the exercise of discretion by administrative authorities, without deciding whether the courts or other external agencies should be given the power to review allegedly arbitrary exercise of their discretion?

THE STATE COMPENSATION LAW

Already the skeletal principles governing private tort actions against administrative agencies have been expanded by the State Compensation Law (SCL), enacted in May 1994 and put into effect on January 1, 1995.[130] The law provides that organs of the state are liable for damages for injuries caused by the illegal exercise of authority by state functionaries; individual officials are personally liable if they "intentionally committed errors or [if they] committed grave errors."[131] The SCL appears to distinguish between two types of negligence, ordinary and serious. The latter involves failure of the officials to notice that their behavior was wrong, along with failure to take preventive action to avoid damages.[132] These damages may be either direct or indirect, and the amount may be comprehensive or calculated on a daily basis. Plaintiffs must first formally demand compensation from the agency involved and may only file an action in the People's Courts if they are dissatisfied with the administrative decision. The SCL apparently applies to all administrative actions subject to scrutiny under the ALL and, in fact, claims under the two statutes may be combined.[133]

Claims may be filed against the agencies that administer the criminal process (police, Procuracy, courts, and prisons). If the claimant is dissatisfied with the initial decision on his claim, he must appeal to the next higher level of the agency involved before initiating a suit in a People's Court. Several commentators have raised an obvious question about the dubious likelihood of success that a claimant would encounter in pursuing internal review within the police or in any judicial proceeding against the police or the courts.[134]

The SCL reveals a disinclination to use judicial review as the dominant form of dealing with claims for compensation under the statute. As already noted, claimants may go to the courts only after they have been unsuccessful at the agency. Upon reaching court, however, the claimant may also apply to the "compensation committee" of the court, which appears to be yet another form of administrative decision-making and a means of avoiding an adjudication.

THE ADMINISTRATIVE PUNISHMENT LAW

The extensive range of punishments that are administered by administrative agencies without court involvement has already been mentioned, as has the Administrative Punishment Law (APL), which should also be noted in this discussion of the emergence of Chinese administrative law. The Administrative Punishment Law was promulgated by the National People's Congress in 1996.[135] It sets forth procedural rules applicable to all administrative punishments, provides for the invalidation of punishments that lack legal basis or fail to meet the procedural requirements of the Law, and specifies rights of appeal both to administrative authorities and to the courts. The APL partially addresses the legislative confusion among different levels of laws, specifying that punishments that restrict personal freedom may only be stated in those normative rules that are classified as "laws," not "administrative regulations." It also states certain rights of the defendant, to be notified of the punishment and the basis for the decision, and to participate in his defense. The law goes beyond other Chinese legislation in requiring that agencies must hold hearings before they issue orders to cease business, cancel a permit, or impose a "relatively large fine."

The APL is noteworthy for its attempt to bring transparency to an area of administrative discretion notorious for its absence. The procedures that it specifies are not complete, and their significance is not made entirely clear. For example, although a hearing is required before certain punishments are imposed, as noted above, the law is silent on whether the decision of the administrative agency must be limited to evidence presented at the hearing.[136] More basically, its spirit conflicts with the mentality and past practice of agencies such as the police. As is true with so many other areas in which legal culture must be changed to breathe life into the enforcement of new laws, the concept of procedural justice will have to be promoted as a political matter if the APL is to have real force.

ADMINISTRATIVE RECONSIDERATION

The last major area that I will discuss is "administrative reconsideration," the subject of regulations adopted by the State Council in 1990 and superseded by law in 1999.[137] The legislation establishes external, nonjudicial review of certain administrative acts. Provisions for administrative reconsideration had previously been scattered through many pieces of legislation, but without specificity on such critical matters as procedure and jurisdiction.

The law permits aggrieved parties affected by a "specific act" of an administraive organ to seek reconsideration. Under the previous regulations, only administrative actions that directly affected the rights and obligations of the complainant could be challenged, not "abstract administrative acts" such as rules with general binding effect. The new law provides that rules issued by departments of the State Council, village and town governments, and departments of local governments above the county level may also be challenged. The complaint must, in principle, be addressed to the department at the next level above the one whose act has been challenged.[138] Although previously review cases were dealt with internally, the new law permits appeals to the courts or to the State Council when the agencies involved are local governments or departments of the State Council. This new law marks an expansion of Chinese administrative law, especially since rules of general application may now be attacked.[139] The involvement of the State Council reflects the continued appeal of non-judicial remedies.

THE MINISTRY OF SUPERVISION

The Ministry of Supervision, abolished during the Cultural Revolution, was reestablished in 1986. Its function is to investigate violations of laws, regulations, and policies and to investigate complaints against officials. It may "suggest" punishment of offending officials, and it may also "suggest" cancellation, suspension, or amendment of the norms or policies in question. The ministry has established thousands of local supervisory organs at the level of county or above, but it should be noted that these bodies are responsible to local governments (the very organs that they are supposed to supervise) as well as to higher-level supervisory agencies.

Further blurring the lines between state and Party, in 1993 the ministry was merged with the Central Commission for Discipline Inspection of the CCP, although each continues to operate under the regulations that created them. At each level in the system at which there is a Party committee there is a discipline committee, which is supposed to check on cadres' fulfillment of their duties. They have considerable investigative powers, but their decisions on sanctions are subject to the approval of the local Party committees of which they are part. It should be clear, though, that although laws provide for punishments by officials for criminal acts, separate rules and sanctions apply to Party members who have engaged in criminal activity.

Concluding Thoughts on Administrative Law

The statutes noted here are only weak initial steps toward the control of administrative illegality. As one scholar notes, omission of the Party from the organizations whose decisions may be challenged means that the one entity that is the ultimate maker of decisions in every government organization at the present time, the Party Committee, remains unchallengeable by the courts.[140] In the meantime, two critical weaknesses impair the use of the ALL and the SCL—the quality of personnel and the influence of local government and Party officials over what is emphatically not an independent judiciary.

Administrative law and procedure form an arena in which critical struggles over the depth and reach of Chinese law may take place in the future. Chinese leaders have long wrestled with the choice between controlling the use of administrative discretion through internal administrative devices or through external agencies such as the Ministry of Supervision,[141] but only recently has this been considered a legal problem. Hampered by the shallow Marxism-Leninism that has dominated Chinese legal thinking, Chinese law has not developed a clear classification for external controls of administrative agencies. Common law and civil law systems alike distinguish between public and private law, but Chinese doctrine continues to deny this distinction.[142]

The capacity of the legislation to bring about meaningful review of abuses of discretion by officials remains largely potential rather than actual, and the prospects for enlarging or deepening the scope of review are poor. Recent experience with various other laws, themselves innovations during the 1980s, suggests that the increasing web of legislation and judicial implementation causes a thickening of the texture of bureaucratic rules. This has been true, for example, in the growth of rules and practice governing Sino-foreign joint venture contracts. Such progress suggests that future legal reformers, having begun to establish administrative law in China, may be able to work to strengthen it without trying to fit it into a preexisting scheme of legal theory.

Soon after the Administrative Punishment Law was promulgated, a provincial governor (concurrently provincial deputy Party secretary) wrote an article in which he invoked the speech by Jiang Zemin in February 1996 on the rule of law that has been discussed in the previous chapter. Identifying the mentality that is a formidable obstacle to the expansion of administrative legality, he said:

To govern the country in accordance with the law . . . administrative organs must conscientiously abide by the law and act within the bounds prescribed by law. . . . [S]ome comrades misinterpret "governance in accordance with the law" as "exercising management over the common people through the law," and regard "law" as a means by which "officials" exercise management over the "people." It is as if state organs had a right to "apply the law" but not a duty to abide by the law . . . some comrades stress substance over procedure, thinking that they can do things as long as they have power and make light of the way things are done. They even view legally prescribed procedures as too troublesome and restrictive. In reality, we should follow procedures in everything we do. . . . Legally prescribed administrative procedures only serve to restrict and check abuse of power while safeguarding and guaranteeing the exercise of power in a correct manner.[143]

He further called for administration with greater "openness" and "transparency." It would be too much to expect these views to be widespread in the near future. If they do become more influential, they would promote wider judicial review of administrative activity than is now possible, which, in turn, would extend the scope of legality to yet another area of Chinese life from which it presently remains largely distant.

At the base of the problem of administrative arbitrariness is a failure of vision on the part of the Party and its leaders. The Party could once claim legitimacy not only because it boasted of having a unique ear for the voice of History, but because it successfully made a revolution and won the support of a large portion of the Chinese people. In recent years, with its legitimacy fading, it has tried a number of tactics to bolster that legitimacy. It has attempted to increase popular support by advocating modernization and economic reform and, to a certain extent, legal reform as well. Party leaders, aware of the decline in the morality of cadres and the increase in corruption, have tried to modify cadre participation in administration by increasing the separation of government and Party, advancing younger cadres, and compelling older ones to retire. The approach has been characterized as an "appeal to virtue."[144] In view of the gravity of the social and legal problems that challenge the stability of Chinese society, an attempt to control official behavior and enhance individual citizen participation by recalling the fabled purity of the revolution will surely fail. An expanded administrative law, vigorously promoted, seems absolutely necessary if further meaningful steps are to be taken toward the rule of law.

The examples discussed in this chapter should serve to demonstrate the considerable efforts that have been made to reform the economy and to create a legal infrastructure that promotes not only economic reform but other non-economic interests of the Chinese people. It is difficult not to be impressed with the volume and scope of the legislation that has been adopted since the decision of the CCP Central Committee in 1978 to embark on market-oriented reforms, despite the weak state structure on which new legal institutions must be built, the weak ideological justification for them, and political limits on the reach of legal reform. Despite constraints imposed by history and harsh current political reality, the enacted legislation has created a platform that could support further reform.

It is important to consider how deeply the initial efforts of the first twenty years have been implemented. To do that, I will focus on dispute resolution, which is surveyed in the next two chapters and which necessarily involves the assertion of rights that the new laws purport to create. By analyzing how disputes are handled, particularly by the courts, we may begin to appraise the extent to which the organization of the institutions charged with handling this variety of social conflict and their methods of decision-making condition the assertion and vindication of these rights.

CHAPTER 8

Mediation After Mao

CHINESE INSTITUTIONS for dispute resolution are being reshaped by the same forces that have launched the extraordinary transformations of China's planned economy and society. The reforms of the 1980s gave birth to a great surge of commerce, entrepreneurship, and corruption—and to more disputes and the need to resolve them. China's law reformers have been challenged to generate rules to govern transactions that in the West would lie in the realm of civil law, to build institutions that apply legal rules in specific disputes, and to adapt previous dispute resolution procedures to different circumstances. These institutions now depart widely from pre-reform assumptions about how the Party-state should address social conflict, but they also bear weighty legacies of pre-reform organization and habits of thought.

Institution-building for dispute resolution has taken place since 1979 in three principal areas: mediation, arbitration, and adjudication, which I examine in this chapter.

In 1989 new regulations on people's mediation committees replaced the rules dating from 1954. The Ministry of Justice has revived the nationwide network of rural mediators as an instrument to maintain public order and to alleviate an otherwise intolerable burden on the courts. These committees are supervised and supported by judicial assistants and by township and village legal service offices that augment the resources for rural dispute resolution. At the same time, the social and economic effects of reform have reduced the scope and authority of mediation.

As contract disputes under economic reforms multiplied, a variety of new organizations were improvised to arbitrate such disputes. These have been replaced by a nationwide system of local arbitration commissions, whose gradual establishment began in 1995.

Courts, once only tokens of Chinese Party-state legitimacy, have been revived, expanded, and developed. A civil procedure law was adopted on a trial basis in 1982, then revised in 1991. Civil litigation has grown steadily. At the same time, persistent and formidable political forces constrain the power and authority of the courts.

This chapter analyzes extra-judicial (i.e., "people's") mediation as it operates today and notes recent reforms in arbitration. Chapter 9 turns to the operation of the courts.

Extra-Judicial Mediation

The people's mediation committees described in chapter 3 came under attack from the left in the Chinese leadership during the latter part of the 1950s. Although they were briefly incorporated into grass-roots crime prevention and security organizations, they survived; during the Cultural Revolution, however, they were entirely suspended or abolished along with other legal institutions. The apparatus of urban control—of which the mediation committees were a part—was reconstituted during the 1970s and early 1980s. Rural people's mediation committees had not been as affected by the upheavals and violence of the late 1960s; with the disappearance of the rural people's communes, the rural village has regained some of the importance it had before the communes were organized in 1958–1960.

POLICY: CONTINUING EMPHASIS
ON EXTRA-JUDICIAL MEDIATION

China's leadership evidently remains attached to the urban people's mediation committees. Throughout the 1970s I and other visitors to China who were interested in law were permitted to visit residents' committees and the mediation committees under them that specialized in handling disputes. The latter were invariably exhibited as embodiments of a uniquely Chinese Communist approach to handling minor disputes. In 1973, 1978, and 1979 I visited urban neighborhoods, and on each occasion my hosts described the activities of mediators in a way that uncannily resembled, in theme and emphasis, the sources I had worked with when I wrote on mediation in 1967. Aunty Wu, the model mediator of the 1950s extolled in the newspaper article quoted at the beginning of chapter 3, had formerly been only remotely known to me, but after meeting women mediators in Beijing and Shanghai who echoed her words two decades later, I felt that I had come to know her a good deal better. My inquiries into the processes of dispute resolution were limited during these visits, however, because my hosts were unwilling to depart from superficial descriptions of dispute resolution practice.

After the Cultural Revolution ended, the Ministry of Justice, reestablished in 1979, not only revived mediation but emphasized that it was to
be the primary avenue for resolving civil disputes.[1] The formulation of
that policy has changed somewhat over the years. Before 1982, the policy
was expressed as "mediation first, litigation second"; the Civil Procedure
Law of 1982 changed this to an injunction to "emphasize mediation";
when the Civil Procedure Law was revised in 1991 it provided that the
courts should "conduct mediation in accordance with the principles of
voluntary participation by the parties."[2] The shift has been explained as a
change in focus from extra-judicial to judicial mediation,[3] which will be
discussed below. The growth and increasing complexity of more formal
institutions for dispute resolution challenge people's mediation committees to remain relevant to the lives of the Chinese populace, especially in
the cities, where economic life has changed markedly since 1979 and
where residents no longer live under the political constraints that made
the neighborhood committee a forum that could not be avoided.

By 1981 there were 5,575,000 mediators working throughout China.
In the countryside, training had been increased and new mediators re-
cruited. The role of mediation grew as economic disputes over economic
contracts and over such matters as rights over land, water, and agricultural
implements multiplied. By the end of 1992, the number of mediators had
almost doubled to more than ten million, working in over one million
mediation committees. From 1985 to 1992 committees handled over 5.26
million cases, almost five times the number received by the courts during
the same period and, according to one observer, they achieved a "success
rate" of 91.6 percent.[4]

Mediation is often characterized in the controlled press as a product of
Chinese traditions, both prerevolutionary and Communist,[5] which meets
the needs of the state for civil dispute settlement and prevention of social
disorder; it is also responsive to cultural preferences.

Civil Dispute Settlement

Mediation is deemed suited for resolving minor disputes, such as marital and family problems, real property, debts, and demands for compensation for injuries after fights.

Preventing Social Disorder

People's mediation has long been viewed by the leaders of the Party-
state as helping to prevent social disorder and crime. In 1957, Liu Shaoqi,
China's prime minister before the Cultural Revolution, called people's
mediation the "first line of defense" in the work of "political-legal construction." More recently the Department of Grass-Roots Work, the Min-

istry of Justice agency responsible for mediation activities, has repeated Liu's characterization of mediation as an important defense, adding that it prevents disputes from "becoming acute and causing crimes," promotes family unity, and enhances "social stability and unity." The ministry continues to describe mediation as an expression of the "people's democratic dictatorship" and as an appropriate means for dealing with "contradictions within the people."[6]

Responding to Cultural Preferences

Although the formal legal system has been developed, litigation is expensive and time-consuming, and the legal system cannot handle all disputes that arise. Many among the populace are wary of litigation, dare not sue in the courts, and feel more comfortable settling disputes in the traditional manner of using intermediaries. One Chinese author writes:

Since the 1980s this situation has been changing, but traditional consciousness cannot be thoroughly changed within a short period of time, unless there is really no other alternative, [Chinese people] simply are not willing to litigate in the courts. People's mediation is just right for satisfying the hopes of the masses for solving disputes without litigation.[7]

The pragmatic, depoliticized rhetoric of this last quotation is representative of discussion in recent years. Political language is also all but absent from the most recent legislation under which mediation is carried out.

THE CHANGING LEGISLATIVE FRAMEWORK OF PEOPLE'S MEDIATION

Regulations on People's Mediation Committees

The revival of mediation was underscored when new regulations (Mediation Regulations) were issued in 1989, replacing the original regulations that had governed the mediation committees since 1954.[8] Although there are continuities, some differences between the two sets of rules are evident.

The Goals of Mediation Have Become Less Didactic and Less Politicized. In addition to resolving disputes, the old rules aimed at "strengthening the people's education in patriotic observance of the law, and promoting internal unity of the people in order to benefit production by the people and construction by the state" (Art. 1). The new rule omits reference to "patriotism" but retains the explicit educational function expressed in the old regulations, although it is now more closely related to law. The old regulations referred to "conducting propaganda-education" (Art. 3), but the new ones speak of "propagandizing state laws, regulations, rules and policies through mediation work" and "educating citizens to obey law and discipline, and to respect social ethics" (Art. 4). The purpose of the mediation committees, in addition to mediating civil disputes, is said to be "promoting the unity of the people, maintaining social stability, and benefiting the construction of socialist modernization" (Art. 1).

Legal Rules More Prominently Shape Outcomes. The old regulations stated that mediation had to be conducted "in compliance with the policies, laws and decrees of the people's government" (Art. 6[1]). The new regulations state that the guiding principles for the mediation committees are to be "laws, regulations, rules and policies." They add that "where there are no clear stipulations in laws, regulations, rules or policies," the mediators must rely on "social morality" (Art. 6[1]). The role of law is now elevated, and policy is last among authoritative norms emanating from the Party-state. At the same time, as shown below, dispute settlement, like other law-related institutions, nonetheless remains an instrument of policy.

Formality Has Been Increased. The new regulations add formality to the procedures of mediation committees by providing, as earlier regulations did not, for registering and recording mediation proceedings in writing.

Mediation Is Less Explicitly Tied to Politics. People's mediators elected to the committees are to be "adult citizens who are fair-minded, linked with the masses, enthusiastic about mediation work and who have a certain level of legal knowledge and a certain level of understanding about policies" (Art. 4). This clause has replaced the requirement for a correct "political attitude" that was previously an expressed prerequisite for a proper "understanding of policies." The need for some legal knowledge has also been added.

Mediation Committees Are More Closely Supervised by the People's Courts. Both the 1954 and 1989 regulations state that the local people's governments and the courts supervise the mediation committees, but the new Mediation Regulations state that the daily supervision of their work shall be done by Judicial Assistants, administrators attached to the local bureaus of the Ministry of Justice (see below), who are also charged with mediating difficult cases themselves.

Mediation Regulations Provide More Support for the Mediation Committees. The Mediation Regulations provide that "appropriate subsidies" may be given to mediators (Art. 14).

Voluntariness Is Still Fostered. Like the old regulations, the new ones warn against coercing the parties to agree to a settlement and state that mediation is not a prerequisite to bringing suit in the courts. Parties may not be prevented from filing suit because they have not gone through mediation or because mediation has been unsuccessful (Art. 6[1]). In practice, coercion remains a concern, as discussed below.

Standards Have Been Set for Mediators' Behavior. The new regulations are more comprehensive in their requirements that mediators avoid acting out of personal considerations or committing fraud, suppressing disputes, retaliating against or insulting the parties, disclosing their private matters, or accepting bribes or gifts.

Mediation Committees No Longer Have Sanctioning Powers. The mediation committees' power to deal with minor criminal cases under the 1954 regulations has been omitted from the more recent regulations.

The Rules Reflect Changing Demands on Mediation. These rules, while looking backward to earlier practice, also hesitantly look a bit forward as well. They reiterate the preference for voluntary non-adjudicated settlement that has long informed Chinese approaches to law and continues to be embedded in all Chinese institutions for dispute resolution. At the same time they shift the mediation committees away from their previous role as vehicles for overtly disseminating propaganda and declare more explicitly than before that their mission is to resolve disputes by applying legal rules.

Other Mediation-Related Legislation

Judicial Assistants. The renewed emphasis on people's mediation committees brought with it the need to regularize their supervision, and as early as 1979, courts were transferring responsibility for that supervision to Judicial Assistants.[9] The Ministry of Justice promulgated provisional rules on the work of these Judicial Assistants in November 1981,[10] but only in April 1990 did it issue regulations explicitly addressing their work, describing them as "judicial administrative workers at the basic level of People's Government, specifically responsible for the work of handling people's disputes" (Art. 2). They supervise and participate directly in mediation, bridging the workings of the people's mediation committees and local government administration. Two scholars who studied rural mediation indicated in discussion in Beijing in 1995 that Judicial Assistants were able to function effectively in villages, although their legal training was limited to taking short-term classes. They noted that mediators were often village committee members and, unlike many of their counterparts in the cities, were usually not retired from other careers. The Judicial Bureau organizes classes for them and conducts legal propaganda and publicity. It appears that their efficacy rests less on legal training than on their relationships with local élites.[11]

Methods for Handling Disputes Among Citizens. The "Methods for Handling Disputes among Citizens" (Methods) were promulgated in 1990 by the Ministry of Justice.[12] They outline how the Judicial Assistants are to deal with disputes "over personal or property rights or other disputes arising in the course of daily life" (Art. 3) by directing the parties to a mediation committee if they have not already gone to one; by directly mediating cases in which mediation has not resulted in settlement; or by declaring void a settlement that violates law, regulations, administrative rules, or policies (Art. 18). Mediation is clearly the preferred method for dealing with disputes, but when it fails, the local government may "decisively handle" them. If one of the parties wishes to repudiate a settlement, it must apply to a court within fifteen days after the agreement has been signed. If after fifteen days the agreement has neither been carried out nor made the subject of application to the court, one of the parties may apply to the court to "take the necessary measures to carry out [the agreement]." As in the Mediation Regulations, voluntariness and legality have been emphasized. The Methods also underscore the mediation committees' ties to the Ministry of Justice—rather than to the courts—by making the Judicial Assistants the managers of mediation.

Township and Village Legal Service Offices (TVLSOs). With the advent of the contract-responsibility system came a burgeoning need for legal expertise in rural areas that has continued to grow. New legal service organizations arose, and their operations were formalized in May 1987 in the "Provisional Rules for Township and Village Legal Service Offices." But only in September 1991 did the Ministry of Justice issue comprehensive regulations governing the conduct of all rural legal service work,[13] which effectively clarified the status of those organizations.[14] Under the leadership of local People's Governments and Judicial Assistants, these offices act both as mediators and as agents for parties in mediation and other legal actions. The ministry's 1992 "Opinion on Reforms in Basic Level Legal Service Work" makes it clear that the agencies are expected to operate as private service enterprises rather than as any form of governmental or mass organization.[15] In practice, they have indeed evolved into the general service offices they were intended to be, supporting but not displacing existing dispute resolution entities.

The legislation surveyed here seeks to preserve existing resources for informal dispute resolution and to provide additional resources. However, economic changes caused by reform may also create demands that the institutions defined by that legislation cannot meet. It may be possible to infer future trends from the current operation of these institutions, which are described below.

THE MEDIATION COMMITTEES AT WORK

Volume and Type of Disputes

The extent of extra-judicial mediation and the types of cases that it handles may be best understood against the background of recent statistics (see Tables 4 and 5).

Although the number of cases mediated by the mediation committees each year declined by more than 25 percent between 1990 and 1997, and is now below the number handled in 1985, the committees still handle more civil cases than the courts. In 1990, TVLSOs handled 15 percent of all cases of extra-judicial mediation, a number which rose to 18 percent in 1997. In the meantime, by comparison, the number of civil cases handled by the courts went from 1.85 million in 1990 to 3.24 million in 1997.

These figures show that family and minor civil disputes remain at the core of the work of the mediation committees. In 1996 and 1997 they constituted 41 percent of the cases handled by mediation committees, an increase of 8 percent from 1990. Disputes arising out of the economic contracts have for the most part been channeled to new arbitration organs and the courts. (In the meantime, the number of economic disputes that have been taken to the courts has been rising, from slightly more than 500,000 in 1990 to three times that number in 1997 (see Table 6, p. 254).)

As noted earlier, the delineation between "civil" and "economic" cases is not precise. Among the principal types of disputes that one Supreme Court notice classified as "economic" are those involving contracts between persons or between juristic persons and individuals or "specialized households," trade-related contracts with foreigners or Chinese counterparts in Hong Kong and Macao, and disputes involving the claims of juristic persons for damages for tortious conduct related to "production and circulation."[16] "Civil" contracts and other "civil" matters, by default, are those that have not been included in the Economic Contract Law or in various notices of the Supreme People's Court, such as the one quoted above on jurisdiction.

During the reform years, official media accounts of the cases handled by the mediation committees have remained quite consistent, stating that "most civil cases involved marriage, love affairs, inheritance, support of parents, housing, family disputes, relations between neighbors and debt."[17] They can be grouped into three primary categories: personal, production-related, or property-related (in cases in which kin ties are not relevant).[18]

Personal disputes related to marriage can involve demands for the return of betrothal gifts after broken engagements and for divorce, including questions of custody, child support, and the division of marital property. They may involve disputes within households, often between co-resident kin; regarding inheritance; and concerning obligations to support and care for the elderly, for spouses, and for children of one's extended family. Because Chinese law requires younger generations to support elder generations, complications may occur when middle generations die leaving young couples to care for elderly grandparents.

Production-related disputes include those which arise out of responsibility contracts that allocate managerial rights to households and to larger social units over property such as land, forests, water, livestock, and farm implements. Typical of the more difficult cases encountered by mediators are disputes over rights and property arising out of contracts under which the management of an enterprise is contracted to a designated individual. Conflicts may occur between two contract-managers, between one contract-manager and private citizens or households, or within a single managerial unit. Other production-related disputes can arise, such as:

within partnerships, in which partners' mutual and joint rights and obligations are often only dimly articulated, even when written contracts exist;

over rent/lease agreements, whether for residential or commercial property or for equipment used in production and transportation; or

over commodity quality and quantity, including disputes between manufacturer and reseller or between reseller and customer.

As the Chinese economy has grown more complex, the level of technical knowledge necessary to determine whether products, services, or financial obligations meet contractual requirements has also increased, and some cases are becoming too difficult for mediators.

Property disputes can arise over ownership of land, often when parties seek to reclaim land taken over during state campaigns or unlawfully occupied during periods of social upheaval. The subsequent sale, rental, or use as collateral of such land and the addition of improvements further complicates these disputes. The number of disputes over land intended for property construction—especially survey disputes—has risen sharply. Finally, mediating disputes over debts, whether involving money or goods such as grain, is complicated, especially when they involve illegal profiteering. Certain miscellaneous cases such as those involving uninvited stewardship—when one party without solicitation causes benefit to another party and then demands recompense—suggest that mediators may have to rely heavily on Chinese ideals of social ethics when resolving disputes.

A final category of dispute involves damage to "civil rights" that would

TABLE 4. Cases Handled by People's Mediation Committees in 1985 and 1990–1997

	1985	1990	1991	1992	1993	1994	1995	1996	1997
Marriage	1,072,116	1,222,214	1,333,026	1,183,317	1,187,687	1,191,925	1,146,769	1,091,703	1,031,489
Succession	206,943	284,979	295,794	280,448	295,766	296,227	311,159	305,336	308,321
Support and Fostering	347,377	445,963	472,188	413,476	434,085	440,621	451,490	432,931	416,127
Houses and Residential Sites	1,035,618	894,349	859,857	721,004	687,822	659,980	641,074	591,567	556,670
Debt	254,669	498,564	435,016	415,558	463,727	462,539	477,318	480,662	465,281
Production and Management	900,093	751,651	744,818	623,492	626,722	611,555	636,018	602,932	570,754
Damages	570,596	528,148	531,927	464,736	442,967	492,325	415,886	414,518	394,960
Other Family	463,167	1,167,792	723,154	602,351	587,173	570,404	544,425	534,102	522,131
Neighbors	508,476	989,827	1,074,351	946,080	947,589	899,226	883,281	838,157	800,775
Other Non-Family	973,858	625,735	599,110	522,747	549,420	498,927	509,563	510,322	476,650
Total	6,332,913	7,409,222	7,069,241	6,173,209	6,222,958	6,123,729	6,016,983	5,802,230	5,543,166
Family	2,089,603	3,120,948	2,824,162	2,479,592	2,504,711	2,499,177	2,453,843	2,364,072	2,278,068
Non-family	4,243,310	4,288,274	4,245,079	3,693,617	3,718,247	3,624,552	3,563,140	3,438,168	3,265,090
Family (% of total)	33.0%	42.1%	40.0%	40.2%	40.2%	40.8%	40.8%	40.7%	41.1%
Non-Family (% of total)	67.0%	57.9%	60.0%	59.8%	59.8%	59.2%	59.2%	59.3%	58.9%

SOURCES: Department of Grass-Roots Work, *People's Mediation in China*; *Zhongguo falü nianjian* (Law Yearbook of China) 1991 (p. 956), 1992 (p. 956), 1993 (p. 875), 1994 (p. 1047), 1995 (p. 1081), 1996 (p. 977), 1997 (p. 1075), 1998 (p. 1257). Discrepancies in figures appear in originals.

TABLE 5. Work of Township and Village (and Street Committee) Legal Service Offices, 1990–1997

	No. of organs	No. of personnel	TVE consultancies	Cases mediated	Represent client in civil litigation	Represent client in civil non-litigation	Legal advising	Organize propaganda tableaus	Lecture on the law
1990	31,758	98,293		1,300,700	163,500	334,200	4,335,000	582,100	4,899,300
1991	32,193	102,254	227,953	1,295,200	202,300	613,500	4,834,200		1,013,800
1992	32,750	103,848	291,801	1,144,500	236,600	906,700	5,142,500		613,100
1993	33,652	107,398	322,545	1,167,300	263,800	735,200	5,046,700		595,500
1994	34,952	110,770	364,414	1,169,300	322,600	926,300	5,143,200		563,700
1995	35,038	111,295	412,542	1,144,200	385,500	998,900	5,256,000		546,900
1996	34,554	113,612	477,527	1,252,500	491,700	1,154,400	6,092,900		740,500
1997	35,207	119,115	488,569	1,234,800	532,000	1,138,200	8,187,200		508,000

SOURCES: *Zhongguo falü nianjian* (Law Yearbook of China): 1991 (p. 956), 1992 (p. 875), 1993 (p. 956), 1994 (p. 1047), 1995 (p. 1081), 1996 (p. 977), 1997 (p. 1075), 1998 (p. 1257).

be classified in Anglo-American law as torts, involving claims for monetary damages for injury to person, property, or reputation.

The Organizational Context

Urban Neighborhoods. Dispute resolution continues to be a core activity of neighborhood committees. First established in the 1950s and revived after the Cultural Revolution, these remain the essential basic-level units in the urban apparatus of control. In new regulations issued in 1990 on the neighborhood residents' committees, a list of functions prominently includes "mediating in nongovernmental disputes."[19]

Before reforms, this system of urban control was capable of levels of efficiency and intrusiveness into residents' lives unsurpassed by any other twentieth-century totalitarian regime. In 1989 one observer noted, "virtually nothing escapes the notice of the street committee,"[20] and as recently as 1991 residents' committees were described "at times . . . as therapist, at times as utility company, at times as patrol unit, always trying to prod, scold, nudge and push the Government's policies down to the masses."[21]

Most recently, however, the urban control network is showing signs of decay, and the CCP may not be able to maintain it in the face of changing social values and economic pursuits.[22] The population to be served by each committee has increased, but the quality and quantity of committee members have declined. Interviews with legal scholars and judges suggest most urban mediators are still primarily retired workers or housewives, as they were before the Cultural Revolution,[23] although an increasing number of mediators are drawn from the ranks of retired cadres. A survey of twenty residents' committees conducted in Beijing in 1990 indicated that most members were housewives who had been members for decades and were "illiterate or only semi-literate."[24] Stipends paid to residents' committee members have stayed at the same low levels for forty years, and even in the residents' committees that are working well, running profitable businesses has become more important than performing duties related to maintaining social order.[25] In Shanghai in 1997 some street committees were reported to have become part of Coca-Cola's distribution network.[26] In the 1950s and 1960s, police were involved in resolving disputes, but police are now more occupied with fighting crime and generally may have less authority than they did in the Maoist era.[27] Charlotte Ikels, studying Guangzhou in the 1990s, finds that serving the people is no longer a meaningful ideal.[28] Former volunteers now work elsewhere for pay or help with the work of their employed or enterprising family members; the volunteers who remain are overworked, and it is not clear who will be their successors.

Changes in the physical configuration of large Chinese cities lessen the neighborhood committees' ability to play a role in the affairs of urban residents simply by making it more difficult for committee members to pry and spy.[29] New spatial organization is accompanied by a growing sense of privacy, fostering resentment of neighborhood busybodies.

Before reforms, urban residents were closely tied to their residences through China's household registration system. During the reform years, however, personal mobility has steadily increased. Despite efforts to contain them, urban residents in the huge "floating population" often operate outside the network control.

Rural Villages. When the rural people's communes were disbanded and their functions transferred to townships and villages,[30] more resources and functions were given to rural committees than to urban residents' committees. In an environment of "uneven institutionalization," the powers of the CCP and government are not clearly separated.[31] Today village heads and Party secretaries still exercise much power over many matters, including dispute resolution. The justice they dispense may depend on whether economic reform has made the villagers wealthy and, therefore, less dependent on officials, or whether the parties or the official who must decide the dispute belong to powerful families.[32] The official press disregards such distinctions and continues to celebrate rural mediators much as they do their urban counterparts.

In the countryside, in addition to economic changes caused by reform, some very traditional forces have reappeared. For centuries clans were a primary social unit in the Chinese countryside, and until 1949 their powerful role in organizing rural society was expressed in part by their participation in mediation and control over the suppression of local disputes. Central-state power historically shared a Confucian interest in permitting clan leaders to enjoy some degree of autonomy over clan disputes.[33] Since 1949, however, the construction of basic-level people's governmental institutions was predicated on the eradication of clan organizations. Whether clans were in fact uprooted, or whether their roots simply lay dormant in the chill economic climate of collectivization, clan organizations have flourished in the post-reform period and clan mediation is now on the rise in areas with a strong clan tradition.[34] In some areas disputes over property are first mediated by clan leaders and brought to people's mediation committees only after clan mediation fails. Clans also exercise influence over dispute mediation indirectly by co-opting existing state-sponsored vehicles for mediation. Fu Hualing observes that experiments in the 1980s to contract responsibility for dispute settlement (and public order generally) to village leaders led to "the contract security system [being] hijacked by clan organizations."[35]

Mediation at Work Units. Although people's mediation was intended to be operative in the workplace as well as in residential areas, little has appeared in the Chinese press about this form of mediation. The work-unit's dominance over many aspects of the lives of its members has declined with reforms and consequently fewer disputes are likely to be mediated in the workplace, but its continued presence is significant. In one industrialized town a factory oversaw 48 mediation committees comprising over 2,000 mediators, who served 55,000 employees and their additional 20,000 dependents.[36] But only when work-unit leaders supervise their workers' residential environment do they also oversee mediation, and then for the usual range of disputes arising in the course of social life. A separate regime has been created for labor disputes: under the Labor Law promulgated in 1995, labor disputes are initially dealt with by mediation conducted by commissions set up for the purpose and, if mediation fails, by labor dispute arbitration commissions, whose decisions may be appealed to the courts.[37]

Mediational Style in Practice

In one recent study of the operation of people's mediation committees and Chinese legal culture, authors Liu Guangan and Li Cunpeng distinguished three styles of mediation according to the principal bases for the outcomes: (1) emotion and reason, (2) law, and (3) a combination of feeling (*ganqing*) and law.[38] It is striking that they omit policy as a source of standards for decision since it is difficult to imagine that policy has become totally irrelevant to mediation. On the other hand, just as traditional and other non-policy factors could formerly hide behind a facade of policy, the reverse is also possible.

Mediation Based on Emotion and Reason ('Qingli'). The Mediation Regulations of 1989 require that mediation be carried out according to "law, regulations, rules and policies," and that in the absence of "clear stipulations" in these sources, mediators shall rely on "social morality" (*shehui gongde*). Liu and Li suggested that outcomes linked to law were often based on social morality.[39] They cited the following examples:

Two brothers disputed over the division of family property for 14 years. The mediation committee director engaged in heart-to-heart talks with the brothers, assisted them with their needs and recalled their goodwill in the past. They reconciled and renounced their bitterness, and continued their business relationship.

When a husband wanted to divorce his wife because she was childless, the mediator reminded him of the good care his wife gave him. The couple adopted a child.

In these cases mediators did not focus on the rights of the parties, their views of the facts, or any laws at all. They "departed from the dispute itself," emphasizing instead the relationships involved and the desirability of reconciliation. Two other cases illustrated the same approach:

A retired worker named Ho had only two small rooms for his nine-member family. Cramped conditions contributed to the failure of his 26-year-old youngest son in wooing several girlfriends. The young man pestered the father to build a new house—materials had already been purchased—but Ho could not obtain a construction license. Aware of the situation, the director of the mediation committee made four trips to the district Urban Construction Bureau. Within days a permit for the house was issued. The parents were so moved that they kowtowed to the mediator to express their appreciation.

An eighty-year-old woman intended to commit suicide because none of her four sons would support her. A mediator talked with them many times, but they would not listen to him. The mediator himself took care of the woman for months, and his deeds moved her sons to acknowledge their wrongdoing. They divided responsibility for their mother's care.

In all of these cases the mediators caused the dispute to subside by calming the parties, not by explaining or analyzing any gain or loss of rights by the parties. This approach is more than dispute suppression because it aims at achieving a new social equilibrium. And while it may work to resolve difficult problems, it may not promote legality. Also, a political dimension still remains: when the mediators sacrifice time and effort to solve a dispute, they illustrate the Party-state's solicitousness for the masses.

Mediation Based on Law: Legal Rules as Sources of Standards for Decision. Mediation outcomes are increasingly expressed in terms of formal legal rules. For example, ownership disputes over land are settled on the basis of rights recorded in local property registers or on whether or not a certificate of ownership had been issued by the local government.[40] Liu and Li do not indicate whether disputants *themselves* think in terms of rights, and, if so, what they view as the basis of their rights. They state only that legal rules are invoked less frequently than principles derived from reason or custom. Liu and Li nonetheless see mediation today as a force for "persuasion and education" about individual rights.[41]

One impediment to the application of legal rules within mediation lies in mediators' personal limitations. Liu and Li write that the educational level of mediators is low, and even state propaganda avoids mention of any rise in the legal sophistication of mediators. Many lack substantial formal education and receive only short-term training. Liu and Li also suggest that law-based mediation is less frequent because it fails to protect the "face" (*qingmian*) of the disputants after the dispute is settled. They note that most mediated disputes involve divorces or disagreements among neighbors that cannot easily be settled on legal grounds.

Policy now favors resolving disputes according to the legal rights of the parties and no longer emphasizes learning from the masses. The long-standing preference for compromise has also been allowed to re-emerge—although policy still sets limits. Policy considerations no longer dominate mediation but are still sometimes relevant to outcomes. One manual for mediators instructs the reader that in contract disputes the mediator must consider whether the contract in question is within the economic plan. The mediator is told that the collective represents the national interest in contracts between a collective and one or some of its members.[42] The shrinking of the plan and the rise of localistic forces in the countryside make it difficult to think that such emphases, so central to the pre-reform Party-state, continue to retain vitality.

Mediation Based on Combining "Emotion, Reason, and Law." The relative depoliticization of mediation in recent years is illustrated by the endorsement that the traditional Chinese value of "yielding" (*rang*) now receives.[43] Frowned upon under Maoism as a relic of "feudalism," yielding is central to the most widely used style of mediation, "mediation concurrently using feeling and law." Liu and Li characterize the style as seeking to "influence by appealing to emotion, instruct by appealing to reason, and make judgments according to law" (*dong zhi yi qing, xiao zhi yi li, ming zhi yi fa*). This compressed summary, elegantly balancing three elements, expresses the essence of thousands of years of traditional views of dispute resolution. It will reappear in the discussion of Chinese legal culture in chapter 9.

Some mediators seek to avoid the burden of investigating, but succeed only in "plastering over" (*huo xini*)[44] the dispute. Liu and Li are unsympathetic to mediation that simply focuses on suppressing disputes without clarifying the legal interests involved or dealing with the feelings of the parties. The Supreme People's Court has also expressly disapproved *huo xini* and the unwillingness to determine liability for breaches of contract.[45]

THE CONTEMPORARY FUNCTIONS OF PEOPLE'S MEDIATION

In earlier writings on mediation under Mao, I identified four functions of mediation in Chinese society prior to the Cultural Revolution: dispute settlement, mobilizing mass support for CCP policies, dispute suppression, and social control. Not surprisingly, reform has changed these functions significantly. Dispute settlement was the least important in the Maoist era, when extra-judicial mediation was cast as an adjunct to political mobilization and social control. Maoist mediation did not aim to resolve a dispute in terms of issues and concepts most relevant to the disputants but rather in terms of policy. For example, one couple seeking a divorce was told they owed it to the task of "national construction" to stay married, although building socialism per se was presumably less important to them than resolving their personal conflicts. A party with "good" class status very often prevailed over one with "bad" class status regardless of the specific issues that had caused the dispute. Mediators were instructed to view disputes as disruptions of social order that interfered with national goals. At the same time, even though mediation committees often expressed solutions in terms of Maoist concepts and slogans, other forces, such as the traditional preference for compromise, also influenced outcomes.

Civil Dispute Settlement

The prime function of mediation today has shifted to resolving civil disputes in nonpolitical terms, although other functions continue to compete with and may sometimes overwhelm this basic function. Also, as economic relationships grow more numerous and more complex, claims couched in terms of claimants' views of their rights derived from promulgated laws are on the rise and laws increasingly provide the referents for the settlement of mediated disputes.

When market-oriented economic reforms began in 1979, some legal scholars assumed that mediation was still a useful way to resolve contract disputes and argued that mediation was appropriate in disputes between state-owned enterprises because all were working for socialism.[46] Such sentiments are noticeably absent today. Instead, in the growing nongovernmental sectors of the economy, an individualistic and competitive mentality has displaced past notions of socialist harmony; litigation over civil and economic matters has increased; mediation is receding.

Because mediation is less politicized than before, its vocabulary has changed. Post-Maoist mediation can settle the dispute in terms of the issues disputants themselves might raise such as whether a husband mistreated a wife, whether a debt is owed, or who started a fracas and why. Moreover, law and policy require, relatively more strongly than before reform, that mediation be voluntary: disputants need not carry out mediation at all, and, if they do, they need not abide by its outcome if they wish to go to court. At the same time, mediation remains available to the Party-state as an instrument of policy. As already noted, mediators may still decide that a particular outcome is required when it contributes to some policy goal regardless of the rights of the parties.

Dispute Suppression and Social Control

Dispute suppression remains a key goal of mediation policy, but because of concern to prevent crime and disorder rather than to promote political aims. Liu and Li summarize the official line as one that still "propagandizes people's mediation work from the angle of protecting social stability and strengthening comprehensive management of social order."[47] Official policy continues to emphasize the prevention of crime, in the sense of preventing minor disputes from escalating into larger ones involving injury or death.[48] Reports regularly calculate the number of crimes prevented, and one high official stated that the 14 million civil disputes mediated in 1987 "could have resulted in some 140,000 murders and suicides" or 210,000 personal injury cases.[49] By and large, class struggle is no longer emphasized, although some commentators have clung to old rhetoric.[50] Some discussions suggest that the people's mediation committees should act as eyes and ears for the police, as they did when they were organized in 1950 by recording disputes, keeping statistics, and reporting upward all cases that might escalate.[51]

Liu and Li ascribe governmental support of mediation to the official concern for stability. They cite a 1994 newspaper article describing a "war of annihilation" launched by officials in Zhejiang, who mobilized 1,290 county mediators in a rural area and sent them to the countryside for five days, during which time they and others disposed of 180 cases. The authors note that while this method may be useful to calm (pingxi) some disputes, these mediators would not pay attention to special questions or to the demands of parties that their rights be protected.[52]

Mobilization

The use of mediation to focus the attention of the populace on a particular problem of policy has become less noticeable than in the Maoist era, but mediation is still sporadically linked to specific policies. In the mid-1980s, for example, recourse to both mediation and the courts was urged in order to uphold peasants' contracts. In early 1993, the Guangzhou Municipal CCP Committee was concerned about a rise in rural land disputes and sent work teams to "launch education on law and discipline in the villages and to mediate land and mountain forest disputes."[53] The teams were expected to stay in the villages for three to six months to investigate problems, educate the villagers on relevant laws and regulations, and mediate disputes. Soon after the Tiananmen tragedy, press articles fell back on an older rhetoric of struggle, discussing mediation as a vehicle for propagandizing policy and educating the masses on correct political thought.[54] More recently, mediation is consistently praised in connection with preventing crime.

THE FUTURE OF PEOPLE'S MEDIATION

In other modernizing societies such as Taiwan, the penetration of society by the state has caused traditional institutions for dispute resolution to decline and state institutions to grow.[55] On the mainland, extra-judicial mediation will probably decline for the same reasons it has done so in other modernizing societies. The discussion that follows first assesses some of the conflicting forces that are shaping mediation today and then assesses the future of mediation and its importance relative to other forms of dispute resolution.

Forces Promoting Continuation of People's Mediation

Concern for Social Control. People's mediation can be expected to remain significant in the foreseeable future because of the Party-state's strong interest in using people's mediation committees to detect and deter crime and social disorder and to lighten the workload of the courts, which is likely to grow.[56]

The Ministry of Justice is primarily interested in maintaining mediation in order to preserve its sphere of bureaucratic authority. Also, the Party has sought to maintain symbols of socialism even while it undoes the planned economy and may be reluctant to abandon yet another symbol of the Maoist past, especially one that is grounded in Chinese tradition and not borrowed from the Soviet Union. The mediation committees have a participatory form familiar to older generations of Chinese leaders and bureaucrats, and one that provides some basis for the argument that the mediation committees represent an exercise in popular democracy.

Chinese Legal Culture and Mediation. Mediation is also deeply rooted in traditional Chinese culture because it emphasizes the desirability of maintaining personal relationships. Chinese social networks, especially in the countryside, are based on acquaintances (*shuren*) from one's residence or workplace. In such contexts, "people do not want to use law to handle ordinary disputes and injure relationships. They would rather renounce some rights, if it serves emotion and reason, in order to improve social relations around them."[57] Mediation still offers opportunities for face-saving compromise as an alternative to an all-or-nothing outcome. Also, some problems are just too small to warrant adjudication and are not even perceived as raising legal issues. According to one judge:

Attitudes are changing, but many people still want to go to the mediation committees. Family matters, disputes between neighbors . . . residents still go to the mediation committees, which have a function for these kinds of disputes. Many disputes do not involve law but morality (*daode*), like dumping water out of a window onto the street, small assaults, thefts and the like.[58]

Popular perceptions of litigation also buttress people's mediation. Many Chinese are ignorant about the courts and their functions; the courts have long been characterized in propaganda as instruments to exercise dictatorship over class enemies rather than to settle disputes among the people.[59] The low level of the courts, popular cynicism about the influence of *guanxi* on outcomes, and a general lack of confidence in judicial fairness further combine to deter potential litigants. Uncertainty about costs is another factor. Finally, mediation fills a need when legal assistants in the villages are unable to provide effective legal assistance.

Forces Promoting the Decline of People's Mediation

Changing Nature of Disputes. As reforms create a more differentiated society, new kinds of disputes do not fall within the jurisdiction of the mediation committees. Labor disputes and disputes arising out of economic contracts, for example, are channeled to arbitration commissions and to the courts. In the past, mediation most often involved transactions among inhabitants of the same neighborhood or village. Today contracts increasingly may involve parties from different locales, parties without prior relationships, and higher monetary stakes than disputes centered on residence, family, or small transactions among relatives or acquaintances. Under these circumstances, effective mediation seems less possible and litigation has increased.

Changing Values. As emphasis on materialism and personal advancement grows among the Chinese populace, interest in contributing to a common wealth, socialist or otherwise, has declined. The decline of interest in community matters is most noticeable among the young, the well-educated, and other persons most exposed to Western influence.[60] Urban residents are both apathetic about serving on local residents' committees and less willing to submit their disputes to them. One judge comments:

The scope of mediation has shrunk, and the function of the street committees has changed. There is a new emphasis on privacy, and disputants may not want the intervention. Retired workers and old women now have less education than the parties, who would prefer to go to lawyers and courts, at least in the cities.[61]

In the countryside other factors may discourage disputants from using mediation committees. Rural people's mediation committees are still often seen as the grass-roots representatives of state administrative power and, once involved, villagers may feel subject to that power.[62]

Growing Rights-Consciousness. Fundamental changes in Chinese society brought on by reforms have also stimulated rights-consciousness and the use of courts to protect rights and seek compensation for infringement of rights.[63] The use of contracts has increased, as have the interests given explicit legal protection—by creating rights in intellectual property and in reputation—and the number of cases brought to the courts. One scholar at the Chinese Academy of Social Sciences noted that while the number of disputes brought to the courts has increased, the number of cases brought to mediation organizations has not.[64] The number of cases brought to mediation committees fell below six million for the first time in 1996.[65]

Research by scholars at the Institute of Law of the Chinese Academy of Social Sciences indicates that villagers are slowly becoming more willing to bypass local leaders and to seek redress directly in the courts, just like their counterparts in the cities, who are increasingly willing to bypass the local residents' committees.[66] Among the more than five thousand people surveyed, considerable numbers stated that in the event of an assault by a boss or a law enforcement employee, they would be willing to sue, although many said that they would feel shame if they were to institute a lawsuit in some kinds of cases—especially when a family member was involved.

Of course these changes in values can occur only slowly. One influence inhibiting the growth of rights-consciousness is the traditional notion that rights are granted by the state rather than inherent to the individual. Other influences include the necessity and the practice of submitting to greater power, reluctance to seek formal redress for grievances, and the long-standing emphasis on collective harmony rather than individual rights. Ignorance of rights and the slowness of the law to keep up with social developments further impede the expansion of rights-consciousness.

Decline in Authority of the Mediation Committees. The general loosening of the Party-state's control over citizens' lives seems to be weakening the authority of urban mediation committees. Fu Hualing argues that reform has eroded the mediation committees' rationale for existence. Formerly their members were chosen because they were activists and wanted to serve the revolution. Now that mediation must be conducted according to law, mediators cannot actually exercise state power because they cannot enforce their own decisions. Fu concludes that "[t]he reform has created a cultural and structural imperative that makes mediators powerless and their job meaningless. . . . The legalization and professionalism of people's mediation itself remains largely rhetoric."[67]

Continuing Issues for the Future

Recent discussions of mediation in Chinese journals and newspapers illustrate some of the contradictory forces tugging at mediation today. People's mediation, like many Chinese institutions, embodies traces of a Maoist conception of society on which the Chinese leadership no longer

relies. With the ideological justifications for the economic reforms themselves unclear, it is not surprising that policy toward mediation, other than
emphasizing its usefulness in maintaining social order, is no more coherent than Chinese policy generally. Some sources continue to praise people's mediation as an instrument of mass self-government and extol the
voluntariness of parties' participation as an expression of democracy. Other
sources look less to theory than to practical arguments for mediation. They
cite its flexibility and the familiarity of mediators with the milieu in
which disputes arise, and they praise it for leading to the direct and timely
resolution of disputes and saving the time and energy of the courts.[68]

Some academics insist that mediation should be more closely associated
with law. Before the Mediation Regulations were adopted in 1989, some
Chinese observers had expressed concern that mediation was not linked
closely enough to the law.[69] More recently, others argue that as the disputes change, the style of mediation must also change; taking reasonableness as a standard may lead to rights being neglected.[70] Criticisms of coercion and of "plastering over" disputes reflect the view that the mediation process slights legal rules. An article co-authored by Jiang Wei, one of
China's leading scholars of civil procedure, argues that although mediation
is appropriate when laws are general or vague, as civil law develops, the
rights and obligations that it creates should receive greater protection in
dispute-settling processes.[71] Although Jiang is concerned with judicial mediation (which will be discussed in chapter 9), his reasoning is broad
enough to apply to mediation generally. Other scholars also urge that adjudication should increase in importance over mediation, particularly in
economic cases.[72]

Writers less concerned about legal rights seek autonomy for mediation.
They seem to prefer to consider the people's mediation as not constituting
part of the legal system at all because it is based on voluntary mediation
agreements,[73] and they criticize attempts to apply to mediation rules of
procedure like those used in the courts, presumably because they do not
wish to curb its spontaneity.[74] Still others take an intermediate position.
Recognizing that economic reform has changed both the nature of the disputes that arise and the social context of mediation, they argue that the
function of mediation has shifted from serving economic construction indirectly—by maintaining stability and order—to serving it directly.[75] They
argue that mediation should be expanded and be more closely supervised.

The two contrasting schools of thought in Chinese legal circles have
been characterized as "Populists" and "Legalists."[76]

Populists argue that since mediation is a form of popular justice, it
should be left alone by the state; even if abuses exist, they can be corrected
by "scientific management."[77] They further argue that it is unrealistic to

expect mediators to represent parties in economic transactions or to provide a wider range of legal services, given their low levels of education and legal sophistication.[78]

Legalists, mindful of the coercive power that people's mediation exercised before the Cultural Revolution, would limit its scope. When the mediation regulations were revised, Legalists succeeded in formally removing minor criminal cases from the jurisdiction of the mediation committees. Rejecting mediation's intrusiveness, they argue that mediators should not become involved unless specifically requested by the disputants.[79]

One problem, however, is that although courts might provide an accessible alternative to mediation committees, the courts sometimes refuse to accept small disputes.[80] In any event, defining the authority of the mediation committees remains problematic. Fu argues that to make the mediation committees meaningful they must be given additional authority to enforce their decisions, but this seems unlikely in view of the tendency to stress supervision of the mediation committees by the courts and the judicial assistants.

Even if people's mediation somehow becomes more "legalized," Chinese disputants may still avoid it. Donald Clarke suggests that, to many, mediation threatens to combine the potential for coercion with the weakness of the courts. He adds that, "as mediation becomes institutionalized, it becomes an arm of the state, and the Chinese state is generally uncomfortable with the idea of letting individuals make their own deals, whether in dispute resolution or in the market place."[81]

It may be that mediation in cities and in the countryside will evolve differently. Fu Hualing proposes that mediation be allowed to decay in the cities, where he views its power and prestige as declining, but that the countryside be treated differently:

Due to the cultural and physical distance between the state-supported law and the peasants, rural societies are different from cities, and should be treated as such. Accordingly, local features should be considered, local customs and regulations respected, and local élites given authority to resolve certain civil and criminal matters within their communities. At the same time, however, the basic principles of criminal law should be upheld.[82]

Too many factors that have already been discussed warn against delegating power to local élites. I have already emphasized that central power has weakened as a result of reform; further delegation of power to maintain order could mean even greater weakening, not only of the center, but within localities as well.[83] At the moment, there seems to be no serious interest in changing the link between courts and mediation committees. If formal legal institutions gain further credibility, the contrast between adjudicating rights in courts (or in arbitration tribunals) and effecting compromises and repairing relationships in mediation committees may be intensified. At the same time, local authorities as well as the Ministry of Justice may modify the make-up of the committees to add legally sophisticated members to the urban residents who have previously been the only class of members. Such experimentation is suggested by a Chinese press release that not only presented yet another model mediator, 68-year-old "Aunt Huang," as a peace-keeper in Shanghai's busy streets, but added that civil mediators are "judicial assistants, clerks of neighborhood committees and some senior citizens."[84]

Yet another problem in defining the function of people's mediation is the need to define the values it should promote. Laura Nader has analyzed "ideologies of harmony" in dispute resolution, noting that they may be used defensively by a community to resist domination by other groups in the society (such as colonizers) or offensively as part of an ideology that justifies the exercise of control by one group over others.[85] Mediation under Mao was most unambiguously suffused with an ideology of control: It required that the outcomes of mediated disputes be "correct" according to politicized criteria. Today, however, the basis of that ideology of control has been seriously eroded. The need for social order may rationalize maintaining the apparatus of control, but Maoist ideology's loss of legitimacy still requires the Chinese leadership to decide what values they will want mediation to affirm.

While they are deciding, however, Chinese society will not wait; values are emerging independent of the Party-state. Current mediation regulations explicitly recognize "social morality" as one of the bases on which mediated solutions to disputes rest. That social morality will inform solutions to disputes in neighborhoods and villages where values are shared, including whatever ideology about harmony may exist in popular culture.

In attempts to understand Chinese legal culture and institutions, we should not treat "mediation" as a unitary concept. It had no single style or form in traditional China;[86] under Maoism it was a more complex institution than it was portrayed in the official press, and it promoted a mixture of traditional and modern values that were not always mutually consistent. Today, styles of mediation and the values mediation promotes vary greatly when practiced in settings as diverse as urban neighborhood mediation committees, factories, city offices for settling housing disputes, arbitration commissions for settling contract disputes, and the courts themselves. The status and power of mediators, particularly in the countryside, are also bound to affect the outcomes of disputes and perceptions of the process by both disputants and observers.[87]

The research discussed here suggests that attitudes toward assertion of claims in the courts range along a spectrum from traditionally motivated reluctance to state-promoted aggressiveness, with traditional values still dominant. Neither rights nor traditional attitudes toward those rights are unitary or fixed, however, and the continuous rise in contract litigation suggests changes in traditional values. At the same time, the concepts of rights held by litigants may be less rigid than those of Western counterparts. Chinese claimants may expect less than American litigants when they assert that their "rights" have been violated, suggesting some continuity with the "softness" of concepts of rights in earlier times. Even notions of rights that seem diluted by comparison to Western ideal types could, however, still be useful—and be perceived by Chinese claimants as being useful—in bringing about results considered to be just or fair in a Chinese context.

Larger developmental processes not unique to the PRC will also affect dispute settlement. Economic growth on Taiwan made values associated with tradition become increasingly fragmented and easily manipulated in the settlement of disputes,[88] and, as private and collective economic activity grows in the PRC, similar fragmentation of values will occur. Finally, an even broader perspective suggests that although mediation everywhere professes to restore or establish social harmony, if its functions are to be understood, the "harmony ideologies" underlying mediation must be clearly identified.[89]

For the moment, all the alternatives available to disputants will have some relationship to the Party-state, which has not displayed a willingness to foster or permit "non-state" mediation. The Chinese view of law appears to be so rooted in social control that mediators may continue to effect compromises that conform to "the values embodied in state norms," rather than play a facilitative role for private economic actors. Disputants may prefer to look for mediation that is more truly "nonstate mediation,"[90] and the Party-state may be unable to prevent the growth of informal practices of dispute resolution in whatever version of civil society that emerges in China in the future.

The destiny of people's mediation is linked to that of the courts, especially if the latter become more professionalized in the struggle to increase autonomy. The emergence of rights-consciousness will turn partly on perceptions among the general population of how the courts resolve disputes that are brought to them.

Arbitration

The new arbitration commissions provide an additional alternative to formal adjudication that is more rigorous than people's mediation and could, therefore, enhance rights-consciousness.

THE ABSENCE OF ARBITRATION BEFORE REFORM

Arbitration is a relatively new addition to the ensemble of Chinese vehicles for dispute settlement. Early in the history of the PRC an arbitral organ was established to handle international commercial disputes on the model of the Soviet Union.[91] Arbitration otherwise received little serious consideration in the pre-reform period, as I suggested in chapter 4. Illustrating what Chinese law-makers later recognized to be a confusion of roles, a notice of the State Council in 1962 provided that disputes among state enterprises should be "arbitrated" by local branches of the State Economic Commission, which was charged with executing the five-year and yearly plans. As a quasi-official commentator later put it, "although the term 'arbitration' appeared, in reality this was not arbitration but rather administrative handling."[92] Thereafter, the Cultural Revolution intervened, preventing further experimentation with legal institutions, and arbitration mechanisms did not reappear until twenty years later.

POST-REFORM EXPERIMENTATION WITH ARBITRATION, 1980–1994

As new commercial transactions were defined by legislation in the early 1980s, arbitration bodies were created to deal with a growing number of disputes. These arbitral bodies were created on an ad hoc basis and lacked unifying concepts or principles. Confusion between administration and dispute settlement grew, and contradictory views of the function of arbitration contended. Was arbitration to emphasize mediation and conciliation or was it to be more like adjudication? Was it to be final? If not, should a decision be appealable? If appealable, should the appeal go to an administrative body (if so, which one?) or to a court? The relations between the new arbitration organizations and the courts differed considerably among the various arbitration schemes, as did the finality of the arbitral decisions.

After more than ten years of experimentation, the Arbitration Law of the PRC (Arbitration Law), which became effective on September 1, 1995, was adopted with the aim of establishing a coherent and internally consistent arbitral system. The problems and the hodgepodge which that legislation was intended to correct ought to be understood for what they tell the observer about the emergence of arbitration; in addition, the problems illustrate some of the most fundamental difficulties that the PRC faces today in ordering a legal system. A few examples will suffice.

For economic contracts, arbitration was conducted by Economic Contract Arbitration Commissions created by the vast State Administration of Industry and Commerce (SAIC) in 1983. Either party to a contract had the choice of taking a dispute to an arbitration organization or to a court. If the matter went to arbitration first and one of the parties was dissatisfied with the result, he could begin suit in the courts. This process became known as the "one arbitration, two adjudication" system. The system was extended to new types of economic contracts such as those dealing with construction and the sale of mineral products and various kinds of insurance.

When the State Council adopted measures intended to strengthen the autonomy of state-owned enterprises in disputes arising out of "lease management" (*zuling jingying*), the parties could apply for arbitration to the Economic Contract Arbitration Commission mentioned above; if either party was dissatisfied with the decision, it could appeal to the next highest level of Arbitration Commission, whose decision would be final. Later the State Council, which had established rules for "contracted management" of state enterprises, provided that if the parties had included an arbitration clause in their contract the system of "reconsideration" (*fuyi*) previously described could apply to these contracts as well.[93]

Yet another variation was provided in the Product Quality Law, adopted in 1993. It called for arbitration by the Economic Contract Arbitration Commission if the parties had previously agreed in their contract to that mode of dispute settlement, but if they had not, either party could initiate suit in the courts. This was dubbed "arbitration by agreement" or "either arbitration or adjudication."

Not all economic contracts were arbitrated by the commissions of the SAIC. Controversies over authors' rights were arbitrated by special commissions established by the Ministry of Cultural Affairs; controversies arising out of technology contracts were arbitrated by commissions established by the Science and Technology Commissions; controversies over transactions in real property were arbitrated by real estate arbitration commissions established under local real estate management bureaus. In large cities, city-level and urban district commissions shared and sometimes overlapped jurisdiction; in some places an agreement between the parties was a prerequisite to arbitration, while in others it was not. Legislation on whether suit in the courts was possible after an arbitral decision was issued was not consistent from city to city and also varied on whether municipal commissions could revise decisions of district commissions. Patterns were even less discernible in commissions established under the consumer protection law, although the arbitrators were often concurrently administrators from the SAIC.

By the end of the 1980s, the situation was chaotic. One observer counted twenty-four different laws that created arbitration mechanisms for purely domestic matters. The sources of those laws varied from the State Council, State Planning Commission, State Economic Commission, and the SAIC to highly specialized agencies such as those responsible for fishing, harbors, labor, and inspection of medical products. Multiple local arbitration laws existed on such matters as contracts, product quality, prices, environmental matters, and housing, to cite some prominent examples. In this legislative welter some twenty different types of arbitration organizations existed, all varying on such fundamental issues as the requirement of an agreement between the parties as a prerequisite to arbitration and the relationship of arbitration to mediation; moreover, in some cases the parties could go directly to the courts.

There was also a basic contradiction between administration and arbitration. Although many disputes by their nature might better have been dealt with as matters involving legal rights and duties, they were being handled by administrative agencies accustomed to ordering bureaucratically. However, bureaucratic means of handling disputes seemed more appropriate to a planned economy than to the market that Chinese policy aspired to attain. When administrative agencies acted as arbitration organizations, they generated uncertainty about the jurisdiction and the legal effect of their decisions. ·

ARBITRATION UNDER THE ARBITRATION LAW
OF 1994: GENERAL PROVISIONS

Against this background extensive research was done, and in 1994 a new law, the Arbitration Law, was promulgated in order to create a new nationwide system. It defined arbitrable transactions, established a nationwide and uniform system of arbitration to replace the previous unsystematized assortment of institutions, provided a procedural code for the conduct of arbitration, aimed at professionalized arbitration personnel, went a long way toward endowing arbitral awards with finality, and set the outlines of relationships between arbitration organizations and the courts.[94] Because the new law has become effective so recently and mandated the dissolution of all former arbitration organizations and establishment of new commissions, little information is available on practice under the new system. Throughout this book, I have emphasized the need for skepticism about the extent to which Chinese laws and Chinese practice correspond, and here, too, the reader should regard this legislation as a plan whose effectiveness will turn on its implementation. The new law is noteworthy because it promises to be a significant expansion of the available resources. It is also a welcome systematization of earlier ad hoc arrangements.

The disputes to be arbitrated were defined by the new law as arising out of "contract disputes" and other disputes involving rights and interests in property among citizens, legal persons, and other organizations that are of equal legal status, that is, not government departments. Since the new commissions are intended to replace all previously existing domestic contract arbitration mechanisms, they will probably exercise jurisdiction over all types of economic disputes, such as torts, even if they are not specifically named in the Arbitration Law itself. Disputes over family-related matters, namely those involving "marital, adoption, guardianship, support for the elderly and inheritance disputes," are not arbitrable, and neither are administrative disputes.

In place of the many different organizations that previously existed, the new law establishes arbitration commissions in cities including those governed directly by the central government (Beijing, Shanghai, and Tianjin), cities in which provincial or autonomous governments are situated, and cities with established districts. The new system does not have multiple levels of jurisdiction. It is independent of all administrative departments and subject only to the general disciplinary supervision of a China Arbitration Commission that was to be created after the law came into effect. The commission had not yet been created when the law was promulgated. Each commission is to have a "supervisory commission," a secretariat, and a panel of arbitrators. By March 1997, around 110 such commissions had already been created, but it is unclear how many will be established altogether.[95]

The commissions shall "engage" arbitrators to comprise the panel of each arbitration commission. To qualify, candidates must have eight years of experience as arbitrators, lawyers, or judges, or else have comparable stipulated qualifications; officials of administrative departments may be appointed if they are qualified. Lists of the members of the panels are to be published.

The new law centers on the importance of the agreement of the parties, either at the time they signed their contract or after the dispute arose, to submit their dispute to arbitration. An agreement must express the intent of the parties to submit to arbitration, it must identify the matters to be arbitrated, and it must specify the arbitration commission that the parties have chosen (Art. 16). The jurisdiction of the commissions is not based on any territorial principle, and, in an attempt to combat the "local protectionism" that hinders the courts, the law permits the parties to select any arbitration commission in China to hear their disputes. If the parties disagree on the validity of the agreement, either the Arbitration Commission or a court may rule on the issue. If their agreement is valid, the designated PRC arbitration organization has exclusive jurisdiction over the matter unless one party files suit before the arbitration begins and the other does not object.

The procedures established by the legislation are very simple. Unless the parties agree to appoint a single arbitrator, their dispute will be heard by a tribunal composed of three arbitrators. Each party may choose one arbitrator from the panel; the third, the presiding arbitrator, is chosen by the commission or the parties if they agree. Rules for disqualification of arbitrators are stated, including *ex parte* meetings with the parties or acceptance of entertainment or gifts. Written submissions of the parties' arguments must be made and the commission must conduct a hearing (which is not public unless the parties agree otherwise), at which lawyers may participate. The tribunal may mediate the dispute if the parties agree. Decision is by majority opinion of the arbitrators, and the decision must be expressed in a written statement. The award becomes effective on the date it is rendered.

Like the procedure in the courts, the arbitration rules provide for mediation to be conducted by the tribunal only if the parties are willing. If through mediation the parties agree to settle the dispute, the tribunal must prepare a written mediation agreement or award, which has binding legal effect and, therefore, is enforceable in the courts if necessary; if mediation does not succeed, the tribunal must make an award "in a timely fashion."

The award may be challenged in the local intermediate-level people's court for certain limited reasons, which include the following:

no arbitration agreement was reached;

the award covered matters not within the scope of the agreement or the jurisdiction of the commission;

the composition or the procedure of the tribunal violated the law;

the evidence on which the award was based was fabricated;

one party concealed evidence that affected the impartiality of the arbitration; or

the arbitrators accepted bribes or practiced favoritism.

An additional basis for overturning an award, however, is a potential threat to the finality of arbitration awards, since it is simply that arbitrators "subverted the law." This provision would seem to be another compromise with those who did not want to diminish the power of the courts, and it remains to be seen whether it will have a significant effect in reducing the effectiveness of arbitration under the new law.

Execution of the award can be carried out by the courts if one party resists implementation of the award; in defending against enforcement, a party may raise objections to the award that are broader than those mentioned above that can serve as the basis for a direct attack on an award.

They are the grounds that were established by the Civil Procedure Law as the basis for nonenforcement of an arbitral award:

the parties did not conclude an arbitration agreement;

the matters arbitrated exceeded either the arbitration agreement or the jurisdiction of the arbitration commission;

the composition of the tribunal violated the Arbitration Law;

the main evidence on which the facts were ascertained was insufficient;

the law was incorrectly applied.

The first three grounds are identical with the permissible bases for challenges to an award under the Arbitration Law, but the last two are troubling. Although the grounds under the Arbitration Law relating to evidence ("fabricated" or "concealed") or law ("perverted") for directly challenging an award were obviously intended to be relatively limited, the broadly expressed basis for refusing to enforce an award permits the court to engage in a wide-ranging reinvestigation of the arbitral proceedings.[96] As will be shown in chapter 9, the lack of finality that is embedded in the arbitration process is a prominent defect of adjudication by the courts as well.

A threat to the success of the new arbitration system is posed by "local protectionism," a serious problem currently critically hampering the judicial system that I will discuss in chapter 9. Although, as we have seen, the parties to a contract may agree to submit their disputes to any commission, suits to enforce arbitration awards must be brought in the courts of the place where the losing party resides or possesses assets.[97] These are the places, of course, in which a party can most effectively muster the support of government and Party officials to pressure the local courts. This possibility will work directly against the intention of the drafters of the Arbitration Law to elevate the arbitration commissions above local pressures, as demonstrated by the previously noted fact that the law bases the jurisdiction of the arbitration commissions not on any territorial principle but solely on the agreement of the parties.

The Arbitration Law sets forth principles of legality and method consistent with a market economy, including the following:

Voluntariness. The parties have the freedom to agree to arbitrate and to choose the arbitral organ and the composition of the arbitral tribunal.

Independence of arbitration. The arbitral commissions and tribunals are not subordinate to administrative agencies or to the courts (except to the extent that the courts can pass on arbitral awards within the scope of legislation as stated above); moreover, the arbitral tribunals, in deciding specific cases, are independent both of the arbitration commissions that appoint them and of the China Arbitration Association, which is styled as a "self-regulatory organization of arbitration commissions" and is responsible for maintaining professional discipline among the commissions; the tribunals are free, too, from internal administrative review of their decisions.

Observance of principles of legality. The tribunals must clarify facts, correctly apply the law, and be fair to all parties.

Exclusivity of arbitration. Once the parties have agreed to arbitration, a party may not take the dispute to a court or to another arbitral organization.

SINO-FOREIGN DISPUTES NEWLY ADDED TO THE JURISDICTION OF DOMESTIC ARBITRATION COMMISSIONS

The tasks of the new Arbitration Commissions were already complicated when it was thought that they would deal only with domestic contract disputes, and, in July 1996, the State Council provoked some surprise when it decided that the new commissions would also have jurisdiction over disputes involving foreigners (*shewai*) if the foreigners agree.[98] This decision meant that the monopoly over such disputes that had been enjoyed by CIETAC for forty years was ended; CIETAC would now share that jurisdiction with the Arbitration Commissions, although the Arbitration Law itself had not indicated that such a change was intended. If the parties do not agree to use either type of arbitration tribunal, their dispute can be resolved only by the Chinese courts. This development carries with it some reasons for anxiety for foreign traders. CIETAC, however, has fought back: although previously there was some doubt whether CIETAC would take jurisdiction over disputes between FIEs and Chinese parties when the only "foreign-related" element was foreign investment in the FIE, in May 1998 CIETAC announced that it would hear any disputes between FIEs and between FIEs and Chinese parties.[99]

The commissions are brand-new, in a country in which the rule of law is at best nascent and tentative. Not only do they lack any experience in handling international disputes, but many of them are located in places where there are unlikely to be many arbitrators sophisticated about international trade or investment. Also, although CIETAC awards cannot be reexamined by Chinese courts except for certain exceptional reasons (consistent with international practice), decisions by the new commissions may be reexamined by the courts, which can refuse to enforce them because of errors in weighing evidence or applying the law. Arbitration before the local commissions could thus be only a prelude to involvement in the local Chinese courts rather than an alternative to it.

Extra-judicial dispute resolution and judicial mediation now exist in a very different social and economic environment from that of China before reform. Although extra-judicial mediation has faded in prominence, it still offers a compelling model for dispute resolution to many in the society and in the courts themselves, and it remains an attractive alternative to adjudication that can dilute emerging conceptions of rights as well as blunt growing rights-consciousness. In the chapter that follows, we will move to the courts and explore their approaches to dispute resolution.

CHAPTER 9

The Courts Under Reform

Courts throughout the country are vigorously advocating the "Iron Judge" spirit of making selfless contributions in upholding the law impartially, causing an outpouring of good judges in the style of Tan Lin. In the court of Zhangjiagang, in Jiangsu province, studying Tan Lin begins with the leaders. Members of the court's Party organization take the lead, handling several important cases each month. . . . Throughout the three levels of courts in Beijing, officials promote the Tan Lin spirit that "People's Court officials . . . carry the scales of justice on their shoulders, we absolutely cannot permit one case in our hands to be handled incorrectly," and participate actively in the "Strike Hard" struggle.[1]

TODAY, CHINA'S JUDGES adjudicate disputes by applying promulgated laws and follow rules of civil procedure quite familiar to Western observers. The contrast with their activity before reform is great. The imprint of the pre-reform past lingers, however, and very different philosophies of law and organization continue to contend for dominance in defining judges' tasks and their methods of work. New forces generated by reform also greatly complicate attempts to strengthen the courts and their influence in Chinese society.

A majority of the disputes that reach the courts, for example, still end in mediated rather than in adjudicated outcomes. Also, policy and propaganda continue to emphasize an overt political dimension in the work of the courts. This is symbolized, for example, by the resemblance between the praise of a model judge in 1996 that is quoted above and the celebration of a model Maoist mediator in 1955 quoted at the beginning of chapter 3. Mediator and judge alike are praised because they perform their work in a politically correct manner, and, as we will see below, state propaganda still commonly views judges as soldiers in struggles, such as in the "Strike Hard" campaigns against crime that have for years been thrust into the Chinese courts.

This chapter analyzes the operation of the courts from a variety of perspectives. It introduces the judicial hierarchy, surveys the education, selection, and promotion of judges; and discusses the values that they are supposed to embody and the ethical dilemmas that they constantly encounter. It then examines the operations of the judicial process, the sources of the rules that judges apply in their decisions, and reported judicial decisions. I conclude the chapter by proposing an interpretation of Chinese conceptions of the role of courts and some of its implications for the rule of law.

The Chinese Judicial System

For the first thirty years of the People's Republic, Chinese courts essentially existed in form but not in substance, and they all but disappeared during the Cultural Revolution. The judicial system has been extensively rebuilt since 1979, and its organization is summarized here.

THE JUDICIAL HIERARCHY

The Chinese judicial system includes courts of general jurisdiction as well as specialized courts.[2] The courts of general jurisdiction are organized hierarchically by location. At the top is the *Zuigao renmin fayuan*, or Supreme People's Court (SPC) in Beijing, below which are three levels. The first consists of thirty *Gaoji renmin fayuan*, or Higher-Level People's Courts (HLPC). This "higher level" includes centrally administered cities like Beijing and Shanghai and autonomous regions like Tibet and Xinjiang, in addition to each of China's provinces. At the next level are 389 *Zhongji renmin fayuan*, or Intermediate-Level People's Courts (ILPC). This "prefectural level" includes provincially administered cities (*shi*), as well as prefectures (*diqu*) directly beneath the provinces and districts within centrally administered cities. At the lowest level, that of rural counties and urban districts, are 3,067 *Jiceng renmin fayuan*, or Basic Level People's Courts (BLPC). In large rural counties with dispersed populations the county BLPCs often establish People's Tribunals (*Renmin fating*) in outlying areas; they are technically at the same administrative level as their parent BLPC, rather than at a subordinate fifth level. In 1994, excluding the People's Tribunals, of which there are approximately 18,000, People's Courts at all four levels totaled 3,486.[3] There are also over 100 specialized courts, including railway, forestry, maritime, and military courts, whose jurisdiction is not limited by the administrative boundaries discussed above.

This jurisdictional pyramid is not as neat as it would appear, however, because higher-level courts may sometimes exercise primary jurisdiction over cases that would have an influence in their district.[4] In economic cases, the stated criteria for determining whether higher-level jurisdiction should be exercised include the level in the governmental hierarchy of the departments involved, the amount of money involved, and the complexity of the case.

ORGANIZATION OF THE COURTS

Courts of general jurisdiction at all levels are administered by general administrative and personnel offices. They are organized into separate divisions (*ting*) for criminal, administrative, civil, and economic matters, and for enforcement. Administrative divisions handle cases involving disputes of individuals, organizations, or enterprises with governmental agencies. Civil divisions tend to focus on family and inheritance law, and on contract, property, and tort disputes between natural persons. Almost half of all cases brought before the People's Courts in 1996 concerned marriage and family (*hunyin jiating*), with debts running a close second.[5] As reform of real estate ownership and management has been instituted, disputes over rights to real property have appeared. Economic divisions focus on contract disputes among state-owned enterprises and between those enterprises and a variety of new economic actors that have appeared as a result of economic reform.[6] Tort litigation, involving such matters as accidents and product liability, has also been growing. Most basic-level and intermediate courts also have enforcement and appeals divisions.[7] Also, various specialized divisions have been set up in recent years, including, notably, one for intellectual property matters.

Each court has a president, one or more vice presidents, an Adjudication Committee (*shenpan weiyuanhui*), judges who work in the divisions, and clerks. The court president has three types of duties: substantive case work, internal administration, and external affairs, discussed here in order. First, because all decisions in cases within Chinese courts must be approved by either the court president, a vice president, or a division chief (*tingzhang*), the president is usually involved in his court's most important cases. Second, the president is responsible for the court's finances and personnel matters. This task is closely tied to his third and most important duty, external relations. Chinese judges lack tenure of any kind and are therefore beholden to local government and Party officials for their positions and their courts' finances. Local Party secretaries and their Political-Legal Committees (*zhengfa weiyuanhui*) routinely review the disposition of court cases (their involvement in the work of the courts is discussed in detail below). Relations with such local power-holders are a vital, if informal, aspect of the court president's job.[8]

Because the court president is busy dealing with local officials, many of his administrative and case approval duties fall to his vice presidents, who supervise the work of the divisions. Each division has a chief judge, judges, assistant judges, and clerks. Cases are heard by a three-judge panel called a collegiate bench (*heyiting*), with one judge in charge.[9] Some cases are also heard by a panel of one judge and two People's Assessors (*renmin peishenyuan*). While each member of such committees formally has equal say, in practice People's Assessors are expected to follow the ruling of the presiding judge.[10]

THE TYPES OF CIVIL AND ECONOMIC CASES HANDLED BY THE COURTS

Tables 6 and 7 display the types of civil and economic cases that the courts handle. The data reflect the increasing commercialization of the Chinese economy: marriage and family disputes did not increase much during the seven-year period considered here, whereas the number of debt cases in the civil category and the number of economic cases and contract disputes more than doubled during the same period. The rising number of cases also reflects the governmental policy of encouraging use of the courts.[11]

The Chinese Courts at Work

THE JUDGES

Judicial Qualifications

The size of the Chinese judiciary has grown dramatically since the reforms began. One survey estimates that it increased from 58,000 court cadres in 1979 to 292,000 in 1995, of whom 156,000 were judges, with the remainder court police and other court staff.[12] By 1997, the number of judges had reached 250,000.[13] Throughout the 1980s most of China's judges came to their positions through transfer from Party and military posts. Most lacked a university education, and very few had received formal legal instruction.

Demobilized soldiers have been a major pool from which judges have been drawn since the early 1950s. According to one judge,[14] PLA officers were considered good candidates for judgeships because they, like police, had been engaged in enforcing proletarian dictatorship and possessed the appropriate ideological outlook on their work. Some were made vice presidents of the courts even without legal education. The former PLA officers were instructed in "basic legal knowledge" and "legal practice" in special spare time training courses instituted at the courts to make up for their low educational level.[15]

More formal training programs have been established by the Supreme People's Court at Beijing University and at People's University, where judges attend courses for from one to three years. There are also one-year programs for assistant judges, who can be promoted to senior judge if they are successful on an examination, and six-month programs for judges from intermediate courts and the Supreme People's Court.[16] A Judicial Training College was established in Beijing in 1997.[17] Although these training ef-

TABLE 6. First Instance Economic Dispute Cases Decided, 1990-1997

	Total	Contract	Damages	Labor	Bankruptcy
1990	598,317	553,540	1,134	521	
1991	583,771	535,799	1,613	547	
1992	648,018	595,510	2,392		265
1993	883,681	814,842	2,707		710
1994	1,045,440	964,302	2,682		1,156
1995	1,271,434	1,178,311	3,742		1,938
1996	1,504,494	1,393,275	3,629		4,400
1997	1,478,139	1,367,560	3,801		5,697

SOURCE: *Zhongguo falü nianjian* (Law Yearbook of China) 1991 (p. 935), 1992 (p. 855), 1993 (p. 936), 1994 (p. 1028), 1995 (p. 1065), 1996 (p. 959), 1997 (p. 1056), 1998 (p. 1239).

forts have raised the educational level of judges considerably,[18] overall levels remain low. In 1994, a provincial higher court president wrote that "about half of the judges in the country have not reached the level of university level legal education."[19] In 1993 almost 30 percent of chief judges of HLPCs lacked a university or college background.[20] A study noted that in 1994 the Ministry of Justice entertained the hope that by 1997 general diplomas from part-time universities would have been awarded to 70 percent of court employees, 80 percent of judges, and 90 percent of court presidents.[21]

Whether or not a judge has a degree may not be very meaningful. Some college degrees were granted after only short periods of study during the early 1980s, and some of the degrees earned were not in law. The content and the effectiveness of the courses intended to raise the legal sophistication of the judges is questionable. One judge who had completed a two-year part-time course told an interviewer that "many of the students, including me, at that time wanted only to get a diploma. . . . At present, few verdicts or reports summarizing cases are well written."[22]

Although law schools are producing graduates in unprecedented numbers, only 500 to 600 of these new law graduates were assigned to courts each year throughout most of the 1980s.[23] Some of these were appointed to staff positions such as secretaries, rather than judges. Moreover, the recent law graduates are still too young and too few to play a significant role in the system. The shortage of legally trained judges makes judicial ignorance of the law a real danger, particularly because of the legislative incoherence that has been mentioned above.

The Judges Law

Objective qualifications for all judges were not formally established until a Judges Law[24] was promulgated in 1995, and judges then in office who did not meet the qualifications were given an undetermined amount of time to attain them.[25] Nonetheless, the Judges Law helped to raise standards by requiring academic qualifications for judges. It provides that Chinese citizens who have reached the minimum age of twenty-three, uphold the Constitution, and "possess good political and professional quality and good conduct" may become judges if they have graduated from an institution of higher learning where they specialized in law as undergraduates or graduates or, if they have graduated from such an institution with a specialization other than law, have "professional legal knowledge" and have worked for two years.[26]

Provision was made in the Judges Law for examinations of judges, with grades on such examinations to be the basis for "rewards, punishments, training, dismissals and readjustment of grades and wages" (Art. 13). Each People's Court is required to establish examination and appraisal committees, and the committee at the Supreme People's Court is to organize national examinations for newly appointed judges and assistant judges (Art. 46). Judges face annual performance reviews and can be dismissed for,

Table 7. First Instance Civil Cases Handled, 1990–1997

	Civil	Marriage and family	Debt	Tort	Housing
1990	1,849,728	935,831	568,016	169,919	58,095
1991	1,910,013	1,007,901	543,322	184,878	57,747
1992	1,948,949	1,042,880	565,880	190,073	59,052
1993	2,091,651	1,096,164	638,318	197,606	67,036
1994	2,382,174	1,197,343	783,007	213,455	80,868
1995	2,714,665	1,314,678	939,927	245,004	93,147
1996	3,084,464	1,398,396	1,156,431	275,233	108,760
1997	3,242,402	1,428,722	1,243,159	296,633	117,816
	Civil	Marriage and family	Debt	Tort	Housing
1990	1,849,728	50.6%	30.7%	9.2%	3.1%
1991	1,910,013	52.8	28.4	9.7	3.0
1992	1,948,949	53.5	29.0	9.8	3.0
1993	2,091,651	52.4	30.5	9.4	3.2
1994	2,382,174	50.3	32.9	9.0	3.4
1995	2,714,665	48.4	34.6	9.0	3.4
1996	3,084,464	45.3	37.5	8.9	3.5
1997	3,242,202	44.1	38.3	9.1	3.6

Source: *Zhongguo falü nianjian* (Law Yearbook of China): 1991 (p. 934), 1992 (p. 855), 1993 (p. 936), 1994 (p. 1028), 1995 (p. 1064), 1996 (p. 958), 1997 (p. 1056), 1998 (p. 1239).

among other reasons, having been rated as "incompetent" in two consecutive years.

Appointment, Removal, and Reward of Judges

Appointment and removal of chief judges at each level in the hierarchy is made by decision of the legislative body at the same level. Thus, the Supreme People's Court president is appointed by the National People's Congress, and lower courts' presidents are elected and removed by the people's congresses at the corresponding level. Judicial personnel above the rank of assistant judge (i.e., judges, deputy chief judges, members of the Adjudication Committee, and deputy court presidents) are selected by the chief judges at each level and approved by the Standing Committees of local people's congress at that level. Assistant judges are selected by chief judges.

The Judges Law places a value on formal educational qualifications. However, nonprofessional criteria are widely used in selecting judges, and, in practice, local Party organizational departments have the final say over all judicial appointments.[27] Strikingly, few lawyers have been selected to be judges. One judge, interviewed before the law was enacted, admitted that "[o]ur organization department has an express provision, that those who have not tempered themselves in departments of politics and law, who have no experience in handling cases, who have not majored in the legal profession, including those with [an academic level of] middle school or high school—of course primary school is too low—people like that can become judges."[28] CCP officials determine for local People's congresses which candidates to select for the judiciary, and often value *guanxi* and political orthodoxy over professional standards.

The Chinese Judiciary: Performance Criteria

The Judge as Soldier of the State. He Weifang, a law professor at Beijing University who has written insightfully about the Chinese courts, cautions that although public emphasis on recruiting PLA officers as judges has declined, the outlook and the cast of mind associated with the program have not completely changed. Analyzing the content of an internal judicial system newspaper, He finds that model judges are commended for fighting in support of the PRC on the civilian front. Demobilized soldiers are disproportionately singled out for commendation in the performance of judicial duties, when compared with university and college graduates, and their accomplishments are often described using militaristic imagery. When judges with formal education are commended, they are praised for "work-style" and dedication rather than for their experience or legal knowledge. Articles analogize courts to fighting units; one report told of a night raid on a Jilin town by court cadres and policemen to round up persons who had failed to obey verdicts or court orders "as if on a battlefield instead of in a dignified but solemn court."[29] Writing in January 1998, He Weifang complained in a newspaper article about the persistence of the practice of placing demobilized soldiers in the courts as judges.[30]

Criteria for Rewards. Further insight into the contemporary Chinese conception of the judge is the provision in the Judges Law on rewards (Art. 28), which enumerates the "outstanding performances" that may be rewarded with three grades of merit citations. The first three, understandably, are for "enforcing the law fairly," "summing up practical experience in trials and playing a guiding role in judicial work," and proposing suggestions for judicial reform that achieve "outstanding results." Improving judicial work and assisting people's mediation committees are also commendable deeds. Also listed, however, are "safeguarding state, collective and individual interests to prevent major losses," "courageously struggling against criminal activities," and "protecting state secrets and secrets in judicial work."

These last examples of exemplary conduct represent qualities desirable in administrators of social or political programs. They bespeak overt responsibilities of Chinese judges to promote the interests of the state. In the West judicial systems are hardly beyond politics; in the United States, politics has a heavy influence on the nomination and election of judges. The Western judge also personifies the authority of the state and has the duty of promoting it, but there is a qualitative difference between the political colorations of judges in China and their Western counterparts.

Politicized Criteria of Judicial Excellence. He Weifang notes that judges are also frequently praised for devotion to the Party. Like innumerable political models in the PRC, a judge of peasant origin who had served in the PLA and upon demobilization was sent to work as a People's Court judge is quoted as saying: "I am a lucky fellow among tens of thousands of peasant children. I am grateful to the Party for its nurture and education, so I will never slacken my efforts in whatever work the Party assigns me to do."[31]

These words echo the politicization of the courts under Mao, when judges were deliberately undifferentiated from other cadres and all were supposed to remain close to the masses. During the 1950s and 1960s, as I suggested in chapter 4, discussions of the courts reflected two overtly competing conceptions of bureaucracy. The Maoist concept was deliberately fluid and consultative and rejected professional expertise; the more rational and professionalized alternative that was articulated only briefly during 1956–1957 remained unacceptable from the late 1950s until the onset of reform.[32] The rule of law was essentially irrelevant to both, except to the extent that regularity in bureaucratic decision-making could overlap with controls over arbitrariness. Before reform, model Communist judges were celebrated for going to the masses to solve their problems on the spot.[33] He Weifang's observation that the current propaganda on the correct behavior of judges echoes this earlier line can be confirmed by reading similar reports in the Legal Daily (*Fazhi bao*), published by the Ministry of Justice.

THE JUDICIAL PROCESS

Examination of the work of the Chinese courts commences here by surveying trial procedure, beginning with the judicial process in courts of first instance and then passing to the multiple methods used to review court decisions and the problems of enforcing judgments. I then examine judicial mediation and discuss judicial ethics.

Trial Procedure: An Overview

Trial procedure is conducted according to the 1991 Civil Procedure Law (CPL), which builds on ten years of practice under the predecessor "trial" civil procedure law.

Commencement of a Civil Action. Parties to disputes may act on their own behalf or by agents *ad litem* who may be lawyers or any citizen approved by the court.[34] After a would-be plaintiff files a written complaint at a court, litigation is formally begun. The court, acting through a clerk or judge who has ascertained that the court has jurisdiction and that the complaint states the facts and the nature of the dispute, accepts the case. The plaintiff must pay a "case acceptance fee" and other fees "according to regulations" (Art. 107).[35] Communications are generally conducted via the court, which is responsible for serving documents on the parties under specific rules on the service of process.

After the case has been accepted, a judge is assigned by the chief of his division (*tingzhang*) to handle the case, first with regard to all pretrial issues, and then to act as the presiding judge if a three-judge panel is formed to conduct the trial. The methods of determining assignments vary in each court, and often assignments are not made strictly by rotation. The *tingzhang* may make assignments based on the weak and strong points of various judges. If the case is "complicated," additional judges may be assigned, or the matter may be referred to the Adjudication Committee of the court, which I discuss in greater detail below. The *tingzhang* may continue to oversee the judges throughout the process.

Pretrial Procedure. The judicial personnel (which may include People's Assessors, although as noted above the collegial panels are generally composed of three judges) "must conscientiously read and examine case materials and investigate necessary evidence" (Art. 116). If the investigating judges encounter problems, they may discuss them with the *tingzhang*, singly or at a meeting. Although the CPL makes no provision for pretrial hearings, sometimes the court will hold hearings to clarify facts or issues. Judicial mediation would occur at this stage if the parties agree, either willingly or if pressed by a judge.[36] Also during the pretrial stage the court may hear and decide on any application by a party to preserve evidence or property, or to provide security if the court is satisfied that a judgment might otherwise be impossible or difficult to execute.

Gathering of Evidence. Each party bears responsibility for coming forward with evidence supporting its position (Art. 64). The CPL enumerates the various types of evidence, but it says nothing about how parties may collect evidence. In practice, the parties conduct their own investigations, which may involve deposing witnesses. The law makes no reference to anything resembling pretrial discovery. The courts have the primary task of gathering evidence from any individuals or organizations and may also obtain assistance on specialized issues from an "appraisal authority."[37] Evidence in the possession of banks or state agencies cannot be obtained by parties directly, and as a result it is sometimes necessary for judges to travel to collect evidence. Although they are allowed a *per diem* travel allowance out of the court's budget, it is regularly supplemented by the litigants, which, as one observer wryly notes, "may influence the eventual judicial decision."[38] The courts must examine evidence for "veracity and validity" (Art. 65). Judicial style has been active, with courts frequently conducting their own investigations, but in recent years they have shown considerable interest in placing the burden of investigation on the parties.[39]

Trial Procedure. The Chinese trial is marked by the judge–dominated civil law model that the Republic of China first began to use before the PRC was established, and which it continues to use on Taiwan. Under the CPL, judges consider evidence in the following order:

presentation of statements by the parties;

testimony by witnesses and reading of statements by absent witnesses;

presentation of documentary and material evidence;

reading of testimony of expert witnesses;

reading records of inspections.

The parties may introduce new evidence at trial, including evidence that differs from evidence previously introduced. The court, and afterward the parties with permission of the court, may question witnesses or present other evidence.[40]

The next stage of the trial is the "debate," when each party formally argues its views; after each has stated its views they may then debate with each other, often with the participation of the court, which may continue to ask questions of all the parties. The formal proceedings end with concluding statements by each party. The CPL provides that after the debate has ended, the court shall make its judgment. Consistent with the general preference for mediation previously discussed, the CPL states that if mediation is possible before the rendering of a judgment, "mediation procedures may be undertaken. If mediation is unsuccessful, a judgment shall be made without delay" (Art. 128).

The trial procedure outlined here makes considerable demands on judges that present difficulties to a judiciary that is not completely professionalized. For example, one court reported that cadres are reluctant to participate in open trials of economic disputes because they are used to deciding only on the basis of the file in the case and interviews of the parties, lack confidence, and are unqualified.[41]

This general framework for the conduct of trials may vary significantly in practice due to what one observer has called "advocacy outside the courtroom":

It is considered normal practice for judges to meet with counsel in the judges' office, without opposing counsel being present. This is not considered to violate the prohibition in the Judges Law on judges meeting privately with litigants or their agents. Although prohibited by the Civil Procedure Law, a frequent practice in many areas is for lawyers to meet with the judges involved in their case over the dinner table or at other places of entertainment.[42]

Other problems of professional responsibility that litigation presents to the emerging Chinese bar include the creation of business joint ventures between law firms and courts, pressures on clients to use law firms in which a government official has a financial interest, and bribery of judges or regulatory officials.[43] In late 1998 the central government in Beijing ordered all courts, as well as military units, to divest themselves of commercial activities, but thorough implementation of the new policy remained problematical.[44]

The Judicial Process Prior to Judgment

Internal Review of Judge's Decisions at the Courts of First Instance. The decision-making process at the trial court level involves, often decisively, the participation of judges other than those initially charged with handling cases. Before the court's judgment is issued it may be reviewed and approved by other judges, judicial superiors, and higher courts, in a manner very different from practice in either Anglo-American or Continental civil courts to which Chinese sometimes claim affinity. Most striking is the fact that the outcome of the case may be shaped by the extra-judicial influence of local Party or government officials.

Interviews with five judges[45] indicate that opinions are normally reviewed twice in civil cases and three times in criminal cases. After the collegiate bench (*heyiting*) has heard the case, the judge in charge will write a report and a draft opinion, which he sends to the chief or deputy chief of his chamber (*tingzhang* or *fu tingzhang*). Practice is not uniform, and one judge stated that in his court review stopped at the level of the deputy president of the court. Two judges stated that in some courts, if the matter is simple, the *heyiting* will reach a decision that will not have to be approved by the *tingzhang*. The factors that require approval before a judgment is issued include the amount of money involved, whether there are legal problems involved such as doubt over the applicability of a particular rule, the possible influence or effect of the case, and of course the ease with which a disposition can be reached. As will be seen below, the possible effect of a judgment one way or the other on local enterprises may also be taken into account; caseload, too, is a factor. Draft opinions on all but the simplest cases are likely to be reviewed and revised, perhaps a number of times. In criminal matters the case would be sent higher, perhaps to the president of the court.

Internal Review of Cases by the Adjudication Committee. The judges interviewed all agreed that if a case is "complicated" it would be sent to the Adjudication Committee of the court, either by the various *tingzhang* or the president of the court. The Adjudication Committee includes the senior judges such as the *tingzhang* in addition to the chief judge. The Organizational Law of the People's Courts requires courts to establish Adjudication Committees, whose tasks are to "sum up judicial experience, discuss major or difficult cases and discuss other issues of judicial work."[46] Published Chinese sources give only limited explication of the role of the Adjudication Committees. According to one recent book on court administration,[47] "doubtful" cases are those in which the facts are in issue, whereas "difficult" cases involve interpersonal relationships, such as differing opinions within the court or between judges of higher and lower courts. A Western observer notes that "more often a case is 'difficult' due to the complex personal and institutional relationships involved."[48]

Although in principle cases are supposed to be submitted to the Adjudication Committee only after they have been heard by a panel of judges, sometimes Adjudication Committees discuss cases *before* trial, making for a pithy summary of the consequences: "Those who try the case do not decide it, and those who decide the case do not try it."[49] This practice has been questioned as a violation of legality because it denies a party the right to a public trial. Just as troubling is the problem that arises if the decision of the Adjudication Committee differs from that of the panel of judges initially charged with deciding the case. There is a clear tension between the basic responsibility of the panel of judges and the administrative realities of the courts. One writer states that, contrary to claims that the decision of the Adjudication Committee should not be substituted for that of a panel, in practice, the decision of the Adjudication Committee must be carried out.[50] One judge offers a simple explanation: "the authority of the Adjudication Committee is too great."[51]

Internal review of cases by senior judges or Adjudication Committees, while it departs from Western ideals of judicial independence, is entirely consistent with the Chinese view of judicial autonomy. The Judges Law (reiterating the Constitution) provides that judges shall not be subjected to interference from "administrative bodies, social organizations, [or] individuals" while judging cases according to law.[52] The People's Courts are required to "independently exercise the right of adjudication by law,"[53] but in the current Chinese view this means that the court *as a whole entity* is independent, not the individual judge.[54] This *collective responsibility* is derived from the principle of democratic centralism, which has often been stated to be as basic as an administrative principle for the judiciary as it is for all the other organs of the Party-state[55]—and which means that the work of the Chinese courts is conceived of quite differently from adjudication in Western courts.

To the eyes of Western lawyers, it seems probable that the Adjudication Committee serves to coordinate judicial decisions at each court with current interpretations of state and Party policy.[56] A provocative alternative view is suggested by a Chinese scholar, Professor Zhu Suli of Beijing University.[57] On the basis of interviews with judges, he suggests that the Adjudication Committee supports rather than interferes with judicial independence, because it is an effective safeguard against corruption and improper outside influence, and it unifies practice within the jurisdiction. Furthermore, the low professional level of basic-level judges makes internal review of their work necessary. At the same time, he notes some problems: Many court presidents and vice-presidents lack legal sophistication, and the Adjudication Committees are overworked because too many judges pass difficult cases on to the Committees rather than accept responsibility for handling the cases themselves. Zhu suggests further that in the face of the many sources of outside influence on judges (many poorly trained), the Committees could function to maintain rather than weaken judicial independence. Given the impossibility of making fundamental changes, he concludes that it is necessary to consider the Committees as a Chinese response to current Chinese conditions rather than to regard them entirely negatively from the viewpoint of Western ideals of judicial independence.

Internal Review: Requesting Instructions from Higher Level Courts. Although the Chinese system limits appeals so that they can ascend only to the next higher judicial level above the trial court, appeals may be effectively short-circuited by the practice of not hearing or deciding a case until the court of first instance has requested instructions on deciding the specific matter from its superior-level court. As one Chinese judge has noted, there should be no need for this practice, but courts "have traditionally been managed by administrative methods," the quality of judicial personnel has not been high, and requesting instructions from higher courts helps bring about the correct application of the law.[58] The quality of personnel is improving but the practice continues, often because lower courts seek guidance owing to the generality or incompleteness of legislation.[59] Interviews with judges suggest that because they are concerned that their decisions might be reversed, they continue to request instructions from superior courts, a practice that lower-court judges call "buying insurance."[60] When a lower court requests instructions on interpreting a law that is involved in a case pending before it, the proceedings will be suspended. Whether the court notifies counsel is at the discretion of the court.[61]

Lower courts also seek instruction from others. When the court must interpret a rule that requires the action of a nonjudicial administrative agency to implement its interpretation, it will consult with the highest level of that agency beforehand. That administrative superior might then issue instructions within its own hierarchy or bureaucratic system, informing its lower-level agencies of the interpretation, and instructing them to comply.[62]

Involvement of the Local Party-State. Numerous extra-judicial influences, of which the CCP is only one, often affect the outcomes in specific cases. The vulnerability of the Chinese courts to interference in their work by local representatives of the Party-state has been frankly discussed by insiders and closely studied by foreign scholars.[63] At the beginning of the reforms, an effort to remove CCP organizations at the courts from involvement in daily judicial work was aborted,[64] and the evidence of continuing involvement of Party officials in the work of the courts is compelling. For example, a book written by a judge on managing the work of the courts advises courts to rely heavily on the Party Committee:

[The court] must take the initiative to ask for instruction from and report work to the Party Committee of the same level. Issues related to the ideology and organization of the court, the implementation of judicial principles and important policies . . . important and new social developments discovered in the course of adjudication, individual cases involving important social and political influences should be actively reported to the Party Committee to seek guidance and support.[65]

One county court judge offers a strong indictment of the power that local officials wield over the courts. As a result of the power concentrated in local Party Committees and exercised by First Secretaries, he says, "courts cannot avoid being manipulated by senior officials," in a system in which the weakness of the courts is exacerbated by the "unified leadership" of the court by the localities, which control the courts' personnel, finances, and housing.[66] This control leads to improper pressures on the courts to persuade complaining parties to withdraw suits, to issue judgments not in accord with law and facts, and to transfer judges who try to be impartial.

The extent to which the CCP remains embedded in Chinese legal institutions has been closely studied by He Weifang, whose research strongly suggests that the principal affairs of the court are directed by the Party organization within the court, which is itself subject to the leadership of the local Party committee. Party leadership over the courts is reflected both in selecting judges (in which the local Party committee and its personnel department as well as the Party committee at the court are likely to be involved) and in the handling of some important and "difficult" cases. In such cases: "[the court] often reports . . . to the local Party committee and solicits opinions for solution . . . and if contradictions arise among different judicial organs, the Party's political-legal committee often steps forward to coordinate."[67] Political-legal committees are in charge of the courts, police, and Procuracy, as well as civil affairs at each level of organization, and these committees also deal with "important and difficult cases."[68] Local Party secretaries regularly reviewed cases before legal reform began,[69] and they continue this practice, which can affect the outcome of specific cases. In criminal matters they may use their political influence to exert pressure to fulfill goals that have been enunciated (although not numerical targets or percentages like those used in campaigns during the 1950s).[70] Several judges who were interviewed suggested that direct CCP influence in noncriminal matters may be lessening slowly.

In noncriminal cases, however, the *financial* interests of the local Party-state are strong and growing and are as potent as crude political influence. Interviews and published discussions indicate that in economic cases officials of the local Party-state frequently seek to influence outcomes, either to prevent local enterprises from suffering losses that would reduce the revenue of the local government or to protect parties to the dispute with whom they have personal or economic relationships.

Some basic characteristics of the non-state economic sector that has been the engine of reform, highlighted in chapter 5, often significantly affect the work of the courts. Decentralization has not meant a lessening of state control. It has rightly been observed that "there is nothing particularly non-state about this sector. In China's cities and counties, the two ownership types of state and collective overwhelmingly dominate, and are both managed by the state structure *at that level*."[71]

As I noted earlier, whether through partnership, clientelistic relations, or bribery, business in the private sector is advancing by promoting particularistic relationships with local government units. Local enterprises must enter into a variety of arrangements with local governments in order to obtain the desired status of collectives and receive protection from the local cadres.[72] The need for these relationship arises, as has already been explained, because the enterprises lack well-defined legal rights that protect their property and officials may perceive it to be in their interests to keep property rights weak.

The courts are funded by local governments, not the central government, as we have seen. As a result, when local courts deal with legal problems arising out of reform, local officials can use the absence of a strong legal system to their advantage. For example, the courts must sometimes decide which entities should be made parties to litigation involving the debts of defunct enterprises, and it may be difficult to hold government departments liable for their failure to pay in capital as required by law or for improper management practices.[73] Patron-client relations directly affect the application of legal rules[74] and shape the strategies adopted by economic actors to protect themselves.[75] Local protectionism, often inspired by courts' reluctance to impose measures that may inflict serious economic harm on a local enterprise involved, such as forcing it into bankruptcy, leads courts to refuse to aid other courts, to procrastinate in handling cases brought by outsiders, and to decide cases unfairly against them.[76]

One judge interviewed by He Weifang illustrated local protectionism with the following example: If the courts are asked by local officials to unfreeze a bank account that they were required to freeze by law, they must comply. A higher-level court might admonish the lower court for unfreezing the account, but not the local leadership, which would have had no direct administrative relationship with the higher court. In this kind of situation, "you cannot make the party secretary, mayor or [municipal] district head accountable to others. What they say counts, they have the power, but yet they are not responsible."[77] The judicial newspaper has stated that in poor areas the shortage of funds for courts influences their work and the chief judge's independence. The courts must placate local power-holders, because "Everything the judge does, he has to ask for help."[78] Another judge is explicit on the consequences of this judicial dependence: "If the Bureau of Finance is offended by [your handling of] a case, the new Procuracy building next door will get built all right, but your [court] building won't."[79]

Influence can be exerted on the courts from many quarters. According to one judge interviewed in 1995, inquiries may be directed anywhere in the judicial hierarchy as well as to the local government, the local People's Congress, the NPC, or the Procuracy, at any stage of the proceedings—even after the case has been decided.[80] One estimate is that some twenty to thirty "proposals" from members of the NPC are submitted yearly to the Supreme People's Court, which replies with reports to the NPC member on each matter.[81]

Discussing the problem in a book edited by the Economic Division of the Supreme People's Court,[82] the authors recognize that cadre interference must be eliminated for the courts to be independent, although they also recognize that the courts cannot solve such problems themselves. In the face of the political realities that presently constrict judicial autonomy, the authors turn timid. They say that "comprehensive handling" is required and that it is necessary to "improve and adjust certain (*mouxie*) relationships"[83] involved with the bureaucratic system, so that courts can resist the pressure from administrative cadres. More specifically, the authors recommend that when cadres from the Party, government, or NPC ask for reports on pending cases, the judges should explain the law, noting that often an interested party has related the facts incorrectly. They add the pious view that if the judges sincerely handle the case, report on it accurately, and explain the law clearly, in practice the majority of leaders will support the right of the courts to carry out independent adjudication. It has also been suggested that local officials may cease their pressure to influence particular outcomes if lower courts are acting according to instructions from higher-level courts, because lower-level officials understand that lower courts, like themselves, must obey higher-level instructions.[84]

Judgments and Enforcement; Local Protectionism

The increasing impact of local governments on the judicial process is most visible in efforts to collect judgments. The formal requirements for judgments are easily summarized: Judgments must be publicly pronounced. Once pronounced in court, a written judgment must be issued within ten days; if pronounced later, the written judgment must follow immediately. In any event the parties must be informed of their rights to appeal and the court to which appeal must be addressed.

Even when parties overcome traditional reluctance to sue and persevere through litigation to obtain a favorable judgment, they may fail to vindicate their claim because of difficulties in enforcing court judgments. In 1988, Supreme People's Court President Zheng Tianxiang acknowledged that "about 30 percent of the economic dispute cases on which courts made decisions last year were not enforced, and the ratio exceeded 40 percent in some provinces." Zheng blamed "local protectionism and selfish departmentalism, which make it difficult to execute court rulings."[85] Adequate statistics are not available, although Donald Clarke suggests that in 1992, around 35 to 40 percent of all civil and economic disputes were referred to enforcement divisions, and that the reported success rate in such referrals is 80 percent. The statistics cannot be relied on except to indicate that the problem is considerable.[86]

The original court of first instance normally carries out execution of its judgments through its enforcement division, but if the losing party either is domiciled or has property outside the district in which the judgment is rendered, the court that has awarded the judgment must request the assistance of other courts to reach the defendant's person or property. If a party fails to comply with a judgment, the other party may apply to the court for execution within specified time limits, or the court itself may initiate execution proceedings. The CPL arms the courts with the power to order "compulsory execution measures" such as freezing bank accounts, confiscating or withholding part of a party's income, or ordering the confiscation or sale of a party's property (Arts. 221, 222).

Judgments may be unenforceable for a variety of reasons. The economic reforms have brought about changes that make Chinese organizations less powerful over the persons who work in them. As Clarke points out, when all workers are state workers it is easy to garnish the salary of those who are judgment debtors, but that becomes impossible when the debtor in question is a private business person with no wages to garnish.[87] But more serious problems arise out of fundamental changes in the Chinese Party-state that were introduced in chapter 5 in the survey of economic reform and its consequences. Ren Jianxin, president of the Supreme People's Court for over a decade until he retired from that post in 1998, enumerated the following causes of nonenforcement of judgments:[88]

enterprises "deep in the red" are unable to pay their debts;

localities or departments protect local units and refuse to cooperate with the courts;

parties that lack "a strong sense of law" avoid their obligations; and

a small number of decisions are "unfair" and cannot be enforced.

To these a number of other reasons have been added by Donald Clarke:[89]

a genuine reluctance to use coercion in civil cases that flows from the Maoist notion that these disputes are contradictions "within the people" and not with an "enemy";

the lack of finality in the Chinese system that arises out of the

multiplicity of avenues that unsuccessful parties can use to reliti-
gate a case (discussed below); and

the immunity in practice of certain enterprises, such as those run
by the military.

Of these, the most serious may be local protectionism. The same political and economic forces that influence the outcome of judgments can also
create formidable obstacles to enforcing a judgment against a local individual or enterprise. Economic reform has increased the dependence of
local governments on revenue from local enterprises and has consequently
increased their inclination to defend such enterprises against economic
damage.[90] Local governments possess considerable resources to defend
themselves, for example by employing the local police and Procuracy to
resist the enforcement of judgments against local enterprises.[91] Some reports have told of clans resisting enforcement.[92]

Sometimes local protectionism combines with the financial weakness
of state-owned enterprises. Many SOEs are unable to pay their debts, including their judgment debts. In addition, however, local governments
have sometimes helped to make them judgment-proof. When government
credit was tightened in the late 1980s in an effort to restrain inflationary
economic growth, the working capital of many enterprises shrank and
they became technically insolvent. But, as Clarke notes, some government
departments that run enterprises escaped liability by closing businesses
down or by using subterfuges to avoid the impact of legislation that imposed liability on them.

"Local protectionism" is an ominous reason for nonenforcement of
judgments because it testifies so strongly to the weakness of the central
government and the fragmentation of the legal system. Some law enforcement officials and judges have called for the need to employ a national
perspective in order to protect legality, fairness, and the national interest.[93]
Sometimes local courts are congratulated in the judiciary newspaper for
soliciting or seeking instructions from local Party and government leaders
when presented with important cases involving enforcement problems.[94]
Appeals to judges to consider national interests that transcend those of
their localities, however, seem unlikely to succeed in a political culture in
which each hierarchy makes vigorous efforts to protect its turf. An authoritative Chinese source mentions "agency protectionism" (bumen baohu
zhuyi) and "local protectionism" side by side,[95] and both reflect a fragmentation of authority that obstructs the growth of regularity and legality. For
example, courts seeking to enforce judgments might discover that agencies
whose action is required to assist the courts will not cooperate. Such dis-
obedience to court orders arises, in part, because in the Chinese bureau-

cratic scheme courts do not possess greater authority than the banks but merely belong to a hierarchy, or *xitong* ("system") that exists *parallel* to banks and all other agencies. "Protectionism," it is clear, pervades the judicial process and constrains the growth of judicial autonomy. The extent to which it can be reduced will depend on many factors outside the legal institutions themselves.

Review of Lower-Court Decisions After Judgment

Every judicial system has to strike a balance between reviewing the outcomes of cases for consistency with law and policy and assuring their finality so that expectations will be made secure. A striking aspect of the Chinese judicial system is the low degree of finality that judicial decisions—and successful litigants—are permitted to enjoy because of a variety of means that allow cases to be reviewed and reopened.

Appeal. When a case is appealed, the court of second instance may consider all relevant issues of fact and law, regardless of what issues were raised by the parties either in the lower court or on appeal. Chinese practice diverges from that of common law jurisdictions, in which appeals are limited to the issues raised by the parties and factual issues are not reexamined. In this aspect, Chinese appellate courts are more like courts in civil law jurisdictions. The appellate court forms a collegiate bench, as in the lower courts, and in addition to reviewing the record may also conduct its own investigations and question the parties. After having done so, it may consider the facts of the case to be verified and render a judgment without a hearing (Art. 152); however, it may also collect new evidence and hold an entirely new hearing. The court may reject the appeal, set aside the lower court judgment and remand it for a retrial, or modify the judgment. Appeals may be made only to the next highest level; consequently, judgments of courts of second instance are final and further appeal is barred, although the CPL also provides that parties "may appeal against a new judgment or ruling rendered after a retrial of their case" (Art. 153).

Lower-court judges know that appeals from their decisions can affect their record and chances of promotion, and their resulting concern to avoid reversals impels many to encourage mediation of cases that come to their courts. Judges may also exert pressure on the parties not to appeal.[96] Concern may run in the opposite direction as well: higher-level courts may sometimes refrain from reversing lower-court judgments out of concern for the feelings of the lower-court judges, or focus only on the substantive result reached by the lower court while overlooking procedural irregularities. Sometimes, for the same reason, the higher court may send the case back for retrial rather than reverse the lower-court decision.

Petition. In addition to review by appeal, the CPL provides that for up to two years after a judgment or ruling has become legally effective, a party may petition either the court that originally heard the case or a higher-level court for a retrial (Arts. 178, 182). Such a retrial may be ordered if:

new evidence compels reversal of the original judgment;

the evidence on which the original judgment was based is insufficient;

the original judgment misapplied the law;

the court of first instance committed a procedural violation that affected the correctness of its judgment;

judicial personnel "accepted bribes, practiced favoritism for personal benefit or perverted the law" (Art. 179).

One judge has described the handling of petitions.[97] Many courts have offices that handle visits from the people. When a person presents a matter that he claims was handled wrongly, the staff and some judges discuss it. If the staff member who investigates finds errors, the matter will be discussed informally at a higher level, such as with a section chief (*zuzhang*). If the petition is presented to a higher court, that court may decide that a mistake had been made that did not critically affect the result, or send a memorandum to the original trial court, indicating that the litigant had claimed that the court erred and had requested a review. The higher court would then decide that the original decision was correct, should be modified, or should be reversed. The procedure, to this point, can be characterized, as the judge interviewed put it, as an "informal administrative proceeding." It becomes more formal when the matter is returned to the trial court, which may not wish to change its decision. In that event, the upper-level court would issue a formal finding that the possibility of error exists and order that the matter be formally reopened. After this opinion is drafted and before it is sent to the lower court it would be reviewed internally by the group leader, then a *tingzhang*, who will then refer it to the Adjudication Committee for decision.

Supervision. Judgments may also be reviewed and reopened without any request by the parties, as an administrative matter, either by the court that rendered the original judgment or by a higher-level court. The CPL provides that if a chief judge finds a "definite error" in a legally effective judgment or ruling, he shall refer the matter to the Adjudication Committee of the court (Art. 177).[98] Similarly, if the Supreme People's Court finds a "definite error" in the decision of any lower-level court or if a higher-level court discovers such an error in a lower-level court, the higher courts may either review such matters themselves or order retrial at a lower level (Art. 177).

A group of judges interviewed in late 1995 expressed differing views on how cases are selected to be reviewed. One stated that his court reviewed cases on which they received a lot of public comment. A small percentage of cases were also selected randomly for quality control, targeted by subject matter or by lower court. A Beijing judge said that in reviewing cases, notice was taken not only of major errors that required reversal or modification of lower court opinions, but also of less serious errors that had not in themselves caused the decision to be wrong. These would be recorded and discussed by the reviewing judges at periodic meetings with the lower-level judges who had been involved.

One judge at a high-level court interviewed in 1995 stated that readjudication is highly flexible, and that the courts have great discretion to decide whether to review a case. If a lower court decision is questioned by the lawyers or parties know the judges personally, such relationships could influence the decision to review. Judges exercise enormous discretionary power, and procedure is so informal that it lends itself to unreviewable decisions. Interviews with two practicing lawyers, also in 1995, corroborated this assessment.

Procuratorial Review. The People's Procuracy was established in the early years of the PRC. Like the Soviet institution on which it was modeled, it was formally entrusted with two roles, carrying out the duties of a public prosecutor and supervising the legality of the organs of the state. In practice, the "general legal supervision" function withered and died during the 1950s, but with the advent of reform it has been revived. Under legislation promulgated in 1992, the Procuracy at each level may protest to the court at the same level judgments that have already become legally effective.[99] An exception is that when judgments of basic level courts are protested, the Procuracy at that level must request a higher-level Procuracy to handle the matter. Protests may be on the grounds of insufficient evidence, errors of law, violations of procedure that affect the correctness of the judgment, or the same types of misconduct by judicial personnel that may be the foundation of parties' protest.

Multiple Avenues of Review and Finality: Implications. The multiplicity of means of review of trial court judgments and the resulting detraction from the finality of their decisions suggest a considerable difference between Chinese and Western conceptions of a judicial system. In the Western view, as long as the parties have had a fair and full hearing, they should not obtain a second hearing of the same facts and issues. Procedural justice is so important that some substantive injustice will be tolerated in the interests of stability. The Chinese system, by contrast, displays "a [broad] reluctance to allow any aspect of procedure to dictate a substantive result, a reluctance that finds expression throughout the legal system."[100]

The multiplicity of avenues of review has obvious implications for the attainability of the rule of law in China. In the West, that concept expresses the aspiration for society to be governed by laws that are prospective, ascertainable, uniformly applied, and stable. Opening judicial decisions to scrutiny long after they become effective introduces instability and variability that runs counter to the Western ideal of the rule of law, especially if outcomes are revised for political reasons.

Judicial Mediation

The predominance of mediation does not end at the doors of Chinese courts. Some of the forces that shape extra-judicial mediation—cultural tradition, Maoist political roots, and limits on available resources—also lead courts to rely heavily on mediating civil disputes. Because mediation at the courts is so extensive, it deserves close examination.

Judicial Mediation as a Major Mode of Dispute Resolution. We begin with a basic fact: well over half of all civil and economic disputes brought to the courts are mediated. In the mid-1980s the Ministry of Justice *expected* the courts to conclude no less than 80 percent of all civil disputes by means of mediated settlement.[101] Statistics for recent years indicate that although the percentage is now lower, it is still closer to 60 percent and mediation retains its dominant position[102] (see Table 8).

Mediation Procedure. The Chinese Law on Civil Procedure provides very generally for mediation. All civil cases, once accepted by the courts, can be mediated (Art. 85). Judicial mediation must be initiated on the basis of the parties' voluntary participation and conducted by "ascertaining the facts and distinguishing right from wrong" (Art. 85). Mediation may be done by one or more judges and "as far as possible" should be done outside the courtroom, "on the spot" (Art. 86). The courts may invite relevant units and people to assist the mediation (Art. 87). Mediation may not be coerced, and the parties should reach agreement voluntarily (Art. 88). If mediation ends with an agreed settlement, it must be recorded in a formal agreement, prepared by the court and signed by the judge. It becomes legally effective when delivered to the parties. Such agreements are required in all but divorce actions that end in reconciliation and adoption cases that end with the maintenance of the adoptive relationship, or in other cases in the discretion of the judges (Arts. 89 and 90). If mediation is not effective or a party decides not to carry out such an agreement, the court must "promptly" adjudicate the matter (Art. 91). Mediation can be

TABLE 8. Civil Cases by Disposition, 1990–1997

Year	Cases concluded	Mediated	Adjudicated or decided by ruling	Other	Transferred
1990	1,849,728	1,194,350	353,940	301,438	
1991	1,910,013	1,128,465	456,000	325,548	
1992	1,948,989	1,136,970	460,932	351,047	
1993	2,091,651	1,224,060	854,227		13,364
1994	2,382,174	1,392,114	977,773		12,287
1995	2,714,665	1,544,258	1,156,823		13,584
1996	3,084,464	1,672,892	1,395,061		16,511
1997	3,242,202	1,651,996	1,574,278		15,928

Year	Cases concluded	Mediated	Adjudicated or decided by ruling	Other	Transferred
1990	1,849,728	64.6%	19.1%	16.3%	
1991	1,910,013	59.1	23.9	17.0	
1992	1,948,989	58.3	23.6	18.0	
1993	2,091,651	58.5	40.8		0.6
1994	2,382,174	58.4	41.0		0.5
1995	2,714,665	56.9	42.6		0.5
1996	3,084,464	54.2	45.2		0.5
1997	3,242,202	51.0	48.6		0.5

SOURCE: *Zhongguo falü nianjian* (Law Yearbook of China): 1991 (p.934), 1992 (p. 855), 1993 (p. 936), 1994 (p. 1028), 1995 (p. 1064), 1996 (p. 958), 1997 (p. 1056), 1998 (p. 1239).

carried out at any time before a judgment is rendered (Art. 128). Mediation is also possible on appeal.

Common Problems of Judicial Mediation. Within this general framework, is mediation inside the courts conducted any differently than it is outside them? Although procedure in the court could arguably be "more rigorous, structured and weighty than that relied on in extra-judicial mediation,"[103] considerable evidence suggests that judicial mediation is often as amorphous and open to abuse as extra-judicial mediation. The authority and responsibilities of judicial mediators are greater than those of extra-judicial mediators, judicial mediation may deal with more complicated issues, and the judges' participation is probably more active than that of extra-judicial mediators. Chinese scholarly commentary and interviews with judges alike suggest that the differences between the two kinds of mediation may be less than might be expected, and that judicial mediation not only exhibits some of the same problems that surround extra-judicial mediation but others as well. A variety of sources suggest that in practice judicial mediation raises serious issues of legality.[104]

Mediation and Adjudication Are Not Rigorously Separated. If mediation fails and the court elects to try the case, it may without further investigation rely solely on the information acquired by the judge while he acted as a mediator. Often, critics say, a clerk will be assigned to mediate and will propose a solution, but if it is not accepted, that proposal then becomes the basis for the decision without any judicial participation. One judge who was interviewed agreed that sometimes secretaries mediate, explaining that they often have a better legal education than judges.

Judges May "Plaster Over" the Dispute. Another complaint is that the mediating judge often forgoes investigation and superficially compromises the dispute in the name of reasonableness but without defining and resolving the parties' rights and duties. This style should be distinguished from the combination of law with "emotion and reason" that was mentioned in discussing people's mediation. The Chinese phrase "to do work (on)" is often used to describe the judge's conduct toward parties and connotes a range of techniques that bureaucrats engage in to persuade, cajole, and coerce the person who is the object of the "work" to agree or submit to the speaker. Liu Guangan and Li Cunpeng have argued that this process is inimical to the protection or exercise of rights and also undermines the legal system.[105] It affects the trust that parties place in the court and disappoints their hope that judicial mediation will be better than village mediation, and they become reluctant to return to the courts. Furthermore, they argue, if many citizens become disappointed, the growth of such a mentality may endanger social stability because it could encourage attempts at self-help.

Coercion by the Courts. In some cases a judge may conduct mediation and then, if the parties do not accept his proposed solution, adjudicate the case on the basis of the rejected proposal. This process creates much pressure on the parties, who are afraid that they will lose in the adjudication. The Civil Procedure Textbook states that when the CPL was modified by substituting the phrase "carry out lawful mediation based on voluntarism and law" for the previous injunction to "emphasize carrying out mediation," this change was not intended to weaken mediation as an institution but was aimed at "one-sidedly" raising the number of mediated cases, and at reducing coerced and illegal mediation.[106]

Interviews with judges add further detail.[107] A judge who served in a basic-level court during the mid-1980s stated that at that time, all cases were routinely mediated. These were civil matters, usually divorces, and the rate of settlement was high. The judges "mobilized" the parties, indicating that if they did not come to a reconciliation the dispute might take as long as a year or more to adjudicate. After a notice was issued by the Supreme People's Court in 1987 emphasizing voluntariness, the number of cases settled by mediation declined. But as changes in economic policy affecting legal rights and obligations swelled courts' caseloads, pressure to mediate has increased.

A second judge who had served in a basic-level court during the late 1980s said that the Civil Procedure Law's emphasis on mediation had been revised because the law was not being applied and too much time was being taken by mediation in the courts. There was much "stirring up the mud," that is, disputation that does not attain settlement.

A third judge, who had served both in district (basic-level) and intermediate-level courts in Beijing during the mid-1980s, said that although some 80 percent of cases in rural counties were dealt with by mediation, only 60 percent were handled in this manner in the cities. Coercion was a problem against which there was little protection. The judges liked mediation because it was simple and required only one judge, not three, since a court secretary could conduct the mediation. Reflecting a general inattention to procedure that has been remarked on by Chinese legal scholars in conversations on the subject, many thought they could violate the law when conducting mediation because they regarded it as entirely extra-legal.

These interviews suggest that coercion remains as much of a problem inside the courts as it is outside of them. Indeed, because the courts are more authoritative than mediation committees, the problem may be worse. There are, moreover, some factors that impel judges to press for mediation, which are discussed immediately below.

Gaps in the Law. Judges often encounter novel disputes whose subject matter has not been addressed by legislation. In these circumstances they see no choice but to mediate.[108]

Bureaucratically Generated Pressures on Judges to Mediate. One thoughtful Chinese observer traces problems to the bureaucratic setting of judicial dispute settlement.

In practice, judges prefer to use mediation because the successful rate of mediation is used as a quota in evaluating the achievements of the court. The more cases the judges successfully mediate, the more praise they will receive from their superiors. As a result, delays frequently occur due to the judge's insistence on using mediation in spite of the fact that the dispute in question is not likely to be resolved through mediation. This kind of practice has received much criticism in recent years.[109]

Although these words were written in 1984, some of the same pressures on judges to mediate have persisted. Mediation can be used to avoid the possibility of appeals. One judge stated that in basic-level courts, judges' chances for promotion are influenced by the number of their cases that are subsequently reversed or retried. Because appeals from their decisions are considered to reflect badly on them if they are reversed, judges do not wish to write opinions that might risk reversals. Another judge said that during the mid-1980s cases settled through mediation, as opposed to adjudication, were required to meet a standard percentage that varied from court to court but sometimes could be as high as 80 to 90 percent. Adherence to or deviation from this standard would be noted in their record, and would affect their chances for promotion.

Pressure on Courts to Mediate Because of Difficulty of Enforcing Civil Judgments. "Local protectionism," which was identified above in the context of enforcement as a critical weakness of the current Chinese judicial system, may also influence judges' choices of the mode of resolution. Courts often simply wish to mediate rather than adjudicate a dispute because they believe that to enforce a judgment against a local party would be difficult.[110] One judge in Yangzhou reports that *whenever* a litigant from outside the province appears, his court always attempts to settle the dispute through mediation rather than to risk encountering opposition to a judgment that resulted from an adjudicated end to the dispute.[111]

Mediation at the Second Instance. Mediation can be conducted at all stages of a dispute and is built into appellate procedure as solidly as in trial procedure. This feature further contributes to the lack of finality in the judicial process because it gives the parties an opportunity to renegotiate even those lower-court decisions that clarified the facts and applied the law correctly. According to Palmer, sometimes a party who resists mediation and loses in the trial court appeals, and accepts mediation at the appellate level, reasoning that he will do better because the result reached by the court is compromised.[112]

Pressure on the Courts to Mediate Generated by Rising Workload. As economic reform created new economic relationships, the number of disputes inevitably increased. At the beginning of the 1980s disputes were handled only by the mediation committees and the courts, which created economic divisions in 1979. Numerous ad hoc organizations to arbitrate economic disputes were created throughout the 1980s, but they have since been replaced by a nationwide arbitration system, as described in chapter 8. By the mid-1980s, the rapid growth of contract disputes seemed to require the creation of additional mechanisms.

One experiment, apparently short-lived, illustrates the persistence of devotion to mediation.[113] At the instigation of Ren Jianxin, then president of the Supreme People's Court, economic dispute mediation centers (*jingji jiufen tiaojie zhongxin*, hereafter EDMC) were established, first experimentally in Shenzhen and at other courts. All economic disputes brought to the courts had to be mediated at the new centers. Although they were very speedy in processing cases, many scholars criticized them. Even though this innovation was reported to the NPC for approval, no legislation was ever promulgated to formalize the creation of the new centers. Their procedure was not governed by law; when mediation failed, the parties had again to pay court fees for the adjudication phase that followed; their power was great, and opportunities for corruption were greater.[114]

To some extent, opposition to the centers arose out of changing notions about rights. New economic policies gave enterprise managers more power over the property of their enterprise, and the managers became more personally interested in the economic outcomes of their disputes. If a dispute was taken to the EDMC, both parties to the dispute anticipated that they would have to compromise if the dispute was mediated, yet they were reluctant to abandon positions based on their view of their rights under the contract in question. The use of lawyers in economic disputes has grown, especially in the cities. Lawyers are used in 90 percent of "large" cases, according to a Chinese judge with whom I discussed the centers. Most recently, the Chinese press has stopped referring to the EDMCs, which have declined in favor of new arbitration tribunals established under the Arbitration Law.

Contending Views of Legality. Rights-oriented solutions and solutions more obviously based on compromise are likely to continue to compete. Will mediation endure because of culturally dictated preferences? As I suggested in chapter 3, although traditional influences lent some support to the use of mediational forms favored by Communist ideology, those influences also diluted the politicization of mediation. As the foregoing discussion has shown, some preferences for mediation over adjudication have lingered within the courts themselves, despite the decline of Communist ideology generally and the frequent extolling of rights-related adjudication in the courts as a matter of policy.

At the same time, judicial mediation is being reexamined, at least by some judges and legal scholars who criticize its excessive use and would like to reduce the proportion of disputes that are mediated after they reach the courts. Two scholars have suggested that mediation is not the best way to define and protect the rights that have been created by the economic reforms,[115] and another has criticized it for wasting time, producing "plastered-over" or coerced outcomes and one-sidedly promoting judges' skills at mediating rather than adjudicating.[116] By compromising cases mediation allows parties who breach contracts to escape full liability for their breach; by restricting appeals it encourages substandard work by judges and it exposes judges to the possibility of corruption.[117] The increased use of lawyers by some litigants, especially in the cities, expresses their resistance to diluting legal rights by compromise. One judge commented in an interview:

The lawyers make it difficult for the judges to mediate. A basic feature of mediation is to ask each party to give up some portion of their legal rights, while lawyers will emphasize the rights of the parties. Maybe now in the cities [in economic disputes] some 50 percent of the parties would have lawyers, and all legal persons have lawyers. In civil and adoption cases over 60 percent of the disputants might not have lawyers, but this is changing, too.

Mediation also allows external reasons to influence the disposition of the matter. Some judges do not want to waste time on mediation, they have strong legal educations and want to judge cases according to law. These are the younger, better educated judges. There is a hopeful trend here.

These remarks suggest that at least in the cities there is an emergence of a new rights-consciousness that prompts disputants to seek adjudication rather than mediation.[118] While this may be a trend, it has begun to emerge only slowly: litigants were represented in less than a quarter of the cases heard by the courts in 1997.[119]

Judicial Ethics

Judges may be subjected to powerful pressures that often affect their decisions. The pressures come from both within and outside the courts, and the judges' tasks are made difficult because their domain is not separated from the world, bureaucratic and otherwise, outside the courts. Quite apart from being asked to accept bribes and otherwise benefit from clearly corrupt conduct, they are the objects of other not-so-subtle pulls on their judgments and emotions by the governments that appoint them and pay their salaries and by connections (*guanxi*) with interested parties—third persons such as relatives or administrative superiors. The high value that Chinese culture places on enduring human relationships denoted by the two Chinese concepts of *guanxi* and "human feelings" (*renqing*) often leads to behavior that in the West would be considered corrupt. For example, one judge has observed that when high government officials, who appoint, remove, and pay the judges, inquire about a pending case, "[these] leaders don't have to give you gifts, because they are your superiors. But to handle the case the way they ask, that's doing them a favor. In the future, if your court has some kind of problem, you find those leaders and they can fix things for you."[120]

The judges' lack of distance from their communities, together with their low salaries, makes them susceptible to misconduct that greatly influences their impartiality. One commentator has noted that "the relative social acceptability of supplemental financial payments [such as for travel to collect evidence] means that bribery of judges is a widespread phenomenon."[121]

He Weifang has noted that although current policy stresses objective adjudication, it is difficult to ascertain how deeply it is taking hold. He notes that the media rarely report cases of serious violations of judicial ethics and that the judges he interviewed were generally reluctant to discuss corruption and violation of ethics. He assumes, though, that such conduct is extensive, and conversations with Chinese lawyers, judges, and law professors corroborate.[122] In one case, a judge self-reportedly refused a large number of bribes and banquet invitations. For that, "She was ridiculed by her neighbors, treated coldly by her friends and was even the object of revenge and abuse by scoundrels, but in the end she won the trust and praise of the masses."[123] After giving other examples, he suggests that the frequency of such articles shows how serious bribery has become and concludes that China lacks a "comprehensive system of standards, of judicial professional ethics," as well as a system for enforcing such ethics.

Courts are being enmeshed in relationships among officials and private enterprises that involve both traditional values and the newly respectable profit motive. Pressures on judges to accept bribes or to favor local parties are generated by low salaries and financial dependence on local governments. A Chinese legal scholar quotes a statement made at a meeting of high-level court presidents: "In the past two years some problems among court personnel have already become quite serious, the phenomenon of corruption has been growing ferociously and developing quickly. In some places it is relatively common for court workers to accept favors and presents, it is done almost half-openly."[124] More fundamentally, he observes that the work of judges has not been distinguished in kind from that of other officials, and consequently they have not been expected to maintain a greater distance from their local communities than other officials. Finder comments:

[Judges] generally work in their home district, where they have long-standing ties with classmates or friends who are lawyers, business people and government officials. Certain aspects of the Chinese social environment also influence the way Chinese judges approach cases. In particular, Chinese society places a high value on the maintenance of proper relations, both among institutions and individuals. Therefore, Chinese judges may accommodate their decisions to maintain good relations with powerful persons, institutions, or companies.[125]

Relationships and corruption, then, in a society increasingly without moral compass, pose a strong threat to judicial independence, perhaps as serious as that of political control by the CCP.[126]

In the midst of these difficult circumstances, Chinese judges are deciding disputes brought to them by growing numbers of litigants. Further
insight into the judicial process may be aided by considering, as I do immediately below, the sources of the legal rules that judges apply in their
decisions, and the support the rules seem to provide for assertions of the
new rights that have been created by legislation implementing the economic reforms.

Sources of Law

Chinese constitutional rules and doctrine are deceptively and superficially
clear about the allocation of the power to generate rules of society-wide
application, as we saw in chapter 6. Nonetheless, issues of fundamental
importance have emerged vis-à-vis the sources of the rules that Chinese
courts apply in the cases that come before them.

THE SUPREMACY OF POLICY REVISITED:
THE INSTRUMENTAL BACKGROUND

I have already suggested that an instrumental concept of law continues
to influence the implementation of policies and have pointed to the en-
listment of the courts in widely publicized campaigns against crime as the
most obvious example. There are more subtle manifestations of instru-
mentalist direction of the work of the courts to implement policies.[127]
Courts are sometimes given specific tasks; for instance, campaigns may
mobilize them to help enterprises not only by assisting them to collect
debts but by taking the initiative to advise enterprises to file suit.[128]
Courts have been lauded for assisting specific economic policies, including
one that promoted spring plowing and won the support of the masses and
rural cadres by organizing groups of judges to visit peasants during the
plowing seasons and conduct public trials of criminals who "sabotaged
rural social security." Another court worked with peasants to help them
discover "seven ways to get rich." Yet another seized the mood of the
Spring Festival, a time when families wish to be united, and conducted
mediation work among estranged couples. The extent to which courts are
part of the local administrative apparatus is also reflected in the expecta-
tion that court personnel can be mobilized to help deal with problems
that confront local governments such as helping with the poor or conducting socialist education.[129]

Although the close ties of the courts to policy and Party have been
criticized and greater judicial autonomy has been sought by some judges
and legal scholars, the mind-set of many judges may accept as proper the
interrelationships of policy and law that have been sketched here. One
Western observer notes: "many officials involved in the development of

Chinese law appear content that the legal system should derive consistency and coherence primarily from the dictates of Party and state policy and perhaps even the commonly held values of Chinese society."[130]

CHINESE COURTS AND LEGISLATIVE SUPREMACY

More than policy situates the courts in a subservient position to other organs of the Party-state. I have already noted that the legislature is viewed as the sole source of law. That doctrine is being quietly challenged by the Supreme People's Court in a manner that echoes long-standing and ongoing Western problems of defining the relationship of the courts and the legislature. In China two different conceptions of the functions of the courts have emerged. In the first, the courts are faithful servants of the legislature and only "apply" laws; the second would permit them to make interpretations that are capable of influencing similar cases in the future not only because the outcomes may be relevant in other cases, but because they articulate legal rules to meet changing circumstances in society. These two conceptions are bound to collide, as they have throughout Western legal history.

Every legal and political system has its own doctrine of the sources of law. In all countries that belong to the two great families of Western legal systems, there is a tension between the authority of legislatures and administrative agencies to make rules and the freedom of judges to interpret rules. Each system defines in its own way the powers that courts exercise when they apply rules, whether the rules emanate from legislatures, administrative agencies, or other courts. In the United States, for example, the distribution of power established by federal and state constitutions defines the authority of federal, state, and local legislation and the jurisdictions and powers of federal and state courts.

The fundamental allocations of power in Western democracies have not averted controversies over the power of courts to interpret legislation in situations in which the applicability of a rule is unclear or was unforeseen by the legislator. For the civil law systems, the French Revolution established a concept of separation of powers that limited the courts to *applying* the rules enacted by the legislature; courts were otherwise "completely forbidden to intrude upon the policy-making function of the legislature. In theory, courts were prohibited even such interstitial creativity as is required by the interpretation of statutes."[131] Indeed, at the very beginning of the French Revolution, when courts were in doubt about legislative intent, they were required to refer matters back to the legislators.

As one scholar has noted, "similar unrealistic bans on judicial interpretation were imposed by absolutist rulers from Justinian to Frederick II of Prussia to Joseph II of Austria. . . . It hardly needs saying that all such prohibitions were of short duration."[132] In civil and common law jurisdictions alike, no amount of legislation or administrative rules has been able to eliminate judicial discretion. In common law countries, judicial "activism" may tend toward doctrinal innovation—and inspire controversy about its appropriateness.[133] In civil law jurisdictions, the interpretative role of the courts came to be recognized despite strong doctrinal insistence that courts could only "apply" the law. China today seems destined to follow the path of those earlier unsuccessful attempts in the West to restrain interpretative activity of the courts. I have already noted that Chinese doctrine views central and local-level legislation and administrative regulations as the sole sources of legal rules, insisting that only the legislative or administrative body that promulgated a rule may interpret it. This position leaves no room for an interpretative role for China's courts, whose decisions have no formal precedental value, although other courts deciding later cases may use them as "reference." Economic reforms, however, are generating pressures on the courts to depart from these doctrines, and the Supreme People's Court is engaged in an effort to promote the coherence of promulgated laws and to provide guidance to a judicial hierarchy whose authority is badly splintered.

DEVELOPMENT OF PROCESSES OF INTERPRETATION

The Limited Authority of the Supreme People's Court to Interpret the Law

The basic power to interpret legislation, as explained in chapter 6, is divided between the Standing Committee of the NPC and the State Council, with only limited roles assigned to the Supreme People's Court and the Procuracy. As I noted in chapter 6, under the applicable State Council resolution, the Supreme People's Court has been given only the power to interpret "problems of the concrete application of laws or regulations in the course of litigation," while the Procuracy may interpret only "questions involving the specific application of laws and decrees in the procuratorial work of the procuratorates." In this scheme, laws "unrelated" to either the courts or the Procuracy may be interpreted only by the State Council or "competent departments."[134]

As the language of the resolution suggests, the Court's interpretative powers differ from legislative interpretation by the NPC Standing Committee and the State Council. As one observer has explained it, the Standing Committee "may supplement and amend laws if necessary. In contrast, the Court's interpretive function is limited to clarifying and strengthening the laws without changing their original meaning."[135] The Court is further limited to interpreting only laws promulgated by the NPC and the State Council. It may not interpret any other laws, nor may it invalidate any laws at all. These limits on the Court's interpretative power flow from its nature as an administrative organ that supervises the courts in their "adjudication work" under legislation promulgated by the law-making bodies of the central government. When the courts apply rules made by other agencies, such as ministries under the jurisdiction of the State Council, *these agencies' own interpretations of such rules must be followed.* The courts must consult other agencies when a case involves interpretation of their rules.

Despite these limits on its power, in practice the Supreme People's Court has begun to interpret laws and regulations independently. These interpretations are expressed in many types of documents, which are in form identical with the administrative documents issued by every other government department. In these documents the Court, as administrative organ, applies legislated rules to situations that they did not address directly and sets down general rules with broad prospective application.[136]

The range of these interpretations demonstrates the extensive interpretative power the Court has gained since 1979. The broadest and most wide-ranging are official opinions (*yijian*) or interpretations (*jieda* or *jieshi*), which are general statements of normative rules not made in connection with pending litigation. They may be opinions either on an entire law, or on specific sections, and in practice they may sometimes establish new rules or even contradict NPC legislation.[137] Opinions and interpretations published in the Court's official gazette become authoritative sources of rules for decision in cases. Official replies and letters (*pifu, fuhan*, or *dafu*) are issued in response to requests for advice from lower courts on the interpretation of a law. Official notices (*tongzhi* or *tonggao*) contain interpretations of law that are binding and are sometimes issued jointly with other agencies. The Court also issues summaries of conferences at which important matters were discussed (*yiyao*); in practice these are treated by the lower courts as weightily as the other more formal documents.

What one scholar has called "the chaos of forms of judicial interpretation" inspired the Supreme People's Court to issue its "Rules on Interpretation Work" in June 1997 (the Rules).[138] The Court classified judicial interpretations as "interpretations," "rules," and "responses." "Interpretations" can be either detailed interpretations of a comprehensive law such as the General Principles of Civil Law or directives on how to apply a rule to a particular case or group of cases. "Rules" cover judicial procedures, and "responses" are answers to questions raised by the lower courts. Despite this attempt to clarify the interpretative documents issued by the Court, others remain, as Wang Chenguang points out: "notifications," "minutes" of meetings, speeches, regulations issued by the Court and other agencies such as the Ministry of Public Security, answers to questions conveyed by telephone or correspondence, and the judicial decisions published in the Gazette of the Court (case law is discussed below).

Problems Presented by the Court's Exercise of Its Interpretative Role

The evolving practice of the Supreme People's Court raises a number of issues: First, in practice the Court often legislates, and therefore exceeds the scope of its legal authority. When the generality of Chinese legislation creates difficulties for lower courts, the Supreme People's Court provides rules that serve as the sources of their decisions. Illustratively, the Court's opinion on the General Principles of Civil Law laid down many rules to supplement the code.[139] In one case, although the General Principles requires partners to draw up a written partnership agreement, the Court issued a rule that permits courts to validate oral agreements in cases in which partners had fulfilled all other requirements of a partnership and their relationship could be proven by evidence from two or more persons.[140] In the criminal area, the Court ruled that individuals who were not state officials could be charged with corruption if they colluded with a state official engaged in corrupt conduct.[141] No legislative authority exists for this practice, and it has been suggested that its justification lies in the supremacy of the CCP within the Party-state and the consequent use of the Court to issue interpretations that will keep the application of law consistent with policy.[142] Presumably such extra-legal considerations justify the Court's occasional practice of issuing interpretations jointly with administrative agencies, such as the Ministry of Public Security, with which it is only coequal in status.

A second problem is that practice is not standardized, and not all interpretations are published. The relative authority of different kinds of documents is unclear. For example, notices and conference summaries are not supposed to be interpretations, but are taken as such by lower-court judges. The Court has also been inconsistent in its policy toward the power of the lower courts to interpret laws. A more serious problem of legality is that many interpretations are never published at all; of those that are, some appear in the Court's official gazette, while others can be found only in publications that circulate within the court system.[143]

The Emergence of Case Law

Published accounts of decided cases have emerged as another source of law without formal legislative authorization. Chinese doctrine firmly rejects the doctrine of precedent (*pan li*), denying any binding force to judicial decisions. Although prior cases may be considered instructive examples (*an li*), they are not binding and are not supposed to be considered a source of law.[144] In practice, the Supreme People's Court has been publishing decisions in its Gazette since 1985 for their "reference" and "educational value." Most are lower-court decisions that were carefully chosen and substantially rewritten in order to transmit to the lower courts the Court's views on the issues involved.[145]

Other reports of decisions circulate to the lower courts through internal channels, but only the most "mature" and "representative" are selected for open publication. Although the lower courts may not cite them (by published order of the Court), Nanping Liu argues that the Court intends these published cases to carry the same weight as precedents, and reports that a growing number of Chinese legal scholars believe that they should be treated as such. He sees them as a "regulatory effort" on the part of the Court to create a "governing vehicle" through an administrative device. Since the Court alone may publish decisions, its choice of provincial cases is intended to establish centralized precedents for the judicial system as a whole.[146] The Court's claim that these cases are merely for the "guidance" of the lower courts is, in Liu's interpretation a "gesture toward other political branches,"—in other words, to avoid the appearance of acting too aggressively as a judiciary asserting a bourgeois concept of the separation of powers.[147]

The Supreme People's Court has a high awareness of the significance of publicly reporting decisions. The editor of the Gazette, Liang Huixing, expressed it clearly in a 1995 talk.[148] Chinese law, he said, was undergoing the same kind of evolution that the civil law systems of Europe had experienced. As European society became more complex in the nineteenth and twentieth centuries, judges began to create "important legal principles . . . despite the fact that the civil law system still did not admit the validity of precedent." The Supreme People's Court, by deciding to publish decisions in the Gazette, "has moved our country's legal system from nineteenth-century traditional legal theory into modern legal theory." The reported cases, Liang added, will both guide the courts and create legal norms (*guize*), thereby filling many of the gaps in Chinese law.

How should the role of the Court be assessed? It is certainly performing a necessary role in filling gaps in vague and generally drafted legislation at a time of remarkable social change. As Wang Chenguang observes, judicial interpretations are sometimes needed because the implementation of rules is uncoordinated.[149] (Although he adds that the interpretations may sometimes be produced hastily.) The current distribution of power among Party and state entities limits the Court's ability to introduce a doctrine of judicial precedent. Yet as Nanping Liu has suggested, it may also be performing a very different function by coordinating the application of law with current Party policy.

The Effect of Legislative Incoherence

The interpretative activity of the Supreme People's Court adds much-needed coherence to Chinese legislation, but its powers remain limited.

Less limited are the activities of administrative agencies in interpreting laws and regulations. Anthony Dicks has closely examined some examples of interpretation by courts and administrative agencies and finds that the current system permits different bureaucratic agencies to produce "logically inconsistent rules of substantive law."[150] This modern practice—understandable in terms of both traditional Chinese legal culture, which did not recognize the separation of powers, and Marxism-Leninism, which insists that only legislatures may interpret legislation—has had unfortunate consequences. When the courts are presented with issues that involve an overlap between their own jurisdiction and that of administrative agencies, they may negotiate joint interpretations, follow administrative interpretations, or even refuse jurisdiction altogether, deferring instead to an administrative agency to decide on the interpretation of a law or regulation.

I have touched on administrative rule-making in chapter 7, but its impact on the courts deserves emphasis here. Dicks has characterized the arrangement as "legal fragmentation." It leads, he continues, to "some of the worst disadvantages of federal legal systems without the appropriate legal and political machinery even to resolve the resulting conflicts and tensions, far less to unify the law." This analysis "throws doubt on the authority of the courts as exponents of a [China-wide] generalized and universally applicable view of the law." Dicks suggests that "the traditional limits on the power of the People's Courts, imposed by the jurisdictional claims of other authorities, have survived the reforms of the 1980s largely unimpaired."[151]

The need for Chinese courts to interpret legislation seems likely to grow, but the courts cannot by themselves bring about greater predictability, certainty, and consistency in judicial decision-making. A larger political solution that raises their status above that of other agencies is required, but such a change implies the need to revise arrangements of fundamental importance that are enshrined in the Chinese Constitution. In the near term at least, economic and legal reform are likely to continue to create pressure to expand the interpretative power of the courts, while the current configuration of political institutions will inhibit their ability to respond to the challenge.

Perspectives on the Chinese Courts

This survey of the structure and operation of the courts has reviewed the considerable difficulties they encounter. Despite the difficulties, however, litigants are bringing suits to the courts to assert rights. The rising caseload, impressionistic evidence (little more is presently available), and reported decisions from a heavily edited Chinese source combine to suggest that the courts have begun to develop an ability to vindicate private rights that are asserted by litigants. The increase in judicial effectiveness is relative, to be sure, compared to the powerlessness of courts, the legislative vacuum, and the hostility to law itself in the not-so-distant past. Nevertheless, the trend is discernible in press and court reports that reflect the legislative creation and the judicial enforcement of rights.

JUDICIAL ENFORCEMENT OF RIGHTS

New Rights, New Means of Asserting Them

In order to define the new legal relationships and transactions created by the economic reforms, an enormous amount of legislation has been adopted. Chinese law-makers have created a framework for contract and other commercial transactions and have defined new rights in many other areas. In the realm of property, for example, one of the principal aims of an inheritance law that took effect in 1985 is the protection of private rights over property that not long ago would have been considered "means of production" and, therefore, could be owned only by the state.[152] The articulation of principles of tort liability has already been mentioned.[153] Legal scholars and press reports alike tell of successful lawsuits in which these new rights have been asserted, and a leading scholar has elaborated on the increasing use of the General Principles of Civil Law as the basis for suits for injury to a variety of personal rights including rights to life and health, personal names, image, and reputation.[154] He notes, too, that the interpretation of that code by the Supreme People's Court has expanded the definition of rights arising under its provisions, as by listing examples of conduct that should be deemed injurious to reputation.[155] Consumers have asserted their rights to sue a retail seller for knowingly selling counterfeit goods.[156]

Notably, too, class actions have been brought to enforce a wide and growing range of rights, such as failure to pay dividends, breach of contract, damage to crops caused by inferior seed or fertilizer, and violation of environmental antipollution regulations.[157] Such lawsuits impose burdens on the courts, already suffering from a lack of resources and trained judges. Judges, whose performance assessments are based in part on the number of cases they process, may discourage such cases as too time-consuming. Lawyers, too, may not welcome class actions because of their complexity or difficulty and because the regulations on legal fees give them little incentive to take on such cases. Despite these obstacles, the use of class actions is growing, with interesting implications. Class actions are a means by which citizens can try to force local governments to obey national laws; more generally, they suggest that "the ways in which litigants use the legal system to pursue their own interests may be increasingly important in shaping the evolution of law in China."[158]

Published Decisions

Published decisions of the courts provide additional evidence of judicial responsiveness to attempts to enforce rights. The evidence is of limited and uncertain value, however, for a number of reasons. Only a small number of cases are published in the sole official publication, the Bulletin of the Supreme People's Court, which has been discussed earlier. Some are published for propaganda purposes.

Increasingly, though, collections of cases are being published under semiofficial auspices. They appear to be intended to give guidance to the courts.[159] One such semiofficial collection provides glimpses of the courts as they deal with rights arising out of economic transactions. Since 1992 the *Anthology of Adjudicated Cases in China* (*Zhongguo shenpan anli yaolan*, hereafter referred to as Anthology) has been published in Chinese annually by the Senior Judges Training Center of the Supreme People's Court and the Law Faculty of People's University. The first volume, containing cases decided in 1991, has been translated into English as *China Law Reports* and has been used for reference here. The Anthology is not representative of ordinary judicial decisions because it is a compilation of decisions submitted from courts all over China that have been chosen, edited, and often extensively rewritten by law professors before publication.[160] It can be taken, however, to illustrate what Chinese legal scholars and high-level judges think they would want Chinese judicial decisions to look like and is discussed as such below.

The Style of Judicial Decisions. A major limitation on the usefulness of reported decisions as sources of insights into the judicial process is the conclusory and formalistic style in which they are written. Each reported decision in the *China Law Reports* contains substantial summaries of the claims asserted by the parties and the findings of fact by the court. The CPL provides that judgments shall state "facts on which the judgment is based" and "the reasons in support" of the decision (Art. 138), paralleling civil law codes. However, in most decisions the courts state only that the facts supported a finding that the case did or did not fall within a specific rule, which is expressed in formulaic invocations of the applicable laws (e.g., "in accordance with . . . plaintiff's claim is dismissed") that reveal little about the court's reasoning. The decisions give no hint that they are interpreting legislation or interpretations of the Supreme People's Court. One reviewer of the Anthology has rightly observed that the courts' reasoning and analysis "tends to be all too laconic, and this criticism has been expressed by Chinese scholars as well."[161]

Representative Outcomes. Despite these limitations, some of the cases in the Anthology are interesting because of the types of issues that they present. Some decisions illustrate the application of very elementary legal principles. In the nonstate sector, many economic transactions have been entered into either in a legal vacuum or between parties unaware of the legal significance of their acts. Decisions in such cases might apply rules no more complicated than that parties to contracts must adhere to them, including agreements to pay damages in the event of breach.[162] When a buyer used most of the goods purchased before complaining about their quality, a higher court ruled it improper for a lower court to uphold the buyer's quality claim.[163] Other decisions apply formal legal distinctions that a party to a transaction did not understand, in one case, for instance, affirming the validity of a contract signed by an authorized representative of a local government even though he was succeeded by another person.[164] Reported cases like these may seem almost primitive to a Western lawyer, but the court's buttressing of the distinction between individuals acting in representative as opposed to personal capacities is of basic commercial significance. Quite a few cases involve decisions on the effects of contracts that were illegal under restrictive legislation, such as a contract for a transaction not comprehended within a party's business license[165] or one that violated a directive related to the state plan.[166] These illustrate the continuing existence of administrative limitations on the power of economic actors to enter into contracts.

Other decisions illustrate the creative role of the Supreme People's Court. One decision relied on an interpretation by the Court directed against lower court formalism, holding that although two parties had not complied with the required procedures for forming a partnership, the facts showed that their relationship "possessed the essential elements" of one and treated it as such.[167] Another Court interpretation that defined legal duties to third persons was invoked when a manufacturer was held liable for personal injuries to the retail purchaser of a product.[168]

Some cases apply broad general standards of fairness. In one decision,[169] a plaintiff in the early 1950s agreed to buy the defendant's husband's house, took possession after paying two-thirds of the purchase price, and then left China for Taiwan without paying the balance. He returned thirty years later to reclaim the house, and the court upheld his claim in a one-sentence decision, citing without discussion Article 4 of the General Principles of Civil Law, which states that "Civil activities must be carried out in accordance with the principles of voluntariness, fairness, exchange of equivalent values, and good faith." The court to which this decision was appealed agreed in a three-sentence decision that emphasized that the plaintiff had been given control of two floors of the house by the deceased seller.[170] In another case, a hotel and a peasant traveling with a pig and a donkey had to share responsibility for the hotel's loss by theft of the peasant's animals overnight. The court decided that both parties knew that their agreement that the hotel would keep them overnight was invalid, and that they should therefore bear liability in proportion to their fault under Article 61 of the General Principles of Civil Law, which allocates legal liability for invalid contracts according to the degree of the parties' fault.[171]

The political convulsions of the 1950s and 1960s continue to generate disputes over property in the lower courts and have led the Supreme People's Court to issue interpretations for their guidance. The Court has favored upholding determinations of property rights made during the land reform movement (1949–1952), presumably to avoid destabilizing long-established expectations. In disputes involving problems that arose after land reform, however, property interests dating back to the mid-1950s have been revisited and overturned.[172]

Award of Damages. Because of the limitations in the reported decisions that I have noted here, I can offer no more sophisticated conclusion than that the limited number of reported decisions in the 1992 compilation that have been used as a source suggests that courts are increasingly providing remedies for claimants seeking damages for violation of their rights. The reports offer no insight into the courts' reasoning about the amount of damages awarded. The relative fault of parties is explicitly mentioned in some cases, such as the dispute mentioned above over the animals that disappeared from a hotel overnight, but in numerous cases damages less than the amount claimed by the successful plaintiff are awarded without any explanation. Still, in a large number of the reported decisions, successful plaintiffs recovered all or substantial percentages of the amounts they requested.

The failure of the decisions to offer guidance on the theories that underlie the damage awards is understandable, perhaps, in light of the state of development of the Chinese market. When the plan was dominant, specific performance was the primary remedy. As discussed in chapter 7, the Economic Contract Law provides for damages but also permits the injured party to demand specific performance as well, and the draft Unified Contract Law modifies the rule. Chinese economic reform has not yet created the markets whose existence is assumed by Western courts, which presuppose that a party injured by a breach of contract will be able to purchase on the market the performance that he was promised.[173]

Implications

The publication of these cases under the authority of the Court is an expression of the growth of the courts and of the lengthening of the reach of the laws they apply. It demonstrates—as it is no doubt intended to demonstrate—that the courts are enforcing legal rights. These cases must be seen, however, in light of the evidence of strong local government involvement in the outcomes of court decisions that has been mentioned above. Two studies by Western scholars of dispute resolution during the 1980s concluded that the courts treated current policies and the views of local officials as more important to the outcomes than relevant laws.[174] One study, while concluding that the courts emphasized contractual rights, stressed that this emphasis derived "from an insistence upon observing the Party's current policy, not from an inalienable right to due process under law."[175] Since the research for these studies was completed, the nonstate sector has grown continuously and the number of contract disputes brought to the courts has risen. At the same time, the Chinese sources discussed in this chapter underline the existence of fundamental problems in the quality of Chinese adjudication and the ability of the courts to enforce their decisions. On balance, although it seems appropriate to treat these published reports of judicial decisions as evidence of some development of the courts during the past decade, they should not be taken as accurate representations of the daily work of the judicial system.

These cases suggest other issues. The Anthology provides notice, at least theoretically, to other economic actors in society about the rules applicable to business transactions. Although other collections of cases have been published commercially since the mid-1980s, the semiofficial Anthology was first published in 1992. However, transmission of the rules by the courts is, as Marc Galanter has argued, "only part of the process." It is necessary to ask: "Who gets which messages? Who can evaluate and process them? Who can use the information?"[176] We know nothing yet about the impact of these reported cases, which are not supposed to have any precedental value, and which private conversations with a small number of judges and law professors suggest are not frequently consulted by lower courts. As for the lawyers, since cases are not supposed to have precedental value, might they feel less need to keep abreast of Chinese court decisions than their Western counterparts? My conversations with Chinese lawyers suggest that some, in litigation, are beginning to cite previous cases in their arguments to the courts.

The publication of decided cases reflects the accretion of experience by the courts. However, the formalism of their opinions not only gives no hint of their reasoning but also conceals doctrinal and structural difficulties that have been addressed in my examination of the sources of the rules and standards that Chinese courts apply in their decisions.

Other evidence suggests that regardless of how many legalisms Chinese courts invoke in their opinions, the broad range of values that currently coexist in Chinese society—traditional, Maoist, reformist—shapes both the arguments of parties to civil litigation and the judicial decisions that resolve disputes. One study of litigation indicated that not only was the percentage of litigants represented by lawyers small but, even when lawyers participated in courtroom debate, they asserted arguments based not on law but on values derived from traditional society or even pre-reform "collectivist society."[177] Not one but numerous Chinese legal cultures will continue to shape the articulation and enforcement of rights in China.

The courts have only limited power to adapt Chinese legislation to the needs of a society undergoing extraordinary changes. Whether the function of the courts will be broadened and the limitations on their powers reduced cannot be foreseen at this time. It seems possible nonetheless to hazard a perspective on the Chinese courts that could be useful in shaping foreign understanding not just of courts, but of the developmental path that Chinese law could take in the future.

CHINESE COURTS AS BUREAUCRATIC INSTITUTIONS

The Problem

The ambiguities in the roles of judges are clear. Although current policies present judges as administrators of justice, long practice treats them as cadres whose functions are not distinct from those of other officials. They have not yet been trained to prize procedural justice. This appraisal is not an exclusively Western one: At a meeting I attended with a group of judges in late 1995, a Chinese law professor criticized judges for overemphasizing substantive results while neglecting the need for procedural regularity. His point was clear. Procedural justice and the rule of law are linked in Western outlooks, but for the link between them to become ingrained in the mentalities of Chinese judges will take a long time. Discussion here has illustrated the considerable pressures that face them: policy and popular sentiment insist that judges mete out even-handed justice, but irresistible claims are made on them by local governments—on whose payrolls and at whose pleasures they serve. The Party demands loyalty and adherence to Party policy. Many judges, particularly older ones, have limited legal educations and outlooks inconsistent with an independent judiciary. Corrupt litigants or officials may influence their decisions.

Since the early 1980s, the activities of judges have become increasingly regularized and rights-consciousness among the populace has grown slowly. Some Chinese judges do recognize the need to insulate the courts from pressures generated by the Party-state. Both among legal professionals and the general population, an incipient belief in the *legitimacy* of formal institutions for dispute resolution has begun to evolve. For these trends to continue, they must be nourished by popular perceptions that the courts function meaningfully to foster substantive justice. Policy, however, remains unclear about the functions that courts should perform; little in Chinese history suggests any model for an appropriate relationship among courts, the government that created them, and the society they serve. This analysis suggests a perspective on the Chinese courts that, although inspired by Western scholarship, also resonates both in Chinese scholarship and in the views of articulate Chinese judges.

A Western Perspective on Chinese Courts

The description of the organization, ethos, and decision-making processes of the courts in this chapter highlights some significant ways in which Chinese courts differ from Western courts, both in ideals and in practice. What emerges is the weakness of the concept of *adjudication* as that function is performed when Chinese courts decide cases. A model of analogous Western institutions, even if it is necessarily abstract and idealized, may supply a useful comparative perspective. Such a model has been proposed by Marc Galanter, who has enumerated criteria of the phenomenon known as "adjudication." The elements of his "adjudication prototype" are contrasted below with Chinese conceptions and practice.[178]

Intake: The forum addresses "delimited controversies" between identified persons rather than general situations and gives individuated treatment to each case in deciding each case on its merits. Such criteria would apply to Chinese courts in many but not all cases. When courts are used in conjunction with campaigns to promote policy, and as adjuncts to local administrative bureaucracy, they sometimes seek out cases in order to join the efforts of other elements of the Party-state's bureaucracy in furtherance of certain stated goals.

Process: The disputants participate by presenting proofs and arguments, the rules of the forum govern, and the case is "defined by claims that specific events, transactions or categories should be measured by application of some delimited conceptual categories." The central conceptions of adjudication under Chinese civil procedure would meet this criterion. But courts often move away from this aspect of classic adjudication, and mediation or decision-making takes into account matters that involve events or transactions beyond the conduct out of which the claim arises, such as personal relations between the parties.

Basis for decision: The basis for decision is formally rational and the parties' claims are "assessed in the light of some bounded body of preexisting authoritative normative learning, to which the forum is committed in advance." Decisions of Chinese courts are often shaped by political or localistic considerations external to the body of legal rules that courts are supposedly engaged in applying, and as such they are not "formally rational." Also, this criterion assumes that the courts apply publicly available rules, whereas some rules applied by Chinese courts are available only in internal publications. Further, the vagueness that marks the language of China's normative rules weakens their clarity and suggests a lack of differentiation from general policies.

Decision: The forum renders a decision on the merits in the form of a final award or remedy to one party, "rather than engaging in therapeutic reintegration of the parties," and norms render readjudication difficult. As I have shown, the Chinese courts often engage in mediation and can do so at any stage of their proceedings. The Chinese system's encouragement of, and tolerance for, readjudication weakens the finality of judicial decisions. A range of alternatives is available to parties who wish to challenge judicial decisions even after they have become legally effective, including review initiated at the request of government or Party officials.

Differentiation: Adjudication is differentiated from other activities, is conducted by professional specialists, and in general is "insulated from general knowledge about persons and their histories and status." As I have discussed in this chapter, Chinese adjudication remains closely tied to politics and policy, and considerations other than formal-legal ones may decisively influence the courts' decisions. The Party-state's policies can affect the outcomes of specific decisions, and its officials influence outcomes for personal and localistic reasons. Until the Judges Law was promulgated, the criteria used in selecting judges apparently did not differ significantly from the criteria used in selecting other bureaucratic personnel. Recent discussions with Chinese legal scholars suggest that the Judges Law has not yet been thoroughly implemented.

Chinese adjudication has a special characteristic thrust on it by political doctrine. Adjudication is not a societywide phenomenon, since most of the activities of other Chinese agencies lie beyond the reach of the courts. Most controversies arising out of the exercise of power by a Chinese agency of government, central or local, to which affected persons may wish to object as a matter of law, may not and do not come to the attention of the courts at all. Other agencies of the Party-state deal with—or do not deal with—issues that are often the ordinary work of courts elsewhere.[179]

Impartiality and independence: The forum is impartial and "is not the agent of any entity outside the forum, with responsibility to further policies other than those crystallized in the decision." One deputy president of the Supreme People's Court stated explicitly in 1994 that when higher courts carry out adjudication supervision, they are not only carrying out the law but "concretely expressing the democratic centralism of the CCP in the work of the courts."[180] The responsibility of the Chinese courts to support and advance policies of the Party-state and their dependence on local governments has been sufficiently reviewed above to warrant no further discussion here.

Today Chinese courts and law are much less politicized than at any time since the PRC was founded—otherwise there would be no point in writing about them in such detail—but they still remain so functionally undifferentiated from the rest of the Party-state that they should be characterized as bureaucratic rather than adjudicatory organs. Courts everywhere have bureaucratic characteristics, more so in the civil law systems than in the Anglo-American systems because "the emphasis on career service, explicit hierarchy of posts, precise application of codes, the elaboration of files, and correction and supervision by superiors matches the bureaucratic model fairly closely."[181] It is instructive to consider the Chinese courts in light of the distinctions between courts and bureaucracies in Anglo-American jurisdictions:

Appellate courts are usually not hierarchic superiors to trial courts . . . [t]hey may overrule trial court decisions [but their] review . . . is initiated by litigants. It is not motivated by a policy focus of the higher court, nor does it constitute a systematic quality control of the work of the trial courts. . . . Supreme courts often promulgate procedural rules that govern trial courts, but they exercise no continuous supervision over day-to-day trial work and almost none over the flow of cases that courts process. They almost never hire, transfer, or fire trial judge or other trial courtroom personnel. They have little or no influence over trial court budgets.[182]

By contrast, the Chinese courts exaggerate each of these enumerated features. The extent of hierarchical review of judicial decisions, within and between courts—often before decisions are final—suggests that Chinese judicial decision-making is more of an administrative process than a judicial one, especially if the criteria are judicial independence and the judge's individual responsibility for the decision.[183]

These aspects of the judicial hierarchy reflect its position as only one of many bureaucratic "systems" (*xitong*), existing in parallel with, but not superior to, all others. This integration of courts into the entire Chinese bureaucracy[184] causes adjudication, *which is the means by which the rule of law must be implemented continuously if it is to be meaningful*, to be no different in kind from the act of any other governmental agency—such as issuing permits, establishing production targets for state-owned enterprises, or making safety rules for the roads.

A Chinese Perspective on Chinese Courts

The appropriateness of the view of Chinese courts that has been proposed here is suggested by recent research by He Weifang that captures the views of some judges on the position of their courts in Chinese society. One interview, with a county court judge before enactment of the Judges Law, is particularly telling. Although a major concern was selection of judges, the judge looked to underlying problems:

The management style of our courts is a kind of unprofessionalized form of management. Why is it so difficult to reform the style of adjudication? Because Chinese law is mass-oriented (*qunzhong hua*) and anti-professionalized. . . . Judges of grass-roots and intermediate courts with low levels of legal professionalization handle many cases. . . . why is it for a long time there has been no change in the situation in which a large number of demobilized soldiers become judges? I once worked in a county. . . . the director of the county personnel department said: "What is the PLA for? It serves as a tool of proletarian dictatorship. And what is a judicial organ for? It is also a tool of proletarian dictatorship. It's the same thing." Apart from this, anyone from any profession can join judicial organs. . . . the best cadres will not be assigned to work at the court, only those without a profession will be assigned to the courts because anyone can do the job. Can this profession have any authority?. . . . This is a systemic problem, and cannot be solved by the judicial organs alone.[185]

Based on such interviews, He Weifang concludes that "as long as the judge fulfills a kind of administrative or non-judicial function, there will be no possibility or necessity to attain professionalism in the selection of judges."[186] He goes on to note the current problems faced by one vice president of a provincial court:

The operational mechanism of the court isn't scientific, it's "just a copy from the same old Political-Legal department mold"; [it] lacks a mechanism that would guarantee independent adjudication by law and mixes Party and governmental functions with adjudication; [it provides] no legal guarantee of occupation, position, or salary for the judge, [and] no legal guarantee of financial support, [so that] the courts are restricted by administrative agencies.[187]

These last interviews emphatically indicate the continuing impact of the values and institutions of the Maoist period and further highlight the complexities of defining the function of Chinese courts.

The current situation reflects the continuing challenge to legal reform presented by organizational patterns antedating reform. I have already emphasized that under Mao, Chinese law was assimilated to administration and became an arena of contention between two different views of bureaucracy, as shown by the contrast and conflict between "Red" and "Expert." Today Chinese law reformers must make fundamentally different distinctions. As totalitarianism ebbs and functional specialization increases, speculation has begun in China about a view of judicial activity centered on upholding the rule of law and about the professional orientation that is appropriate to the courts in light of this goal. An alternative to viewing courts in terms of bureaucracy is emerging.

The nature of that alternative is still obscured by considerable continuous confusion of law with bureaucracy and by the failure thus far to adopt the rule of law in practice. In both Chinese tradition and Communist practice, law was regarded as an ensemble of rules for administering a society rather than as an arrangement of norms that create rights in the persons and entities in that society. This view further helps explain the generality of much Chinese legislation, its resemblance to statements of policy, and the lodging of vast discretion in the administrative agencies that administer often mutually indistinguishable laws and policies.

The Chinese courts can currently foster legality only within limits imposed by a hostile ideology and by institutions faithful to it. The courts could function to strengthen the rule of law but only if a Chinese leadership adopts, or yields to, a different philosophy of governance. The rule of law *is* an ideology.[188] Courts truly dedicated to promoting that ideal cannot be instruments of a government that uses them to promote changing political tasks; they must have a more passive interest in solving conflict to attain a social equilibrium.[189] Because the rule of law implies a very different view of the state, movement in the PRC toward legality remains hobbled. It puts into question a fundamental element of current Party policy—insistence that the boundaries of reform must be set by the CCP without changing its position in the Party-state. A metaphor that may be appropriate here was suggested early in the reforms by the call of a senior Chinese economist to keep the nonstate sector of the economy as a "bird in a cage." That expression no longer fits the economy, but it does describe law reform today, which is still enclosed by the bars of a cage.

CHAPTER 10

Conclusion

> The political and civil laws of each nation must be proper for
> the people for whom they are made, so much so that it is a very
> great accident if those of one nation can fit another. . . . They
> must agree . . . with the customs [of the people].

> —*Montesquieu*[1]

THIS FINAL CHAPTER considers the likely future of China's legal reforms
and the political, institutional, and cultural obstacles that must be overcome if China is to progress toward establishing and maintaining a stable
rule of law. The accomplishments of China's legal reformers have been
impressive despite the limitations set by policy on the role of law itself, the
flux of China's ongoing social and economic transformations since 1979,
and the continuing strength of traditional legal culture. The future growth
of legal institutions depends critically on the support that they receive,
both from the government that creates them and from the society they
must serve; Chinese legal institutions must overcome the mistrust of both.

For the achievements of law reform to be deepened, a number of
forces must operate favorably: Economic growth and economic reform
(extending also to SOEs and the banking system) must continue, and the
leadership must also perceive Chinese society to be stable enough and
their control secure enough to encourage the growth of legality. If, under
such circumstances the leadership promotes further legal reform, the reformers should be able to continue their steady and undramatic efforts to
support and strengthen the institutions they have created. Even in the
most favorable political context, however, to be effective the institutions
will have to become more rooted in Chinese society than they are today:
The changes in Chinese legal culture that have begun to occur will have
to go farther. The processes of change that are involved necessarily

require a long period of time. Given these difficulties, the best that can be hoped for is incremental reform, and it would be wise for Western observers to take, as China must, a long view.

It should be clear, though, that building and consolidating legality, however, are primarily political tasks. Regardless of how much legislation is promulgated and how many judges are trained and installed in the courts, legality will not grow unless the Party-state fosters and maintains a commitment to it and alters the allocation of power between the courts and the rest of the Party-state. That cannot be done without the Party abandoning its dominance.

This chapter draws together some implications of the preceding chapters, as of the end of 1998, for Chinese legal development and for US-China relations. I first consider a mix of forces that seem likely to constrain the further development of legal institutions. I have not revisited many aspects of the work of the courts that have already been discussed in detail. Of particular concern, however, are problems arising out of new patterns in relations between state and society. I characterized them in the beginning of chapter 5 as essential elements of the context in which the legal reforms are taking place. I have returned to these problems below in order to speculate about the possible influence of emerging new institutional and cultural patterns.

The final section of the chapter is concerned with some implications for the United States of the likely slow growth in Chinese legality. American involvement with China promises to become more intense because of the increasing volume of Sino-American economic relations and because China's growing power requires that the United States "engage" China on a wide variety of regional and global issues. As long as China's political system remains an authoritarian one, however, the United States will have to manage relations with a government of which many Americans disapprove. Many also care a great deal about law, legality, and related issues of human rights—all the more reason why American perceptions of Chinese legal institutions should be clarified. I have ended by suggesting implications for US policy toward China, specifically on human rights and on China's membership in the WTO, which should flow from a clear understanding of the current state of Chinese legal institutions and from realistic expectations about the prospects for their further development.

Some Major Influences on Legal Development

PARTY POLICIES

Some current limits on legal reform derive from pre-reform policies that remain in place. Most notably, although Chinese leaders declare that the rule of man must be replaced by the rule of law, they have not changed methods of governance that obstruct institutionalization of the rule of law, such as insistence that it must serve policy generally and respond to specific demands by the central Party-state. The most visible expression of these demands has been in the repeated campaigns against crime and consequent intensification of criminal punishments during such campaigns, and the obedience shown by the courts to the Party when dissidents are accused. Other intrusions of policy into the daily work of the courts, less obvious but requiring no less subordination of the courts to implementation of policies, have been noted in chapter 9.

In practice, too, policy about the function of law continues to reflect ambiguities. Chinese leaders as well as legal scholars have articulated a view of law that is quite recognizable in the West. They have repeatedly said that for Chinese legal development to be meaningful, rules enforced by the power of the Chinese state must protect the expectations of individual citizens, groups, enterprises, and organizations arising out of economic transactions. This view is expressed in legislation on civil and economic law and in the work of building institutions to settle disputes arising out of civil and economic transactions. Continued economic development will intensify pressures to employ and expand legal institutions and to develop additional ones. Contracts are being used more widely in China, and rights claimed to arise out of them are being asserted more frequently. Both the consciousness and the security of those rights can be expected to grow, albeit slowly, if citizens perceive that the Party-state supports vindication of their rights by both policy and practice. It remains to be seen what content such rights or their analogues will possess.

By what standards will attempts to exercise rights be understood? In the West, private law establishes a framework for individuals to pursue their interests autonomously, with the state creating "the means whereby, if necessary, those individuals can secure the interest in question by calling upon the state's judicial and law-enforcement apparatus."[2] It is not yet clear, however, how comprehensively the Chinese Party-state will permit law to function as a framework to facilitate private transactions. Both long before and since the PRC was established, law has been regarded in China exclusively as an instrument of control and discipline. In the nonstate sector, as I noted earlier, there is a lingering adherence to the notion of contract law as an administrative device to "manage" contracts. Policy that requires functionaries of the Party-state to leave "private" behavior alone departs radically from long-established injunctions to punish "speculation." This dilemma is especially confusing because economic reform has often caused officials much difficulty in distinguishing lawful "private" economic activity from criminal "speculation."

THE STATE BUREAUCRACY AND THE COURTS

Expansion of the power of courts is critically limited by the absence of effective restraints on the Chinese bureaucracy, whose grip on Chinese society will be difficult to dislodge. The limited reach of laws that institutionalize citizen challenges to administrative arbitrariness has already been discussed, as have the major obstacles to the growth of the rule of law that are presented by current Chinese administrative practices. Adoption of the Administrative Litigation Law (1989), the State Compensation Law (1994), and the Administrative Punishment Law (1996) reflected recognition of the need to protect individuals and entities against official arbitrariness by creating rights to challenge arbitrary exercise of bureaucratic discretion. As the millennium approached, further efforts were being made to draft additional legislation intended to control administrative acts by defining and regularizing administrative procedures. That was the hope of Chinese legislative drafters at the National People's Congress as well as legal scholars with whom these problems were discussed on several occasions in 1998. However, simply promulgating new laws that create rights to challenge arbitrary officials in the courts will not remove the major obstacles that current Chinese governmental practices present to the growth of the rule of law. Legislation and administrative rules are often so generally drafted that they resemble statements of policy, which are "clarified" through interpretations and applications by bureaucrats exercising their discretion. Foreign investors commonly note this problem as one of the more troubling features of the Chinese investment environment, and we may be sure that it is a fact of life for Chinese.

Changing the language of Chinese law will be especially difficult, because not merely drafting techniques but also attitudes toward power must change. As long as Chinese administrative agencies enjoy the power both to write their own rules as broadly as they do now and to interpret them, they have a license to be arbitrary. To change this situation, the domain of law would have to be enlarged and the powers of bureaucrats diminished. At present, doing so seems beyond the will of the current leaders of the Party-state. A senior Chinese judge with whom I discussed these problems agreed, saying, "there is much that has to be changed from outside, not from within the courts."

Judicial powers will also not expand as long as the judicial hierarchy remains only one among many bureaucratic hierarchies, existing coordinate with them but possessing no greater authority than any of them. The rule of law will not advance as long as the courts (or some other functional equivalent within the administration) lack the power to interpret and decide on the validity of legislation and of administrative rules. As I have already emphasized, major political decisions will be required in order to change the position of the courts vis-à-vis the rest of the Party-state. Absent such decisions, reform can only be piecemeal and incomplete.

THE RISE IN THE POWER OF THE LOCAL PARTY-STATE

In sketching some of the major changes brought about by the economic reform in chapter 5, I stressed the importance of the devolution of power to the localities that allowed them to create a parallel marketized economy. Although this vibrant sector of the economy has been the engine of reform, as I emphasized earlier, its growth may retard and deflect Chinese legal development. The weakening of central power creates difficulties for efforts to construct and strengthen a unified national legal system. The efforts of the Supreme People's Court to "guide" the lower courts by circulating authoritative interpretations of legislation and significant court decisions are not sufficient to meet the needs for legal coherence and consistency. As noted earlier, the Court's role is limited by reason of the position of the judicial hierarchy itself and the Court's interpretative activity raises constitutional issues with ideological and powerful political implications. At the same time its "gap-filling" role may also be a reflection of "democratic centralism" in serving to implement CCP policies.

Viewed from the local level, the development of relationships based on administrative power and on economic reciprocity seems inimical to the growth of legality. I need only refer here to the discussion earlier of the power of local Party and government officials over the courts and the difficulties that "local protectionism" has created for the courts. The interpenetration of business and government at the local level promotes particularistic relationships that do not seem conducive to the strengthening of concepts of law and legality. Although one optimistic view suggests that proliferation of such relationships is but a step toward the breakdown of the vertical bureaucracies of the Party-state and a preliminary step not only to the building of markets but to the construction of universalistic legal rule,[3] current tendencies do not suggest such a trend.

At the moment of writing, it is striking that Western scholarly perspectives greatly emphasize that although the reforms have led to a lessening of central control, the local manifestations of the state have not been in retreat. One writer notes, "despite the political leeway that currently exists in China, it is notable that few anecdotes reveal substantial social activity that is wholly independent of the state."[4] The changes do not suggest "a 'society' detaching itself from, and gaining greater autonomy and power vis-à-vis the 'state'," but rather "the lower reaches of a state structure gaining increased autonomy from higher reaches and forging new kinds of political and economic ties with individuals and enterprises outside."[5] As a result, courts are involved in relationships among officials and business that both echo traditional values and practices and also reflect outright contemporary profit-seeking. Judicial independence is threatened by the strength of these relationships, which are more tenacious than political control by the CCP because they are so rooted in Chinese society.[6]

Moreover, personal relationships are embedded in the economic relationships of commerce in the nonstate sector (they also flourish, differently, in the state sector). Even though the central Party-state's ideology has become more noticeably hospitable to autonomous private economic activity, the integrity and universality of the legal framework for such activity are threatened by local-level interests. One aspect of the problem, which looms critically large in the future of legal reform, is the current ambiguity of rights over the acquisition, management, and disposition of property. One scholar, writing in 1997, noted that although local firms and governments were beginning to retain lawyers, "perhaps it is these social ties and the credible expectations that are embedded within them, rather than any hard and fast laws, that have made it possible to have growth without clear and secure property rights in the western sense of the term."[7]

How might these institutions evolve? It is impossible to predict the outcome of any contest between nationwide legal rules and the patron-client relationships on which many businesses rely today. At the present, the contest seems so likely to endure for a long time that its outcome cannot be foreseen. Conventional Western theory teaches that in a marketizing economy, participants desire legal certainty and that an increasingly complex economy ought to generate more precise conceptions of rights. The slow emergence of rights-consciousness in China suggests that formal legal institutions—legal rules and the courts that can enforce them—can gain importance. Their relative power, however, could long be blunted by other Chinese institutions and by certain components of traditional Chinese culture.

THE RULE OF LAW AND CHINESE LEGAL CULTURE

A striking characteristic of Chinese legal culture has been the primacy of interpersonal relations over legal relationships. This is not only a theme that has been echoed in research, but it has been demonstrated to me in twenty-five years of negotiating Sino-Western transactions in China, as well as in many conversations with Chinese. It would be wrong to draw too strong a contrast between Westerners who conceive of their business relationships in terms of legal rights and duties and Chinese who are concerned only with personal qualities and relationships. After all, considerable Western legal scholarship shows that significant economic relationships are managed entirely outside the law[8] and that parties to contracts are very often willing to forgo their legal rights on the basis of other considerations.[9] Nonetheless, the Chinese emphasis on relationships (*guanxi*) seems to have had a strength and durability for thousands of years that make it more powerful and pervasive than comparable Western emphases.

Although in this book I have focused on legal institutions that in the West are at least formally independent of personal relationships, such relationships are so important in Chinese culture that no assessment of Chinese law should fail to weigh heavily the interactions between law and traditional forms of *guanxi* and its modern manifestations. This theme has emerged in this book although I had no intention to emphasize it when I began writing. It is impossible, however, to escape noticing the importance of status relationships in traditional China, the use of personal relationships in Maoist times to overcome rigidities in the administrative apparatus and the state sector of the economy, and the obvious growth of powerful *guanxi* relationships among businesses and officials at the local level as a result of economic reform. It therefore seems appropriate to recall here the likely continuing importance of such relationships in the future of Chinese law.

The depth of traditional values presents a considerable obstacle to the deepening of legal consciousness and the strengthening of legal institutions. Two scholars who studied the resolution of contract disputes throughout the 1980s wrote persuasively of the cultural "embeddedness" of the emphasis on personal relationships.[10] Although they suggested that the deepening of economic reforms would expand both contract relations and legal concepts of contract, the continuing strength of *guanxi* relationships suggests that such changes in values will occur only slowly.[11]

Guanxi, to be sure, is not unchanging. Rather, the "production of *guanxi*" is the outcome of behavior that is conditioned both by past traditions and by current practical concerns.[12] Although the influence of the past is considerable, Chinese economic actors are confronted by new challenges that include, among others, the increasing importance of economic exchange in relationships affected both by *guanxi* and by increasingly important legal institutions. We have already seen that although law is a recent addition to the configuration of rules and institutions that govern

China, it has become more visible in shaping relationships and managing conflict. Signs of these changes include the relative decline of extra-judicial mediation and the increase in litigation of all major types, such as class actions, challenges of administrative arbitrariness, and suits by employees against their work units.[13] Less obvious are changes in the attitudes of Chinese engaged in economic activities, who may come to want the stability of their expectations protected by legal rules as well as by interpersonal relationships with their counterparts.[14]

OVERSEAS CHINESE INFLUENCE

The force of tradition is strong, however, and China's current crisis of values reinforces the need to rely on personal relationships in order to stabilize expectations. Moreover, the potency of traditional values is sustained by a powerful and unique source of support. Unlike all other post-totalitarian Communist societies, a vast number of its ethnic compatriots residing abroad make massive contributions to China's economic reform. As much as 80 percent of all foreign investment may be attributable to overseas Chinese.[15] Overseas Chinese bring to China not only their remittances and expertise, but also ideas about how businesses and governments ought to work. Some, especially from Southeast Asia, may also carry with them values that may not be conducive to the growth of a legal system.

It has been observed, for example, that overseas Chinese fit very well into the corporatist trend toward alliances between local businesses and officials.[16] One trenchant summary notes that overseas Chinese "are relatively untroubled by the absence of a legal and accounting framework or of reliable market research" and assume that they need "to co-opt political support to get anything done."[17] A well-known Hong Kong Chinese businessman has been quoted as saying "Western companies take a long time to make decisions; they need a lot of lawyers. The bureaucracy is too heavy for this part of the world. overseas Chinese know not to create such deterrents."[18]

The lengthy contracts that are usually preferred by many multinational corporations and their lawyers often strike their PRC counterparts as too wordy, legalistic, and unfamiliar. The major concern among overseas Chinese businessmen, however, may not be lawyers but rather the use of law itself. An American banker in Hong Kong was quoted in this pointed observation: "'You need a partner for the local flavor when you negotiate . . . and to take care of things behind the scenes.' By that he means that sometimes necessary transactions foreign firms need to distance themselves from."[19]

The practices and business ethics of overseas Chinese vary and are not being subjected to close analysis here. All businesspeople, regardless of their ethnicity must, especially if they work in multinational corporations, conduct businesses in conformity with the legal environment in which they operate.[20] Even with this caveat, however, it is still apparent to many observers inside and outside China that overseas Chinese from Southeast Asia operating in China often value legal rules and the formal arrangements fashioned to conform with them very differently than many Western and Japanese businessmen.[21] These attitudes inevitably color those of Chinese in the PRC and seem, further, likely to influence the development of Chinese legal institutions.[22] As long as the motherland continues to welcome "overseas compatriots," some overseas Chinese will continue to bring with them cultural values that are not conducive to the elevation of Chinese legal consciousness.

The Asian financial crisis that began in 1998 provoked some reconsideration, both among overseas Chinese investors and Chinese officials, of methods of doing business and the need for transparency, but it is too early to tell whether business practices will actually change.[23] Regardless of whether events outside China will change patterns of behavior among overseas Chinese, changes in official policy and practice within China could have a powerful effect if they provoked overseas Chinese and other investors to believe that adherence to legal rules was important.

The Rule of Law as an Alternative Ideology

In the face of policies and institutional forces that limit the growth of legality that we have looked at here, other and newer forces support law reform.

THE DESIRE FOR JUSTICE

As both Communist ideology and official virtue decline, the rule of law could fill the growing vacuum of belief, despite the absence of a strong rights-based tradition in Chinese history. The refusal to recognize rights that could be asserted by individuals and vindicated by legal institutions was not a Communist innovation. In traditional China, as noted at the outset of this book, law was undifferentiated from administration and was guarded by an élite charged with governing by means of noble example and deep wisdom.

The rule of law challenges that tradition and the decaying ideology that has been used to justify the Party-state. When its validity becomes generally recognized, the rule of law itself functions as an ideology that legitimates the exercise of a distinct form of power.[24] When Chinese individuals participate in litigation they *experience* the rights-consciousness dimension of law. Institutions interact with legal culture, and the legitimacy of the Party-state itself would be bolstered if the legal institutions that it has created are perceived by the populace as operating in the manner in which they are advertised.

Legal reform and its heavily propagandized popularization have heightened individuals' consciousness in China about legal concepts, legal rights, and substantive justice. This heightening of consciousness is due partly to the influx into China of Western ideas and partly to the legal reforms themselves. On numerous occasions in China, especially in the last ten years, I have repeatedly heard ordinary Chinese express values consistent with Western ideals of equality, justice, and legality, and research provides additional albeit impressionistic evidence of belief in those values.[25] Other observers have concluded that what Chinese today mean when they say that there is no law "is something very specific: the government is not restrained by its own rules, *and it should be*."[26] In the face of the forces that constrict legality and the weaknesses in the institutions that have been described in detail here, it is difficult to be optimistic. But my own and others' personal impressions suggest that among the Chinese populace are many who have considerable desire for a government that will give them justice.

At the same time, we should anticipate that Chinese will not necessarily seek justice in the same places and in the same manner as they would be sought in the West. For example, there is a deep Chinese tradition of complaining to higher levels of authority, which was even echoed in Mao's "mass line" political style that encouraged officials to maintain close contacts with the populace.[27] In the PRC today, many citizens seek direct contact with officials on policy issues, especially when they seek protection from application of a policy that damages their interests. Such contacts may involve efforts at the working level or at higher levels, the Party or the Young Communist League, deputies to the local People's Congress, letters to newspapers, or local offices for "letters and visits," which act as complaint bureaus. The complaint bureaus have existed since the first days of CCP rule, and the results they reach after receiving complaints are decidedly mixed. The existence of this extra-legal route for redress of grievances against authority indicates the persistence of a traditional approach that is likely to continue to condition future institutional experimentation. The tendency to seek justice elsewhere than the courts is likely to remain strong.

LEGAL REFORM AND POLITICAL REFORM

What we learn from analyzing the Chinese courts in their social and cultural context has implications for assessing the possible influence of legal reforms on more extensive system-wide political reform. The rhetoric of legal reform often aims at nothing less than fundamental reversal of previous policies. Deng Xiaoping himself said that "to realize democracy and the rule of law is the same as realizing the four modernizations."[28] Many Chinese legal scholars conceive of a role for law that is distinctly post-totalitarian and see law as an instrument for change.[29]

The growth of Chinese law may also resonate with other aspects of reform. Law, William Alford points out, has a "peculiar, if limited capacity to stimulate and consolidate other types of change, while, at least implicitly, diminishing claims of its autonomy."[30] Legal reform shapes and disseminates concepts about relations between state and society that affect individuals' relationships with each other as well as with the state. Although many Chinese do not yet distinguish between the courts and other state agencies, some are bringing suits to force local cadres to comply with national laws.[31] In addition, peasants angered by predatory cadre behavior use government laws and regulations as the basis for protest, sometimes violent.[32] The village elections that have been promoted by the Ministry of Civil Affairs in order to reassert weakening central control over policy implementation in the countryside could also generate institutionalized practices that limit government powers.[33]

The weakening of Beijing's control over the rest of the country since the late 1980s suggests that even if the Chinese leadership decided to promote a more integrated legal system and the rule of law, it would encounter great difficulty. Local and provincial governments that gain in strength may seek to build stronger legal institutions in the areas they rule,[34] but the relative strengths of central and local governments are presently in flux, and so too is their capacity to build stable legal institutions. Moreover, the power of local élites to evade and blunt policies aimed at reinforcing legality should not be underestimated.

Movement for political reform may receive varying degrees of support among intellectuals and some officials,[35] but Western-style pluralism is outside Chinese experience: "What legitimizes government is not pluralism and participation but moral rectitude and administrative performance," notes Andrew Nathan, summarizing the results of a public-opinion survey conducted in China in 1990.[36] China's leaders publicly avow their opposition to Western-style democracy,[37] and although they seem to have loosened controls over expression of politically unorthodox views, their opposition to activities that smack of organized protest was dramatized in late 1998 by the arrest and speedy conviction of dissidents who advocated establishment of a new political party.[38] Appraising the major forces in Chinese society, one Western observer concluded that the holders of political power were committed to restraining reform, economic actors who might favor reform preferred to operate within the corporatist framework that linked them to the Party-state, and the majority of the Chinese populace was satisfied with the improvement in their material well-being that economic reform had brought them.[39]

Regardless of the reluctance of the Chinese leadership to promote political reforms and the apparent passivity of the Chinese populace, some optimistic Western observers have predicted that continued and sustained economic development will lead to China's becoming a democracy. Henry Rowen, extrapolating from the recent history of Taiwan and South Korea, has asserted that "a richer China will become more democratic" and even suggests that this will happen by the year 2015.[40] Minxin Pei, although more cautious, points to the strengthening of the NPC and legal reform, in which he sees "the potential to evolve from a system of law into a rule of law."[41] Rowen does not discuss how he believes the current configuration of state-society relations could evolve, and no clear trends seemed apparent as of January 1999.[42]

What we have seen in preceding chapters of this book about the operation of the courts and the limits on legal reform suggests that these views are excessively optimistic. Moreover, the greater weight of Western scholarship on China suggests a high probability of the continuation of some form of authoritarianism and a great unlikelihood of the establishment of a true parliamentary democracy.[43] The effects of the Southeast Asian economic crisis that began in late 1997 were unclear as of the writing of this book. The smaller Asian dragons with which China was formerly often compared were further along the path of economic development than China, and the crisis could promote legal development in at least some of them because of the need for greater transparency in each of the nations involved. The harm done all over Southeast Asia by "crony capitalism" possibly could spur Chinese leaders to accelerate both economic and legal reform, since China has its own form of relation-based finance. One noticeable emphasis in Chinese leadership statements that linked the Asian economic crisis with law was a call for additional regulation of financial activities.[44] Until now, however, China has been the most hesitant dragon of all to deepen legal reforms because of their serious political implications.

Suggestions for US Policy

Chinese legal institutions do not concern only China. They have generated considerable interest abroad because of what they portend for the development of the Chinese state and the manner in which it will exercise its power within and outside its borders. Analysis of the institutions of dispute resolution and the context in which they operate suggests some implications for US policy toward China on law-related issues.

HUMAN RIGHTS: LESS AMERICAN MORALIZING

In the view of Lawrence Friedman, "One of the most striking aspects of American society, to natives and foreigners alike, is the way law and the legal system seem to dominate public life."[45] The contrast between the United States and China in this regard marks one of the sharpest differences between the two societies, and the difference is accentuated by the American tendency to stress legal concepts in international relations. George Kennan, a wise student of US foreign policy, has remarked that "the tendency to achieve our foreign policy objectives by inducing other governments to sign up to professions of high moral and legal principle appears to have a great and enduring vitality in our diplomatic practice."[46]

An obvious manifestation of what Kennan calls the American "legalistic-moralistic approach to international problems" is US policy on human rights. The United States has taken the lead, among all nations of the world, in judging other governments' treatment of their own people in accord with standards of human rights that it regards as universal.

After June 1989, the United States made Chinese human rights violations a major issue in US-China relations. Such violations caused annual debates in Congress over whether China should receive most-favored-nation (MFN) treatment from the United States until 1994, when President Clinton "delinked" the two issues. Human rights issues continue to figure not only in debates on MFN[47] but, more importantly, in overall US policy toward China. From 1990 until 1997, the United States led efforts to make the UN Human Rights Commission criticize China for human rights violations. The PRC, in turn, has responded angrily to what it has characterized as an attack on Chinese sovereignty and a culture-bound attempt to project Western values onto a China with different traditions and difficult economic circumstances.[48] The issue declined somewhat as a point of contention when the United States and the European Union decided in 1998 not to introduce a condemnatory resolution, and the PRC announced that it would sign the International Covenant on Civil and Political Rights.[49] China signed the covenant in late 1998,[50] but harsh treatment of dissidents and concern among some American groups about repression of religious activity are bound to fuel continued concern among many Americans about human rights violations in China.

The human rights debate has generated heat and emotion on both sides of the Pacific because

It touches some of the core values in each society: the American values of freedom, individualism, and democracy, and the Chinese values of sovereignty, national pride, and self-determination. It evokes each society's core myths: American missionary responsibility to carry freedom and democracy overseas, and China's struggle against foreign intervention in its internal affairs.[51]

In addition, the American critique of China is based on concepts that have found only a fragile foothold in post-Mao China. The notion of rights generally is extremely underdeveloped in China today and is only beginning to be accepted. A concept of inherent rights is even more alien. Sino-Western differences on this issue are understandable in light of the fundamental problems in Chinese legal reforms that have been discussed here.

The American human rights critique of China also involves the projection of other American values, such as due process.[52] Some observers are reluctant to accept such culture-bound intellectual categories, arguing that because China is a poor and developing country, "economic and social rights may be much more important than political and civil rights,"[53] or that Chinese undervalue individual rights because of the importance in Chinese tradition placed on individual behavior in groups. In this view, the assumption that a legal system should protect human rights is not relevant to understanding Chinese law and Chinese society. Analyses derived from Anglo-American concepts of legal procedure also overlook a historical Chinese lack of concern for procedural justice.

Despite these critiques, there is evidence that whatever the differences in the starting points from which Chinese and Westerners begin when formulating concepts of governance or limits on official power, concern for due process values has been increasingly voiced in recent years in China, by Chinese. Chinese leaders have been consistently concerned about the need to curb official arbitrariness. Some Chinese legal scholars, officials, and intellectuals have called for a legal system that embodies standards of procedural fairness. Since 1978, published discussions of political and legal reform as well as demonstrations by Chinese students in the name of democracy have increasingly called for the rule of law.[54] These are Chinese sentiments, not the creations of Western scholars, and they signify that the rule of law is becoming a Chinese problem. Such developments suggest, as Jerome Cohen urged as early as 1977, that the argument that "such due process values, as we call them, are irrelevant to China . . . is [an argument] of extreme cultural and political relativism."[55]

At the other extreme, some Americans insist on pronouncing censorious judgments on China and would require the United States to place at the center of US policy relentless insistence that China must become a law-based society.[56] These views are often no more than simplistic calls to punish the Chinese leadership because China fails to live up to American ideals.[57] Another observation by George Kennan is enlightening here:

I am extremely skeptical of the relevance and applicability of *our* moral principles to the problems and outlooks of others, and I suspect that what passes as the 'moral' approach to foreign policy in our country is often only another expression of the serious American tendency to smugness, self-righteousness and hypocrisy.[58]

The difference between Chinese and Western ideas—and ideals—of law has long vexed Sino-Western relations generally, and different ideas about rights under law will continue to trouble Sino-American relations. American policy-makers who wish to press China to move more decisively toward the rule of law should take into account the constraints on China's capacity to change its legal institutions, which stem not only from the determination of the CCP to retain its rule and power, but from the lasting influences of tradition and the pre-reform Communist past, limited resources, and structural developments in state-society relations that have been caused by economic reform. Awareness of these ought to temper American impatience and help place law-related issues in perspective.

Moreover, the United States obviously lacks the power to muster international support for a policy of aggressive pressure on the Chinese government to modify Chinese institutions. As one China specialist has noted, when the United States has threatened sanctions because of trade, military sales, and human rights issues, "in almost every instance the other G-7 countries have not supported America's threats [which] has made Washington's claim that it is acting on behalf of widely accepted international norms ring hollow."[59]

The United States should no longer pursue rights-related issues as publicly or as sanctimoniously as it has done in recent years. Its past pressure for condemnation of the PRC by the United Nation Commission on Human Rights has produced noisy posturing by both nations. It should, however, quietly but insistently remind the Beijing leadership that the world is watching its treatment of its own people, and that foreign images of China are shaped in large part by perceptions of Chinese democracy. Rather than projecting American due process ideals, the United States should appeal to the concepts articulated in the Universal Declaration of Human Rights that are not rooted in any particular philosophy, ideology, or social system.[60]

Many observers over the years have pointed out that US policy has been equivocal toward some of the most important international covenants that express the human rights that it condemns China for denying to its citizens. The United States signed the International Covenant on Civil and Political Rights in 1992 only after insisting on many reservations, and (like China) it has not signed the International Covenant on Economic, Social, and Cultural Rights, which would also express American willingness to recognize concepts of human rights that go beyond the legal and political rights that are at the core of American policy. If the United States is to be credible and not merely moralistic, it should improve its own record.[61]

Chinese legal culture is surely relevant to American insistence on rights-based changes in Chinese behavior. In the mouths of moralistic critics of China, "human rights" has become a slogan that allows no room for "the burden of the past which any major change in the character of the Chinese rights system will have to overcome."[62] William Alford points out the narrowness of American rights-based arguments, noting that it reminds many Chinese of one hundred fifty years of exploitation and bullying by the West. Nineteenth-century Chinese perceptions that law was used as a weapon to justify violating Chinese sovereignty still echo in Chinese memories. To the extent that US policy projects or relies on American visions of how a legal system ought to work, it may generate resistance and resentment of a powerful Western nation hectoring China.

The conduct of the Chinese Party-state is unlikely to change significantly in response to foreign pressure unless rights-consciousness among Chinese rises considerably above its present level. The Sino-American disagreement on protection of the intellectual property of Americans is suggestive here. Absent what William Alford has described as "a belief that individuals are endowed with rights that they are entitled to assert even with respect to those in positions of authority,"[63] American pressure on China to toughen its laws on intellectual property protection is unlikely to succeed. Alford further points out that "massive threats" to bring about changes in the internal laws of another country are "incapable of generating the type of domestic rationale and conditions needed to produce enduring change."[64] He argues that the "institutions, personnel and values needed to undergird a rights-based legality" must support the laws themselves, and his argument applies to human rights as well as other legal issues. The forces supporting legality to which Alford refers can only come, most importantly, from within China itself. The quotation from Montesquieu at the head of this chapter carries a lesson that seems apposite today.

PROMOTING LEGALITY IN CHINA

The restraint that I urge here on US pressure on China to modify its human rights practices does not mean that the United States should abandon concern about promoting legality in China. United States policy should support long-term institutional reform in order to enhance the protection afforded to individual rights. The US government, American foundations, and the American business community should provide assistance to programs that aim at fostering the growth of legality in China. Such programs must necessarily start with an understanding of the Chinese legal environment—because simply sending foreigners to lecture in China or inviting Chinese legal professionals to the West for training is not enough. Training programs might be established in China, although they could be expensive and difficult to run, but such programs would have to proceed from an understanding of Chinese needs and a nuanced consideration of the extent to which foreign institutions could be adapted to Chinese circumstances.

Presidents Clinton and Jiang Zemin agreed in October 1997 to establish a Sino-American program of legal exchanges, and this useful initial understanding should be followed up by choosing from among the broadly phrased areas mentioned in the agreement and energetically elaborating long-term programs to implement the agreement.[65] Whether Congress would lend its support, after years of refusing to appropriate funds for US programs to foster the rule of law in China, remains to be seen. Congress refused in 1998. The Asia Foundation and the US-China Business Council provided limited funding for a small number of projects, but little other financial support for Sino-American legal cooperation and exchanges was available. One area that cries out for immediate close attention is improvement of Chinese administrative law. The underdevelopment of Chinese administrative law and the breadth of the discretion wielded by Chinese bureaucrats, which have been noted in this book, impede the further development of Chinese legality. Sino-Western consultation on improving Chinese systems for review of administrative acts, therefore, should be a high priority. This area could be highly relevant to Chinese participation in the World Trade Organization (WTO), as I discuss below.

POLICY ON CHINA'S INTERNATIONAL CONDUCT

In General

In domestic US politics, debate over China policy has become too narrowly focused on the dichotomy between trade and human rights, which human rights activists have cast as a struggle between Greed and Morality. Not only has debate within the United States become both narrow and shrill, but the need to place law-related issues in perspective has also been lost. Regardless of differences between the United States and the PRC on law-related issues, the United States must try to engage China in dialogue on strategic and other international issues of concern to both nations such as peaceful settlement of international boundary disputes; control of carbon monoxide emissions, which threaten the environment of all peoples; missiles and nuclear proliferation; and resolution of strategic issues, such as those involved in keeping and assuring peace on the Korean Peninsula.

The tone of US policy toward China merits more attention and subtlety than it has received. Concern for tone is especially necessary because of the moralizing about legal principles that has marked US policy. The tone of the dialogue is especially important because the two nations are unlikely to influence each other's domestic institutions very much. Under these circumstances, tone becomes substance; thus the United States should not preach but should attempt to persuade and to project quiet authoritativeness.

China, the WTO, and the Rule of Law

China's courts and other legal institutions raise long-range concerns for the international community in one notable context, China's participation in the WTO. China's application to join the WTO was the subject of international negotiation throughout much of the 1990s. There was little doubt about the desirability of China's joining, because membership would multilateralize China's economic relations with the rest of the world and thereby enable China to manage its international economic relations on the basis of agreed-to and enforceable rights and obligations, and to participate in writing the trade rules for the next century.[66] Membership should permit other nations to exert international pressure on China to abide by the rules of the WTO as "a way of pushing China to accelerate its efforts to introduce the rule of law at least into economic affairs."[67]

The operation of Chinese legal institutions has clear implications for US policy because it illustrates the difficulties that China will encounter if it must adjust its institutions to meet the requirements that membership in the WTO imposes on all members. Human rights considerations are irrelevant, because membership in the WTO is not a prize earned for acceptable political behavior but a status bestowed on nations willing to abide by trade and economic rules agreed on by most of the world's nations and expressed in the General Agreement on Tariffs and Trade (GATT).[68] Issues will arise, as during the accession negotiations, over the PRC's willingness and ability to adhere to these rules after it joins the WTO. Abundant evidence exists of trade and investment-related practices that permit Chinese officials to discriminate against and among foreigners in a manner that violates the central GATT principles of most-favored-nation and national treatment.[69] Of equal concern ought to be China's ability to meet the requirements of another basic GATT principle, that of transparency. The operation of Chinese legal institutions, as they have been discussed in this book, calls into question China's ability to meet the GATT requirement of transparency.

Article X of the GATT requires that member nations must publish their laws on trade and administer them in a "uniform, impartial and reasonable manner."[70] The analysis in this book suggests that China is far from meeting this standard at the present time and is unlikely to be able to meet it in the foreseeable future. The standard is only very general, of course, and it is certainly not consistently maintained by other GATT members.[71] The precise measures that China must take to address transparency issues, like others, must be addressed specifically in the Protocol of Accession that will eventually be agreed on by the PRC and the Working Party that has been charged by the WTO with carrying out negotiations, and in which Chinese obligations will be defined.

The issues raised by Article X have been the subject of lengthy negotiations. As of early 1997 the text of the Draft Protocol on Chinese accession to the WTO contained, among others, a clause to which the PRC has agreed, providing that:

China shall establish or designate, and maintain, tribunals, contact points, and procedures for the prompt review of all disputes relating to the implementation of laws, regulations, judicial decisions and administrative rulings of general application . . . the tribunals shall be independent of the agencies entrusted with administrative enforcement.[72]

This clause and the treaty standard quoted above imply that the PRC should be required to establish goals for the increased effectiveness of its legal institutions as a condition of membership, including at least a long-term commitment to build administrative law and to reduce "local protectionism" in the courts. In the short term, in order to establish nominal adherence to the agreement to maintain tribunals to hear disputes under the above-cited paragraph of the Draft Protocol, and in the absence of a comprehensive body of administrative law rules, it might be appropriate to establish administrative law tribunals in Beijing and two or three other cities. A crucial prerequisite would be enactment of a law articulating the procedural standards that Chinese bureaucrats would have to meet, as well as meaningful measures to implement such legislation. Although my discussions with Chinese legislative drafters in late 1998 suggested that they hoped to draft such a statute in the future, it is impossible to predict when it might appear, the extent to which it could be deemed to meet the standard of Article X, and, worse yet, how much time might have to elapse before it becomes a practical reality.

These problems raise a further disquieting issue, of whether China possesses the state capacity to meet the standard of Article X or the Draft Protocol. The "fragmented authoritarianism" of Chinese governance and weakened central control are causes for concern about whether, even if the central government made a commitment to develop Chinese legal institutions so that they came closer to meeting the treaty standard, it would be able to carry out such a commitment.

These concerns suggest that regardless of when China becomes a member of the WTO, the United States and the other major trading nations must entertain clear and realistic expectations about the limited results that can be attained by even the most energetic and sincere Chinese efforts to create and operate the judicial institutions required by the GATT. They should also anticipate that if other members of the WTO seek to use the WTO dispute resolution process to secure Chinese compliance with agreed-upon goals and schedules, the WTO panels could become seriously overloaded. Writing in early 1999 while China's membership in the WTO was being negotiated I thought that it seemed desirable for the EU and the United States to make clear to Beijing, before Chinese accession, the types of violations that would most provoke them to invoke the dispute settlement process.[73] After accession, whenever that might come, the same issues are likely to arise. Overall, the institutional transformations that will be required of the PRC on legal issues alone may be so difficult that focusing international concern on Chinese legality as part of enforcing China's obligations under the WTO is likely to be a long and time-consuming process.

In this conclusion, it seems desirable to emphasize two themes. First, although in this book I have been entirely concerned with China's attempts to build legality within its own borders, the international implications of these efforts are both considerable and inescapable. I believe that I have demonstrated convincing evidence for my statement in the preface that because of the absence of a unifying concept of law and a considerable fragmentation of authority, China does not have a legal *system*. I have noted elsewhere in this book other reasons for this view, which include the weak differentiation of the courts from the rest of the Chinese bureaucracy, organizational methods in the courts, and a cast of mind among judges that distinguish the courts little from the rest of the bureaucracy. Structural weakness, ideology, rigidity, entrenched interests, localism, and corruption limit the functions and autonomy of the courts and undermine their legitimacy. In this chapter I have noted that difficulties of the courts in applying Chinese law and enforcing their judgments raise an issue of the very capacity of the Chinese state. The current problems of the courts raise critical issues for the Chinese leadership and populace if they hope to continue economic reform and build strong and stable institutions. These issues, moreover, are not China's alone, because they concern other nations that would live with China peacefully and constructively.

Among examples of domestic laws with international implications, the difficulties that beset Chinese litigants in the courts also impede the enforcement of China's environmental laws.[74] As long as China lacks an effectively functioning legal system, China's ability to fulfill international obligations, even after they have been freely undertaken by representatives of the central government, will be impaired. This weakness promises to create difficulties in China's international relations and will retard Chinese efforts to participate constructively in the international community.

My second theme in closing is the difficulty, raised in chapter 2, of clearly defining foreign perspectives on Chinese legal institutions. The problem of China's state capacity also exists in the eyes of its beholders, foreign observers for whom it is difficult to form realistic expectations about Chinese legal institutions. The weaknesses of Chinese legal institutions are bound to cause concern abroad, and not only in trade-related matters that will come before the WTO. Legal reforms even complicate the problem, because they have begun to make it possible to discuss law using a vocabulary that is common both in the West and in China. That newly shared vocabulary conceals, however, underlying differences in meanings that stem from profound contrasts between historical and current Chinese and Western notions about law and governance.

It is essential, for example, to remain mindful of the ease with which Americans insist on comparing foreign legal institutions against oversimplified models of American institutions. Thus, as one student of Japanese law has noted, it is common in the United States to "exaggerate the importance of law and neglect other means for social ordering."[75] Americans, especially policy-makers for whom the rule of law provides a rhetorical device with irresistible appeal, are not accustomed to expect that the functions discharged by formal legal institutions in the United States might be found in institutional configurations unfamiliar to Americans. On Taiwan, for example, where democratic institutions have matured in recent years, law has been said to be "marginalized," because economic development has been fostered by a combination of modern legal institutions, networks of relationships, and enforcement by organized crime.[76]

Foreign observers must continue to question and clarify their assumptions. For example, some in the West assume that newly emerging groups and strata in Chinese society, once freed from the grip of totalitarianism, will seek autonomy from the state. As I noted in considering the future of the Chinese bar in chapter 9, it is not clear whether lawyers will seek autonomy more aggressively than they have in the past or prefer to ally themselves with governing élites; the same issue has been raised about businessmen, as I noted in chapter 5. When exploring links between these emerging strata and local power-holders, we must clarify the theoretical assumptions about development that may be implicit in our questions. For example, a recent study points out that although in the West the idea is popular that law grew out of medieval representative assemblies wresting concessions from kings, scholarship shows that they cooperated with kings in state-building and only slowly evolved away from being instruments of royal rule.[77] Viewed from this perspective, Western observers should not expect Chinese lawyers and local legislatures to seek autonomy in the early stage of the post-Deng history of China, because their hopes may rest on a distortion of Western history.[78]

No single perspective on Chinese law can prevent uncritical judgments based solely on Western development—or on myths about Western development. It is necessary to improvise an assortment of perspectives in order to interpret an unruly and continuing mix that includes Western concepts of legality, also contested, with sometimes incompatible Chinese values and institutions. Moreover, whatever our perspectives, the two decades of reform are only a historical instant, Chinese legal institutions are not transparent, and Chinese society is undergoing dramatic ongoing change. We should, therefore, attempt only restrained interpretations of our disorderly impressions. No matter how long we search, though, while we seek to enhance our understanding of China, we must remember to understand ourselves as well.

Reference

ABBREVIATIONS USED IN NOTES AND WORKS CITED

CCH   CCH Australia Ltd., ed. *China Laws for Foreign Business, Business Regulation*. North Ryde, NSW: CCH Australia

FBIS   Foreign Broadcast Information Service China—Daily Report

FGHB   *Zhonghua renmin gongheguo fagui huibian* (Compilation of Laws and Regulations of the People's Republic of China)

FLHB   *Zhongyang renmin zhengfu faling huibian* (Compilation of Laws and Regulations of the Central People's Government)

JPRS   Joint Publications Research Service translations

SCMM   U.S. Consulate, Hong Kong, *Selections from Chinese Mainland Magazines*

SCMP   U.S. Consulate, Hong Kong, *Selections from Chinese Mainland Periodicals*

Xinhua   Xinhua News Agency

ZRFG   *Zhonghua renmin gongheguo zuigao renmin fayuan gongbao* (Bulletin of the Supreme People's Court of the People's Republic of China)

PREFACE

   1. Lubman, "Peking Placing New Emphasis."

CHAPTER I

   1. Edwards, "Ch'ing Legal Jurisdiction."
   2. Quoted in Naughton, "Growing Out of the Plan," 120.
   3. Harry Harding, "Breaking the Impasse."
   4. "White House Releases Joint U.S.-China Statement."

CHAPTER 2

1. Gernet, "Introduction," xv. For a useful comparative discussion see Bünger, "Foreword."

2. The same metaphor has been used by Victor Li in *Law Without Lawyers*, 17.

3. Dicks, "Chinese Legal System," 542.

4. Alford, *To Steal a Book*, 4–5.

5. Lawrence M. Friedman, *Legal System*, 2.

6. Elton, *F. W. Maitland*, 21.

7. See Berman, *Law and Revolution*; Strayer, *Medieval Origins*.

8. Strayer, *Medieval Origins*, 21.

9. Strayer, *Medieval Origins*, 23.

10. Poggi, *Development of the Modern State*, 120.

11. The abbreviated discussion in this chapter of philosophical attitudes toward claims and disputes relies principally on Ch'ü, *Law and Society*; Needham, *Science and Civilisation* 2: 526–532, 543–583; Van Der Sprenkel, *Legal Institutions*; Bodde, "Basic Concepts of Chinese Law"; Dull, "Evolution of Government"; Turner, "Sage Kings"; MacCormack, *Spirit of Traditional Chinese Law*; and Bodde and Morris, *Law in Imperial China*.

12. Chang Wejen, "Traditional Chinese Attitudes," 1. A slightly different formulation by Professor Chang is cited in Alford, *To Steal a Book*, 10.

13. For a discussion of the specific differentiations in conduct dictated by the *li*, see Ch'ü, *Law and Society*, 230–239; Bodde, "Basic Concepts of Chinese Law," 383. A lucid discussion of the *li* is Mayfair Mei-hui Yang, *Gifts, Favors, and Banquets*, 222–229.

14. Alford, *To Steal a Book*, 10.

15. Liang Zhiping, "Explicating 'Law'," 87.

16. Chang Wejen, "Traditional Chinese Attitudes," 10.

17. The application of code provisions by analogy also illustrates a difference between Western and Chinese views: The analogical application of a penal provision by a magistrate could not be done as a matter of discretion, but had to be approved by "superior magistrates" and by the emperor himself. Bodde and Morris, *Law in Imperial China*, 520. But the motive for control of judicial discretion was not because it was unfair to defendants, but to assure that judges did not reach decisions that were contrary to imperial will. MacCormack, *Traditional Chinese Penal Law*, 55.

18. Poggi, *Development of the Modern State*, 23.

19. W. Friedmann, *Legal Theory*, 35.

20. Roberto Mangabeira Unger, *Law in Modern Society*, 85.

21. Poggi, *Development of the Modern State*, 73.

22. Roberto Mangabeira Unger, *Law in Modern Society*, 158–166.

23. Schwartz, "Primacy of the Political Order," 1–2.

24. Schwartz, "Primacy of the Political Order," 4.

25. Schwartz, "Some Polarities," 50, 56. As one scholar has observed, the term *fa* connotes a "model or standard imposed from above, to which the people must conform." Bodde, "Basic Concepts of Chinese Law," 379.

26. Wang Guangwu, "Powers, Rights, and Duties."

27. The brief discussion of traditional Chinese society that follows relies, in addition to the works cited below, on two excellent discussions of administration during the Qing dynasty, Ch'ü, *Local Government*, and Hsiao, *Rural China*. The Qing was not only China's last dynasty but the one that interacted most with the West. Focusing on the Qing, however, greatly foreshortens the view of Chinese state and society that I take here by failing to consider centuries of history of the institutions described and extensive variations in their operation.

28. Hsiao, *Rural China*, 6.

29. Max Weber, *Religion of China*, 121.

30. The clerks drafted, checked, and filed documents and records; the runners were court attendants, watchmen, policemen, guards, coroners, and turnkeys; personal secretaries coordinated the activities of clerks and runners and had key responsibility for such activities as preparing for judicial proceedings, supervising trials, collecting information for tax records, and collecting taxes and grain tribute. The private secretaries were also administrative experts on specialized matters such as law and taxation and supplied the magistrates with the knowledge of the detailed codes and precedents necessary to administer the law.

31. Some persons acquired gentry status not by passing examinations, but by purchasing degrees and offices from the state, especially in the declining years of successive dynasties. Until the mid-nineteenth century, success in the examinations was the primary means of obtaining an official appointment, but after the Taiping Rebellion in 1851, sale of offices by the financially hard-pressed government became more important. See Ho Ping-ti, *Ladder of Success*, 46–51.

32. Scholarly opinions differ considerably on the extent to which the gentry assisted the common people by exercising their influence with officials. Some see the gentry as deeply involved with the welfare of the people in their area, e.g., Chung-li Chang, *Chinese Gentry*, 51–70, while others stress the gentry's selfishness and concern with their own personal interests, e.g., Hsiao, *Rural China*, 505–508. The CCP, not surprisingly, emphasized the gentry's oppression of the peasantry. Certainly China's peasantry was miserably poor, and the gentry took advantage of their prestige and power to protect themselves against economic misfortune. The gentry's conduct was conditioned to some, and often a considerable, extent by their Confucian beliefs and the unseemliness of overt aggression. When they were successful in modulating official demands on themselves and their localities, they eased the burdens that lay on the common people even though they did not generally act as spokesmen for China's vast population of tillers, laborers, artisans, and merchants.

33. On the "bare sticks" or "village bullies," see Hsiao, *Rural China*, 454–462 and authorities there cited.

34. Hui-chen Wang Liu, "Analysis," 68–72.

35. On the functions of the clans, see generally Freedman, *Lineage Organization*; Hui-chen Wang Liu, *Traditional Chinese Clan Rules*; Martin C. Yang, *Chinese Village: Taitou*, 134–142.

36. On the guilds, see Burgess, *Guilds*; Fried, *Fabric of Chinese Society*, 146–153; MacGowan, "Chinese Guilds."

37. C. K. Yang, "Some Characteristics," 135.

38. This view is elegantly presented in Alford, *To Steal a Book*, 9–12.

39. This paragraph is based on Bünger, "Concluding Remarks," 313–319.

40. The imperial Censorate exercised surveillance over other officials but could also remonstrate with the emperor, with varying degrees of effectiveness. See, generally, Hucker, *Censorial System*. Although decidedly in the minority, one Western scholarly view maintains that law was regarded as embodying standards that the monarch was required to obey. See Turner, "Sage Kings."

41. Metzger, *Internal Organization of Ch'ing Bureaucracy*, is invaluable both on law-making and on administrative punishment of officials; concern in the Qing for clarity and consistency in the laws is also emphasized by Turner, "Rule of Law Ideals?," 26–37, who also emphasizes that imperial concern about arbitrariness did not arise from any concern to safeguard individual rights but from concern to "[preserve] human and material resources" for use by the state. Turner, "Rule of Law Ideals?," 40. On liability for incorrect decisions, see MacCormack, *Traditional Chinese Penal Law*, 91–95, 138–143.

42. Meijer, "Abuse of Power," 203.

43. Nathan, *Chinese Democracy*, 113.

44. Nathan, *Chinese Democracy*, 116. Consistent with this view, Paul A. Cohen, "Post-Mao Reforms," perceives a common thread of authoritarianism in political reforms advocated by Chinese leaders as diverse as the Empress Dowager, Chiang Kai-shek, and Deng Xiaoping.

45. Lawrence M. Friedman, *Republic of Choice*, 39.

46. Lawrence M. Friedman, *Legal System*, 21.

47. Berman, *Law and Revolution*, 5.

48. W. Friedmann, *Legal Theory*, 478–479.

49. See, e.g., Glendon, "Sources of Law," 238.

50. Peerenboom, "What's Wrong with Chinese Rights?," 47.

51. Peerenboom, "What's Wrong With Chinese Rights?," 47.

52. See generally, MacCormack, *Spirit of Traditional Chinese Law*, 48–50.

53. Chinese customary law is discussed in Weggel, *Chinesische Rechtgeschichte*, 170–191. The most extensive study of Chinese customary law as it was illustrated in the Republican compilation was done by Eduard Kroker, whose articles are cited in Weggel's bibliography. The Japanese compilation on Taiwan has been studied by Rosser H. Brockman, whose illuminating article on customary contract law, "Commercial Contract Law," has been relied on here. The Japanese compilations are cited in Brockman, 130 n. 1.

54. Weggel, *Chinesische Rechtgeschichte*, 172.

55. Fu-mei Chang Chen and Ramon H. Myers, "Customary Law (Parts 1, 2)."

56. Brockman, "Commercial Contract Law."

57. This discussion of *dian* is based on Feinerman, "Dian Transaction."

58. Feinerman, "Dian Transaction," 20–21.

59. Van Caenegem, *Birth of the English Common Law*, 93.

60. Van Caenegem, *Birth of the English Common Law*, 9.

61. Strayer, *Medieval Origins*, 36.

62. Regarding the power to tax and to dispense justice: "both assertions of

royal authority could be justified as logical extensions of doctrines implicit in feudal relationships." Strayer, *Medieval Origins*, 43.

63. Milsom, *Historical Foundations*, 1–3.

64. Milsom, *Historical Foundations*, 19.

65. Van Caenegem, *Birth of the English Common Law*, 102–103.

66. Van Caenegem, *Birth of the English Common Law*, 24.

67. Van Caenegem, *Birth of the English Common Law*, 56: "Royal will and coercion were the historic mainsprings of Common Law actions and accounted for the unmistakable police flavour of its civil actions in later times."

68. On the evolution of juries in royal courts see Van Caenegem, *Birth of the English Common Law*, 62–84; Shapiro, *Courts*, 77–78; Milsom, *Historical Foundations*, 1–25.

69. Shapiro, *Courts*, 78.

70. Van Caenegem, *Birth of the English Common Law*, 91.

71. Dawson, *History of Lay Judges*, 301; Strayer, *Medieval Origins*, 53: "France was a mosaic state, made up of many pieces, and the bureaucracy was the cement which held all the pieces together. If the cement sometimes got so thick that it obscured the pattern of government, this was better than letting it get so thin that the state fell apart. French methods did make it possible to create a state out of provinces and regions with widely divergent characteristics. And because most of the European states which eventually emerged were mosaic states like France, they tended to follow the French model."

72. Von Mehren et al., *Civil Law System*, 16–17, and sources there cited.

73. Roberto Mangabeira Unger, *Law in Modern Society*, 50.

74. Roberto Mangabeira Unger, *Law in Modern Society*, 53.

75. Bodde and Morris, *Law in Imperial China*, 4.

76. Rheinstein, ed., *Max Weber*, 264.

77. Such codes were primarily but not exclusively penal. Shapiro, *Courts*, 165–166; on the codes, law-making, and sources of law in general, see MacCormack, *Traditional Chinese Penal Law*, 48–71.

78. On the operation of the criminal process, particularly appellate review, see generally Alford, "Of Arsenic and Old Laws."

79. See C. K. Yang, "Some Characteristics," 150–156.

80. Jerome A. Cohen, "Chinese Mediation," 1212. C. K. Yang, "Some Characteristics," notes (at 145) that "only the generalist with *proven practical ability* was promoted," and that "the impractical scholar, the bookworm, and the inept devotee of literary form were met most frequently at the low level of county magistrate," rather than at upper levels (emphasis added).

81. Hui-chen Wang Liu, *Traditional Chinese Clan Rules*, 155.

82. Jerome A. Cohen, "Chinese Mediation," 1213.

83. See the long list in Ch'ü, *Local Government*, 47–48.

84. See, e.g., Ch'ü, *Local Government*, 49: "The opening of a case could be purposely delayed if the defendant offered a clerk a bribe. Or the clerk charged with writing a deposition, the chao-shu, could make some changes in the records" (footnotes omitted). For accounts of how magistrates' employees could conspire to extort money under threat of involvement in litigation, see Doolittle, *Social Life*

1: 305–306; Smith, *Village Life*, 218–219; Byron, "Office of District Magistrate," 49–50.

85. For a description of the positions of witnesses and parties before the magistrate, see John Henry Gray, *China: A History* 1: 35; Holcombe, *Real Chinaman*, 201–205 and 211; Van Gulik, trans., *T'ang-yin-pi-shih*, 55–58; Byron, "Office of District Magistrate," 51–52.

86. Van der Sprenkel, *Legal Institutions*, 123.

87. Douglas, *Society in China*, 104.

88. See, e.g., Gamble, *North Chinese Villages*, 246–247; Smith, *Chinese Characteristics*, 224–225.

89. See, e.g., Van Gulik, trans., *T'ang-yin-pi-shih*; Van Der Sprenkel, *Legal Institutions*, 79 (litigation "exceptional"); Jerome A. Cohen, "Chinese Mediation," 1216; Ch'ü, "Book Review." In addition to these sources, this discussion relies on two excellent surveys of traditional dispute resolution, Van Der Sprenkel, *Legal Institutions*, and Jerome A. Cohen, "Chinese Mediation," 1209–1225.

90. On the clans, see Freedman, *Lineage Organization*, 115; Hui-chen Wang Liu, "Analysis," 67.

91. On guilds, see Van der Sprenkel, *Legal Institutions*, 89–96 and sources therein cited. On clans, see Hui-chen Wang Liu, *Traditional Chinese Clan Rules*, 156–158.

92. Jerome A. Cohen, "Chinese Mediation," 1223.

93. Freedman, *Lineage Organization*, 115. Sometimes disputes were mediated first by elders of a clan subdivision; the subdivisions were based on descent from different sons of the common male ancestor considered to be the founder of the clan. If mediation was unsuccessful, first individual clan elders, then the clan council, would attempt to settle the dispute. C. K. Yang, *Chinese Village*, 97.

94. See, e.g., Gamble, *North China Villages*, 83–96; Kulp, *Country Life* 1: 127, 320–322; Smith, *Village Life*, 228–229.

95. See, e.g., Van Der Sprenkel, *Legal Institutions*, 92.

96. Van Der Sprenkel, *Legal Institutions*, 117.

97. For a description of this process, see Martin C. Yang, *Chinese Village: Taitou*, 165–166.

98. See Van Der Sprenkel, *Legal Institutions*, 85, and sources cited.

99. See, e.g., Freedman, *Lineage Organizations*, 115; John Henry Gray, *China: A History* 1: 219–220.

100. For an account of such a hearing, see Gamble, *Peking*, 194.

101. See, e.g., Kulp, *Country Life* 1: 322–323. See Ch'ü, *Local Government*, 189: "True, there were gentry members who helped the innocent for the sake of justice. But more frequently their actions were motivated by nepotism or by financial gain." Scholarly opinion on the extent to which the gentry took advantage of their position or benefited local inhabitants is widely divergent. A considerable body of commentary by nineteenth-century travelers is highly critical of the gentry's alleged impartiality. See, e.g., Smith, *Village Life*, 219, who classes with the "village bullies" who instigated lawsuits and conspired with *yamen* clerks "the most expert of all this dreaded class," the "bullies" who had passed one of the literary examinations and misused their status "to make use of this leverage as a

means of raising themselves and of harming their neighbors. Any Chinese bully is greatly to be feared, but none is so formidable as the literary bully."

102. Van der Sprenkel, *Legal Institutions*, 119–120.

103. On the strength of public opinion in villages, see, e.g., Martin C. Yang, *Chinese Village: Taitou*, 150. See also Douglas, *Society in China*, 112–113. On similar pressures in the clan, see Hui-chen Wang Liu, *Traditional Chinese Clan Rules*, 157. Even when civil cases were brought to the magistrate, he would sometimes encourage extra-judicial mediation by refusing to hear the dispute, "suggesting that the matter was too trifling for the courts and that the parties might best settle the matter themselves by conciliation." Buxbaum, "Chinese Family Law," 623.

104. Jerome A. Cohen, "Chinese Mediation," 1223.

105. Fried, *Fabric of Chinese Society*, 226: "*Ganqing* differs from friendship in that it presumes a much more specific common interest, much less warmth and more formality of contact, and includes a recognized degree of exploitation." For examples and further analysis, see Fried, *Fabric of Chinese Society*, 102–109, 116–123, 144–145, 152–153, 170–176, 206–209, 223–228. Gallin, *Hsin Hsing*, 303 n. 2, adds that "it is basically a matter of structured obligation. The feeling or sentiment results from satisfied or disappointed expectations of appropriate behavior, and the expected behavior is behavior appropriate to the formal relationship of the two individuals within the social structure."

106. On the concept of face, see Hsien Chin Hu, "Chinese Concepts of 'Face'," quoted in Van der Sprenkel, *Legal Institutions*, 99–100; Martin C. Yang, *Chinese Village: Taitou*, 167–172.

107. Huang, *Civil Justice*, 13.

108. Huang concludes that because the courts made it possible for many, "even simple peasants," to assert and enforce their claims, they were exercising "rights in practice, even if not in theory." Huang, *Civil Justice*, 235. His conflation of rights with the claims that were actually enforced tends to reduce the contingency of the claims and assimilate them rather unrigorously to Western analogues. Nonetheless, his mapping of "semi-formal" justice is a valuable addition to the scholarship, and one that would have greatly enriched the discussion of traditional mediation in chapter 3 had it been available when the article that is now chapter 3 was originally published.

109. Melissa Macaulay, "Civil Reprobate," 78.

110. See generally Melissa Macaulay, *Social Power and Legal Culture*.

111. The measures are summarized in Ch'ien, *Government and Politics*, 226–232.

112. C. K. Yang, *Chinese Village*, 106. Gamble, *North Chinese Villages*, 41–44, noted slow but marked changes during 1929–1933 in villages due to increased government control.

113. See, e. g., text below at n. 142.

114. "[The Chinese people] used to consider going to court, that is bringing law suits before the hsien magistrate, as lacking in respectability. That sentiment still lingers to some degree. The lack of easy accessibility of the courts and the high cost of modern law suits also discourage an essentially poor people from resorting to litigation to solve their disputes. Many disputes are settled out of court,

sometimes to the advantage of both parties, but more often to the advantage of the local gentry." Ch'ien, *Government and Politics*, 257.

115. Shapiro, *Courts*, 93.

116. Shapiro, *Courts*, 95.

117. Van Caenegem, *Historical Introduction*, 72–73, describes how Roman law was rediscovered in the twelfth century and spread by means of universities and commentators. Although it was older, Roman law reflected a stage of social evolution more advanced than that of Europe at the time. Rome had been cosmopolitan and sophisticated with a developed urbanized economy, while Europe was feudal and agrarian, and in a state of primitive intellectual development.

118. Van Caenegem, *Historical Introduction*, 73: "For the sovereigns of the late Middle Ages, the *Corpus* was above all an inexhaustible reserve of arguments to reinforce their positions."

119. See Von Mehren et al., *Civil Law System*, 3–96, for a comparative survey of civil and common law traditions. See Van Caenegem, *Historical Introduction*, 45–85, on the reception, the scholars, and the universities.

120. Merryman, *Civil Law Tradition*, 65.

121. Van Caenegem, *Historical Introduction*, 24.

122. Whitman, "Why Did the Revolutionary Lawyers?," discusses the basis of law changing from custom to natural law.

123. Van Caenegem, *Historical Introduction*, 104: "During the first centuries of the Middle Ages as well as in Germanic antiquity, the people had taken a direct and active part in decisions; sometimes the judges had sought assistance, and the people had been asked to express agreement with, or disapproval of, the decisions proposed by the judges who had 'found' the applicable law."

124. MacCormack, *Spirit of Traditional Chinese Law*, 11. See also Van der Sprenkel, *Legal Institutions*, 1.

125. Before the eleventh century, emphasis throughout Europe had been on settling disputes through compromise and reconciliation. See, e.g., Clanchy, "Law and Love." Of the English of Anglo-Saxon times, it was said that they would "take every opportunity of ending civil suits by compromise between the parties," and had a conception of law "which prefers peaceful settlements under the authority of a court to judicial decisions." Stenton, *English Justice*, 7, quoted in Van Caenegem, *Birth of the English Common Law*, 97. The royal courts offered an attractive alternative to disputants. In England, disputes were settled by ordeal and by compurgation, which involved a disputant swearing to the rightness of his position or his innocence of a crime, assisted by "oath-helpers," who added their own oaths to his. Local landholders made up juries that decided whom to believe. However, the great risk of losing the oath-taking encouraged the disputants to settle. See generally Berman, *Law and Revolution*, 75.

126. Elton, *F. W. Maitland*, 53.

127. Paul A. Cohen, *Discovering History*, 80, quoting Rudolph and Rudolph, *Modernity of Tradition*, 4–6.

128. Upham, "Place of Japanese Legal Studies," 650–651.

129. Edward Powell, "Settlement of Disputes," 24. For discussions emphasizing that the history of the courts is not the entire history of dispute settlement in

England, see Van Caenegem, *Birth of the English Common Law*, xi, and Shapiro, *Courts*, 15–16.

130. The fifteenth-century Crown lacked the resources with which to maintain either a standing army or a police force, and, consequently, "where the coercive apparatus serving the courts was weak and the influence of the local community powerful, it was inevitable that the mediatory, restitutive functions of justice would prevail over the punitive." Edward Powell, "Arbitration and the Law," 50–51, argued that there was a vigorous and durable tradition of extra-judicial arbitration. Enforcement, however, was difficult in the common law courts, and equitable remedies expanded. Often arbitration occurred in conjunction with litigation that was begun as a tactical prelude to negotiation.

131. See, e.g., Arthurs, "Special Courts, Special Law," 380.

132. Bloch, *Feudal Society*, 360.

133. One study notes that arbitration took into account the relationships of the parties and helped reconcile them, often creating compromises that "were . . . regarded as being if anything, firmer, more binding and more just than the court judgments that might sometimes have been rendered in the same cases." White, "Pactum . . . Legem Vincit," 308, quoted in Kuehn, *Law, Family and Women*, 21. In the hierarchical society of the time, rural justice "rested as much on clientage and fidelity as on the basic human solidarities, which were intensified in a closed economy by collective constraints on work and life." Castan, "Arbitration of Disputes," 258–259. Although urbanization and capitalism broke down the patterns of relations that were hospitable to mediated justice, "one solid reason for the peasant's abiding suspicion of all comers lay in the devastating intrusions of the alien law and its representatives into his world. . . . All that had to do with 'justice' was a cause for fear." Eugen Weber, *Peasants Into Frenchmen*, 50.

134. "The Common Law took no interest in the unfree peasants who were harshly excluded and even amerced if they tried to use its benefits." Van Caenegem, *Birth of the English Common Law*, 96–97.

135. Cotterell, *Sociology of Law*, 30.

136. Shapiro, *Courts*, 11–12, 15–16.

137. See, e.g., Commission on Extra-Territoriality in China, *Report of the Commission*.

138. See Bünger, "Die Rezeption," 166.

139. Jean Escarra, a French legal scholar who visited China in 1933 and 1934, found Chinese legal education both at home and abroad to be abstract and probably useless for Chinese conditions. Escarra, *Le Droit Chinois*, 345–431.

140. Conner, "Lawyers."

141. Ch'ien, *Government and Politics*, 254; see also Gamble, *Ting Hsien*, 127.

142. "A judge who is faithful to his work may not be as rapidly promoted or as favorably transferred as one who has the proper connections," Ch'ien, *Government and Politics*, 255.

143. Zelin, "Merchant Dispute Mediation," 249.

144. Huang, *Civil Justice*, 48, 52.

145. These views have rightly been criticized. Alford, "Inscrutable Occidental?"; Alford, *To Steal a Book*, 10–12; Huang, *Civil Justice*.

146. Alford, *To Steal a Book*, 10–12.

147. Brockman, "Commercial Contract Law." In an earlier time, state officials may have been more involved; see Scogin, "Between Heaven and Man," 1402: "As the first long-lasting, unified Chinese empire, [the Han] extended the principle of state responsibility for the adjudication of disputes."

148. Compare Watson, *Legal Transplants*, 11: "Comparative Law can scarcely be systematic . . . any study of Comparative Law will be subjective, and no objective test will demonstrate that the aspects considered were the most appropriate and the only ones appropriate."

149. See, e.g., Lampton et al., *Relationship Restored*, concluding (165): "social and natural scientists have been hampered by restrictions on field research in China, and these restrictions have substantially reduced the benefits of exchanges from the American perspective."

150. See, e.g., Phyllis Chang, "Deciding Disputes," 116: "Access to primary judicial materials and judicial personnel is extremely limited. The Chinese judicial system remains essentially a closed institution, largely impenetrable not only to foreigners but also to most Chinese." The author conducted research in China in 1985–1986 on judicial decision-making in rural contract disputes.

151. I have relied here on Fallon, "Rule of Law," 8–9, and Lawrence M. Friedman, "Rule of Law," 7–8.

152. Peerenboom, "Ruling the Country," 1.

153. See Fallon, "Rule of Law."

154. See chapter 10, p. 316.

155. Alford, *To Steal a Book*, 4–5.

156. In the United States, the problem is aggravated, because student-edited law reviews publish articles that do little more than discuss Chinese laws and regulations without reference to practice.

157. To the extent that the new laws are promulgated to implement new policies before such policies are considered to have been tested in practice, their use is novel. See Sun Guohua, "On Bringing Reform Into the Orbit of the Rule of Law," 19, suggesting that laws can be "effective weapons pointing the direction of reform."

158. Discussing the Chinese civil law textbook that he translated, Jones says "there is very clear support for the notion that China's industrialization will be achieved by permitting individuals to make contracts on their own and to organize collective entities—juristic persons or corporations—that will act independently and in accordance with the market. The function of the civil law is to further and protect this development. Whether this aim will be achieved is anyone's guess." Jones, "Editor's Introduction," xvi.

159. On these characteristics of the Chinese bureaucracy as they affect policy implementation, see, e.g., Lampton, "Implementation Problem," 11–17, and references there cited; Lieberthal and Oksenberg, *Policy Making*, 160–167.

160. Cotterell, *Sociology of Law*, 99.

161. See Gordon, "Critical Legal Histories," 63–65. For a summary of recent challenges to functionalist thinking in American legal theory see Kelman, *Guide to Critical Legal Studies*, 228–233, and sources there cited.

162. See, e.g., Glendon et al., *Comparative Legal Traditions*, 11–12, and authorities there cited.

163. Illustrating the level of generality at which leading comparatists have been content to formulate their functional outlook, see, e.g., Gutteridge, *Comparative Law*, 174: "the laws must be examined in the light of their political, social or economic purpose, and regard must be paid to their dynamic rather than their static or doctrinal aspects"; Zweigert and Kötz, *Introduction to Comparative Law*, 11: "Comparative lawyers have long known that only rules which perform the same function and address the same real problem or conflict of interests can profitably be compared. They also know that they must cut themselves loose from their own doctrinal and juridical preconceptions and liberate themselves from their own cultural context in order to discover 'neutral' concepts with which to describe such problems or conflicts of interests." Zweigert and Kötz further state (at 11) that the comparatists must "force themselves to be sufficiently receptive to the non-legal forces which control conduct, and here they have much to learn from the more open-minded sociologists of law." Criticizing comparative functionalism, particularly that of Zweigert and Kötz, is Frankenberg, "Critical Comparisons," 434–440.

164. Cotterell, *Sociology of Law*, 99.

165. Kaplan, "Civil Procedure," 431, quoting Association of American Law Schools, *Summarized Proceedings*, 111.

166. Lubman, "Methodological Problems," 258. Similarly, Alford has suggested that we deepen our analysis of the "intended function and actual operation" of the traditional criminal justice process, of the social context in which it operated, and of the standards we use to evaluate the criminal justice system of a society "removed from our own both culturally and temporally." Alford, "Of Arsenic and Old Laws," 1245, 1248.

167. The distinction between manifest and latent functions is derived from Merton, *Social Theory*, 51.

168. Lubman, "Form and Function," 565–572; Lubman, "Emerging Functions."

169. Lawrence M. Friedman, *Legal System*, 15; see also Lawrence M. Friedman, "Concept of Legal Culture."

170. See Rosen, *Anthropology of Justice*, xiv: "the analysis of legal systems, like the analysis of social systems, requires at its base an understanding of the categories of meaning by which participants themselves comprehend their experience and orient themselves toward one another in their everyday lives." Rosen studied dispute settlement under Islamic law in Morocco by *khadis*, who have been treated in Western jurisprudence as the archetype of subjective and irrational judges since they were so styled by Max Weber. Rosen found their decisions, however, to be grounded in and limited by ideas and values widely held throughout the culture.

171. A recent discussion by a Chinese scholar is Liang Zhiping's "Explicating 'Law'."

172. Geertz, "Thick Description."

173. See chapter 9, text at n. 177.

CHAPTER 3

1. "Model Mediation Committee Member Aunty Wu."

2. Lubman, "Mao and Mediation."

3. Barnett, *Cadres*, 437–438; Johnson, "Building a Communist Nation," 47.

4. Mao Zedong, "On the People's Democratic Dictatorship," 417; Schurmann, *Ideology and Organization*, 109–110, 115–118; Townsend, *Political Participation*, 66–67.

5. Mao Zedong, "On New Democracy," 351–352; Mao Zedong, "On the People's Democratic Dictatorship"; Mao Zedong, "On the Correct Handling of Contradictions."

6. On the "mass line" see John Wilson Lewis, *Leadership in Communist China*, 70–100; and Townsend, *Political Participation*, 72–74.

7. Townsend, *Political Participation*, 73–74.

8. Vogel, "Voluntarism," 168.

9. Townsend, *Political Participation*, 81.

10. On the concept and role of the cadre see John Wilson Lewis, *Leadership in Communist China*, 185–195, and Schurmann, *Ideology and Organization*, 162–172.

11. "A cadre is a leader who is supposed to lead in a certain way. The ideal cadre is supposed to act as combat leader, in intimate relationship with his followers, yet always responsive to higher policy." Schurmann, *Ideology and Organization*, 162.

12. The basic philosophical ingredients of Maoism summarized here are perceptively and systematically analyzed in John Wilson Lewis, *Leadership in Communist China*, 35–69, and Schurmann, *Ideology and Organization*, 17–57. On Mao's insistence on transforming the thought of individuals, see Schram, *Political Thought*, 52; Schwartz, "Modernisation," 11–12.

13. The standard translation of *sixiang* is "thought," but it is used in the Communists' lexicon to mean ideological thought. Schurmann, *Ideology and Organization*, xvii.

14. Thought reform has been described as follows: Essentially, the technique consists in the usually temporary alienation of a single member from the group through the application of collective criticism. One member is singled out for criticism, either because of faulty ideological understanding, poor work performance, or some other deviance. He is not only subjected to a barrage of criticism from the members, but also joins in and begins to criticize himself. The avowed purpose of the procedure is to "correct" (*gaizao*) the individual. Under normal circumstances, the individual is "reintegrated" into the group after the "temporary" alienation. Schurmann, "Organization and Response," 57.

15. In 1949 it ruled 90 million Chinese. John Wilson Lewis, *Leadership in Communist China*, 6.

16. Leng, "Pre-1949 Development," 105.

17. See, e.g., "Decision on Mediation of Cases"; "Instruction on Strengthening Village Mediation Work"; Leng, "Pre-1949 Development," 106, n. 65, cites legislation for the Shaanxi-Gansu-Ningxia and Shanxi-Chahar-Hubei regions.

18. See, e.g., "Comrade Ma Xiwu's New Method"; "Use Mediation More."

For a summary of developments at this time, see Leng, "Pre-1949 Development," 106–107.

19. This and the following paragraph are based on "General Condition of Judicial Work," 2–13.

20. "General Condition of Judicial Work," 8.

21. For convenience, the Chinese term "public security" (*gongan*) is freely rendered here as "police." The central police authority in a city is a "bureau"; there is one "subbureau" in each district.

22. The legislation establishing the police stations is "Organizational Regulations for Public Security Stations." My summary of police station organization is a composite based on interviews with former policemen and police detainees from Guangdong, Guangxi, and Fujian. The legislation establishing the street business offices is "Organizational Regulations for Street Business Offices."

23. For more on the importance of these dossiers, see Vogel, "Voluntarism," 172.

24. See also Schurmann, *Ideology and Organization*, 373: "He is generally not armed, is well acquainted with the people of the neighborhood, and has some of the qualities of a 'local cop'."

25. For more on the history and activities of Residents' Committees, see Schurmann, *Ideology and Organization*, 374–380, and Townsend, *Political Participation*, 158–165.

26. "Organizational Regulations for Urban Residents' Committees," 3(1).

27. On small groups generally, see John Wilson Lewis, *Leadership in Communist China*, 156–160; Townsend, *Political Participation*, 174–176; Schurmann, "Organization and Response."

28. On small group leaders, see Schurmann, "Organization and Response.".

29. The "security defense committees" were organized under the "Temporary Regulations on the Organization of Security Defense Committees." The Chinese *zhian baowei weiyuanhui* might be rendered more literally as "committees for the protection of public order."

30. On Party organization and leadership the literature is voluminous; see generally John Wilson Lewis, *Leadership in Communist China*, 101–144; Schurmann, *Ideology and Organization*, 139–162.

31. For a description of Party "organizational life" and "study," see Barnett, *Cadres*, 25–26, 30–32; Barnett and Vogel, "County," 161–166.

32. See, e.g., "Revolutionary Stories."

33. The Lus will also normally encounter other persons with authority. Mr. Lu will come into contact with them at his place of employment, as will his wife if she is employed. Their children will also have significant contacts with such persons at their schools.

34. See, e.g., "Laws and Decrees Combined with Facts."

35. See Beijing renmin fayuan mishi chu, *Renmin sifa gongzuo juyu*, 47–48, a report on the work of the People's Court in Beijing during the first year of Communist rule.

36. See, e.g., "Progressively Strengthen Mediation Work"; "Mediation Small Group."

37. See, e.g., "Reform of Judicial Work"; "Judicial Work Must Be Thoroughly Reformed"; Shi Liang, "Report on Reform" (Shi Liang was minister of justice); "CCP Central-South Bureau"; "Judicial Reform in Central-South." For discussions of a more theoretical nature, see, e.g., Li Jianfei, "Criticism"; Li Guangcan and Wang Shui, "Criticisms."

38. China's economy was not yet nationalized in 1952.

39. See, e.g., "Firmly Put Into Effect the Spirit of the Masses."

40. See, e.g., "Mediation Small Group"; "Closely Relying on the Masses"; He Pingran, "People's Judicial Work"; "Organize the Masses"; "Strengthen Mediation Work."

41. For discussions, see, e.g., "Strengthen Mediation Work."

42. On this last error, see "Instructions of the People's Government of Sinkiang Province."

43. See, e.g., "People's Judicial Work"; "Closely Relying on the Masses"; "Progressively Strengthen Mediation Work."

44. "2nd All-China Judiciary Conference"; "Renmin tiaojie weiyuanhui zanxing zuzhi tongze."

45. The *xiang*, "administrative village," is a rural administrative unit composed of several natural villages.

46. "Do Well People's Mediation Work."

47. In a 1956 debate on whether to retain or disband the committees, it was argued that disputants often preferred to ask a cadre or some other person known to them to settle a dispute, rather than to involve the mediation committee. No one argued for increasing judicial responsibility for dispute settlement, although several judges argued that mediation was specialized work that should be guided by the courts.

In opposition, cadres argued that settlement of such disputes would interfere with cadres' duties to supervise production and would take up too much of their time. Their views prevailed, and the mediation committees have continued to exist. See "Should Mediation Committees in the Cities and Countryside Continue to Exist?"

48. See Deng Zhixiu, "Yuejin zhong de anhui renmin tiaochu gongzuo"; Jiang Shimin et al., "Zhengque chuli," 28–30, describing an assortment of devices that can be used to "educate" persons, including "large wall posters," "large discussions," "democratic debates," "family meetings," "persuasion" by friends and families, negotiations, and mediation.

49. Of one model committee, it was reported: "Primary in the work of [the committee] was to be able to have closer relations with the basic-level street organizations." So close were its relations with other organizations that in a divorce case, the committee consulted with the local Women's Association. See "How the Mediation Committee." For another typical description, see "A Ball of Thread," reporting that "after the mediation committee of Penglai Street learned [of a dispute between neighbors over a minor debt] it forthwith met with the Women's Association to carry out criticism and education of the two parties."

50. See text accompanying n. 1 of this chapter.

51. "Model Mediation Committee Member Aunty Wu."

52. "Mediation Chairman." The author has directly translated only the quoted material and has summarized the rest.

53. "Mediation Committee Member Zhu Xizhen."

54. Townsend, *Political Participation*, 164. Further illustrating that activism may be very weak indeed are the many émigrés who have told researchers that they greatly improved their chances of obtaining approval of their applications to leave China for Hong Kong by feigning activism for an extended period of time before applying for permission to leave.

55. Unpublished interviews by Professor Victor Li, then of Michigan Law School, which he was kind enough to make available to me, make this clear.

56. See, e.g., Ye, "Fully Develop the Role," 16.

57. See, e.g., "Work Report of Higher People's Court of Jilin."

58. A graduate of the Beijing Political-Legal School described a typical divorce case: A spouse who wanted a divorce would not go to a court, but went to the mediation committee or residents' committee in the couple's neighborhood. The mediator would call on the couple's family, neighbors, and fellow workers to assist in resolving the dispute. If, after several attempts at reconciliation, the complaining spouse still sought a divorce, he or she could go to the court, but a judge, before deciding the case, would speak first with the parties, their families, friends, neighbors, and fellow workers. Frequently, too, the complaining spouse's place of work would be notified, and a meeting would be called there to persuade the complainant to desist. Only after all of these devices were exhausted would the court decide the case.

59. Chome, "Two Trials," 163.

60. Greene, *Awakened China*, 199–209. See also Woodsworth, "Family Law."

61. For Party members who are also full-time employees of the Party at Party Committee offices, Party and organization are, of course, synonymous.

62. See, e.g., "Tientsin No. 4 State Cotton Mill"; consider this passage in "Make the Collective Dormitory Work a Success": "Dormitories are places for rest and sleep but are not only places for rest and sleep. Having labored, worked and studied, people will naturally talk about questions of general interest in the dormitories. . . . These activities and manifestations of spare-time life or extracurricular life often reflect the thought deep in one's mind. For this reason . . . we must attach great importance to dormitory work, talk with those living in the dormitories about various questions from time to time . . . and correctly solve various ideological and practical problems."

63. See, e.g., "Correctly Develop People's Mediation Work"; "This City Holds Meeting."

64. For a detailed study of Party control in a Beijing ministry, see Barnett, *Cadres*, 18–37.

65. See, e.g., "Communist Party Committee of May 3 Factory"; "An Important Matter," 10: "The trade union is a bridge linking the Party and the masses." Unions not only engage in propaganda work and efforts to mobilize workers to increase production or fulfill economic plans but also administer educational, cultural, and welfare programs including the labor insurance scheme of compensation for injuries. See, e.g., "Labour Insurance Regulations," Arts. 21, 25–31. After na-

tionalization of China's industries was completed in 1957, the trade unions lost to Party committees some of the supervisory and administrative functions they had performed in privately owned enterprises. Their mobilizational role continued to exist.

66. Note that the level of authority between the citywide administration and the factory itself is ambiguously denominated as "intermediate." In some cases, units within the factory would be linked to a territorial superior, for example, a district government; in other cases, it would be linked with a functional superior. For instance, the Party committee in a large textile factory would be responsible to a Party committee for the textile industry in that city.

67. At the time, trials conducted in open courts were heard by a single judge sitting with two "people's jurors," who were elected by their organizations or residential units to serve for a period of several years.

68. The number of communes, brigades, and teams fluctuated. One official Communist Chinese figure put the total of communes at 74,000; one Nationalist source estimated there were over 700,000 production brigades. See Skinner, "Marketing," 397, 399 n. 279. On commune organization see John Wilson Lewis, *Leadership in Communist China*, 204–243; Schurmann, *Ideology and Organization*, 474–497; and Skinner, "Marketing," 382.

A large commune in South China studied by Barnett had 11,000 households and a total population of more than 60,000 people. See Barnett, *Cadres*, 339. It was made up of sixteen brigades; a typical brigade had between 500 and 600 households formed into twenty-four production teams. See Barnett, *Cadres*, 363.

69. See Barnett, *Cadres*, 390.

70. Barnett, *Cadres*, 390.

71. Barnett, *Cadres*, 345, 366, 368–370, 381.

72. See Barnett, *Cadres*, 343–349, 364–365, 367–372, 418–419.

73. Discussions of commune cadres' roles have specifically mentioned dispute settlement. See, e.g., Ye, "Fully Develop the Role"; "Showing Concern." "At Yangdan Commune Headquarters," 19–20, states: "The [commune office] was sometimes like an extempore judge's chambers. Two or three persons would come to lay complaints or get a quarrel or dispute settled. The commune cadres mediated, calmed the excited and soon everyone departed satisfied. . . . Minor problems are settled on the spot; larger ones go to the Commune Management Committee."

74. Barnett, *Cadres*, 403: "It was symptomatic and symbolic of the pervasive way in which the Party and public security authorities had intruded into people's lives in Commune C that they had come to dominate even the function of mediation, a function which traditionally in China had been fairly informal and autonomous and was generally independent from the more powerful formal instruments of state power."

75. See Barnett, *Cadres*, 35–36: "According to a former non-Party cadre . . . a clear 'psychic distance' was consistently maintained between the Party members and non-Party cadres. Non-Party cadres were fully conscious of the power and authority conferred by Party membership, whatever the salary rank of an individual. The regular closed Party meetings and Party members' special access to certain classified Party materials were constant reminders of their special position.

Non-Party cadres felt, moreover, that Party members were continuously judging them. Party members were wary about forming close personal relationships, even within the office, with non-Party cadres . . . [o]utside the office there was relatively little social contact between Party members and non-Party cadres, even though they often lived in close proximity."

76. See generally Walker, *Planning in Chinese Agriculture*.

77. See, e.g., Chen Guanhua, "Experience"; "People's Mediation Committee of Xianhe Village"; "Positively Serve Mutual Aid."

78. See, e.g., "A Village People's Mediation Committee."

79. See, e.g., "Haideng County's More than Four Hundred Mediation Committee Members"; "Mediation Committees Are 'Peacemakers'"; "People's Mediation Committees Everywhere."

80. See, e.g., Zhang Rongji, "Zhunque daji diren"; Cui Chengxuan, "Women shi zenme yang baowei."

81. Ye, "Fully Develop the Role," 16.

82. Until the Cultural Revolution, it was common for absentee overseas Chinese to continue to own urban dwellings, which they were permitted to rent through local agents. See, e.g., "Overseas Chinese Dependents."

83. See, e.g., nn. 50 and 52 above.

84. Vogel, "Voluntarism," 171.

85. See Jerome A. Cohen, *Criminal Process*, 20–21, for a description of the variety of sanctions.

86. See the account of a tenant-landlord dispute in this chapter at p. 61.

87. "How I Carried Out Mediational Work." In another dispute, the same mediator succeeded in turning a quarreling family into a "harmonious family."

88. See chapter 2 at p. 24, on the Chinese virtue of *rang*.

89. See, e.g., Skinner, "Marketing," 386: "As of 1958 . . . despite a decade of preachment about proper socialist or, if you will, universalistic principles, bonds of common origin (*tongxiang*) were still invoked by the peasant in seeking favors from the authorities, kinship ties (*tongxing*), for instance, still elicited cooperation where more rational appeals failed, classmates (*tongxue*) were often truer comrades than fellow Party members, and within the cooperative-farm-cum-village, the local leader who could manipulate these particularistic allegiances was often more effective than the outside cadremen." On the tension between the mass line and particularistic relationships, see John Wilson Lewis, "Leadership Doctrine."

90. Schwartz, "On Attitudes," 37.

91. See Jerome A. Cohen, "Chinese Mediation," 1208; Schwartz, "On Attitudes," 29–30.

92. Cf. Max Weber, *Religion of China*, 101–102.

93. Schwartz, "On Attitudes," 34.

94. Max Weber, *Religion of China*, 149.

95. Henderson, *Conciliation and Japanese Law* 2:241.

96. Henderson, *Conciliation and Japanese Law* 2:216.

97. See, e.g., Hart and Sacks, *Legal Process*, 155–179.

98. The literature on Weber's theory of bureaucracy is immense. The core notion of the theory stressed in the text, of "modern" bureaucracy as the most dif-

ferentiated, is derived from his distinction between charismatic, traditional, and rational authority and the bureaucratic structure characteristic of each. Max Weber, *Theory of Social and Economic Organization*, 328–392. For a discussion of Weber's theory as it relates to modernization, see LaPalombara, "*Bureaucracy*," 48–55.

99. See, e.g., Holdsworth, *History of English Law* 1: 231–242, on the separation of legal and administrative functions of the Exchequer in the thirteenth century.

100. See, e.g., Beck, "Bureaucracy and Political Development"; Fainsod, "Bureaucracy and Modernization"; Vogel, "Politicized Bureaucracy."

101. See Henderson, *Conciliation and Japanese Law* 1: 4–5.

102. For an analysis of the psychological pressure to which individuals were subjected, especially through "criticism" and "encouragement" to engage in "self-criticism," see Lifton, *Thought Reform*; Mu, *Wilting of the Hundred Flowers*, 153–159, 208–247.

103. Schurmann, *Ideology and Organization*, 8.

104. Vogel, "From Friendship to Comradeship."

105. See Northrup, "Mediational Approval Theory," 360, arguing that mediation aimed at compromise cannot remain unchanged in a modernizing country in which the modernizers seek to substitute national values for more particularistic ones.

106. Jerome A. Cohen, "Chinese Mediation," 1226.

107. Jerome A. Cohen, "Chinese Mediation," 1226. Rejection of a "succession" between traditional and Communist mediation does not amount to a refusal to find continuities between the two modes, as should be clear from the selective continuities identified here.

108. For Japan, see Henderson, *Conciliation and Japanese Law*, Vol. 2. For Taiwan, see "Regulations on Mediation"; Gallin, *Hsin Hsing*, 185, describes informal mediation of an intervillage dispute on Taiwan.

109. Gallin, "Conflict Resolution"; Fried, "Some Political Aspects of Clanship," 298: "This probably is an area of great change, for the clans formerly functioned as quasi-legal courts, keeping disputes out of formal courts. From a traditional posture of avoidance with regard to former legal apparatus, the Chinese, at least those observed in Taiwan, seemed positively litigious. A great volume of cases is being taken to the courts, with a consequent atrophy of the clans' adjudicative functions."

CHAPTER 4

1. The discussion that follows reprints substantial portions of Lubman, "Form and Function."

2. Another analysis written shortly before this one and from which I benefited was Jerome A. Cohen, "The Criminal Process in the People's Republic of China, 1949–1963: An Introduction," *Harvard Law Review* 79, no. 3 (1966): 469–533, later published in Jerome A. Cohen, *Criminal Process* (all page references herein refer to this latter work). Cohen's book, the first major scholarly work on the criminal process in the PRC, is an excellent collection of documentary sources and émigré interviews. My own interpretations differed from Cohen's in a number of respects. I stressed the importance of the formative influence on Chinese legal in-

stitutions of the CCP's experience in ruling many millions of people before they gained power over the entire country. I argued that the practical importance and the real influence of Soviet models during the years 1954–1957, when the Chinese were supposedly looking to such models, were less than was commonly believed. I emphasized the disorderliness of police-administered sanctions, and I was more hesitant to find direct continuities between traditional and Communist Chinese legal institutions. Most important, I was reluctant to treat Communist policies toward legal institutions separately from those for other bureaucratic institutions.

3. Thus, a 1946 report from a "Liberated Area" said: "The masses demand that the government immediately announce a punishment of the offenders according to the law. But we have some comrades who have a fixed rule in their thought. They think that the only way to decide a case is by having a trial in court. Sometimes, we still don't understand that a big mass meeting, where the complainant makes his accusations, the witnesses testify, and the accused answers and defends, is merely the holding of a big public session of court." "General Condition of Judicial Work," 18.

4. Barnett, *Cadres*, 405.

5. He Shanggao, "Strive to Build a Complete Revolutionary System."

6. "Constitution"; "Organizational Law of the People's Courts"; "Organizational Law of the People's Procuracy"; "NPC Promulgates New Regulations."

7. Mao Zedong, "Question of Agricultural Cooperation," 101.

8. In April 1957, a critic of the rigid and dogmatic teaching in Chinese law schools complained, "In the class, the teacher reads the Soviet textbook word by word and students takes notes accordingly. Some students suggested that the teacher was like a recording machine and the students like a typewriter." *Guangming ribao* (Apr. 30, 1957), quoted in Chu-yuan Cheng, *Science and Engineering Manpower*, 256.

9. See, e.g., "Ministry of Internal Affairs Directive."

10. Ma, "Guanyu dangqian shenpan gongzuo."

11. Xiao and Shen, "People's Court Judgment."

12. Bao, "My Understanding."

13. Lu Dingyi, "Let a Hundred Flowers Blossom."

14. Liu Shaoqi, "Political Report," 82.

15. "Speech by Comrade Tung Pi-Wu," 87.

16. "Speech by Comrade Tung Pi-Wu," 88.

17. "Speech by Comrade Tung Pi-Wu," 88, 89, 90, 92.

18. "What Is the 'Legal System'?"

19. Jerome A. Cohen, *Criminal Process*, 48.

20. "Security Administration Punishment Act." The Chinese term *zhian* is often rendered as "security administration"; I prefer the freer but more descriptive "public order."

21. "Decision of the State Council of the PRC Relating to Problems of Rehabilitation Through Labor."

22. Police-administered sanctions during the reform era are discussed in chapter 6.

23. "Provisional Measures of the PRC for Control of Counter-Revolutionaries," Art. 3.

24. "Decision of the State Council of the PRC Relating to Problems of Rehabilitation Through Labor," Art. 1(2).

25. See, e.g., "Act . . . for Punishment of Corruption," and the report of Peng Zhen (then deputy chairman of the Political-Legal Committee of the Government Administration Council of the Central People's Government) on the act, discussing the campaigns it followed. Peng Zhen, "Explanation."

26. See, e.g., Wechsler, "Challenge of a Model Penal Code," 1122–1123.

27. Jerome A. Cohen, Criminal Process, 20–21.

28. Jerome A. Cohen, Criminal Process, 27.

29. Damaska, Faces of Justice, 199.

30. Donnelly et al., Criminal Law, 3 n. 3.

31. Ma, "Guanyu dangqian shenpan gongzuo."

32. See, e.g., Zhang Cipei, "Several Problems," 17–18.

33. Packer, "Two Models." Richard Pfeffer used Packer's dichotomy to urge us not to use an idealized "due process" model of the American criminal process when we study its Chinese analogue. Pfeffer, "Crime and Punishment," 163–173.

34. Packer, "Two Models," 61.

35. Vogel, "From Revolutionary to Semi-Bureaucrat," 37.

36. Schurmann, Ideology and Organization, 162.

37. Schurmann, Ideology and Organization, 166–167.

38. John Wilson Lewis, "Leader, Commissar and Bureaucrat," 466–467.

39. The views in this paragraph are based on interviews conducted in Hong Kong in 1965–1967 with eight former police cadres and four law school graduates, two with first-hand experience in the courts.

40. Zhuang, "Xingshi susong."

41. The use of models and campaigns to exemplify values that the Party wishes to promote has been a fundamental characteristic of mass line administration. On the Chinese use of models, see Munro, "Dissent"; for a discussion of one emulation campaign see Ralph Powell, "Commissars."

42. Wang Wanfeng, "Advanced Experience."

43. "Questions of Popularizing Advanced Experience," 5.

44. The discussion that follows reprints substantial portions of Lubman, "Methodological Problems."

45. See generally Loeber, "Plan and Contract Performance," 128; see also sections 2 and 3, both on Contracts of Delivery, in Soviet Economic Law.

46. See, e.g., Ji Meng, "Discussion."

47. This paragraph is based on Zhang Jiayong, "Notarial Work."

48. See, e.g., "Many Cities."

49. "Announcement of the People's Congress of Canton."

50. See, e.g., "Protect the Rightful Interests of Overseas Chinese," for a Xiamen resident disposing of property in Southeast Asia, and "Protect the Legal Interests of Citizens," for a son in China unable to succeed to his deceased father's property in Indonesia without sending a certificate from a notarial bureau to Indonesia.

51. "Canton Gradually Develops Notarial Work," "The People's Courts of Various Counties," "Protect the Rightful Interests of Overseas Chinese."

52. See, e.g., "Protect the Legal Interests of Citizens."

53. See, e.g., "Protect the Legal Interests of Citizens"; "Notarial Work in Canton."

54. Albert H. Y. Chen, *Introduction to the Legal System*, 144.

55. Institute of Civil Law, *Basic Problems*. Pfeffer, "Institution of Contracts (Part 2)," 115, summarizes well the chapters on contracts, although it underestimates the extent to which the contract in China departed from Soviet patterns.

56. See "Should Mediation Committees in the Cities and Countryside Continue to Exist?" and "Is It Necessary for Us to Retain People's Mediation Committees?"

57. See, e.g., Fan, "Interview."

58. See my discussion of notarial work above.

59. The 1958 civil law textbook by the Institute of Civil Law, *Basic Problems*, was, according to an editor's note, compiled in the spring of 1957 and revised both later that year and in 1958; the criminal law text was apparently completed in April 1957, although printing and circulation were delayed until August of that year because of a change in policy.

60. Institute of Civil Law, *Basic Problems*, 16.

61. Institute of Civil Law, *Basic Problems*, 28.

62. Institute of Civil Law, *Basic Problems*, 178.

63. Institute of Civil Law, *Basic Problems*, 180.

64. Institute of Civil Law, *Basic Problems*, 196–197.

65. Institute of Civil Law, *Basic Problems*, 196

66. Institute of Civil Law, *Basic Problems*, 85–88.

67. Institute of Civil Law, *Basic Problems*, 86.

68. Institute of Civil Law, *Basic Problems*, 86.

69. Institute of Civil Law, *Basic Problems*, 87.

70. On "bureaucratism," see Schurmann, *Ideology and Organization*, 112, 316–318; on "commandism," see Schurmann, *Ideology and Organization*, 113, 246.

71. The relation between the use of contracts and major changes in policy is discussed in Pfeffer, "Institution of Contracts (Part 1)."

72. For a more recent discussion of the use of contracts as an administrative device, see Feinerman, "Legal Institution."

73. "Temporary Procedures for the Signing of Contracts."

74. Related, of course, to what has been said here is our need to avoid using Western legalisms in studying Chinese institutions. Otherwise, we risk placing fluid Chinese patterns into an overly rigid mold of Western legal concepts. When the Chinese use an administrative agency, not a mediating or a quasi-adjudicatory agency, to decide contract disputes, they may use the term *chuli* to describe the disposition of the dispute. The term can be rendered into English as, *inter alia*, "decide," "dispose of," or "handle." There is something to be said for using the admittedly vague "handle," which suggests the vagueness of Chinese administrative techniques rather than the precision of Western adjudication.

75. "Temporary Procedures for the Signing of Contracts," Art. 10.

76. Ministry of Heavy Industry, "Temporary Basic Clauses."

77. Ministry of Heavy Industry, "Temporary Basic Clauses," sections 31–38.

78. Ministry of Heavy Industry, "Temporary Basic Clauses," section 36. A liberal rendering is given here, to avoid translating the term as *force majeure*.

79. E.g., the clause on avoidance of fines in cases in which nonperformance is caused by certain circumstances is phrased to mean: "If the contract is not performed, then liability follows, unless higher orders or unavoidable natural disasters caused the nonperformance."

80. Ministry of Heavy Industry, "Temporary Basic Clauses," section 43.

81. See Ren Jianxin, "Jiaqian jingji hetong gongzuo." Ren later became the head of the legal affairs department of the China Council for the Promotion of International Trade and, in 1988, the president of the Supreme People's Court.

82. Institute of Civil Law, *Basic Problems*, 212.

83. Jing, "Plot of the Top Ambitionist," 1.

84. Jing, "Plot of the Top Ambitionist," 4.

85. "Notice of the Central Committee."

86. See generally Donnithorne, *China's Economic System*, 423.

87. Of course, if the respective customers disagreed, the matter would then become a conflict between the customer's and the supplier's banks.

88. Li Chengrui and Zuo Chuntai, *Shehui zhuyi de yinhang gongzuo*, 185. A Chinese textbook on commercial finance also refers to the authority of bank personnel to ascertain and decide whether rejection of payment is based on "lawful reason." See "Commercial Finance."

89. Li Chengrui and Zuo Chuntai, *Shehui zhuyi de yinhang gongzuo*, 185.

90. Song Jishan, "Brief Discussion."

91. Song Jishan, "Brief Discussion." On direct contracts between enterprises, see also Deng Zhanming, "On Economic Cooperation"; Weng, "Developing Permanent Cooperation."

92. Song Jishan, "Brief Discussion," 65 (translation modified).

93. Deng Zhanming, "On Economic Cooperation," 45.

94. Christine Wong, "Material Allocation," 256; Shirk, *Political Logic*, 29–30.

95. See, e.g., "Place Even More Subsidiary Agricultural Products."

96. See, e.g., Meng Chaocheng, "Some Thoughts."

97. Meng Chaocheng, "Some Thoughts."

98. E.g., Guan, "On the System of Contracts."

99. See, e.g., Qin Baohong, "All-round Application"; Xie, "Lun hetong zhidu."

100. Guan, "On the System of Contracts"; Institute of Civil Law, *Basic Problems*, 225.

101. E.g., "Place Even More Subsidiary Agricultural Products." This article mentions investigations, loans, "resolution of problems, of production" (presumably supplying fertilizer and tools), and sending cadres to "aid" teams in planning tasks.

102. Meng Chaocheng, "Some Thoughts."

103. "Strengthen the Ideological Education," criticizing cadres who, instead of signing contracts and educating peasants about their obligations, simply called meetings and assigned production tasks.

CHAPTER 5

1. *China 2020*, 12.

2. The discussion in this and the following paragraph is based on Jean Oi, *Rural China Takes Off*.

3. Naughton, *Growing Out of the Plan*, 157.

4. Jefferson and Rawski, "How Industrial Reform Worked," 131.

5. Lieberthal, *Governing China*, 264–265.

6. Goldstein, "China in Transition," 1115, citing Yang-Ling Liu, "Reform From Below," 313.

7. Oi, "Fiscal Reform." See also Goldstein, "China in Transition," 1121, describing the local enterprises as "part of a Soviet-style political economy, protected . . . by the political tools at the disposal of their local government patrons to promote their economic success."

8. Oi, "Role of the Local State," 1141.

9. Oi, "Fiscal Reform," 125. See also Oi, *Rural China Takes Off*, chapter VII.

10. Goldstein, "China in Transition," 1120.

11. Naughton, *Growing Out of the Plan*, 307.

12. Oi, "Fiscal Reform," 124.

13. Walder, "Local Governments," 266 and references there cited; see also Naughton, "What Is Distinctive?," 486.

14. See Oi, "Evolution of Local State Corporatism"; Walder, "County Government," especially at 64.

15. James Harding, "Chinese Collectives' Pace Checked."

16. See, e.g., "China: Township Enterprises Report," a Ministry of Agriculture report on the situation of TVEs in April 1997: "Some enterprises fail to clearly define their property rights, separate their management from government administration, have a weak mechanism, and experience the loss of collective assets. . . . In many localities, township and town enterprises have to shoulder heavy and unreasonable burdens because [of] such phenomena as arbitrary requisition of donations, unwarranted collection of fees and fines, as well as unwarranted pooling of funds." (Translation modified by the author.)

17. Oi, *Rural China Takes Off*, chapter 4. Although this view emphasizes the power of the local Party-state, another interpretation regards TVEs not as necessarily strengthening formal state power at the local level but as a form of local "dictatorship" dominated by "family links." Zweig, *Freeing China's Farmers*, 24, summarizing the conclusions of Nan Lin, "Local Market Socialism." On the increase in privatization of local enterprises, see, e.g., Yatsko, "New Owners."

18. See, e.g., *China 2020*, 25.

19. This paragraph draws on Naughton, *Growing Out Of the Plan*, 204–227.

20. Jefferson and Rawski, "How Industrial Reform Worked," 132.

21. The problems are summarized in Sachs and Woo, "Understanding China's Economic Performance," predicting (at 29–30) that "privatization would continue under the protection of a terminological haze." See also Lardy, *China's Unfinished Revolution*, 21–58, especially his assessment of the mixed results of privatizing small-scale SOEs (at 54–55) and his conclusion that "there is little evidence of sig-

nificant changes in the governance of the medium and large state-owned firms that have converted to limited liability shareholding ownership"(p. 55). Illuminating case studies of three large SOEs are in Steinfeld, *Forging Reform*.

22. This discussion of the state sector draws on Naughton, "Hierarchy."

23. Walder, "Local Bargaining Relationships," 331.

24. Naughton, "Hierarchy," 268.

25. Naughton, "Hierarchy," 270.

26. This paragraph is based on Shaoguang Wang, "Rise of the Regions." See also Naughton, "Decline of Central Control," 77.

27. *China 2020*, 28–29.

28. The decree is discussed in Baum, *Burying Mao*, 355–356, and at n. 74, citing *Beijing Review* 35, no. 32 (Aug. 10–16, 1992): 7. On Deng Xiaoping's southern strategy, see *Burying Mao*, 341–368.

29. Yuanzheng Cao et al., "From Federalism," 22.

30. "Full Text of Jiang Zemin's Report." See Faison, "Great Tiptoe Forward." On Premier Zhu's announcement, see Eckholm, "New China Leader Promises Reforms."

31. Lieberthal, *Governing China*, 126–127.

32. Naughton, *Growing Out of the Plan*, 180.

33. Naughton, *Growing Out of the Plan*, 288–289.

34. The distinction is used by Dernberger, "China's Transition," 58.

35. On the matters discussed in this paragraph, see Lampton, ed., *Policy Implementation*.

36. Shaoguang Wang, "Rise of the Regions," 109.

37. Solinger, "Despite Decentralization."

38. Walder, "China's Transitional Economy," 975, citing Shaoguang Wang, "Rise of the Regions," and Shaoguang Wang and Hu Angang, "Zhongguo guojia nengli baogao."

39. Lieberthal, "Introduction."

40. Lampton, "Plum for a Peach," 35.

41. Yan, "Everyday Power Relations."

42. Yan, "Everyday Power Relations," 238.

43. Yan, "Everyday Power Relations," 229.

44. See Baum, *Burying Mao*, 377.

45. Rozelle, "Decision-Making," 123.

46. Odgaard, "Entrepreneurs."

47. Oi, "Fate of the Collective," 35–36.

48. See Lianjiang Li and Kevin J. O'Brien, "Villagers and Popular Resistance," and sources cited therein.

49. Zweig, "Urbanizing Rural China," 358–359.

50. See, e.g., Baum, *Burying Mao*, 377–378.

51. Lianjiang Li and Kevin J. O'Brien, "Villagers and Popular Resistance," 40.

52. Lianjiang Li and Kevin J. O'Brien, "Villagers and Popular Resistance," 53.

53. O'Brien and Li, "Politics of Lodging Complaints," 782.

54. O'Brien, "Rightful Resistance," 43.

55. O'Brien, "Rightful Resistance," 52–55.

56. See O'Brien, "Implementing Political Reform," on which this paragraph draws.

57. O'Brien, "Implementing Political Reform," 37–41. In Lianjiang Li and Kevin J. O'Brien's forthcoming "Struggle Over Village Elections," the authors describe the powerful impetus given to the Organic Law by Peng Zhen and Bo Yibo, who were concerned with rural decay, and the debate that led to endorsement of the law by the Central Committee of the CCP in 1990.

58. O'Brien, "Implementing Political Reform," 50–58.

59. Kelliher, "Chinese Debate," 63. This paragraph follows Kelliher's analysis.

60. Jennings, "Political Participation," and O'Brien, "Rightful Resistance," which, written in the spring of 1996, saw the reforms gaining in momentum. While power relationships between populace and officials are changing, so are relations among the populace. In the countryside, for example, there is evidence that peasants are forming social networks to meet their needs for cooperative financial aid and for social connections. The result is that "a larger web of personal relations provides a stronger protective network for peasants when they come in conflict with village cadres or agents of the local government." Yan, "Everyday Power Relations," 222–223.

61. Wank, "Bureaucratic Patronage." See also a later study by the same author, emphasizing that the dependence is mutual and assumes the importance of a "political coalition." Wank, Commodifying Chinese Communism, 176–203.

62. Oi, "Fiscal Reform."

63. Bruun, "Political Hierarchy."

64. Yan, "Culture of Guanxi," 22.

65. Mayfair Mei-hui Yang, "Modernity of Power," 411.

66. Goldstein, "China in Transition," 1129–1130.

67. Wank, "Institutional Process."

68. See the discussion above of rural economic reform. Pearson, in China's New Business Elite, refers to "socialist corporatism," while Oi refers to "state corporatism."

69. Walder, "Corporate Organization," 62, citing excellent articles by Oi and Christine P. Wong on the Chinese countryside.

70. Solinger, "Urban Entrepreneurs," 136.

71. See, e.g., Walder, "Quiet Revolution," 14–17.

72. Oi, "Fiscal Reform," 101.

73. Whyte, "Urban China," 73.

74. Baum, "Modernization," 102.

75. Lieberthal, Governing China, 298.

76. Whyte, "Urban China," 97.

77. Wakeman, "Civil Society," 134.

78. Lieberthal, Governing China, 302.

79. Baum, optimistic on this question ten years previously, has more recently noted the "virtual lack of any viable Chinese institutional framework of civil society." Burying Mao, 309.

80. Goldstein, "China in Transition," 1124.

81. See Wank, "Private Business"; Pearson, China's New Business Elite.

82. Pearson, *China's New Business Elite*, 119.

83. Jonathan Unger, "Bridges"; see also Gordon White, "Dynamics of Civil Society."

84. Baum and Shevchenko, "State of the State." The growing corporatist trend does not exclude the emergence of other trends favorable to pluralism and political reform. See, e.g., Kathy Chen, "China's Press and Politics."

85. Nevitt, "Private Business Associations," 43.

86. Jonathan Unger and Anita Chan, "China, Corporatism and the East Asian Model."

87. Oi, *Rural China Takes Off*, chapter 7.

88. Goldstein, "China in Transition," 1131, quoting Christine Wong, "China's Economy," 52.

89. Jefferson and Rawski, "How Industrial Reform Worked," 133–134.

90. Dernberger, "China's Mixed Economic System," 94.

91. David D. Li, "Theory of Ambiguous Property Rights."

92. See Walder and Oi, "Property Rights."

93. Putterman, "Role of Ownership," 1052.

94. Naughton, *Growing Out of the Plan*, 322.

95. Oi, "Fiscal Reform," 123.

96. See Wank, "Social Networks."

97. See chapter 2 at text following n. 54.

98. Wank, *Commodifying Chinese Communism*, 207.

99. At the same time, lest Western celebrators of the triumph of capitalism over the state in China exult prematurely, one observer has noted the possibility that marketized Chinese enterprises may reproduce some elements of the *danwei* system and promote dependence on them by their employees. Francis, "Reproduction of Danwei Institutional Features."

100. See Shue, "State Sprawl"; Shaoguang Wang, "Politics of Private Time."

101. Lieberthal, *Governing China*, 305–308.

102. Baum, *Burying Mao*, 380. For a description of the problems of communities of provincials who have moved to large cities from the countryside, see Wang Chunguang, "Communities," and the accompanying series of articles. See also Elisabeth Rosenthal, "Poverty Spreads."

103. This is well expressed in Thurston, "Society at the Crossroads."

104. Baum, *Burying Mao*, 376–380.

105. Lieberthal, *Governing China*, 268.

106. Bruun, "Political Hierarchy," 204–205. See also the assessment in US-China Business Council, "China's Political Developments," at 5: "The corruption problem seems only to worsen. So tightly knit are corrupt practices into the fabric of modern Chinese society that they are almost invisible. Invoice fraud, diversion of government investment capital, bribery and misappropriation of central and local government funds all seem to have become a way of life. . . . The universal assumption that all officials and corporate managers are corrupt is probably responsible for the speed with which disgruntled workers take to the streets; civil protest, mostly peaceful, is reported almost daily by the foreign (not Chinese) press in China."

107. Lieberthal, *Governing China*, 269.

108. For comprehensive discussions, see Hao and Johnston, "Reform at the Crossroads"; Johnston and Hao, "China's Surge of Corruption."

109. Yan, "Everyday Power Relations," 223.

110. Liu Binyan, *China's Crisis*, 22. The same conditions that provoke despair and alienation feed the revival of nationalism, which has also been encouraged by the leadership. See Barmé, "To Screw Foreigners Is Patriotic."

111. Han Youtong, "Smash Spiritual Shackles."

112. See, e.g., Hu Qiaomu, "Act in Accordance with Economic Laws."

113. Dicks, "Chinese Legal System," 544: " . . . there appears to be an unspoken veneration for the foundations of the new socialist legal system which were laid in the first 5 or 6 years after 1949 . . . and there is a real sense in which much of the law-making of the past decade can be regarded either as the completion of the unfinished work of that earlier era, or the reversion to legal forms which commended themselves to the legislators of that period" (footnotes omitted).

114. Deng Xiaoping, *Selected Works*, 18.

115. See, e.g., "Jiang Zemin, Qiao Shi Address Judicial Meeting."

116. An example of a Soviet-educated Chinese jurist arguing for the class nature of law is Sun Guohua, "Laws Cannot Be Understood in Isolation"; on recent assertions by Chinese scholars that human rights are universal, see Keith, *China's Struggle*, 64.

117. See, e.g., "Government by Law."

118. "Zhongguo fazhi gaige." Similar views are expressed in the lead article by Wang Jiafu et al., "Lun fazhi gaige," written by three senior leaders of the institute.

119. Keith's *China's Struggle* relies almost exclusively on scholarly discussions to conclude that China has accepted the rule of law. Although the conclusion is wildly optimistic, the legal scholarship on which he relies displays strong commitment to the ideal of legality. See Lubman, "Book Review."

120. Pitman B. Potter, "Riding the Tiger," 352–357.

121. "Deng Xiaoping on Upholding the Four Cardinal Principles."

122. "Jiang Zemin, Qiao Shi Address Judicial Meeting."

123. "Jiang Zemin, Qiao Shi Address Judicial Meeting," 17.

124. Fewsmith, "Neoconservatism."

125. See, e.g., "Party Plenum Communiqué"; Forney, "Patriot Games."

126. "Yifa zhiguo"; Liu Hainian, "Yifa zhiguo."

127. Liu Hainian, "Yifa zhiguo."

128. See Keith, "Post-Deng Jurisprudence." The author concludes (at 56): "If there is a widespread abstract support for the rule of law that acts as a predicate in the socialist marketplace, there is a dialectical tension between the factors favoring autonomy and pluralism and those that might well lead into a soft reformist state corporatism."

129. "Jiang Zemin Addresses Legal System Forum."

130. See, e.g., "Jiaqiang fazhi xuanchuan." On Peng Zhen's concern for using law to legitimize CCP rule, see Pitman B. Potter, "Peng Zhen: Evolving Views," and Pitman B. Potter, "Curbing the Party." Potter argues in both that although

Peng viewed law as the expression of Party policy, he went beyond other leaders in considering the implications of using law not only to embody Party policy, but to serve as the "organizational framework for the enforcement of policy" ("Peng Zhen: Evolving Views," 22). Potter further describes Peng's views on the relationship between the Party and law, i.e., that the Party has overall supervision but should not be involved in the disposition of individual cases, and that Party members should not be treated differently from ordinary citizens. He also notes Peng's increasing interest in codifying and following procedures.

131. Peng Zhen, "Guanyu zhengfa gongzuo."

132. See, e.g., Yu Xingzhong, "Legal Pragmatism," 47: "law is always an expression of policy and has no independent status of its own."

133. Shen, *Bijiao fa*, 363–364.

134. Tong, "Shenli jingji hetong jiufen anjian," 35.

135. Keller, "Sources of Order," 729.

136. Keller, "Sources of Order," 731.

137. Alford, "Double-Edged Swords," 65 n. 8.

138. "Anhui Holds Telephone Conference."

139. "Shandong Launches Campaign."

140. This paragraph draws on Exner, "Convergence."

141. Epstein, "Law and Legitimation," 35.

142. Jiang Hua, "Earnestly Perform People's Court Work Well."

143. "State Council Directive on Crackdown"; "Fighting Economic Crimes."

144. See, e.g., "Fujian Government Issues Circular"; "Hangzhou Import Controls."

145. "NPC Adopts Resolution."

146. "CCPCC, State Council Decision."

147. On the campaigns of the early 1980s, see "Concepts of Law."

148. "Ren Jianxin: Problems Still Exist."

149. "Supreme People's Court Work Report," 18.

150. "Ren Jianxin Addresses Crime Issue," 15.

151. "Work Report of the Supreme People's Court."

152. "Supreme Court President on Law Enforcement," 26.

153. See, e.g., Gilley, "Rough Justice"; "Xinjiang Populace."

154. "Security Ministry Unveils 'Winter Action' Campaign."

155. See Lubman, "Form and Function"; Jerome A. Cohen, *Criminal Process*; Barnett, *Cadres*, 142.

156. "China Campaigns to Enforce Laws."

157. Meng Qinguo, "Some Issues."

158. Fu Hualing, "Bird in the Cage," 282.

159. "Fighting Economic Crimes."

160. "Xinhua Comments on Punishing Economic Criminals."

161. "CCPCC, State Council Decision," K4.

162. The use of campaigns to focus the work of the courts is further discussed in chapter 8.

163. The literature is enormous. See, for example, Amnesty International, *Political Imprisonment*; Leng, *Criminal Justice*, 3–34.

164. See, e.g., Amnesty International, *China—Violations*, 5–51.

165. See, e.g., Oksenberg et al., eds., *Beijing Spring*.

166. "Criminal Law Expert."

167. "Socialist Democracy Requires Discipline."

168. "Renmin Ribao Article on Freedom of Speech," L4.

169. "Renmin Ribao Article on Freedom of Speech," L5.

170. "Gongren Ribao Article on Freedom of Speech," L15; see also "People's Daily Editorial"; "Peking Daily Explains Why Counter-Revolutionaries Do Not Enjoy Free Speech."

171. "Hongqi Article Discussing Freedom of Speech."

172. "Visit to China," 10.

173. See, e.g., Lawyers Committee for Human Rights, *Criminal Justice*, 77–81.

174. See, e.g., Amnesty International, *Political Imprisonment*; Amnesty International, *China—Violations*; Kent, *Between Freedom and Subsistence*.

175. See Eckholm, "In Drive on Dissidents," reporting that a labor activist was sentenced to ten years in prison for giving an interview to Radio Free Asia about farmer protests, and that three other men who tried to organize a new political party were convicted of subversion and sentenced to terms of eleven to thirteen years. Prospective lawyers for the defendants in this case "had been warned off by the police or detained," it was reported in Eckholm, "China Sentences 3." The conviction of the defendant who gave out the computer addresses is reported in Faison, "E-Mail to U.S."

CHAPTER 6

1. On Chinese legislative processes, see the excellent recent research in the following works: Tanner, "Organizations"; Tanner, "How a Bill Becomes a Law"; Keller, "Sources of Order"; Keller, "Legislation"; Tanner, *Politics of Lawmaking*; Dowdle, "Constitutional Development."

2. One Chinese scholar has observed that "in the past, the ultimate meaning of the phrase basic law was never very clear conceptually, which caused . . . some legislative dislocations." Li Buyun, "Guanyu qicao 'Zhonghua renmin gongheguo lifa fa'," 13.

3. Tanner, "Organizations," 59.

4. See, e.g., "Qiao Shi Interviewed"; "Qiao Shi Discusses Political Issues." He was replaced in March 1998 by Li Peng.

5. Kynge, "China's People's Congress," quoting Zhou Wangsheng, a Beijing University law professor.

6. Tanner, "Organizations," 88. See also O'Brien, "Legislative Development," 382, characterizing the NPC as a supporter of the institutionalization of legitimacy and moderate reform. An early and over-optimistic appraisal in this vein, but with a detailed study of the legislative process at work on one law, is Ta-kuang Chang's "Making of Chinese Bankruptcy Law."

7. Until he ceased in 1998 to be chairman of the Standing Committee of the NPC, Qiao Shi vigorously promoted the role of the NPC in drafting legislation and in exercising its powers under the Constitution to supervise legality in en-

forcing enacted laws. See, e.g., "Qiao Shi Interviewed"; "Qiao Shi Discusses Political Issues."

8. Tanner, "Organizations," 89: "In the long run, given the common tendency for legislatures in developing countries to become politically powerful before they become democratic, this may be a very modest source of optimism."

9. Tanner, "How a Bill Becomes a Law."

10. O'Brien, "Legislative Development," 379. Kevin O'Brien has noted that some members of national and local people's congresses take on roles of "remonstrators" on behalf of their constituencies, rather than acting as "agents" of the central government. "Agents and Remonstrators." In the same vein, specifically on the NPC, see Tanner and Chen, "Breaking the Vicious Cycles," 44: "many NPC officials are gradually changing their constituency orientations and increasingly taking their 'representative' title seriously."

11. O'Brien, "Legislative Development," 372.

12. Jiang Ping, "Chinese Legal Reform," 74.

13. This and the following paragraph draw on Seidman and Seidman, "Drafting Legislation for Development."

14. Keller, "Legislation."

15. See Li Buyun, "Guanyu qicao 'Zhonghua renmin gongheguo lifa fa'," 13. See also Corne, "Legal System Reforms." The author discusses a draft Law on Legislation that was circulated in 1996 but was not adopted.

16. Corne, *Foreign Investment*, 56.

17. Keller, "Sources of Order," 735: "Developing a principle of exclusive NPC authority over certain substantive matters is not entirely impractical, but would require greater discipline than has so far been evident in Chinese legislative or judicial practice."

18. See generally Corne, *Foreign Investment*, 68–83.

19. Corne, *Foreign investment*, 125–126.

20. Keller, "Sources of Order," 742; Dicks, "Compartmentalized Law," 87–90.

21. Li Buyun, "Guanyu qicao 'Zhonghua renmin gongheguo lifa fa'," 14.

22. Dicks, "Compartmentalized Law."

23. Keller, "Sources of Order," 740.

24. Galanter, "Adjudication," 173.

25. See Cai, "Constitutional Supervision," 245.

26. Finder, "Supreme People's Court," 164, citing "Resolution of the Standing Committee of the NPC Providing an Improved Interpretation of the Law" (June 10, 1981), in *Laws of the People's Republic of China 1979–1982* Vol. 1, 251. This section on judicial interpretation draws on Finder; Shizhou Wang, "Judicial Explanation"; and Nanping Liu, "Ignored Source."

27. Li Buyun, "Guanyu qicao 'Zhonghua renmin gongheguo lifa fa'," 18.

28. Li Buyun, "Guanyu qicao 'Zhonghua renmin gongheguo lifa fa'," 17–18. On the courts, see, e.g., Keller, "Legislation," 668; Nanping Liu, *Judicial Interpretation*.

29. Keller, "Sources of Order," 745.

30. Zuckerman, "End to Chinese Inscrutability."

31. For numerous examples see Corne, *Foreign Investment*, 71–77.

32. Keller, "Sources of Order," 750–752.

33. This helpful catalogue is from Corne, *Foreign Investment*, 95–104.

34. Pitman B. Potter, "Riding the Tiger." For other definitions of formalism that might also apply, see Schauer, "Formalism," 509–510.

35. In addition to a yearly compilation of laws and regulations enacted by the National People's Congress and its Standing Committee, the *Zhonghua renmin gongheguo fagui huibian* (Collection of Laws and Regulations of the PRC), laws and regulations have been published with increasing frequency in compilations. Some of these are cited in Keller, "Sources of Order," 711 n.1.

36. See, e.g., Hsia and Johnson, "Law Making." Arguing for giving greater weight to cases is Cao Pei, "Borrowing the Case Law Method." Case law is discussed further in chapter 9.

37. "Qiao Shi Interviewed." Wan Li, chairman of the NPC Standing Committee, earlier had urged: "We can transplant or learn from mature laws of Hong Kong and foreign countries on the development of commodity economy. There is no need for us to start from scratch in everything." "Commentary on Applying Hong Kong, Foreign Laws."

38. See Jones, "Editor's Introduction," xvi–xvii, pointing to the reliance of the General Principles of Civil Law on basic concepts and terminology of the German Civil Code, and to examples demonstrating that Chinese legal scholars "are quite willing to look outside Chinese legal sources for the answers to problems for which there are no Chinese answers."

39. See Seidman and Seidman, "Drafting Legislation for Development," 10–13.

40. Keller, "Sources of Order," 711.

41. See Li Buyun, "Guanyu qicao 'Zhonghua renmin gongheguo lifa fa.'"

42. Keller, "Sources of Order."

43. O'Brien, "Chinese People's Congresses"; O'Brien, "Agents and Remonstrators." Tanner, "Politics of Lawmaking"; Dowdle, "Constitutional Development."

44. Corne, *Foreign Investment*, 90.

45. Meng Qinguo, "Some Issues."

46. Keller, "Sources of Order."

47. This section is based primarily on Alford and Fang, "Legal Training." On legal education at the beginning of the 1980s, see Gelatt and Snyder, "Legal Education." A more recent article is Kraus, "Legal Education," which, though sometimes overly optimistic (132: "China has embraced the need to produce more lawyers . . . while recognizing that a stronger judiciary and growth in the role of law are beneficial aspects of its more liberal internal policies") is informative not only about curricula but also student attitudes. See also Hom, "Legal Education."

48. Pitman B. Potter, "Class Action," 17.

49. Epstein, "Law and Legitimation," 34.

50. Pitman B. Potter, "Class Action," 17.

51. Alford and Fang, "Legal Training," 17.

52. Alford and Fang, "Legal Training," 30–37.

53. "CLEEC Ford Proposal," rev. Nov. 3, 1992, in the author's files.

54. See generally Gelatt, "Lawyers in China"; and Lawyers Committee for Human Rights, *Lawyers in China.*

55. "Provisional Regulations on Lawyers."

56. "Criminal Procedure Law," Art. 28.

57. Alford and Fang, "Legal Training," 7.

58. Lawyers Committee for Human Rights, *Lawyers in China*, 65.

59. See Lawyers Committee for Human Rights, *Lawyers in China*, 34–35.

60. "Roundup: China Stressing Lawyers' Role by Law."

61. Lawyers Committee for Human Rights, *Lawyers in China*, 29, 37, citing Chen Yanni, "Legal Sector Opening Wider," *China Daily* (Feb. 21, 1998), at 1. On the growth and regulation of foreign law firms, see Lawyers Committee for Human Rights, *Lawyers in China*, 36–38.

62. *Zhongguo falü nianjian* 1997, 1055, 1074.

63. Peerenboom, "China's Developing Legal Profession."

64. "Lawyers Law." The Law is exhaustively discussed in Lawyers Committee for Human Rights, *Lawyers in China*, on which this discussion draws.

65. Alford and Fang, "Legal Training."

66. See generally Luo Qizhi, "Legal Aid Practices."

67. "Lawyers: A Profession in Flux," 8–10.

68. See Luo Qizhi, "Legal Aid Practices," 59.

69. Alford, "Tasselled Loafers," 31 (footnotes omitted).

70. See the discussion below of the criminal process.

71. In 1995, in 496,082 criminal cases concluded, 1,886 persons (0.38 percent) were found not guilty. "Zuigao renmin fayuan gongzuo baogao," 45.

72. Alford, "Tasselled Loafers," 36.

73. Alford, "Tasselled Loafers," 37.

74. See Article 7 of the Ministry of Justice's 1996 "Decision Concerning the Strict Enforcement of the Lawyers Law and the Further Strengthening of the Establishment of the Lawyer Force," as cited in Lawyers Committee for Human Rights, *Lawyers in China*, 51 at n. 177.

75. Gao Zongze, "Zhongguo lüshi," 18.

76. Zhou Min, "Xianwei zuzhibu." See Lawyers Committee for Human Rights, *Lawyers in China*, for accounts of violent physical attacks on lawyers (at 31–33) and for examples of regulations prohibiting interference with the work of lawyers, including their courtroom activities (at 81–84).

77. Zhou Min, "Xianwei zuzhibu," 12.

78. See, generally, Alford, "Tasselled Loafers."

79. "Criminal Law."

80. Berman et al., "Comparison," 257.

81. See, generally, Lawyers Committee for Human Rights, *Wrongs and Rights,* a detailed review of the 1997 revisions by Professor Donald C. Clarke of the University of Washington School of Law; Finder and Fu, "Tightening up Chinese Courts' 'Bags'."

82. See especially on these issues, Lawyers Committee for Human Rights, *Wrongs and Rights*, 34.

83. "Criminal Law"; "Criminal Procedure Law."

84. Albert H. Y. Chen, *Introduction to the Legal System*, 110.

85. Wang Dexiang, "Correct, Lawful and Timely."

86. "Jiang Links Strong Legal System, Successful Reform."

87. "Decision of the Standing Committee of the NPC on the Question of the Implementation of the Criminal Procedure Law"; "Decision of the Standing Committee of the NPC Concerning the Question of Time Limits."

88. "Decision of the Standing Committee of the NPC Concerning the Procedure for Rapid Adjudication."

89. "Supplementary Provisions . . . Concerning . . . Time Limits."

90. "Concepts of Law."

91. Lawyers Committee for Human Rights, *Opening to Reform?*, 5. This study is highly recommended for its detailed analysis of the issues and institutions that have been summarized here.

92. Wang Minyuan, "Xingshi beigaoren quanli yanjiu," 506–507.

93. See Kam C. Wong, "Police Powers," and on pre-trial detention generally, consult Lawyers Committee for Human Rights, *Opening to Reform?*, 20–43, and Epstein, ed., "Legal Documents."

94. Lawyers Committee for Human Rights, *Opening to Reform?*, 45.

95. Fazhi gongzuo weiyuanhui, "Zuigao renmin fayuan," 6.

96. Wang Minyuan, "Xingshi beigaoren quanli yanjiu," 531–533. Wang arrives at the conclusion after a careful analysis of official statistics that report a higher number of criminal cases in which defense counsel participated.

97. Wang Minyuan, "Xingshi beigaoren quanli yanjiu," 532.

98. Wang Minyuan, "Xingshi beigaoren quanli yanjiu," 535.

99. Wang Minyuan, "Xingshi beigaoren quanli yanjiu," 521, 543.

100. Lawyers Committee for Human Rights, *Opening to Reform?*, 5–13. The discussion of the reforms and their shortcomings that follows is based on this excellent analysis.

101. "Decision of the NPC on the Revision of the 'Criminal Procedure Law'."

102. Lawyers Committee on Human Rights, *Opening to Reform?*, 27, citing the revised Criminal Procedure Law, Art. 126.

103. Lawyers Committee for Human Rights, *Opening to Reform?*, 30

104. Lawyers Committee for Human Rights, *Opening to Reform?*, 26, citing the revised Criminal Procedure Law, Art. 60.

105. Lawyers Committee for Human Rights, *Opening to Reform?*, 57.

106. Hecht, "Book Review," 320. Hecht is the author of *Opening to Reform?*

107. "China: Regulations on Criminal Procedure Law."

108. Lawyers Committee for Human Rights, *Opening to Reform?*, 48–49.

109. Lawyers Committee for Human Rights, *Opening to Reform?*, 43.

110. See Gelatt, "PRC and the Presumption of Innocence."

111. Lawyers Committee for Human Rights, *Opening to Reform?*, 65.

112. Lawyers Committee for Human Rights, *Opening to Reform?*, 63.

113. See, e.g., "Ren Jianxin Speaks."

114. Lu Zhongya, "New Criminal Procedure Law," 17.

115. Wang Ren, "Trial Procedure."

116. See chapter 5, n. 171.

117. Lawyers Committee for Human Rights, *Opening to Reform?*, 79; see also H. L. Fu, "Criminal Defence," at 48: "Amending the [Criminal Procedure Law] will not make the rights real unless they can be effectively enforced. While the Amendment may have laid a foundation for improvement, there is little likelihood that the legislation will bring about meaningful change in the practice of criminal defence in the near future."

118. "Security Administration Punishment Regulations."

119. These sanctions are discussed in Amnesty International, *China—Punishment Without Crime*; Lawyers Committee for Human Rights, *Criminal Justice*; "Visit to China," 36–38.

120. See, e.g., *China Law Reports* 1991 Vol. 3, 1–40; *Zhongguo shenpan anli yaolan* 1994, 1396–1427, 1430–1455, 1458–1461. Suits have been brought against the police to challenge administrative sanctions under the Administrative Litigation Law, which is discussed in chapter 7.

121. See, generally, Lawyers Committee for Human Rights, *Criminal Justice*, 71–76; Epstein, ed., "Legal Documents"; "Visit to China," 36–38.

122. "Guowuyuan guanyu laodong jiaoyang de buchong guiding"; "Laodong jiaoyang shixing banfa"; "Laodong jiaoyang guanli."

123. Clarke and Feinerman, "Antagonistic Contradictions," 142–143.

124. See "Visit to China," 44.

125. Ying, "Administrative Punishment System." On police arbitrariness in particular, see "Article Views Law Enforcement Organs."

126. "Administrative Punishment Law." See also Cai, "Introduction to the Administrative Penalty Law."

127. See the discussion in chapter 7 of administrative law.

128. Cabestan, *L'Administration*, 434–443.

129. "Anti-Corruption Drive Starts."

130. "Radio Beijing: Party Cadres Not Above State Law."

131. "Guangming Ribao on Dismissal as Punishment."

132. See, e.g., "Cadres Accused of Violating Law." After a commune brigade Party branch secretary was accused of stealing trees that belonged to the collective and reprimanded, he falsely denounced the commune member who exposed his theft. The cadre was sentenced to five years in prison for misusing his authority. However, the commune Party secretary at all times tried to shield the offender, wrote the Party committee later, as a result of which "the masses completely lost their confidence in the integrity of our Party organization."

133. See, e.g., Baum, *Burying Mao*, 176–177, 378.

CHAPTER 7

1. "Tian Jiyun on Laws for Market Economy"; see also "Accelerated Law-Making."

2. "Qiao Shi on Market Socialism," 19.

3. "Qiao Shi on Legal System," 37.

4. "Xinhua on Socialist Market Economy Laws," 19 (emphasis supplied).

5. "Commentator on Market Economy."

6. See, e.g., Berman, "Protection of Rights," 217–218: "In the American market economy, most breaches of economic contracts are not the subject of litigation but are settled amicably between the parties. This is partly because a lawsuit, including resort to arbitration, tends to create hostility between the parties and thus to impede their future business relations. Also enterprises which sue for breach of contract acquire the reputation of being litigious, and others will not wish to deal with them. Finally, litigation is apt to be expensive in time and money. It is quite common, therefore, for the parties to seek to 'keep the contract going' despite a breach or, if that is impossible, to accept the breach as inevitable and perhaps to share the losses resulting from it." A suggestive case study is Stewart Macaulay, "Non-Contractual Relations."

7. Stewart Macaulay, "Reliance Interest," 287.

8. See, generally, Feinerman, "Backwards into the Future."

9. See, e.g., Solinger, *China's Transition*, 112–113.

10. "Economic Contract Law." Pitman B. Potter, *Economic Contract Law*, provides invaluable background on this law.

11. Pitman B. Potter, *Economic Contract Law*, 62–66.

12. "Provisional Regulations of the PRC on Notarization."

13. Tung-pi Chen, "Chinese Notariat," 77.

14. "Foreign Economic Contract Law."

15. "Lianhe guo guoji huowu xiaoshou hetong gongyue."

16. "General Principles of Civil Law." On earlier drafting efforts and the doctrinal issues discussed here, Jianfu Chen, *From Administrative Authorisation to Private Law*, 33–68, is useful.

17. Pitman B. Potter, "Riding the Tiger"; most of a Chinese law textbook on civil law published in 1987 has been translated into English as Jones, ed., *Basic Principles*.

18. Dicks, "Chinese Legal System," 560: "the adoption of the General Principles may prove to have further significance, for, based upon reasoning which owes more to Gaius than to Marx, these generalized abstractions give Chinese law—economic and administrative law as well as civil law in the narrower sense—a conceptual strength and coherence it has long lacked."

19. Jones, "Some Questions."

20. "General Principles of Civil Law," Art. 71.

21. Soileau, "Past Is Present," 348.

22. Albert H. Y. Chen, *Introduction to the Legal System*, 197.

23. Jones, "Editor's Introduction," xv.

24. See Epstein, "Theoretical System."

25. On the revision of the ECL, see "Standing Committee of the NPC, PRC, Economic Contract Law Amendment Decision," and especially Pitman B. Potter's "editor's notes" afterword at 46–48. The new Contract Law is "Contract Law of the People's Republic of China."

26. But Rubenstein, in "Legal and Institutional Uncertainties," 513, doubts that the contracts of individuals ("natural persons") were intended to receive the same protection as those of "legal persons."

27. Pitman B. Potter, "Riding the Tiger," 343–344 nn. 91–93. For an example, see *China Law Reports* 1991 Vol. 3, 595–599, Business Department of Shanghai

General Shenjiang Enterprise Corp. v. Shenxi Woolen Sweaters Factory of Ying County, overturning a profit-sharing agreement between investors as unfair.

28. The last draft, published in 1998, is "Zhonghua renmin gongheguo hetong fa (caoan)." The law that was finally adopted in March 1999 is "Contract Law of the People's Republic of China." For discussions of the draft, see Jiang Ping, "Drafting the Uniform Contract Law"; Harpole, "Proposed New Contract Law"; Paglee, "Contract Law."

29. "Economic Contract Law," Art. 31.

30. Rubenstein, "Legal and Institutional Uncertainties," 522.

31. "Economic Contract Law," Art. 51. The discussion in this paragraph draws on Rubenstein, "Legal and Institutional Uncertainties," and Rubenstein, "Transaction Costs."

32. See section entitled Arbitration in chapter 8.

33. See, e.g., "Guanyu chachu liyong hetong jinxing de weifa xingwei de zanxing guiding"; "Guojia gongshang xingzheng guanli ju guanyu yifa yanli chachu . . . de tongzhi."

34. Zhang Shouqiang, ed., *Zhonghua renmin gongheguo hetong fagui*, 3–8.

35. "Guojia gongshang xingzheng guanli ju guanyu guanche luoshi . . . de yijian."

36. *Gongshang xingzheng guanli.*

37. Albert H. Y. Chen, "Developing Theory of Law," 6.

38. Qian, "Hetong guanli," 23.

39. "Negotiable Instruments Law."

40. As is common when legal institutions are transplanted, some wrinkles have appeared. Thus, the principle of negotiability is qualified by the rule that a holder of a negotiable instrument may be prevented from enforcing the obligation if he knew of circumstances that would have made the instrument in question void. The courts will have to elaborate standards of "knowledge," and "it remains unclear precisely what level of inquiry, if any, is required of a holder if he has, or reasonably should have, causes to suspect a defect in his transferor's title." Xu and Caldwell, "Analytical Perspective," 2.

41. Sommers and Phillips, "P.R.C.'s Negotiable Instruments Law," 320–322, 340–341.

42. "Security Law."

43. "China Enacts Constitutional Amendments."

44. See Epstein, "Theoretical System," 184–185.

45. Dicks, "Chinese Legal System," 555, nn. 76–77.

46. "Provisional Regulations of the PRC Concerning the Grant and Assignment of the Right to Use State Land in Urban Areas." See also Howson, "Law of the Land."

47. Hanstad and Li, "Land Reform." The 1993 decision was reiterated in 1995.

48. "Provisional Measures on Administration of Allocated Land Use Rights."

49. On the subject of this paragraph see, generally, Soileau, "Past Is Present."

50. Soileau, "Past Is Present," 385.

51. Soileau, "Past Is Present," 387.

52. "Law of the PRC on the Administration of Urban Real Estate"; see Clarke and Howson, "Developing P.R.C. Property"; "PRC, Land Administration Law (Revised)."

53. Epstein, "Theoretical System."

54. "Provisional Regulations of the PRC on Private Enterprises." For discussion of private enterprises before the Regulations were promulgated, see Chao and Yang, "Private Enterprise"; Epstein and Ye, "Individual Enterprise."

55. See Yu Guanghua and Zhang Xianchu, "Law of Business Organizations," 343–346, supplemented by Yu Guanghua, "Emerging Framework"; "Provisional Regulations of the PRC on Private Enterprises."

56. See, generally, Halper, "Partnership Enterprises Law."

57. "Law of the PRC Governing Partnership Enterprises." The law is summarized in Yu Guanghua, "Emerging Framework," 49–53.

58. Halper, "Partnership Enterprises Law," 21.

59. "Regulations on Rural Collective Enterprises"; "Regulations on Urban Collective Enterprises"; Augustin-Jean, "Rural Enterprises"; "China: Township Enterprises Report."

60. See Lichtenstein, "Enterprise Reform," 8–9.

61. Naughton, *Growing Out of the Plan,* 157. See also the other sources on property rights mentioned in chapter 5.

62. Augustin-Jean, "Rural Enterprises," 7.

63. "Zhonghua renmin gongheguo xiangzhen qiye fa."

64. "Law of the PRC on Industrial Enterprises."

65. *China's Management of Enterprise Assets,* 22. An excellent analysis of the failure of SOE reform for a variety of reasons including the continued power of local governments to interfere in their operation and extract revenues from them is Steinfeld, *Forging Reform.*

66. "Company Law."

67. Simon, "Legal Structure," 292. Another observer has noted that, given the frequency with which the application of laws turns on local interpretations of very general provisions, the generality of the provisions on directors' responsibilities has the effect of depriving shareholders of some protection. Osgathorpe, "Critical Survey," 502.

68. Anna M. Han, "China's Company Law," 477–478.

69. "The state will maintain the ultimate control and majority ownership of the largest enterprises." Art and Gu, "China Incorporated," 275; the same authors make a similar argument in Gu and Art, "Securitization."

70. Anna M. Han, "China's Company Law," 488.

71. *China's Management of Enterprise Assets,* 53.

72. Howson, "China's Company Law," 172–173.

73. The literature on the subject of this section is vast and growing. I have drawn on Pitman B. Potter, "Legal Framework"; Jianfu Chen, *From Administrative Authorisation to Private Law,* 197–235; and, especially, the analysis in Fang Liufang, "China's Corporatization Experiment."

74. Jay Zhe Zhang, "Securities Markets," 626 (notes omitted).

75. Naughton, *Growing Out of the Plan*, 298.

76. Fang Liufang, "China's Corporatization Experiment," 208–209.

77. Palmer, "China's New Inheritance Law," 193.

78. Epstein, "Tortious Liability"; Force and Chen, "Introduction to Personal Injury and Death Claims"; "Chinese Discover Product-Liability Suits."

79. "Law of the PRC on the Protection of Minors."

80. Among the principal English-language sources for PRC legal materials on foreign investment is a loose-leaf service published by CCH Australia, Ltd., *China Laws for Foreign Business*. The magazine *China Law and Practice* is indispensable, and another magazine, *China Law for Business*, is also very useful. A survey of the legislation up to 1994 can be found in Pitman B. Potter, "Foreign Investment Law." Pearson, *Joint Ventures*, reviews and analyzes Chinese government policies toward FDI during the 1980s. An overview of the accomplishments and problems of Chinese policy on FDI since 1979 is Lubman, "Legal and Policy Environment." See also Stross, *Bulls in the China Shop*, for insightful comments on encounters between different business cultures on FDI issues.

81. See generally, Mo, "Taxation Power."

82. See e.g., Pitman B. Potter, *Foreign Business Law*, 47, and sources there cited.

83. Pitman B. Potter, "Foreign Investment Law," 170–172.

84. See generally, Pitman B. Potter, *Foreign Business Law*.

85. See Guanxi Zheng and H. L. Fu, "New *Investment Catalogue* Disappoints."

86. "Firms Seek Official Help."

87. "MOFTEC Clarifies Extension Process."

88. See, e.g., "New Duty Exemptions."

89. Silver, "Removing the Rose-Colored Lenses," 11.

90. "PRC Tax Administration."

91. Lubman and Wajnowski, "Technology Transfer"; Markel and Peerenbloom, "Technology Transfer Tango."

92. Markel and Peerenboom, "Technology Transfer Tango."

93. Pitman B. Potter, *Foreign Business Law*, 31.

94. "Passion for Profit," 55.

95. Pitman B. Potter, *Foreign Business Law*, 33.

96. Feinerman, "Chinese Law Relating to Foreign Investment," 832–833.

97. "Administration of the Appraisal of Assets."

98. David Ho and Nancy Leigh, "Retail Revolution."

99. See "Jurassic Park"; Steven Shi and Anne Stevenson-Yang, "Retail Roundabout."

100. The "official check-up" was announced in "China to Shut Down"; the order limiting foreign ownership is reported in James Harding, "Foreign Investors."

101. Childs, "Exercising Strong Direction." (Emphasis added.)

102. Feinerman, "Chinese Participation," 194.

103. On foreign investor attitudes, see Lubman, "Legal and Policy Environment," at §3.04(2).

104. See, e.g., Overholt, "China After Deng," a choice piece of rosy-colored optimism. For an optimistic view of the legal system, see "Gelatt Forum," in

which NYU Professor Jerome Cohen is quoted as saying "China is second to the U.S. in attracting foreign investment. Law has played an important role. We have heard complaints about the legal system, but the overwhelming number of prob-lems investors have are settled informally. I think foreign investors have little to feel insecure about in China, even though the legal system is still a work in progress." Daniel H. Rosen, in *Behind the Open Door,* a study based on interviews with expatriate managers of FIEs in China from thirteen foreign firms, presents (at 203–229) a nuanced account of their need to cope with legal uncertainty, weak or corrupt mechanisms for dispute resolution, and the desirability of culti-vating bureaucratic support. The author concludes that an important tactic of the firms that he studied was to secure "superlegal privileges" such as "failure to en-force laws, deliberate failure to reform laws, patron-client protection, and market share allocation" (221).

105. See, e.g., Gordon Chang, "GITIC Lenders"; Landler, "Bankruptcy."

106. Song Bing, "Assessing China's System," at 2 n. 4, notes that by 1989 over 130 laws and regulations expressed the right to sue administrative organs.

107. "Administrative Procedure Law Adopted"; "Administrative Procedural Law Text."

108. See, e.g., "Circular Implements Administrative Procedure Law"; "Yao Yilin on Administrative Procedures Law"; Chang Hong, "Law Gives the People Power."

109. See, generally, Finder, "Like Throwing an Egg."

110. This section relies on Pitman B. Potter, "Administrative Litigation Law"; Song Bing, "Assessing China's System"; Meng Shang, *Contrôle des Actes Adminis-tratifs.*

111. One noteworthy case in 1992 involved a suit under the ALL by Guo Luo-ji, a professor forced to leave Beijing University after having been singled out by Deng Xiaoping as a "bourgeois liberal." After he transferred to Nanjing Univer-sity, the Party Committee at that university decided that he should not be allowed to teach. He sued in the Jiangsu HLPC but that court refused to accept the case on the grounds that a CCP organization cannot be sued under the ALL. Song Bing, "Assessing China's System," 11–12.

112. "Administrative Litigation Law," Art. 12. See Pitman B. Potter, "Admin-istrative Litigation Law," 283.

113. "Administrative Litigation Law," Art. 11. See also "Opinions of the Supreme People's Court on Some Issues Relating to the Implementation of the Administrative Litigation Law (For Trial Implementation)," in Lin Feng, *Adminis-trative Law,* 322–345.

114. Pitman B. Potter, "Administrative Litigation Law," 279.

115. "Administrative Litigation Law," Art. 54.

116. See, however, Weller, "Bureaucratic Heavy Hand," 31–38, which cites some procedural standards and a few cases in which they have been applied but makes note of commentators who have emphasized the absence of procedural due process standards.

117. See "Administrative Litigation Law," Art. 12 (iv) and the interpretation of the Supreme People's Court cited in n. 108 above.

118. See *China Law Reports* 1991 Vol. 3, 229–233, for the case of Shi Lichang v. People's Government of Laoqiao Township, and at 214–219 for the case of Wu Weilin and Anor v. Fishery Administrative Office of Changshu City, as cited and discussed in Weller, "Bureaucratic Heavy Hand," 36–39 and 42–43, respectively.

119. Pitman B. Potter, "Administrative Litigation Law," 283. It has been suggested that this is an excessively narrow reading of the ALL. Weller, "Bureaucratic Heavy Hand," 28.

120. Pitman B. Potter, "Administrative Litigation Law," 288.

121. Tanner, "How a Bill Becomes a Law," 54, citing Pitman B. Potter, "Administrative Litigation Law." Tanner also reports that ministries frequently seek exemptions from the coverage of new legislation.

122. Pei, "Citizens v. Mandarins," 842–845.

123. The single source that Pei uses is *Zhongguo shenpan anli yaolan* (Anthology of Adjudicated Cases in China), which publishes reported judicial decisions selected and edited by an independent panel and published by the Senior Judges' Training Center of the Supreme People's Court. The opinions are selected by a board of editors, and readers can only guess at their criteria for selection; the decisions are also often extensively rewritten. These cases are described at greater length, and cases involving contract disputes discussed, in chapter 9.

124. The first of the volumes, for 1992, has been translated into English and published in a three-volume set as *China Law Reports* 1991. This volume and the Chinese original of the 1994 volume were reviewed in search of administrative law cases. Of the 350 decisions published in 1991, 38 are administrative cases in which plaintiffs complained about an administrative decision; in 1994, 60 out of 429 are administrative cases. Plaintiffs won 9 of the 13 cases against the police reported in the 1991 volume, even though the actual ratio of quashed police punishments for 1991 was slightly over 19 percent (1,464 out of 7,464). In 1994, plaintiffs won 15 of 16 reported cases, whereas only 16 percent (1,343 out of 8,454) of all plaintiffs nationwide fared so well.

125. *Zhongguo falü nianjian* 1998, 134.

126. Pei, "Citizens v. Mandarins," 844.

127. Administrative case no. 2, *China Law Reports* 1991 Vol. 3, 9–13.

128. Administrative case no. 10, *China Law Reports* 1991 Vol. 3, 59–65.

129. Administrative case no. 12, *China Law Reports* 1991 Vol. 3, 71–75.

130. "State Compensation Law."

131. Lin Feng, *Administrative Law*, 300.

132. Lin Feng, "Examination," n. 61, citing Hu Kangsheng, ed., *Zhonghua renmin gonghe guo guojia peichangfa shiyi*.

133. See Weller, "Bureaucratic Heavy Hand," 48–49, discussing whether the standard of illegality may differ under the ALL and the State Compensation Law.

134. Lin Feng, "Examination," 17.

135. Lin Feng, *Administrative Law*, 346–355. This discussion of the APL follows Corne, *Foreign Investment*, 207–214.

136. Luo Wenyan, "Tingzheng zhidu."

137. "Administrative Reconsideration Law," FBIS 1999–0512 (Apr. 29, 1999);

see generally Lin Feng, *Administrative Law,* 51–110, and Corne, *Foreign Investment,* 260–282.

138. On procedure under the regulations, see Corne, *Foreign Investment,* 260.

139. By making rules appealable, the 1999 law goes beyond the ALL.

140. Song Bing, "Assessing China's System."

141. See, for example, on the 1970s, Harry Harding, *Organizing China,* 78–86. Recent legislation further formalizing activity in this area by the Ministry of Supervision is the Administrative Supervision Law of the People's Republic of China, adopted by the Standing Committee of the Eighth People's Congress, May 9, 1997, "China: PRC Administrative Supervision Law." See Lin Feng, "Administrative Supervision Law."

142. Wang Chenguang and Liu Wen, "Shichang jingji."

143. Yang Zhengwu, "Earnestly Implementing Administrative Punishment Law."

144. Goodman, "Democracy," 308–311.

CHAPTER 8

1. The statistical information and summary of main policy currents in the following two paragraphs are drawn from Jiang Yue, *Renmin tiaojie zhidu,* 8–16; Zhang Yunqing and Zhang Yushan, eds., *Renmin tiaojie,* 8–13; Li Chunlin and Pan Xiaming, "Renmin tiaojie wenti," 18–19.

2. "Civil Procedure Law (for Trial Implementation)," Art. 6, and "Civil Procedure Law," Art. 85.

3. Jiang Wei and Li Hao, "Lun shichang jingji."

4. Jiang Yue, *Renmin tiaojie zhidu,* 1–2.

5. The traditions in which mediation is rooted are commonly expressed in two ways. In the first, a preference for mediation long antedating the advent of Communism is celebrated. For example, "Ministry Explains Communities' Role" states: "The Chinese people have a tradition of solving civil disputes through neighbors' mediation. The tradition dates back more than 1,000 years." In the second, links to revolutionary institutions in the 1920s and in later Communist-administered Revolutionary Bases are emphasized; see, e.g., Department of Grass-Roots Work, *People's Mediation,* 87–88.

6. Department of Grass-Roots Work, *People's Mediation,* 92.

7. Jiang Yue, *Renmin tiaojie zhidu,* 48.

8. For the old rules see "Renmin tiaojie weiyuanhui zanxing zuzhi tongze." For the new rules see "Renmin tiaojie weiyuanhui zuzhi tiaoli."

9. Fu, "Understanding People's Mediation," 233 n. 94, citing Wang Hongyan and Yang Yuanzhong, "Shilun renmin tiaojie."

10. For these provisional rules and their explanation, see Liu Zhitao, *Renmin tiaojie shiyong daquan,* 819–823.

11. Liu Guangan and Li Cunpeng, "Minjian tiaojie."

12. "Minjian jiufen chuli banfa."

13. Zhang Yunqing and Zhang Yushan, eds., *Renmin tiaojie,* 394–415.

14. These regulations and their explanation are available in Liu Zhitao, *Renmin*

tiaojie shiyong daquan, 824–826. For a fuller discussion of these offices see Jiang Wei and Yang Rongxin, eds., *Renmin tiaojiexue*, 112–114.

15. For excerpts from this opinion, see Liu Guangan and Li Cunpeng, "Minjian tiaojie," 291.

16. "Circular of the Supreme People's Court on Strengthening the Economic Trial Work."

17. "Mediation in Shanghai." In 1986, a spokesman of the Ministry of Justice stated that of 3.5 million cases solved through mediation, 577,000 had involved marital matters, 540,000 were housing and land disputes, and 121,000 concerned inheritance. Zhong Hua, "System of Mediating Disputes."

18. Jiang Wei and Yang Rongxin, eds., *Renmin tiaojiexue*, 168–179.

19. "Organic Law on Urban Neighborhood Committees."

20. Gup, "Granny as Big Brother."

21. WuDunn, "In the Cities of China."

22. Fu, "Understanding People's Mediation," 223.

23. See Benewick, "Political Institutionalisation," 255: "Our own research reinforces the conventional view of an organisation of housewives and retired workers, mainly women, tied to the neighbourhood because of the demands of their circumstances."

24. Fu, "Understanding People's Mediation," 224, citing *Fazhi ribao* (Aug. 20, 1990).

25. Fu, "Understanding People's Mediation," 224–226. See, e.g., Langfitt, "Neighborhood Watchdogs."

26. "Distribution Is It."

27. Fu, "Understanding People's Mediation," 222–223.

28. Ikels, *Return of the God of Wealth*, 43.

29. "As more apartment buildings go up in Chinese cities, tenant and property management associations are replacing neighborhood committees faster than they can form." Langfitt, "Neighborhood Watchdogs."

30. "Organic Law of Village Committees."

31. Benewick, "Political Institutionalisation," 261.

32. See, e.g., Clarke, "Dispute Resolution," 269–270.

33. Shi Fengyi, "Renmin tiaojie zhidu suyuan," 45–46.

34. Liu Guangan and Li Cunpeng, "Minjian tiaojie," citing an investigation documenting clan mediation activities in the 1980s.

35. Fu, "Understanding People's Mediation," 242.

36. See Palmer, "Revival of Mediation: (1) Extra-Judicial," 257.

37. "Labor Law," Arts. 77–84. Before then, regulations now superseded and not relevant here dealt with labor disputes in state-owned enterprises.

38. A fourth type of mediation identified by Liu and Li is based on custom, because some customs among minorities "still play a role in contemporary civil mediation" (299). They cite one case in which violence was averted in a dispute between two minority villages over ownership of agricultural land when the mediator used a minority custom to settle disputes over wine. In another, minority custom was invoked to require that the owner of an ox pay compensation for vegetables that the ox had eaten. The force of the custom was moderated, how-

ever, when the two villages agreed that it would be too costly to slaughter the offending ox and share its meat. Liu Guangan and Li Cunpeng, "Minjian tiaojie," 299.

39. The following discussion of the use of emotion and reason in settling disputes is based on Liu Guangan and Li Cunpeng, "Minjian tiaojie," 294–306.

40. Liu Guangan and Li Cunpeng, "Minjian tiaojie," 297–300.

41. Liu Guangan and Li Cunpeng, "Minjian tiaojie," 293–294.

42. Zhang Yunqing and Zhang Yushan, eds., *Renmin tiaojie*, 125.

43. See e.g., Sun Pizhi and Wang Wei, *Renmin tiaojie zhishi*, 60: "in accordance with law and policy, mediators should persuade parties to promote peace and unity, and to yield and reconcile (*huliang hurang*)."

44. Zheng Qixiang et al., "Zhuozhong tiaojie," 26.

45. Pitman B. Potter, "Riding the Tiger."

46. Liang Qinhan, "Chuli jingji jiufen anjian."

47. Liu Guangan and Li Cunpeng, "Minjian tiaojie," 323.

48. See, e.g., Zhang Lin, "Mediators Urged to Help"; "Civil Mediators Successful in Beijing"; "Community Mediators Heal Family Discord."

49. "More Mediation in Civil Disputes Called For." Michael Palmer has referred to "a shift in concern from households with doubtful class backgrounds to households which are quarrelsome." Palmer, "Revival of Mediation: (1) Extra-Judicial," 261.

50. For example, see the discussion of the need for socialist legality to strengthen the people's democratic dictatorship in Zhang Yunqing and Zhang Yushan, eds., *Renmin tiaojie*, 174.

51. Jiang Yue, *Renmin tiaojie zhidu*, 247; Jiang Wei and Yang Rongxin, eds., *Renmin tiaojiexue*, 192–198.

52. Liu Guangan and Li Cunpeng, "Minjian tiaojie," 306. Liu and Li summarize two cases to illustrate the combination of rights-based argument and the invocation of sentiments such as the desirability of reconciliation. In each, disputants had been on the point of committing violent acts, and in each there was less emphasis on analyzing legal issues than on the human and emotional problems that provoked and deepened the dispute. Although in both of the illustrative cases mediators prevented crimes from being committed, the authors express concern (at 301–303) about encouraging ordinary mediators to take on such responsibilities, which are beyond the capacities of most.

53. "Guangzhou Teams to Arbitrate Land Disputes."

54. "Mediators Help Ensure Social Stability."

55. Moser, *Law and Social Change*.

56. Liu Guangan and Li Cunpeng insert a note of doubt. They observe that although the number of mediation committees increased from 1980 to 1992, the ratio of mediated cases to those heard in the courts dropped from almost 11:1 to a little over 3:1 and the absolute number of mediated cases stayed steady at between six and seven million cases annually. The statistics for 1990–1994 (see above) show that the totals for 1993 and 1994 were 6.22 and 6.12 million, respectively. "Minjian tiaojie," 307–308. Table 4 shows a continued decline.

57. Liu Guangan and Li Cunpeng, "Minjian tiaojie," 305.

58. Interview on file with the author.

59. "Many people cannot, dare not, do not know or are not willing to choose legal proceedings, but must rely on mediation while waiving or injuring the exercise of rights to legal proceedings." Liu Guangan and Li Cunpeng, "Minjian tiaojie," 308.

60. Chu and Ju, *Great Wall*, 149–168.

61. Interview on file with the author.

62. Liu Guangan and Li Cunpeng, "Minjian tiaojie," 324.

63. Gao Hongjun, "Zhongguo gongmin quanli yishi."

64. Gao Hongjun, "Zhongguo gongmin quanli yishi," 33–34.

65. *Zhongguo falü nianjian* 1997, 1075. See Table 4.

66. Liu Guangan and Li Cunpeng, "Minjian tiaojie."

67. Fu, "Understanding People's Mediation," 243.

68. Jiang Yue, *Renmin tiaojie zhidu*, 18–19; similar views are expressed in Zhang Yunqing and Zhang Yushan, eds., *Renmin tiaojie*, 1–2; Kong, "Renmin tiaojie zhidu," 20–23.

69. See e.g., Sun Pizhi, "Renmin tiaojie," 16–20.

70. Jiang Wei and Yang Rongxin, eds., *Renmin tiaojiexue*, 58–59.

71. Jiang Wei and Li Hao, "Lun shichang jingji," 189.

72. Wang Yaxin, "Lun minshi, jingji shenpan."

73. Li Chunlin and Pan Xiaming, "Renmin tiaojie wenti," 17–18.

74. Li Chunlin and Pan Xiaming, "Renmin tiaojie wenti," 19–20.

75. Wen, "Jiaqiang renmin tiaojie gongzuo."

76. The distinction is Fu Hualing's, although Palmer's comparison of extrajudicial with judicial mediation suggests the same. See Fu, "Understanding People's Mediation," 230–233; and Palmer, "Revival of Mediation: (2) Judicial," 153–156.

77. Fu, "Understanding People's Mediation," 230–231.

78. Jiang Yue, *Renmin tiaojie zhidu*, 256–257.

79. Fu, "Understanding People's Mediation," 232.

80. Zhang Youyu, "Tantan renmin tiaojie."

81. Clarke, "Dispute Resolution," 294–295.

82. Fu, "Understanding People's Mediation," 245–246.

83. Fu himself has observed that attempts during the 1980s to contract with villages for maintenance of public order have led to local élites expanding their control over the countryside ("Understanding People's Mediation," 241). To endow local governments with greater power, whether alone or in corporatist alliances with a growing class of entrepreneurs, might further weaken the center and worsen the prospects for a nationwide rule of law.

84. "China: Civil Mediation System Ensures Harmony." The article also noted that "more than 10,000 community dispute mediation centers have been set up in Shanghai. These centers gather together personnel from the police, housing administration, and administration of industry and commerce organs to tackle unexpected occurrences in the communities with the help of the civil mediators." This new hybrid organization also echoes the familiar desire to use mediation to preserve social order. The article notes that when 58 households refused to demol-

ish illegal structures after being told to do so by authorities, "the resulting furor was settled with the help of mediators."

85. Nader, *Harmony Ideology*.

86. See, e.g., Shapiro, *Courts*, 182–193.

87. See Sulamith Heins Potter and Jack M. Potter, *China's Peasants*, 296–312, discussing "a caste-like system of social stratification" in the countryside.

88. See Moser, *Law and Social Change*, 184: "for individual disputants in search of vindication, revenge, self-gain or face [Confucian ideology] constitutes a rich vocabulary of shared symbols by which private action may be justified in the public arena."

89. See Nader, *Harmony Ideology*, especially 291–322.

90. Clarke, "Dispute Resolution," 295: "just as non-state mediation institutions in traditional China grew from the desire of individuals to avoid the loss of control associated with complaints to the magistrate, so we may expect that there will continue to be a demand in China for the kind of mediation that can be found only beyond the horizon of official 'mediation' institutions."

91. See generally, Lubman and Wajnowski, "International Commercial Dispute Resolution."

92. "Zhonghua renmin gonghe guo zhongcai fa jieshuo," 9. This section is based on an excellent and thorough review of the situation before the enactment of the Arbitration Law and of the aims of that legislation found in Donald Lewis and Karen Ip, "Domestic Commercial Arbitration," supplemented with references to foreign laws and practice.

93. Donald Lewis and Karen Ip, "Domestic Commercial Arbitration," 88.

94. See Donald Lewis, "New Arbitration Law."

95. Private communication to the author from a local arbitration commission.

96. A more reassuring view of the scope of review in an enforcement proceeding is taken in Jiang Wei and Li Hao, "Lun renmin fayuan," 38. The authors argue that because the Arbitration Law does not require that arbitration awards contain precise findings of fact and conclusions of law, the courts can only review awards for any violation of "national and public interests."

97. Donald Lewis and Karen Ip, "Domestic Commercial Arbitration," 90 n. 78, citing "Opinion of the Supreme People's Court on Several Questions Concerning the Civil Procedure Law," Paragraph 256.

98. "Guowuyuan bangongting . . . de tongzhi," 702. See also Lubman, "Setback for China-Wide Rule of Law."

99. "China to Handle Foreign-Funded Enterprise Disputes."

CHAPTER 9

1. "Activities Underway Everywhere."

2. For an admirable summary of the structure of the Chinese courts and a particularly thoughtful analysis of the Chinese judicial system see Clarke, "Power and Politics." An excellent, detailed study of the courts and civil procedure, with considerable emphasis on aspects of particular interest to foreign litigants in the Chinese courts, is Kolenda et al., "People's Republic of China."

3. "Renmin fayuan zai gaige kaifang zhong," 2.

4. "Zuigao renmin fayuan guanyu shiyong 'Zhonghua renmin gongheguo minshi susong fa' ruogan wenti de yijian."

5. Of a total of 3,277,572 civil cases received in 1997, 1,435,194 involved marriage and family disputes, while 1,259,797 concerned debts. *Zhongguo falü nianjian* 1998, 1239.

6. Of a total of 1,483,356 economic dispute cases received in 1997, 1,373,355 involved domestic contract disputes. *Zhongguo falü nianjian* 1998, 1239.

7. Of a total of 347,651 appeals received in 1997, half involved civil cases, with the remainder divided fairly equally between criminal (19 percent) and economic (25 percent) disputes. *Zhongguo falü nianjian* 1998, 1240.

8. See, e.g., Clarke, "Dispute Resolution," 261–263; Fang Chengzhi, "Renmin fayuan," 15–16.

9. Finder, "Inside the People's Courts," 67–68.

10. Clarke, "Dispute Resolution," 255 n. 29.

11. Fu, "Understanding People's Mediation," 217.

12. He Weifang, "Tongguo sifa," 220. This essay by He Weifang, a law professor at Beijing University, presents a remarkable view into the legal culture of judges.

13. Wang Chenguang, "Banan xiaolü."

14. Interview on file with the author.

15. Chinese informants were often dismissive of the former PLA officers, but one Chinese judge, himself not a law graduate, who had learned "on the job" and in spare-time courses, expressed a kinder view of demobilized soldiers in the courts. He said that ten years ago many judges were demobilized PLA officers, but now even these are more experienced; many have studied and have received degrees and can handle the normal burdens of a judge.

16. For more on judicial training programs see Alford and Fang, "Legal Training," 20–23.

17. See "China: Leaders Attend Opening."

18. The percentage of judges with "college or higher academic credentials" rose from 17.1 percent in 1987 to 66.6 percent in 1992, according to a report by the president of the Supreme People's Court, Ren Jianxin. "Supreme People's Court Work Report," 24.

19. He Weifang, "Tongguo sifa," 228, citing Zhou Dunhe, "Cong 'zhongshi jiaoyu'."

20. He Weifang, "Tongguo sifa," 238.

21. Alford and Fang, "Legal Training," 21.

22. He Weifang, "Tongguo sifa," 241.

23. Alford and Fang, "Legal Training," 21.

24. "Law of the PRC on Judges."

25. Clarke, "Dispute Resolution," 258 n. 44.

26. Some judges, in private conversation, regretted the failure to adopt other obvious methods of raising standards such as paying judges more and employing a nationwide competitive examination. Interview on file with the author.

27. Clarke, "Power and Politics," 8.

28. He Weifang, "Tongguo sifa," 240
29. He Weifang, "Tongguo sifa," 236.
30. He Weifang, "Fuzhuan junren."
31. He Weifang, "Tongguo sifa," 249–250, quoting from *Renmin fayuan bao* (May 21, 1993).
32. Lubman, "Form and Function," 544–551.
33. See, e.g., Lubman, "Mao and Mediation," 1307.
34. China is one of the few countries in the world that permits class actions, which are analyzed in Liebman, "Note: Class Action Litigation."
35. Fees in matters other than divorce are generally charged according to the amount in issue. Rules and practices with regard to fees have been criticized on a number of grounds: Fees are not generally returnable, which is a disincentive to settlement, and courts sometimes seek out cases to resolve in order to earn fees. See He Weifang, "Fayuan gaishou duoshao fei?"
36. Judicial mediation is examined in detail below.
37. Art. 72. See generally Kolenda et al., "People's Republic of China," A9.89–A9.108.
38. Finder, "Inside the People's Courts," 71.
39. See, e.g., Wang Liming and Yao Hui, "Renmin fayuan jigou," 23–25.
40. Informal discussions with Chinese lawyers suggest that sometimes the parties prefer not to present witnesses in court because they would like to avoid unexpected answers by witnesses to questions posed by opposing counsel or the judge.
41. Qinghai sheng gaoji renmin fayuan, "Quanmian tuixing," 67.
42. Finder, "Inside the People's Courts," 72.
43. Alford, "Tasselled Loafers," 33.
44. See, e.g., "China: Circular Bans Businesses."
45. Interviews on file with the author.
46. Art. 11, "Organic Law of the People's Courts."
47. Wen, *Fayuan shenpan yewu guanli*, 103–105. This work was written while the author was studying at the Training Center for Higher Judges.
48. Finder, "Inside the People's Courts," 68.
49. Clarke, "Dispute Resolution," 260.
50. Wen, *Fayuan shenpan yewu guanli*, 107.
51. Zhou Dao, "Shiying shehui zhuyi." The revised Criminal Procedure Law provides that the collegiate bench must carry out the decree of the Adjudication Committee (Art. 149). No such rule is explicitly stated in the Civil Procedure Law.
52. Art. 8 (2).
53. "Constitution," Art. 126.
54. Wen, *Fayuan shenpan yewu guanli*, 36–37.
55. See Tang, "Quanmian jiaqiang jingji shenpan gongzuo," 143.
56. Woo, "Adjudication Supervision," 107.
57. Zhu Suli, "Jiceng fayuan."
58. Wen, *Fayuan shenpan yewu guanli*, 91.
59. For example, one case involved liability for breach of contract made by an

association of enterprises created before "partnerships" and "legal persons" had been defined in the GPCL. The provincial higher people's court to which a lower court decision was appealed requested instructions from the Supreme People's Court, which advised analysis of the facts, including the written agreement of association and the law, in order to decide whether the association was a legal person. Zuigao renmin fayuan jingji shenpan ting, ed., *Zuigao renmin fayuan*, 373–392, Rectification Leading Group of Shanxi Industrial Group v. Guangxi Lingchuan Feroalloy Factory.

60. Wen, *Fayuan shenpan yewu guanli*, 90.

61. On procedure in the Supreme People's Court, see Finder, "Supreme People's Court," 174.

62. See Finder, "Supreme People's Court," 176.

63. Clarke, "Dispute Resolution," 260–268; Clarke, "Power and Politics," 8 n. 23. To offer one representative foreign view: "There is no doubt that the Party, and not the court, was, and is, the real decision-maker in P.R.C. adjudication. The Party is clearly the center of judicial power." Koguchi, "Some Observations," 202.

64. Koguchi, "Some Observations."

65. Wen, *Fayuan shenpan yewu guanli*, 43.

66. Zhou Dao, "Shiying shehui zhuyi," 10.

67. He Weifang, "Tongguo sifa," 249.

68. Clarke, "Dispute Resolution," 261, especially n. 56.

69. Clarke, "Dispute Resolution," 261–262.

70. Interview on file with the author.

71. Goldstein, "China in Transition," 1116. The author further notes (at 1118): "The 'non-state' sector is not to be confused with separateness from administrative control."

72. Oi cautions that "[The term] contracting suggests a degree of autonomy and allocation of property rights that simply is not present. In contrast to agriculture and land, the property rights of township and village firms remain in the hands of local governments." Oi, "Role of the Local State," 1136.

73. Yangzhou shi zhongji renmin fayuan, "Kefu difang baohu zhuyi," 122–123.

74. Oi, "Role of the Local State," 1136.

75. See, e.g., Wank, "Bureaucratic Patronage."

76. See generally, Clarke, "Power and Politics," 40–49, and the detailed discussion in "Local Protectionism and Law Enforcement"; see also Faison, "Razors, Soap, Cornflakes," in which a representative of the State Administration of Industry and Commerce explained that he did not want to seek to impose high penalties for counterfeiting trademarked goods because of the harm to society that would be caused if the counterfeiting enterprise was forced into bankruptcy as a result.

77. He Weifang, "Tongguo sifa," 255.   78. He Weifang, "Tongguo sifa," 261.

79. He Weifang, "Tongguo sifa," 259.   80. Interview on file with the author.

81. Finder, "Supreme People's Court," 153.

82. Zuigao renmin fayuan jingji shenpan ting, comp., *Jingji shenpan canyue ziliao*, 106–112.

83. Zuigao renmin fayuan jingji shenpan ting, comp., *Jingji shenpan canyue ziliao*, 111.

84. Finder, "Supreme People's Court," 173.

85. Liang Huixing, "Minfa de fazhan," 8.

86. Clarke, "Power and Politics," 34. Clarke notes a study suggesting that in 11 New Jersey counties in 1987 only 25 percent of all writs of execution in civil cases were returned fully satisfied.

87. Clarke, "Power and Politics," 86.

88. "Supreme People's Court Work Report," 20. This catalog by China's chief judge is sufficient evidence of the gravity of the problem. An even more detailed and scathing review is "China: Protectionism Rampant."

89. Clarke, "Power and Politics," 35–37, 38–40, 63–64.

90. See, e.g., Clarke, "Power and Politics," 41–42.

91. See, e.g., Zhou Dao, "Shiying shehui zhuyi"; "Procuratorates Told Not to Overstep Authority."

92. See, e.g., Yu Bo, "Guidong baoli."

93. See, e.g., Tang, "Quanmian jiaqiang jingji shenpan gongzuo."

94. He Weifang, "Tongguo sifa," 256.

95. *Zhongguo falü nianjian* 1995, 98.

96. Wen, *Fayuan shenpan yewu guanli*, 90–91.

97. Interview on file with the author.

98. Criticizing this practice is Wang Liming and Yao Hui, "Renmin fayuan jigou," at 28.

99. "Zuigao renmin jiancha yuan."

100. Clarke, "Power and Politics," 83.

101. Palmer, "Revival of Mediation: (2) Judicial," 145.

102. Jiang Wei and Li Hao, "Lun shichang jingji," 189.

103. Palmer, "Revival of Mediation: (2) Judicial," 153.

104. Wang Huaian, ed., *Zhongguo minshi susong fa* (a text for part-time study by judicial cadres); Liu Guangan and Li Cunpeng, "Minjian tiaojie," 316–320 (a report based on research by two scholars at the Institute of Law of the Chinese Academy of Social Sciences).

105. Liu Guangan and Li Cunpeng, "Minjian tiaojie," 318–319.

106. Wang Huaian, ed., *Zhongguo minshi susong fa*, 178.

107. Summaries of these interviews, conducted by the author in 1995 in New York and Beijing, are in the author's files.

108. Li Hao, "Minshi shenpan zhong de tiaoshen fenli," 60.

109. Wang Jianping, "Judicial and Administrative Mediation," 18.

110. Palmer, "Revival of Mediation: (2) Judicial," 149–151.

111. Yangzhou shi zhongji renmin fayuan, "Kefu difang baohu zhuyi," 15.

112. Palmer, "Revival of Mediation: (2) Judicial," 163.

113. This discussion is based on interviews by the author with three legal scholars in Beijing in late 1995 and early 1996.

114. One scholar has suggested in discussions that mediation was a means of increasing the revenue earned by the courts because the court retained 20–30 per-

cent of the fees. Lawyers, too, favored the new centers because they were used as mediators as well as judges. In the absence of jurisdictional rules, lower courts began to create such centers. There was also doubt as to whether the centers could, like the courts, use compulsory measures to protect property during a dispute. The relationship between the new centers and the economic divisions of the courts was unclear. According to the scholars interviewed, legal scholars opposed the EDMCs and a negative report was written by staff at the Supreme People's Court. The court decided that the system should be rationalized, but no specific measures were adopted. At a conference of economic judges in 1993 the centers were discussed and the experiment was allowed to continue, although negative opinion continued to be expressed. As already noted, the rising number of cases presents a problem. In 1994, slightly more than one million economic cases were decided by the courts. By 1996, the yearly total had risen by 50 percent and remained close to 1.5 million in 1997. See Table 6, p. 254.

115. Jiang Wei and Li Hao, "Lun shichang jingji."

116. Zheng Qixiang et al., "Zhuozhong tiaojie," 26.

117. Jiang Wei and Li Hao, "Lun shichang jingji."

118. Some foreign visitors to China during the 1980s, including Chief Justice Warren Burger, uncritically praised China for reducing litigation through the use of mediation and advocated that the West study China in this regard. See "U.S. Chief Justice." Palmer found increasing interest in having the Chinese courts operate in a more rigorous manner than that infused with "the popular-participatory approach that dominated during the more radical years of socialist rule [and move] to a more professional orientation." See Palmer, "Revival of Mediation: (2) Judicial," 168. "Serious consideration" has been given to "restricting the role of judicial mediation," Palmer wrote at 169; it has declined somewhat since he wrote.

119. In 1997, 5,722,455 cases of all types were heard by the courts; lawyers represented clients in 1,162,416 cases, or 20 percent. *Zhongguo falü nianjian* 1998, 1256.

120. He Weifang, "Tongguo sifa," 279.

121. Finder, "Inside the People's Courts," 69.

122. See He Weifang, "Tongguo sifa," 272–273, noting the blatant behavior of two litigants who went to judges' offices to offer bribes.

123. He Weifang, "Tongguo sifa," 266–267.

124. Li Hao, "Lun fayuan tiaojie," 12, citing "Miandui gaige de xin xingshi—quanguo gaoji fayuan yuanzhang huiyi fangtan lu (Facing a new style of reforms—Interviews from the National Meeting of High-Level People's Court Presidents)," *Renmin sifa* 2 (1994).

125. Finder, "Inside the People's Courts," 69. On the strength of the influence on judges of their relationships outside the courts, see also Zhu Suli, "Jiceng fayuan."

126. The pervasiveness of corruption in the courts was given top-level attention in 1998, when the leadership ordered an "educational rectification campaign" that focused specifically on the courts. Among the activities that were denounced were many that have already been described here as customary: "accepting offers of money, gifts or dinners from litigants, secretly handling lawsuits without com-

plying with legal procedures or refusing to open a trial that should be opened, introducing lawyers to litigants or privately meeting with a litigant and his attorney." "China: Supreme Court's New Measures." Newspapers reported that judges and other court personnel were punished for egregious misconduct, and emphasized the need to build stronger institutions that would improve the quality of justice. Representative articles are "China: Guangxi Senior Judge Jailed"; "China: Beijing Judicial Officials Punished"; see also Zhou Dewei, "Fighting Corruption," reviewing cases uncovered and measures taken in the course of the "hard struggle waged by courts across the country over . . . the past five years."

127. See, for example, a report in 1994 by a deputy president of the Supreme People's Court praising the courts for promoting the independence of enterprises, preventing losses of national capital, promoting the establishment of markets and lawful trade, controlling illegal conduct, protecting fair competition, and promoting new transactions. Tang, "Quanmian jiaqiang jingji shenpan gongzuo," 143.

128. One court, cited as a model, assigned staff to "look for cases," and had them visit a paper mill that was owed 15 million RMB by almost 300 enterprises. They spent "over 100 days and nights" seeking out debts in over 12 provinces and cities, and their success in recovering 4.6 million RMB inspired the praise of the local Party secretary: "this is service, this is efficiency." He Weifang, "Tongguo sifa," 251.

129. For these cases see He Weifang, "Tongguo sifa," 251–253. Similarly, in a collection of essays for judges assembled by the Judge's Training Center of the Supreme People's Court, one article instructs judges to "adopt an attitude that actively and with initiative" takes jurisdiction over cases that endanger social stability. It relates how the courts dealt with a sudden rise in cases in Sichuan arising out of failure by buyers of nutrias to honor their contracts to purchase the animals from "tens of thousands" of households that had raised them in the hope of getting rich quickly. In the face of considerable public agitation over the losses and responding to instructions of the provincial higher court, lower courts acted quickly to begin hearing cases, sending "swindlers" to the police, and advising breeders on where to file cases. They then quickly decided some cases that served as "models," and thereby brought hope to the breeders. Sichuan sheng gaoji renmin fayuan, "Fahui jingji shenpan zhineng zuoyong," 7–8. For the text of a document issued by the Supreme People's Court intended to mobilize the courts to carry out a CCP Central Committee decision to punish economic crimes seriously, see Nanping Liu, *Judicial Interpretation*, 51–54.

130. Keller, "Sources of Order," 729.

131. Damaska, *Faces of Justice*, 37.

132. Damaska, *Faces of Justice*, 37 n. 38.

133. See, e.g., Galanter, "Adjudication, Litigation and Related Phenomena," 179–181.

134. Finder, "Supreme People's Court," citing "Resolution of the Standing Committee of the National People's Congress Providing an Improved Interpretation of the Law" (June 10, 1981), in *Laws of the People's Republic of China 1979–1982* 1: 251. This section on judicial interpretation draws on Finder,

"Supreme People's Court"; Shizhou Wang, "Judicial Explanation"; and Nanping Liu, "Ignored Source."

135. Nanping Liu, *Judicial Interpretation*, 30.

136. Finder, "Supreme People's Court," 167, enumerates nine different types of documents, but the number is even larger. See Wang Chenguang, "Increasing Judicial Activism."

137. Finder gives examples, such as the definition of a crucial term or one instance in which the Court changed a rule to make it conform to "reality." Finder, "Supreme People's Court," 168.

138. "Zuigao renmin fayuan guanyu sifa jieshi gongzuo de ruogan guiding." See also Wang Chenguang, "Increasing Judicial Activism," on which this paragraph relies.

139. Whitmore Gray and Henry Ruiheng Zheng, trans., "Opinion."

140. Whitmore Gray and Henry Ruiheng Zheng, trans., "Opinion," Art. 50.

141. Nanping Liu, *Judicial Interpretation*, 106–107.

142. This is the general argument of Nanping Liu, *Judicial Interpretation*.

143. One estimate is that about half of all of the Court's interpretations issued by the Court between 1985 and 1991 were published in the Gazette. Finder, "Supreme People's Court," 187 n. 160, citing Zhang Jun, "Zuigao shenpan jiguan," 52.

144. Shen, *Bijiao fa*, 466; arguing for giving greater weight to cases is Cao Pei, "Borrowing the Case Law Method."

145. Nanping Liu, "Legal Precedents," 116.

146. Nanping Liu, Legal Precedents," 118.

147. Nanping Liu, "Legal Precedents," 119.

148. Liang Huixing, "Minfa de fazhan," 3.

149. See Wang Chenguang, "Increasing Judicial Activism," 9–13, for a summary of alternative views of the interpretative activity discussed here.

150. Dicks, "Compartmentalized Law," 93.

151. Dicks, "Compartmentalized Law," 84, 109, 108.

152. Palmer, "China's New Inheritance Law," 193.

153. See chapter 7, text at n. 76.

154. Wang Liming et al., eds., *Renge quan fa*. For press coverage of the right to sue for damages over media use of a person's name or likeness, see "Law Professor Discusses Media-Related Torts."

155. Wang Liming, et al., eds., *Renge quan fa*, 18.

156. "He Shan Incident."

157. This discussion of class actions is based on Liebman, "Note: Class Action Litigation."

158. Liebman, "Note: Class Action Litigation," 1541.

159. See, e.g., Zuigao renmin fayuan gongbao bianjibu, comp., *Zuigao renmin fayuan.*

160. *Zhongguo shenpan anli yaolan*. The anthology compiles decisions selected by the courts and sent to Beijing, together with notes and materials from the files in each case, and reviewed, revised, and polished by senior editors. Because the editors found most of the opinions "far too brief" and unstandardized, and be-

cause they wanted to produce a compilation that could serve as a model for judges, they consulted foreign law reports to assure that the collection would not be "a simple assemblage of [original] judgments from the People's Courts." Feng, "Review," 271, citing *Zhongguo fazhi bao* (Legal Daily) (May 26, 1994). The comments were largely written by the editors. A Chinese legal scholar knowledgeable about the editing process has stated in private conversation that heavy editing of the decisions was required, expressed considerable doubt that Chinese judges use the anthology for guidance, and offered the view that the chief value of the publication was as "propaganda."

The Hong Kong publishers have tried to heighten the symbolism of their volume. The single Chinese volume has been transformed into three English-language volumes, one each for criminal and civil cases and a third for administrative and economic cases. Titles stamped in red and gold on the handsome blue cloth binding reinforce a physical resemblance to official English law reports, and exude the dignity that is expected of official court reports in the West. Elaborate headnotes have been added by the Hong Kong translators to the individual reports of each case indicating the principal topics and statutes cited, which lend the decisions an appearance of systematization suggesting far more order and certainty in the system than actually exists. Unfortunately the annotations published in the Chinese original have been omitted from the English edition because, the Introduction states, they were written by the editors and the editors did not want readers to believe that they formed part of the judgment(!). This is a decision to be deplored, because the annotations often provide useful background for understanding the decisions.

161. Feng, "Review," 271. The approach of Chinese courts is suggested by a manual written for judges, Jilin sheng siping shi zhongji renmin fayuan, ed., *Shenpan guanli caozuo guifan*, which defines standards in an effort to improve the quality of judicial work. Based on model courts in Jilin province, it sets forth judicial practice and procedure in a codified form. The portion on civil litigation is long on descriptions of the forms that have to be filled out and the time limits imposed on various stages of procedure (p. 233). When the manual reaches actual judicial decision-making, however, its instructions are limited to the following:

Article 40. Members of the collegial bench are all responsible for the facts of the case and the use of the law. Deliberative work is directed by the responsible judge, who implements the principle of democratic centralism. If there is a division of opinions, the case should be decided through the principle of the minority being subordinated to the majority. The minority's opinions must [however] be recorded in detail.

Article 41. Case deliberations should be based upon the facts and with the law as the yardstick [of determination]. Prevent deliberation based upon subjective assumptions, emotional acts, relying upon the apparently natural, and experience (p. 234).

See Wang Liming and Yao Hui, "Renmin fayuan jigou," 25–26. The authors argue that absent an explanation of a judge's decision, justice is not guaranteed; that when interests of considerable value to the parties are at stake, it is only fair to provide them with a reasoned basis for decision of their dispute; that the need to explain their conclusions holds the judges to standards of quality; and that reasoned opinions make it possible to monitor the quality of the judicial system.

162. *China Law Reports 1991 Vol. 3*, 246–250, Tairi Brickyard of Fengxian County v. Xinchang Xinnan Hardware Factory of Nanhui County.

163. *China Law Reports 1991 Vol. 3*, 286–292, Chemical Plant of Wuhai City v. Soda Plant of Xiadian Town, Dachang Hui Autonomous County.

164. *China Law Reports 1991 Vol. 2*, 206–212, Li Qingni v. People's Government of Huaizhong Township.

165. *China Law Reports 1991 Vol. 3*, 533–538, Shenyang Hongguang Enterprises United Co. v. Lu Songtao.

166. *China Law Reports 1991 Vol. 3*, 604–612, Ninghsia Yinchuan Smeltery v. Huabei Co. of China Color Metal Materials Corp.

167. *China Law Reports 1991 Vol. 2*, 535–539, Li Huixiang v. Li Changping and Dai Hongwei. The court relied on an interpretation by the Supreme People's Court on the implementation of the General Principles of Civil Law that, purporting to interpret the text of the General Principles of Civil Law, actually *changed* the text. Articles 31 and 33 of the General Principles declare that a written agreement and approval and registration (by the State Administration of Industry and Commerce) are necessary prerequisites for the creation of a partnership, and do not provide for any exception in circumstances like those involved in the reported case. The Supreme People's Court actually added the exception to the rule stated in the General Principles. Finder, "Supreme People's Court," 168 n. 98.

168. *China Law Reports 1991 Vol. 2*, 321–325, Gao Pingping v. Guanghua Agency of Arts and Crafts for Everyday Use. The Supreme People's Court had issued a rule permitting suit against either the manufacturer or the seller of a substandard product.

169. *China Law Reports 1991 Vol. 2*, 182–187, Zhu Huiren v. Tan Xihua.

170. Article 4 of the General Principles of Civil Law was also applied in another case: plaintiff lost a cow that was found by the defendants, who demanded cash for its return. The trial court mediated the dispute at the defendants' village, and pursuant to the agreement of the parties ordered that the cow be returned and that the defendants pay the costs of maintaining the cow while the defendants had possession of it. *China Law Reports 1991 Vol. 2, 610–613,* Yang Chengbao v. Ni Fenglan and another.

171. *China Law Reports 1991 Vol. 2*, 337–341, Zhang Fuxiang v. Oriental Hotel.

172. See, for example, *China Law Reports 1991 Vol. 3*, 730–734, Shi Yongming and another v. Sanjie Production Team of Luwu Village, Luwu Town, Lingshan County, in which a court found invalid the confiscation of three lychee trees in 1957 because the "Model Articles of Association of Higher-level Agriculture Production Cooperatives" of the time had been misapplied. Several rulings by the Supreme People's Court on disputes over inheritance of real property in which rights had been allocated in the Maoist era are in Zuigao renmin fayuan gongbao bianjibu, comp., *Zuigao renmin fayuan gongbao dianxing anli he sifa jieshi jingxuan,* 692, 694.

173. Lucie Cheng and Arthur Rosett, "Contract with a Chinese Face," 229.

174. Phyllis Chang, "Deciding Disputes"; Zweig et al., "Law, Contracts, and Economic Modernization." A third study of interest is Ross, "Changing Profile of Dispute Resolution," which predicted a rise in the use of contracts and in the number of contract disputes that would be brought to the courts.

175. Zweig et al., "Law, Contracts, and Economic Modernization," 362.

176. Galanter, "Adjudication," 219.

177. Thireau and Hua, "Legal Disputes."

178. Galanter, "Adjudication," 152.

179. Anthony Dicks has noted that the Chinese courts share their responsibilities "with other 'courts'—ministries, commissions and other bodies." Dicks, "Compartmentalized Law," 86.

180. Tang, "Quanmian jiaqiang jingji shenpan gongzuo," 143.

181. Galanter, "Adjudication," 172.

182. Jacob, "Courts as Organizations," 193.

183. Koguchi, "Some Observations."

184. Keller, "Sources of Order," 753.

185. He Weifang, "Tongguo sifa," 233–234.

186. He Weifang, "Tongguo sifa," 245. See also He Weifang, "Zhongguo sifa guanli," arguing that the courts must be managed and run differently from administrative agencies in the Chinese bureaucracy. He notes the practice, mentioned above, of lower courts seeking guidance from higher courts and, more generally, the higher courts acting as leaders (*lingdao*) rather than supervising (*jiandu*). Also characterizing the courts as bureaucratic agencies is Zhu Suli, "Jiceng fayuan."

187. He Weifang, "Tongguo sifa," 254–255, citing *Renmin fayuan bao*, June 6, 1994. Another indication of the extent to which court operation differs from that in the West is found in the strict regulations defining "state secrets in People's Court work." While much of what is classified as secret would be confidential in any Western legal system, such as internal court deliberations and memoranda, other items are unique. These include statistical reports on criminal cases from intermediate-level courts or higher, "directives or reports which are still under review pertaining to the adjudication of cases of especially great significance for social stability, state unity, ethnic unity or foreign relations," material pertaining to "actions to strike at criminal and economic offenses," statistical and other information on death sentences, and statistical information on non-capital criminal cases from courts at the intermediate level or above. "Renmin fayuan gongzuo zhong guojia mimi."

188. Epstein, "Law and Legitimation."

189. Although it is perfectly obvious, the manner in which the debates within the United States on China policy have been framed overlooks the fact that different societies have devised different institutional frameworks for maintaining the rule of law. Some of the characteristics of the Chinese judicial system, such as audit of lower court opinions by administrative superiors and the provisionality of lower court decisions, also mark some legal systems of Western Europe. See Damaska, *Faces of Justice*.

CHAPTER 10

1. Staunton, *Ta Tsing Leu Lee*, xxv, quoting Montesquieu, *Spirit of the Laws*.

2. Poggi, *Development of the Modern State*, 103.

3. Nee, "Peasant Entrepreneurship."

4. Lieberthal, *Governing China*, 301.

5. Walder, "Quiet Revolution," 16. On resistance to intervention by higher-level governmental authorities, see Bruun, "Political Hierarchy," 206.

6. A Chinese reformer has suggested that to counter local protectionism, regional courts under the direct supervision of the Supreme People's Court should be created to handle disputes between parties from different areas, and that the Supreme People's Court itself should exercise original jurisdiction over such cases. Cao Siyuan, "China's Ailing Courts." Although this suggestion is attractive, especially to Americans familiar with federalism (see, e.g., Jerome A. Cohen, "Reforming China's Civil Procedure," 803–804), quite apart from the obvious political difficulty of negotiating power-sharing among China's central and provincial governments, expanded jurisdiction of the Supreme People's Court could also be a vehicle for assertive Party control over important court decisions.

7. Oi, *Rural China Takes Off*, 341–342.

8. Ellickson, *Order Without Law*.

9. Stewart Macaulay, "Non-Contractual Relations."

10. Lucie Cheng and Arthur Rosett, "Contract with a Chinese Face."

11. Relevant here also is the study of litigation that was mentioned in chapter 9, in which the writers noted that even when litigants were represented by lawyers, most of the argumentation was not centered on legal issues. Thireau and Hua, "Legal Disputes."

12. Kipnis, *Producing Guanxi*, 185.

13. Elisabeth Rosenthal, "Day in Court."

14. See Guthrie, "Declining Significance of Guanxi," 254.

15. Tracey, "Transforming Southern China," 3.

16. Pitman B. Potter, "Foreign Investment Law."

17. "China's Diaspora Turns Homeward."

18. "Woo's New Wave."

19. "Woo's New Wave."

20. As one observer has noted, "Some cultures do, of course, show a remarkable continuity over long stretches of time. But . . . [a] multi-million manufacturing company in Taiwan is not simply a peasant clan writ large. . . . On the contrary, in some situations, people can drastically change their beliefs and their behavior, often in an amazingly short period of time." Berger, "Is Asia's Success Transplantable."

21. Except, of course, when they are treated arbitrarily in China. See "Detained HK Man Vows to Clear Name," quoting a Hong Kong businessman holding an American passport who alleged that he had been illegally arrested in China because of a business dispute with a PRC partner: "I was a so-called China expert, but I have learned more in 40 days in detention than I have in 40 years of academia."

22. A study of the relationships between Taiwan investors and local government officials in a Fujian county illustrates the interplay of overseas Chinese attitudes and extra-legal power relationships of the type that have been described earlier as widespread in the local Party-state: The local officials restrain their rent-seeking activities in return for extra-legal payments for their patronage. Even when government policies change, making it necessary for the local arrangements to change, local informal rules remain influential in shaping relations between the investors and local officials. Jieh-min Wu, "Strange Bedfellows."

23. Some overseas Chinese investors had to reexamine their approach when they had to sell some of their assets in China in order to raise cash needed to finance retrenchment at home. One such was Charoen Pokphand, one of the largest foreign investors in China, which had prided itself on its connections with high-ranking Chinese officials. A company vice-president was quoted as saying, "These days, the connections do not count for much. If you are not doing well, then you should get out." Kahn, "Low on Cash."

24. See Epstein, "Law and Legitimation."

25. See Pitman B. Potter, "Riding the Tiger."

26. Clarke and Feinerman, "Antagonistic Contradictions," 153. For a sophisticated Chinese analysis, see Liang Zhiping, "Law and Fairness."

27. This discussion is based on Tianjin Shi, *Political Participation*, 44–66.

28. Deng Xiaoping, "Emancipate the Mind."

29. Even to the point of believing that "creation of a legal regulatory mechanism can engender the very institution which the law has been created to regulate." Feinerman, "Backwards into the Future," 169.

30. Alford, "Tasselled Loafers," 36.

31. See, e.g., Liebman, "Note: Class Action Litigation."

32. See, e.g., use of the courts by peasants protesting cadre arbitrariness, reported in Croll, *From Heaven to Earth*, 132–133, and Lianjiang Li and Kevin J. O'Brien, "Villagers and Popular Resistance"; of many peasant riots that have been reported in recent years, one was Elisabeth Rosenthal, "Thousands of Farmers."

33. See, e.g., O'Brien, "Implementing Political Reform."

34. See, e.g., Jenner, *Tyranny of History*, 246.

35. See Cabestan, "La Transition Politique."

36. Nathan with Shi, "Left and Right," 192.

37. See, e.g., "Western-style Democracy"; Kynge, "Chinese President."

38. The lines between permissible and impermissible protest are hardly clear. Thus, publication of a book on political reform during the summer of 1998 was noteworthy—see Eckholm, "Chinese Book"—but its circulation was reportedly banned later the same year.

39. Cabestan, "La Transition Politique." 116.

40. Rowen, "Short March," 69.

41. Pei, "Is China Democratizing?," 77.

42. Summarizing uncertainty both about the emergence of civil society in China and the appropriateness of applying the concept to China is Brook and Frolic, "China and the Future of Civil Society."

43. An extensive range of possibilities is considered in Baum, "China After Deng."

44. See, e.g., a statement by Jiang Zemin summarized at length in Cao Jianmin, "Financial Security."

45. Lawrence M. Friedman, *Total Justice*, 1.

46. Kennan, *American Diplomacy*, 46.

47. See, e.g., Gigot, "Engaging China."

48. The literature is extensive. See generally, Ann Kent, *Between Freedom and Subsistence*; Edwards et al., *Human Rights*.

49. See "Justice Prevails in Human Rights Defeat"; Kynge and Harding, "Trade Trumps Human Rights"; "The White House: Press Briefing."

50. See "As China Signs Rights Treaty."

51. Harry Harding, "Breaking the Impasse," 167. Harding advocates (at 174–177), among other policy emphases, that the United States adopt a definition of human rights that includes social and economic rights and that it adopt a long-term perspective toward the issue of democratization. His full discussion of human rights issues in United States–China relations, which includes other policy recommendations, is at 165–184.

52. See, e.g., Jerome A. Cohen, "Due Process?"; Edwards, "Civil and Social Rights."

53. Victor H. Li, "Human Rights," 221.

54. See, e.g., Andrew Nathan's scholarly account of the democracy movement in China before 1989, *Chinese Democracy*, 3–30, 193–232; on the events of spring 1989, see, e.g., Nathan, *China's Crisis*, 171–192. See also Han Minzhu, *Cries for Democracy*, and Walder, "Political Sociology." Among Chinese articles relating law to democracy see, e.g., Chen Pengsheng, "Meiyou falü de zhengzhi," an outspoken call for the rule of law by a scholar at the Institute of Law of the Chinese Academy of Social Sciences.

55. Jerome A. Cohen, "Due Process?," 239.

56. See, e.g., Thomas L. Friedman, "Rethinking China, Part II." In mid-1997 Secretary Albright promised to "shine a spotlight" on Chinese human rights violations. Dolinsky, "Albright Defends China Policy." While visiting Beijing earlier that year, Speaker Gingrich lectured a Chinese group on the need for the rule of law, and he has since declared that "America cannot remain silent about the basic lack of freedom . . . in China." Tyler, "Now, Beijing Hears Another U.S. Voice." Minority Leader Gephardt voted against maintaining China's most-favored-nation status after denouncing China's "free-market Stalinism" as an economy based on "slave labor." Clymer, "Gephardt Will Denounce Trade Policy."

57. See, e.g., Roberta Cohen, "Peoples' Republic of China: The Human Rights Exception"; Wu et al., *Human Rights*; Bernstein, "Break Up the Chinese Gulag"; A. M. Rosenthal, "Muzzled by Beijing."

58. Letter to Philip Jessup, April 9, 1953, quoted in Stephanson, *Kennan*, 183–184.

59. Lieberthal, "China Challenge," 43.

60. Henkin, "Human Rights Idea," 7–13.

61. Van Ness, "Addressing the Human Rights Issue," 328–330.

62. Nathan, "Sources of Chinese Rights Thinking," 164.

63. Alford, *To Steal a Book*, 117.

64. Alford, *To Steal a Book*, 118.

65. "White House Releases Joint U.S.-China Statement."

66. "China and the World Trading System."

67. Perkins, "Prospects for China's Integration," 39.

68. 61 Stat. A3, 55 UNTS 187.

69. A useful survey of the many problems that surround China's admission to the WTO is US-China Business Council, *China and the WTO*. One homely example of the problems that foreign investors regularly encounter will suffice here. In connection with initiation of a policy that may tolerate foreign insurance companies in China, regulations have been issued on licenses to such companies. The regulations specifically state, however, that if a license is denied, the agency in charge does not have to explain its reasons for the denial. Simms, "Waiting for the Other Shoe," 23. Further evidence of practices and habits that are inimical to the transparency that is required by the GATT Treaty is provided by continued use of internal regulations and guidelines and in local departures from central government policy mentioned above. On internal rules see, e.g., Corne, *Foreign Investment*, 110–111; on inconsistency between local and national legislation, see the same work at 124–135.

70. General Agreement on Tariffs and Trade 1947, Art. X.

71. Emphasizing that the requirement of transparency under the treaty is imprecisely defined but agreeing nonetheless that "There is at present a very considerable mismatch between the WTO transparency requirements and the Chinese legal regime" is Ostry, "China and the WTO," 18.

72. "Draft Protocol on China," S-3, at Paragraph D1.

73. This argument is made in Stokes, "Chinese Challenge."

74. Economy, *Case Study of China*; Alford and Shen, "Limits of the Law," 139–143.

75. Haley, *Authority Without Power*, 15.

76. Winn, "Relational Practices."

77. O'Brien, "Chinese People's Congresses," 82–83.

78. See Shklar, *Legalism*, 22: "The ideology of 'the West'. . . . always comes down to a political tradition of freedom under law or the rule of law. The difficulty with this self-congratulatory view of the Western past is that it flies in the face of the most obvious facts of history. There is no *one* Western tradition. . . . To say that *a* political tradition, 'freedom under law', ties [European history] together into a neat pattern is an ideological abuse of the past. It falsifies the past, and renders the present incomprehensible."

Works Cited

"2nd All-China Judiciary Conference Convened in Peking." *Xinhua* May 12, 1953, English language translation in *SCMP* 573 (May 19, 1953): 15–17.

"A Ball of Thread with One Thousand Knots, Mediation Committee Unties Them; City Mediation Committee Performs an Important Function in Handling Cases." *Guangzhou ribao* July 18, 1957.

"A Village People's Mediation Committee Which Serves Production." *Guangming ribao* Oct. 14, 1955.

"Accelerated Law-Making Urged to Boost Market Economy." *JPRS* 94-030 (May 12, 1994): 14–16, translated from *Zhongguo wuzi bao* (China Materials News) Mar. 7, 1994, 4.

"Act of the People's Republic of China for Punishment of Corruption." Promulgated Apr. 18, 1952, *Xinhua* Apr. 21, 1952, in *SCMP* 320 (Apr. 22, 1952): 11–15, and in Jerome A. Cohen, ed., *The Criminal Process in the People's Republic of China, 1949–1963: An Introduction*, p. 308. Cambridge, Mass.: Harvard University Press, 1968.

"Activities Underway Everywhere as Courts Study Tan Lin." *Fazhi ribao*, Oct. 14, 1997.

"Administration of the Appraisal of Assets Invested by Foreign Investors Procedures." *China Law and Practice* 8, no. 8 (Oct. 3, 1994): 39–44.

"Administrative Litigation Law of the People's Republic of China." Adopted Apr. 4, 1989. *CCH* ¶ 19–558.

"Administrative Procedural Law Text." *Renmin ribao* Apr. 10, 1989, in *FBIS* 89-083 (May 2, 1989): 92–102. Originally translated as "Administrative Procedural [or Procedure] Law," this is now uniformly referred to as "Administrative Litigation Law" in both Chinese and foreign English language sources.

"Administrative Procedure Law Adopted." *Xinhua* Apr. 4, 1989, in *FBIS* 89-063 (Apr. 4, 1989): 19–20.

"Administrative Punishment Law of the People's Republic of China." Adopted Mar. 17, 1996. *Xinhua* Mar. 21, 1996, in *FBIS* 96-071 (Apr. 11, 1996): 29–36.

Alford, William P. "Double-Edged Swords Cut Both Ways: Law and Legitimacy in the People's Republic of China." In Tu Wei-ming, ed., *China in Transformation*, pp. 45–69. Cambridge, Mass.: Harvard University Press, 1994.

Alford, William P. "The Inscrutable Occidental?: Implications of Roberto Unger's

Uses and Abuses of the Chinese Past." *Texas Law Review* 64, no. 5 (1986): 915–972.

Alford, William P. "Of Arsenic and Old Laws: Looking Anew at Criminal Justice in Late Imperial China." *California Law Review* 72 (1984): 1180–1256.

Alford, William P. "Tasselled Loafers for Barefoot Lawyers: Transformation and Tension in the World of Chinese Legal Workers." In Stanley B. Lubman, ed., *China's Legal Reforms*, pp. 22–38. Oxford: Oxford University Press, 1996.

Alford, William P. *To Steal a Book Is an Elegant Offense: Intellectual Property Law in Chinese Civilization.* Stanford: Stanford University Press, 1995.

Alford, William P., and Fang Liufang, with Lu Zhifang. "Legal Training and Education in the 1990s: An Overview and Assessment of China's Needs." Unpublished ms. Jan. 31, 1994.

Alford, William P., and Yuanyuan Shen. "Limits of the Law in Addressing China's Environmental Dilemma." *Stanford Environmental Law Journal* 16 (1997): 125–148.

Amnesty International. *China—Punishment Without Crime: Administrative Detention.* New York: Amnesty International, 1991.

Amnesty International. *China—Violations of Human Rights: Prisoners of Conscience and the Death Penalty in the People's Republic of China.* London: Amnesty International, 1984.

Amnesty International. *Political Imprisonment in the People's Republic of China.* London: Amnesty International, 1978.

"An Important Matter." *Gongren ribao* Aug. 29, 1961, English language translation in *SCMP* 3,297 (1961): 8–10.

"Anhui Holds Telephone Conference on Publicizing NPC Laws." *FBIS* (Aug. 15, 1979): O3–O4.

"Announcement of the People's Congress of Canton, Kwangtung Province." *Nanfang ribao* June 24, 1955.

"Anti-Corruption Drive Starts." *Eastern Express* Apr. 20, 1994.

Art, Robert C., and Minkang Gu. "China Incorporated: The First Corporation Law of the People's Republic of China," *Yale Journal of International Law* 20, no. 2 (1994): 273–308.

Arthurs, H. W. "Special Courts, Special Law: Legal Pluralism in Nineteenth Century England." In G. R. Rubin and David Sugarman, eds., *Law, Economy and Society, 1750–1914:* Essays in the History of English Law, pp. 380–411. Abingdon: Professional, 1984.

"Article Views Law Enforcement Organs Abuse of Position." *JPRS* 94-035 (June 3, 1994): 20–21, translating Zhang Jianwei, "Law Enforcement Organs Abuse Office for Profits." *Shanghai faxue* (Mar. 1994): 15–17.

"As China Signs Rights Treaty, It Holds Activist." *New York Times* Oct. 6, 1998: A13.

Association of American Law Schools. *Summarized Proceedings of the Institute in Teaching of International and Comparative Law.* 1948.

"At Yangdan Commune Headquarters." *Peking Review* (Mar. 11, 1966): 18–20.

Augustin-Jean, Louis. "Rural Enterprises and the Law." *China News Analysis* 1,586 (June 1, 1997).

Bao Tinggan. "My Understanding of 'Facts as Basis'." *Guangming ribao* Oct. 28, 1956.

Barmé, Geremie R. "To Screw Foreigners Is Patriotic: China's Avant-Garde Nationalists." *China Journal* 34 (July 1995): 209–234.

Barnett, A. Doak, and Ezra Vogel. "A County." In A. Doak Barnett with Ezra Vogel. *Cadres, Bureaucracy and Political Power in Communist China*, pp. 107–309. New York: Columbia University Press, 1967.

Barnett, A. Doak, with Ezra Vogel. *Cadres, Bureaucracy, and Political Power in Communist China*. New York: Columbia University Press, 1967.

Baum, Richard. *Burying Mao: Chinese Politics in the Age of Deng Xiaoping*. Princeton, N.J.: Princeton University Press, 1994.

Baum, Richard. "China After Deng: Ten Scenarios in Search of Reality." *China Quarterly* 145 (1996): 153–175.

Baum, Richard. "Modernization and Legal Reform in Post-Mao China: The Rebirth of Socialist Legality." *Studies in Comparative Communism* 19, no. 2 (1986): 69–103.

Baum, Richard, and Alexei Shevchenko. "The 'State of the State' in Post-Reform China." In Merle Goldman and Roderick MacFarquhar, eds., *The Paradox of China's Post-Mao Reforms*, pp. 333–362. Cambride, Mass.: Harvard University Press, 1999.

Beck, Carl. "*Bureaucracy and Political Development* in Eastern Europe." In Joseph LaPalombara, ed., *Bureaucracy and Political Development*, pp. 268–300. Princeton, N.J.: Princeton University Press, 1963.

"Beijing Mediation Committees Handle Local Disputes." *Xinhua* Oct. 9, 1979; *FBIS* 79-198 (Oct. 11, 1979): R2–R3.

Beijing renmin fayuan mishu chu (Secretariat of the People's Court of Beijing). *Renmin sifa gongzuo juyu* (Examples of People's Judicial Work). Beijing: n.p., 1950.

Benewick, Robert. "Political Institutionalisation at the Basic Level of Government and Below in China." In Gordon White, ed., *The Chinese State in the Era of Economic Reform*, pp. 243–264. Armonk, N.Y.: M. E. Sharpe, 1991.

Berger, Peter L. "Is Asia's Success Transplantable?" *Asian Wall Street Journal* Apr. 20, 1994.

Berman, Harold J. *Law and Revolution: The Formation of the Western Legal Tradition*. Cambridge, Mass.: Harvard University Press, 1983.

Berman, Harold J. "Protection of Rights Arising Out of Economic Contracts under Socialist Legal Systems: A Comparative Approach." *Osteuropa Recht* 14, no. 4 (1968): 213–220.

Berman, Harold J., Susan Cohen, and Malcolm Russell. "A Comparison of the Chinese and Soviet Codes of Criminal Law and Procedure." *Journal of Criminal Law and Criminology* 73, no. 1 (1982): 238–258.

Bernstein, Robert L. "Break Up the Chinese Gulag." *New York Times* Feb. 17, 1991, E13.

Bloch, Marc. *Feudal Society*. Translated by L. A. Manyon. Chicago: University of Chicago Press, 1961.

Bodde, Derk. "Basic Concepts of Chinese Law: The Genesis and Evolution of Legal Thought in Traditional China." *Proceedings of the American Philosophical Society* 107 (1963): 375.

Bodde, Derk, and Clarence Morris. *Law in Imperial China*. Cambridge, Mass.: Harvard University Press, 1967.

Brockman, Rosser H. "Commercial Contract Law in Late Nineteenth-Century Taiwan." In Jerome Alan Cohen, R. Randle Edwards, and Fu-Mei Chang Chen, eds., *Essays on China's Legal Tradition*, pp. 76–136. Princeton, N.J.: Princeton University Press, 1980.

Brook, Timothy, and B. Michael Frolic. "China and the Future of Civil Society." In Timothy Brook and B. Michael Frolic, eds., *Civil Society in China*, pp. 195–201. Armonk, N.Y.: M. E. Sharpe, 1997.

Bruun, Ole. "Political Hierarchy and Private Entrepreneurship in a Chinese Neighborhood." In Andrew G. Walder, ed., *The Waning of the Communist State*, pp. 184–212. Berkeley: University of California Press, 1995.

Bünger, Karl. "Concluding Remarks on Two Aspects of the Chinese Unitary State as Compared with the European State System." In Stuart R. Schram, ed., *Foundations and Limits of State Power in China*, pp. 313–323. London: School of Oriental and African Studies, 1987.

Bünger, Karl. "Die Rezeption des Europäischen Rechts in China." In Ernst Wolff, ed., *Deutschen Landesreferaten zum III. Internationalen Kongreß für Rechtsvergleichung in London 1950*, pp. 166–189. Berlin-Tübingen, 1950.

Bünger, Karl. "Foreword: The Chinese State Between Yesterday and Tomorrow." In Stuart R. Schram, ed., *The Scope of State Power in China*, pp. xiii–xxv. London: School of Oriental and African Studies, 1985.

Burgess, John Stewart. *The Guilds of Peking*. New York: Columbia University Press, 1928.

Buxbaum, David C. "Chinese Family Law in a Common Law Setting." *Journal of Asian Studies* 25, no. 4 (1966): 621–644.

Byron. "The Office of District Magistrate in China." *Journal of the China Branch, Royal Asiatic Society* 32 (1897–1898): 36–65.

Cabestan, Jean-Pierre. *L'Adminstration Chinoise après Mao: Les Réformes de l'Ere Deng Xiaoping et Leurs Limites*. Paris: Centre National de la Recherche Scientifique, 1992.

Cabestan, Jean-Pierre. "La Transition Politique en Chine Populaire: La Libéralisation Amorcée Peut-Elle Accoucher d'une Démocratisation?" *Revue d'Études Comparatives Est-Ouest* 3 (1997): 95–117.

"Cadres Accused of Violating Law Sentenced to Prison Terms." *JPRS* 76,617 Political, Sociological and Military Affairs, no. 127 (Oct. 14, 1980): 30.

Cai, Dingjian. "Constitutional Supervision and Interpretation in the People's Republic of China." *Journal of Chinese Law* 9, no. 2 (1995): 219–245.

Cai, Dingjian. "Introduction to the Administrative Penalty Law of China." *Columbia Journal of Asian Law* 10 (Spring 1990): 259–262.

"Canton Gradually Develops Notarial Work." *Nanfang ribao* Mar. 9, 1957.

Cao Jianming. "Financial Security and Building of Legal System." *Renmin ribao* June 18, 1998: 10, translated in *FBIS* 98-175 (June 19, 1998) as "China: Article Views Financial Security, Law."

Cao Pei. "Borrowing the Case Law Method to Promote the Construction of the Legal System in Reform." *Renmin ribao* Mar. 3, 1987.

Cao Siyuan. "China's Ailing Courts Need Federalist Medicine." *Asian Wall Street Journal* May 9, 1996.

Cao, Yuanzheng, Yingyi Qian, and Barry R. Weingast. "From Federalism, Chinese Style, to Privatization, Chinese-Style." Unpublished ms. 1997.

Castan, Nicole. "The Arbitration of Disputes under the 'Ancien Regime'." In John Bossy, ed., *Disputes and Settlements: Law and Human Relations in the West*, pp. 219–260. Cambridge: Cambridge University Press, 1983.

"CCP [Chinese Communist Party] Central-South Bureau Calls Conference to Discuss Judicial Reform; Comrade Teng Tzu-Hui Gives Important Instructions." *Nanfang ribao* Sept. 5, 1952, English language translation in *SCMP* 412 (1952): 20.

"CCPCC, State Council Decision on Economic Crimes." *FBIS* (Apr. 14, 1982): K1–K9.

Chang, Chung-Li. *The Chinese Gentry: Studies on Their Role in Nineteenth-Century Chinese Society.* Seattle: University of Washington Press, 1955.

Chang, Gordon G. "GITIC Lenders Learn the Value of Compliance with Foreign Exchange Rules." *China Law and Practice* 12, no. 10 (1998/1999): 21–22, 25–27.

Chang Hong. "Law Gives the People Power to Sue Officials." *China Daily* Sept. 28, 1990.

Chang, Phyllis. "Deciding Disputes: Factors That Guide Chinese Courts in the Adjudication of Rural Responsibility Contract Disputes." *Law and Contemporary Problems* 52, no. 3 (1989): 101–142.

Chang, Ta-kuang. "The Making of the Chinese Bankruptcy Law: A Study in the Chinese Legislative Process." *Harvard International Law Journal* 28, no. 2 (1987): 333–372.

Chang Wejen. "Traditional Chinese Attitudes Toward Law and Authority." Paper presented at the Symposium on Chinese and European Concepts of Law, Mar. 20–25, 1986, organized by the University of Hong Kong, the Goethe-Institut, and the Hong Kong Arts Centre.

Chang Zhen. "The Continued Existence of People's Mediation Committees Is Not Necessary." *Guangming ribao* July 16, 1956.

Chao, Howard, and Yang Xiaoping. "Private Enterprise in China: The Developing Law of Collective Enterprises." *International Lawyer* 19, no. 4 (1985): 1215–1237.

Chen, Albert H. Y. "The Developing Theory of Law and Market Economy in Contemporary China." In Wang Guiguo and Wei Zhenying, eds., *Legal Developments in China: Market Economy and Law*, pp. 3–20. Hong Kong: Sweet and Maxwell, 1996.

Chen, Albert H. Y. *An Introduction to the Legal System of the People's Republic of China.* Singapore: Butterworths Asia, 1992.

Chen, Fu-mei Chang, and Ramon H. Myers. "Customary Law and the Economic Growth of China During the Ch'ing Period (Part 1)." *Ch'ing-shih wen-t'i* 3, no. 5 (1976): 1–32.

Chen, Fu-mei Chang, and Ramon H. Myers. "Customary Law and the Economic

Growth of China During the Ch'ing Period (Part 2)." *Ch'ing-shih wen-t'i* 3, no. 10 (1978): 4–27.

Chen Guanhua. "The Experience of the People's Mediation Committee of San-huai Village." *Guangming ribao* Mar. 29, 1955.

Chen, Jianfu. *From Administrative Authorisation to Private Law: A Comparative Perspective of the Developing Civil Law in the People's Republic of China.* Dordrecht, Netherlands: Martinus Nijhoff, 1995.

Chen, Kathy. "China's Press and Politics Show a Little Gumption as Reforms Speed Up." *Wall Street Journal* Jan. 22, 1998.

Chen Pengsheng. "Meiyou falü de zhengzhi shi weixian de zhengzhi" (Politics Without Law Is Dangerous Politics). *Faxue* 1 (1987): 2–3.

Chen, Tung-pi. "The Chinese Notariat: An Overlooked Cornerstone of the Legal System of the People's Republic of China." *International and Comparative Law Quarterly* 35 (1986): 63–86.

Cheng, Chu-yuan. *Science and Engineering Manpower in Communist China, 1949–1963.* Washington, D.C.: National Science Foundation, 1965.

Cheng, Lucie, and Arthur Rosett. "Contract with a Chinese Face: Socially Embedded Factors in the Transformation from Hierarchy to Market, 1978–1989." *Journal of Chinese Law* 5, no. 2 (1991): 143–244.

Ch'ien Tuan-Sheng. *The Government and Politics of China.* Cambridge, Mass.: Harvard University Press, 1961.

Childs, John. "Exercising Strong Direction." *Financial Times* Nov. 6, 1995.

China 2020: Development Challenges in the New Century. Washington, D.C.: World Bank, 1997.

"'China and the World Trading System': WTO Director-General's Speech at Beijing University." Speech delivered on Apr. 21, 1997. Full text available at http://www.wto.org/wto/press/chipress.htm.

"China Campaigns to Enforce Laws." *China Law for Business* 2, no. 5 (1996): 16.

"China: Beijing Judicial Officials Punished for Corruption." *Xinhua* July 29, 1998, *FBIS* 98-216 (Aug. 4, 1998).

"China: Circular Bans Businesses in Judicial Administration." *Xinhua* July 31, 1998, *FBIS* 98-217 (Aug. 5, 1998).

"China: Civil Mediation System Ensures Harmony in Shanghai." *Xinhua, FBIS* 98-121 (May 1, 1998).

"China Enacts Constitutional Amendments to Entrench Private Business, Rule of Law." *Xinhua* Mar. 16, 1999, in BBC-SWB (Mar. 18, 1999).

"China: Guangxi Senior Judge Jailed for Accepting Bribes." *Xinhua,* July 15, 1998, *FBIS* 98-196 (July 15, 1998).

China Law Reports 1991 Vol. 2, Civil Law. Singapore: Butterworths Asia, 1995.

China Law Reports 1991 Vol. 3, Administrative Law, Economic Law. Singapore: Butterworths Asia, 1995.

"China: Leaders Attend Opening of National Judges College." *FBIS* 97-314 (Nov. 10, 1997).

"China: PRC Administrative Supervision Law." *FBIS* 97-091 (May 9, 1997).

"China: Protectionism Rampant in Legal Enforcement." *FBIS* 97-044 (Feb. 17,

1997), a translation of "Resolutely Eliminate Local and Departmental Protectionism in Law Enforcement." *Liaowang* 7 (Feb. 17, 1997): 4–6.

"China: Regulations on Criminal Procedure Law." *Xinhua*, Jan. 19, 1998, *FBIS* 98-021 (Jan. 21, 1998).

"China: Supreme Court's New Measures to Curb Judicial Corruption." *Xinhua* Sept. 17, 1998, *FBIS* 98-260 (Sept. 17, 1998).

"China to Handle Foreign-Funded Enterprise Disputes in China." *Xinhua* Apr. 10, 1998.

"China to Shut Down Unapproved Foreign-Funded Retail Sector Businesses." *Xinhua* Nov. 14, 1997.

"China: Township Enterprises Report." *FBIS* 97-081 (Apr. 23, 1997).

"China's Diaspora Turns Homeward." *Economist* Nov. 27, 1993: 33–34.

China's Management of Enterprise Assets: The State as Shareholder. Washington, D.C.: World Bank, 1997.

"Chinese Discover Product-Liability Suits." *Wall Street Journal* Nov. 13, 1997.

Chome, Jules. "Two Trials in the People's Republic of China." *Law in the Service of Peace: Review of Contemporary Law* (June 1956): 163.

Chu, Godwin C., and Yanan Ju. *The Great Wall in Ruins: Communication and Cultural Change in China.* Albany: State University of New York Press, 1993.

Ch'ü, T'ung-Tsu. "Book Review." *Pacific Affairs* 35 (1962–63): 396–397.

Ch'ü, T'ung-Tsu. *Law and Society in Traditional China.* The Hague: Mouton, 1961.

Ch'ü, T'ung-Tsu. *Local Government in China under the Ch'ing.* Cambridge, Mass.: Harvard University Press, 1962.

"Circular Implements Administrative Procedure Law." *FBIS* (Jan. 24, 1990): 12.

"Circular of the Supreme People's Court on Strengthening the Economic Trial Work." In *China Law Yearbook* 1987, pp. 428–431. London: Butterworths, 1989.

"Civil Mediators Successful in Beijing." *Xinhua* Nov. 19, 1990.

"Civil Procedure Law (for Trial Implementation) of the People's Republic of China." BBC-SWB (Mar. 17, 1982).

"Civil Procedure Law of the People's Republic of China." Adopted Apr. 9, 1991. *CCH* ¶ 19–201.

Clanchy, Michael. "Law and Love in the Middle Ages." In John Bossy, ed., *Disputes and Settlements: Law and Human Relations in the West*, pp. 47–67. Cambridge: Cambridge University Press, 1983.

Clarke, Donald C. "Dispute Resolution in China." *Journal of Chinese Law* 5 (1991): 245–296.

Clarke, Donald C. "Power and Politics in the Chinese Court System: The Enforcement of Civil Judgments." *Columbia Journal of Asian Law* 10, no. 1 (1996): 1–92.

Clarke, Donald C., and James V. Feinerman. "Antagonistic Contradictions: Criminal Law and Human Rights in China." In Stanley B. Lubman, ed., *China's Legal Reforms*, pp. 135–154. Oxford: Oxford University Press, 1996.

Clarke, Donald C., and Nicolas C. Howson. "Developing P.R.C. Property and Real Estate Law: Revised Land Registration Rules; How They'll Affect Foreign Investors, Lenders, and Real Estate Developers." *East Asian Executive Reports* 18, no. 4 (Apr. 15, 1996): 9–17.

"Closely Relying on the Masses, Do People's Judicial Work Well; An-Shen Ward Mediation Small Group Acquires Preliminary Successful Experience." *Jiefang ribao* (Shanghai) Oct. 29, 1952.

Clymer, Adam. "Gephardt Will Denounce Trade Policy Toward China." *New York Times* May 27, 1997: D11.

Cohen, Jerome A. "Chinese Mediation on the Eve of Modernization." *California Law Review* 54, no. 3 (1966): 1201–1226.

Cohen, Jerome A. *The Criminal Process in the People's Republic of China, 1949–1963: An Introduction.* Cambridge, Mass.: Harvard University Press, 1968.

Cohen, Jerome A. "Due Process?" In Ross Terrill, ed., *The China Difference*, pp. 237–259. New York: Harper and Row, 1979.

Cohen, Jerome A. "Reforming China's Civil Procedure: Judging the Courts." *American Journal of Comparative Law* 45 (1997): 793–804.

Cohen, Paul A. *Discovering History in China: American Historical Writing on the Recent Chinese Past.* New York: Columbia University Press, 1984.

Cohen, Paul A. "The Post-Mao Reforms in Historical Perspective." *Journal of Asian Studies* 47, no. 3 (1988): 519–540.

Cohen, Roberta. "People's Republic of China: The Human Rights Exception." *Human Rights Quarterly* 9, no. 4 (1987): 447–549.

"Commentary on Applying Hong Kong, Foreign Laws." *Xinhua* Dec. 22, 1988, in *FBIS* 88-251 (Dec. 30, 1988): 25–26.

"Commentator on Market Economy, Legal System." Translated from "The Market Economy Is an Economy Based on the Legal System." *Fazhi ribao* Nov. 2, 1992, in *FBIS* 92-227 (Nov. 24, 1992): 31.

"Commercial Finance in Communist China." *JPRS* 19,698 (June 17, 1963).

Commission on Extra-Territoriality in China. *Report of the Commission on Extraterritoriality in China.* Shanghai: Commercial Press, 1926.

"Communist Party Committee of May 3 Factory, How Does the Party Committee Exercise Stronger Leadership Over the Trade Unions?" *Gongren ribao* Sept. 19, 1961, English language translation in *SCMP* 2,602 (1961): 4.

"Community Mediators Heal Family Discord." *Xinhua* Mar. 3, 1989.

"Company Law of the People's Republic of China." Adopted Dec. 29, 1993. *CCH* ¶ 13–516.

"Comrade Ma Xiwu's New Method of Judging." *Jiefang ribao* (Yenan) Mar. 13, 1944.

"Concepts of Law in the Chinese Anti-Crime Campaign." *Harvard Law Review* 98, no. 8 (1985): 1890–1908.

Conner, Alison W. "Lawyers and the Legal Profession During the Republican Period." In Kathryn Bernhardt and Philip C. Huang, eds., *Civil Law in Qing and Republican China*, pp. 215–248. Stanford: Stanford University Press, 1994.

"Constitution of the People's Republic of China." Adopted on Dec. 4, 1982. *CCH* ¶ 4–500.

"Contract Law of the People's Republic of China," *Fazhi ribao* Mar. 22, 1999.

Corne, Peter Howard. *Foreign Investment in China: The Administrative Legal System.* Hong Kong: Hong Kong University Press, 1996.

Corne, Peter. "Legal System Reforms Promise Substantive—But Limited—Improvement." *China Law and Practice* 11, no. 5 (1997): 29–34.

"Correctly Develop People's Mediation Work, Short Comment." *Guangming ribao* Mar. 22, 1954.

Cotterell, Roger. *The Sociology of Law: An Introduction*. London: Butterworths, 1984.

"Criminal Law Expert on Wei Jingsheng Case." *Xinhua* Dec. 29, 1996, in *FBIS* 96-001 (Jan. 2, 1996): 24–25.

"Criminal Law of the People's Republic of China." Adopted July 1, 1979, effective Jan. 1, 1980, translated by Jerome Alan Cohen, Timothy A. Gelatt, and Florence M. Li in *Journal of Criminal Law and Criminology* 73, no. 1 (1982): 138–170.

"Criminal Procedure Law of the People's Republic of China." Adopted July 1, 1979, effective Jan. 1, 1980, translated by Jerome Alan Cohen, Timothy A. Gelatt, and Florence M. Li in *Journal of Criminal Law and Criminology* 73, no. 1 (1982): 171–203. For the Criminal Procedure Law as revised on Mar. 17, 1996, see *Renmin ribao* Mar. 25, 1996, in *FBIS* (Apr. 9. 1996): 24, also in "Amended Criminal Procedure Law." *Xinhua* Mar. 23, 1996, in BBC-SWB Apr. 16, 1996.

Croll, Elisabeth. *From Heaven to Earth: Images and Experiences of Development in China*. London: Routledge, 1994.

Cui Chengxuan. "Women shi zenme yang baowei xingfu renmin gongshe de anquan" (How We Safeguarded the Security of the Welfare People's Commune). *Zhengfa yanjiu* 6 (1958): 61–63, translated in *JPRS* 813-D (1959): 34–38.

Damaska, Mirjan R. *The Faces of Justice and State Authority: A Comparative Approach to the Legal Process*. New Haven, Conn.: Yale University Press, 1986.

Dawson, John P. *A History of Lay Judges*. Cambridge, Mass.: Harvard University Press: 1960.

"Decision of the National People's Congress on the Revision of the 'Criminal Procedure Law of the People's Republic of China'." Adopted Mar. 17, 1996. *Renmin ribao* Mar. 24, 1996: 2.

"Decision of the Standing Committee of the National People's Congress Concerning the Procedure for the Rapid Adjudication of Criminals Elements Who Seriously Endanger Social Order." Adopted Sept. 2, 1983.

"Decision of the Standing Committee of the National People's Congress Concerning the Question of the Time Limits for Handling Criminal Cases." Adopted Sept. 10, 1981.

"Decision of the Standing Committee of the National People's Congress on the Question of the Implementation of the Criminal Procedure Law." Adopted Feb. 12, 1980.

"Decision of the State Council of the PRC Relating to Problems of Rehabilitation Through Labor, Aug. 1, 1957, *FGHB* 6: 243, translated in Jerome A. Cohen, ed., *The Criminal Process in the People's Republic of China, 1949–1963: An Introduction*, pp. 249–250. Cambridge, Mass.: Harvard University Press, 1968.

"Decision on Mediation of Cases by District Offices (Draft)." June 1, 1944. In Jinzhaqi bianqu xingzheng weiyuanhui (Jinzhaqi Border District Administrative Committee), *Xianxing faling huiji* (Collected Current Laws and Decrees) 1: 323. Jinzhaqi: Jinzhaqi bianqu xingzheng weiyuanhui, 1945–1946.

Deng Xiaoping. "Emancipate the Mind, Seek the Truth from Facts and Unite as One in Looking to the Future." In *Selected Works of Deng Xiaoping (1975–1982)*, pp. 157–158. Beijing: Foreign Languages Press, 1984.

Deng Xiaoping. *Selected Works of Deng Xiaoping (1975–1982)*. Beijing: Foreign Languages Press, 1984.

"Deng Xiaoping on Upholding the Four Cardinal Principles and Combating Bourgeois Liberalization." *Beijing Review* (July 17–23, 1989).

Deng Zhanming. "On Economic Cooperation Between Industrial Enterprises." *Jingji yanjiu* 3 (1965): 19, in *JPRS* 31,034 (1965): 38–45.

Deng Zhixiu. "Yuejin zhong de anhui renmin tiaochu gongzuo" (People's Adjustment Work in Anhui During the Leap Forward). *Zhengfa yanjiu* 2 (1960): 33–36.

Department of Grass-Roots Work, Ministry of Justice. *People's Mediation in China.* Beijing: Department of Grass-Roots Work, Ministry of Justice, c. 1991.

Dernberger, Robert F. "China's Mixed Economic System: Properties and Consequences." In *China's Economic Dilemmas in the 1990s: The Problems of Reforms, Modernization, and Interdependence, Study Papers Submitted to the Joint Economic Committee, Congress of the United States* 1: 89–101. Washington, D.C.: Government Printing Office, 1991.

Dernberger, Robert F. "China's Transition to a Market Economy: Back to the Future, Mired in the Present, or Through the Looking Glass to the Market Economy?" In *China's Economic Future: Challenges to U.S. Policy, Study Papers Submitted to the Joint Economic Committee, Congress of the United States*, pp. 57–69. Washington, D.C.: Government Printing Office, 1996.

"Detained HK Man Vows to Clear Name." *South China Morning Post* Oct. 11, 1993.

Dicks, Anthony. "The Chinese Legal System: Reforms in the Balance." *China Quarterly* 119 (1989): 540–576.

Dicks, Anthony. "Compartmentalized Law and Judicial Restraint: An Inductive View of Some Jurisdictional Barriers to Reform." In Stanley B. Lubman, ed., *China's Legal Reforms*, pp. 82–109. Oxford: Oxford University Press, 1996.

"Distribution Is It." *Business China* 23, no. 9 (Apr. 28, 1997): 12.

"Do Well People's Mediation Work to Strengthen the People's Solidarity and Facilitate Production and Construction." *Renmin ribao* Mar. 23, 1954, English language translation in *SCMP* 784 (Apr. 8, 1954): 12–15.

Dolinsky, Lewis. "Albright Defends China Policy in S.F. Appearance." *San Francisco Chronicle* June 25, 1997: A9.

Donnelly, Richard J., Joseph Goldstein, and Richard D. Schwartz. *Criminal Law: Theory and Process.* New York: Free Press, 1962.

Donnithorne, Audrey. *China's Economic System.* New York: Praeger, 1967.

Doolittle, Justus. *Social Life of the Chinese: With Some Account of the Religious, Governmental, Educational and Business Customs and Opinions.* New York: Harper, 1865.

Douglas, Robert Kenneway. *Society in China.* London: A. D. Innes, 1901.

Dowdle, Michael W. "The Constitutional Development and Operations of the

National People's Congress." *Columbia Journal of Asian Law* 11, no. 1 (1997): 1–125.

"Draft Protocol on China." *Inside U.S. Trade* (March 14, 1997): S2–S7.

Dull, Jack L. "The Evolution of Government in China." In Paul S. Ropp, ed., *Heritage of China: Contemporary Perspectives on Chinese Civilization*, pp. 55–85. Berkeley: University of California Press, 1990.

Eckholm, Erik. "China Sentences 3 for Their Dissent." *New York Times* Dec. 22, 1998: A1.

Eckholm, Erik. "Chinese Book on Political Reform Stirs Hopes for More Debate." *New York Times* Aug. 25, 1998: A5.

Eckholm, Erik. "In Drive on Dissidents, China Gives 4th Severe Sentence in Week." *New York Times* Dec. 28, 1998: A9.

Eckholm, Erik. "New China Leader Promises Reforms for Every Sector." *New York Times* Mar. 20, 1998: A1.

"Economic Contract Law of the People's Republic of China." Adopted Dec. 13, 1981, amended Sept. 2, 1993. *CCH* ¶ 5–500.

Economy, Elizabeth. *The Case Study of China, Reform and Resources: The Implications for State Capacity in the PRC*. Cambridge, Mass.: Committee on International Security Studies, American Academy of Arts and Sciences, 1997.

Edwards, R. Randle. "Ch'ing Legal Jurisdiction Over Foreigners." In Jerome Alan Cohen, R. Randle Edwards, and Fu-Mei Chang Chen, eds., *Essays on China's Legal Tradition*, pp. 222–269. Princeton, N.J.: Princeton University Press, 1980.

Edwards, R. Randle. "Civil and Social Rights: Theory and Practice in Chinese Law Today." In R. Randle Edwards, Louis Henkin, and Andrew J. Nathan, *Human Rights in Contemporary China*, pp. 41–75, 167–171. New York: Columbia University Press, 1986.

Edwards, R. Randle, Louis Henkin, and Andrew J. Nathan. *Human Rights in Contemporary China*. New York: Columbia University Press, 1986.

Ellickson, Robert C. *Order Without Law: How Neighbors Settle Disputes*. Cambridge, Mass.: Harvard University Press, 1991.

Elton, G. R. *F. W. Maitland*. London: Weidenfeld and Nicolson, 1985.

Epstein, Edward J. "Law and Legitimation in Post-Mao China." In Pitman B. Potter, ed., *Domestic Law Reforms in Post-Mao China*, pp. 19–55. Armonk, N.Y.: M. E. Sharpe, 1994.

Epstein, Edward J. "The Theoretical System of Property Rights in China's *General Principles of Civil Law*: Theoretical Controversy in the Drafting Process and Beyond." *Law and Contemporary Problems* 52, no. 2 (1989): 177–216.

Epstein, Edward J. "Tortious Liability for Defective Products in the People's Republic of China." *Journal of Chinese Law* 2 (1988): 285–321.

Epstein, Edward J., ed. "Legal Documents and Materials on Administrative Detention in the People's Republic of China." Special edition of *Chinese Law and Government* 27, no. 5 (1994).

Epstein, Edward J., and Ye Lin. "Individual Enterprise in Contemporary Urban China: A Legal Analysis of Status and Regulation." *International Lawyer* 21, no. 2 (1987): 397–436.

Escarra, Jean. *Le Droit Chinois*. Paris: Librairie du Recueil Sirey, 1936.

Exner, Mechtild. "The Convergence of Ideology and the Law: The Functions of the Legal Education Campaign in Building a Chinese Legal System." *Issues and Studies* 31, no. 8 (1995): 68–102.

Fainsod, Merle. "Bureaucracy and Modernization: The Russian and Soviet Case." In Joseph LaPalombara, ed., *Bureaucracy and Political Development*, pp. 233–267. Princeton, N.J.: Princeton University Press, 1963.

Faison, Seth. "A Great Tiptoe Forward: Free Enterprise in China." *New York Times* Sept. 17, 1997: 3.

Faison, Seth. "E-Mail to U.S. Lands Chinese Internet Entrepreneur in Jail." *New York Times* Jan. 21, 1999: A10.

Faison, Seth. "Razors, Soap, Cornflakes: Pirating Spreads to China." *New York Times* Feb. 17, 1995.

Fallon, Richard H., Jr. "'The Rule of Law' as a Concept in Constitutional Discourse." *Columbia Law Review* 97, no. 1 (1997): 1–56.

Fan Zhen. "An Interview with Tsingtao Legal Office." *Renmin ribao* Feb. 22, 1957, in *SCMP* 1,490 (Mar. 15, 1957): 11–13.

Fang Chengzhi. "Renmin fayuan zai guojia jigou zhong de diwei" (The Position of the People's Courts Within the Government Structure). *Faxue zazhi* 4 (1985): 15–16.

Fang Liufang. "China's Corporatization Experiment." *Duke Journal of Comparative and International Law* 5 (Spring 1995): 149–269.

Fazhi gongzuo weiyuanhui xingfa shi (Criminal Law Section, Legal Affairs Committee of the National People's Congress). "Zuigao renmin fayuan, zuigao renmin jianchayuan, gonganbu he sifabu dui xingshi susong fa xiugai de yijian" (Opinions of the Supreme People's Court, the Supreme People's Procuracy, the Public Security Ministry and the Ministry of Justice on Revision of the Criminal Procedure Law). June 19, 1995. This memorandum summarizes the views of participants in a conference held from Mar. 25 to Apr. 24, 1995, copy in the author's files.

Feinerman, James V. "Backwards into the Future." *Law and Contemporary Problems* 52, no. 3 (1989): 169–184.

Feinerman, James V. "Chinese Law Relating to Foreign Investment and Trade: The Decade of Reform in Retrospect." In *China's Economic Dilemmas in the 1990s: The Problems of Reforms, Modernization, and Interdependence, Study Papers Submitted to the Joint Economic Committee, Congress of the United States* 2: 828–840. Washington, D.C.: Government Printing Office, 1991.

Feinerman, James V. "Chinese Participation in the International Legal Order: Rogue Elephant or Team Player." In Stanley B. Lubman, ed., *China's Legal Reforms*, pp. 186–210. Oxford: Oxford University Press, 1996.

Feinerman, James V. "The Dian Transaction: Family, Property and Violence in China." Unpublished ms.

Feinerman, James V. "Legal Institution, Administrative Device, or Foreign Import: The Roles of Contract in the People's Republic of China." In Pitman B. Potter, ed., *Domestic Law Reforms in Post-Mao China*, pp. 225–244. Armonk, N.Y.: M. E. Sharpe, 1994.

Feng, Peter. "Review: China Law Reports (1991)." *Hong Kong Law Journal* 26, part 2 (1996): 268–273.

Fewsmith, Joseph. "Neoconservatism and the End of the Dengist Era." *Asian Survey* 35, no. 7 (1995): 635–651.

"Fighting Economic Crimes." *Beijing Review* Feb. 22, 1982: 3.

Finder, Susan. "Inside the People's Courts: China's Litigation System and the Resolution of Commercial Disputes." In *Dispute Resolution in the PRC: A Practical Guide to Litigation and Arbitration in China*, pp. 63–73. N.p.: Asia Law and Practice, n.d.

Finder, Susan. "Like Throwing an Egg Against a Stone? Administrative Litigation in the People's Republic of China." *Journal of Chinese Law* 3, no. 1 (1987): 1–28.

Finder, Susan. "The Supreme People's Court of the People's Republic of China." *Journal of Chinese Law* 7 (1993): 145–224.

Finder, Susan, and Fu Hualing. "Tightening Up Chinese Courts' 'Bags'—The Amended 'PRC, Criminal Law'." *China Law and Practice* 11, no. 5 (1997): 35–38.

"Firmly Put into Effect the Spirit of the Masses Dealing with Cases: Court Pairs with Mediation Small Groups in Nationally Owned No. 5 Cotton Mill to Handle More than Thirty Accumulated Cases." *Xinwen ribao* Nov. 19, 1952.

"Firms Seek Official Help to Extend Duty Exemptions." *China Joint Venturer* 2, no. 2 (1996): 7–9, 20.

Force, Robert, and Xia Chen. "An Introduction to Personal Injury and Death Claims in the People's Republic of China." *The Maritime Lawyer* 15 (1991): 245–283.

"Foreign Economic Contract Law of the People's Republic of China." Adopted Mar. 21, 1985. *Jingji ribao* Mar. 22, 1985. Translated in *East Asian Executive Reports* May 1985: 27–29. CCH ¶ 5–550.

Forney, Matt. "Patriot Games." *Far Eastern Economic Review* Oct. 3, 1996.

Francis, Corinna-Barbara. "Reproduction of Danwei Institutional Features in the Context of China's Market Economy: The Case of Haidian District's High-Tech Sector." *China Quarterly* 147 (1996): 839–859.

Frankenberg, Gunter. "Critical Comparisons: Re-Thinking Comparative Law." *Harvard Journal of International Law* 26 (1985): 411–485.

Freedman, Maurice. *Lineage Organization in Southeastern China*. London: Athlone Press, 1958.

Fried, Morton H. *The Fabric of Chinese Society: A Study of the Social Life of a Chinese County Seat*. New York: Praeger, 1953.

Fried, Morton H. "Some Political Aspects of Clanship in a Modern Chinese City." In Mark J. Swartz, Victor W. Turner, and Arthur Tuden, eds., *Political Anthropology*, pp. 285–300. Chicago: Aldine, 1966.

Friedman, Lawrence M. "The Concept of Legal Culture: A Reply." In David Nelken, ed., *Comparing Legal Cultures*, pp. 33–39. Brookfield, Vt.: Dartmouth, 1997.

Friedman, Lawrence M. *The Legal System: A Social Science Perspective*. New York: Russell Sage, 1975.

Friedman, Lawrence M. *The Republic of Choice: Law, Authority, and Culture*. Cambridge, Mass.: Harvard University Press, 1990.

Friedman, Lawrence M. "The Rule of Law, Modernization, and the Judiciary." Lectures prepared for delivery in China, June 1997, ms.

Friedman, Lawrence M. *Total Justice*. Boston: Beacon, 1985.

Friedman, Thomas L. "Rethinking China, Part II." *New York Times* Mar. 6, 1996.

Friedmann, W. *Legal Theory*. London: Stevens, 1953.

Fu, H. L. "Criminal Defence in China: The Possible Impact of the 1996 Criminal Procedural Law Reform." *China Quarterly* 153 (1998): 31–48.

Fu Hualing. "A Bird in the Cage: Police and Political Leadership in Post-Mao China." *Policing and Society* 4 (1994): 277–291.

Fu Hualing. "Understanding People's Mediation in Post-Mao China." *Journal of Chinese Law* 6, no. 2 (Fall 1992): 211–246.

"Fujian Government Issues Circular on Smuggling." *FBIS* (Feb. 3, 1981): P3.

"Full Text of Jiang Zemin's Report at 15th Party Congress" (speech delivered by Jiang Zemin at the 15th National Congress of the Communist Party of China on Sept. 12, 1997). *Xinhua* Sept. 21, 1997.

Galanter, Marc. "Adjudication, Litigation and Related Phenomena." In Leon Lipson and Stanton Wheeler, eds., *Law and the Social Sciences*, pp. 151–259. New York: Russell Sage, 1986.

Gallin, Bernard. "Conflict Resolution in Changing Chinese Society: A Taiwanese Study." In Mark J. Swartz, Victor W. Turner, and Arthur Tuden, eds., *Political Anthropology*, pp. 265–274. Chicago: Aldine, 1966.

Gallin, Bernard. *Hsin Hsing, Taiwan: A Chinese Village in Change*. Berkeley: University of California Press, 1966.

Gamble, Sidney D. *North Chinese Villages: Social, Political, and Economic Activities Before 1933*. Berkeley: University of California Press, 1963.

Gamble, Sidney D. *Ting Hsien: A North China Rural Community*. New York: International Secretariat, Institute of Pacific Relations, 1954.

Gamble, Sidney D., with John Stewart Burgess. *Peking: A Social Survey Conducted Under the Auspices of the Princeton University Center in China and the Peking Young Men's Christian Association*. New York: George H. Doran, 1921.

Gao Hongjun. "Zhongguo gongmin quanli yishi de yanjiang" (Lecture on Chinese Citizens' Rights Consciousness). In Xia Yong, ed., *Zou xiang quanli de shidai: Zhongguo gongmin quanli fazhan yanjiu* (Toward a Time of Rights: A Perspective of the Civil Rights Development in China), pp. 3–68. Beijing: Zhongguo zhengfa daxue chubanshe, 1995.

Gao Zongze. "Zhongguo lüshi shi renmin de lüshi: Gao Zongze lüshi zai quanguo youxiu lüshi shiji baogaotuan de yanjiang (Chinese Lawyers Are People's Lawyers: Gao Zongze's Speech before the National Outstanding Model Lawyer Report Group)." *Zhongguo lüshi* (Chinese Lawyer) 3 (1997): 18–19.

Geertz, Clifford. "Thick Description: Toward an Interpretive Theory of Culture." In Clifford Geertz, *The Interpretation of Cultures*, pp. 1–30. New York: Basic, 1973.

"Gelatt Forum Addresses Foreign Investment and Legal Culture." *NYU: The Law School Magazine* (Autumn 1998): 76.

Gelatt, Timothy A. "Lawyers in China: The Past Decade and Beyond." *Journal of International Law and Politics* 23, no. 3 (1991): 751–799.

Gelatt, Timothy A. "The People's Republic of China and the Presumption of Innocence." *Journal of Criminal Law and Criminology* 73, no. 1 (1982): 259–316.

Gelatt, Timothy A., and Frederick E. Snyder. "Legal Education in China: Training for a New Era." *China Law Reporter* 1, no. 2 (1980): 41–60.

"General Condition of Judicial Work in T'ai-Hang District." A translation by Wallace Douglass of the 1946 "Taihang qu sifa gongzuo gaikuang." *Chinese Law and Government* 6, no. 3 (1973): 7–100.

"General Principles of Civil Law of the People's Republic of China." Adopted Apr. 12, 1986, effective Jan. 1, 1987. In *CCH* ¶ 19–150. Also appears translated by W. Grey and H. Zheng, *American Journal of Comparative Law* 34 (1986): 715–743.

Gernet, Jacques. "Introduction." In Stuart R. Schram, ed., *Foundations and Limits of State Power in China*, pp. xv–xxvii. London: School of Oriental and African Studies, 1987.

Gigot, Paul. "Engaging China Doesn't Have to Mean 'Coddling'." *Wall Street Journal* Feb. 21, 1997.

Gilley, Bruce. "Rough Justice: Executions Surge in Tough Anti-Crime Drive." *Far Eastern Economic Review* July 4, 1996: 22–24.

Glendon, Mary Ann. "The Sources of Law in a Changing Legal Order." In Mary Ann Glendon, Michael Wallace Gordon, and Christopher Osakwe, eds., *Comparative Legal Traditions: Texts, Materials and Cases on the Civil Law, Common Law and Socialist Law Traditions, with Special Reference to French, West German, English and Soviet Law*, pp. 232–241. St. Paul, Minn.: West, 1985.

Glendon, Mary Ann, Michael Wallace Gordon, and Christopher Osakwe, eds. *Comparative Legal Traditions: Texts, Materials and Cases on the Civil Law, Common Law and Socialist Law Traditions, with Special Reference to French, West German, English and Soviet Law.* St. Paul, Minn.: West, 1985.

Goldstein, Steven M. "China in Transition: The Political Foundations of Incremental Reform." *China Quarterly* 144 (1995): 1105–1131.

"Gongren Ribao Article on Freedom of Speech." *FBIS* 81-060 (Mar. 30, 1981): L13–L16. Translation of Zhu Jiamu, "Correctly Understand and Exercise the Right to Freedom of Speech." *Gongren ribao* Mar. 16, 1981: 3.

Gongshang xingzheng guanli xingzheng zhifa guifan (Standards for the Administrative Upholding of Law Within the Administration and Management of Industry and Commerce). Beijing: Gongshang chubanshe, 1996.

Goodman, David S. G. "Democracy, Interest and Virtue: The Search for Legitimacy in the People's Republic of China." In Stuart R. Schram, ed., *Foundations and Limits of State Power in China*, pp. 291–312. London: School of Oriental and African Studies University of London, 1987.

Gordon, Robert. "Critical Legal Histories." *Stanford Law Review* 36, no. 1 (1984): 57–125.

"Government by Law and an Open China." *China Daily* Nov. 5, 1988: 4.

Gray, John Henry. *China: A History of the Laws, Manners and Customs of the People.* London: Macmillan, 1878.

Gray, Whitmore, and Henry Ruiheng Zheng, trans. "Opinion (for Trial Use) of the Supreme People's Court on Questions Concerning the Implementation of the *General Principles of Civil Law of the People's Republic of China*." Adopted Jan. 26, 1988, effective Jan. 1, 1987. *Law and Contemporary Problems* 52, no. 2 (1989): 59–87.

Greene, Felix. *Awakened China: The Country Americans Don't Know*. Garden City, N.Y.: Doubleday, 1961.

Gu, Minkang, and Robert C. Art. "Securitization of State Ownership: Chinese Securities Law." *Michigan Journal of International Law* 18, no. 1 (1996): 115–139.

Guan Datong. "On the System of Contracts for the Exchange of Industrial and Agricultural Products." *Renmin ribao* Mar. 9, 1962, in *SCMP* 2,704 (1962): 11–15.

"Guangming Ribao on Dismissal as Punishment." *FBIS* (Dec. 24, 1980): L21.

"Guangzhou Teams to Arbitrate Land Disputes." *Guangzhou ribao* May 15, 1993, in *FBIS* 93-098 (May 24, 1993): 68.

"Guanyu chachu liyong hetong jinxing de weifa xingwei de zanxing guiding" (Temporary Regulations on the Investigation and Handling of Illegal Behavior Undertaken Utilizing Contracts). Promulgated by the SAIC Ministry, Nov. 17, 1995.

"Guojia gongshang xingzheng guanli ju guanyu guanche luoshi 'Guowu yuan bangong ting zhuanfa guojia gongshang xingzheng guanli ju guanyu zai quanguo zhubu tuixing jingji hetong shifan wenben zhidu qingshi de tongzhi' de yijian" (State Administration of Industry and Commerce Opinion on Thoroughly Implementing the 'State Council Office Notice in Response to the State Administration of Industry and Commerce's Request for Explanation of the Gradual Nationwide Promotion of the System of Economic Contract Forms'). Issued May 24, 1990. In Zhang Shouqiang, ed., *Zhonghua renmin gongheguo hetong fagui yu hetong geshi quanshu* (Encyclopedia of PRC Contract Regulations and Contract Forms), pp. 5–6. Harbin: Harbin Press, 1993.

"Guojia gongshang xingzheng guanli ju guanyu yifa yanli chachu liyong jingji hetong jinxing qizha de weifa xingwei de tongzhi" (Notice of the SAIC on Rigorously and According to Law Investigating and Handling Illegal Behavior of Committing Fraud Utilizing Economic Contracts). Mar. 17, 1995.

"Guowuyuan bangongting guanyu guanche shishi 'Zhonghua renmin gongheguo zhongcai fa' xuyao mingque de jige wenti de tongzhi" (Circular of the General Office of the State Council on Certain Issues to Be Clarified on Implementing the 'Arbitration Act of the People's Republic of China'). *Guowuyuan gongbao* (Gazette of the State Council of the People's Republic of China) 18 (July 9, 1996): 701–702.

"Guowuyuan guanyu laodong jiaoyang de buchong guiding" (Supplementary Rules of the State Council on Re-education through Labour), Oct. 29, 1979. In *Zhonghua renmin gongheguo falü quanshu* (Collection of the Laws of the People's Republic of China), p. 1574. Changchun: Jilin renmin chubanshe, 1989.

Gup, Ted. "Granny as Big Brother." *Far Eastern Economic Review* Aug. 17, 1989: 34.

Guthrie, Douglas. "The Declining Significance of Guanxi in China's Economic Transition." *China Quarterly* 154 (1998): 254–282.

Gutteridge, Harold Cooke. *Comparative Law: An Introduction to the Comparative Method of Legal Study and Research*. Cambridge: Cambridge University Press, [2nd ed.] 1949.

"Haideng County's More Than Four Hundred Mediation Committee Members: The Good Consequences of Helping the Masses Settle Disputes." *Fujian ribao* Dec. 4, 1956.

Haley, John Owen. *Authority Without Power: Law and the Japanese Paradox*. New York: Oxford University Press, 1991.

Halper, Andrew. "'Partnership Enterprises Law' Breaks Limited New Ground." *China Law and Practice* 11, no. 3 (1997): 19–22.

Han, Anna M. "China's Company Law: Practicing Capitalism in a Transitional Economy." *Pacific Rim and Policy Journal* 5 (1996): 457–507.

Han Minzhu, ed. *Cries for Democracy: Writings and Speeches from the 1989 Chinese Democracy Movement*. Princeton, N.J.: Princeton University Press, 1990.

Han Youtong. "Smash Spiritual Shackles—Do Legal Work Well." *Renmin ribao* Mar. 16, 1978: 3.

"Hangzhou Import Controls." *FBIS* (Jan. 14, 1981): O3.

Hanstad, Tim, and Li Ping. "Land Reform in the People's Republic of China: Auctioning Rights to Wasteland." *Loyola of Los Angeles International and Comparative Law Journal* 19 (1997): 545–580.

Hao, Yufan, and Michael Johnston. "Reform at the Crossroads: An Analysis of Chinese Corruption." *Asian Perspective* 19, no. 1 (1995): 117–149.

Harding, Harry. "Breaking the Impasse Over Human Rights." In Ezra F. Vogel, ed., *Living with China: U.S.-China Relations in the Twenty-first Century*, pp. 165–184. New York: W. W. Norton, 1997.

Harding, Harry. *Organizing China: The Problem of Bureaucracy 1949–1976*. Stanford: Stanford University Press, 1981.

Harding, James. "Foreign Investors Face New Curbs on Ownership of Stores." *Financial Times* Nov. 10, 1998.

Harding, James. "Chinese Collectives' Pace Checked." *Financial Times* Jan. 6, 1998.

Harpole, Sally A. "Proposed New Contract Law." *China Law Update* 1, no. 4 (1998): 3–7.

Hart, Henry M., and Albert M. Sacks. *The Legal Process: Basic Problems in the Making and Application of Law*. Tentative Edition, Cambridge, Mass.: Harvard University, 1958.

He Pingran. "People's Judicial Work Must Rely on the Masses; Introducing the Work Method of Collective Mediation of a Mass Nature of the Peking People's Courts." *Guangming ribao* Oct. 25, 1952.

"He Shan Incident Represents Consumer Rights Issue." *Zhongguo qingnian bao* Oct. 17, 1996: 1–2, in *FBIS* 96-252 (Oct. 17, 1996).

He Shanggao. "Strive to Build a Complete Revolutionary System." *Guangming ribao* Mar. 27, 1955.

He Weifang. "Fayuan gaishou duoshao fei?" (How Much Should Courts Charge?). *Nanfang zhoumo* (Apr. 24, 1998).

He Weifang. "Fuzhuan junren jin fayuan" (Demobilized Soldiers in the Courts). *Nanfang zhoumo* Jan. 2, 1998.

He Weifang. "Tongguo sifa shixian shehui zhengyi: dui zhongguo faguan xi-anzhuang de yige toushi" (The Realization of Social Justice through Judica-ture: A Look at the Current Situation of Chinese Judges). In Xia Yong, ed., *Zou xiang quanli de shidai: Zhongguo gongmin quanli fazhan yanjiu* (Toward a Time of Rights: A Perspective of the Civil Rights Development in China), pp. 209–284. Beijing: Zhongguo zhengfa daxue chubanshe, 1995.

He Weifang. "Zhongguo sifa guanli zhidu de liangge wenti" (Two Problems of the Chinese System of Judicial Administration). *Zhongguo shehui kexue* (Social Sciences in China) 6 (1997): 117–130.

Hecht, Jonathan. "The Challenge of China and Human Rights," a review of *Between Freedom and Subsistence: China and Human Rights*, by Ann Kent. *Harvard Human Rights Journal* 9 (Spring 1996): 315–322.

Henderson, Dan Fenno. *Conciliation and Japanese Law, Tokugawa and Modern*. Seattle: University of Washington Press, 1964.

Henkin, Louis. "The Human Rights Idea in Contemporary China: A Comparative Perspective." In R. Randle Edwards, Louis Henkin, and Andrew J. Nathan, eds., *Human Rights in Contemporary China*, pp. 7–39. New York: Columbia University Press, 1986.

Ho, David, and Nancy Leigh. "A Retail Revolution." *China Business Review* (Jan.–Feb. 1994): 22–27.

Ho Ping-Ti. *The Ladder of Success in Imperial China: Aspects of Social Mobility, 1368–1911*. New York: Columbia University Press, 1962.

Holcombe, Chester. *The Real Chinaman*. New York: Dodd, Mead, 1895.

Holdsworth, William Searle. *A History of English Law*. 3rd ed. London: Methuen, 1922.

Hom, Sharon K. "Legal Education in the People's Republic of China: A Select Annotated Bibliography of English-Language Materials." *China Law Reporter* 6, no. 1 (1989): 73–85.

"Hongqi, Article Discussing Freedom of Speech." *FBIS* (Apr. 27, 1981): K16.

"How I Carried Out Mediation Work." *Shensi Daily* Mar. 25, 1957.

"How the Mediation Committee of Hebei Yoi in Xifang District Carried Out Its Work." *Qingdao ribao* Apr. 8, 1955.

Howson, Nicholas C. "China's Company Law: One Step Forward, Two Steps Back? A Modest Complaint." *Columbia Journal of Asian Law* 11, no. 1 (1997): 127–173.

Howson, Nicholas C. "The Law of the Land." *China Business Review* 22, no. 6 (1995): 40–45.

Hsia, Tao-tai, and Constance Axinn Johnson. "Law Making in the People's Republic of China: Terms, Procedures, Hierarchy, and Interpretation." Washington, D.C.: Law Library, Library of Congress, 1986, ms.

Hsiao, Kung-Ch'uan. *Rural China: Imperial Control in the Nineteenth Century*. Seattle: University of Washington Press, 1960.

Hu, Hsien Chin. "The Chinese Concepts of 'Face'." *American Anthropologist* 46 (1944): 45–64.

Hu Kangsheng, ed. *Zhonghua renmin gongheguo guojia peichang fa shiyi* (Interpretation of the State Compensation Law of the People's Republic of China). Beijing: Falü chubanshe, 1994.

Hu Qiaomu. "Act in Accordance with Economic Laws, Speed Up the Four Modernizations." *FBIS* (Oct. 11, 1978): E1.

Huang, Philip C. *Civil Justice in China: Representation and Practice in the Qing.* Stanford: Stanford University Press, 1996.

Hucker, Charles O. *The Censorial System of Ming China.* Stanford: Stanford University Press, 1966.

Ikels, Charlotte. *The Return of the God of Wealth.* Stanford: Stanford University Press, 1996.

Institute of Civil Law, Central Political-Judicial Cadres' School. *Zhonghua renmin gongheguo minfa jiben wenti* (Basic Problems in the Civil Law of the People's Republic of China). Beijing: Falü chubanshe, 1958. Complete English language translation in *JPRS* 4,879, Aug. 15, 1961.

"Instruction on Strengthening Village Mediation Work and Establishing Work of Mediation and Handling [Cases] in Districts." In Jinzhaqi bianqu xingzheng weiyuanhui (Jinzhaqi Border District Administrative Committee), *Xianxing faling huiji* (Collected Current Laws and Decrees) 1: 326. Jinzhaqi: Jinzhaqi bianqu xingzheng weiyuanhui, 1945–1946.

"Instructions of the People's Government of Sinkiang Province on Establishing District and Hsiang Mediation Organizations and Developing Mediation Work Among the People." *Xinjiang ribao* Apr. 15, 1953.

"Is It Necessary for Us to Retain People's Mediation Committees?" *Guangming ribao* Sept. 2, 1956, in *SCMP* 1,391 (1956): 7.

Jacob, Herbert. "Courts as Organizations." In Keith O. Boyum and Lynn Mather, eds., *Empirical Theories About Courts*, pp. 191–215. New York: Longman, 1983.

Jefferson, Gary H., and Thomas G. Rawski. "How Industrial Reform Worked in China: The Role of Innovation, Competition, and Property Rights." In *Proceedings of the World Bank Annual Conference on Development Economics* 1994, pp. 129–156. The World Bank, 1995.

Jenner, W. J. F. *The Tyranny of History: The Roots of China's Crisis.* London: Penguin, 1992.

Jennings, M. Kent. "Political Participation in the Chinese Countryside." *American Political Science Review* 91, no. 2 (June 1997): 361–372.

Ji Meng. "Discussion of the Object of Civil Law Regulation." *Renmin ribao* Jan. 6, 1957: 7.

Jiang Hua. "Earnestly Perform People's Court Work Well." *Renmin ribao* Apr. 9, 1980: 3.

"Jiang Links Strong Legal System, Successful Reform." *FBIS* (Dec. 16, 1992): 19.

Jiang Ping. "Chinese Legal Reform: Achievements, Problems and Prospects." *Journal of Chinese Law* 9 (1995): 67–75.

Jiang Ping. "Drafting the Uniform Contract Law in China." *Columbia Journal of Asian Law* 10, no. 1 (1996): 245–258.

Jiang Shimin, Su Meifeng, Li Wencheng, and Yue Jingtang. "Zhengque chuli renmin neibu de jiufen" (Correctly Handle Disputes Within the People). *Zhengfa yanjiu* 4 (1959): 28–31.

Jiang Wei and Li Hao. "Lun renmin fayuan yu zhongcai jigou de xinxing guanxi" (On the New Type of Relationship Between Courts and Arbitration). *Faxue pinglun* 4 (1995): 32–39.

Jiang Wei and Li Hao. "Lun shichang jingji yu fayuan tiaojie zhidu de wanshan" (On the Market Economy and Perfecting the Institution of Judicial Mediation). Reprinted from *Renmin daxue xuebao* 3 (1995): 87–92, in *Faxue* 7 (1995): 187–192.

Jiang Wei and Yang Rongxin, eds. *Renmin tiaojiexue gailun* (An Introduction to People's Mediation Studies). Beijing: Falü chubanshe, 1990.

Jiang Yue. *Renmin tiaojie zhidu de lilun yu shixian* (Theory and Practice of the Institution of People's Mediation). Beijing: Qunzhong chubanshe, 1994.

"Jiang Zemin Addresses Legal System Forum." *Xinhua* Feb. 8, 1996, in *FBIS* 96-030 (Feb. 13, 1996): 12–14.

"Jiang Zemin, Qiao Shi Address Judicial Meeting." *Xinhua* Dec. 16, 1992, in *FBIS* 92-243 (Dec. 17, 1992): 16–18.

"Jiaqiang fazhi xuanchuan shi xinwenjie de zhongyao zhize" (Strengthening Legal Propaganda Is an Important Responsibility of Journalistic Circles). *Renmin ribao* May 12, 1984.

Jilin sheng siping shi zhongji renmin fayuan (Intermediate Level People's Court of Siping City Jilin Province), ed. *Shenpan guanli caozuo guifan* (Operating Standards for the Management of Adjudication). Beijing: Renmin fayuan chubanshe, 1995.

Jing Hong. "The Plot of the Top Ambitionist to Operate 'Trusts' on a Large Scale Must Be Thoroughly Exposed." *Guangming ribao* May 9, 1967, in *SCMP* 3,948 (1967): 1–4.

Johnson, Chalmers. "Building a Communist Nation in China." In Robert Scalapino, ed., *The Communist Revolution in Asia: Tactics, Goals, and Achievements.* Princeton, N.J.: Princeton University Press, 1965.

Johnston, Michael, and Yufan Hao. "China's Surge of Corruption." *Journal of Democracy* 6, no. 4 (1995): 80–94.

Jones, William C. "Editor's Introduction." In William C. Jones, ed., *Basic Principles of Civil Law in China*, pp. xv–xviii. Armonk, N.Y.: M. E. Sharpe, 1989.

Jones, William C. "Some Questions Regarding the Significance of the General Provisions of Civil Law of the People's Republic of China." *Harvard International Law Journal* 28, no. 2 (1987): 309–372.

Jones, William C., ed. *Basic Principles of Civil Law in China*. Armonk, N.Y.: M. E. Sharpe, 1989.

"Judicial Reform in Central-South Penetrates Deeply Step by Step." *Yangtze Daily* Oct. 29, 1952, English language translation in *SCMP* 454 (1952): 19.

"Judicial Work Must Be Thoroughly Reformed." *Renmin ribao,* English language translation in *SCMP* 401 (Aug. 24–25, 1952): 19.

"Jurassic Park." *Business China* 23, no. 12 (June 9, 1997): 6–8.

"Justice Prevails in Human Rights Defeat." *Xinhua* Apr. 24, 1996, in *FBIS* 96-081.

Kahn, Joseph. "Low on Cash, Thai Concern Will Sell China Assets." *New York Times* Mar. 27, 1998.

Kaplan, Benjamin. "Civil Procedure—Reflections on the Comparison of Systems." *Buffalo Law Review* 9 (1960): 409–432.

Keith, Ronald C. *China's Struggle for the Rule of Law.* New York: St. Martin's Press, 1994.

Keith, Ronald C. "Post-Deng Jurisprudence: Justice and Efficiency in a 'Rule of Law' Economy." *Problems of Post-Communism* 45, no. 3 (1998): 48–57.

Keller, Perry. "Legislation in the People's Republic of China." *University of British Columbia Law Review* 23, no. 3 (1989): 653–687.

Keller, Perry. "Sources of Order in Chinese Law." *American Journal of Comparative Law* 42 (1994): 711–759.

Kelliher, Daniel. "The Chinese Debate Over Village Self-Government." *China Journal* 37 (1997): 63–86.

Kelman, Mark. *A Guide to Critical Legal Studies.* Cambridge, Mass.: Harvard University Press, 1987.

Kennan, George F. *American Diplomacy.* Chicago: University of Chicago, 1984.

Kent, Ann. *Between Freedom and Subsistence: China and Human Rights.* Hong Kong: Oxford University Press, 1993.

Kipnis, Andrew B. *Producing Guanxi: Sentiment, Self, and Subculture in a North China Village.* Durham, N.C.: Duke University Press, 1997.

Koguchi, Hikota. "Some Observations About 'Judicial Independence' in Post-Mao China." *Boston College Third World Law Journal* 7 (1987): 195–213.

Kolenda, Helena, Jerome A. Cohen, and Michael R. March. "People's Republic of China." In Sir Anthony Colman, ed., *Encyclopedia of International Commercial Litigation.* London: Kluwer Law International, 1995.

Kong Qinghua. "Renmin tiaojie zhidu shi yixiang juyou zhongguo tese de falü zhidu" (The People's Mediation System Is a Legal System with Chinese Characteristics). *Zhongguo faxue* 3 (1987): 20–23.

Kraus, James. "Legal Education in the People's Republic of China." *Suffolk Transnational Law Journal* 13 (1989): 75–134.

Kuehn, Thomas. *Law, Family and Women: Toward a Legal Anthropology of Renaissance Italy.* Chicago: University of Chicago Press, 1991.

Kulp, Daniel Harrison. *Country Life in South China: The Sociology of Familism, vol. 1, Phoenix Village, Kuangtung China.* New York: Columbia University, 1925.

Kynge, James. "China's People's Congress Wakes Up this Week." *Financial Times* Mar. 3, 1998.

Kynge, James. "Chinese President Takes Hard Line on Dissidents." *Financial Times* Dec. 19–20, 1998.

Kynge, James, and James Harding. "Trade Trumps Human Rights in West's Dealings with China." *Financial Times* Apr. 2, 1998.

"Labor Law of the People's Republic of China." Adopted by the Standing Committee of the National People's Congress, July 5, 1994, and effective January 1, 1995, in *China Law and Practice* 7 (Aug. 29, 1994): 21–40.

"Labour Insurance Regulations of the People's Republic of China." Feb. 23, 1951. *Important Labour Laws and Regulations of the People's Republic of China.* Beijing: Foreign Language Press, 1961.

Lampton, David M. "The Implementation Problem in Post-Mao China." In

David M. Lampton, ed., *Policy Implementation in Post-Mao China*, pp. 3–24. Berkeley: University of California Press, 1987.

Lampton, David M. "A Plum for a Peach: Bargaining, Interest and Bureaucratic Politics in China." In Kenneth G. Lieberthal and David M. Lampton, eds., *Bureaucracy, Politics, and Decision Making in Post-Mao China*, pp. 33–58. Berkeley: University of California Press, 1992.

Lampton, David M., with Joyce A. Madancy and Kristen M. Williams. *A Relationship Restored: Trends in U.S.-China Educational Exchanges*, 1978–1984. Washington, D.C.: National Academy Press, 1986.

Lampton, David M., ed. *Policy Implementation in Post-Mao China*. Berkeley: University of California Press, 1987.

Landler, Mark. "Bankruptcy the Chinese Way." *New York Times* Jan. 22, 1999: C1, C4.

Langfitt, Frank. "Neighborhood Watchdogs Developing Profit Centers." *San Jose Mercury News* Dec. 30, 1998.

"Laodong jiaoyang guanli gongzuo zhifa xize" (Detailed Rules on Implementing the Law in the Administration of Re-education through Labor). Implemented on Aug. 10, 1992. *Guowuyuan gongbao* 26 (Dec. 1, 1992): 1055–1066.

"Laodong jiaoyang shixing banfa" (Trial Measures on Re-education through Labour). Promulgated on Jan. 21, 1982. In *Zhonghua renmin gongheguo falü quanshu* (Collection of the Laws of the People's Republic of China), pp. 1583–1589. Changchun: Jilin renmin chubanshe, 1989.

LaPalombara, Joseph. "*Bureaucracy and Political Development*: Notes, Queries, and Dilemmas." In Joseph LaPalombara, ed., *Bureaucracy and Political Development*, pp. 34–61. Princeton, N.J.: Princeton University Press, 1963.

Lardy, Nicholas R. *China's Unfinished Economic Revolution*. Washington, D.C.: Brookings Institution Press, 1998.

"Law of the People's Republic of China on the Administration of Urban Real Estate." Adopted July 5, 1994. *CCH* ¶ 19–593.

"Law of the People's Republic of China on Industrial Enterprises Owned by the Whole People." Adopted Apr. 13, 1988. *CCH* ¶ 13–534.

"Law of the People's Republic of China on Judges." *BBC-SWB* (Mar. 23, 1995).

"Law of the People's Republic of China on the Protection of Minors." Adopted Sept. 4, 1991. *FBIS* 91-174 (Sept. 9, 1991): 36.

"Law Professor Discusses Media-Related Torts." *FBIS* 95-221 (Nov. 16, 1995), a translation of "Dialogue on Torts in the News Media Between Renmin Ribao Reporter Wang Binlai and Professor of China University of Political Science and Law Jiang Ping." *Renmin ribao* Oct. 6, 1994: 10.

"Laws and Decrees Combined with Facts to Carry Out Persuasion and Education: The Civil Affairs Bureau of the City of Wuhan in the Last Half-Year Mediated 246 Civil Disputes." *Yangtze Daily* Nov. 24, 1950.

"Lawyers: A Profession in Flux." *China News Analysis* Feb. 15, 1996.

Lawyers Committee for Human Rights. *Criminal Justice with Chinese Characteristics: China's Criminal Process and Violations of Human Rights*. New York: Lawyers Committee for Human Rights, 1993.

Lawyers Committee for Human Rights. *Lawyers in China: Obstacles to Independence and the Defense of Rights.* New York: Lawyers Committee for Human Rights, 1998.

Lawyers Committee for Human Rights. *Opening to Reform?: An Analysis of China's Revised Criminal Procedure Law.* New York: Lawyers Committee for Human Rights, 1996.

Lawyers Committee for Human Rights. *Wrongs and Rights: A Human Rights Analysis of China's Revised Criminal Law.* New York: Lawyers Committee for Human Rights, 1998.

"Lawyers Law of the People's Republic of China." Passed May 15, 1996. *Xinhua* May 15, 1996, *FBIS* 96-109 (May 15, 1996).

Leng, Shao-chuan. "Pre-1949 Development of the Communist Chinese System of Justice." *China Quarterly* 30 (1967): 93–114.

Leng, Shao-chuan, with Hungdah Chiu. *Criminal Justice in Post-Mao China: Analysis and Documents.* Albany: State University of New York Press, 1985.

Lewis, Donald. "New Arbitration Law Brings Order to Dispute Settlement." *Asia Law* (Nov. 1994): 19–21.

Lewis, Donald, and Karen Ip. "Domestic Commercial Arbitration in the People's Republic of China." In *Dispute Resolution in the PRC: A Practical Guide to Litigation and Arbitration in China,* pp. 74–89. Hong Kong: Asia Law and Practice, n.d.

Lewis, John Wilson. "Leader, Commissar, and Bureaucrat: The Chinese Political System in the Last Days of the Revolution." In Ping-ti Ho and Tang Tsou, eds., *China in Crisis, Vol. 1, China's Heritage and the Communist Political System,* pp. 449–500. Chicago: University of Chicago Press, 1968.

Lewis, John Wilson. "The Leadership Doctrine of the Chinese Communist Party: The Lesson of the People's Commune." *Asian Survey* 3 (1963): 457.

Lewis, John Wilson. *Leadership in Communist China.* Ithaca, N.Y.: Cornell University Press, 1963.

Li Bian. "Legal System Develops Apace." *Beijing Review* 40, no. 19 (1997): 23–25.

Li Buyun. "Guanyu qicao 'Zhonghua renmin gongheguo lifa fa (zhuanjia jianyi gao)' de ruogan wenti" (On Several Issues Relating to the Drafting of 'PRC Legislative Law [Draft of Experts' Recommendations]'). *Zhongguo faxue* 1 (1997):11–19.

Li Chengrui and Zuo Chuntai. *Shehui zhuyi de yinhang gongzuo* (Socialist Bank Work). Beijing, 1964.

Li Chunlin and Pan Xiaming. "Renmin tiaojie wenti zhengyi zhi wo jian" (Our View of the Debate Over Issues in People's Mediation). *Zhengfa luntan* 2 (1990): 16–21.

Li, David D. "A Theory of Ambiguous Property Rights in Transition Economies: The Case of the Chinese Non-State Sector." *Journal of Comparative Economics* 23, no. 1 (1996): 1–19.

Li Guangcan and Wang Shui. "Criticisms of the Old Legal Viewpoint." *Xuexi* 7 (1952): 16.

Li Hao. "Lun fayuan tiaojie chengxufa yu shitifa yueshu de shuangchong ruanhua: jianxi minshi susong zhong pianzhong tiaojie yu yansu zhifa de maodun"

(On the Double Weakening of Procedural Law and Substantive Law in Judicial Mediation: Analyzing the Contradiction between Emphasizing Mediation and Rigorously Upholding the Law in Civil Litigation). *Faxue pinglun* 4 (July 1996): 11–16.

Li Hao. "Minshi shenpan zhong de tiaoshen fenli" (Separating Mediation and Adjudication in Civil Trials). *Faxue yanjiu* 18, no. 4 (July 1996): 57–68.

Li Jianfei. "Criticism of the Supra-Class View of Law." *Xuexi* 7 (1952): 13.

Li, Lianjiang, and Kevin J. O'Brien. "The Struggle Over Village Elections." In Merle Goldman and Roderick MacFarquahar, eds., *The Paradox of China's Post-Mao Reforms*, pp. 129–144. Cambridge, Mass.: Harvard University Press, 1999.

Li, Lianjiang, and Kevin J. O'Brien. "Villagers and Popular Resistance in Contemporary China." *Modern China* 22, no. 1 (1996): 28–61.

Li, Victor H. "Human Rights in a Chinese Context." In Ross Terrill, ed., *The China Difference*, pp. 219–235. New York: Harper and Row, 1979.

Li, Victor H. *Law Without Lawyers*. Stanford: Stanford Alumni Association, 1977.

Liang Huixing. "Minfa de fazhan yu minfa de fangfalun" (The Development and Methodology of Civil Law). A lecture delivered at the Fourth Meeting of Correspondents of the Supreme People's Court Gazette. 1995.

Liang Qinhan. "Chuli jingji jiufen anjian ying zhuozhong tiaojie" (Mediation Should be Stressed in Dealing with Economic Dispute Cases). *Faxue yanjiu* (Research on Legal Studies) 4 (1981).

Liang Zhiping. "Explicating 'Law': A Comparative Perspective of Chinese and Western Legal Culture." *Journal of Chinese Law* 3, no. 1 (1989): 56–91.

Liang Zhiping. "Law and Fairness at a Time of Change." *China Perspectives* 2 (1995): 30–36.

"Lianhe guo guoji huowu xiaoshou hetong gongyue" (United Nations Convention on Contracts for the International Sale of Goods) *Zhonghua renmin gongheguo guowuyuan gongbao* (June 13, 1990): 290–315.

Lichtenstein, Natalie. "Enterprise Reform in China: The Evolving Legal Framework." Legal Department, The World Bank, Policy Research Working Paper WPS 1198, Sept. 1993.

Lieberthal, Kenneth G. "The China Challenge." *Foreign Affairs* 74, no. 6 (1995): 35–49.

Lieberthal, Kenneth G. *Governing China: From Revolution Through Reform*. New York: Norton, 1995.

Lieberthal, Kenneth G. "Introduction: The 'Fragmented Authoritarianism' Model and Its Limitations." In Kenneth G. Lieberthal and David M. Lampton, eds., *Bureaucracy, Politics, and Decision Making in Post-Mao China*, pp. 1–30. Berkeley: University of California Press, 1992.

Lieberthal, Kenneth G., and Michel Oksenberg. *Policy Making in China: Leaders, Structures and Processes*. Princeton, N.J.: Princeton University Press, 1988.

Liebman, Benjamin L. "Note: Class Action Litigation in China." *Harvard Law Review* 111, no. 6 (1998): 1523–1541.

Lifton, Robert J. *Thought Reform and the Psychology of Totalism: A Study of 'Brainwashing' in China*. New York: Norton, 1961.

Lin Feng. *Administrative Law: Procedures and Remedies in China.* Hong Kong: Sweet and Maxwell, 1996.

Lin Feng. "The Administrative Supervision Law." *China Law for Business* 3, no. 4 (Aug. 1997): 10–12.

Lin Feng. "An Examination of the State Compensation Law." *Hong Kong Law Journal* 25 (1995): 401–416.

Lin, Nan. "Local Market Socialism: Local Corporatism in Action in Rural China." *Theory and Society* 24 (1995): 301–354.

Lin Zhongliang. "Resolutely Eradicate Local Protectionism in Law Enforcement." *Fazhi ribao* Apr. 25, 1995, translated in *FBIS* 95-110 (June 8, 1995): 23–25, as "Local Protectionism in Law Enforcement."

Liu Binyan. *China's Crisis, China's Hope.* Cambridge, Mass.: Harvard University, 1990.

Liu Guangan and Li Cunpeng. "Minjian tiaojie yu quanli baohu" (Civil Mediation and the Protection of Rights). In Xia Yong, ed., *Zouxiang quanli de shidai: Zhongguo gongmin quanli fazhan yanjiu* (Toward a Time of Rights: A Perspective of the Civil Rights Development in China), pp. 285–326. Beijing: Zhongguo zhengfa daxue chubanshe, 1995.

Liu Hainian. "Yifa zhiguo: Zhongguo shehui zhuyi fazhi jianshe xin de lichengbei" (Ruling the Country According to Law: A New Milestone in the Construction of China's Socialist Legal System). *Faxue yanjiu* 18, no. 3 (1996): 24–36.

Liu, Hui-Chen Wang. "An Analysis of Chinese Clan Rules: Confucian Theories in Action." In David S. Nivison and Arthur F. Wright, eds., *Confucianism in Action,* pp. 63–96. Stanford: Stanford University Press, 1959.

Liu, Hui-Chen Wang. *The Traditional Chinese Clan Rules.* Locust Valley, N.Y.: J. J. Augustin, 1959.

Liu, Nanping. "An Ignored Source of Chinese Law: The Gazette of the Supreme People's Court." *Connecticut Journal of International Law* 5 (1989): 271–315.

Liu, Nanping. *Judicial Interpretation in China: Opinions of the Supreme People's Court.* Hong Kong: Sweet and Maxwell, 1997.

Liu, Nanping. "Legal Precedents with Chinese Characteristics: Published Cases in the Gazette of the Supreme People's Court." *Journal of Chinese Law* 5 (1991): 107–141.

Liu Shaoqi. "The Political Report of the Central Committee of the Communist Party of China to the Eighth National Congress of the Party." Delivered on Sept. 15, 1956. In *Eighth National Congress of the Communist Party of China: Documents,* pp. 11–115. Beijing: Foreign Languages Press.

Liu, Yang-Ling. "Reform from Below: The Private Economy." *China Quarterly* 130 (1992): 293–316.

Liu Zhitao, ed. *Renmin tiaojie shiyong daquan* (Practical Compendium on People's Mediation). Changchun: Jilin renmin chubanshe, 1990.

Loeber, Dietrich A. "Plan and Contract Performance in Soviet Law." *University of Illinois Law Forum* 1964 (1964): 128–179.

Lu Dingyi. "Let a Hundred Flowers Blossom, a Hundred Schools of Thought Contend!" In Harvard Center for International Affairs and East Asian Research Center, eds., *Communist China 1955–1959: Policy Documents and Analysis.* Cambridge, Mass.: Harvard University Press, 1962.

Lu Zhongya. "New Criminal Procedure Law Adopts 'Presumption of Innocence' Principle in Conformity with National Conditions." *Shanghai Faxue* 175 (June 10, 1996): 17–18, in *FBIS* 96-187.

Lubman, Stanley B. "Book Review: *China's Struggle for the Rule of Law,* by Ronald C. Keith." *China Quarterly* 142 (1995): 609–611.

Lubman, Stanley B. "Emerging Functions of Formal Legal Institutions in China's Modernization." *China Law Reporter* 2, no. 4 (1983): 195–266.

Lubman, Stanley B. "Form and Function in the Chinese Criminal Process." *Columbia Law Review* 69, no. 4 (1969): 535–575.

Lubman, Stanley B. "The Legal and Policy Environment for Foreign Direct Investment in China: Past Accomplishments, Future Uncertainties." In Carol J. Holgren, ed., *Private Investments Abroad: Problems and Solutions in International Business in 1997,* chap. 3. New York: Matthew Bender, 1998.

Lubman, Stanley B. "Mao and Mediation: Politics and Dispute Resolution in Communist China." *California Law Review* 55, no. 5 (1967): 1284–1359.

Lubman, Stanley B. "Methodological Problems in Studying Chinese Communist 'Civil Law'." In Jerome Alan Cohen, ed., *Contemporary Chinese Law: Research Problems and Perspectives,* pp. 230–260. Cambridge, Mass.: Harvard University Press, 1970.

Lubman, Stanley B. "Setback for China-Wide Rule of Law." *Far East Economic Review* Nov. 7, 1996: 39.

Lubman, Stanley B., and Gregory Wajnowski. "Criminal Justice Process." In William P. Streng and Allen D. Wilcox, eds., *Doing Business in China,* chap. 27. New York: Juris, 1993.

Lubman Stanley B., and Gregory C. Wajnowski. "International Commercial Dispute Resolution in China: A Practical Assessment." *American Review of International Arbitration* 4, no. 2 (1993).

Lubman, Stanley B., and Gregory C. Wajnowski. "Technology Transfer to the People's Republic of China: Law, Practice and Policy." In William P. Streng and Allen D. Wilcox, eds., *Doing Business in China,* chap. 3. New York: Juris, 1993.

Luo Qizhi. "Legal Aid Practices in the PRC in the 1990s: Dynamics, Contents and Implications." *Occasional Papers/Reprints Series in Contemporary Asian Studies* 4 (1997): 1–68.

Luo Wenyan. "Tingzheng zhidu de lifa quexian" (Legislative Flaws in the System of Hearing Evidence). *Faxue* 6 (1997): 22.

Ma Xiwu. "Guanyu dangqian shenpan gongzuo zhong de jige wenti" (On Several Problems in Adjudication Work at the Present Time). *Zhengfa yanjiu* 1 (1956): 3–9.

Macaulay, Melissa. "The Civil Reprobate: Pettifoggers, Property and Litigation in Late Imperial China, 1723–1850." Ph.D. diss., History, University of California at Berkeley, 1993.

Macaulay, Melissa. *Social Power and Legal Culture: Litigation Masters in Late Imperial China.* Stanford: Stanford University Press, 1998.

Macaulay, Stewart. "Non-Contractual Relations in Business: A Preliminary Study." In Lawrence M. Friedman and Stewart Macaulay, eds., *Law and the Behavioral Sciences*, pp. 141–158. Indianapolis, Ind.: Bobbs-Merrill, 1977.

Macaulay, Stewart. "The Reliance Interest and the World Outside the Law School's Doors." *Wisconsin Law Review* (1991): 247–291.

MacCormack, Geoffrey. *The Spirit of Traditional Chinese Law*. Athens, Ga.: University of Georgia Press, 1996.

MacCormack, Geoffrey. *Traditional Chinese Penal Law*. Edinburgh: Edinburgh University Press, 1990.

Macgowan, D. G. "Chinese Guilds or Chambers of Commerce and Trade Unions." *Journal of the North China Branch, Royal Asiatic Society* 21 (1886): 133–192.

"Make the Collective Dormitory Work a Success." *Beijing ribao* May 13, 1964.

"Many Cities in the Nation Begin Notarial Work." *Guangming ribao* June 18, 1955: 1.

Mao Zedong. "On New Democracy." In *Selected Works of Mao Tse-tung* 2: 339–384. Beijing: Foreign Languages Press, 1965.

Mao Zedong. "On the Correct Handling of Contradictions Among the People." In Harvard Center for International Affairs and East Asian Research Center, eds., *Communist China 1955–1959: Policy Documents and Analysis*, pp. 273–294. Cambridge, Mass.: Harvard University Press, 1962.

Mao Zedong. "On the People's Democratic Dictatorship." In *Selected Works of Mao Tse-tung* 4: 411–424. Beijing: Foreign Languages Press, 1961.

Mao Zedong. "The Question of Agricultural Cooperation." In Harvard Center for International Affairs and East Asian Research Center, eds., *Communist China 1955–1959: Policy Documents and Analysis*, pp. 94–105. Cambridge, Mass.: Harvard University Press, 1962.

Markel, Douglas C., and Randall Peerenboom. "The Technology Transfer Tango." *China Business Review* Jan.–Feb. (1997): 25–29.

"Mediation Chairman." *Xinhua* Nov. 24, 1961.

"Mediation Committee Member Zhu Xizhen." *Qingdao ribao* May 20, 1956.

"Mediation Committees Are 'Peacemakers' for the People." *Nanfang ribao* Feb. 27, 1957.

"Mediation in Shanghai." *Xinhua* Apr. 1, 1985.

"Mediation Small Group of Yang-Heng Middle Section." *Jiefang ribao* Nov. 17, 1952.

"Mediators Help Ensure Social Stability." *Xinhua* Oct. 31, 1989.

Meijer, Marinus Johan. "Abuse of Power and Coercion." In Dieter Eikemeier and Herbert Franke, eds., *State and Law in East Asia: Festschrift Karl Bünger*, pp. 184–203. Wiesbaden: Otto Harrassowitz, 1981.

Meng Chaocheng. "Some Thoughts on the Introduction of the System of Combined Purchasing and Marketing Contracts." *Dagong bao* Feb. 9, 1962, in *SCMP* 2,688 (1962): 3–6.

Meng Qinguo. "Some Issues Relating to Policy Law." *Tianjin shehui kexue* 1 (1990): 55–58, translated as "Shortcomings of Policy Law" in *JPRS* 90-038, May 17, 1990: 21–26.

Meng Shang. *Le Contrôle des Actes Administratifs en Droit Chinois et sa Réforme.* Paris: Librairie Générale de Droit et de Jurisprudence, 1991.

Merryman, John Henry. *The Civil Law Tradition: An Introduction to the Legal Systems of Western Europe and Latin America.* Stanford: Stanford University Press, 2nd ed. 1985.

Merton, Robert K. *Social Theory and Social Structure.* Glencoe, Ill.: Free Press, 1957.

Metzger, Thomas A. *The Internal Organization of Ch'ing Bureaucracy: Legal, Normative, and Communication Aspects.* Cambridge, Mass.: Harvard University Press, 1973.

Milsom, S. F. C. *Historical Foundations of the Common Law.* London: Butterworths, 1969.

"Ministry Explains Communities' Role in Mediating Civil Disputes." *Xinhua* Aug. 17, 1985.

Ministry of Heavy Industry of the People's Republic of China. "Temporary Basic Clauses on Contracts for the Supply of Products." In Civil Law Teaching and Research Office, Chinese People's University, ed., *Zhonghua renmin gongheguo minfa cankao ziliao* (Reference Materials on the Civil Law of the People's Republic of China), pp. 243–251. Beijing: Renmin daxue chubanshe, 1956.

"Ministry of Internal Affairs Directive on Provisions for Vagrants." *Xinhua* July 24, 1956, in *SCMP* 1,345 (Aug. 8, 1956): 2.

"Minjian jiufen chuli banfa" (Procedures for Handling People's Disputes). *Guowuyuan gongbao* (Apr. 1, 1990): 597. Reprinted in Zhang Yunqing and Zhang Yushan, eds., *Renmin tiaojieyuan gongzuo shouce* (Handbook of People's Mediators' Work), pp. 391–394. Changchun: Jilin daxue chubanshe, 1992.

Mo, John S. "Taxation Power and Invalidity of Certain Local Tax Concessions in China." *International Lawyer* 26, no. 4 (1992): 933–942.

"Model Mediation Committee Member Aunty Wu." *Guangming ribao* Oct. 14, 1955.

"MOFTEC Clarifies Extension Process for Equipment Imports." *US-China Business Council China Market Intelligence* Feb. 1997: 1.

"More Mediation in Civil Disputes Called For." *Xinhua* July 12, 1988.

Moser, Michael J. *Law and Social Change in a Chinese Community: A Case Study in a Chinese Community.* London: Oceana, 1962.

Mu, Fu-Sheng. *The Wilting of the Hundred Flowers: Free Thought in China Today.* London: Heinemann, 1962.

Munro, Donald J. "Dissent in Communist China: The Current Anti-Intellectual Campaign in Perspective." *Current Scene* 4, no. 11 (1966): 1–19.

Nader, Laura. *Harmony Ideology: Justice and Social Control in Zapotec Mountain Villages.* Stanford: Stanford University Press, 1990.

Nathan, Andrew J. *China's Crisis: Dilemmas of Reform and Prospects for Democracy.* New York: Columbia University Press, 1990.

Nathan, Andrew J. *Chinese Democracy.* Berkeley: University of California Press, 1985.

Nathan, Andrew J. "Sources of Chinese Rights Thinking." In R. Randle Edwards, Louis Henkin, and Andrew J. Nathan, *Human Rights in Contemporary China*, pp. 125–164, 176–182. New York: Columbia University Press, 1986.

Nathan, Andrew J., with Tianjian Shi. "Left and Right in Deng's China." In Andrew J. Nathan, ed., *China's Transition*, pp. 174–197. New York: Columbia University Press, 1997.

Naughton, Barry. "The Decline of Central Control over Investment in Post-Mao China." In David M. Lampton, ed., *Policy Implementation in Post-Mao China*, pp. 51–80. Berkeley: University of California Press, 1987.

Naughton, Barry. *Growing Out of the Plan: Chinese Economic Reform, 1978–1993*. Cambridge: Cambridge University Press, 1995.

Naughton, Barry. "Hierarchy and the Bargaining Economy: Government and Enterprise in the Reform Process." In Kenneth G. Lieberthal and David M. Lampton, eds., *Bureaucracy, Politics, and Decision Making in Post-Mao China*, pp. 245–289. Berkeley: University of California Press, 1992.

Naughton, Barry. "What Is Distinctive about China's Economic Transition? State Enterprise Reform and Overall System Transformation." *Journal of Comparative Economics* 18, no. 3 (1994): 470–490.

Nee, Victor. "Peasant Entrepreneurship and the Politics of Regulation in China." In Victor Nee and David Stark, eds., *Remaking the Economic Institutions of Socialism: China and Eastern Europe*, pp. 169–207. Stanford: Stanford University Press, 1989.

Needham, Joseph. *Science and Civilisation in China*. Cambridge: Cambridge University Press, 1956.

"Negotiable Instruments Law of the People's Republic of China." Adopted May 10, 1995. *CCH* ¶ 19–596.

Nevitt, Christopher Earle. "Private Business Associations in China: Evidence of Civil Society or Local State Power?" *China Journal* 36 (1996): 25–43.

"New Duty Exemptions Conceal Tighter Investment Control." *China Joint Venturer* 3, no. 5 (1998): 1, 4–5.

Northrop, F. S. C. "The Mediational Approval Theory of Law in American Legal Realism." *Virginia Law Review* 44 (1958): 347–363.

"Notarial Work in Canton Develops Gradually." *Nanfang ribao* Mar. 9, 1957: 3.

"Notice of the Central Committee of the Chinese Communist Party and State Council Relating to Strict Adherence to the Procedures for Capital Construction and to the Strict Performance of Economic Contracts." *FGHB* 13 (1962–1963): 62–63.

"NPC Adopts Resolution on Economic Crimes." *FBIS* (Mar. 10, 1982): K1–K3.

"NPC Promulgates New Regulations on Arrests, Detentions." *FBIS* (Feb. 26, 1979): E2–E5.

O'Brien, Kevin J. "Agents and Remonstrators: Role Accumulation by Chinese People's Congress Deputies." *China Quarterly* 138 (1994): 359–380.

O'Brien, Kevin J. "Chinese People's Congresses and Legislative Embeddedness: Understanding Early Organizational Development." *Comparative Political Studies* 27, no. 1 (1994): 80–107.

O'Brien, Kevin J. "Implementing Political Reform in China's Villages." *Australian Journal of Chinese Affairs* 32 (1994): 33–59.

O'Brien, Kevin J. "Legislative Development and Chinese Political Change." In Tahirih V. Lee, ed., *Basic Concepts of Chinese Law*, pp. 369–387. New York: Garland, 1997.

O'Brien, Kevin J. "Rightful Resistance." *World Politics* 49, no. 1 (1996): 31–55.

O'Brien, Kevin J., and Lianjiang Li. "The Politics of Lodging Complaints in Rural China." *China Quarterly* 143 (1995): 756–783.

Odgaard, Ole. "Entrepreneurs and Elite Formation in Rural China." *Australian Journal of Chinese Affairs* 28 (1992): 89–108.

Oi, Jean C. "The Evolution of Local State Corporatism." In Andrew G. Walder, ed., *Zouping in Transition: The Process of Reform in Rural North China*, pp. 35–61. Cambridge, Mass.: Harvard University Press, 1998.

Oi, Jean C. "The Fate of the Collective after the Commune." In Deborah Davis and Ezra F. Vogel, eds., *Chinese Society on the Eve of Tiananmen: The Impact of Reform*, pp. 15–36. Cambridge, Mass.: Council on East Asian Studies, Harvard University, 1990.

Oi, Jean C. "Fiscal Reform and the Economic Foundations of Local State Corporatism in China." *World Politics* 45, no. 1 (1992): 99–126.

Oi, Jean C. "The Role of the Local State in China's Transitional Economy." *China Quarterly* 144 (1995): 1132–1149.

Oi, Jean. *Rural China Takes Off: The Political Basis for Economic Reform*. Berkeley, University of California Press, 1999.

Oksenberg, Michel, Lawrence R. Sullivan, and Marc Lambert, eds. *Beijing Spring, 1989: Confrontation and Conflict, The Basic Documents*. Armonk, N.Y.: M. E. Sharpe, 1990.

"Opinions of the Supreme People's Court on Some Issues Relating to the Implementation of the Administrative Litigation Law (For Trial Implementation)." Adopted May 29, 1991. In Lin Feng, *Administrative Law: Procedures and Remedies in China*, pp. 332–345. Hong Kong: Sweet and Maxwell, 1996.

"Organic Law of the People's Courts of the People's Republic of China." Adopted July 1, 1979, amended Sept. 2, 1983 and Dec. 2, 1986. In Legislative Affairs Commission of the Standing Committee of the National People's Congress of the People's Republic of China, comp., *The Laws of the People's Republic of China, 1983–1986*. Beijing: Foreign Language Press, 1987.

"Organic Law of Village Committees" BBC-SWB 0038 Jan. 1, 1988.

"Organic Law on Urban Neighborhood Committees of the People's Republic of China." Adopted Dec. 26, 1989. *FBIS* 90-011 (Jan. 17, 1990). For Chinese original see "Zhonghua renmin gongheguo chengshi jumin weiyuanhui zuzhi fa." *Fazhi ribao* Dec. 27, 1989.

"Organizational Law of the People's Courts of the People's Republic of China." Sept. 21, 1954. In Albert P. Blaustein, ed., *Fundamental Legal Documents of Communist China*, pp. 131–143. South Hackensack, N.J.: F. B. Rothman, 1962.

"Organizational Law of the People's Procuracy of the People's Republic of China." Sept. 21, 1954. In Albert P. Blaustein, ed., *Fundamental Legal Documents of Communist China*, pp. 144–152. South Hackensack, N.J.: F. B. Rothman, 1962.

"Organizational Regulations for Public Security Stations." Dec. 31, 1954, in *FGHB* (1954–55): 243–244.

"Organizational Regulations for Street Business Offices." Dec. 31, 1954. *FGHB* (1954–55): 171–172.

"Organizational Regulations for Urban Residents' Committees." Dec. 31, 1954. *FGHB* (1954–55): 173–175.

"Organize the Masses to Handle Disputes Within the People—Municipal People's Court in Songshan District Does a Key Experiment." *Jiefang ribao* Oct. 26, 1952.

Osgathorpe, John D. "A Critical Survey of the People's Republic of China's New Company Law." *Indiana International and Comparative Law Review* 6 (1996): 493–515.

Ostry, Sylvia. "China and the WTO: The Transparency Issue." *UCLA Journal of International Law and Foreign Affairs* 3 (1998): 1–22.

Overholt, William H. "China After Deng." *Foreign Affairs* 75, no. 3 (1996): 63–78.

"Overseas Chinese Dependents Work Committees in Canton." *Dagong bao* (Hong Kong) Jan. 14, 1957, English language translation in *SCMP* 1,455 (1957): 16–17.

Packer, Herbert L. "Two Models of the Criminal Process." *University of Pennsylvania Law Review* 113 (1964): 1–68.

Paglee, Charles D. "Contract Law in China: Drafting a Uniform Contract Law." Available at Chinalaw, http://www.qis.net/chinalaw/.

Palmer, Michael. "China's New Inheritance Law: Some Preliminary Observations." In Stephan Feuchtwang, Athar Hussain, and Thierry Pairault, eds., *Transforming China's Economy in the Eighties, Volume 1: The Rural Sector, Welfare and Employment*, pp. 169–197. Boulder, Colo.: Westview, 1988.

Palmer, Michael. "The Revival of Mediation in the People's Republic of China: (1) Extra-Judicial Mediation." In William Elliott Butler, ed., *Yearbook on Socialist Legal Systems*, pp. 219–277. Dobbs Ferry, N.Y.: Transnational, 1987.

Palmer, Michael. "The Revival of Mediation in the People's Republic of China: (2) Judicial Mediation." In William Elliott Butler, ed., *Yearbook on Socialist Legal Systems*, pp. 143–169. Dobbs Ferry, N.Y.: Transnational, 1988.

"Party Plenum Communiqué Stresses 'Spiritual Civilization'." *Xinhua* Oct. 10, 1996 in BBC-SWB Oct. 12, 1996.

"Passion for Profit." *Far Eastern Economic Review* Jun. 23, 1994: 54–56.

Pearson, Margaret M. *China's New Business Elite: The Political Consequences of Economic Reform.* Berkeley: University of California Press, 1997.

Pearson, Margaret M. *Joint Ventures in the People's Republic of China: The Control of Foreign Direct Investment Under Socialism.* Princeton, N.J.: Princeton University Press, 1991.

Peerenboom, Randall. "China's Developing Legal Profession: The Implications for Foreign Investors." Ms. 1998.

Peerenboom, Randall. "Ruling the Country in Accordance with Law: Reflections on the Rule and Role of Law in Contemporary China." Ms., forthcoming in *Cultural Dynamics* 11, no. 3 (1999).

Peerenboom, Randall. "What's Wrong with Chinese Rights?: Toward a Theory of Rights with Chinese Characteristics." *Harvard Human Rights Journal* 6 (1993): 29–60.

Pei, Minxin. "Citizens v. Mandarins: Administrative Litigation in China." *China Quarterly* 152 (1997) 832–862.

Pei, Minxin. "Is China Democratizing?" *Foreign Affairs* 77, no. 1 (1998): 68–82.

"Peking Daily Explains Why Counter-Revolutionaries Do Not Enjoy Free Speech." BBC-SWB (June 18, 1981), excerpted from Chen Weidian and Zhou Xinming, "Socialist Law Does Not Give Counter-Revolutionaries Freedom of Speech." *Beijing ribao* May 25, 1981.

Peng Zhen. "Explanation of the Draft Act of the People's Republic of China for Punishment of Corruption." *SCMP* 320 (Apr. 22, 1952): 15–19, a translation of "Notes on the Draft Regulations for the Punishment of Corruption." *Xinhua* Apr. 21, 1952.

Peng Zhen. "Guanyu zhengfa gongzuo de jige wenti" (Several Questions Concerning Political and Judicial Work). *Hongqi* 9 (1987): 3–6. Translation appears in *JPRS* 87-092 (May 13, 1987): K1–K6.

"People's Daily Editorial on Socialist Democracy." *Xinhua* Feb. 8, 1981.

"People's Judicial Work Must Rely on the Masses; Introducing the Work Method of Collective Mediation of a Mass Nature of the Peking People's Courts." *Guangming ribao* Oct. 25, 1952.

"People's Mediation Committee of Xianhe Village, Haian County, Jiangsi Province." *Guangming ribao* June 5, 1955.

"People's Mediation Committees Everywhere: Positively Serve Agricultural Mutual Aid and Cooperation." *Guangming ribao* Mar. 29, 1955.

Perkins, Dwight. "Prospects for China's Integration Into the Global Economy." In *China's Economic Future: Challenges to U.S. Policy, Study Papers Submitted to the Joint Economic Committee, Congress of the United States*, pp. 34–40. Washington, D.C.: Government Printing Office, 1996.

Pfeffer, Richard M. "Crime and Punishment: China and the United States." *World Politics* 21 (1968): 152–181.

Pfeffer, Richard M. "The Institution of Contracts in the Chinese People's Republic (Part 1)." *China Quarterly* 14 (1963): 153–177.

Pfeffer, Richard M. "The Institution of Contracts in the Chinese People's Republic (Part 2)." *China Quarterly* 15 (1963): 115–139.

"Place Even More Subsidiary Agricultural Products on the Track of Planning." *Nanfang ribao* Apr. 3, 1963.

Poggi, Gianfranco. *The Development of the Modern State: A Sociological Introduction.* Stanford: Stanford University Press, 1978.

"Positively Serve Mutual Aid and Cooperation in Agricultural Production." *Guangming ribao* June 5, 1955.

Potter, Pitman B. "The Administrative Litigation Law of the PRC: Judicial Review and Bureaucratic Reform." In Pitman B. Potter, ed., *Domestic Law Reforms in Post-Mao China*, pp. 270–304. Armonk, N.Y.: M. E. Sharpe, 1994.

Potter, Pitman B. "Class Action: Educating Lawyers in China." *China Exchange News* 22, no. 4 (1994): 16–19.

Potter, Pitman B. "Curbing the Party: Peng Zhen and Chinese Legal Culture." *Problems of Post-Communism* 45, no. 3 (1998): 17–28.

Potter, Pitman B. *The Economic Contract Law of China: Legitimation and Contract Autonomy in the PRC*. Seattle: University of Washington, 1993.

Potter, Pitman B. *Foreign Business Law in China: Past Progress and Future Challenges*. San Francisco, Calif.: The 1990 Institute, 1995.

Potter, Pitman B. "Foreign Investment Law in the People's Republic of China: Dilemmas of State Control." In Stanley B. Lubman, ed., *China's Legal Reforms*, pp. 155–185. Oxford: Oxford University Press, 1996.

Potter, Pitman B. "The Legal Framework for Securities Markets in China: The Challenge of Maintaining State Control, and Inducing Investor Confidence." *China Law Reporter* 7, no. 2 (1992): 61–94.

Potter, Pitman B. "Peng Zhen: Evolving Views on Party Organization and Law." In Carol Lee Hamrin and Timothy Cheek, eds., *China's Establishment Intellectuals*, pp. 21–50. Armonk, N.Y.: M. E. Sharpe, 1986.

Potter, Pitman B. "Riding the Tiger: Legitimacy and Legal Culture in Post-Mao China." *China Quarterly* 138 (1994): 325–358.

Potter, Sulamith Heins, and Jack M. Potter. *China's Peasants: The Anthropology of a Revolution*. New York: Cambridge University Press, 1989.

Powell, Edward. "Arbitration and the Law in England in the Late Middle Age." *Transactions of the Royal Historical Society* 5th ser., 33 (1983): 49–67.

Powell, Edward. "Settlement of Disputes by Arbitration in Fifteenth-Century England." *Law and History Review* 2, no. 1 (1984): 21–43.

Powell, Ralph. "Commissars in the Economy: 'Learn from the PLA' Movement in China." *Asian Survey* 5, no. 3 (1965): 125–138.

"PRC, Land Administration Law (Revised)." Promulgated on August 29, 1998. *China Law and Practice* 12, no. 9 (1998): 27–50.

"PRC Tax Administration Allows Use of Deduction Method." *China Market Intelligence* Jan. (1997): 2.

"Procuratorates Told Not to Overstep Authority." *Xinhua* Aug. 15, 1992, in *FBIS* 92-159 (Aug. 17, 1992): 30.

"Progressively Strengthen Mediation Work of a Mass Nature—Municipal People's Court Starts to Improve Mediation Organs." *Fujian ribao* Nov. 24, 1952.

"Protect the Legal Interests of Citizens." *Beijing ribao* Mar. 31, 1957: 2.

"Protect the Rightful Interests of Overseas Chinese." *Renmin ribao* Oct. 25, 1956: 2.

"Provisional Measures of the People's Republic of China for Control of Counter-Revolutionaries." Approved June 27, 1952. *FLHB* (1952): 53, translated in Jerome A. Cohen, ed., *The Criminal Process in the People's Republic of China, 1949–1963: An Introduction*, p. 277. Cambridge, Mass.: Harvard University Press, 1968.

"Provisional Measures on Administration of Allocated Land Use Rights." Promulgated Mar. 8, 1992, by the State Land Bureau. *CCH* ¶ 14–713.

"Provisional Regulations of the People's Republic of China Concerning the Grant and Assignment of the Right to Use State Land in Urban Areas." Promulgated by the State Council on May 24, 1990. *CCH* ¶ 14–716.

"Provisional Regulations of the People's Republic of China on Notarization." Promulgated by the State Council Apr. 13, 1982. *CCH* ¶ 19–500.

"Provisional Regulations of the People's Republic of China on Private Enterprises." Promulgated June 25, 1988. *CCH* ¶ 13–546.

"Provisional Regulations on Lawyers." Passed on Aug. 26, 1980, translated by Tao-tai Hsia and Charlotte Hambley in *China Law Reporter* 1, no. 4 (1981): 217–221.

Putterman, Louis. "The Role of Ownership and Property Rights in China's Economic Transition." *China Quarterly* 144 (1995): 1047–1064.

Qian Guzhou. "Hetong guanli: fangzhi guoyou zichan liushi de yitiao zhongyao tujing, guojia gongshangju gongping jiaoyi ju juzhang Li Bida fangtan lu" (Contract management: An important approach to preventing the loss of state-property, notes from an interview with Li Bida, National Ministry of Industry and Commerce Fair Trade Bureau Bureau-Chief). *Zhongguo lüshi* (China Lawyer) 8 (1997): 22–23.

"Qiao Shi Discusses Law, Economic Efficiency." *FBIS* 95-106 (June 2, 1995): 25–27.

"Qiao Shi Discusses Political Issues with US Journalists." *Xinhua* Jan. 16, 1997, in *FBIS* 97-012.

"Qiao Shi Interviewed on Role of NPC." *Xinhua* Dec. 14, 1996, in *FBIS* 96-242.

"Qiao Shi on Legal System for Market Economy." *Xinhua* Jan. 13, 1994, in *FBIS* 94-014 (Jan. 21, 1994): 36–38.

"Qiao Shi on Market Socialism Legal Framework." *China Law* Dec. (1994): 8–11, in *FBIS* 95-034 (Feb. 21, 1995): 18–21.

Qin Baohong. "All-Round Application of Commercial Purchasing and Sales Contracts." *Dagong bao* Feb. 9, 1962: 1.

Qinghai sheng gaoji renmin fayuan (Qinghai Provincial Higher-Level People's Court). "Quanmian tuixing ershen jingji jiufen anjian gongkai shenpan de jidian zuofa" (Several Methods of Work in the Comprehensive Promotion of Public Trials for Economic Dispute Cases at the Second Instance). In Zuigao renmin fayuan jingji shenpan ting (Supreme People's Court Economic Adjudication Division), ed., *Jingji shenpan canyue ziliao yu xin leixing anli pingxi* (Economic Adjudication Reference Materials and Critical Analysis of New Types of Cases), pp. 66–73. Beijing: Renmin fayuan chubanshe, 1994.

"Questions of Popularizing Advanced Experience in Judicial Work: Interviews with Responsible Officials of the Ministry of Justice." *Guangming ribao* Aug. 8, 1956, in *SCMP* 1,354, pp. 3–5.

"Radio Beijing: Party Cadres Not Above State Law." *FBIS* 80-166 (Aug. 25, 1980): L15.

"Raise People's Mediation Work to a Higher Plane." *Renmin ribao* Dec. 31, 1985.

"Reform of Judicial Work Under Planning by All Judicial Organs." *Xinhua* Aug. 17, 1952, in *SCMP* 401 (Aug. 24–25, 1952): 17–19.

"Regulations on Mediation in Hsiang Market Towns." Jan. 22, 1956. In Zhang Jinbei, ed., *Liufa quanshu* (Complete Book of the Six Laws). 1967.

"Regulations on Rural Collective Enterprises." State Council, June 10, 1990.

"Regulations on Urban Collective Enterprises." State Council, June 21, 1991.

Ren Jianxin. "Jiaqiang jingji hetong gongzuo cujin guomin jingji jihua de shunli zhixing" (Strengthen the Work of Economic Contracts and Promote the

Smooth Implementation of National Economic Planning). *Zhengfa yanjiu* 1 (1957): 31–34.

"Ren Jianxin: Problems Still Exist." *Xinhua* Dec. 9. 1992, in *FBIS* 92-237 (Dec. 9, 1992): 15–16.

"Ren Jianxin Addresses Crime Issue." *Xinhua* Dec. 27, 1993, in *FBIS* 94-008 (Jan. 12, 1994): 14–16.

"Ren Jianxin Speaks on Reforming Judicial Procedures." *Xinhua* July 15, 1996, in *FBIS* 96-149.

"Renmin fayuan gongzuo zhong guojia mimi jiqi miji juti fanwei de guiding (Regulations on State Secrets and the Concrete Scope of Secrecy Grades in People's Court Work)." In Zuigao renmin fayuan jijian zu (Supreme People's Court Discipline and Inspection Unit) and Zuogao renmin fayuan jianchazu (Supreme People's Court Supervision Unit), eds., *Jijian jiancha gongzuo shouce* (Discipline and Inspection, and Supervision Work Handbook). Beijing: Renmin fayuan chubanshe, 1991.

"Renmin fayuan zai gaige kaifang zhong quanmian fazhan—fang zuigao renmin fayuan yuanzhang Ren Jianxin" (People's Courts are Developing in All Areas in the Course of Opening and Reform—An Interview with President of the Supreme People's Court Ren Jianxin). *Zhongguo falü* 2 (June 15, 1995): 2–8.

"Renmin Ribao: Article on Freedom of Speech." *FBIS* (Feb. 17, 1981): L4–L5.

"Renmin tiaojie weiyuanhui zanxing zuzhi tongze" (Provisional Organizational General Rules for People's Mediation Committees). Promulgated on Mar. 22, 1954. In *Zhongyang renmin zhengfu faling huibian*, 1/54–9/54 (The Collected Laws and Decrees of the Central People's Government, Jan.–Sept. 1954), p. 55. English translation in Cohen, *Criminal Process*, pp. 123–135.

"Renmin tiaojie weiyuanhui zuzhi tiaoli" (Organizational Regulations for People's Mediation Committees). Promulgated by the State Council on June 17, 1989. Reprinted in Zhang Yunqing and Zhang Yushan, eds., *Renmin tiaojieyuan gongzuo shouce* (Handbook of People's Mediators' Work), pp. 388–391. Changchun: Jilin daxue chubanshe, 1992.

"Resolution of the Standing Committee of the National People's Congress Providing an Improved Interpretation of the Law." June 10, 1981. In *Laws of the People's Republic of China 1979–1982 Vol. 1*, 251.

"Revolutionary Stories Popular in Chinese Cities." *Xinhua* July 30, 1965, in *SCMP* 3,511 (1965): 23.

Rheinstein, Max, ed. *Max Weber on Law in Economy and Society*, translated by Edward Shils and Max Rheinstein. Cambridge, Mass.: Harvard University Press, 1954.

Rosen, Daniel H. *Behind the Open Door: Foreign Enterprises in the Chinese Marketplace*. Washington, D.C.: Institute for International Economics, 1999.

Rosen, Lawrence. *The Anthropology of Justice: Law as Culture in Islamic Society*. Cambridge: Cambridge University Press, 1989.

Rosenthal, A. M. "Muzzled by Beijing." *New York Times* Feb. 21, 1997: A35.

Rosenthal, Elisabeth. "A Day in Court, and Justice, Sometimes, for the Chinese." *New York Times* Apr. 27, 1998.

Rosenthal, Elisabeth. "Poverty Spreads, and Deepens, in China's Cities." *New York Times* Oct. 4, 1998: A3.

Rosenthal, Elisabeth. "Thousands of Farmers Protest in China; 1 Dies in Police Clash." *New York Times* Jan. 16, 1999.

Ross, Lester. "The Changing Profile of Dispute Resolution in Rural China: The Case of Zouping County, Shandong." *Stanford Journal of International Law* 26, no. 1 (1990): 15–66.

"Roundup: China Stressing Lawyers' Role by Law." *Xinhua* May 27, 1996.

Rowen, Henry S. "The Short March: China's Road to Democracy." *National Interest* 45 (1996): 61–70.

Rozelle, Scott. "Decision-Making in China's Rural Economy: The Linkages Between Village Leaders and Farm Households." *China Quarterly* 137 (1994): 99–124.

Rubenstein, Daniel. "Legal and Institutional Uncertainties in the Domestic Contract Law of the People's Republic of China." *McGill Law Journal* 42 (1997): 495–536.

Rubenstein, Daniel. "Transaction Costs and Market Culture Under China's Contract Law Reform," Ph.D. diss., University of Minnesota, 1996.

Rudolph, Lloyd I., and Susanne Hoeber Rudolph. *The Modernity of Tradition: Political Development in India*. Chicago: University of Chicago Press, 1972.

Sachs, Jeffrey D., and Wing Thye Woo. "Understanding China's Economic Performance." *National Bureau of Economic Research Working Paper* 5935 (1996).

Schauer, Frederick. "Formalism." *Yale Law Journal* 97, no. 4 (1998): 509–548.

Schram, Stuart R. *The Political Thought of Mao Tse-Tung*. New York: Praeger, 1963.

Schurmann, Franz. *Ideology and Organization in Communist China*. Berkeley: University of California Press, 1966.

Schurmann, Franz. "Organization and Response in Communist China." *Annals of the American Academy of Political and Social Science* 321 (1959): 51–61.

Schwartz, Benjamin. "Modernisation and the Maoist Vision—Some Reflections on Chinese Communist Goals." *China Quarterly* 21 (1965): 3–19.

Schwartz, Benjamin. "On Attitudes Toward Law in China." In American Council of Learned Societies, ed., *Government Under Law and the Individual*, pp. 27–39. Washington, D.C.: American Council of Learned Societies, 1957.

Schwartz, Benjamin. "The Primacy of the Political Order in East Asian Societies: Some Preliminary Generalizations." In Stuart R. Schram, ed., *Foundations and Limits of State Power in China*, pp. 1–10. London: School of Oriental and African Studies, 1987.

Schwartz, Benjamin. "Some Polarities in Confucian Thought." In David S. Nivison and Arthur F. Wright, eds., *Confucian Theories in Action*, pp. 50–62. Stanford: Stanford University Press, 1959.

Scogin, Hugh T., Jr. "Between Heaven and Man: Contract and the State in Han Dynasty China." *Southern California Law Review* 63 (1990): 1325–1404.

"Security Administration Punishment Act of the People's Republic of China." Promulgated Oct. 22, 1957. In *FGHB* 6 (Jul.–Dec. 1957): 245, English translation in *SCMP* 1,646 (Nov. 6, 1957): 1–7, and also in Jerome A. Cohen, ed., *The Criminal Process in the People's Republic of China, 1949–1963: An Introduction*, interspersed with other material at 205–237. Cambridge, Mass.: Harvard University Press, 1968.

"Security Administration Punishment Regulations of the People's Republic of China." Effective Jan. 1, 1987. This appears as amended in *Guowuyuan gongbao* (Gazette of the State Council of the People's Republic of China) 11 (June 27, 1994): 440–448.

"Security Law of the People's Republic of China." Adopted June 30, 1995. English translation in *China Banking and Finance* 7 (1995): 9–16.

"Security Ministry Unveils 'Winter Action' Campaign as Successor to 'Strike Hard'." *Xinhua* Nov. 18, 1996.

Seidman, Ann, and Robert B. Seidman. "Drafting Legislation for Development: Lessons from a Chinese Project." *American Journal of Comparative Law* 44, no. 1 (1996): 1–44.

"Shandong Launches Campaign to Publicize New Laws." *FBIS* (Aug. 16, 1979): O3.

Shapiro, Martin. *Courts: A Comparative and Political Analysis.* Chicago: University of Chicago Press, 1981.

Shen Zongling. *Bijiao fa zonglun* (General Theory of Comparative Law). Beijing: Beijing daxue chubanshe, 1987.

Shi Fengyi. "Renmin tiaojie zhidu suyuan" (The Origins of the System of People's Mediation). *Zhongguo faxue* 3 (1987): 44–49.

Shi Liang. "Report on Reform and Reorganization of People's Courts." *Xinhua* Aug. 22, 1956, English translation in *SCMP* 404 (1952): 5.

Shi, Steven, and Anne Stevenson-Yang. "Retail Roundabout." *China Business Review* 25, no. 1 (1998): 43–49.

Shi, Tianjian. *Political Participation in Beijing.* Cambridge, Mass.: Harvard University Press, 1997.

Shirk, Susan L. *The Political Logic of Economic Reform in China.* Berkeley: University of California Press, 1993.

Shklar, Judith. *Legalism: Law, Morals, and Political Trials.* Cambridge, Mass.: Harvard University Press, 1964 [1986].

"Should Mediation Committees in the Cities and Countryside Continue to Exist?" *Guangming ribao* July 16, 1956: 2.

"Showing Concern Over the Livelihood of the Masses, Consulting Them When Problems Arise." *Women of China* 2 (1961), English language translation in *ECMM* 261 (1961): 22–23.

Shue, Vivienne. "State Sprawl: The Regulatory State and Social Life in a Small Chinese City." In Deborah S. Davis, Richard Kraus, Barry Naughton, and Elizabeth J. Perry, *Urban Spaces in Contemporary China: The Potential for Autonomy and Community in Post-Mao China*, pp. 90–112. Washington, D.C.: Woodrow Wilson Center Press, 1995.

Sichuan sheng gaoji renmin fayuan (Sichuan Provincial High-level People's Court). "Fahui jingji shenpan zhineng zuoyong, wei weihu shehui wending fuwu" (Develop the Functions of Economic Adjudication Work to Serve the Protection of Social Stability). In Zuigao renmin fayuan jingji shenpan ting (Supreme People's Court Economic Adjudication Division), ed., *Jingji shenpan canyue ziliao yu xin leixing anli pingxi* (Economic Adjudication Reference Materials and Critical Analysis of New Types of Cases), pp. 3–11. Beijing: Renmin fayuan chubanshe, 1994.

Silver, Kimberly. "Removing the Rose-Colored Lenses." *China Business Review* 24, no. 3 (1997): 10–13.

Simms, Larry L. "'Waiting for the Other Shoe': A Critical Analysis of the PRC's Laws on Insurance." *China Law and Practice* 11, no. 2 (1997): 20–24.

Simon, William H. "The Legal Structure of the Chinese 'Socialist Market' Enterprise." *Journal of Corporation Law* 21, no. 2 (1996): 267–306.

Skinner, G. William. "Marketing and Social Structure in Rural China, Part III." *Journal of Asian Studies* 24, no. 3 (1965): 363–399.

Smith, Arthur Henderson. *Chinese Characteristics.* New York: F. H. Revell, 1894.

Smith, Arthur Henderson. *Village Life in China: A Study in Sociology.* New York: F. H. Revell, 1899.

"Socialist Democracy Requires Discipline." *JPRS* 77,590, Political, Social and Military Affairs, no. 170 (Mar. 16, 1981): 13.

Soileau, William D. "Past Is Present: Urban Real Property Rights and Housing Reform in the People's Republic of China." *Pacific Rim Law and Policy Journal* 3, no. 2 (1995): 299–387.

Solinger, Dorothy J. *China's Transition from Socialism: Statist Legacies and Market Reforms.* Armonk, N.Y.: M. E. Sharpe, 1990.

Solinger, Dorothy J. "Despite Decentralization: Disadvantages, Dependence and Ongoing Central Power in the Inland—the Case of Wuhan." *China Quarterly* 145 (1996): 1–34.

Solinger, Dorothy J. "Urban Entrepreneurs and the State: The Merger of State and Society." In Arthur Lewis Rosenbaum, ed., *State and Society in China: The Consequences of Reform,* pp. 121–141. Boulder, Colo.: Westview Press, 1992.

Sommers, Amy L., and Kara L. Phillips. "The P.R.C.'s Negotiable Instruments Law: An Instrument for Facilitating Private Economic Activity or Monetary Control?" *Houston Journal of International Law* 20, no. 2 (1998): 317–351.

Song Bing. "Assessing China's System of Judicial Review of Administrative Actions." *China Law Reporter* 8, no. 1–2 (1994): 1–20.

Song Jishan. "A Brief Discussion of the Nature and Function of Economic Contracts in Industry." *Jingji yanjiu* 2 (1965): 33–34, in *JPRS* 31,033 (July 12, 1965): 59–65.

Soviet Economic Law. Vol. 2 of the series *Soviet Statutes and Decisions.* New York: International Arts and Sciences Press, 1965–1966.

"Speech by Comrade Tong Pi-Wu." In *Eighth National Congress of the Communist Party of China: Speeches.* Beijing: Foreign Languages Press, 1956.

"Standing Committee of the National People's Congress, PRC, Economic Contract Law Amendment Decision." Adopted Sept. 2, 1993. English translation with notes by Pitman B. Potter in *China Law and Practice* 8, no. 9 (1993): 40–48.

"State Compensation Law of the People's Republic of China." Adopted May 12, 1994. Translation in Reuter Textline BBC Monitoring Service Far East.

"State Council Directive on Crackdown on Speculation, Smuggling." *Xinhua* Jan. 16, 1981: 6.

Staunton, Thomas George. *Ta Tsing Leu Lee.* London: Cadell and Davies, 1810.

Steinfeld, Edward S. *Forging Reform in China: The Fate of State-Owned Industry.* Cambridge: Cambridge University Press, 1998.

Stenton, Doris M. *English Justice between the Norman Conquest and the Great Charter,* 1066–1215. Philadelphia: American Philosophical Society, 1964.

Stephanson, Anders. *Kennan and the Art of Foreign Policy.* Cambridge, Mass.: Harvard University Press, 1989.

Stokes, Bruce. "The Chinese Challenge." *Financial Times* Aug. 29, 1997.

Strayer, Joseph R. *On the Medieval Origins of the Modern State.* Princeton, N.J.: Princeton University Press, 1970.

"Strengthen Mediation Work, Implement Giving a Mass Nature to Judicial Work." *Xinwen ribao* Jan. 12, 1953.

"Strengthen the Ideological Education of Cadre and Commune Members on the Concept of the State: Cheng-ch'eng Concretizes Purchasing Duties and Promotes the High Tide of Production." *Nanfang ribao* Mar. 2, 1963.

Stross, Randall E. *Bulls in the China Shop and Other Sino-American Business Encounters.* New York: Pantheon, 1990.

Sun Guohua. "Laws Cannot Be Understood in Isolation." *Guangming ribao* Dec. 28, 1986: 3. Translated as "Guangming Ribao Analyzes Class Nature of Law," in *JPRS* (Jan 16, 1987): K21–K25.

Sun Guohua. "On Bringing Reform Into the Orbit of the Rule of Law." *Guangming ribao* Feb. 7, 1989: 2, translated as "Article Views Reform, Rule of Law." *FBIS* 89-031 (Feb. 16, 1989): 19–21.

Sun Pizhi. "Renmin tiaojie xuyao zhiduhua falühua" (People's Mediation Must Be Systematized and Legalized). *Zhongguo Faxue* (Chinese Legal Studies) 3 (1987): 16–20.

Sun Pizhi and Wang Wei. *Renmin tiaojie zhishi* (People's Mediation Knowledge). Harbin: Heilongjiang Publishing House, 1985.

"Supplementary Provisions of the Standing Committee of the National People's Congress Concerning the Time Limits for the Handling of Criminal Cases." Adopted July 7, 1984.

"Supreme Court President Gives Report to NPC: Notes Failure to Enforce Decisions." *Xinhua* Apr. 2, 1988, in *FBIS* 88-064 (Apr. 4, 1988): 18–19.

"Supreme Court President on Law Enforcement." *Liaowang* July 17, 1995: 4–5, in *FBIS* 95-164 (Aug. 24, 1995): 25–28.

"Supreme People's Court Work Report." *Xinhua* Apr. 4, 1993, in *FBIS* 93-0065 (Apr. 7, 1993): 17–25.

Tang Dehua. "Quanmian jiaqiang jingji shenpan gongzuo, wei jingji jianshe he shehui zhuyi shichang jingji tizhi de jianli tigong sifa baozhang" (Comprehensively Strengthen Economic Adjudication Work, Provide Legal Safeguards for Economic Construction and the Establishment of the Socialist Market Economy System). Work report delivered on Oct. 21, 1994 at the Third National Economic Adjudication Work Meeting, excerpted in *ZRFG* 4 (Dec. 20, 1994): 142–144.

Tanner, Murray Scot. "How a Bill Becomes a Law in China: Stages and Processes in Lawmaking." In Stanley B. Lubman, ed., *China's Legal Reforms*, pp. 39–64. Oxford: Oxford University Press, 1996.

Tanner, Murray Scot. "Organizations and Politics in China's Post-Mao Law-Making System." In Pitman B. Potter, ed., *Domestic Law Reforms in Post-Mao China*, pp. 56–96. Armonk, N.Y.: M. E. Sharpe, 1994.

Tanner, Murray Scot. *The Politics of Lawmaking in Post-Mao China: Institutions, Processes, and Democratic Prospects.* Oxford: Oxford University Press, 1998.

Tanner, Murray Scot, and Chen Ke. "Breaking the Vicious Cycles: The Emergence of China's National People's Congress." *Problems of Post-Communism* 45, no. 3 (1998): 29–47.

"Temporary Procedures for the Signing of Contracts by Organs, State-managed Enterprises and Cooperatives." Promulgated Oct. 3, 1950. In Civil Law Teaching and Research Office, Chinese People's University, ed., *Zhonghua renmin gongheguo minfa ziliao huibian* (Collection of Materials on the Civil Law of the People's Republic of China), vol. 1. Beijing: Renmin daxue chubanshe, 1954.

"Temporary Regulations on the Organization of Security Defense Committees, Aug. 11, 1952. *FLHB* 1952: 62–64.

"The People's Courts of Various Counties of Jinjiang Special District Protect the Rights of Overseas Chinese." *Xinhua* Mar. 9, 1957.

"The White House: Press Briefing by Mike McCurry." *M2 Presswire* Mar. 16, 1998.

Thireau, Isabelle, and Hua Linshan. "Legal Disputes and the Debate about Legitimate Norms." In Maurice Brosseau, Kuan Hsin-chi, and Y. Y. Kueh, eds., *China Review* 1997, pp. 349–378. Hong Kong: Chinese University Press, 1997.

"This City Holds Meeting of Representatives of Advanced Mediation Workers; 10 Advanced Units and 74 Advanced Workers Reap the Benefits of the Meeting." *Qingdao ribao* Apr. 24, 1956.

Thurston, Anne F. "A Society at the Crossroads." *China Business Review* 21, no. 3 (1994): 16–20.

"Tian Jiyun on Laws for Market Economy." *FBIS* 93–140 (July 23, 1993): 36–37.

"Tientsin No. 4 State Cotton Mill Guides Spare-Time Activities of Workers in an Earnest Manner and Enables Them to Lead a Rich and Colorful 'After-Work' Life." *Renmin ribao* Jan. 19, 1961, English language translation in *SCMP* 2,426 (1961):13.

Tong Zhaohong. "Shenli jingji hetong jiufen anjian shiyong falü de jige ruogan wenti" (Several Questions on the Application of Laws in Adjudication of Economic Contract Dispute Cases). In Sun Posheng, ed., *Jingji shenpan zhuanti yanjiu* (1) (Research on Special Topics in Economic Adjudication, vol. 1), pp. 30–61. Beijing: Zhongguo zhengfa daxue chubanshe, 1993.

Townsend, James R. *Political Participation in Communist China.* Berkeley: University of California Press, 1967.

Tracey, Noel. "Transforming Southern China: The Role of the Chinese Diaspora in the Era of Reform." In Howard Davies, ed., *China Business: Context and Issues*, pp. 1–21. Hong Kong: Longmans Asia, 1995.

Turner, Karen. "Rule of Law Ideals in Early China?" *Journal of Chinese Law* 6, no. 1 (1992): 1–44.

Turner, Karen. "Sage Kings and Laws in the Chinese and Greek Traditions." In

Paul S. Ropp, ed., *Heritage of China: Contemporary Perspectives on Chinese Civilization*, pp. 86–111. Berkeley: University of California Press, 1990.

Tyler, Patrick E. "Now, Beijing Hears Another U.S. Voice." *New York Times* Mar. 29, 1997.

Unger, Jonathan. "'Bridges': Private Business, the Chinese Government and the Rise of New Associations." *China Quarterly* 147 (1996): 795–819.

Unger, Jonathan, and Anita Chan. "China, Corporatism and the East Asian Model." *Australian Journal of Chinese Affairs* 33 (Jan. 1995): 29–53.

Unger, Roberto Mangabeira. *Law in Modern Society: Toward a Criticism of Social Theory*. New York: Free Press, 1976.

Upham, Frank K. "The Place of Japanese Legal Studies in American Comparative Law." *Utah Law Review* 2 (1997): 639–656.

"U.S. Chief Justice in Shanghai." *Xinhua* Sept. 8, 1981 in BBC-SWB Sept. 10, 1981.

US-China Business Council. *China and the WTO: A Reference Guide*. Washington, D.C.: US-China Business Council, 1996.

US-China Business Council. "China's Political Developments." In US-China Business Council, comp., *China Operations '98*. Unpublished materials from China Operations '98, a conference held in Beijing, Feb. 17–18, 1998.

"Use Mediation More and More Among the People." *Jiefang ribao* (Yenan) June 14, 1944.

Van Caenegem, R. C. *The Birth of the English Common Law*. 2d ed. Cambridge: Cambridge University Press, 1988.

Van Caenegem, R. C. *An Historical Introduction to Private Law*. Translated by D. E. L. Johnston. Cambridge: Cambridge University Press, 1992.

Van der Sprenkel, Sybille. *Legal Institutions in Manchu China: A Sociological Analysis*. London: Athlone Press, 1962.

Van Gulik, R. H., trans. *T'ang-yin-pi-shih, Parallel Cases from under the Pear Tree: A Manual of 13th Century Jurisprudence and Detection*. Leiden: E. J. Brill, 1956.

Van Ness, Peter. "Addressing the Human Rights Issue in Sino-American Relations." *Journal of International Affairs* 49, no. 2 (1996): 309–331.

"Visit to China by the Delegation Led by Lord Howe of Aberavon, Report." London: HMSO, 1993.

Vogel, Ezra. "From Friendship to Comradeship: The Change in Personal Relations in Communist China." *China Quarterly* 21 (1965): 46–60.

Vogel, Ezra. "From Revolutionary to Semi-Bureaucrat: The 'Regularisation' of Cadres." *China Quarterly* 29 (1967): 36–60.

Vogel, Ezra. "Politicized Bureaucracy: Communist China." Unpublished ms.

Vogel, Ezra. "Voluntarism and Social Control." In Donald W. Treadgold, ed., *Soviet and Chinese Communism: Similarities and Differences*, pp. 168–184. Seattle: University of Washington Press, 1967.

Von Mehren, Arthur Taylor, and James Russell Gordley. 2d ed. *The Civil Law System*. Boston: Little, Brown, 1977.

Wakeman, Frederic, Jr. "The Civil Society and Public Sphere Debate." *Modern China* 19, no. 2 (1993): 108–138.

Walder, Andrew G. "China's Transitional Economy: Interpreting Its Significance." *China Quarterly* 144 (1995): 963–979.

Walder, Andrew G. "Corporate Organization and Local Government Property Rights in China." In Vedat Milor, ed., *Changing Political Economies: Privatization in Post-Communist and Reforming Communist States*, pp. 53–66. Boulder, Colo.: Lynne Rienner, 1994.

Walder, Andrew G. "Local Bargaining Relationships and Urban Industrial Finance." In Kenneth G. Lieberthal and David M. Lampton, eds., *Bureaucracy, Politics, and Decision Making in Post-Mao China*, pp. 308–333. Berkeley: University of California Press, 1992.

Walder, Andrew G. "Local Governments as Industrial Firms: An Organizational Analysis of China's Transitional Economy." *American Journal of Sociology* 101, no. 2 (1995): 263–301.

Walder, Andrew. "The Political Sociology of the Beijing Upheaval of 1989." *Problems of Communism* (Sept.–Oct. 1989): 30–40.

Walder, Andrew G. "The Quiet Revolution from Within: Economic Reform as a Source of Political Decline." In Andrew G. Walder, ed., *The Waning of the Communist State: Economic Origins of Political Decline in China and Hungary*, pp. 1–24. Berkeley: University of California Press, 1995.

Walder, Andrew G., and Jean C. Oi. "Property Rights in the Chinese Economy: Contours of the Process of Change." In Jean C. Oi and Andrew G. Walder, eds., *Property Rights and Economic Reform in China*. Cambridge, Mass.: Harvard University Press, forthcoming.

Walker, Kenneth R. *Planning in Chinese Agriculture: Socialisation and the Private Sector, 1956–1962*. Chicago: Aldine, 1965.

Wang Chenguang and Liu Wen. "Shichang jingji he gongfa yu sifa de huafen" (Market Economy and the Demarcation of Public Law and Private Law). *Faxue* (Beijing) 1 (1994): 37–45.

Wang Chenguang. "Banan xiaolü yu fayuan neibu yunxing tizhi de gaige: shenpan fangshi gaige zhong yi ge bu ke hushi de fangmian" (Case-Handling Efficiency and the Reform of the Internal Operating System of Courts: An Aspect of Adjudication Method Reform Which Cannot be Overlooked). *Faxue* 10 (1998): 46–51.

Wang Chenguang. "Increasing Judicial Activism in China." Draft of paper presented at the Conference on Comparative Judicial Systems, Hong Kong, June 2–3, 1998.

Wang Chunguang. "Communities of 'Provincials' in the Large Cities: Conflicts and Integration." *China Perspectives* 2 (1995):17–21.

Wang Dexiang. "Correct, Lawful and Timely—Several Thoughts on Studying China's Criminal Law and Law of Criminal Procedure." *Renmin ribao* July 17, 1980: 3, excerpts translated in *FBIS* (July 27, 1979): L1.

Wang Guangwu. "Powers, Rights, and Duties in Chinese History." In Wang Guangwu, ed., *The Chineseness of China: Selected Essays*, pp. 165–186. Hong Kong: Chinese University Press, 1991.

Wang Hongyan and Yang Yuanzhong. "Shilun renmin tiaojie zhidu de fazhan"

(On the Development of the People's Mediation System). *Faxue yanjiu* 2 (1988): 72.

Wang Huaian, ed. *Zhongguo minshi susong fa jiaocheng* (Textbook of Chinese Civil Procedure Law). Beijing: Renmin fayuan chubanshe, 1994.

Wang Jiafu, Liu Hainian, and Li Buyun. "Lun fazhi gaige" (On Reform of the Legal System). *Faxue yanjiu* (Studies in Law) 2 (1989): 1–9.

Wang Jianping. "Judicial and Administrative Mediation in the People's Republic of China." Ms. May 1984.

Wang Liming, Yang Lixin, and Zhao Hui, eds. *Renge quan fa*. Beijing: Falü chubanshe, 1997.

Wang Liming and Yao Hui. "Renmin fayuan jigou shezhi ji shenpan fangshi gaige wenti yanjiu (xia)" (Research on Problems of Establishing Institutions Within the People's Courts and Reforming Trial Methods, Part 2). *Zhongguo Faxue* 3 (1998): 23–32.

Wang Minyuan. "Xingshi beigaoren quanli yanjiu" (Research on the Rights of Criminal Defendants). In Xia Yong, ed., *Zou xiang quanli de shidai: Zhongguo gongmin quanli fazhan yanjiu* (Toward a Time of Rights: A Perspective of the Civil Rights Development in China), pp. 500–550. Beijing: Zhongguo zhengfa daxue chubanshe, 1995.

Wang Ren. "Trial Procedure with Chinese Characteristics in New Criminal Procedure Law." *Shanghai faxue* 175 (June 10, 1996): 22, in *FBIS* 96-187.

Wang, Shaoguang. "The Politics of Private Time: Changing Leisure Patterns in Urban China." In Deborah S. Davis, Richard Kraus, Barry Naughton, and Elizabeth J. Perry, eds., *Urban Spaces in Contemporary China: The Potential for Autonomy and Community in Post-Mao China*, pp. 149–172. Washington, D.C.: Woodrow Wilson Center Press, 1995.

Wang, Shaoguang. "The Rise of the Regions: Fiscal Reform and the Decline of Central State Capacity in China." In Andrew G. Walder, ed., *The Waning of the Communist State: Economic Origins of Political Decline in China and Hungary*, pp. 87–113. Berkeley: University of California Press, 1995.

Wang Shaoguang and Hu Angang. "Zhongguo guojia nengli baogao" (Report on China's State Capacity). Shenyang: Liaoning renmin chubanshe, 1993.

Wang, Shizhou. "The Judicial Explanation in Chinese Criminal Law." *American Journal of Comparative Law* 43 (Fall 1995): 569–579.

Wang Wanfeng. "Advanced Experience in Judicial Work." *Guangming ribao* Dec. 23, 1955.

Wang Yaxin. "Lun minshi, jingji shenpan fangshi de gaige" (On Reforming the Method of Civil and Economic Adjudication). Reprinted from *Zhongguo shehui kexue* (Chinese Social Science) 1 (1994): 3–22. in *Faxue* 4 (1994): 137–156.

Wank, David L. "Bureaucratic Patronage and Private Business: Changing Networks of Power in Urban China." In Andrew G. Walder, ed., *The Waning of the Communist State*, pp. 153–183. Berkeley: University of California Press, 1995.

Wank, David L. *Commodifying Chinese Communism: Business, Trust, and Politics in Xiamen*. Cambridge UK; Cambridge University Press, 1998.

Wank, David L. "The Institutional Process of Market Clientelism: *Guanxi* and Private Business in a South China City." *China Quarterly* 147 (1996): 820–838.

Wank, David L. "Private Business, Bureaucracy, and Political Alliance in a Chinese City." *Australian Journal of Chinese Affairs* 33 (Jan. 1995): 55–71.

Wank, David L. "Social Networks and Property Rights: Enforcement, Expectations, and Efficiency in the Urban Non-State Economy." In Jean C. Oi and Andrew G. Walder, eds., *Property Rights and Economic Reform in China*. Cambridge, Mass.: Harvard University Press, forthcoming.

Watson, Alan. *Legal Transplants: An Approach to Comparative Law*. Charlottesville: University of Virginia, 1974.

Weber, Eugen. *Peasants Into Frenchmen: The Modernization of Rural France, 1870–1914*. Stanford: Stanford University Press, 1976.

Weber, Max. *The Religion of China: Confucianism and Taoism*. Translated and edited by Hans H. Gerth. Glencoe, Ill.: Free Press, 1951.

Weber, Max. *The Theory of Social and Economic Organization*. Translated by A. M. Henderson and Talcott Parsons. Edited with an Introduction by Talcott Parsons. Glencoe, Ill.: Free Press, 1947.

Wechsler, Herbert. "The Challenge of a Model Penal Code." *Harvard Law Review* 65, no. 7 (1952): 1097–1133.

Weggel, Oskar. *Chinesische Rechtsgeschichte*. Leiden: E. J. Brill, 1980.

Weller, David L. "The Bureaucratic Heavy Hand in China: Legal Means For Foreign Investors to Challenge Agency Action." *Columbia Law Review* 98 (1998): pp. 1238–1282.

Wen Jing. *Fayuan shenpan yewu guanli* (Management of Court Adjudication Work). Beijing: Falü chubanshe, 1992.

Wen Jing. "Jiaqiang renmin tiaojie gongzuo de kexue xing" (Strengthen Scientific Administration of People's Mediation Work). *Zhongguo faxue* 3 (1987): 23–27.

Weng Zhan. "Developing Permanent Cooperation and Fixed Supply Sources in Local Industry?" *Jingji yanjiu*, no. 4 (1965): 1, in *JPRS*, 31035 (1965): 1.

"Western-Style Democracy Not an Option." *FT Asia Intelligence Wire* (Dec. 1, 1998).

"What Is the 'Legal System'?" *Gongren ribao* Dec. 20, 1956.

"White House Releases Joint U.S.-China Statement." *U.S. Newswire* Oct. 29, 1997.

White, Gordon. "The Dynamics of Civil Society in Post-Mao China." In Brian Hook, ed., *The Individual and the State in China*. Oxford: Clarendon Press, 1996.

White, Stephen D. "'Pactum . . . Legem Vincit et Amor Judicium': The Settlement of Disputes by Compromise in Eleventh-Century Western France." *American Journal of Legal History* 22 (1978): 281–308.

Whitman, James Q. "Why Did the Revolutionary Lawyers Confuse Custom and Reason?" *University of Chicago Law Review* 58 (1991): 1321–1368.

Whyte, Martin K. "Urban China: A Civil Society in the Making?" In Arthur Lewis Rosenbaum, ed., *State and Society in China: The Consequences of Reform*, pp. 77–101. Boulder, Colo.: Westview, 1992.

Winn, Jane Kaufman. "Relational Practices and the Marginalization of Law: Informal Financial Practices of Small Businesses in Taiwan." *Law and Society Review* 28, no. 2 (1994): 193–232.

Wong, Christine. "China's Economy: The Limits of Gradualist Reform." In Willam A. Joseph, ed., *China Briefing, 1994*, pp. 35–54. Boulder, Colo.: Westview, 1994.

Wong, Christine. "Material Allocation and Decentralization: Impact of the Local Sector on Industrial Reform." In Elizabeth J. Perry and Christine Wong, eds., *The Political Economy of Reform in Post-Mao China*, pp. 253–278, 315–319. Cambridge, Mass.: Council on East Asian Studies, Harvard University, 1985.

Wong, Kam C. "Police Powers and Control in the People's Republic of China: The History of Shoushen." *Columbia Journal of Asian Law* 10, no. 2 (1996): 367–390.

Woo, Margaret Y. K. "Adjudication Supervision and Judicial Independence in the P.R.C." *American Journal of Comparative Law* 39 (1991): 95–119.

"Woo's New Wave." *Far Eastern Economic Review* Dec. 23, 1993: 38–39.

Woodsworth, K. C. "Family Law and Resolution of Domestic Disputes in the People's Republic of China." *McGill Law Journal* 13, no. 1 (1967): 169–177.

"Work Report of Higher People's Court of Jilin." *Jilin ribao* July 22, 1958, English language translation in *SCMP* 1,874 (Oct. 14, 1958): 18–25.

"Work Report of the Supreme People's Court Presented by Ren Jianxin." *Xinhua* Mar. 22, 1995, in BBC-SWB Mar. 29, 1995.

Wu, Jieh-min. "Strange Bedfellows: Dynamics of Government-Business Relations Between Chinese Local Authorities and Taiwanese Investors." *Journal of Contemporary China* 6, no. 15 (1997): 319–346.

Wu, Yuan-li, et al. *Human Rights in the People's Republic of China*. Boulder, Colo.: Westview, 1988.

WuDunn, Sheryl. "In the Cities of China, the Busybodies Are Organized and Are Busy Indeed." *New York Times* Mar. 13, 1991.

Xiao Yongqing and Shen Zongling. "People's Court Judgment Based on Facts and Law." *Guangming ribao* Oct. 18, 1956, translated in *SCMP* 1,404 (Nov. 5, 1956): 2–4.

Xie Ming. "Lun hetong zhidu" (On the Contract System). *Zhengfa yanjiu* 2 (1959): 41–43.

"Xinhua Comments on Punishing Economic Criminals." *FBIS* (Apr. 1, 1982): K14–K15.

"Xinhua on Socialist Market Economy Laws." *FBIS* (July 7, 1993): 18–20.

"Xinjiang Populace Reportedly Handing Criminals Over to Authorities." *Xinjiang ribao* Oct. 7, 1996.

Xu, Xiangmin, and Robert Caldwell. "An Analytical Perspective on China's Negotiable Instruments Law." *China Banking and Finance* 10 (1995/1996): 1–5.

Yan, Yunxiang. "The Culture of *Guanxi* in a North China Village." *China Journal* 35 (Jan. 1996): 1–25.

Yan, Yunxiang. "Everyday Power Relations: Changes in a North China Village." In Andrew G. Walder, ed., *The Waning of the Communist State*, pp. 215–241. Berkeley: University of California Press, 1995.

Yang, C. K. *A Chinese Village in Early Communist Transition*. Cambridge, Mass.: Technology Press, 1959.

Yang, C. K. "Some Characteristics of Chinese Bureaucratic Behavior." In David S. Nivison and Arthur F. Wright, eds., *Confucianism in Action*, pp. 134–164. Stanford: Stanford University Press, 1959.

Yang, Martin C. *A Chinese Village: Taitou, Shantung Province.* New York: Columbia University Press, 1945.

Yang, Mayfair Mei-hui. *Gifts, Favors, and Banquets: The Art of Social Relationships in China.* Ithaca, N.Y.: Cornell University Press, 1994.

Yang, Mayfair Mei-hui. "Modernity of Power in the Chinese Socialist Order." *Cultural Anthropology* 3, no. 4 (1988): 408–427.

Yang Zhengwu. "Earnestly Implementing Administrative Punishment Law and Improving the Standard of Administration in Accordance with the Law in an All-Around Manner." *Hunan ribao* Sept. 30, 1996: 1–2, in *FBIS* 96-200 (Sept. 30, 1996).

Yangzhou shi zhongji renmin fayuan (Yangzhou Municipal Intermediate Level People's Court). "Kefu difang baohu zhuyi, jianchi yansu gongzheng zhifa" (Overcome Local Protectionism, Resolve to Seriously and Justly Uphold the Law). In Zuigao renmin fayuan jingji shenpan ting (Supreme People's Court Economic Adjudication Division), ed., *Jingji shenpan canyue ziliao yu xin leixing anli pingxi* (Economic Adjudication Reference Materials and Critical Analysis of New Types of Cases), pp. 113–125. Beijing: Renmin fayuan chubanshe, 1994.

"Yao Yilin on Administrative Procedures Law." *FBIS* (Sept. 4, 1990): 32.

Yatsko, Pamela. "New Owners: Privatization Comes to China's Township Enterprises." *Far Eastern Economic Review* Feb. 5, 1998: 52–53.

Ye Gulin. "Fully Develop the Role of People's Mediation Work for Serving the Construction of Socialism." *Zhengfa yanjiu* 4 (1964): 12–16, English language translation in *SCMM* no. 461 (1965): 1–8.

"Yifa zhiguo jianshe shehui zhuyi fazhi guojia xueshu yantao hui jiyao" (Summary of Forum on Ruling the Country According to Law and Constructing a Nation of Socialist Legality). *Faxue yanjiu* 18, no. 3 (1996): 3–23.

Ying Songnian. "Administrative Punishment System Ineffectual and Subject to Abuse." *Fazhi bao* Sept. 28, 1995: 7, in *FBIS* 95-237 (Dec. 11, 1995): 16–17.

Yu Bo. "Guidong baoli kangju zhifa anjian shimo" (The Beginning and End of a Violent Obstruction of Justice in Eastern Guangxi). *Falü yu shenghuo* 3 (1995): 31–35.

Yu, Guanghua. "The Emerging Framework of China's Business Organizations Law." *Transnational Lawyer* 10, no. 1 (1997): 39–76.

Yu Guanghua and Zhang Xianchu. "Law of Business Organizations." In Wang Chenguang and Zhang Xianchu, eds., *Introduction to Chinese Law*, pp. 341–366. Hong Kong: Sweet and Maxwell Asia, 1997.

Yu Xingzhong. "Legal Pragmatism in the People's Republic of China." *Journal of Chinese Law* 3 (1989): 29–51.

Zelin, Madeleine. "Merchant Dispute Mediation in Twentieth-Century Zigong, Sichuan." In Kathryn Bernhardt and Philip C. Huang, eds., *Civil Law in Qing and Republican China*, pp. 249–286. Stanford: Stanford University Press, 1994.

Zhang Cipei. "Several Problems Relating to the Use of Evidence to Determine the Facts of a Case in Criminal Litigation." *Zhengfa yanjiu* 4 (1962): 11–18, in *JPRS* 19,646, p. 16, partial translation in Jerome A. Cohen, ed., *The Criminal Process in the People's Republic of China, 1949–1963: An Introduction*, pp. 404–405. Cambridge, Mass.: Harvard University Press, 1968.

Zhang, Jay Zhe. "Securities Markets and Securities Regulation in China." *North Carolina Journal of International Law and Commercial Regulation* 22 (1997): 557–629.

Zhang Jiayong. "Notarial Work Can Effectively Supervise the Performance of Contracts." *Renmin ribao* Mar. 25, 1955.

Zhang Jun. "Zuigao shenpan jiguan xingshi sifa jieshi gongzuo huigu yu sikao, 1980–1990" (Review and Thoughts About Judicial Interpretation of the Criminal Law by the Highest Judicial Organs, 1980–1990). *Faxue yanjiu* 3 (1991): 46–53.

Zhang Lin. "Mediators Urged to Help Cut Crime." *China Daily* July 14, 1988.

Zhang Rongji. "Zhunque daji diren, jishi tiaochu jiufen, baowei renmin gongshe de gonggu he fazhan" (Strike Incisive Blows at the Enemy, Handle Disputes Promptly, and Safeguard the Solidarity and Development of the People's Communes). *Zhengfa yanjiu* 6 (1958): 59–61, in *JPRS* 813-D (1959): 28–31.

Zhang Shouqiang, ed. *Zhonghua renmin gongheguo hetong fagui yu hetong geshi quanshu* (Encyclopedia of PRC Contract Regulations and Contract Forms). Harbin: Harbin Press, 1993.

Zhang Youyu. "Tantan renmin tiaojie gongzuo de jige wenti" (Discussing Several Issues in People's Mediation Work). *Faxue yanjiu* 2 (1987): 69–71.

Zhang Yunqing and Zhang Yushan, eds. *Renmin tiaojieyuan gongzuo shouce* (Handbook of People's Mediators' Work). Changchun: Jilin daxue chubanshe, 1992.

Zheng, Guanxi, and H. L. Fu. "New *Investment Catalogue* Disappoints." *China Law and Practice* 12, no. 1 (1998): 51–53.

Zheng Qixiang, Wu Tongzhang, and Chen Guohua. "'Zhuozhong tiaojie' de tifa yingyu xiugai: dui minshi susong tiaojie zhidu de zai shentao" (The Wording of 'Emphasizing Mediation' Should Be Amended: Re-examining the Institution of Mediation in Civil Lawsuits). *Faxue* 2 (1990): 26–28.

Zhong Hua. "System of Mediating Disputes Examined." *China Daily* Dec. 12, 1986.

Zhongguo falü nianjian 1991 (Law Yearbook of China 1991). Beijing: Zhongguo falü nianjian she, 1991.

Zhongguo falü nianjian 1992 (Law Yearbook of China 1992). Beijing: Zhongguo falü nianjian she, 1992.

Zhongguo falü nianjian 1993 (Law Yearbook of China 1993). Beijing: Zhongguo falü nianjian she, 1993.

Zhongguo falü nianjian 1994 (Law Yearbook of China 1994). Beijing: Zhongguo falü nianjian she, 1994.

Zhongguo falü nianjian 1995 (Law Yearbook of China 1995). Beijing: Zhongguo falü nianjian she, 1995.

Zhongguo falü nianjian 1996 (Law Yearbook of China 1996). Beijing: Zhongguo falü nianjian she, 1996.

Zhongguo falü nianjian 1997 (Law Yearbook of China 1997). Beijing: Zhongguo falü nianjian she, 1997.

Zhongguo falü nianjian 1998 (Law Yearbook of China 1998). Beijing: Zhongguo falü nianjian she, 1998.

"Zhongguo fazhi gaige xueshu taolun hui fayan zhaiyao" (Summary of Speeches at Conference on Reform of China's Legal System). *Faxue yanjiu* (Studies in Law) 2 (1989): 10–35.

Zhongguo shenpan anli yaolan 1992 (Anthology of Adjudicated Cases in China 1992). Compiled by Zhongguo gaoji faguan peixun zhongxin (Senior Judges Training Center of the Supreme People's Court) and Zhongguo renmin daxue faxueyuan (Law Faculty of People's University). Beijing: Zhongguo renmin gongan daxue chubanshe, 1992.

Zhongguo shenpan anli yaolan 1993 (Anthology of Adjudicated Cases in China 1992). Compiled by Zhongguo gaoji faguan peixun zhongxin (Senior Judges Training Center of the Supreme People's Court) and Zhongguo renmin daxue faxueyuan (Law Faculty of People's University). Beijing: Zhongguo renmin gongan daxue chubanshe, 1994.

Zhongguo shenpan anli yaolan 1994 (Anthology of Adjudicated Cases in China 1994). Compiled by Zhongguo gaoji faguan peixun zhongxin (Senior Judges Training Center of the Supreme People's Court) and Zhongguo renmin daxue faxueyuan (Law Faculty of People's University). Beijing: Zhongguo renmin gongan daxue chubanshe, 1995.

"Zhonghua renmin gonghe guo zhongcai fa jieshuo" (Explanation of the Arbitration Law of the PRC). In Quanguo renda changweihui fazhi gongzuo weiyuanhui minfa shi (National People's Congress Standing Committee Legal Affairs Committee Civil Law Chamber) and Zhongguo guoji jingji maoyi zhongcai weiyuanhui mishu ju (Secretarial Bureau of the Chinese International Economic and Trade Arbitration Commission), comps., *Zhonghua renmin gongheguo zhongcai fa quanshu* (Encyclopedia of Arbitration Law of the People's Republic of China), pp. 1–69. Beijing: Falü chubanshe, 1995.

"Zhonghua renmin gongheguo faguan fa" (Law on Judges of the People's Republic of China). Effective July 12, 1995. *Fazhi ribao* Mar. 3, 1995.

Zhonghua renmin gongheguo fagui huibian (Collection of Laws and Regulations of the People's Republic of China). Beijing: Renmin chubanshe.

"Zhonghua renmin gongheguo hetong fa (caoan)" (Contract Law of the People's Republic of China, Draft). Xinhua release (Sept. 4, 1998), *FBIS* 99-017 (Jan. 17, 1999) as "China: Text of PRC Contract Law."

"Zhonghua renmin gongheguo xiangzhen qiye fa" (Law on Town and Township Enterprises of the People's Republic of China). In Guowuyuan fazhibu, comp., *Zhonghua renmin gonghe guo xin fagui huibian* 1996 (4), pp. 1–9. Beijing: Zhongguo fazhi chuban she, 1996.

Zhou Dao. "Shiying shehui zhuyi shichang jingji tizhi xuyao jiakuai fayuan tizhi gaige bufa" (To Adapt to the Socialist Market Economy, the Pace of Reform of the Court System Must Be Quickened). In *Zhongguo sifa zhidu gaige zongheng tan: quanguo fayuan xitong diliu jie xueshu taolun hui lunwen xuan* (A Free Discussion of the Reform of China's Judicial System: A Collection of Essays from the Sixth Academic Conference of the National Court System), pp. 1–12. Beijing: Renmin fayuan chubanshe, 1994.

Zhou Dewei. "Fighting Corruption: Rightfully Enforcing Law to Display the Might of Laws." Fazhi ribao (Sept. 25, 1997), translated in FBIS 98-170 (June 19, 1998) as "China: Court Role in Anticorruption Campaign."

Zhou Dunhe. "Cong 'zhongshi jiaoyu, zhongshi rencai' tan faguan jiaoyu, peixun wenti" (Discussing Education and Training of Judges from the Perspective of "Emphasizing Education, Emphasize Human Resources"). Renmin fayuan bao May 12, 1994.

Zhou Min. "Xianwei zuzhibu bu rang wo dang lüshi" (The County Organizational Department Won't Let Me Be a Lawyer). Minzhu yu fazhi 11 (1996): 11–12.

Zhuang Huichen. "Xingshi susong zhong shenpan yu zhencha qisu de guanxi wenti" (Problems of the Relationship Between Trial, Investigation and Prosecution in Criminal Procedure). Zhengfa yanjiu 3 (1957): 28–29.

Zhu Suli. "Jiceng fayuan shenpan weiyuanhui zhidu de kaocha ji sikao" (Investigations and Reflections on the Adjudication Committee System in Basic-Level Courts). Paper presented at the Conference on Comparative Judicial Systems, Hong Kong, June 2–3, 1998.

Zuckerman, Lawrence. "An End to Chinese Inscrutability." Time Dec. 18, 1988: 65.

Zuigao renmin fayuan gongbao bianjibu, comp. Zuigao renmin fayuan gongbao dianxing anli he sifa jieshi jingxuan (Selections of Model Cases and Judicial Explanations from the Supreme P.eople's Court Bulletin). Beijing: Zhonghua gongshang lianhe chubanshe, 1993.

"Zuigao renmin fayuan guanyu sifa jieshi gongzuo de ruogan guiding (Several Rules by the Supreme People's Court on Judicial Interpretation Work)." Issued June 23, 1997. Zhonghua renmin gongheguo zuigao renmin fayuan gongbao 3 (Sept. 20, 1997): 96.

"Zuigao renmin fayuan gongzuo baogao" (Supreme People's Court Work Report). Delivered by Ren Jianxin on Mar. 12, 1996. In Zhongguo falü nianjian 1997 (Law Yearbook of China 1997), pp. 44–50. Beijing: Zhongguo falü nianjian she, 1997.

"Zuigao renmin fayuan guanyu shiyong 'Zhonghua renmin gongheguo minshi susong fa' ruogan wenti de yijian" (Opinion of the Supreme People's Court on Several Issues Concerning the Application of the 'Civil Procedure Law of the People's Republic of China'). Promulgated July 14, 1992. ZRFG 1992: 70–94.

Zuigao renmin fayuan jingji shenpan ting (Supreme People's Court Economic Adjudication Division), comp. Jingji shenpan canyue ziliao yu xin leixing anli pingxi (Economic Adjudication Reference Materials and Critical Analysis of New Types of Cases). Beijing: Renmin fayuan chubanshe, 1994.

Zuigao renmin fayuan jingji shenpan ting, ed. Zuigao renmin fayuan shenli de ershen zaishen jingji jiufen anli xuanbian (Collection of Cases Decided by the Supreme People's Court Involving Second Level Trial and Retrial of Economic Disputes). Beijing: Renmin chubanshe, 1994.

"Zuigao renmin jiancha yuan guanyu minshi shenpan jiandu chengxu kangsu gongzuo zanxing guiding" (Interim Provisions of the Supreme People's Procuracy Concerning the Work of Civil Adjudication Supervision Procedure and Protest). In Zhongguo falü nianjian 1993 (Law Yearbook of China 1993), p. 733. Beijing: Zhongguo falü nianjian she, 1993.

Zweig, David. "Urbanizing Rural China: Bureaucratic Authority and Local Autonomy." In Kenneth G. Lieberthal and David M. Lampton, eds., *Bureaucracy, Politics, and Decision Making in Post-Mao China*, pp. 334–363. Berkeley: University of California Press, 1992.

Zweig, David. *Freeing China's Farmers: Rural Restructuring in the Reform Era*. Armonk, N.Y.: M. E. Sharpe, 1997.

Zweig, David, Kathy Hartford, James Feinerman, and Deng Jianxu. "Law, Contracts, and Economic Modernization: Lessons from the Recent Chinese Rural Reforms." *Stanford Journal of International Law* 23, no. 2 (1987): 319–364.

Zweigert, Konrad, and Hein Kötz. *Introduction to Comparative Law, Volume 1, The Framework*, 2nd rev. ed., translated by Tony Weir. Oxford: Clarendon Press, 1987.